CONCORDIA'S COMPLETE

Bible Handbook

Second Edition

CONCORDIA'S COMPLETE

Bible Handbook

Second Edition

Introductions by Jane L. Fryar

Other contributors include
Carla Fast, Abigail Genig, Deborah Henry,
Judith E. Meyer, Cynthia Schilf, Susan Schulz,
Julie Stiegemeyer, Thomas A. Nummela, and Suzanne Yelkin

Edward A. Engelbrecht, General Editor

3558 S. Jefferson Avenue, St. Louis, MO 63118-3968
1-800-325-3040 • www.cph.org

Introductions by Jane L. Fryar

Edited by Edward A. Engelbrecht

Manufactured in East Peoria, IL / 63692 / 160356.

1 2 3 4 5 6 7 8 9 10 22 21 20 19 18 17 16 15 14 13

Table of Contents

Charts, Maps, Diagrams

Preface

What's your favorite story?

It's hard to imagine life without stories. As long as there have been people, they have been telling stories. Some stories are fictional, cooked up in the mind of the storyteller. Maybe you know the story of the Greek hero Odysseus and his ten-year journey home after the fall of the city of Troy. That story is known as *The Odyssey*, and it has fascinated hearers for countless generations. Or maybe when you were younger, you enjoyed fairy tales from Sweden or Germany or folk tales from Africa or Central America. Stories like these live on because they inspire us, intrigue us, challenge us, and sometimes even teach us.

This handbook will help you read and understand the world's most important story. It will help you see the Bible not as a collection of unrelated stories and poems, but as the Holy Spirit–inspired source of one uniquely momentous story—the story of salvation. All of the accounts you have likely called "Bible stories" are instead really chapters in this unique story; they are part of the one, much longer story through which Jesus has redeemed you and all people. The accounts of Noah's ark, David and Goliath, Daniel in the lions' den, and all the rest are simply episodes in the story—the history—of how the Creator of the universe has brought salvation to His children, to undeserving sinners here on earth.

An Astonishing Book

Everything in the Bible—the poetry, the prophecy, the proverbs, and the panoply of other literature there—fits together to create one astonishing and moving account. Word by word, verse by verse, chapter by chapter, those elements combine to make one—and only one—Bible story. It's the story of sin and grace, the story of Law and Gospel, the story of our need and God's plan to meet that need through our Savior, Jesus. Best of all, this story is not fiction. It's not fantasy. It's true! It's real! And the hope that's found there is for you—personally!

Even the best human stories have a shelf life. People read them for a generation or two or three. Then the story no longer applies. Individuals read their favorite book or poem once, twice, ten, or even thirty times. But eventually it goes stale. The reader has milked all the meaning, and the book goes back on the shelf. It no longer challenges, inspires, or comforts.

Not so the Bible! For generation after generation, people have been reading and studying the Bible. Century after century, millennia after millennia, God's story of grace stays fresh. Month by month, year after year, individuals who come prayerfully to the Scriptures find that our Lord meets them there every time—just as He has promised. The deeper we plunge, the more the meaning grows. Far from becoming stale, the story keeps on getting richer and more intriguing.

My prayer is that *Concordia's Complete Bible Handbook for Students* will guide you as you continue a lifelong pursuit: learning to know your Savior-God as you read what He tells you about Himself in His book. I pray you will learn to know what the Bible says, what it means, and especially what it means for you each new day.

A Current Book

The story of the Bible is true. The details are true. Every word in the Bible is God breathed. The story is real. It really happened. Much of it is still happening. You're caught up in the middle of it right now, whether you realize it or not. It's an adventure of truly heroic proportions, and it's building toward an incredible ending.

May the Holy Spirit fill your heart with a deeper faith, firmer hope, and holier life as you use this Means of Grace and take your place among the saints whose life stories, by God's grace, proclaim the Savior's love!

—Dr. Jane L. Fryar

What's the Bible All About?
An Introduction

Each year, more than 275,000 new books are published in the United States. If you wanted to read them all, you'd need to read more than 450 of them every day, all year long. Then you'd need to start all over again on the next year's publications!

That's a lot of reading! Many books are worth reading; some, probably not. But one book returns to the top of the best-seller list every year, decade after decade: the Bible. It's an extraordinary book. It's changed literally millions of lives. It can change yours. Maybe it already has.

Some people—even some Christians—see the Bible as "God's Book of Rules." For them, the stories become moral tales, like Aesop's fables, and the characters are heroes—or villains. These people respect the Bible, but they don't really understand it.

Other people—even some Christians—treat the Bible like a book of mysteries that help one uncover higher spiritual truths. They think that by meditation or speculation, they will uncover these higher truths and gain an advantage in life and with God. These people also respect the Bible, and yet they don't really understand it.

The Bible does contain rules and describe mysterious things, as you will see. But Jesus Himself told us how to interpret the Bible. Read His words carefully:

> *You search the Scriptures because you think that in them you have eternal life; and it is they that bear witness about* Me.
>
> *John 5:39 (emphasis added)*

When the resurrected Christ met the disciples on the road to Emmaus on the first Easter evening, the three talked about what had happened on the cross and in the now-empty tomb:

> *Beginning with Moses and all the Prophets, [Jesus] interpreted to them in all the Scriptures the things* concerning Himself.
>
> *Luke 24:27 (emphasis added)*

Later that evening, Jesus appeared to all the disciples. He told them:

> *"These are My words that I spoke to you while I was still with you, that everything written* about Me *in the Law of Moses and the Prophets and the Psalms must be fulfilled." Then He opened their minds to understand the Scriptures.*
>
> *Luke 24:44–45 (emphasis added)*

From start to finish, Genesis to Revelation, the Bible is about Jesus! Abraham, Isaac, and Jacob point us to Jesus! Noah, Samuel, and David point us to Jesus! The tabernacle and the temple point us to Jesus! All the sacrifices, all the wars, all the poems, and even all the genealogies point us to Jesus! Matthew, Mark, Luke, John, Paul, and all the other human authors of the Holy Scriptures point us to Jesus! He's the true hero—the *only* hero—of the Bible.

Unless you realize this and read the Bible looking for your Savior, you will miss the main thing God intends to communicate in His book. You may even come to believe things about God and about His purposes for your life that simply aren't true! So keep Christ in mind no matter what you're reading in Holy Scripture. The Bible is all about Jesus and the salvation God made possible for us through Jesus. That story is the one true story on which Christians base their lives!

Who wrote the Bible?

Scripture itself answers this question:

> *No prophecy was ever produced by the will of man, but men spoke from God as they were carried along by the Holy Spirit.*
> *(2 Peter 1:21)*

God used human beings to write the Bible. The prophets wrote the books of the Old Testament, and the apostles and evangelists wrote the books of the New Testament. In all, many authors contributed books to this unique library.

We say the Bible was "inspired" by God. This means:

- The Holy Spirit moved the authors to write and guided them as they wrote. Yet He also worked with the authors' emphases and styles so that the books are true expressions of those authors.
- The Holy Spirit's inspiration was not partial, but full and complete. Thus, we often refer to *plenary verbal inspiration*. By this, we assert that God inspired the complete text of the Bible.
- We can trust not just the doctrinal content of Scripture, but also the historical and scientific data included in it, understanding that ancient people wrote about these things in different ways than historians or scientists might write about them today.
- The Bible is *inerrant*. This means it is accurate, truthful, and free of error.

The Holy Spirit inspired a wonderful book, one on which we can fully rely! That does not mean God dictated the text. Rather, He gave the human authors the freedom to let their personalities shine through. John writes differently than Moses does. Isaiah's poetry differs from David's. In fact, God used the backgrounds, interests, and knowledge of the human authors, incorporating it into the text while still excluding errors and mistakes. For example, Luke was a physician, and his profession influenced some of the details he chose to use as he reported on some of Jesus' healing miracles.

Divine. Human. The Scripture is uniquely both.

Random Facts about Chapter and Verse

- There are 929 chapters in the Old Testament and 260 chapters in the New Testament. This makes a total of 1,189 chapters.
- Psalm 117 is the middle chapter of the Bible. Psalm 117 is also the shortest chapter of the Bible.
- Psalm 119 is the longest chapter of the Bible.
- There are 23,145 verses in the Old Testament and 7,957 verses in the New Testament. This makes a total of 31,102 verses.
- 1 Chronicles 1:25 ("Eber, Peleg, Reu;") is the shortest verse in the Hebrew Old Testament.
- 1 Thessalonians 5:16 ("παντοτε χαιρετε," "Rejoice always,") is the shortest verse in the Greek New Testament.
- John 11:35 ("Jesus wept.") is the shortest verse in most English translations.

How is the Bible organized?

The Bible is not really one book, but a library of sixty-six shorter books. Not all of these books are written in the same genre. Some are history, some poetry, some are letters, some prophecy. A few books are *apocalyptic*—a special kind of literature. The word *apocalypse* means "unveiling or revealing." Parts of Daniel, Ezekiel, Zechariah, and Revelation are written in apocalyptic style. They reveal Christ and the new heavens and new earth His second coming will bring. (See, for example, Revelation 1 and 21.)

The Old Testament includes thirty-nine books. All were written in Hebrew, though a few chapters of Daniel and Ezra were penned in a language called Aramaic. The twenty-seven books of the New Testament were written in Koine Greek—the Greek of the marketplace during Jesus' earthly life and the decades that followed.

The Old Testament documents the history and experiences of God's people before Jesus was born. It points forward to the Messiah, the Savior, God promised to send.

The New Testament focuses on that Savior, documenting the life of Jesus and the history of the Church in the decades that followed His resurrection from the dead and ascension into heaven.

After Malachi wrote the last book of the Old Testament, God gave no further revelation for about four hundred years. God was still at work in and for

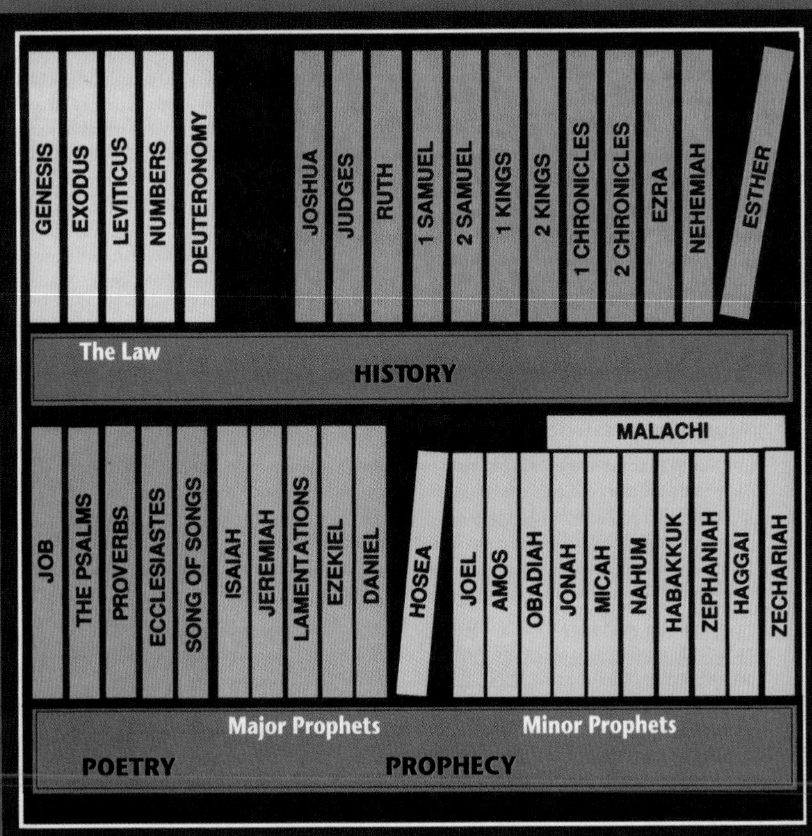

His people during this "intertestamental period." Other historians of that time tell us some of what happened during those years. But Scripture itself is silent between the Book of Malachi and the first of the New Testament writers.

The original text of the Bible did not contain chapters and verses. These were added later to make finding specific sentences and paragraphs easier.

What's up with all those translations?

The authors of the Old Testament wrote primarily in Hebrew; the authors of the New Testament wrote in Greek. If all Christians today would learn Hebrew and Greek, we wouldn't need translations at all. But even if we could do that, we might want a Bible in our own language anyway. There's something powerful about reading or hearing God's Word in our own "mother tongue" or "heart language." It's why missionaries around the world

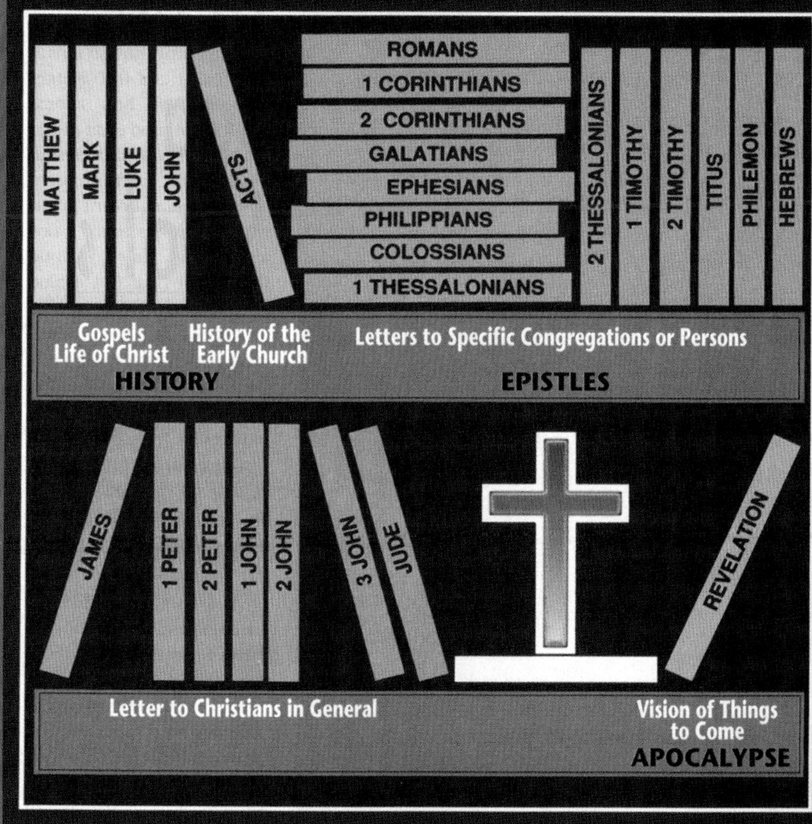

make every effort to translate part or all of the Bible into the language of the people they serve.

No one knows for sure who made the first Bible translation, but among the most famous early translations was the Septuagint. Scholars working in Alexandria, Egypt, during the second and third centuries before Christ translated the entire Hebrew Old Testament into Greek. Some of the New Testament writers—and maybe even Jesus Himself—read and studied this translation. It's quoted several times in the New Testament letters and in the sermons of the apostles in the Book of Acts.

Early in the sixteenth century, William Tyndale translated the entire Bible from Hebrew and Greek into English, becoming the first scholar to do so. When the authorities found out about his project, they sent bounty hunters and inquisitors to find him so they could put him on trial and execute him! Tyndale fled to Germany from England so he could continue his work in relative safety.

The first printed copies of Tyndale's English New Testament were smuggled into England in 1525. He based his work largely on the example of Martin Luther's German translation of the Bible from the original languages (1522).

The history of early Bible translation is fascinating, filled with the dangers and intrigue of a great adventure. To learn more about it, type "history of Bible translations" into your Internet search engine. You may be surprised at how hard Christians had to work and fight down through the centuries so that we can read and own copies of the Holy Scriptures!

Bibles in English today fall along a spectrum from paraphrases to word-for-word translations. Which Bible should you use? If you're looking to carefully study the Bible, consider a scholarly translation like The English Standard Version (ESV), The New King James Version (NKJV), The New American Standard (NASB), or the New International Version (NIV). Helpful editions include *The Lutheran Study Bible* (ESV), *Concordia Self-Study Bible* (NIV), and *Faith Alive Bible* (NIV). On the other hand, if you're new to Bible reading and want to read devotionally, you might find a paraphrase like *The New Living Translation* (NLT) or even *The Message* (MSG) helpful.

Don't let the idea of so many translations frighten you, though. If you lay all the major translations side by side, you will notice some differences in meaning among them. Of course, there is no perfect translation. If you're studying a major or controversial doctrine, you'll want to consult several versions before you make up your mind.

However, if you are memorizing Scripture, choose one major translation and stick with it. Jumping from translation to translation will make memorization harder, and it will make it more difficult to use a concordance to find specific verses later on.

Is the Bible reliable and trustworthy?

In a word, yes! Absolutely! God the Holy Spirit not only inspired His written Word, He watched over it down through the centuries, ensuring that no one—not even Satan himself—could destroy or change what it had to say.

From time to time, an excited reporter bursts onto the scene to announce the discovery of a "new" Bible book or even some kind of archeological evidence that supposedly proves that the Bible contains errors. These "discoveries" have never been proven true, and they won't! If you wonder about them, do the research! Ask your pastor or someone else you trust to point you to resources that will tell the whole story.

Over the past few decades, many people have explored and written about various questions in apologetics, including questions about Scripture's reliability and authenticity. Some have even started out intending to disprove the Bible and have become Christians in the process! If you have questions, look for valid answers. The evidence for the Bible's credibility is already overwhelming, and it is growing year by year.

When it comes right down to it, though, we believe the Bible because we believe Jesus Himself. He is the heavenly Father's final Word to us sinners, and He points us to the Scriptures as the record of what the triune God has done down through history to rescue us and bring us into His very own family.

How can I get the most out of the Bible reading I do?

That's a great question. Below are some thoughts many Christians have found helpful. The *Bible Handbook* will teach you more about how to apply them.

- Come to the Scripture with an open heart. Expect God to speak through His Word. He has promised to do so!
- Pray for God's help. (See the "Prayer to See God's Ways.")

The Prayer to See God's Ways

Speak, Lord, for Your servant hears. Please show me now Your ways, that I may gain Christ and be found in Him, not having a righteousness of my own that comes from the Law, but that which comes through faith in Christ. Your Word is a lamp to my feet and a light to my path. Give me life, O Lord, according to Your Word, and I will declare Your greatness. Amen.

- Schedule a regular time every day to be with Jesus in His Word. Choose a time and place where you won't be interrupted. Have a plan. Do you want to read all four Gospels this year? The entire New Testament? Key "Bible reading plan" into an Internet search engine, and choose one of the plans that pop up.

- Read whole passages and books, not just a verse here and a verse there. Reading larger passages helps you gain the best understanding of what a writer is trying to express.
- Look for Jesus in the teaching, even when you read the Old Testament. Clues pointing to the salvation He has won for us appear on nearly every page.
- Frame the message in terms of Law and Gospel. Ask yourself, "Where do I see my sin in this text? What disobedience do I need to confess?" Then ask, "What promise of forgiveness in Christ's cross does God give in this text?"
- Don't worry if you don't understand everything you read. Not even the world's greatest Bible student understands everything! Think about what you *do* understand. As you keep reading, day by day, year by year, your understanding will grow. Count on it! The Holy Spirit Himself is your teacher! (See John 14:25–26.) Ask Him to deepen your insight.

Want to plog?

Do you txt? Tweet? Blog? DQMOT, but IMNSHO some of the acronyms can leave U ROF ROR! Whether you IM or not, whether you txt or not, whether U R BWL by now or not, you can learn to *plog*. It's a way to grow closer to Jesus and deeper in His Word.

Think of *plogging* ("prayer logging") like you would blogging, except when you plog, you focus on our Savior. Think of it as one way to get in touch with Him—instantly!—every day.

Whether you write it out longhand in a journal or use your computer and every txt shortcut you know, you'll want to write down what you learn. Why? We all note what's important to us. When new friends give us their phone number or e-mail address, we write it down. When someone asks us to come to a party, we write it down. Our brains process the information that passes from our eyes and ears to the pen in our hand and onto the paper we're holding.

When we plog on a regular basis, we can look back on what our Lord has been saying to us over days, months, and years. Patterns will pop out. Victories Jesus has won for us will emerge. Our Lord's answers to our prayers will become obvious. Our confidence in our faithful God will grow as He uses His Word to strengthen our faith.

How do you plog? Here's one way you might want to try.

1. Buy a notebook; 5½ × 8½ inches is a good size. Or set up a file on your computer, if you prefer to work electronically.

2. Get familiar with **SNAP**:

***S**cripture:* Read the text assigned for the day. Notice when a particular word, phrase, verse, or section "pops" off the page. The Holy Spirit works. Anticipate it. When you finish the day's reading, write out the phrase/verses that seemed most powerful or meaningful to you.

***N**otes:* What do you notice about the Scripture selection you wrote out? Is it Law? (In His Law, God tells us what we are to do or avoid doing. The Law also accuses us of sin.) Is it Gospel? (In the Gospel, God reminds us of His grace and forgiving love, particularly in our Savior, Jesus, and His cross.)

***A**pplication:* Why do you think your Lord called your attention to these particular words? What is He saying to you about your need for His help? What is He promising to do for/in you? Based on this passage of Scripture, if Jesus were sitting across the table from you, what would He say to you?

***P**rayer:* Respond to the Scripture you just thought about (meditated on). What do you want to say to God about it? What sin(s) will you confess? What promise will you rely on? What will you ask Jesus to do for you? What praise and thanks will you offer?

1. Date each entry. Then, when you finish your prayer, go back and title that day's plog. It will help you summarize what you've seen/learned. And when you return to the page later, you'll more easily remember the key idea. *Tip: The Lutheran Study Bible Journal* includes a helpful indexing system that lets you return to earlier thoughts you have recorded.

2. You need a *time*, a *place*, and a *plan*. The steps above are your plan. Now all you need is a time and place where you will not be interrupted! Jesus Himself wants to make a daily appointment with you! Walk through the door He is opening, and you'll never be the same again!

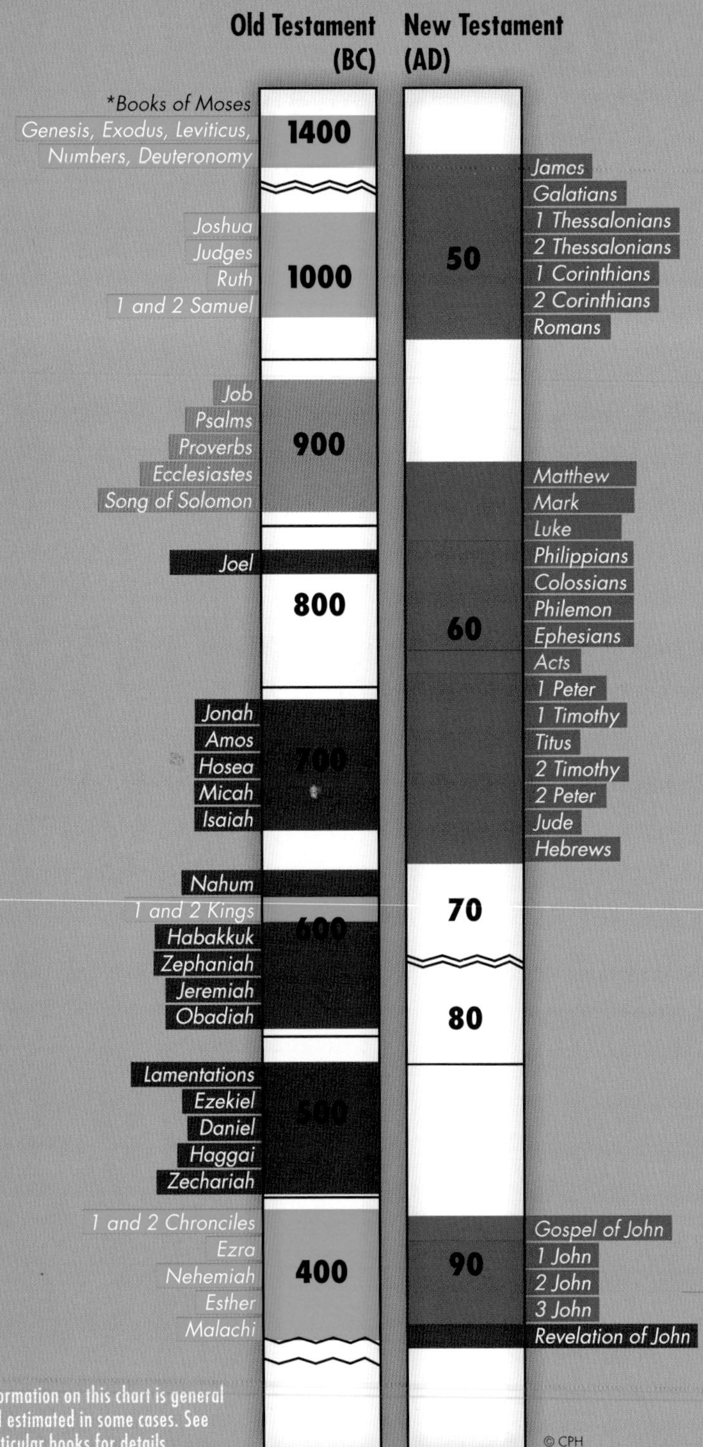

Information on this chart is general and estimated in some cases. See particular books for details.

Writing the Scriptures Timeline

2 Peter 1:21

Psalm 119:105

John 20:31

The Bible is called "the Holy Scriptures" because God the Holy Spirit gave to His chosen writers the thoughts that they expressed and the words that they wrote. This is called verbal inspiration. The Bible is God's own Word and truth, without error. God gave the Old Testament in Hebrew and Aramaic and the New Testament in Greek.

Psalm 119:105 says that God's Word "is a lamp to my feet and a light to my path." (2 Peter 1:21 and John 20:31 tell more about the inspiration of Scripture and why God gave the Scriptures.)

Exact dates of scriptural writings, especially of the Old Testament, are difficult to date. Even highly educated scholars have different opinions. The dates on this timeline are only approximate.

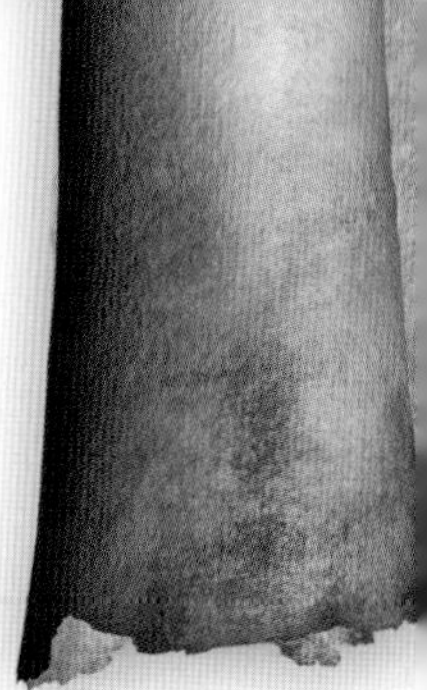

Writing and Printing

Books, magazines, and newspapers are so common today that it may be hard to imagine when they were not readily available. Just six hundred years ago, almost all books and other writing were *manuscripts* ("manual writing," that is,

3000 BC	2000 BC	1000 BC
2500 BC People in Asia wrote on animal skins	**2400 BC** A papyrus scroll was used for writing	**900 BC** Leather used for scrolls

Highlights in the history of printing:

- As early as 3500 BC, clay tablets were used to record words in Sumer, a region of Babylonia.
- People in Asia wrote on animal skins as early as 2500 BC.
- Made with an early form of paper, a papyrus scroll was used for writing around 2400 BC.
- Leather was used for scrolls starting about 950 BC.
- Until the time of Jesus, all books—including the Old Testament Scriptures—were in the form of papyrus or leather scrolls rolled onto wooden spindles.
- About AD 100, *codices* (the plural form of *codex*) came into common use; these were books made from pages of leather.

We are now in an age when printed material is sometimes being replaced by electronic texts—writing preserved in computers and sent over phone lines and broadcast without wires. How times have changed! Each innovation has become

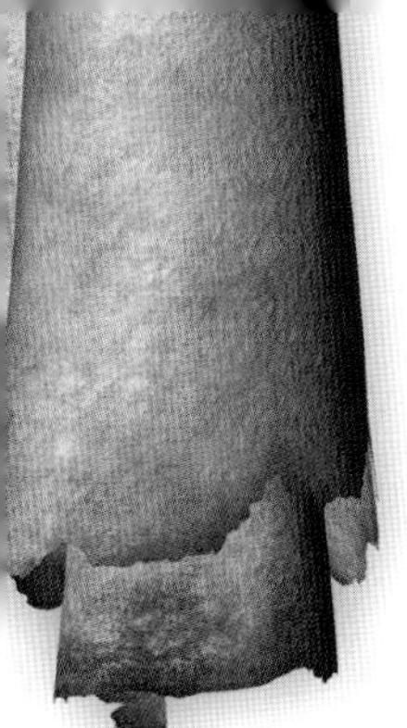

prepared by hand). During the lives of the apostles, all writings—including all copies of the Scriptures—were handwritten by scribes and generally bound in the form of scrolls.

BC / AD	AD 1000	AD 1500
AD 100	**AD 868**	**1450 BC**
Codices came into common use	Earliest known wood-block printing came from China	Johannes Gutenberg created a movable-type press

- In the Middle Ages, scribes copied books by hand in *scriptoria*. Scriptoria, or copying rooms, were often located at monasteries or religious communities, where copies of God's Word were prepared.
- The earliest known wood-block printing comes from China and is dated AD 868.
- Almost all books were written by hand until after AD 1000.
- The kind of paper we know today was invented in China about AD 100, but it was not common in Europe until after AD 1000.
- Movable type was used in printing in China as early as AD 1041.
- Around AD 1450, Johannes Gutenberg created a movable-type press. In the mid-1450s, he printed the Bible in the German language.

a new tool by which God's Word can be shared so that people can come to know Jesus as their Savior.

Depiction of the First Council of Nicaea.

Summarizing the Bible in Creeds

Because the Bible is such a large book, Christians have appreciated summaries of biblical teaching. Most Christians accept three *creeds*, statements of what the Bible teaches about God. These are the Apostles' Creed, the Nicene Creed, and the Athanasian Creed.

The Apostles' Creed

The exact origin of the shortest of the creeds is not entirely clear. It would appear to be based on an older Roman creed that existed in the second century AD. Although the apostles did not write the Apostles' Creed, it reflects their basic teachings. This creed has, from its beginnings, been linked to the Sacrament of Baptism.

The Apostles' Creed in its present form, though with the omission of a few phrases, dates to the middle of the fifth century.

The Nicene Creed

Early Christians debated several issues about Jesus, including whether or not Jesus was truly God. A meeting was called in Nicaea in AD 325 to combat the *heresy*, or false teaching, called "Arianism"—that Jesus, though the Son of God, was not eternal and was subordinate to the Father. The result was the Nicene Creed, which states that Jesus is "God of God, Light of Light, very God of very God, begotten, not made, being of one substance with the Father by whom all things were made."

Public Domain

The First Council of Nicaea presenting the Nicene Creed.

The Athanasian Creed

The Athanasian Creed is named after Athanasius, bishop of the Christian Church in Alexandria, Egypt, who emphasized a number of things recorded in this creed. This church was a major center of Christianity in the second, third, and fourth centuries. Athanasius, known for his defense against Arianism, died in AD 373. This creed is significantly longer than either the Apostles' or Nicene Creed. It is a detailed explanation of truths about the triune God, three equal persons in one God. This creed is now rarely used in the Divine Service. In many churches, it is heard only on Trinity Sunday.

Today, there still exist many misunderstandings and false beliefs about who God is and what He desires for us. Some deny that Jesus is the only way to the Father (John 14:6). Some think that God requires something of us before we can deserve salvation (Ephesians 2:8–9). The Christian creeds offer a clear summary of what the Bible teaches about God. While we cannot understand the mystery of the Three in One, as Christians, we confess that the Father is true God, the Son is true God, and the Holy Spirit is true God.

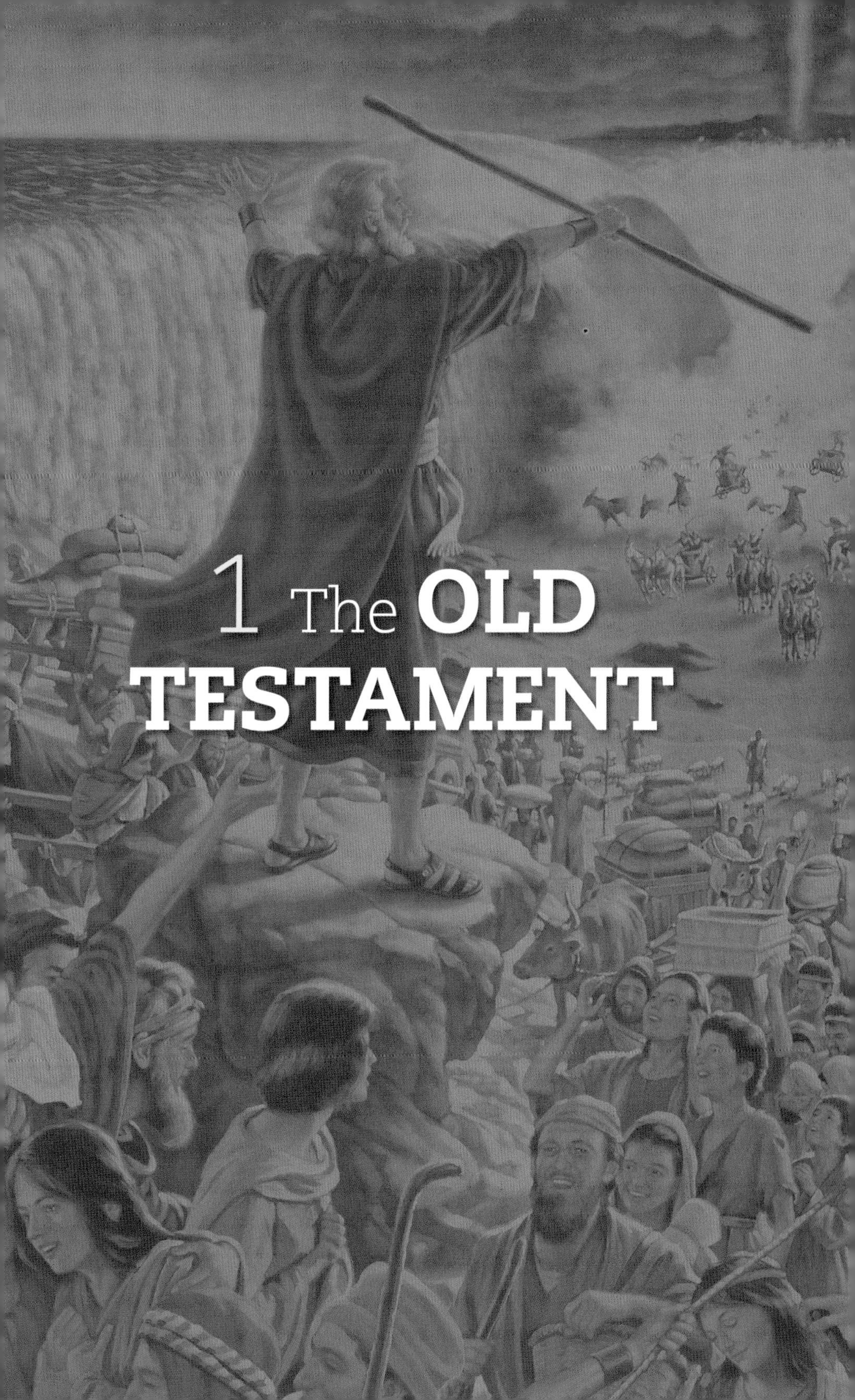

1 The OLD TESTAMENT

Into the Old Testament

What's a "testament"?

We use this term today in legal documents, as in "last will and testament." It means "agreement" or "covenant." The term *Old Testament* refers to the thirty-nine books of the Bible in which God revealed Himself and His will to His people before the Savior, Jesus Christ, was born. The term *New Testament* refers to the twenty-seven books of the Bible inspired by God after Jesus came. A third set of books were written during the time between the

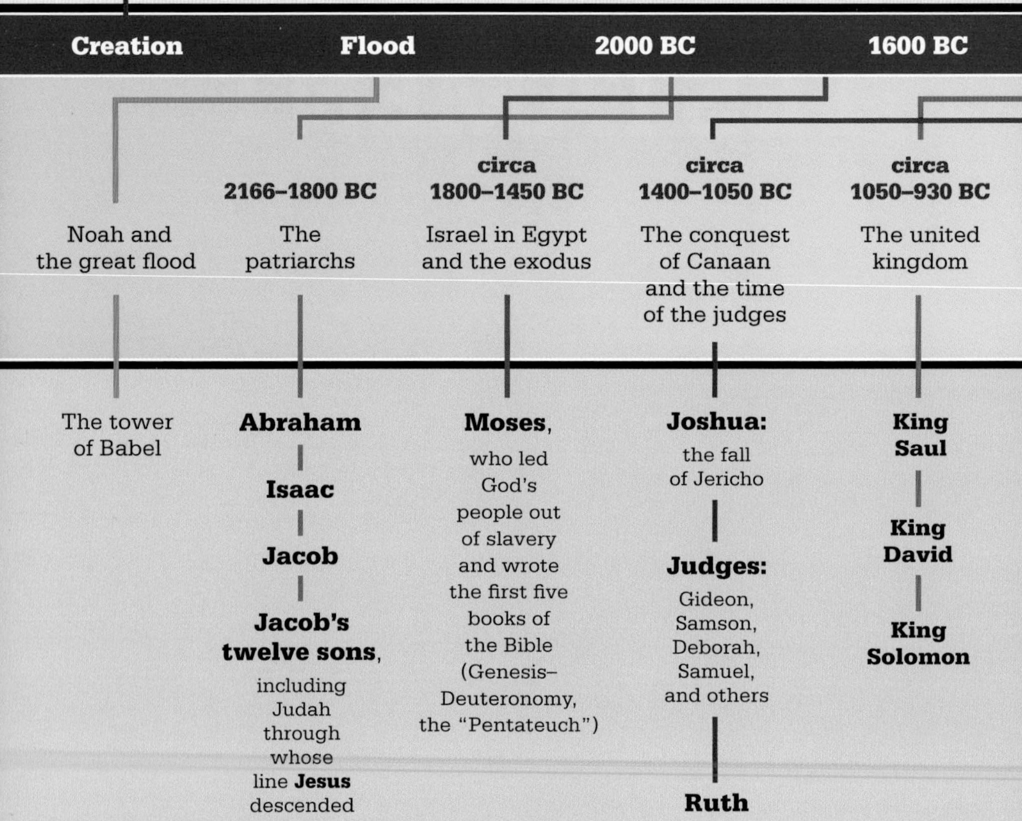

Old Testament and the New Testament. They are called "the Apocrypha." They are good to read and are included in some Bible translations. But they are not the same as the Holy Scriptures.

The Old Testament is sometimes also called "the Hebrew Scriptures" because Christians and Jewish believers both recognize the divine origin and authority of these books.

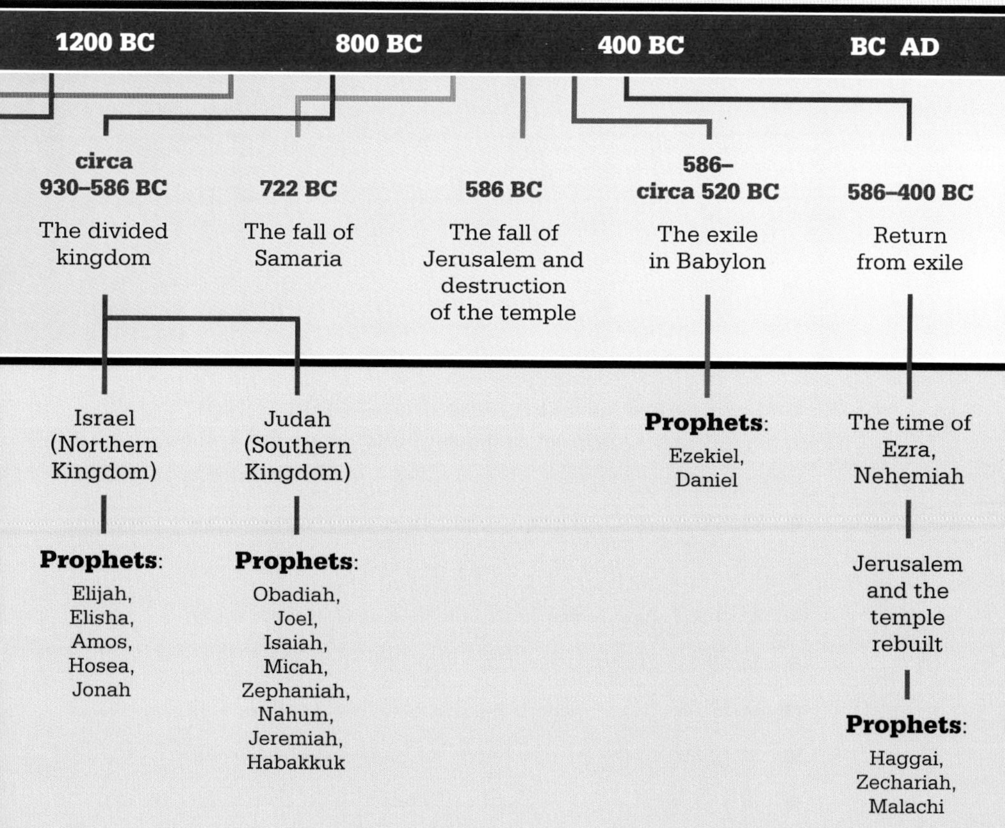

How did God reveal Himself in the Old Testament?

The more you read the Bible, the more you will understand how wonderful, majestic, powerful, holy, and magnificent God is. In fact, human beings cannot understand Him fully. We can't even come *close* to understanding Him!

Add to that the fact that human sin creates fear in our hearts. Not only can't we know God, we don't *want* to know Him! His holiness and power terrify us.

Still, despite our rebellion and disobedience, God keeps on loving us! He still wants us to belong forever in His family. And so, down through history, He's taken steps to make that possible. The Old Testament records the many ways He revealed Himself to human beings:

- In the creation, we see God's wisdom, power, and care. (See Genesis 1; 2; Psalm 19:1–6; 139:13–18.)
- In promising a Savior after Adam and Eve sinned, we see God's mercy and compassion. (See Genesis 3:15.)
- In choosing Abraham and promising to send the Savior ("Messiah") through Abraham's descendants, God shows us His grace, His undeserved love for sinners. (See Genesis 12; 15; 17.)
- In preserving the covenant people through whom He would enact His plan of salvation, God reveals His almighty power and fatherly care. (See especially the Books of Exodus, Joshua, 1 and 2 Chronicles, and Ezra, but all the books of the Old Testament underscore the hand of God at work in the history of His people.)
- God used various names in making Himself known, such as the seven redemptive names found below. God reveals His holiness, majesty, power, goodness, kindness, and grace by His names:
    - *YAHWEH–Yireh*—The Lord Our Provider (Genesis 22:13–14)
    - *YAHWEH–Rophe'*—The Lord Our Healer (Exodus 15:26)
    - *YAHWEH–Nissi*—The Lord Our Banner (Exodus 17:15)
    - *YAHWEH–Shalom*—The Lord Our Peace (Judges 6:24)
    - *YAHWEH–Ro'eh*—The Lord Our Shepherd (Psalm 23:1)
    - *YAHWEH–Tsidkenu*—The Lord Our Righteousness (Jeremiah 23:6)
    - *YAHWEH–Shammah*—The Lord Present with Us (Ezekiel 48:35)

The Mighty Tetragrammaton

It sounds like something out of a sci-fi novel: the Mighty Tetragrammaton! But actually, the term refers to God's Old Testament covenant name: the Lord.

Tetra means "four" in Greek. *Grammaton* refers to "letters," as in letters of the alphabet. *Tetragrammaton*, then, refers to a four-letter name that Bible translators render "YHWH," "Yahweh," or "Jehovah." In many Bibles, the tetragrammaton appears as "the Lord" (all capital letters). This is the covenant name God revealed to Moses on Mount Sinai (Exodus 3:14).

In Hebrew, this word comes from a verb. While we often think of this word as meaning "I AM," it could be translated "He causes to happen" or, more loosely, "the One Who Makes It So." When we read Exodus 34:4–7 and note all the mercy and goodness of God revealed there, we can see how the name came to imply "The One Who Makes the Good Thing Happen."

The *Yah* part of the tetragrammaton forms the first part of the Hebrew name *Joshua,* the Old Testament version of *Jesus*. So one could say that Jesus' name means "the One Who Makes Salvation Happen."

Look for the tetragrammaton as you read the Old Testament. It will add to the meaningfulness of the text as you remember what God says about Himself in His covenant name!

- In the Old Testament, God tied words of promise to physical objects (proto-sacraments) to strengthen the faith of His people. God revealed His care, kindness, and His understanding of His children's needs. (See, for example, the serpent on a pole in Numbers 21:6–9, the ceremony of circumcision in Genesis 17:10–11, and the Passover Seder in Exodus 12.)
- In sending the prophets by whom "the Word of the Lord came," God demonstrated His concern for all humanity and His heart's desire that sinners turn to Him for life and salvation. That phrase—"the Word of the Lord came"—occurs more than a hundred times in the Old Testament, particularly in the prophetic books. The Word came and came and kept on coming. It comes to us still today, changing hearts and lives.

God's self-revelation came most fully and perfectly in Jesus Christ, the God-man and Savior of the world:

> *Long ago, at many times and in many ways, God spoke to our fathers by the prophets, but* in these last days He has spoken to us by His Son, *whom He appointed the heir of all things, through whom also He created the world. [Jesus] is the radiance of the glory of God and the exact imprint of His nature, and He upholds the universe by the word of His power. After making purification for sins, He sat down at the right hand of the Majesty on high.*
>
> *Hebrews 1:1–3 (emphasis added)*

How does the Old Testament look forward to Jesus?

The reformer Martin Luther once called the Old Testament "the cradle for the Christ." We see Jesus throughout, from Genesis to Malachi:

- Jesus was present at the creation, participating fully in it. (See Genesis 1; 2; Proverbs 8:22–32; Colossians 1:15–17; Hebrews 1:1–3.)
- Jesus' work for our salvation is pictured in the Old Testament sacrifices, in the fixtures and arrangement of both the tabernacle and the temple, and even in the way the nation of Israel set up camp in the wilderness after the exodus. (See Exodus; Leviticus; 1 Kings; and 2 Chronicles 3–7.)
- The Lord sometimes appeared in a bodily form to walk across the pages of the Old Testament before the incarnation, or so many Bible scholars think. (See, for example, Joshua 5:13–15.)
- Jesus is the faithful, obedient child of God pictured in the Psalms, the only one who can confidently pray them. But because He has connected us to Himself through faith in His cross and empty tomb, the comfort God gives and the promises He makes to Jesus in the Psalms now belong to us!
- Jesus is the servant of the Lord, the true "Israel" described by Isaiah in chapters 42, 49, 50, and 53. (See also Galatians 6:16.)
- Jesus is pictured in the lives of several Old Testament believers. That picture is cloudy and incomplete, but it is there nonetheless. These people foreshadow His person and work. Abraham, David, and Joshua have all been called "types of Christ." The Bible itself compares Melchizedek to Jesus (see Genesis 14:18–20; Psalm 110:4; and Hebrews 7:1–17).

These are just some of the places we see Jesus in the Old Testament when we read the texts through the lens of our Christian faith. Look for Him as you study the text!

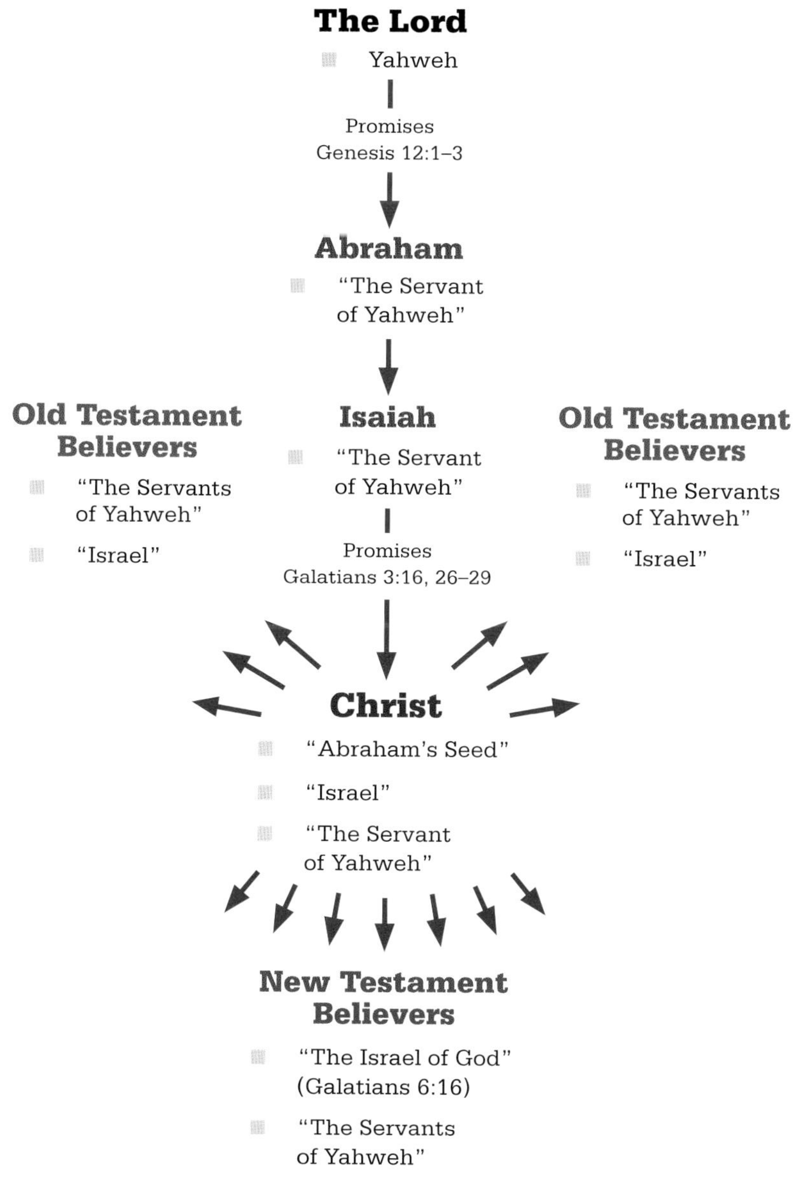

2 The Books of MOSES

Genesis

Exodus

Leviticus

Numbers

Deuteronomy

Genesis

Into Genesis

Genesis means "beginnings."
Theme: What it means to live by faith

©CPH

Who wrote Genesis?

Moses wrote Genesis as well as Exodus, Leviticus, Numbers, and Deuteronomy. Together, these five books are called "the Pentateuch"—*penta* meaning "five" and the entire word itself meaning, roughly, "five-volume book." More than thirty times in the Gospels[1] Jesus quotes the Pentateuch and credits Moses as its author. Other New Testament books also refer to Moses as the author of these books (see, for instance, Romans 10:5). Other rabbis and leaders in the Early Church attested to the Pentateuch's Mosaic authorship.

Genesis closes more than three hundred years before Moses was born. So how did Moses know what to write? God may have revealed it to him directly. Moses may have had records from faithful writers available to him (for example, "the book of the generations of Adam," Genesis 5:1). Or the Holy Spirit may have used the faithful testimony of His people as they passed the history of the human family down from parents to children, generation after generation. (Keep in mind that people in cultures without written records often memorize—word for word—material that would fill many pages if it were written out. Still today, children in some Islamic cultures succeed in memorizing the entire Qur'an!)

Whatever method the Holy Spirit chose to use as He inspired Moses to write, the resulting text is God's Word for us still today:

---

[1] The "Gospels"—Matthew, Mark, Luke, and John—are the four biographies of our Savior, Jesus Christ, included in the New Testament. See the introductions to the Gospels for more detail.

© Corel

All Scripture *is breathed out by God and profitable for teaching, for reproof, for correction, and for training in righteousness, that the man of God may be competent, equipped for every good work.*

(2 Timothy 3:16–17; emphasis added)

When was Genesis written? Why?

© Corel

The Bible doesn't plainly tell us when. But it seems likely that Moses wrote Genesis (and the other four books of the Pentateuch) after God rescued His people Israel from slavery in Egypt and while Israel wandered for forty years in the wilderness (ca. 1446–1406 BC).

If so, Genesis would have provided much encouragement to the nation as they struggled to understand their identity and their place in God's plan to save the world. They had been slaves in Egypt for nearly four hundred years! Think of what that would have done to the way they saw themselves and the way they saw their God.

And yet, Genesis assured Israel of their God-given destiny:

- They could trace their ancestry back to Adam and Eve, the world's first people and God's unique creation. In fact, their God had created the universe as a home for them!

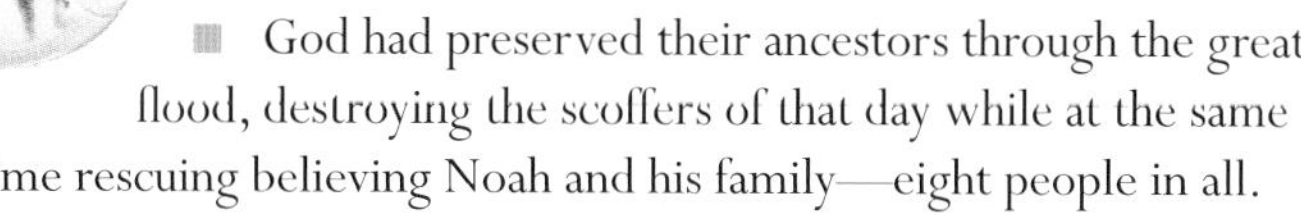

© Corel

- God had preserved their ancestors through the great flood, destroying the scoffers of that day while at the same time rescuing believing Noah and his family—eight people in all.
- They were children of Abraham, the patriarch to whom God spoke, revealing His plan to send the world's Savior through one of Abraham's descendants.
- The time of slavery in Egypt had not taken God by surprise; He had, in fact, told Abraham all about his descendants' enslavement and its duration in an unusual but amazingly exact vision (Genesis 15:12–20).

God's Family Tree

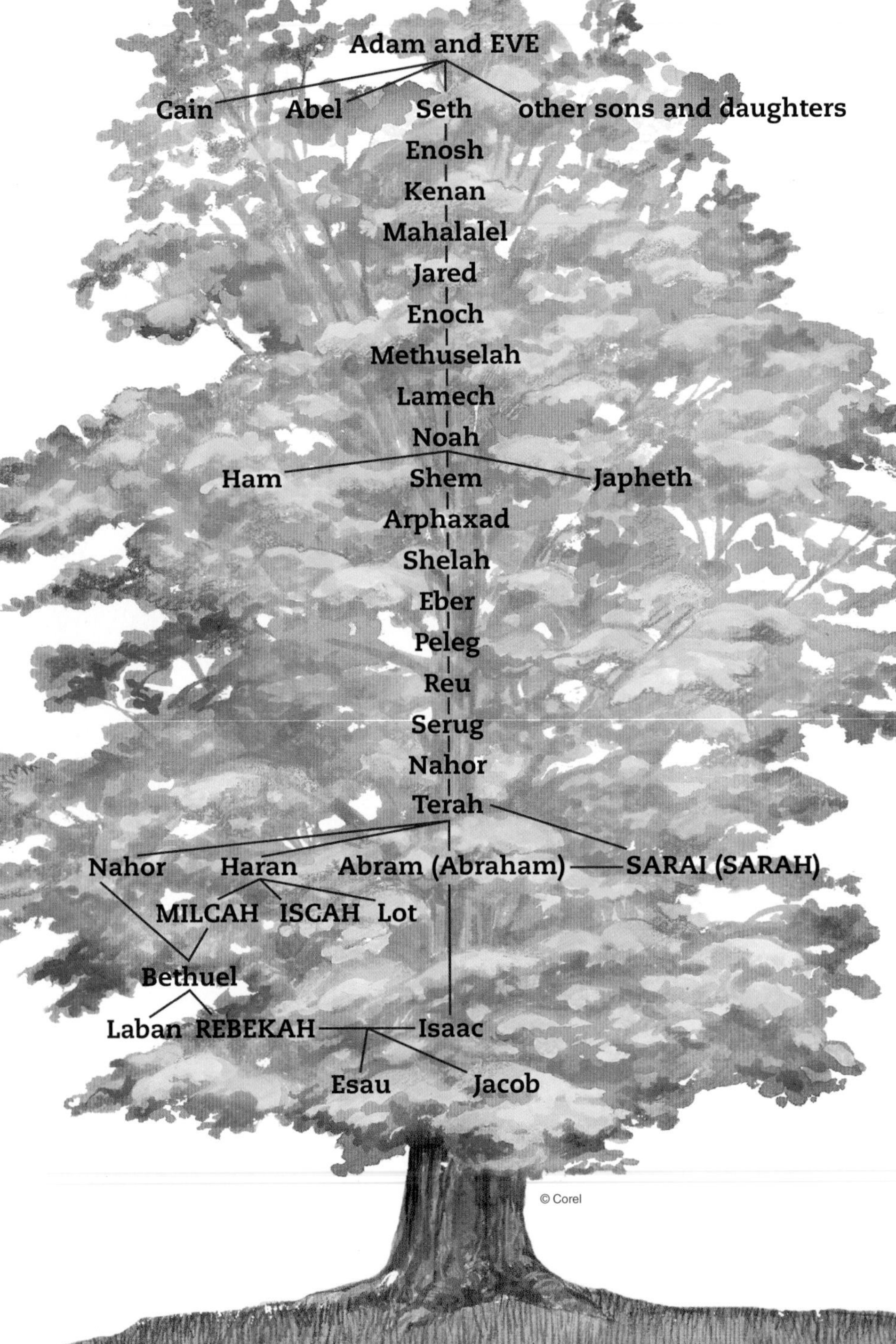

- Abraham, Isaac, Jacob, and their family had endured many hardships, but the Lord had delivered them out of every trouble. Just as He had guarded and protected the patriarchs, so He would guard and protect the nation of Israel that had now descended from them.

In the same way, Genesis assures God's people still today of His unchanging love for us. Despite our sins and failures, He forgives—just as He forgave Adam, Eve, Abraham, Sarah, Isaac, Rebekah, Jacob, Rachel, Tamar, and the other saints whose lives Genesis records. Just as God protected them, so still He guards, protects, warns, and cherishes us today.

How is Genesis classified?

Genesis is one of the Books of Moses in the Old Testament. Most of it is written as factual narrative and should be interpreted that way. However, it does include text that is obviously poetry; see, for example, the blessings Jacob pronounces on his sons in Genesis 49.

Noah's ark was shaped like a box or similar container. The word in Genesis for ark is the same word used for Moses' basket when, as a baby, he floated in the river.

"Make yourself an ark of gopher wood. Make rooms in the ark, and cover it inside and out with pitch."(Genesis 6:14)

Fascinating Facts about Noah's Ark

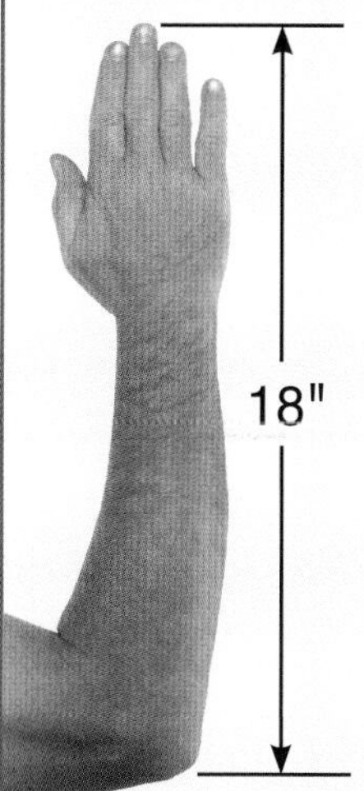

© CPH

How big was Noah's ark?

- 300 cubits long × 50 cubits wide × 30 cubits high **(Genesis 6:15)**

How long is a cubit?

A cubit is the length of a man's forearm, from fingertips to elbow, which is about 18 inches long. So, if a cubit roughly equals 18 inches, or 1 1/2 feet, Noah's ark was:

- 450 feet long × 75 feet wide × 45 feet high

That means **the deck of Noah's ark was 33,750 square feet!** That's larger than twelve tennis courts lined up side by side!

Did Noah's ark look like this?

© CPH

No! A boat shaped like this would never have survived over a year at sea!

> *The flood continued forty days on the earth. The waters increased and bore up the ark, and it rose high above the earth. The waters prevailed and increased greatly on the earth, and the ark floated on the face of the waters. And the waters prevailed so mightily on the earth that all the high mountains under the whole heaven were covered.*
>
> *(Genesis 7:17–19)*

© CPH

© Corel

Which animals did Noah take on the ark?

> *Take with you seven pairs of all clean animals, the male and his mate, and a pair of the animals that are not clean, the male and his mate, and seven pairs of the birds of the heavens also, male and female, to keep their offspring alive on the face of all the earth.*
>
> *(Genesis 7:2–3)*

Creatures that lived in the water didn't need to board the ark.

What are the key divisions of Genesis?

- **Genesis 1–11** The history of our world before the patriarchs. In these chapters, we read of the creation, the fall into sin, the great flood, and the tower of Babel. These chapters provide a quick overview of how our world came to be. They also explain that although in the beginning, God pronounced His creation "very good" (1:31), evil has invaded and is on the rampage. Sin, trouble, and death have marred the universe, and every human being bears some of the responsibility for this.
- **Genesis 12–50** The history of God's grace in working with sinful human beings to rescue us from our rebellion and the eternal death it brings. These chapters focus on the family of Abraham and how God gave him faith, nurtured that faith, and allowed him to pass that faith down to his children and his children's children. An especially important note in these chapters is God's ongoing promise that He would send a Savior through the family of Abraham, Isaac, Jacob, and Judah.

How does Genesis point to Jesus?

Genesis often points to Jesus! Here are a few examples:

- God's first promise to send a Savior[2] is found in Genesis (3:15).
- The animals God sacrificed to cover Adam and Eve's sin and shame foreshadow Jesus' death on Calvary (Genesis 3:21).
- The altars of sacrifice that dot Genesis point forward to the altar of Christ's cross, where God Himself would make the one, final, perfect Sacrifice for our sins (e.g., Genesis 8:20; 12:7; 13:18; 35:3).
- Melchizedek is a "type," or picture, of Christ, picturing Jesus as both King and Priest, bringing peace. (Compare Genesis 14:17–24 with Psalm 110 and Hebrews 7.)
- Abraham is a "type" of Christ as he prays for sinful Sodom (Genesis 18:22–33). He foreshadows Jesus, our great High Priest, interceding for us.
- Sometimes called "The Sacrifice of Isaac," Genesis 22 foreshadows the Savior's death for us. God commands that a ram die in Isaac's place. Thousands of years later, God the Father did what He would not ask Abraham to do—sacrifice His Son in atonement for sin.

---

[2] This is sometimes called the *protoevangel*, a word coming from the Greek language and meaning literally "first good news."

- Jesus appears to Jacob in a dream (Genesis 28:10–17) at a time of great sin and need in Jacob's life. Compare the text in Genesis with John 1:51. These two texts were the inspiration behind the American spiritual song "We Are Climbing Jacob's Ladder."
- Jesus' kingly role is foretold in Jacob's blessing of Judah (Genesis 49:8).
- Joseph's forgiveness of his brothers (Genesis 50:15–21) pictures Jesus' mercy on us.

What are the key chapters in Genesis?

- **Genesis 1–2** The creation of the universe.
- **Genesis 3** The first sin and the first promise of the Savior.
- **Genesis 6–11** The great flood and the escape God provided Noah.
- **Genesis 12** God calls Abram and brings him to faith.
- **Genesis 17** Circumcision is introduced as a sign of God's covenant. (This corresponds to the New Testament Sacrament of Baptism; compare Colossians 2:11–15.)
- **Genesis 22** The "sacrifice" of Isaac.
- **Genesis 41** Joseph's ascent to power in Egypt.
- **Genesis 46** Jacob's family comes to live in Egypt as guests of Pharaoh during a drought in the Promised Land.

In the Book of Genesis, we learn about Jacob, whose name was later changed to Israel (35:10). From his twelve sons—Reuben, Simeon, Levi,

Firsts in Genesis

- The creation (1:1–2:3)
- The first people (2:4–25)
- The sin (3:1–7)
- The first promise of a Savior (3:15)
- The first murder (4:1–15)
- The first city (4:17)
- The first agriculture (4:2)
- The first musical instruments (4:21)
- The first smelting of metals (4:22)
- The first polygamy (4:23)
- The first destruction of the world (6:9–8:22)
- The first rainbow (9:12–17)
- The first communication gap (11:1–9)
- The first family of faith . . . and how it grew (12:1–50:26)

Judah, Zebulun, Issachar, Dan, Gad, Asher, Naphtali, Joseph, and Benjamin—came the twelve tribes of Israel who dwelled in the Promised Land. Joshua 13–22 tells about the land assigned to each of the tribes. (The numbers below match the numbers of the chart on p. 19; to see where each tribe settled, see the map on p. 20.)

Twelve Sons—Twelve Tribes

1. Reuben

Reuben was Jacob's first son. His mother was Leah (Genesis 29:32). He was the firstborn of Jacob, and as such, he normally would have received the birthright. But his sin caused Jacob to give the birthright to his brother Judah instead (49:3–4). Reuben's tribe was linked with Gad's, and they occupied territory east of the Jordan River.

2. Simeon

Simeon was the second son of Jacob, and his mother was also Leah (Genesis 29:33). Simeon and his brother Levi took part in a cruel massacre of the men of Shechem for dishonoring their sister, Dinah. For that reason, Simeon and Levi both were denied blessing from their father (49:5–7). Simeon's territory lay south of Judah.

3. Levi

Levi was Jacob's third son, and his mother was Leah (Genesis 29:34). To Levi, no territory was given. His descendants became priests for the Israelites.

4. Judah

Judah was Jacob's fourth son, and his mother was Leah (Genesis 29:35). Of Judah, Jacob said, "Your brothers shall praise you; your hand shall be on the neck of your enemies; your father's sons shall bow down before you" (49:8). Most important about Judah is the fact that he is an ancestor of Jesus (Luke 3:33; Hebrews 7:14). His territory was in southern Canaan, to the west of the Dead Sea.

5. Dan

Dan was the fifth son of Jacob. His mother was Rachel's maidservant, Bilhah. His name may mean "to judge" because Rachel said of his birth, "God has judged me, and has also heard my voice and given me a son" (Genesis 30:6). He was blessed by his father, who said, "Dan shall judge his people as one of the tribes of Israel" (49:16). The small territory of Dan lay to the west of the tribe of Benjamin.

The World of the Patriarchs

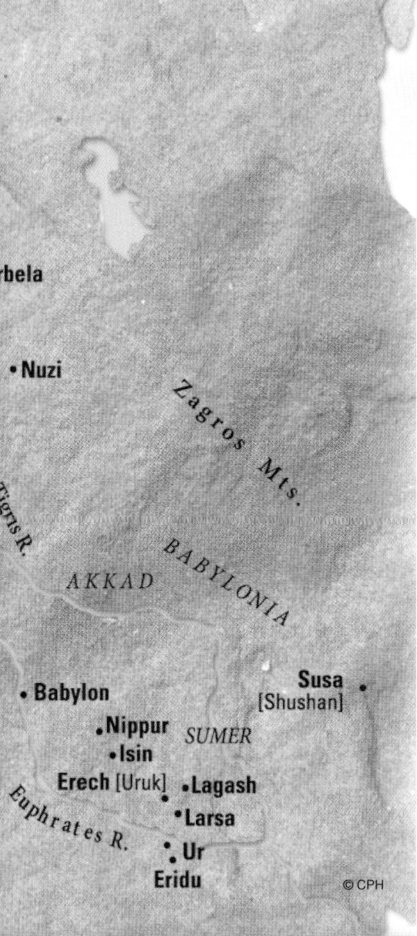

6. Naphtali

Naphtali was Jacob's sixth son. His mother was Rachel's maidservant, Bilhah (Genesis 30:7–8). Naphtali was blessed by his father, who said of him, "Naphtali is a doe let loose that bears beautiful fawns" (49:21). He would live a free and fruitful life. His large territory was farthest north in the land of Canaan.

7. Gad

Gad was Jacob's seventh son. His mother was Leah's maidservant, Zilpah. At his birth, Leah said, "Good fortune has come!" (Genesis 30:11), so she named him "Gad." The name *Gad* sounds like the Hebrew word for "good fortune." He was blessed by his father, who said of him, "Raiders shall raid Gad, but he shall raid at their heels" (49:19). Gad's territory was south of that of Manasseh to the north end of the Dead Sea.

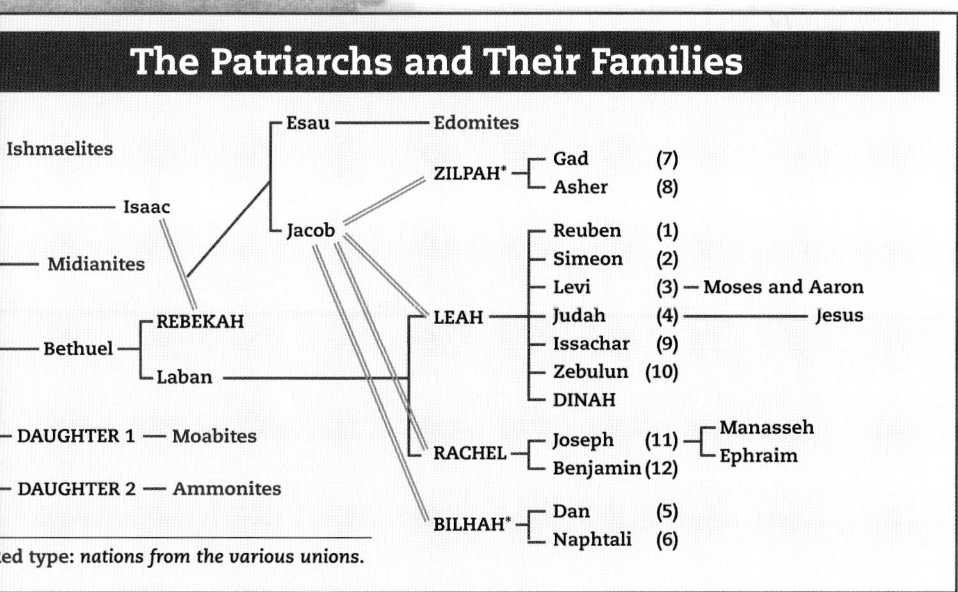

The Twelve Tribes in the Promised Land

The twelve sons of Jacob became great tribes of Israel and eventually settled in Canaan, as described in the Book of Joshua.

ARAM
ASHER
NAPHTALI
EAST MANASSEH
SEA OF KINNERETH
ZEBULUN
ISSACHAR
Jordan River
THE GREAT SEA
MANASSEH
EPHRAIM
GAD
DAN
BENJAMIN
AMMON
REUBEN
JUDAH
MOAB
SALT SEA
(DEAD SEA)
SIMEON
NEGEB
EDOM
EGYPT

8. Asher

Asher was the eighth son of Jacob. His mother was Zilpah, Leah's maidservant. Jacob blessed Asher on his deathbed, saying, "Asher's food shall be rich, and he shall yield royal delicacies" (Genesis 49:20). The territory of Asher was on the sea coast, north of Mount Carmel.

9. Issachar

Issachar was Jacob's ninth son. His mother was Leah (Genesis 30:14–18). Jacob blessed him by saying that "he bowed his shoulder to bear, and became a servant at forced labor" (49:15). His territory, south and west of the Sea of Galilee, was rich, fertile land. Issachar's descendants would work hard at farming and shepherding.

10. Zebulun

Zebulun was the tenth son of Jacob. His mother was Leah (Genesis 30:19–20). Jacob's blessing to Zebulun was that he would occupy a large piece of land in southern Galilee, between Asher and Naphtali (49:13).

11. Joseph

Joseph was the eleventh son of Jacob, and his mother was Rachel (Genesis 30:22–24). He was greatly blessed by his father, who called all sorts of blessings onto Joseph, saying, "May they be on the head of Joseph, and on the brow of him who was set apart from his brothers" (Genesis 49:26). Joseph had been sold into slavery to Egypt, falsely accused, and wrongly imprisoned before he finally became Pharaoh's governor who helped to rescue his own family from famine. There is no region on the map for Joseph. Instead, his sons, **Ephraim** and **Manasseh**, received large territories in Canaan.

12. Benjamin

Benjamin was the twelfth son of Jacob. His mother was Rachel. His name means "son of my right hand." Next to Joseph, he was Jacob's favorite son. Jacob later blessed Benjamin while on his deathbed, calling Benjamin "a ravenous wolf, in the morning devouring the prey and at evening dividing the spoil" (Genesis 49:27). Benjamin's territory, north and west from the Dead Sea, was directly north of the territory of Judah.

Tent Dwelling

In Abram's day, many people lived as nomads. They moved from place to place, living where their livestock and herds could eat, and then moving to a new place. Nomads might grow crops for a season or two, but then they would move on.

Because of their way of life as nomads, and because of the hot, dry climate, people in Abram's time lived in tents that could be packed up and moved, or sometimes they lived in caves. Canaan's limestone hillsides were full of natural caves that became refuges for shepherds and their flocks, as well as shelter for the poor and sick.

Nomads often lived in tents, which kept the inhabitants shaded from the sun, sheltered from the dust, and warmed in the desert's cold night air. Tent cloth was made from woven goat or camel hair.

Cave dwelling.

A goat hide.

Large Bedouin tents in Jordan.

Many preferred to use black goat hair for their tent cloth.

A small tent, no larger than a blanket, could become protection for a single individual for a night. Depending on their size, large tents could provide protection for a family, many families, or even a whole clan.

Inside the Tent

Because the tent cloth was so thick, the tent was cool and shady inside. In fact, it was sometimes so dark inside the tent that even during the day, lamps were needed.

On the floor, tent dwellers used mats and rugs made from goats' hair. How wealthy or poor a family was would determine how many and how fancy these rugs were.

During the day, the rugs would often be rolled up and placed around the walls of the tent. These then could become couches to sit on.

Learning more about Abram's way of life helps us to understand parts of the Bible that compare our bodies to tents. St. Paul writes in 2 Corinthians 5:1: "For we know that if the tent that is our earthly home is destroyed, we have a building from God, a house not made with hands, eternal in the heavens." Like Abram, we have temporary homes here on earth. Our permanent home is in heaven with our Savior, Jesus.

Small Bedouin tents.

Special Names

In Israelite culture, the name of a person represented the character, or essence, of the person. The giving of the name was more than just giving a child a label. It was an occasion for giving a blessing as well. The names given to certain Old Testament people and places were important, especially the new names given by God after a significant event.

Abram means "exalted father." God changed it to *Abraham* as a sign of the covenant God made with him, promising that Abraham would be the "father of many nations." Abraham's wife's name was changed from *Sarai* to *Sarah*. After the wrestling match at Jabbok, God gave Jacob (a name meaning "He who grabs by the heel") the new name of *Israel* (meaning "He who struggles with God and wins").

The patriarchs set up altars of stone as places to worship God and remember His divine presence and protection on a specific occasion. Some of those special places were also given new symbolic names. For example, the place where Jacob had his dream (Genesis 28) was renamed *Bethel*, which means "house of God." Jacob called the place where he wrestled with the divine stranger *Peniel*, or "face of God," acknowledging that God had been there and that Jacob had seen Him face-to-face. During the struggle, Jacob (Israel) asked the stranger to tell His name, but the stranger refused. Jacob came away from that wrestling match with a blessing, but God did not reveal His name.

God would later reveal His name to Moses only as "I AM" (Exodus 3:14). Israel pronounced the name "Yahweh." This was the name by which He wanted to be known and worshiped by the people of Israel because it expressed His character as dependable and faithful.

Exodus

Into Exodus

Exodus means "going out" or "departure."
Theme: What it means to have a God and worship Him

Who wrote Exodus?

Moses wrote Exodus, as well as Genesis, Leviticus, Numbers, and Deuteronomy. For more information, see "Who wrote Genesis?" (p. 2).

When was Exodus written? Why?

Moses likely wrote Exodus after God rescued His people Israel from slavery in Egypt and while Israel wandered for forty years in the wilderness (ca. 1446–1406 BC).

Exodus records the rescue of God's people from slavery in Egypt. Hearing this book read aloud for the first time would have reminded Israel of all that God, in mercy, had done for them. In addition, the Book of Exodus served as a permanent record of the covenant of God made with Israel after their rescue and of the obligation it imposed to obey Him in return:

> *You yourselves have seen what I did to the Egyptians, and how I bore you on eagles' wings and brought you to Myself. Now therefore, if you will indeed obey My voice and keep My covenant, you shall be My treasured possession among all peoples, for all the earth is Mine; and you shall be to Me a kingdom of priests and a holy nation.*
> *(Exodus 19:4–6)*

This covenant is a key feature of Exodus. God made this covenant with Israel while the nation camped at the foot of Mount Sinai. (They spent a year there after their escape from Egypt.)

The New Testament sharply contrasts the covenant God made with Abraham—a covenant of pure grace, accessed by faith—and the covenant of Sinai—a covenant of the Law, demanding obedience:

> *The law was given through Moses; grace and truth came through Jesus Christ.* (John 1:17)

> *For all who rely on works of the law are under a curse; for it is written, "Cursed be everyone who does not abide by all things written in the Book of the Law, and do them." Now it is evident that no one is justified before God by the law, for "The righteous shall live by faith." But the law is not of faith, rather "The one who does them shall live by them." Christ redeemed us from the curse of the law by becoming a curse for us—for it is written, "Cursed is everyone who is hanged on a tree"—so that in Christ Jesus the blessing of Abraham might come to the Gentiles, so that we might receive the promised Spirit through faith.* (Galatians 3:10–14)

The New Testament book of Galatians, especially chapters 3 and 4, tells us why God gave the covenant of Sinai: to help the people mature and to prove to His people that they could not obey so that they would cling in faith to the coming Savior, the One who could and would obey the Law of God in their place and then die the death they deserved because of their sins. The Law does that same thing for God's people today. It shows us our sin and our need for the Savior.

Exodus includes much Law. But the Gospel shines from its pages too.

How is Exodus classified?

Exodus is one of the Books of Moses in the Old Testament. Most of it is written as factual narrative and should be interpreted that way.

Even so, Exodus does contain sections of poetry, Exodus 15 most notable among them. This "Song of Moses" appears again in Revelation 15. We will likely sing it in heaven, forever!

What are the key divisions of Exodus?

In Exodus, Moses records both the birth of the nation of Israel and her marriage to the Lord. (Later on, the prophet Ezekiel would summarize the entire Book of Exodus in just 14 verses. See Ezekiel 16:1–14.)

- **Exodus 1–6** Moses' birth and his call to lead God's people.
- **Exodus 7–13** The conflict between Egypt's ruler, Pharaoh, and God Himself, as God demands that Pharaoh release His people; the ten plagues and the first Passover.

- **Exodus 14–15** Israel's release from slavery; the miracle at the Red Sea, and their joy in the Lord's rescue.
- **Exodus 16–18** God works miracles to preserve His people early in their wilderness experience.
- **Exodus 19** A preface of grace—a preamble—to the covenant of Sinai.
- **Exodus 20** The Ten Commandments.
- **Exodus 21–24** An explanation of the Law with examples.
- **Exodus 25–31** God commands His nation to build the tabernacle, including descriptions of its furnishings, and duties of the priests who would serve there. These would be necessary because the people would find perfect obedience to the Law (chapters 20–24), even outward obedience to the Law, impossible. Sacrifice was necessary, and so the tabernacle became a place of sacrifice, which pointed forward to the sacrifice Jesus would offer at the cross.
- **Exodus 32–34** Israel's disobedience: the golden calf; God's amazing grace: He pardons their sin.
- **Exodus 35–40** Construction of the tabernacle and ordination of the priests.

How does Exodus point to Jesus?

In many ways Exodus points forward to Jesus! Here are a few examples:

- Moses is a "type," or picture, of Christ, pleading the people's case before both Pharaoh (Exodus 7–13) and God (32–34).
- Aaron, the high priest, represents Jesus in His service as our High Priest.
- Jesus is the Passover Lamb (Exodus 12; John 1:29), the final, perfect Sacrifice for our sins.
- The manna that fell from heaven, sustaining Israel throughout their journey through the wilderness (Exodus 16:1–5), represents Jesus, the Bread of Life (John 6:35).
- The apostle Paul compares the rock in Exodus 17:1–7 with Christ (1 Corinthians 10:1–4). See also John 7:37.

Moses	Jesus
Spared in infancy when king ordered baby boys killed. Exodus 2:1–10	**Spared in infancy when king ordered baby boys killed.** Matthew 2:1–18
Rescued by an Egyptian princess. Exodus 2:5–10	**Taken to Egypt to escape Herod.** Matthew 2:13–16
Crossed Red Sea and spent forty years in desert.	**Baptized in the Jordan River and spent forty days in desert.** Matthew 4:2
Sent by God. Exodus 3	**Sent by the Father.** John 17:3, 21
His own people did not recognize and welcome him as rescuer. Exodus 2:14	**His own people did not recognize Him.** John 1:10
Willing to give up his life for his people. Exodus 32:32	**Gave up His life for His people.** Hebrews 9:14, John 3:16
Received the Ten Commandments. Exodus 20	**Kept all the commandments.** John 8:29
Faithful as a servant in God's house. Hebrews 3:5	**Faithful as a Son over God's house.** Hebrews 3:6
Primary character in the Book of Exodus—God's rescue and call of His people.	**Completion of what the Book of Exodus is all about—God's rescue and call of His people.**

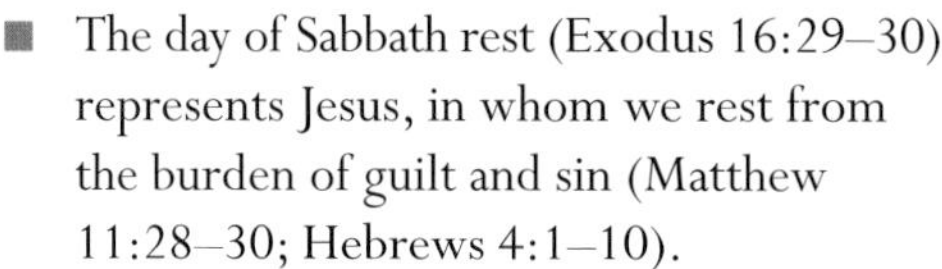

- The day of Sabbath rest (Exodus 16:29–30) represents Jesus, in whom we rest from the burden of guilt and sin (Matthew 11:28–30; Hebrews 4:1–10).
- Jesus is the Mercy Seat described in Exodus 37:6; we run there to find hope, pardon, and help in every time of need. (See also Hebrews 4:16.)
- Jesus is the light of the world, depicted by the lampstand in the tabernacle (Exodus 37:17–24; John 8:12).
- Jesus sacrificed Himself on the altar of the cross, which corresponds to the altar of burnt offering (Exodus 38:1–7).

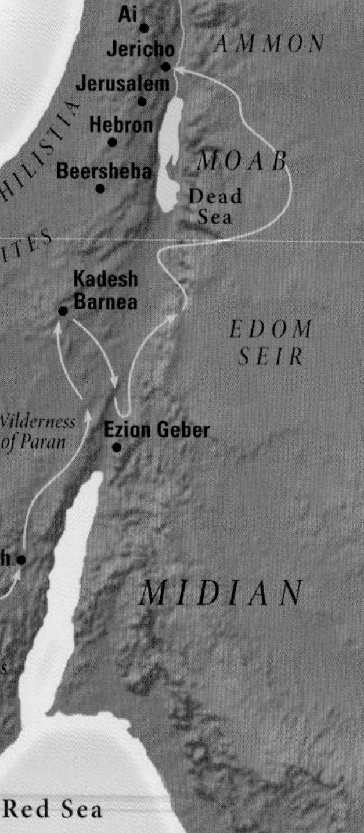

What are the key chapters in Exodus?

- **Exodus 3** The burning bush and God's call of Moses.
- **Exodus 7–11** The ten plagues precede the exodus.
- **Exodus 14** Israel crosses the Red Sea.
- **Exodus 20** God gives the Ten Commandments.
- **Exodus 32** The golden calf and Israel fall into idol worship.
- **Exodus 40** The tabernacle is completed, and God's glory settles there to live among His people.

Ancient Egypt

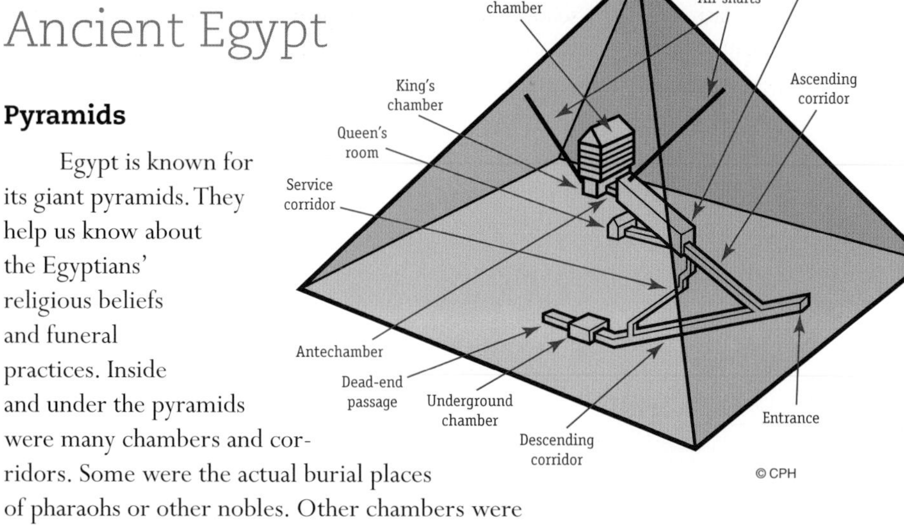

Pyramids

Egypt is known for its giant pyramids. They help us know about the Egyptians' religious beliefs and funeral practices. Inside and under the pyramids were many chambers and corridors. Some were the actual burial places of pharaohs or other nobles. Other chambers were galleries or chapels.

Most historians think the pyramids were built by the Egyptians, though it is not known for certain *how* they were built. It has been suggested that they used ramps, ropes, and many, many people to build the massive structures.

Religion

Ancient Egyptians were *polytheistic* (POL-ee-thee-IS-tik), which means they worshiped many gods and goddesses. They bowed down before the sun, the moon, and even their own pharaohs.

Mummies

Egypt is known for its mummies. The mummification process was used to keep bodies from decaying after burial. The process was long and complicated. The body organs were removed. The body was put in mineral salts for seventy days. Then the body was wrapped in linen strips for burial. As a result, mummified bodies have been found with the face, hair, and eyelashes intact thousands of years later.

Hieroglyphics

Egyptians communicated through picture words known as *hieroglyphics*. Each picture, or hieroglyph, stood for a word or idea. Scribes were the few people in Egypt who could read and write. They mastered hieroglyphics and also learned *hieratics*, a kind of cursive writing. Later, a simpler form of writing developed, called *demotic*.

© Vladimir Korostyshevskiy/Shutterstock, Inc.

For many years, scholars knew that hieroglyphics and demotic script were types of written communication, but they could not decipher the languages. Then, in 1799, a black, four-foot-tall stone inscribed with writing in three languages (hieroglyphics, demotic, and Greek) was found in the mud near a town called Rosetta. The Rosetta Stone was the key scholars used to translate these languages for the first time.

Have you ever wanted to see your name in hieroglyphics? Search for a Web site that translates English letters into hieroglyphics.

What did ancient Egyptians eat?

© CPH

Egyptians at the time of Joseph ate a variety of different foods. Wheat and barley, grown along the Nile River, were ground into flour and baked into bread.

Herds of cattle provided meat and milk. (They also carried heavy loads and did other difficult work.) Other sources of meat were goats, sheep, geese, and ducks. Nobles, who were wealthier people, ate gazelle and antelope. Some wild birds were captured by net and eaten; others were kept to provide Egyptians with eggs. The poorest Egyptians ate fish. However, their religious beliefs forced them to avoid certain types of fish.

Egyptians enjoyed a variety of fruits and vegetables. They ate cucumbers, beets, sweet onions, radishes, turnips, and garlic. They also enjoyed lettuce, chickpeas, beans, lentils, and peas. They ate figs, grapes, raisins, plums, dates, and watermelon.

What did ancient Egyptians drink?

Egyptians drank beer sweetened with honey, dates, or fruit juices. Most families brewed beer in their kitchen by baking a loaf of bread and then soaking it in water to allow it to ferment. After a period of time, this would become beer. Egyptians also enjoyed red wine made from fermented palm sap or grapes.

Did Egyptians like sweets?

The typical Egyptian had a sweet tooth, just like many modern people. The Egyptians sweetened their beer and wine. They made a honey-based candy flavored with the thick, sticky sap from marshmallow plants, which grow in salt marshes. This plant was the source of marshmallow candy until the mid-nineteenth century.

Egyptians also enjoyed licorice. The root was sometimes chewed as a special sweet treat, but it was also used as a medicine.

A supply of licorice root was found in the tomb of the boy king, Tutankhamen (you might know him as "King Tut").

© Gordana Sermek/Shutterstock, Inc.

The Ten Plagues

"Let My people go!" This is what God demanded of Pharaoh through Moses. But Pharaoh's heart was hardened. He refused to release the Israelites from slavery. Because of Pharaoh's hardened heart, God demonstrated His almighty power by sending the plagues to Egypt so that people would know and believe in Him.

The Plague of Water Turned to Blood (Exodus 7:14–24)

When Pharaoh first refused to release the Israelites, God told Moses to strike the Nile with his staff. When he did, the water in the Nile River turned into blood. God told Moses that Aaron should stretch his hand across all of the water in Egypt, and all of the other water turned to blood too. There was no water to drink anywhere. The fish died, and the smell was awful. But Pharaoh's magicians then did the same thing, using evil or ungodly magic or probably a trick, so Pharaoh went back into his palace and ignored them all.

© CPH

The Plague of Frogs (Exodus 7:25–8:15)

Frogs, frogs, frogs everywhere! When Pharaoh again said no to God's demand a week later, Aaron raised his staff, and frogs came to Egypt from everywhere. There were frogs in the palace, frogs in homes, frogs in the kitchen, even frogs in beds. No one could take a step without stepping on frogs. But Pharaoh's magicians could also make frogs appear. Then Pharaoh asked Moses to get rid of the frogs, promising that if he did, Pharaoh would let the Israelites leave. The Lord answered Moses' cries and the frogs died. They smelled bad! But when they were gone, Pharaoh hardened his heart, and the Israelites remained in Egypt.

© Nikolay Stefanov Dimitrov/Shutterstock, Inc.

© Shutterstock, Inc.

The Plague of Gnats (Exodus 8:16–19)

Gnats are tiny flies. They cluster around the eyes, ears, and mouths of people and animals. They buzz in ears. They are real pests. When Aaron struck the ground, the dust turned to millions and millions of gnats. The air was so full of them that it was hard to breathe. Pharaoh's magicians could not make gnats appear. They said, "This is God's work!" But Pharaoh still would not listen.

The Plague of Flies (Exodus 8:20–32)

After the gnats went away, the flies came—big flies, little flies, just like the flies that disrupt a picnic. But there were so many! There were as many flies as there had been gnats. But the flies only came to Egypt. There were no flies in Goshen, where the Israelites lived. Pharaoh promised to let the Israelites go if Moses made the flies go away. Moses prayed, and the flies left. But Pharaoh changed his mind again, and the Israelites had to stay.

The Plague on Livestock (Exodus 9:1–7)

Egypt and Goshen were filled with livestock—cattle, sheep, goats, camels, horses, and donkeys—because the people raised them for food and clothing and used them for work. When Pharaoh refused again to let God's people go, all of the Egyptians' livestock died. But the Israelites' livestock lived. And yet, Pharaoh still would not let the Israelites go.

The Plague of Boils (Exodus 9:8–12)

Boils are another name for ugly, open sores on the skin. God told Moses to throw soot from the furnace into the air near Pharaoh. The soot settled on all of the Egyptians, both people and animals, and their skin broke out with boils. The magicians were too sick to try to do this as a trick. But the Israelites didn't get sores. Still, Pharaoh did not let the people go.

The Plague of Hail (Exodus 9:13–35)

When Moses told Pharaoh that God would send a hailstorm, some of Pharaoh's servants listened to Moses' warning to bring their livestock and slaves in from the fields. When the storm came, it was worse than any storm that had ever been in Egypt before. There has never been such a storm since. Any slaves or livestock left in the fields were killed. The Egyptians' crops of flax and barley were ruined. But no hail fell in Goshen. Pharaoh confessed his sin against God and promised to let the people go if Moses prayed for the storm to stop. Moses prayed. The storm stopped. But then Pharaoh hardened his heart, and the Israelites remained slaves.

© Olga Bogatyrenko/Shutterstock, Inc.

The Plague of Locusts (Exodus 10:1–20)

When Moses said the locusts would come, Pharaoh's servants begged him to listen to God. Pharaoh said only the Hebrew men could leave Egypt. The locusts came. Locusts were everywhere. Locusts ate every green thing that had survived the hailstorm. Locusts covered all of Egypt—except Goshen, where God's people were. Goshen had no locusts. Again Pharaoh begged, so Moses prayed, and the locusts went away. And again Pharaoh hardened his heart, and the Israelites were still slaves.

The Plague of Darkness (Exodus 10:21–29)

Pharaoh still refused to listen to Moses, so for three days, darkness covered the land of Egypt. There was no sun, no stars, no moon—nothing! But the Israelites had light. God was with them. Pharaoh told Moses that the people could go if the animals stayed behind. When Moses insisted the animals come, too, Pharaoh threatened to kill Moses if he ever saw him again.

© CPH

The Plague of Death of the Firstborn (Exodus 11:1–10)

God instructed Moses to tell Pharaoh of one last plague on Egypt. The Israelites were to ask their neighbors for silver and gold and prepare to leave, because this would be the plague to convince Pharaoh to release the Israelites from slavery. Moses told Pharaoh that at about midnight, God would move through Egypt, and every firstborn male would die, and the firstborn of the cattle would die too. By now, many Egyptian people regarded Moses as a great man, but Pharaoh remained stubborn. Even the threat of this great horror did not move him—but the plague itself did. God's people were set free.

Passover

God commanded the Israelites to celebrate the Passover each year for generations to come. God wanted His people to remember how He delivered them from their slavery to the Egyptians. God also intended the Passover to point ahead to—or foreshadow—the perfect Lamb of God, who would sacrifice His life to deliver all people from slavery to sin and death: Jesus.

© CPH

The Passover Table

A place is set for each person. An extra place is set for Elijah. This symbolizes the return of Elijah to proclaim the coming of the Savior predicted in Malachi 4:5. Jesus called John the Baptist the "Elijah who is to come" (Matthew 11:14) to prepare His way.

The Foods of Passover and Their Significance

The Seder plate was not used in the original Passover celebration, but it is used today.

A roasted egg reminds the people of the sacrifices brought to the temple.

A roasted shank bone of lamb symbolizes the perfect lamb sacrificed and eaten by the Israelites before they left Egypt.

Charoset, a mixture of chopped apple, nuts, cinnamon, and wine, symbolizes mortar. When they were slaves in Egypt, the Israelites used bricks and mortar to build for Pharaoh.

Maror is a bitter herb, like horseradish. The bitterness reminds the people of their difficult lives as slaves. Our lives of sin also leave a bitter taste.

Parsley is dipped twice in salted water. The first dipping represents the tears shed during slavery. The second dipping represents the drowning of the Egyptian army in the Red Sea.

The sixth place on the Seder plate gives the appearance of the Star of David. It can be filled with red horseradish.

© Shutterstock, Inc.

Matzo Bread

Matzo (or Matzoh) is bread made without yeast.

Christians see much symbolism in this traditional Passover bread. Three pieces of matzo are folded inside a napkin. The three pieces of matzo might represent the Trinity—Father, Son, and Holy Spirit. The middle matzo is broken in half. One half is placed back in the napkin; the other half is hidden, just as Jesus was broken on the cross and hidden in the tomb.

First, each person eats horseradish spread on matzo; then, they eat charoset spread on matzo. Later, the children find the hidden piece of matzo, called the *afikomen*, and each family member is given a piece to eat.

It is at this point in the ritual that Jesus probably instituted the Lord's Supper by saying, "This is My body, which is given for you" (Luke 22:19).

The Cups of Passover

During the Passover ritual, four cups of wine are used.

Cup of Sanctification: As the participants drink from the cup, they are setting apart this special celebration to the Lord.

Cup of Plagues: As the participants drink from the second cup, they thank God for deliverance from the plagues. Christian Jews thank God for deliverance from the plague of sin.

Cup of Redemption: God's people remember with this cup that they were brought out of slavery by the blood of the perfect lamb. We were bought out of a life of slavery to sin and death by the blood of Jesus.

At the Last Supper, Jesus used one of the cups of wine—perhaps this third cup—to institute Holy Communion. "Drink of it, all of you; this cup is the new testament in My blood, which is shed for you for the forgiveness of sins. (Luther's Small Catechism, The Sacrament of the Altar).

Cup of Praise: As they drink this last cup of wine, those present praise God that they are His people. Jesus taught that His disciples would celebrate this meal anew with Him in His Father's Kingdom (Matthew 26:29), therefore, the Passover and the Lord's Supper always point Christians to the coming of Jesus and His promise of everlasting life.

The Four Questions of Passover

During Passover the youngest child asks the father four questions that explain why Passover is celebrated. The account of the first Passover is also read from Exodus 12.

The Tabernacle

The Garden of Eden was the perfect place for humans to live. Plants and animals abounded in glorious array. After the fall of humankind into sin, God desired to stay close to His people in order to show them His mercy. We have learned that through the lives of the patriarchs—Abraham, Isaac, and Jacob—God's plan of salvation is revealed more and more.

Aaron the Priest

In the exodus from Egypt, Moses became God's spokesperson to the people of Israel in conjunction with his brother, Aaron. Aaron became the first high priest, who interceded for the people at the tabernacle. Aaron pleaded with God for mercy, and God delivered His grace to the people. However, God did not communicate His message with words alone. He instructed Moses to build a tabernacle, a place where He would dwell in the middle of His chosen people.

© Hugh Claycombe

Sacrifices for Sin

When Adam and Eve sinned, God clothed them in animal skins—the first sacrifice for sin. At the east entrance to the tabernacle, there was a massive bronze altar that was used for animal sacrifice, burnt offerings, and grain offerings. The animals that died on the altar at the tabernacle were a vivid reminder that sin has a price: death.

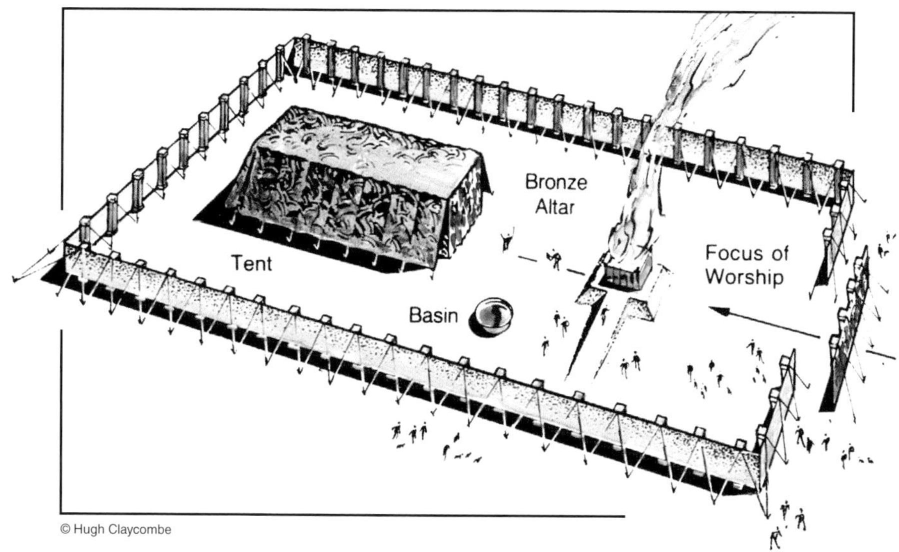

© Hugh Claycombe

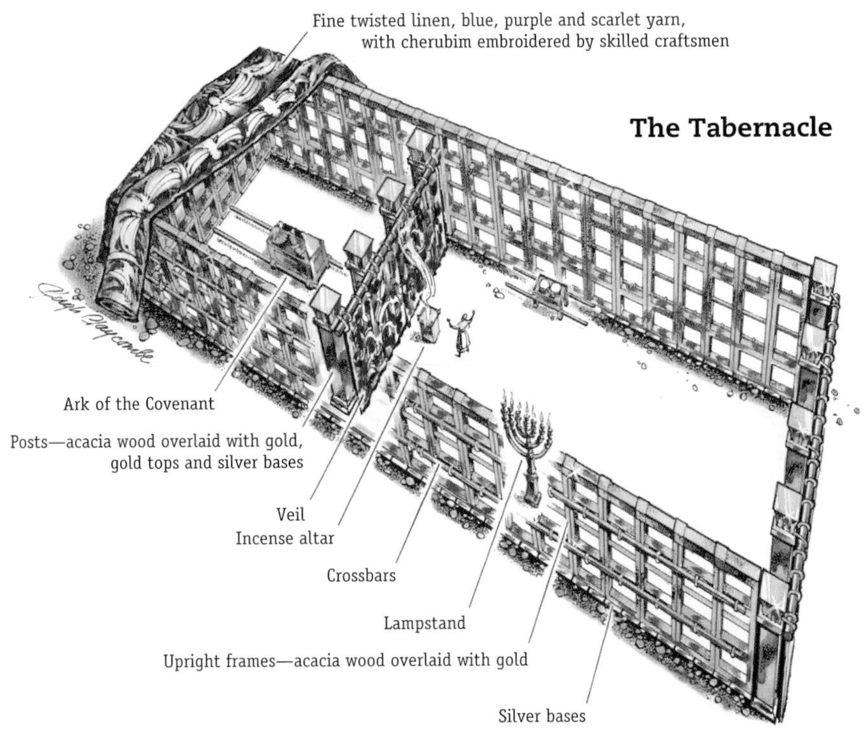

A Picture of Heaven

We read in Exodus that the tabernacle was richly appointed with gold and silver pillars (Exodus 26, 36), utensils, and lampstands engraved with almond blossoms (Exodus 25–26; 36–38). Curtains of luxurious red, blue, and purple cloth (Exodus 26) were woven with designs of *cherubim*—angels of the Lord. The priests wore splendid pure gold in their headdresses and robes, which were bordered with pomegranates and gold bells (Exodus 28:33; 39:24–25). The pomegranate and almond blossom are symbols of heaven to this day. There was a gold altar in front of the ark of the testimony where sweet-smelling incense was burned. All this added up to provide a picture of heaven on earth.

The people gladly gave their precious metals to the building project so that the tabernacle would be visible proof of God's grace among them. Moses built the tabernacle and everything in it exactly according to the Lord's instructions. God intended it to be a reflection of heaven.

God is a God of order. He has a precise plan to save us. His Son, Jesus, came to earth to dwell with us as true man and true God. The tabernacle where God located Himself among the Israelites, the priests who interceded for the people, the incense, and the animal sacrifices all pointed to the perfect sacrifice on Calvary. Jesus is that sacrifice that leads all believers to heaven.

Redemption of the Firstborn

The redemption of the firstborn was the second ritual performed for firstborn Jewish baby boys. It followed circumcision on the eighth day of the child's life. The redemption of the firstborn took place about a month after birth. In the ceremony, the father presented his newborn son to the priest. The father gave five silver coins to symbolically redeem, or buy back, the baby. In biblical times, the price paid was five silver shekels.

© CPH

Redeeming the firstborn was done in obedience to the command God gave after He brought the Israelites out of Egypt. In the Passover, the Lord destroyed all the firstborn sons in Egypt, but passed over the homes of the Israelites who had obeyed God's command and sprinkled lamb's blood on their doorposts. To remember this event, God ordered the Israelites: "Consecrate to Me all the firstborn. Whatever is the first to open the womb among the people of Israel, both of man and of beast, is Mine" (Exodus 13:2).

Mary also was required to make a sacrifice for her purification after childbirth. This sacrifice was made forty days after giving birth. In Luke 2:22–40, it is evident that Mary and Joseph performed both of these rituals during the same trip to Jerusalem.

Through the ritual of redemption, firstborn sons were thus sanctified (that is, set apart as holy) as belonging to God. From the exodus, God desired that the firstborn males of Israel would serve Him as priests. However, God later chose the tribe of Levi over the firstborn for this sacred role (Numbers 8:14–18). Even though firstborn sons are no longer obligated to serve as priests, according to Jewish custom, the firstborn sons of Israel hold a very special place in the family, including receiving extra responsibilities for the preservation of the family and its property.

> *Everything that opens the womb of all flesh, whether man or beast, which they offer to the* Lord, *shall be yours. Nevertheless, the firstborn of man you shall redeem, and the firstborn of unclean animals you shall redeem. And their redemption price (at a month old you shall redeem them) you shall fix at five shekels in silver, according to the shekel of the sanctuary, which is twenty gerahs. (Numbers 18:15–16)*

© CPH/Phil Howe and Cheri Bladholm

So what is "holiness"?

On a very simple, surface level, *holy* means "sinless and hating sin." But as we study Scripture, we see that its meaning goes much deeper. Holiness is a characteristic of God Himself. "Holy" people and "holy" things were set aside as God's own possessions, dedicated for His glory. So, for instance, the innermost room of the tabernacle was the "Most Holy Place." Outward from there, like a series of ever-larger rings of decreasing holiness, lay the following:

- the Holy Place
- the tabernacle court
- the camp of the Levites
- the camp of Israel's other tribes
- the nations outside Israel

This arrangement spoke Law in a graphic way to the hearts of sinners. It pointed out the terrible dangers of sin and what God's wrath over human sin means for us!

In Isaiah 6, for example, the prophet finds himself suddenly caught up into God's presence. Isaiah sees the Lord's holiness and his own sinfulness. Terror floods his heart! He exclaims, in essence, "I'm a dead man! Woe to me, for my eyes have seen the King, the Lord of glory!" (See Isaiah 6:5—and God's gracious rescue of Isaiah in his need, vv. 6–7.)

But the holiness code also shows God's mercy. It established a kind of "quarantine zone" to protect sinners from coming accidentally into God's holy presence (compare Exodus 19). And it allowed God's people access to His presence through the work of the priests, who brought sacrifices on the people's behalf into God's holy presence—sacrifices that represented Jesus' coming sacrifice on Calvary.

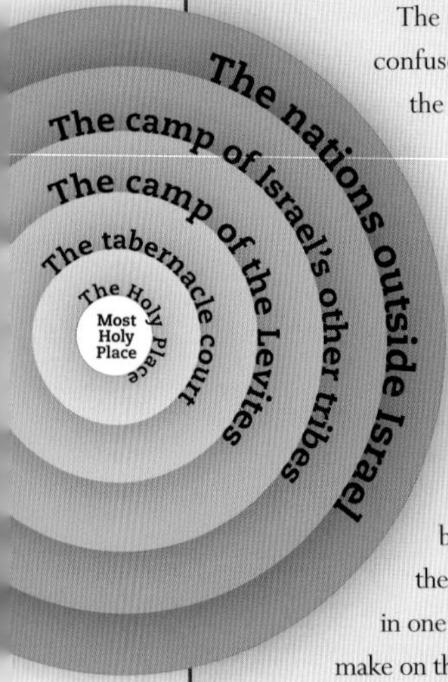

The God of Leviticus is *not* "my pal in the sky" or a kindly, somewhat confused grandfather who lives upstairs. He is the awesome Creator of the universe, the Holy God, the merciful God in Jesus Christ.

The last three books of Moses continue the story of the Israelites' journey to the Promised Land, a journey that lasted forty years.

Leviticus emphasizes the awesome holiness of Israel's God. It describes the covenantal rituals and stipulations by which unholy, sinful people could enter His presence to worship Him.

The people's lives centered around various sacrifices, the priesthood, laws of purification, and special days, such as the great Day of Atonement. The book's English title relates to the Levites, who were intimately involved in these activities. (Like the other books of the Pentateuch, its Hebrew title is from the first sentence of the book: "And He Called.") Every aspect of the sacrificial system spoke in one way or another about the sacrifice our Lord Jesus would one day make on the altar of the cross.

When holiness meets unholiness, the unholy is incinerated instantly. In one sense, the "holiness code" of Leviticus was meant to teach Israel the terrible dangers of sin. In another sense, it set up a system of what we might call quarantine. It protected Israel and the nations around her from death.

Leviticus

Into Leviticus

Leviticus means "concerning the Levites"; members of the tribe of Levi led Israel in worship.

Theme: What it means to live as God's holy people

Who wrote Leviticus?

Together with Genesis, Exodus, Numbers, and Deuteronomy, Moses also wrote Leviticus. He belonged to the tribe of Levi, as did his brother Aaron, Israel's first high priest. For more information, see "Who wrote Genesis?" (p. 2).

When was Leviticus written? Why?

Leviticus serves as a kind of worship handbook for the priests and other members of the tribe of Levi who led God's people in worship. It describes the offerings, the duties of the priests, various ceremonial laws, and other rituals.

Moses wrote Leviticus during Israel's forty-year wilderness wanderings, perhaps during the year the nation camped at Mount Sinai just after leaving Egypt (ca. 1446–1406 BC).

How is Leviticus classified?

Leviticus is one of the Books of Moses in the Old Testament.

What are the key divisions of Leviticus?

- **Leviticus 1–7** Sacrifices and holiness
- **Leviticus 8–10** Holy priests to serve a holy God
- **Leviticus 11–15** Rituals to maintain holiness ("cleanness")

- **Leviticus 16** The Day of Atonement
- **Leviticus 17–20** More rituals and moral holiness
- **Leviticus 21–22** Holy priests remaining holy
- **Leviticus 23–25** Holy days for rest and worship
- **Leviticus 26–27** The blessings of holiness and the consequences of unholiness

As you study this outline, notice how it builds up to the Day of Atonement in chapter 16 and how similar topics are repeated, one by one, on either side of that chapter: chapters 11–15 and 17–20 focus on rituals for holiness; chapters 8–10 and 21–22 focus on holiness for priests; and chapters 1–7 and 23–25 describe the worship expected of all the people of Israel.

	Day of Atonement Leviticus 16	
Chapters 11–15	**Rituals for Holiness**	Chapters 17–20
Chapters 8–10	**Holiness for Priests**	Chapters 21–22
Chapters 1–7	**Worship Expected of All People of Israel**	Chapters 23–25

Moses seems to have arranged his text to emphasize the importance of the Day of Atonement. As we read, it's as though we were climbing steps toward chapter 16; then, in chapter 17, we begin to descend again. Chapters 26–27 form a kind of conclusion.

How does Leviticus point to Jesus?

Here are a few examples:

- As in the rest of the Pentateuch, Aaron, the high priest, represents Jesus in His service as our High Priest. To cite just one example, twelve precious stones were attached to the *ephod*, a kind of apron that Aaron wore as part of his priestly clothing. These jewels represented the twelve tribes: God's people. Aaron—and the high priests who came after him—carried the needs of God's people on his heart each time he entered God's presence in the tabernacle. Today, Jesus carries our needs to the heavenly Father too, as He intercedes for us (Hebrews 4:14–16).

- Each sacrifice described in Leviticus 1–7 pictures facets of Jesus' sacrifice of Himself for us.
- The Day of Atonement (Leviticus 16) foreshadowed Good Friday.
- The Year of Jubilee points forward to the blessings Jesus' death and resurrection would win for us.

What are the key chapters in Leviticus?

- **Leviticus 1–7** details the offerings that formed the centerpiece of Israel's worship in both the tabernacle and, later, the temple.
- **Leviticus 16** is the high point of the book. It describes the work Jesus would complete for His people in exquisite detail. The symbolism (and its fulfillment) are astonishing!
- **Leviticus 23** summarizes the seven observances and festivals that Israel followed year by year. Each of them points in one or more ways to Jesus.

Feasts Appointed by the Lord

In Genesis 2 and Exodus 20, the Lord hallowed the seventh day as a day of rest so that God's people could learn of God's blessings, celebrate them, and be strengthened for further service. During the exodus, the Lord added other feasts (Exodus 12; 23:10–19; 34:18–26) and required the men of Israel to gather annually for special celebrations. In this way, the Lord hallowed time so the people could share in His holiness. The chart below provides an overview of the feasts as listed in Leviticus 23 and how the people observed them at the tabernacle.

Reference	Date	Occasion	Lay Observance	Work Prohibition	Offerings/Gifts to the Lord
23:3	Sabbath			Total	
23:5	14th day of first month	Passover			
23:6, 8	15th–21st days of first month	Feast of Unleavened Bread	Eating of unleavened bread		Yes
23:6–8	15th day of first month	First day of Feast of Unleavened Bread, a holy day	Eating of unleavened bread	Partial	Yes
23:8	21st day of first month	Last day of Feast of Unleavened Bread, a holy day	Eating of unleavened bread	Partial	Yes
23:9–14	16th day of first month	Feast of Firstfruits	Presenting the first sheaf of barley harvest		Yes
23:15–21	50th day after elevation of first sheaf	Feast of Weeks, a holy day (Day of Pentecost)		Partial	Yes
23:24–25	First day of seventh month	Feast of Trumpets, a holy day		Partial	Yes
23:27–32	10th day of seventh month	Day of Atonement, a holy day	Fasting	Total	Yes
23:34–43	15th–21st days of seventh month	Feast of Booths, Feast of the Lord, holy days	Going on pilgrimage, residing in booths, rejoicing		Yes
23:35	15th day of seventh month	First day of Feast of Booths, a holy day	Going on pilgrimage, residing in booths, rejoicing	Partial	Yes
23:36	22nd day of seventh month	Closing ceremony of Feast of Booths, a holy day		Partial	Yes

Start of Israelite year

As Jews, the earliest Christians followed the Israelite calendar and its feasts as observed by first-century Judaism. However, as more and more Gentiles came to faith in Jesus as their Savior, a new yearly pattern of worship emerged: the Church Year, which most Christians continue to observe today. The Israelite year was organized around the rhythm of the agricultural seasons in Israel and national events. By contrast, the Church Year was organized around the life and teachings of Jesus.

Two Church festivals descend directly from Israelite feast days: Easter and Pentecost. For centuries, the early Christians referred to Easter as *Pasch*, from the Hebrew word for Passover. The name *Pentecost* comes from the Greek word for fifty, since Israelites and Christians celebrated this feast fifty days after Passover. These annual celebrations remind us of the Old Testament roots of the Church as well as the transformation of worship in view of the life, death, and resurrection of Jesus. Study the chart below to grow in your understanding of the Jewish and Christian calendars.

OT and Jewish Feasts	Celebration	Season	Church Year	Celebration
Start of Israelite year Rosh Hashanah Lv 23:23–25; Nu 29:1–6	Completion of agricultural year and beginning of new year	September/October	Sundays after Pentecost	During the "Half-Year of the Church" (*Semester Ecclesiae*), worship focuses on the teaching of Jesus for the Church.
Day of Atonement/Yom Kippur Lv 16; 23:26–32; Nu 29:7–11	A day of national fasting and sacrifice during which the high priest entered the Most Holy Place in the tabernacle	September/October		
Booths/Tabernacles/Ingathering Ex 23:16; Lv 23:33–43; Nu 29:12–39; Dt 16:13–17	Harvest and commemoration of Israelite wanderings	September/October		
Hanukkah Mentioned in Jn 10:22 as the Feast of Dedication	Purification of the temple from Seleucid rulers (165–164 BC)	December	Start of Church Year Advent/Christmas	The "Half-Year of the Lord" (*Semester Domini*) focuses on the life of Jesus.
Purim Est 9:18–32	National deliverance through Queen Esther at time of Babylonian exile	February/March	Epiphany	
Passover/Unleavened Bread Ex 12; 23:15; Nu 9; Dt 16:1–8	National redemption from Egypt	March/April	Lent/Easter	
Weeks/Pentecost/Harvest Lv 23:15–22; Nu 28:26–31; Dt 16:9–12	Firstfruits of the wheat harvest	May/June	Ascension/Pentecost	

Why did God command the "Sabbath Day"?

The Third Commandment requires that we "Remember the Sabbath Day by keeping it holy" (Luther's Small Catechism). The word *Sabbath* means simply "rest." Each time God's Old Testament people observed the Sabbath, He intended that it would remind them of the coming Savior.

The Book of Hebrews makes it clear that Jesus Himself is our Sabbath. In Him, we find relief from the burden of our guilt. In Him, we can relax from trying to earn salvation by trying hard to obey God. See Hebrews 4:9.

But that "rest" included more. People who lived around Israel in ancient times thought God's people were lazy. No one except the Israelites took a whole day off once a week! There was work to do! Crops to raise! Metals to smith!

But God's people could relax because they knew their heavenly Father's promise to care for them, to provide for them. While those who didn't know the true God slaved away seven days a week and worried about where their next meal might come from, the Lord's power and love released His people from all that.

So, too, it is for us today:

> My God will supply every need of yours according to His riches in glory in Christ Jesus. (Philippians 4:19)

> Humble yourselves, therefore, under the mighty hand of God so that at the proper time He may exalt you, casting all your anxieties on Him, because He cares for you. (1 Peter 5:6–7)

Sacrifices

Sin separated people from God. God commanded His Old Testament people to atone for their sins by making offerings or sacrifices. The Books of Moses tell about these laws. To atone for each sin, there was a specific requirement. Some sins required offerings of grain, oil, or wine, while others required the sacrifice of an animal. The animal must have been one that was raised for food and belonged to the person who was making the offering. It also had to be perfect and pure. The animal was killed, its blood was sprinkled on the horns of the altar, and part of its meat was burned in the fire on the altar.

Sin still separates people from God. But we are His New Testament people. Today, we no longer have to make blood sacrifices. God gave His Son, the Lamb of God, as the perfect, final sacrifice. Jesus' death and resurrection atoned for our sins. He fulfilled the requirements of the Law for us. God forgives our sin for Jesus' sake, bringing us to Him through His Word and Sacraments.

Priestly Duties

A priest's job was to represent the people to God. Priests offered sacrifices to atone for the sins of the people, according to God's command (some priestly customs may have changed as they served in different sanctuaries during Israel's history). The priests took turns offering sacrifices. People wanting to make a sacrifice—usually men, but sometimes women—brought the animal to the priests and stood at the front gate to watch the presentation of the sacrifice. The priest chosen to make that day's offering would kill the animal outside the temple at sunrise, when the gate leading to the sanctuary was opened. A part of the meat from the sacrifice was taken into the temple and placed on the ramp leading up to the altar. Other offerings, including flour, cakes, and wine, all prepared according to God's laws, were also left on the ramp for placement on the altar.

After the offering was left there, the priests had several other duties to perform. They collected ashes from the inner altar, trimmed the wicks of the candelabrum, and brought glowing-hot coals from the outer altar to the inner altar. One priest was selected for a special privilege. He would burn incense on the golden incense altar in the temple. The heavy fragrance filled the temple. Then the priests raised their hands and recited the Aaronic blessing: "The Lord bless you and keep you; the Lord make His face to shine upon you and be gracious to you; the Lord lift up His countenance upon you and give you peace" (Numbers 6:24–26). Finally, blood from the sacrifice was sprinkled on the horns of the altar.

After fulfilling these duties, the priests cast lots for the privilege of carrying the sacrificial offerings up the ramp to the fire. After witnessing the sacrifices, the people paid their tax of a half shekel. They might also make an extra donation to pay for the frankincense, firewood, and other temple necessities.

The Disease of Leprosy

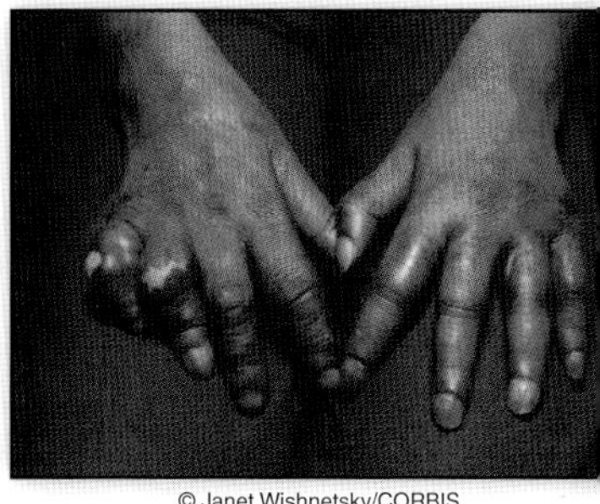
© Janet Wishnetsky/CORBIS

Leprosy (Hansen's disease) is a disease caused by a germ that discolors patches of skin and causes those areas to lose feeling. After feeling is lost in a certain area, other damage often occurs to that part of the body. For example, if someone loses feeling in his fingertips, then his fingers could more easily be injured. He could bump his fingers or burn them without feeling pain. The injury could be quite severe before he even realized it. These secondary injuries are what often cause the most problems. Leprosy does not cause fingers and toes to fall off, but sometimes the secondary injuries cause this to happen.

Is pain a blessing?

© CPH

Our bodies protect themselves through pain. Pain forces you to move away from the source of the pain. Imagine that you accidentally put your finger on a hot stove. The pain you feel in your finger forces you to quickly remove your finger from the heat. Your finger may be burned, but the pain you felt prevented a worse injury.

Why did people with leprosy have to live outside the city?

Before treatment begins, leprosy is a contagious disease, which means that it can be passed from person to person through close physical contact. In the past, before medicines were developed to treat it, the only way to avoid leprosy was to stay away from people who had it. Jesus went to those with sicknesses—even people with leprosy—to heal them and to love them.

© Vishal Shah/Shutterstock, Inc.

Although the germ for leprosy was discovered in the 1870s, it wasn't until the 1940s that a successful treatment was discovered. Today, most people with leprosy can be cured if they receive the right combination of medicines. Unfortunately, there are still many people around the world who have leprosy because they don't have access to medicine. In 2004, more than 400,000 new cases of leprosy were reported. Most of the people sick from leprosy lived in Southeast Asia.

The Practice of Fasting

To fast is to purposely go without food and/or drink for a period of time. Usually, people who fast for religious reasons are allowed to drink water, and they sometimes eat food after sunset on the day of fasting.

Many religious groups—Jews, Hindus, Muslims, Roman Catholics, Eastern Orthodox Christians, and some Protestant denominations—encourage fasting as part of their practice and to help a person focus on God.

Fasting in the Jewish tradition requires a person to avoid all food and drink, including water, on seven specific days of the Jewish calendar. Five of these, called "minor fast days," allow the person to eat and drink after sunset and before sunrise. The other two days, the "major fast days," require fasting from sunset of one day until sunset of the next day. Jews never fast on the Sabbath—which is observed from sundown on Friday until sundown on Saturday—unless Yom Kippur falls on the Sabbath.

Jews fast to remember events in Jewish history, to show thanks to God, and to ask for forgiveness. If a person dropped the scrolls of the Torah, for example, he could fast to obtain forgiveness. Jewish people also believe that doing good deeds could shorten the length of a required fast.

Fasting is difficult for the body. Without water or other drink, the body will dehydrate (that is, dry up). A person who is dehydrating may feel dizzy and nauseated, get a headache, faint, and have low blood pressure. The skin gets dry and turns red. Breathing and heart rate get very fast. The person may get very sleepy, and the arms and legs might tingle. A person can die from dehydration in three days.

Without food, a person can survive for up to three weeks. After about three days, feelings of hunger go away. But not taking in vitamins and nutrients can cause people to be tired and irritable, develop diarrhea and skin rashes, and experience swelling in their arms and legs. Without vitamins, internal organs can be damaged. People who don't eat enough food also have a harder time paying attention, caring about themselves and others, and making good choices. They might not want to be around people, and they can get depressed, anxious, or angry.

When a person doesn't eat food for energy, his or her body makes energy from glucose (sugars) and fats already in the body. The human brain requires glucose to function. When the existing supplies of glucose are used up, the body makes energy out of protein tissues, like muscles. When the protein in the body is used up, the brain can't get the glucose it needs. Too little protein in the body can cause death.

The next time you are hungry or thirsty, think about how Jesus fasted, going for forty days and forty nights without food or water. Because Jesus kept the Law perfectly for us, we no longer need to fast or do anything else for ourselves to keep God's Law. Jesus has done it all for us. We are saved by faith in Him.

People in the Bible Who Fasted

Moses, while on the mountain with God (Exodus 34:28)

King David, to save the life of his son (2 Samuel 12:15–23)

King Jehoshaphat, seeking God's deliverance from attacking tribes (2 Chronicles 20:3)

Elijah, while at Mount Horeb (1 Kings 19:8)

The people of Nineveh, in repentance (Jonah 3:5–10)

Pharisees, to keep Jewish laws (Matthew 9:14; Mark 2:18; Luke 18:11–12)

Anna, to honor God (Luke 2:36–38)

Members of the Early Christian Church, to honor God (Acts 13:2–3)

Clean and Unclean Animals

In the Books of Moses, called "the Pentateuch," God gave His people laws regarding clean and unclean animals. Clean animals were animals that were acceptable to be used as sacrificial offerings. Unclean animals were not acceptable to be used as offerings. Also, God's people could only eat clean animals.

Clean animals were animals that had both cloven (split) hooves and chewed their cud (Leviticus 11:3).

Unclean animals were any animals that were not clean (Leviticus 11:4–8). Leviticus 11:13–19 lists different kinds of birds that are unclean. Seafood that did not have scales and fins was considered unclean (Leviticus 11:10–12). Even certain insects were clean or unclean (Leviticus 11:20–21).

People who even touched an unclean animal after it died were also considered unclean until sundown. They had to wash themselves and their clothes in a certain way to become clean again. If an unclean animal fell on an article of wood, cloth, or animal skin, the article became unclean until evening and had to be put into water. Other surfaces touched by an unclean animal or insect had to be destroyed. Pottery had to be broken if anything unclean fell into it (Leviticus 11:31–33).

Clean and

Clean Leviticus 11:3, 9
cattle
sheep
goats
chickens
geese
ducks
fish with scales and fins
locusts

Many modern Jews continue to observe the practice of eating only clean, or *kosher*, foods. In order for food to be kosher, it must be only from a clean animal, must not be mixed with unclean foods, and must be prepared in a special way. Even clean animals have certain parts that are considered unclean. Dietary laws also forbid eating dairy and meat in the same meal. It is very difficult to remain kosher.

Scripture doesn't say why some animals were deemed clean and others were unclean. Some modern Jews believe it was simply to give God's people a way to obey Him. Following the Law exactly was very important to Jews. They believed that by keeping the Law, they would please God.

When Jesus came to fulfill the Law, He fulfilled *all* of the Law, including laws about clean and unclean animals. Today, God's people are free to eat meat from any animal. Jesus said, "It is not what goes into the mouth that defiles a person, but what comes out of the mouth; this defiles a person" (Matthew 15:11). People are sinful by nature, not just by what they do. They are forgiven for all sins through faith in Jesus Christ, who kept His Father's Law perfectly.

n Animals

Unclean
ticus 11:4–8, 10–19, 20–21

pigs

camels

hares

bats

winged insects
that go on all fours

rodents

reptiles

amphibians

lobster

crabs

clams

crayfish

New Year Festivals

© IsraelImages.com

Israel's Calendar

Israel lived by a calendar of twelve lunar months. God's Law decreed that Israel should consecrate each month to the Lord at the new moon festival with special sacrifices and the blowing of trumpets on the first and second days of the month. Because the months were strictly lunar, beginning when the first crescent of a new moon became visible, their months always include parts of two of the months on our contemporary calendar. This lunar system also had to be adjusted frequently to accommodate the eleven-day difference between twelve lunar cycles and one solar cycle. Every three years, Israel added an extra month, repeating the twelfth month of the sacred calendar.

Another confusing point is that Israel numbered the months with two different systems. A sacred system numbered the months beginning each New Year with the Passover—days that would be included in our months of March or April. A civil, or commercial, system numbered the months from the beginning of the planting season at the beginning of the seventh sacred month, usually in late September or early October.

Israel's New Year Celebrations

The sacred New Year for Israel began with the Passover. The civil New Year was marked by trumpet blasts blown on rams' horns as a signal all across the land that the new season had begun.

Today, Jews call this festival Rosh Hashanah, the Jewish New Year. In Jewish synagogues, notes are still sounded on the ram's horn, or *shofar*, as a call to repentance. For Jews today, no work is permitted on Rosh Hashanah. Much of the day is spent worshiping in the synagogue.

Numbers

Into Numbers

The title comes from the two censuses it records.
Theme: What it means to grow in faith

Who wrote Numbers?

Moses wrote all five books of the Pentateuch, including Numbers. For more information, see "Who wrote Genesis?" (p. 2).

When was Numbers written? Why?

The Book of Numbers is, in essence, a diary, journal, or perhaps even an adventure log, detailing Israel's forty-year journey through the wilderness on their way to the Promised Land (ca. 1446–1406 BC). Numbers includes all the events that happened after the nation broke camp and left Mount Sinai. (They stayed at Sinai for about a year immediately following the exodus.)

The picture isn't always pretty. Aaron, Miriam, Moses, and the nation as a whole all fall into doubt, disobedience, and despair from time to time. The ground opens up to swallow Korah, Dathan, and Abiram, and fire falls from heaven to destroy their followers when they rebel against Moses' leadership! Many Israelites are enticed into worshiping an idol-god (Baal), just as the nation stands on the brink of entering Canaan. In short, the people are often faithless.

But God remains faithful despite His people's sin. He is at work to bring them to repentance and to fulfill His promises to them. And He is at work to fulfill His promise to Adam, to Abraham, to Isaac, to Jacob, and to us! He will bring a Savior to redeem His sinful people from both the guilt and the power of our sins.

How is Numbers classified?

Numbers is one of the Books of Moses in the Old Testament; it contains a large amount of historical information and should be read that way.

What are the key divisions of Numbers?

Numbers may be divided into these major sections:

- **Numbers 1–10** Israel prepares to break camp at Sinai; the first census
- **Numbers 11–12** The wilderness journey: Sinai to Kadesh
- **Numbers 13–20:13** The twelve spies; the nation rebels
- **Numbers 20:14–19; 21** The wilderness journey: Kadesh to Moab
- **Numbers 22–25** Israel at Moab; Balaam's blessing and curse
- **Numbers 26–32** A new generation; the second census
- **Numbers 33–36** Closing appendix; various details

How does Numbers point to Jesus?

Here are a few examples:

- Like Jesus, Moses repeatedly intercedes for the people, asking God to pardon their sins. See, for example, Numbers 14:13–20.
- In John 3:14–16, Jesus compares the bronze serpent of Numbers 21 with His own saving work.
- Balaam describes in detail the coming of the "Star" and "Scepter" from Israel in Numbers 24:17–19.
- Each of the worship practices reviewed and summarized in Numbers 28–29 depicts the coming Savior and the peace He would bring.
- Jesus is our "city of refuge" (Numbers 35:9–15), the place where we can flee for refuge from the guilt and shame of our sins. (See also vv. 25, 28.)

What are the key chapters in Numbers?

- **Numbers 1** The first census in Israel.
- **Numbers 6:22–27** Aaron pronounces a benediction on God's people. (This blessing is still used in Christian churches today.)
- **Numbers 10** Israel breaks camp at Sinai and sets out in the wilderness, toward the Promised Land.
- **Numbers 13–14** Spies are sent out and return; the people's fearful, faithless response to the spies' report; the consequence of their rebellion—forty years of wandering in the wilderness.

- **Numbers 19** The ritual for purification from death, the ceremony of the "red heifer" (Many Bible scholars believe it points forward to Baptism.)
- **Numbers 20:1** Miriam's death.
- **Numbers 20:10–13** A second "water from the rock" episode; Moses' disobedience.
- **Numbers 21** Israel's victories over King Sihon (vv. 21–30) and King Og (vv. 31–35). (The Old Testament writers call these names to mind again and again throughout the rest of the Old Testament as examples of God's faithfulness to His people.)
- **Numbers 22** Balaam and his talking donkey.
- **Numbers 26** Moses takes a second census of the people.
- **Numbers 27** God appoints Joshua to succeed Moses and take Israel into the Promised Land.
- **Numbers 33** Israel's wilderness wanderings under Moses' leadership, campsite by campsite.

Why did God command war?

Several times in Exodus and Numbers, God ordered His people into battle against other people groups, His enemies. Other Old Testament books record similar instances. Joshua and Judges focus on little else. In the books of Samuel and Kings, King Saul and King David repeatedly battle the Philistines. The prophet Samuel condemned King Saul for not completely destroying the Amalekites (1 Samuel 15).

God's Old Testament commands about war are puzzling—perhaps even frightening—to God's people today, especially in light of the idea of *jihad* ("holy" war) taught by radical Islam and the devastation jihad has caused worldwide for decades.

So what's up with its inclusion in our Bible?!

To understand it, we need to know several key facts:

- The old covenant and new covenant differ. Under the old covenant, God focused on a specific family of people in a specific location—the nation of Israel. Under the new covenant, God focuses on His Church—all believers of every nation, language, and location on earth.
- Under the old covenant, church and state were united. Not so today! In the past, the Church has sometimes twisted God's will and caused great damage to the Gospel message by trying to use political

or even military means (for instance, abuses during the Crusades and the Inquisitions) to deal with the enemies of Christ.

- God cannot ignore evil or pretend it doesn't matter. In holiness and justice, He must destroy it. He knows the power of evil to hurt His people.

God commanded that ancient Israel remove every trace of idols and idol worshipers from the Promised Land because He knew His people would be tempted to worship these same false gods, which would compromise their relationship with Him. Worse still, they would endanger the plan of salvation—His promise to send the Messiah as a descendant of Abraham, Isaac, and Jacob.

God warned His people clearly in Numbers 33:55:

> *If you do not drive out the inhabitants of the land from before you, then those of them whom you let remain shall be as barbs in your eyes and thorns in your sides, and they shall trouble you in the land where you dwell.*

His words of warning eventually came true in Israel, and His people's failure to obey Him led to all kinds of trouble, just as He had foretold.

Evil lives on in our world. But it will be completely erased on the Last Day, when Jesus comes again. Then our Savior-God will cast everything unholy into the eternal fire of His judgment. For now, we share Jesus' love and promised forgiveness with everyone around us—even those who consider themselves enemies of God. And we live in the certain hope that fear, pain, poverty, sin, temptation, injustice, Satan, and death itself will one day disappear from our lives forever. God will swallow them up!

> *"O death, where is your victory?*
> *O death, where is your sting?"*
> *The sting of death is sin, and the power of sin is the law.*
> *But thanks be to God, who gives us the victory*
> *through our Lord Jesus Christ. (1 Corinthians 15:55–57)*

Food in the Old Testament

God provided for Israel in marvelous, miraculous ways, by sending them manna and quail in the wilderness on their way to Canaan. But what else did people in Bible times eat?

© Shai Ginott/Israelimages.com

Bread

Just as you might eat bread at different meals, God's people in Bible times also ate a lot of bread. Grains are an important part of a healthy diet, and God gave the Israelites both wheat and barley for bread. Bread made with wheat was softer; bread made with barley was harder and more difficult to chew. Today, most people get their bread in a clean plastic bag in the supermarket. However, in Bible times, people had to make their own bread. After harvesting and threshing the grain, the people ground it by hand into flour. It took up to three hours just to produce enough flour for five or six people for one day. After the flour was ground, water and yeast were added. The mixture was set aside to rise. It was kneaded once or twice by hand and then baked over hot coals or in a clay oven.

© Willem Tims/Shutterstock, Inc.

Meat and Fish

Israelites enjoyed many different types of fish, usually grilling it over a fire. They also ate lamb, goat meat, and a small amount of beef.

© Gala Kan/Shutterstock, Inc.

Vegetables

People in Bible times enjoyed cucumbers, carrots (although they were white instead of orange), celery, olives, onions, leeks, and garlic.

Fruits

The Israelites enjoyed many kinds of fruits, including pomegranates, dates, figs, melons, and a fruit called *citron*. The citron is a citrus fruit (in the family of oranges, lemons, and limes). It is a large, light-green fruit, similar in shape to a lemon.

© Shutterstock, Inc.

Nuts and Sweets

The Israelites also ate almonds and walnuts and enjoyed all sorts of sweets. They made cake with almonds and honey. They used honey to sweeten a variety of foods.

© Shutterstock, Inc.

© Israelimages.com

Drinks

In the dry climate of Israel, water was extremely important. Sometimes eight months went by with no rain. People drew water from wells and stored it in large jars or in underground cisterns. Because water was stored so long, scientists are quite certain that bacteria developed and made it unsafe to drink. However, some believe that storing it in dark underground cisterns would have prevented the growth of bacteria. Water was often mixed with a little wine before drinking. The wine in the water may have killed bacteria.

Winemaking was a lengthy process. After harvesting the grapes, people used their feet to crush them in a big vat. The mashed grapes fermented into wine. Wine was a common beverage at meals, but it also was served at special celebrations.

John, the son of Zechariah and Elizabeth, who was called "the Baptizer" or "the Baptist," lived and preached in the wilderness (Luke 1:80), in an area called the Desert of Judea. This uninhabited region stretched for about twenty miles from Jerusalem down to the Jordan River and the Dead Sea. It was a lonely, rugged place.

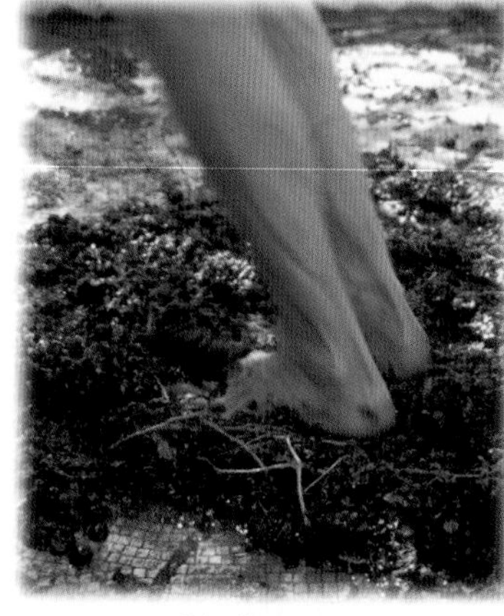

© Israelimages.com

© Eyal Bartov/Israelimages.com

Women draw water from a well (upper left); rocks (left) and feet (above) are used to crush grapes.

The Wilderness

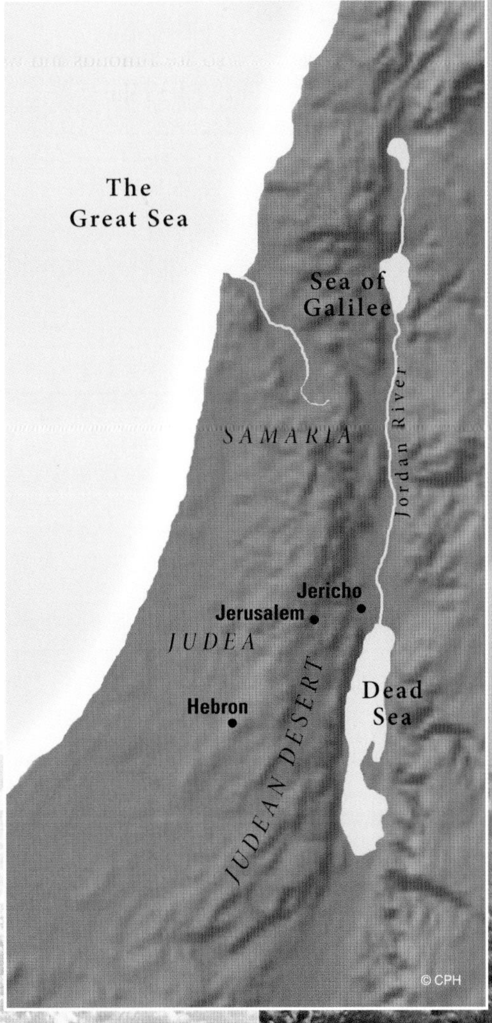

The wilderness was important in Jewish worship. Once a year, on the Day of Atonement, the high priest offered a special sacrifice for all the people of Israel (Leviticus 16). He placed his hands on the head of a goat and confessed the sins of all the people. This symbolically transferred all of the peoples' sins onto the *scapegoat*, which was then removed from the temple and sent out into the wilderness to die. John the Baptizer would later introduce Jesus by saying, "Behold, the Lamb of God, who takes away the sin of the world!" (John 1:29). Jesus is the perfect sacrifice to save us from sin. Our Lamb took all of our sins on Himself, died on the cross, and rose again, crushing sin, death, and the power of the devil once and for all.

In Jesus' time, many devout Jewish people would go to the desert to seek spiritual renewal in the quiet and solitude. This was a tradition dating back to Moses and the prophet Elijah. Jesus Himself "was led up by the Spirit into the wilderness to be tempted by the devil" for forty days and forty nights (Matthew 4:1).

Christians today often go to remote places to be alone in order to fast and pray, following the example of Jesus and the prophets.

Manna and the Ark of the Covenant

In Exodus 16:32–34, Moses describes a command from God that an *omer* (about two quarts) of manna should be placed in a jar and kept "'throughout your generations.' . . . before the testimony."

The manna, of course, was the bread from heaven that God sent to feed His people during their forty years of wandering in the wilderness of Sinai (Exodus 16:35). "It was like coriander seed, white, and the taste of it was like wafers made with honey" (Exodus 16:31). Coriander is a large herb that grows to a height of about two feet and yields a gray-white seed. Both the seed and the leaf of the coriander were used as cooking spices by the Israelites.

The "testimony" to which Moses refers in verse 34 is the stone tablets on which God had written the Ten Commandments, the second copy that God prepared to replace the original tablets that Moses broke in anger (Exodus 31:18; 32:19; 34:1). The Ten Commandments were placed in the ark of the covenant—also called "the ark of the testimony" (Exodus 25:22)—after it was constructed (Exodus 25:16). The ark was a type of chest made of acacia wood covered inside and out with pure gold. There was gold molding around the outside. God directed exactly how it was to be made. It was two and one half cubits long, one and one half cubits wide, and one and one half cubits high. There were two gold rings on each side. Poles made of acacia wood covered in gold were slipped through the rings in order to carry the ark. They were not to be removed. It was overlaid with a *mercy seat* (Exodus 25:17; some Bible translations call it an "atonement cover") of pure gold. Hammered gold cherubim were placed at each end with their wings spread upward, overshadowing the cover. The mercy seat signified the reconciliation of God to the people. He had mercy on them.

The manna, in a golden jar (see Hebrews 9:4), and the testimony were placed inside the ark along with the budding staff of Aaron (Numbers 17:1–11). The Ten Commandments were not given and the ark was not built until several months after God began sending manna to His people. Moses, the author of the first five books of the Bible, evidently wrote the account of God's gift of manna and quail with full knowledge of the instructions that God gave later for the construction of the ark and the tabernacle.

The ark was the throne of the true God, who chose to dwell among His people. It was the presence of God on earth. The ark is considered to be a "type" of the presence of Christ in the midst of His people. His body is incorruptible; it did not see decay. The gold represents purity, wisdom, and love. The jar of manna foreshadows Christ's body given for the forgiveness of sins as part of God's plan of salvation. Priestly Aaron's staff shows that Christ is a priest forever. The stone tablets of the Law signify that Jesus is the accomplishment of the Law. Together, the ark and its contents were a powerful image of "God with us."

Spies

Spies Today

© Jose Asreyes/iStockphoto.com

According to the official Web site of the Central Intelligence Agency (CIA) of the United States, intelligence is information needed by a nation's leaders to keep a country safe. When a leader has a question about a foreign country's possible threat, he or she needs good, reliable information.

A lot of intelligence gathering simply involves reading newspapers from other nations to see what is happening there. Sometimes spies are sent to find out things that are not public knowledge.

Spies need to be able to adapt to any situation in any culture. They need to know other languages. They need to be courageous and self-disciplined.

Of course, one of the main traits they need is loyalty to their country. Spies usually do not reveal the work they do or receive public credit for their service. Often, even their families don't know the contributions they have made to the safety of others.

Spies in Canaan

It was common in the ancient Near East to use spies to find out about an enemy's strengths and resources. Israel was probably influenced by this practice, and its people wanted to know what to expect when they entered the Promised Land. Moses himself instructed the spies to report on the crops, the people, and the cities. God had not required Israel to send out spies, but He allowed Moses to give in to their wishes (see Deuteronomy 1:22–23). God's plan didn't need spies, only faith in Him on the part of the Israelites.

Later, when Joshua and Caleb finally led the people into Canaan, they sent spies out as well. This time, Israel didn't rebel against God. By God's grace and under Joshua's leadership, they had faith and didn't cower at the strength of their enemy. This time, God used Israel's spies in His plan to bring His people to the Promised Land. What's more important, He used the Israelites in His plan of salvation for all people. (Read Joshua 2 and 6 and Hebrews 11:30–31 to learn more.)

Deuteronomy

Into Deuteronomy

Deuteronomy means "second law," in part because the Ten Commandments are repeated in chapter 5.

Theme: What it means to have a covenant with the Lord

Who wrote Deuteronomy?

Moses wrote all five books of the Pentateuch, including Deuteronomy. For more information, see "Who wrote Genesis?" (p. 2).

Deuteronomy 34 records Moses' death and burial. It's likely that another human author, perhaps Joshua, added these final words to the Pentateuch.

When was Deuteronomy written? Why?

Deuteronomy records three sermons Moses preached to the nation Israel as they lay camped on the east bank of the Jordan River across from Jericho. At this time, Moses was 120 years old and was ready to enter the promised land of heaven. The year was about 1405 BC.

Joshua would soon assume leadership of the nation and would take God's people into Canaan, the land He had promised to Abraham more than four hundred years earlier (Genesis 12:1–9; 15:1–21; 17:8). Before this new generation crossed the Jordan to begin their conquest of the territory then occupied by idol worshipers, Moses spoke to warn Israel of the spiritual dangers and to encourage them in the grace of their covenant-making, covenant-keeping Lord.

How is Deuteronomy classified?

Deuteronomy is counted among the Books of Moses in the Old Testament. It differs from the other books in that it's mostly a book of sermons, all preached by Moses.

Especially in his first sermon (chapters 1–4), Moses recounts all God has done for His people from the time they broke camp at Sinai to the day they arrived on the banks of the Jordan.

In his second sermon—by far the longest and most detailed (chapters 5–26)—Moses repeats the Ten Commandments, the moral law first given on Mount Sinai forty years earlier. He explains in detail what the Lord expects of Israel as they conquer Canaan and settle down to live there.

In his third and final sermon (chapters 27–30), Moses prophesies about Israel's future.

What are the key divisions of Deuteronomy?

Deuteronomy may be divided into five major sections:

- **Deuteronomy 1–4** Moses' first sermon: what the Lord has done for Israel in the past.
- **Deuteronomy 5–26** Moses' second sermon: what the Lord expects from Israel in the present.
- **Deuteronomy 27–30** Moses' third sermon: what the Lord will do for Israel in the future.
- **Deuteronomy 31** Moses commissions Joshua to lead Israel.
- **Deuteronomy 32–33** Moses' song and final blessing on Israel.

How does Deuteronomy point to Jesus?

Here are a few examples:

- Moses is a "type," or picture, of Christ as he acts as a mediator between a holy God and His sinful, fearful people in Deuteronomy 5:22–33.
- Centuries after Deuteronomy was written, Jesus draws from Moses' words, quoting verses from this book as He faces—and defeats—Satan's temptations. See Deuteronomy 6:13, 16 and 8:3.
- In Deuteronomy 18:15–19, Moses prophesies directly about the coming Savior who would be a prophet greater than Moses.
- "A hanged man is cursed by God," declares Deuteronomy 21:23. Paul applies this verse to Jesus:

Christ redeemed us from the curse of the law by becoming a curse for us—for it is written, "Cursed is everyone who is hanged on a tree"—so that in Christ Jesus the blessing of Abraham might come to the Gentiles, so that we might receive the promised Spirit through faith.
(Galatians 3:13–14)

- Mount Ebal (Deuteronomy 27:1–8), the "mountain of blessing," foreshadows Mount Calvary and the blessings we receive by God's grace through the Savior who bled and died there for us.

What are the key chapters in Deuteronomy?

- **Deuteronomy 5** The Ten Commandments, God's moral law given on Mount Sinai to all human beings as God's will for all time.
- **Deuteronomy 6:4** The *Shema*: "Hear, O Israel: The LORD our God, the LORD is one." (This became a kind of "creed" throughout Old Testament history and remains so among Jews today.)
- **Deuteronomy 11:18–25** Parents commanded to teach their children to know, love, and obey the Lord.
- **Deuteronomy 17:14–20** Instructions for Israel's future kings in how to behave toward the Lord and toward His people.
- **Deuteronomy 18:15–22** The coming Messiah described as the Prophet of the Lord.
- **Deuteronomy 32** A song of Moses, taught to the nation just before his death. (Its words teach the people about sin and repentance in a memorable format. Centuries later, when the people were exiled in Babylon because of their rebellion against the Lord, they could sing this song and remember His love and His willingness to forgive His repentant children.)
- **Deuteronomy 34** Moses' death and burial by God on Mount Pisgah. (Jude 1:9 records an interesting—and mysterious—footnote on this burial. Look it up!)

The Ten Commandments

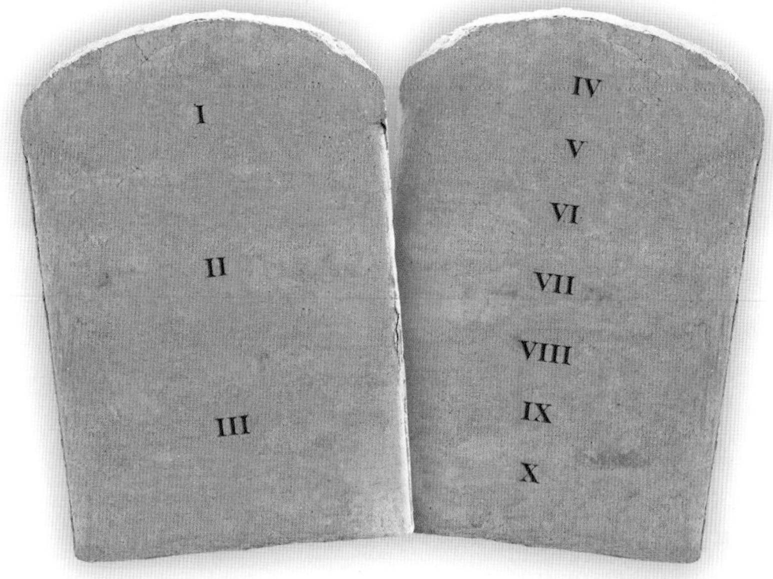

© DuckyCards/iStockphoto.com

During the first year of their forty-year journey through the Sinai wilderness, while the people of Israel camped at the base of Mount Sinai, Moses ascended the mountain and received from the hand of God two tablets of stone—flat pieces of stone suitable for engraving—on which God personally wrote the Ten Commandments. "And He gave to Moses, when He had finished speaking with him on Mount Sinai, the two tablets of the testimony, tablets of stone, written with the finger of God" (Exodus 31:18). Moses broke these tablets in anger when he discovered Israel's sin of idolatry with a golden calf (32:19); God replaced them shortly thereafter (34:1). This second set of tablets was kept in the ark of the covenant, first in the tabernacle and later in the temple, but was apparently lost when Nebuchadnezzar destroyed the temple in 586 BC.

In Hebrew and Latin, they are called "the Ten Words"—*Decalogue*. We don't know for sure how or even *if* the Commandments were numbered on the stone tablets God gave to Moses. You may talk with a friend who belongs to a different church and find out that when you talk about the Fifth Commandment, you are referring to different words. Since the Bible does not number the Commandments, various church bodies have numbered them differently based on their traditions. There were even different divisions of the Commandments among the ancient Jews. Some Jews make Exodus 20:2 the First Commandment, vv. 3–6 the Second, and Exodus v. 17 the Tenth. The Eastern Orthodox and the Reformed Churches make Exodus 20:2–3

In Deuteronomy 31, Moses commissioned Joshua to lead Israel since Moses knew his death was near.

the First, Exodus vv. 4–6 the Second, and Exodus v. 17 the Tenth. Lutherans and Roman Catholics draw the Second Commandment from Exodus 20:7, the Third from vv. 8–11, and make v. 17a the Ninth and v. 17b the Tenth.

We often refer to "the two tables of the Law." Here, too, church bodies have differed in their approach. Jews today divide the Ten Commandments into two groups of five each. Lutherans and Roman Catholics assign three commandments to the First Table and seven to the Second Table. Eastern Orthodox and Reformed Churches assign four commandments to the First Table of the Law and six to the Second Table.

For Lutherans, the First Table deals with our relationship with God. The Second Table deals with our relationships with our neighbors. Jesus said, "You shall love the Lord your God with all your heart and with all your soul and with all your strength and with all your mind, and your neighbor as yourself" (Luke 10:27). The first three commandments, as we number them, talk about our love for God—putting Him first, honoring His name, and worshiping Him faithfully. The remaining commandments describe love for our neighbor.

God did not give His people—believers—the Ten Commandments so that we could earn His favor. He knows that we are sinful and cannot keep the Law as He desires. These Commandments, and all the Law, serve us as (1) a curb, helping to control violent outbursts of sin and keeping order in the world; (2) a mirror, showing us how sinful we are and preparing us to seek a Savior; and (3) a guide, showing us what God expects and guiding us in our life as God's children.

Jesus said, "Do not think that I have come to abolish the Law or the Prophets; I have not come to abolish them but to fulfill them" (Matthew 5:17). Through His perfect life on earth and His sacrificial suffering and death for us, Jesus fulfilled the Law for us. Through faith in Him, we have forgiveness of sins, new life, and salvation.

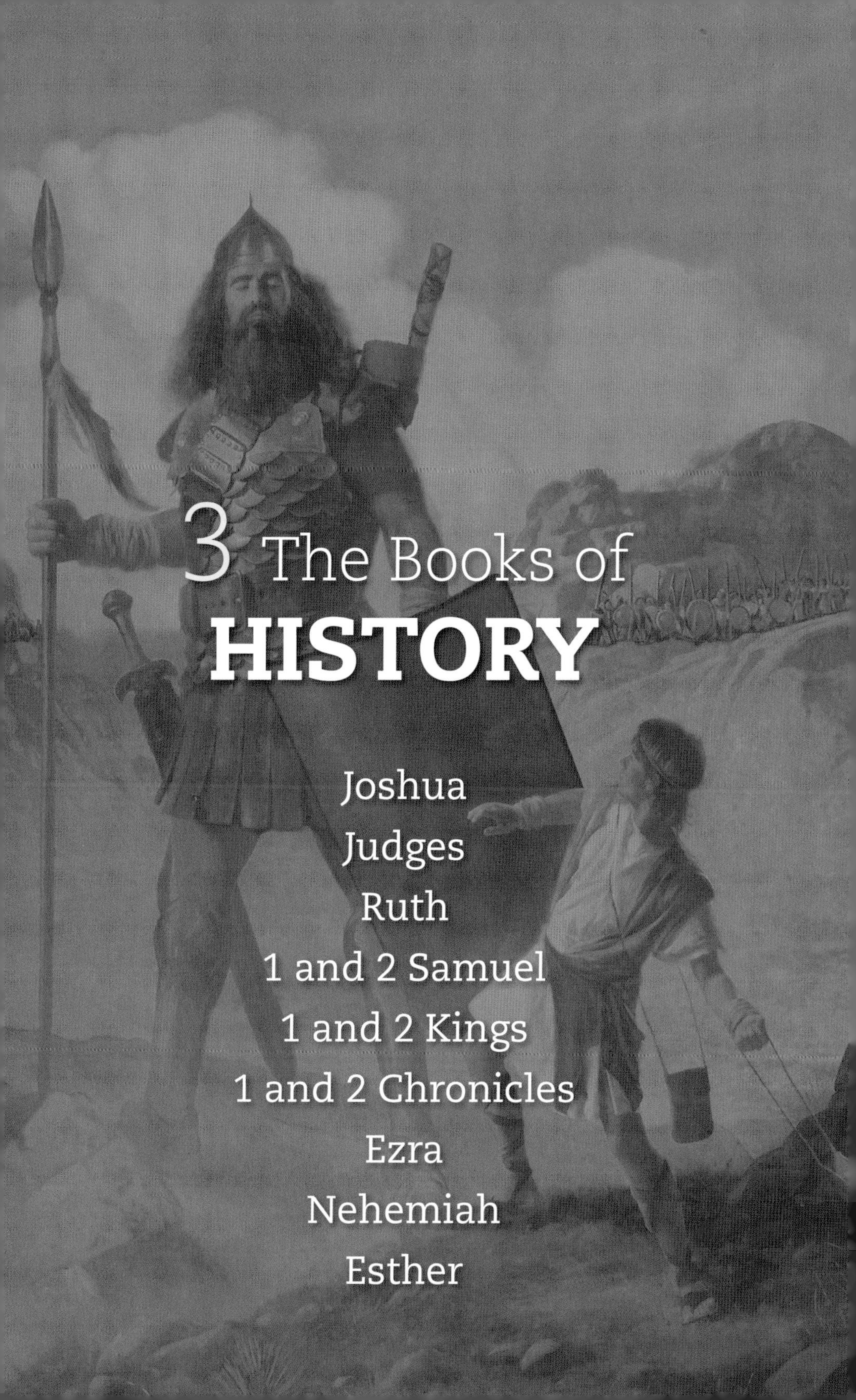

3 The Books of HISTORY

Joshua
Judges
Ruth
1 and 2 Samuel
1 and 2 Kings
1 and 2 Chronicles
Ezra
Nehemiah
Esther

Joshua

Into Joshua

Joshua means "the Lord saves" or "the Lord is salvation." Joshua is an Old Testament form of the name Jesus; Joshua is the English rendering of the Hebrew name, and Jesus is the English rendering of the Greek spelling.

Theme: Be strong and courageous; the Lord fights for you!

When was Joshua written? Why?

Many Bible scholars credit Joshua himself with writing the book, and much of the material in the book does appear to be eyewitness testimony. Other scholars have suggested Samuel as the author. Joshua 24:29–33, the account of Joshua's death, was almost certainly written by someone other than Joshua.

The dating of the book is also unknown. However, there's good evidence to suggest it may have been written at about the same time the events of Joshua occurred.

Questions about the authorship and the dating of Joshua, however, do not take away from the power of the book, the encouragement it has given God's people throughout history, and the encouragement it continues to give us today.

It clearly shows God's faithfulness to His promises and His people, and it warns against the dangers of worshiping any false gods.

Joshua picks up the history of ancient Israel immediately after the death of Moses. It records the history of Israel's conquest of Canaan from 1406 to about 1380 BC.

How is Joshua classified?

Joshua is counted among the Books of History in the Old Testament. As noted previously, much of it is eyewitness testimony.

What are the key divisions of Joshua?

Joshua falls into roughly two parts:

- **Joshua 1:1–13:7** The battles by which Israel took Canaan, driving out the idol-worshiping nations that lived there
- **Joshua 13:8–24:33** Israel settles in Canaan, and the land is divided among eleven tribes of Israel

Note: The tribe of Levi received no land; instead, they inherited

- their service in the nation's worship;
- cities scattered throughout the territory of the other eleven tribes; and
- the pasture lands surrounding those cities. See **Joshua 14:4**.

See also Numbers 18:20–24 and Deuteronomy 10:8–9, which explain the tribe of Levi's inheritance in more detail. Note that the Lord Himself was Levi's inheritance—as He is ours! All New Testament believers are now God's "royal priesthood" (1 Peter 2:9).

How does Joshua point to Jesus?

Here are a few examples:

- Joshua himself is a picture, or "type," of Jesus. Just as Joshua led the conquest that gave the land of Canaan to Israel, so Jesus, by His life, death, and resurrection, has conquered death and given all believers the eternal promised land. (See Joshua 1:6–7.)
- Like Jesus, Joshua is the "servant of the LORD" (Joshua 24:29).
- In Joshua 2, we read the story of the Gentile prostitute Rahab. In grace, God brought her to Himself and enfolded her in the ancestry of the Savior! (See Matthew 1:5.)
- God gave the land of Canaan to Israel as part of His plan of salvation. There, He would keep them as safe as possible from the influence of the idolatry all around them. He would keep them in true faith and prepare them to receive Jesus, the Savior of the world.

What are the key chapters in Joshua?

- **Joshua 1** We are encouraged to find strength and courage in God's Word, minute by minute throughout life.

- **Joshua 3** The parting of the Jordan River and Israel's crossing over into the Promised Land (This parallels the parting of the Red Sea forty years earlier as the nation left slavery in Egypt; see Exodus 14.)
- **Joshua 5** As Israel enters Canaan, the manna they had eaten during their wilderness wanderings stops falling. (They could now eat the fruit and other food that grew in abundance in Canaan.)
- **Joshua 6** The fall of Jericho
- **Joshua 10** The sun stands still during a battle, allowing Israel's army to gain full victory over their enemy.
- **Joshua 18:1** The tabernacle is set up at Shiloh. The nation would continue to use the tabernacle as its place of central worship for about five hundred years, until Solomon built the temple (around 970 BC).
- **Joshua 24** Joshua's final words to the nation, including this famous charge:

  Now therefore fear the Lord and serve Him in sincerity and in faithfulness. Put away the gods that your fathers served beyond the River and in Egypt, and serve the Lord. And if it is evil in your eyes to serve the Lord, choose this day whom you will serve, whether the gods your fathers served in the region beyond the River, or the gods of the Amorites in whose land you dwell. But as for me and my house, we will serve the Lord. (Joshua 24:14–15)

Israel's Idols

Despite the warnings of both Moses and Joshua, the people of Israel did adopt many of the idols worshiped by the people groups they displaced in Canaan.

In some ways, these gods seem very strange to us today. For example, many of Canaan's gods were considered territorial—they had power on a particular mountain or valley, but only there. Contrast this with the Lord's claim to rule the whole earth (see, for instance, Psalm 148)! It must have sounded outrageous to the nations outside Israel.

In other ways, the gods of the Old Testament peoples seem strangely familiar. Gods of silver and gold still attract us today, though not in exactly the same way. Some of the idols encouraged sexual sins; some promised power to their followers. Such "gods" are still popular today.

Scripture tells us something about ancient idolatry; archeology fills in some of the blanks too. Here are a few of the more prominent false gods mentioned in Scripture:

- **Baal** appears most often of all the idols in the Old Testament. The word *ba'al* means "lord" or "master." People thought of this idol as a storm and fertility god. His female consort was known as *Ashtoreth*. Worship of both these idols seriously infected the nation of Israel as early as the time of the judges (Judges 6; see also 1 Kings 11:5; 2 Kings 23:13). In Jeremiah 7:18 and 44:17, Ashtoreth is called "the queen of heaven." *Baal-zebub* was worshiped as a god who caused and cured diseases; he is mentioned in connection with King Ahaziah's injury in 2 Kings 1:6. Jesus used this name to refer to Satan (Matthew 10:25—*Beelzebul*). See also 1 Corinthians 10:19–20.
- **Chemosh** was the god worshiped as an idol by the people of Moab. He may have been a god of war. In 2 Kings 3:27, we read about the king of Moab sacrificing his firstborn son to Chemosh. (See also Jeremiah 48:7, 13, 46.) Solomon built an altar for Chemosh (1 Kings 11:7) in addition to the other idol altars he erected, in part to please his pagan wives.
- **Dagon** was worshiped by the Philistines. Many of his worshipers considered him Baal's father. During Samson's lifetime, Dagon was worshiped at Gaza (Judges 16:21–23). See 1 Samuel 5:2–7 for an interesting (and even humorous) demonstration of the Lord's superiority over this false god.
- **Molech** was a Canaanite deity whose worship demanded the sacrifice of children and infants. There is evidence that parents would place live babies in the arms of a Molech idol-altar, then the baby would be burned alive. The Lord found sacrifices to Molech especially detestable. In Molech we see the grisly image of a god who devours infant sons and daughters—a total contrast to the Lord's revelation of Himself as our kind, wise heavenly Father!

Scripture everywhere assumes demons stood behind each pagan idol. (See, for instance, Deuteronomy 32:17; Psalm 96:5; and Zechariah 13:2.) There's a warning in this for us today. Any "spirituality" that lies outside the means the Holy Spirit uses—the Word and Sacraments—does indeed put us into contact with real spirit beings. But they're not the kind of "spirits" any child of the true God wants to meet!

The One True God

God created the world—including the sun, the elements, and weather—and He commands them. The Israelites knew that their God was the living Lord of heaven and earth. He was not present only in a statue of wood, stone, or metal, and, in fact, He forbade His people to make such idols.

God's people worshiped the true God according to His commands.

Unlike the lumps of stone or wood created by the worshipers of the false gods, the God of Israel spoke to His people through His priests and prophets. God listened to, cared for, and wanted to be reconciled with His people.

Jesus Christ, the Son of God and the Word of God, became a living human being—the Word became flesh and dwelled among us (John 1:14). He came to reconcile us through His death on the cross and His resurrection. Now He is with us through His Word and Sacraments. He is not dead, inanimate, or far away, like many false gods that people still believe in today. He lives and reigns to all eternity!

Heathen Nations in the Land of Canaan

> *And they told him, "We came to the land to which you sent us. . . . However, the people who dwell in the land are strong, and the cities are fortified and very large. And besides, we saw the descendants of Anak there. The Amalekites dwell in the land of the Negeb. The Hittites, the Jebusites, and the Amorites dwell in the hill country. And the Canaanites dwell by the sea, and along the Jordan." But Caleb quieted the people before Moses and said, "Let us go up at once and occupy it, for we are well able to overcome it." (Numbers 13:27–30)*

Who were these idolaters over whom God promised the Israelites victory?

Descendants of Anak

Anak's descendants were a race of giants who lived near Hebron. Not much is known about their religion, but their large, fierce appearance frightened the Israelites. Goliath, the Philistine David fought, was a descendant of Anak (1 Samuel 17:4, 23).

Canaanites

Canaanites were many different groups of people who lived in the land of Canaan. They were descendants of Canaan, who was Noah's grandson, the son of Ham. Canaanites fished, hunted, farmed, built ships, and produced a written language. They worshiped many false gods called "Baals." Their worship practices were horrible and included sacrificing their own children to the gods and doing things that were sexually impure.

Amalekites

The nomadic Amalekites were related to the Edomites, descendants of Esau. They became known as the enemies of Israel because they often attacked the Israelites. Even after hundreds of years of living near the Israelites, they continued to reject God and clung to their idols.

Hittites

The Hittites, relatives of the Canaanites, were known for their ability to build and use chariots. They made things out of iron and traded with other tribes. One well-known Hittite was the soldier Uriah (2 Samuel 11). Punishments for severe crimes among Hittites, even for murder, were usually only fines. The Hittites had many gods, and when they conquered another group of people, they added the gods of the conquered people to their own. Later, some of the Hittites also worshiped Yahweh alongside their idols, which is a violation of the First Commandment.

Jebusites

The Jebusites, a Canaanite tribe, were probably related to the Amorites and the Hittites. They lived at Jebus, in the mountains where Jerusalem is today. There were probably fewer of the Jebusites than of other Canaanite tribes. Their religion had many gods and similar immoral practices.

Amorites

The Amorites were tall, fierce, nomadic herdsmen from the hills, often taking over land they needed to graze their herds. They had settled in the city of Babylon but spread to other regions. Their false gods were also gods in Mesopotamia.

© Mike Ganor/Israelimages.com
© Duby Tal/Israelimages.com

Archaeology and the Promised Land

What is archaeology?

Archaeology is the study of ancient peoples. Archaeologists carefully dig around and unearth artifacts, monuments, and ruins. They clean and study them in order to learn more about the culture and way of life of people in that area. This article tells more about biblical archaeology in the Promised Land, using Jericho for an example.

Jericho

The ancient city of Jericho has a very low elevation. It is surrounded by sun-baked desert, and yet it flourishes as an oasis full of wells and springs.

Archaeologists trace structures in Jericho back to around 8000 BC. Evidence of palaces, towers, walls, and other structures has been found in the last two hundred years. They have also excavated pottery, wooden tables, stools, beds, baskets, and many other items that were well preserved inside many of the tombs.

When Joshua and the Israelites entered the Promised Land and overtook Jericho, the city was surrounded by a tall wall to protect the population from attacking armies. "Now Jericho was shut up inside and outside because of the people of Israel. None went out, and none came in" (Joshua 6:1). The large gate, which permitted people to go in and out of the city, was closed. With the wall surrounding the entire city, there was no way in or out.

Jericho Quick Facts

- Five miles to the west of the Jordan River
- Located about ten miles northwest of the place where the Jordan River flows into the Dead Sea
- Sometimes called the "city of palm trees"
- One of the oldest continuously inhabited cities in the world

What is a *shofar*?

A *shofar* is made from a ram's horn and is a type of trumpet. Israelite priests blew the shofar to call the people to worship, much like some Christians use church bells today.

Who is Rahab?

After the Israelites crossed the Jordan River into the Promised Land, Joshua sent spies ahead to Jericho to see what they were up against. Rahab protected the spies. She was promised she would be spared when the city of Jericho was destroyed. God showed His grace to her by saving her from destruction. She is a distant ancestor of Jesus.

> *Come, behold the works of the LORD, how He has brought desolations on the earth. . . . The LORD of hosts is with us; the God of Jacob is our fortress. Psalm 46: 8, 11*

Entering the Promised Land

© CPH

We see so many pictures while reading Joshua 3–5 that connect to our lives as God's people. In many ways, the story of the Israelites is our story.

The Wilderness

The Israelites had wandered for forty years while waiting to receive the land God had promised to their fathers. This generation barely remembered the escape from slavery in Egypt. They only knew their harsh life the desert. However, the entire time of their journey and wandering, God was with them, feeding them manna and taking care of them. They camped for three days beside the Jordan (Joshua 3:2), waiting for God, through his servant Joshua, to lead them across the river. Jesus was in the grave for three days—crucified for the sins of the world—before He rose victorious and opened paradise to the new Israel, His Church. We might say that here on earth, we are in the desert of sin, death, and Satan, waiting to cross to the promised land of heaven, following our leader, Jesus.

Crossing the Jordan

When the priests stepped into the Jordan River, it stopped flowing (Joshua 3:15–17). The waters piled up on the upstream side so that Israel could cross. Does this remind you of the crossing of the Red Sea, when Israel escaped the evil slavery under the Egyptians and came under God's care in the desert? Israel crossed the Jordan from the desert to the land of plenty, flowing with milk and honey (Joshua 5:6).

© Jeffrey Borchert/Israelimages.com

Baptismal site on the Jordan River.

When we hear accounts about water, we are reminded of Baptism. The Jordan River holds much significance for the Christian. In these waters, Jesus was baptized, taking upon Himself all the sin of the world for our sake so that He could put it to death on the cross. In our Baptism, the old Adam, our sinful nature, is drowned and the new man appears. We have put on Christ; we are in Christ.

All the males of Israel were circumcised at Joshua's command (Joshua 5:2). Did you know that circumcision was the means God used to bring new people into His chosen people of Israel? Baptism is the means God uses to bring us into the Church (Colossians 2:11–15).

The Bread of Life

God gave the bread of life—manna—to the Israelites in the desert. He traveled with them through His presence in the ark of the covenant, and He cared for them. When they crossed into the Promised Land, they didn't need the manna any longer. They ate the fruit of the land (Joshua 5:11–12). Even though we live in a sinful world, we are cared for by God. Daily, He gives us all we need for this life. He also keeps us in the faith through the means He provides—His Word and Sacraments. We hear the Word of God preached in the Divine Service, as well as in other services of the Church. We eat the manna of Jesus' body and drink His blood in the Sacrament of the Altar. This is a foretaste of the banquet we will feast on in heaven, where we will not need the elements of Holy Communion, just as the Israelites no longer needed manna. There, we will see God face-to-face.

The Passover

© Shutterstock, Inc.

The people once again celebrated the Passover when they entered the Promised Land (Joshua 5:10). This meal, established by God some forty years before, helped the Israelites recall their escape from Egypt. At the first Passover, they ate the sacrificed lamb and painted its blood on their doorposts so that the angel of death would pass over their houses. This blood protected their firstborn from death. The sacrificed lamb reminds us of the Lamb of God—Jesus, who delivers us from death and brings us to life with Him forever in heaven.

© Duby Tai/Israelimages.com

More Jericho Facts

The city of Jericho is thought to be one of the oldest continuously inhabited cities in the world. It is still quite famous worldwide—not as a powerful fortress standing above all others, as its citizens might have desired, but as the city whose walls fell down. The remains of the Old Testament Jericho have been located, along with interesting artifacts of the period.

© Duby Tai/Israelimages.com

Tell es-Sultan

The fall of Jericho occurred in the time period of the Late Bronze Age (1550–1200 BC). The city was located on a spot known today as *Tell es-Sultan*. *Tell* means "mound" in Arabic. Over the course of centuries, many cities are destroyed by war or other calamity and then are rebuilt, with new construction taking place on the rubble of the previous construction. A detectable mound results as each new city is built on ground that is a few feet higher than its predecessor. The mound of ancient Jericho is approximately a mile northwest of modern Jericho.

The mound itself measures approximately four hundred by two hundred yards. As archaeologists have discovered, many cities had been built on top of Jericho. The remains of more than twenty-four reconstructions have been discovered, including two sets of walls. Which level is the remains of the Jericho destroyed in Joshua 6 has not been determined, though archaeologists report that part of the mound—and its history—was washed away by erosion.

Center for Trade

Jericho was located at the entrance to the Canaanite hills, positioned on several trade routes. Because of the city's ideal location, the people who lived there most likely controlled the trade of items such as salt, sulfur, and bitumen. In addition, the town also may have been important for worship, since the name *Jericho* means "moon city." The Canaanites worshiped a moon god. No doubt, the destruction of Jericho also caused the Canaanites to wonder whether their god was really a god.

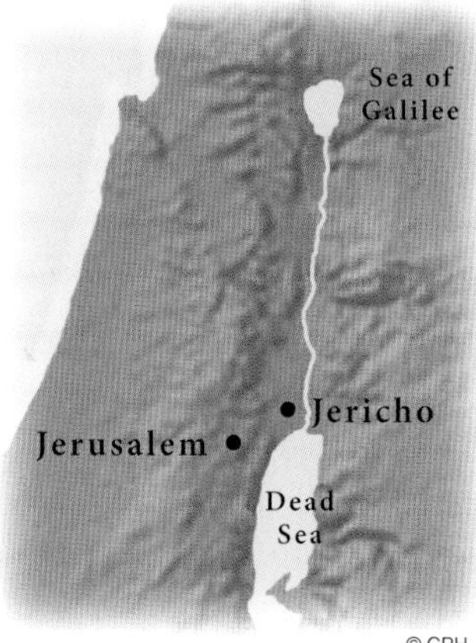

Jericho in the Bible

Jericho was the first city God's people conquered as they entered the Promised Land (Joshua 6). Joshua, who himself once had been a spy, had sent spies to that specific destination to search out the land (Joshua 2:1–3). Jericho is also the site of several New Testament events. It is near this city that Jesus healed blind men on several occasions (Matthew 20:29–34; Mark 10:46–52; Luke 18:35–43). In Jericho, Jesus greeted and then dined with the not-so-tall Zacchaeus (Luke 19:1–9). Jericho was also the intended destination of the traveler who was attacked by robbers in Jesus' parable of the Good Samaritan in Luke 10:29–37.

Judges

Into Judges

Judges is named after the leaders whose work the book describes. These "judges" were not primarily people who settled legal disputes or punished criminals. Instead, they were deliverers who rescued God's people from oppression by invading armies.

Theme: "Everyone did what was right in his own eyes" (Judges 21:25).

When was Judges written? Why?

Although Joshua chronicles a period of about fifteen years, Judges describes more than three hundred years of Israel's history—a very sad three hundred years that start out bad and grow worse as time goes on.

No one knows for sure who wrote Judges, though many scholars have attributed it to the prophet Samuel.

Judges focuses on the years of decline after Joshua's death—about 1380–1050 BC.

As you read Judges, keep in mind that no judge ruled over the entire territory God had given to Israel. They seem to have operated in various localized parts of the land. Far from being a unified nation, Israel was at this time a kind of loose confederacy. The book's closing sentence sums up the time of the judges: "In those days there was no king in Israel. Everyone did what was right in his own eyes" (Judges 21:25).

How is Judges classified?

Judges is counted among the Books of History in the Old Testament. As stated earlier, much of it relates information that would only have been available to an eyewitness of the events described.

What are the key divisions of Judges?

Judges falls into roughly three main parts:

- **Judges 1:1–3:6** A general description of Israel under the Judges
- **Judges 3:7–16:31** The cycle of sin-judgment-repentance repeats itself again and again
- **Judges 17–21** Examples of Israel's increasing depravity

How does Judges point to Jesus?

Judges shows us primarily how very much we need Jesus! It reveals what happens in hearts and societies when God's Law is ignored and God's love is not lived out.

- **Judges 2:16–19** summarizes a pattern repeated again and again in Judges—and too often in the lives of God's people today:

  Step 1: "The LORD raised up judges, who saved them out of the hand of those who plundered them" (v. 16).

  Step 2: "Yet they did not listen to their judges, for they whored after other gods and bowed down to them. They soon turned aside from the way in which their fathers had walked, who had obeyed the commandments of the LORD, and they did not do so" (v. 17).

  Step 3: "Whenever the LORD raised up judges for them, the LORD was with the judge, and He saved them from the hand of their enemies all the days of the judge. For the LORD was moved to pity by their groaning because of those who afflicted and oppressed them" (v. 18)

  Step 4: "But whenever the judge died, they turned back and were more corrupt than their fathers, going after other gods, serving them and bowing down to them. They did not drop any of their practices or their stubborn ways" (v. 19).

Despite the terrible sin of His people, God did not give up on them. Still today, because of Jesus, God does not give up on us. He keeps bringing us to repentance and assuring us of the forgiveness Jesus won for us on the cross.

What are the key chapters in Judges?

Chapter after chapter, Judges grows more and more dismal. There are highlights, however, if we consider God's mercy in using flawed human beings to rescue His people and to preserve the nation of Israel as the covenant people through whom He one day would send the Savior.

- **Judges 4–5** The story of Deborah, Israel's courageous (and poetic) female deliverer
- **Judges 6–8** The account of Gideon, God's "mighty man of valor" (6:12), who is famous for "putting out a fleece" (twice!) (6:36–40) and who defeated the army of Midian using only trumpets and torches as weapons
- **Judges 13–16** The account of Samson's life. Although some have thought that Samson's strength was in his hair, in reality that strength was God given. See Judges 16:28–31.

Judges

1. Othniel, Israel's first deliverer (Judges 1:11–15; 3:1–11; Joshua 15:16–19; 1 Chronicles 4:13)
2. Ehud, the left-handed deliverer (Judges 3:12–30; 4:1)
3. Shamgar, the "ox goad deliverer" (Judges 3:31; 5:6)
4. Deborah, the woman deliverer, and Barak (Judges 4:1–5:31; Hebrews 11:32)
5. Gideon, the "mighty man of valor" (Judges 6:1–8:32; Hebrews 11:32)
6. Abimelech, the wicked "anti-judge" (Judges 8:33–9:57; 2 Samuel 11:21)
7. Tola (Judges 10:1–2)
8. Jair (Judges 10:3–5)
9. Jephthah, the "historian-scholar deliverer" (Judges 10:6–12:7; Hebrews 11:32)
10. Ibzan (Judges 12:8–10)
11. Elon (Judges 12:11–12)
12. Abdon (Judges 12:13–15)
13. Samson, the "strong deliverer" (Judges 13:1–16:31; Hebrews 11:32)
14. Samuel and sons, Joel and Abijah (1 Samuel 8:1)

Deborah

Gideon

Samson

Who Were the Ishmaelites and Midianites?

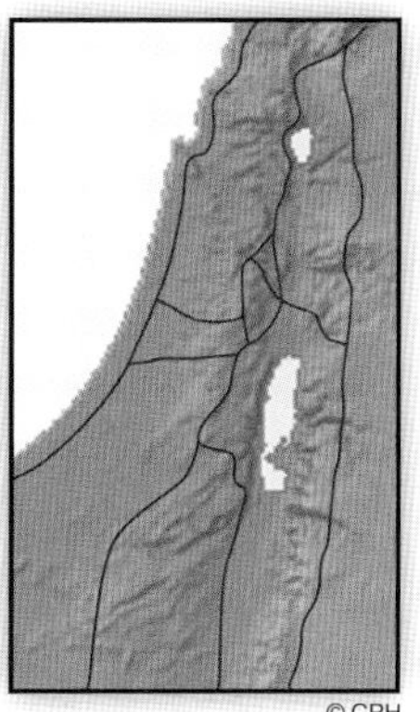

© CPH

Red lines indicate common trade routes in Israel.

In the Book of Genesis, Joseph is sold by his brothers to traders on their way to Egypt. Genesis 37 uses the names *Ishmaelite* and *Midianite* to describe the same group of traders. Bible scholars think they were probably the same general group known to have descended from Abraham.

> *Then Midianite traders passed by. And they drew Joseph up and lifted him out of the pit, and sold him to the Ishmaelites for twenty shekels of silver. They took Joseph to Egypt. (Genesis 37:28)*
>
> *Meanwhile the Midianites had sold him in Egypt to Potiphar, an officer of Pharaoh, the captain of the guard. (Genesis 37:36)*
>
> *Now Joseph had been brought down to Egypt, and Potiphar, an officer of Pharaoh, the captain of the guard, an Egyptian, had bought him from the Ishmaelites who had brought him down there. (Genesis 39:1)*

Ishmael was born to Abraham through Hagar (Genesis 16), Sarah's handmaiden. God promised to bless Ishmael and make him fruitful and the father of twelve princes who would become a great nation (Genesis 17:20). The Arab tribes of today are considered to be the descendants of Ishmael.

The Midianites were descendants of Midian, a son of Abraham and his servant girl Keturah (Genesis 25:1–2). "Midianite" probably identified a group of tribes descended from Abraham that roamed far beyond their homeland. Jethro and Zipporah, Moses' father-in-law and wife, were Midianites, but apparently faithful to the true God. Other Midianites engaged in the false religious practices of the Moabites and are more often found to be enemies of God's people.

Both groups were nomadic and often involved in commerce, including the transporting and selling of slaves. Their homeland was generally to the east of the Jordan in the regions of Moab, Edom, and the eastern Sinai Peninsula. They are grouped with others in the designation "people of the East" (Judges 6:3).

© CPH/Cheri Bladholm

God Leads His People

From the time that God called Abraham until his grandson Jacob (whom God renamed "Israel") took his household to live with his son Joseph in Egypt, God's people were a family. It was a large family by most standards, consisting of seventy people (Genesis 46:27). The family's affairs were managed or governed by the father of the household.

During their stay in Egypt, God's chosen people—the family of Israel—grew very large. When Moses was called to lead them out of slavery and through the Sinai Desert, he discovered how difficult his position of leadership was. At the advice of his father-in-law, Jethro, he instituted a system of chiefs who managed small units of people and reported to other chiefs who managed larger units, so that only the biggest problems came under Moses' direct supervision (Exodus 18:24–26). In the wilderness, God forged Israel into the nation He ruled through Moses.

When the nation of Israel crossed the Jordan into the Promised Land in about 1406 BC, they numbered more than a million people. (Numbers 1:45–46 lists more than six hundred thousand men older than age 20.) However, the people settled in their assigned portions of the Promised Land as tribes or clans and were presumably led by the head of their respective households, forming alliances between tribes when necessary to defeat their enemies.

About three hundred years later, the people of Israel decided that they needed a king to rule over them "like all the nations" (1 Samuel 8:5).

The Vocation of Judge

Between the time of the conquest of Canaan and the selection of Saul as Israel's first king (1375–1050 BC), there arose a special vocation—judge.

The judges in Israel did more than weigh evidence and resolve disputes as today's judges do. They were called upon to solve community problems. Frequently, Israel's judges served as military advisors, leaders, or warriors. These judges were not elected. Apparently, they served by common consent in the region where they resided because people noticed and valued their godly wisdom.

In the Book of Judges, a cycle is repeated several times: (1) Israel sins, (2) Israel faces oppression, (3) Israel returns to God in repentance, and (4) God sends a judge to deliver His people. Though Israel is repeatedly unfaithful, turning to false gods, God is always faithful to His covenant. The judges, each in his or her own way, foreshadow the coming Deliverer—Jesus, God's Son—who will redeem all who believe in Him from sin, death, and Satan. The Book of Judges mentions thirteen judges in all.

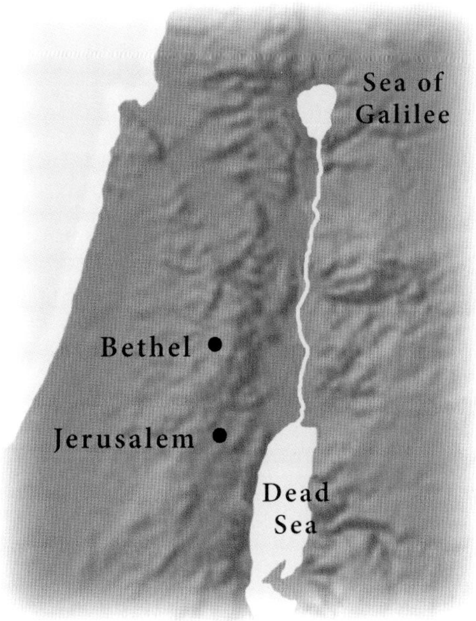

Fear, Fleece, Faith

Gideon was another of the judges of Israel chosen by God before Israel had kings. It was another time of rebellion against God when the Israelites worshiped the false gods of Baal.

Fear

God called Gideon to deliver His people from the Midianites, who were oppressing them by stealing their food and ruining their crops and herds. Gideon responded with fear and doubt, asking, "Please, Lord, how can I save Israel? Behold, my clan is the weakest in Manasseh, and I am the least in my father's house" (Judges 6:15).

© MoonBloom/Shutterstock, Inc.

© Dalibor Sevaljevic/Shutterstock, Inc.

Fleece

A fleece is the large clump of wool that results from the shearing of a sheep. At the end of Judges 6, Gideon sought the will of the Lord by leaving out a fleece overnight and asking the Lord to allow the dew to soak the fleece but leave the ground dry. God granted Gideon's request as proof that He would be with him in battle. Still doubting God, Gideon asked God for another sign the following night. This time, he asked that God confirm His promise by leaving the fleece dry but letting the ground be wet with dew.

People today occasionally speak of "laying a fleece before the Lord" in order to seek His will about a particular situation. Gideon's fear kept him from believing God's promise. He tested God and demanded more signs, even though God had made it clear that He had chosen Gideon for this task and would be with him. Gideon relied on his own understanding of the situation rather than having faith and trusting God.

Faith

On our own, the odds are against us, even as they were against Gideon's army. We become filled with fear, but the Holy Spirit turns fear into faith; miracles are possible. The Holy Spirit helps us conquer our fears and doubts. God promises, "My grace is sufficient for you, for My power is made perfect in weakness" (2 Corinthians 12:9).

God's will is not best discovered by laying out fleeces or asking God for signs. God's will is revealed for us through His Word and the Sacraments. In His Word, God shows us that He is our merciful and loving Creator, and He reveals His plan of salvation—forgiveness and new life through the work of His Son on the cross.

Ruth

Into Ruth

Ruth takes its name from the main character in the book; Ruth was King David's great-grandmother.

Theme: The Lord redeems His faithful people.

Who wrote Ruth? When was Ruth written? Why?

Quite simply, no one knows who authored this book. Because King David's name is mentioned in Ruth 4:17, 22, it's likely the author wrote it during the time of the kings rather than earlier. It focuses on a twelve-year span in the lives of Ruth, her mother-in-law, Naomi, and Ruth's husband, Boaz.

The story takes place during the dark days of the judges. Its tenderness contrasts sharply with the violent, faithless events recorded in the Book of Judges. Even while darkness descended in Israel, the light of God's love continued to shine in some hearts.

The Book of Ruth testifies about God's love for all people and about His faithfulness to His covenant promise to send a Savior. While Israelite society falls apart, the Lord preserves a godly remnant for Himself. Ruth was an unlikely candidate for true faith because she grew up in the idol-worshiping land of the Moabites. Yet God brought Ruth to Himself and even included her in the family tree of the world's Savior (Matthew 1:5).

How is Ruth classified?

Ruth is one of the Books of History in the Old Testament.

What are the key divisions of Ruth?

Ruth may be divided into three parts:

- **Ruth 1** Naomi's widowhood and Ruth's loyalty to her mother-in-law, Naomi
- **Ruth 2–3** Ruth meets Boaz, her kinsman-redeemer
- **Ruth 4** Boaz redeems, marries, and cares for Ruth

How does Ruth point to Jesus?

Here are a few examples:

- Boaz is a picture, or "type," of Christ. In his role as *kinsman-redeemer*, he symbolizes Christ's kindness, care, and deliverance of God's people. (See Deuteronomy 25:5–10; Ruth 2–4.)
- Ruth, a Moabite and almost certainly an idol worshiper, comes to true faith and is grafted into the family tree of our Savior. (See Ruth 4:18–22; Matthew 1:5.)

What are the key chapters in Ruth?

In Ruth 1, we read Ruth's famous pledge of faithfulness to Naomi and her testimony to the God of Israel. These words are often used in Christian wedding services:

> Do not urge me to leave you or to return from following you. For where you go I will go, and where you lodge I will lodge. Your people shall be my people, and your God my God. Where you die I will die, and there will I be buried. May the LORD do so to me and more also if anything but death parts me from you. (Ruth 1:16–17)

Ruth 4:18–22 records a significant genealogy. It connects Ruth and Boaz to their great-grandson, Israel's King David. A thousand years after David, Jesus was born from King David's lineage. Even though the times in which Ruth and Naomi lived were very dark, God still preserved a believing remnant in Israel. The "red thread of salvation history" was winding its way through time at God's direction. God would fulfill His plan to send a Savior!

Harvesting Grain

The harvest of grain is a key part of many stories in the Bible. We read about the grain harvest in the story of Ruth, and Jesus often talks about a spiritual harvest, saying especially to His disciples, "The harvest is plentiful, but the laborers are few; therefore pray earnestly to the Lord of the harvest to send out laborers into His harvest" (Matthew 9:37–38).

When was grain harvested in biblical times?

The time of the harvest varied according to the area of Israel in which crops were grown. The lowlands usually had an earlier harvest than the hilly sections. Barley was harvested in April and May. The wheat harvest began in May and extended into June.

© Milos Luzanin/Shutterstock, Inc.

How was grain harvested?

First, the grain was cut using a tool called a *sickle*. In ancient times, a sickle often was made from half of the lower jawbone of a cow or donkey. Other sickles were made of bronze or iron set in wooden handles. Their sharpness came from small, razor-sharp pieces of flint set into the bone, bronze, or iron. Reapers swung the sickle in an arc to cut down the grain.

© Elnur/Shutterstock, Inc.

Binders came behind the reapers to rake the fallen grain together and bind it into sheaves. Behind the binders came gleaners, who picked up grain that was not gathered into the binders' sheaves. Ruth was permitted to glean behind Boaz's binders.

Finally, the bound sheaves were taken to the threshing floor where they were was stacked to dry. Family members slept with the grain to protect it from thieves.

© Kaspars Grinvalds/Shutterstock, Inc.

© Hanan Isachar/Israelimages.com

What is *threshing*?

Farmers cleared a thirty-foot circular plot of ground for the purpose of threshing. This surface was leveled and rolled until it became as smooth as a modern-day clay tennis court.

The threshing process removes the grain, which is useful for food, from the straw and chaff. Many farmers led cows or donkeys in circles through the grain, allowing their feet to tramp the grain away from the straw and chaff. Some farmers used a paddlelike instrument known as a flail. The grain was now ready for winnowing.

What is *winnowing*?

The winnowing process separates the grain from the straw and chaff. The farmer used an instrument similar to a pitchfork to toss piles of the threshed grain into the air. The chaff, which was of no use to the farmer, was blown away in the wind, while the heavier grain fell to the floor, followed by the straw. Straw was used as bedding and food for the animals in winter.

The farmer then used a sieve to sift and cleanse the grain from dirt and sand, being very careful not to lose any precious grain in the process.

How did the grain get to the farmer's home?

Finally, the grain was measured carefully, packed into sacks or baskets, loaded onto a donkey or other pack animal, and transported home or to market. The grain was further dried and then used for cooking.

© Hanan Isachar/Israelimages.com

Genealogy: Judah to David

Ruth 4:18–22 and Matthew 1:2–6

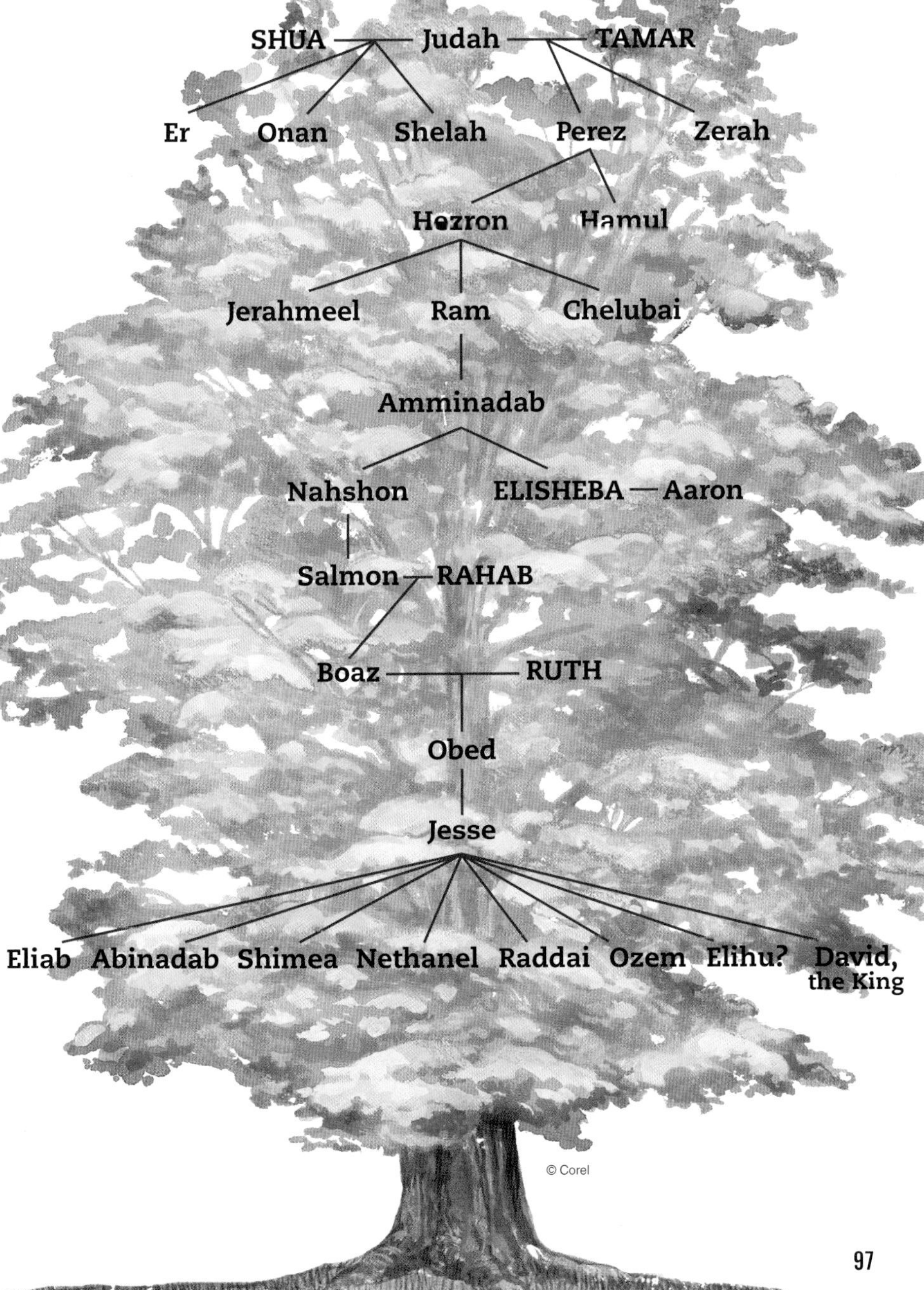

© CPH/Cheri Bladholm

Boaz, the Redeemer

In Ruth 4:13, we read that Boaz takes Ruth to be his wife. In so doing, he provides a secure future for both Ruth and her mother-in-law, Naomi. To understand why this takes place, we must understand two different aspects of the laws that governed the lives of God's people.

Provision for Widows

The laws of Moses, described in Leviticus and Deuteronomy, provide many forms of care and protection for the widows, orphans, foreigners, and Levites, none of whom had rights to property in Israel through which they could support themselves. All those who owned property were to tithe (that is, give 10 percent of) their produce once every three years for the benefit of the less-fortunate people among them (Deuteronomy 14:28–29). The widows, orphans, and foreigners were also allowed to glean in the fields after the property owner completed his harvest, meaning that they could have whatever the first harvesters had missed. Property owners were even instructed (Deuteronomy 24:19–21) not to strip the fields clean in the first harvest so that others might benefit. Ruth was exercising this right when Boaz first saw her (Ruth 2:5).

Widows were accorded an additional means for their welfare. Upon the death of a woman's husband, his nearest male relative (kinsman) was required to take the widow as his wife—an additional wife, if he was already married—to provide for her as part of his family. In this way, the relative became the redeemer of his brother's property and place in Israel. (This law was at the root of one of the questions with which the Sadducees tried to trap Jesus in Matthew 22:23–33.)

Boaz was related to Ruth's deceased husband, Mahlon, though he was not the closest male relative. Mahlon—along with his brother, father, and mother, Naomi—had left Bethlehem due to a famine and had settled in Moab, where Mahlon met and married Ruth. Since Mahlon had died, Boaz had a right and an obligation to marry Ruth if no closer redeemer claimed or accepted that responsibility.

Redeeming Property

Another Hebrew law is also involved, for Mahlon inherited the rights to property in Judah that was his father's before the famine drove the family to Moab. In a sense, no one in Israel owned the land; it was owned by God and given as an inheritance to the twelve tribes of Israel and their descendants. By law, if a man had to sell property that was his through inheritance in order to support his family, he retained a right to redeem it for what it was worth if and when he could afford to buy it back. Every fifty years, in the Year of Jubilee, all property was returned to those who had inherited it.

Mahlon's property could not be redeemed by or returned to him (because he was dead), but it could be redeemed by the closest male relative. In the case of Ruth, the wife and property were a kind of "package deal."

Mahlon's closer male relative declined to exercise his role as redeemer, but Boaz willingly did so. God used Boaz's role of redeemer to arrange for Ruth to become the great-grandmother of David, Israel's greatest king. In that way, she also became an ancestor of Jesus.

In His mercy and love, God has made us members of His family through our Baptism. Jesus is our Kinsman, our Brother. Best of all, Jesus is our Redeemer, who bought us back with His own blood and who freed us from the slavery of sin!

1 and 2 Samuel

Into 1 and 2 Samuel

The books of **1 and 2 Samuel** take their name from one of the main characters, Israel's last judge, and the leader God used to establish the monarchy in Israel.

Theme: The Lord establishes David's "house" forever.

Who wrote 1 and 2 Samuel? When? Why?

Together, the books of 1 and 2 Samuel record the history of God's people from around 1100 BC to 970 BC—from the birth of Samuel to the death of King David. Samuel was the last of Israel's judges (deliverers). David was Israel's second king.

Samuel himself may have written the first part of this work, which is one long account in the Hebrew Bible. (Scribes likely divided the account in two at a later date.) Since 1 Samuel 25 records Samuel's death, he could not have authored the rest. No one knows who wrote the rest.

The two books explain the institution of Israel's monarchy and celebrate God's work through King David who unified the twelve tribes of Israel into a nation with a shared identity and purpose.

Theologically, the two books of Samuel continue to unfold the history by means of which God kept His promises to send the world's Savior from sin through the descendants of Abraham. The prophecy of 2 Samuel 7:8–16 is particularly important as it describes God's plan to establish a dynasty (or "house") for David—an eternal one!

This prophecy is far bigger in scope than the palace and throne in the small, dusty city of Jerusalem. Instead, it focuses on the world's true King and Savior—Jesus Christ Himself, whose throne is eternal and whose reign is everlasting:

> *He will be great and will be called the Son of the Most High. And the Lord God will give to Him the throne of His father David, and He will reign over the house of Jacob forever, and of His kingdom there will be no end.* *(Luke 1:32–33)*

How Are 1 and 2 Samuel classified?

These two books are grouped among the Books of History in the Old Testament.

What are the key divisions of 1 and 2 Samuel?

1 and 2 Samuel may be divided into six main parts:

- **1 Samuel 1–8** The ministry of Samuel the judge in Israel
- **1 Samuel 9–15** The early reign of Israel's first king, Saul
- **1 Samuel 16–31** David is anointed king but lives in exile, hunted by King Saul, who is intent on murdering him
- **2 Samuel 1–4** David learns of King Saul's death and ascends to the throne of Judah
- **2 Samuel 5–21** King David's reign over both Judah and Israel, the united kingdom
- **2 Samuel 22–24** David's accomplishments and his final days

How does 1 and 2 Samuel point to Jesus?

Here are a few examples:

- Samuel serves God's people as prophet, priest, and ruler; in this way, he foreshadows the future work of Christ.
- The prophecy of 2 Samuel 7:4–17 foresees an eternal dynasty, or "house," for King David and his descendants. This is later fulfilled in Jesus. (Compare Luke 1:32–33.)
- David's *psalm*, or worship song, recorded in 2 Samuel 22, foretells Jesus' earthly ministry and the victory He would win for us. All faithful believers enjoy the victory over sin and Satan, hell, and death, which David first described. (See also Psalm 18, which is very similar in approach and wording.)

What are the key chapters in 1 and 2 Samuel?

- **1 Samuel 3** God calls Samuel into His service.
- **1 Samuel 10** Saul is anointed king.
- **1 Samuel 15** Saul is disobedient and the Lord rejects him as king.
- **1 Samuel 16** Samuel anoints David king in a secret ceremony.
- **1 Samuel 17** David's victory over the giant Goliath
- **1 Samuel 31** King Saul and his son Jonathan die in battle.
- **2 Samuel 2** David begins to reign in Judah as king.
- **2 Samuel 5** David's reign is extended to include the ten tribes outside Judah.
- **2 Samuel 7** God's covenant promises to David and his eternal dynasty, or "house"

David	Jesus
Anointed by Samuel; filled with the Holy Spirit 1 Samuel 16	**Anointed by the Father; filled with the Holy Spirit** Matthew 3:13–17; Psalm 45:7
Israel's shepherd 2 Samuel 5:1–2	**Our Good Shepherd** John 10
Defeated Israel's enemies 1 Samuel 17; 2 Samuel 8	**Defeated sin, Satan, hell, and death for us** Hebrews 2:14–15; 10:12; Revelation 1:18
Rules Israel wisely, in kindness and power 2 Samuel 5:12; 8:15	**Rules His church wisely, in self-sacrificing love and power** Ephesians 2:13–22
Led Israel in worship 2 Samuel 6:12–19	**Leads His Church into the Father's presence** Hebrews 4:14–16; 6:19–20
Planned to build the temple 2 Samuel 7:1–17	**Was Himself the temple, the place of God's dwelling among us** John 1:14–16; 2:19–22
Ruled Israel for 40 years 1 Kings 2:11	**Rules His Church forever** Ephesians 3:21

- **2 Samuel 11:1–12:23** David's sin with Bathsheba and his repentance
- **2 Samuel 12:24–25** Solomon's birth
- **2 Samuel 13–19** Absalom's rebellion—its roots, its results, and its resolution in his death
- **2 Samuel 22** David's final psalm of praise
- **2 Samuel 24:18–25** David purchases Araunah's threshing floor as a site for worship (This location, at the top of Mount Moriah, was where Abraham had once "sacrificed" Isaac [Genesis 22]. It would become the site on which King Solomon would build the temple.)

David, the Psalmist of Israel

The psalm titles link many of the psalms to events in the life of David. As you read more about the life of David, you will no doubt find that these psalms take on greater significance. It's easy to see in them David's heart, his longings and faith in the face of joys, trials, sins, and tribulations. And yet, his words remain quite general; we can pray his prayers ourselves as we think about our own joys, trials, praises, sins, and needs.

Escape from Saul.	**1 Samuel 19:1**	**Psalm 59**
David feigns madness.	**1 Samuel 21**	**Psalm 34**
David hiding in the cave.	**1 Samuel 22:1, 24:3**	**Psalms 57 and 142**
Doeg's betrayal of the priests at Nob.	**1 Samuel 22**	**Psalm 52**
The Ziphite informers.	**1 Samuel 23:19**	**Psalm 54**
David in the Judean desert.	**1 Samuel 24:1–2, 22; 2 Samuel 15:13**	**Psalm 63**
Defeat of the Edomites.	**2 Samuel 8:13**	**Psalm 60**
David's sin with Bathsheba.	**2 Samuel 11–12**	**Psalm 51**
Absalom's rebellion.	**2 Samuel 15:13**	**Psalm 3**
David's song of deliverance.	**2 Samuel 22**	**Psalm 18**

Who were the Philistines?

Goliath was one.

David lived among them for awhile.

Philistine armies and raiding parties pillaged, plagued, and plundered the cities of southern Israel for generations during the time of the judges and on into the reigns of both Saul and David. Then, suddenly, their power was broken.

2 Samuel 5:17–25 describes a stinging defeat King David handed the Philistines. After that, the Old Testament speaks about only minor harassments caused by Philistine warriors.

So who were the Philistines, and where did they come from?

- *Palestine* and *Philistine* both come from the same root word. The region was evidently named for them. Palestinians in the Gaza Strip and elsewhere in the Middle East still today can trace their name, at least, back to these fierce warriors.
- The Philistines were not native to Canaan, but evidently migrated there, possibly in several waves over several generations. Scholars think they originally came from the Greek Islands, perhaps as early as the time of Isaac.
- They organized themselves into five city-states, each governed by a different ruler ("the five rulers of the Philistines"—Joshua 13:3). These city-states were Ashkelon, Ashdod, Gath, Ekron, and Gaza.
- The Philistines were technologically advanced. They smelted iron and jealously guarded their knowledge to maintain their monopoly. It gave them advantages both economically and militarily (1 Samuel 13:19–22).
- The Philistines soon came to worship the gods of the Canaanites. They adopted Dagon (1 Samuel 5:1–7), the Ashtoreths (1 Samuel 31:10), and Baal-zebub (2 Kings 1:2).
- Perhaps unfairly, given their advanced technology, the term *philistine* has come to mean in English "someone who opposes progress" or "someone who is uncultured."

Children in Bible Times

Wives Without Children

Several prominent women in the Bible struggled with childlessness. Sarah (Genesis 16:2), Rachel (Genesis 30:1), and Hannah (1 Samuel 1:6) suffered bitterly at their fate of being unable to have children. This is why, for each of these women, their thanksgiving to God was so fervent after they were able to have children.

Teaching Children

During their children's younger years, mothers taught their children God's Word. Little ones heard the stories of God's care for His people. They learned how to pray. They were also taught to love, respect, and obey their fathers and mothers.

© CPH/Cheri Bladholm

What Did Girls Learn?

Mothers taught daughters to become good wives and mothers. A girl learned to cook and perform other household tasks from a young age. She learned to sew and knit, to spin and weave, to grind grain and make bread, to sweep and clean the house. She also learned how to take care of younger children.

What Did Boys Learn?

The training of boys began in their early childhood by their mothers. Later, they were taught to read and write by their fathers. They would learn to read and write well enough to read the Scriptures and take their place in the community. Also, fathers

often taught their boys their own trade. Abraham was a herder and farmer; he would have taught Isaac these same skills. Joseph, Jesus' earthly father, was a carpenter. It is likely that Jesus learned the trade of carpentry from his earthly father.

Babies

Immediately after birth, a midwife would bathe the child in warm water and rub it with salt. The baby would then be tightly wrapped in swaddling cloths. Mothers nursed their babies—bottles weren't used—for two or three years.

What are *Swaddling Cloths*?

Swaddling cloths were merely strips of torn cloth. Swaddling cloths were used to snugly wrap a baby so that his or her feet and hands could not move. It is said that this tight wrapping helped a baby feel calm and reassured, as though he were still in the mother's womb. This reminds us of the Book of Luke, where we learn that our Lord Jesus was wrapped in "swaddling cloths" and that He slept in a feeding trough (2:7).

Weapons of David and Goliath

Helmet

A leather helmet was worn to protect a soldier's head. But Goliath's helmet was made of bronze, a metal containing copper and tin. The helmet probably covered most of Goliath's head, but we know his forehead was left uncovered, because David's stone struck him there.

Shield

A handheld shield was used to protect a soldier from arrows and blows from hand weapons. Shields were either made of metal or of leather stretched over a wooden frame and then oiled. The oil helped preserve the shield and made the enemies' arrows glide off more easily. Sometimes, leather shields were soaked in water so that flaming arrows would be extinguished if they hit.

Coat of Mail

Soldiers wore a coat of mail like a garment. Mail could be made of interlocking chain links or of smaller pieces of metal that resembled fish scales. When Saul was king, only high-ranking leaders wore armor. It was an honor for David to be asked to wear Saul's armor. The coat of mail worn by Goliath weighed 5,000 shekels, or about 125 pounds. Goliath also wore bronze armor on his legs.

Spear

A spear, used for stabbing, had a long, sturdy shaft for a handle and a sharpened metal, bladelike head. Sometimes spears had points at both ends so soldiers could use them against enemies in front of or behind them. Stuck into the ground when not in use, spears were used for war, hunting, and fishing. The spear Goliath carried had a head that weighed 600 shekels, or about 15 pounds. The shaft was quite thick.

Breastplate

A breastplate made of metal covered the soldier's chest and provided protection against arrows, spears, lances, and other weapons.

Javelin

A javelin is similar to a spear, except that it is designed to be thrown, usually by hand. There were some devices for throwing them or shooting them like arrows. Throwing a javelin allowed a soldier to stay at a safer distance from his enemy. Goliath's javelin was made of bronze. He wore it slung across his back to keep it handy for battle.

Sword

Swords, made of copper, bronze, or iron, consisted of a blade attached to a small handle like a knife and were used mainly for stabbing. The sword was a very important weapon in Canaan. Swords are mentioned about four hundred times in the Old Testament. David used Goliath's own sword to cut off Goliath's head.

Sling

A shepherd used a sling to protect his sheep. The sling had two long cords, made of leather or woven goat hair, connected to a leather or woolen pocket that was big enough to hold a stone about 2–3 inches in diameter, or as big as a tennis ball.

The shepherd was skilled at swinging the sling and then letting go of one of the cords. A good slinger could throw a stone at speeds of 100 to 150 miles per hour and as far away as 600 feet. The stone could do quite a bit of damage. Armed only with his sling and several stones, David struck Goliath right in the forehead with the very first stone he threw.

Staff

The shepherd's staff David carried—but didn't use—when confronting Goliath helped him guide sheep and walk along steep and rocky hillsides and valleys. The staff was also used to knock leaves and twigs off of trees for the sheep to eat. It was a straight rod about 6 or 7 feet long that tapered slightly at one end. (Bible story pictures sometimes show a shepherd's staff with a crook at the top, but this kind actually came from Europe, not Israel.) Shepherds also carried a stout shorter stick to use as a club (see Psalm 23:4).

Shepherding Basics

The Bible contains a lesson for us about sheep.

The Lord is my shepherd; I shall not want. (Psalm 23:1)

Psalm 23 was written as if a sheep were telling his friends about his great and loving shepherd who knows him, loves him, and faithfully cares for him.

He makes me lie down in green pastures. He leads me beside still waters. (v. 2)

A good shepherd leads his sheep into green pastures where there is plenty of grass for them to eat. Because they are easily startled and frightened, he talks to them in a soft voice and leads them to quiet waters to drink.

He restores my soul. He leads me in paths of righteousness for His name's sake. (v. 3)

A good shepherd makes sure each of his sheep is accounted for and brings them safely back into the sheepfold, which is like a corral. The sheepfold has only one entrance, or gate, and the shepherd calls the sheep to bring them out and to lead them back in. The sheep recognize their shepherd's voice and will not respond to a stranger's voice.

Even though I walk through the valley of the shadow of death, I will fear no evil, for You are with me; Your rod and Your staff, they comfort me. You prepare a table before me in the presence of my enemies. (vv. 4–5a)

Shepherding can be dangerous, though. Besides the dangers of wolves and other predators, sheep often get themselves into trouble by wandering off. The shepherd carries a club for fighting off animals and a longer walking staff.

You anoint my head with oil; my cup overflows. (v. 5b)

Tending the sheep includes checking their wool every day to keep it clean. A shepherd will pour oil on top of the sheep's head to keep insects away, which might upset the sheep and keep it from feeding properly. In ancient times, oil was applied to the head of an honored guest, as well. This psalm tells us we are treated like honored guests by Jesus, our Good Shepherd.

Surely goodness and mercy shall follow me all the days of my life, and I shall dwell in the house of the Lord forever. (v. 6)

Sheep that are well tended are content and feel safe in the care of their shepherd.

The Nazirite Vow

While they look and sound very much alike, we should not confuse the words *Nazirite* and *Nazarene*. The word *Nazirite* comes from the Hebrew word *nazir*, meaning "to separate" or "keep away from," while *Nazarene* denotes a resident of the city of Nazareth.

© CPH/Corbert Gauthier

The Nazirite vow was a voluntary oath taken before God to abstain from certain things for a certain period of time and to dedicate oneself to the Lord. The vow was usually taken for the purpose of making a special request of God or to give thanks to God. As described in Numbers 6, a man or a woman could take a Nazirite vow. The vow had three parts. First, it required abstaining from all intoxicating grape and alcohol products—"he shall separate himself from wine and strong drink" (Numbers 6:3). Second, it required that one not cut one's hair—"All the days of his vow of separation, no razor shall touch his head. Until the time is completed for which he separates himself to the Lord, he shall be holy. He shall let the locks of hair of his head grow long" (v. 5). Third, the vow required that one avoid any contact with the dead—men or animals—"All the days that he separates himself to the Lord he shall not go near a dead body" (v. 6).

Nazirite vows in most cases only lasted for a few weeks or months. Some people, like Samson (Judges 16:17), were Nazirites from birth. Samuel and John the Baptist may also have been Nazirites from birth. In 1 Samuel 1:11, Samuel's mother vowed to give Samuel to the Lord, stating that his hair would never be cut, one of the provisions of the Nazirite vow. In Luke 1:15, the Lord's angel says that John the Baptist is never to drink wine and that he would be filled with the Holy Spirit from his birth. The vow was a way for people to publicly devote themselves entirely to God and to His work. Of the Nazirites, the Lord said to Moses, "All the days of his separation he is holy to the Lord" (Numbers 6:8). When the time

© CPH/Greg Copeland

of the vow was complete, the Nazirite could then present himself or herself before the priest for purification and a ceremony of release from the vows. The ceremony included offering animal sacrifices as well as cutting his or her hair and burning it on the altar.

Samson's hair was braided into seven sections because in Hebrew, the number seven represents spiritual perfection, completeness, or fullness. When Delilah discovered the secret of Samson's strength, "She made him sleep on her knees. And she called a man and had him shave off the seven locks of his head" (Judges 16:19).

King David

David is one of the most important people in Israelite history. He lived about a thousand years before Jesus. The youngest son of Jesse was born in

Bethlehem and cared for his father's sheep. The prophet Samuel anointed young David to be the second king of Israel because David was God's choice, "a man after His own heart" (1 Samuel 13:14).

David and Jonathan

David's great victory over the Philistine giant Goliath won him great admiration among the people, consequently causing King Saul to hate him. However, it gained him the friendship of King Saul's son, Jonathan. The two young men entered into a covenant friendship, initiated by Jonathan, in which they promised to care for and protect each other and each other's families. Even though as the king's son, Jonathan would rightfully have become king, Jonathan honored God's choice of David, giving David his robe, tunic, and sword. Later, Jonathan risked his own life to protect David from Saul's attempts to murder him. After Jonathan's death in a battle with the Philistines, David kept his promise to Jonathan and cared for Jonathan's crippled son, Mephibosheth, as his own.

David, Warrior and King

As a great warrior king, David defeated Israel's enemies and returned the previously captured ark of the covenant to Jerusalem, the new capital city of Israel. After David became king, he wanted to build a temple in Jerusalem. However, through the prophet Nathan, God told David that *God* would do the building, making a "house," or dynasty, for David. God told David that one of his descendants, the Messiah, would have a kingdom and throne that would last forever (2 Samuel 7:16).

David the Musician

David also loved music and wrote many of the psalms found in the Book of Psalms in the Bible. These songs often expressed his joy and thankfulness for God's protection (Psalm 34) and sometimes spoke of his fears or his sadness about his sins (Psalm 51).

David and Jesus

Jesus, like David, was born in Bethlehem, served as a shepherd for His Father's sheep, and was the King of the Jews. God kept His promise to David, and Jesus was born into David's family. God kept His promise to us and made us part of His family through our Baptism. Every day He keeps His promises to never leave us and to always care for us. We look forward to His promise that our King, Jesus, will one day return in all His glory!

Kings and Governments

The beginning of the monarchy was one of the most important events in Israel's history. For about three hundred years after entering Canaan, the tribes of Israel largely ruled themselves locally. Occasionally, when enemies threatened Israel from without or the remaining Canaanites threatened from within, God provided a deliverer in one of the judges.

God, Israel's King

Throughout the escape from Egypt, the wilderness years, and the period of the judges, God ruled His people directly. He gave Israel His Law in the Ten Commandments for their protection. He dwelled among them in the ark of the covenant and tabernacle. He was to be their King, and they were His people.

Now, however, Israel wanted a human king. They wanted a strong leader like all of the other nations had, who would lead them into battle and defeat their enemies.

God's Warning about Kings

God warned the Israelites about what a human king would do. He told them that a king would have all the power and would use that power for himself, not for them. God said the king would take the Israelites' sons to fight in his armies and their daughters to work by cooking, baking, and making perfume. He would take one tenth of their food and wine for his officers and servants and would take the very best of their flocks and fields for himself. They would be like slaves (1 Samuel 8:10–18).

The people did not heed God's warning and persisted in their demand for a king. God gave them what they asked for by anointing (1 Samuel 10:1) and proclaiming (v. 24) Saul, son of Kish, from the tribe of Benjamin, as their king.

God, Our King

Because we are sinful people, in His love and mercy, God gives us laws, governments, and leaders. Some are good, and some are not; however, God instructs us to obey our laws whether we agree with them or not. We may not like the "no parking" sign in front of the store or the sales tax added on to our purchases, but we are required to comply with them. The Bible teaches us to submit to authority because our laws are there to protect us. We are part of two kingdoms, one spiritual and one earthly. We are part of God's kingdom, fellow heirs with Jesus, through Baptism. We are also citizens of earth, called by God to respect our earthly authorities and follow our elected leaders.

Saul becomes king.

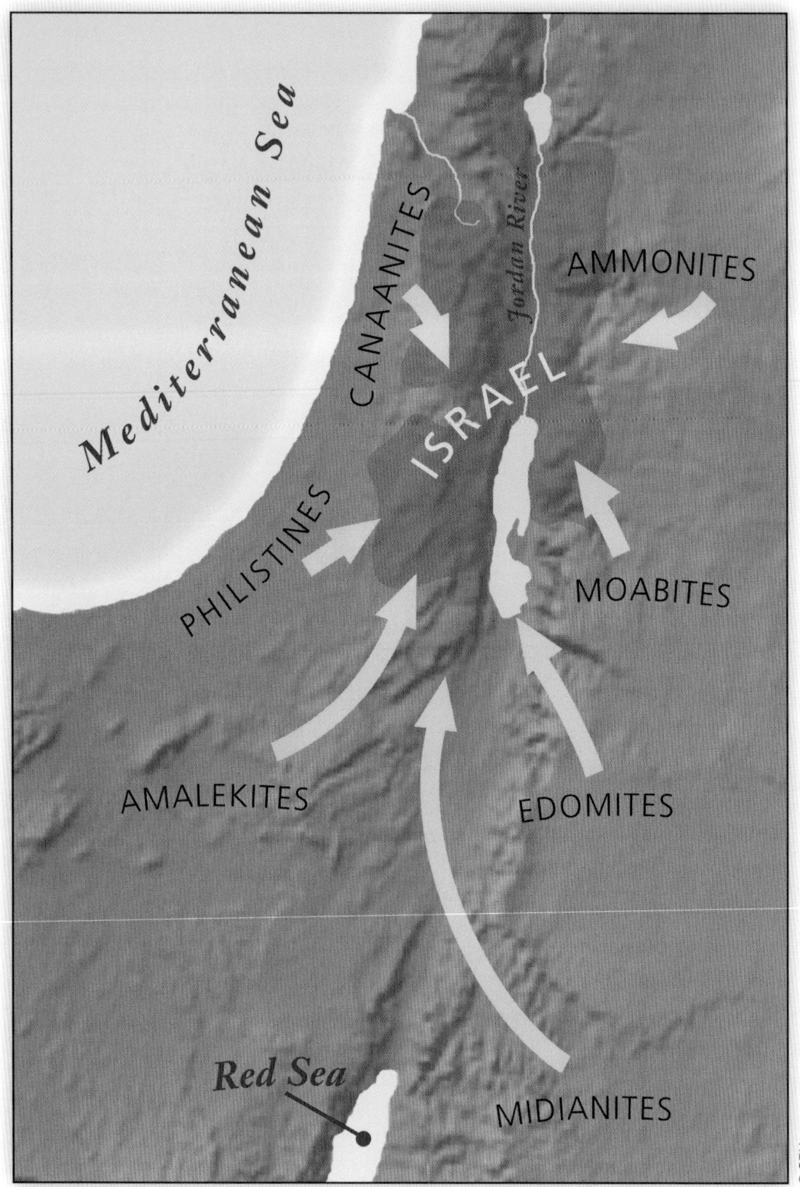

Israel's Enemies

The Promised Land of Canaan is also called "Israel" and "Palestine." It was an important area in the ancient world. It was bounded on the west by the Mediterranean Sea, on the north by the mountains of Lebanon, by the desert on the south, and by the Jordan River to the east. Partly because of its choice location, the people of Israel had many enemies.

Enemies Within

Chief among the enemies that troubled Israel throughout its history were the former inhabitants of the land of Canaan, including the Canaanites, Amalekites, and Philistines. Because these people were not completely destroyed or driven out as God commanded (Numbers 33:51–55), they remained as troublesome threats. Even worse, Israel frequently strayed into the idolatry practiced by these unwanted neighbors.

Enemies Without

The Philistines were Israel's worst enemy, almost constantly at war with the Israelites. They were sea traders who lived in the southwestern part of Canaan along the coast of the Mediterranean. They were known for their cruelty and their powerful weapons made of iron. While digging recently in the areas around the ancient cities of Gaza and Gath, Goliath's hometown, archaeologists (scientists who study fossil relics, artifacts, and monuments to learn how people lived in the past) found several iron weapons, as well as carvings showing helmets and armor. In 1 Samuel 17, we find a description of the giant Goliath's bronze armor, which weighed about 150 pounds.

The Amalekites were nomadic descendants of Esau who lived throughout the Middle East, from Sinai east into Babylon. Many of them, however, settled south of Canaan in the Sinai Peninsula. They attacked the Israelites while the Israelites wandered in the desert on their way to the Promised Land, and they were defeated by Joshua (Exodus 17:8–16).

Occasionally, these various tribes would join together into an alliance to defeat Israel. Who were some of Israel's other enemies? Psalm 83 mentions a few, mostly nomadic tribes who invaded Israel looking for food for their herds.

The Ammonites lived east of the Dead Sea and Jordan River. They were cruel people who worshiped idols. The Moabites lived south of Ammon, east of the Dead Sea, and fought with God's people for most of Israel's history. The Edomites, descendants of Edom—also named "Esau," who was Jacob's older brother—held territory south of Moab and opposed Israel as they traveled to the Promised Land; they attacked the tribe of Judah during Saul's reign. Gideon fought the Midianites, who lived east of the Sinai Peninsula, across the Red Sea.

Our Awesome God

God answered Israel's prayer for help—crushing its enemies through the efforts of Joshua, the judges, and Israel's kings—at least for a time. Later, Assyria would destroy the Northern Kingdom of Israel, and Babylon would take many from the Southern Kingdom of Judah into exile. Israel's enemies taught its people to trust in God and serve Him only.

Jesus defeated our worst enemies—sin, death, and the devil—on the cross. The victory He won for us through His resurrection, as well as His presence in our lives through His Word and Sacraments, gives us the power we need to fight our daily battles with temptations. We belong to Jesus through our Baptism, and no enemy is strong enough to take us away from Him.

Although Jesus' forebear, David, mightily opposed Israel's enemies, he needed God's help with the greatest enemy of all: sin. God provided this help through a prophet.

Nathan, God's Prophet

Nathan's relationship with the king of Israel differed from that of other men in the kingdom. Although he was the subject of David, he had special access to the king because he was a prophet. The word *prophet* comes from the Greek words *pro*, meaning "for," and *phanai*, meaning "to speak"—"to speak for." Prophets had several tasks: preaching, exhorting, explaining God's Word, and sometimes foretelling certain events. However, God's prophets did not speak of their own will. They spoke God's messages for His people. As such, their words could comfort, encourage, strengthen, or even alarm those who heard them.

God's Spokesman

There are three instances in Scripture that record Nathan's talks with King David. At one point, David was planning to build a temple for the Lord in which to house the ark of the covenant. Through Nathan, God told David that David's son Solomon would be the one to do this. Another instance involved the succession of the throne. Adonijah, another of David's sons, set himself up to be the next king upon David's death. Nathan heard of this and advised Bathsheba to approach David with the news. As a result, Solomon secured his claim to the throne.

Call to Confession

Probably the most famous encounter Nathan had with David was when he rebuked the king for the murder of Uriah and adultery with Bathsheba. It is in this account that we see an example of the role that confession may serve in the life of a believer. Nathan comes to David and convicts him of his sin. David repents and receives forgiveness. This same rhythm of confession and absolution is part of Church life today.

1 and 2 Kings

Into 1 and 2 Kings

The books of **1 and 2 Kings** were originally one book in the Hebrew Bible, called simply "Kings." Together, these books record life in Israel during the monarchy from King Solomon to King Jehoiachin.

Theme: The Lord's faithful love for an unfaithful people

Who wrote 1 and 2 Kings? When? Why?

These books were written by anonymous Israelite scribes. A Jewish tradition credited Jeremiah, but scholars today reject that view. The books clearly reveal the need of all people for a Savior and tell how God worked, despite the sins of His people, to preserve His covenant promise to Abraham (Genesis 17:1–8).

The Book of 1 Kings opens about 970 BC as King David is dying. The Book of 2 Kings closes with the release of King Jehoiachin from prison and his elevation to a favored position in the courts of the king of Babylon in around 557 BC. As you can see, then, the books of 1 and 2 Kings record more than four hundred years of the Lord's care and concern for His people.

The writer does not explain why he wrote these books, but we can make an intelligent guess, based on the context. Because of His people's idolatry, God allowed the Babylonian Empire to overrun the kingdom of Judah. The Babylonians captured the Judeans and forced them into exile in Babylon—more than five hundred miles from home.

This timeline details the three waves of conquest that overtook Judah and its people:

- **605 BC** Nebuchadnezzar becomes king of Babylon, invades Judah, loots the temple, and deports the elite members of society—the educated, the leaders, the skilled craftspeople, and the like—to Babylon. This included the prophet Daniel and his three friends of fiery furnace fame, Shadrach, Meshach, and Abednego. (See 2 Kings 17.)
- **601 BC** The Babylonians invade Egypt; both sides suffer. Judah forms an alliance with Egypt, despite the prophet Jeremiah's warnings that this alliance will only lead to destruction. (See 2 Kings 23:36–24:7.)
- **597 BC** Partly in retaliation for Judah's alliance with Egypt, the Babylonians invade Judah again; they besiege and capture Jerusalem. A second wave of exiles—more than ten thousand people in all—are taken back to Babylon, including Ezekiel. Zedekiah becomes a "puppet king" of Nebuchadnezzar in Jerusalem. (See 2 Kings 25:1–17.)
- **589 BC** Zedekiah rebels and Nebuchadnezzar returns to Judah a third time. The Babylonians set up a siege of Jerusalem that lasts for three years. Conditions inside the city are horrific. Many people starve to death. (See 2 Kings 24:20b–25:2.)
- **586 BC** The siege creates such famine that the starving people inside can no longer hold out against the army of Babylon. The walls are breached, and King Zedekiah is captured. Nebuchadnezzar slaughters Zedekiah's sons before his eyes and then blinds him. Yet another wave of captives are deported to Babylon. Jerusalem's walls are demolished; the temple is destroyed and burned. (See 2 Kings 25:3–21.)

Judah's last days weren't pretty. During their seventy years of captivity in Babylon, God's people had time to think about all the horror they had experienced and to ask questions—questions like "Why? Why has this happened to us? Aren't we God's people? Didn't He establish a covenant with our ancestors? Has He forgotten us?"

The author of 1 and 2 Kings writes to answer those questions. The Lord had not broken His covenant with His people. They themselves had broken that covenant, worshiping idols and revolting against the God who had so mercifully and powerfully rescued them from slavery in Egypt.

But all was not lost! There was still hope! The exiles could still return to the Lord, and He would help, heal, and restore them to a right relationship with Himself. The song Moses had taught the nation hundreds of years earlier told them how to repent, and it told them of the forgiveness God would grant. (See Deuteronomy 32:1–43.) The authors of Kings included many examples of reform and restoration, each illustrating the need for repentance and the grace of the Lord Moses had described.

How are 1 and 2 Kings classified?

These two books are grouped among the Books of History in the Old Testament.

What are the key divisions of 1 and 2 Kings?

1 and 2 Kings may be divided into five main parts:

- **1 Kings 1:1–12:24** King David dies; King Solomon rules in wisdom and is succeeded by his son Rehoboam.
- **1 Kings 12:25–16:34** The kingdom of David and Solomon splits into the Northern Kingdom (Israel) and the Southern Kingdom (Judah).
- **1 Kings 17:1–2 Kings 8:15** The Lord sends prophets to call for repentance.
- **2 Kings 8:16–17:41** Deepening unbelief in both kingdoms; Assyria defeats and exiles the people of the Northern Kingdom
- **2 Kings 18:1–25:30** Reforms and rebellion in the Southern Kingdom; Babylon invades and deports the Judeans

How do 1 and 2 Kings point to Jesus?

King Solomon is a "type," or picture, of Christ. (See "Where is Jesus in 1 and 2 Chronicles?")

But there's a larger story in these books—a story of coming rescue in the Savior God had promised to send. Like a red baton passed from runner to runner in a relay race thousands of years long, the covenant promise God first gave to Abraham passed from him to Isaac, then to Jacob, then to Judah, and from Judah, to Perez.

Perez passed that baton of promise to his descendant Salmon. Salmon passed it to Boaz, Boaz to Obed, Obed to Jesse, and Jesse to the shepherd boy, David, who became Israel's second king.

The books of 1 and 2 Kings, then, record the history of how the Lord preserved that "baton" of promise down through successive kings in Israel and Judah—the faithful and the unfaithful, the obedient and the rebels. Finally, centuries later, the Savior would be born from the kingly line of David's "house," or dynasty, just as God had promised (2 Samuel 7:1–16; Matthew 1:1–17).

History shows that none of these kings or their subjects deserved God's kindness. Still, He remained faithful to them, even when they were unfaithful.

We might read right over the words of 2 Kings 25:27–30, seeing them as a footnote of little importance. Who cares that Evil-merodach, king of Babylon, released Jehoiachin from prison and gave him a seat at the king's table?

You and I do! These words give us hope, just as they gave hope to the exiles in Babylon who first read them! God was preserving His covenant promise to send a Savior. He used the most unlikely people, the most unlikely circumstances. But He was at work for us nonetheless. He was at work for His whole family, past, present, and future!

What are the key chapters in 1 and 2 Kings?

- **1 Kings 3** Solomon prays for wisdom—for a "hearing heart"—as he rules God's people.
- **1 Kings 6–8** Solomon fulfills King David's dream of building a temple for the Lord.
- **1 Kings 10** The Queen of Sheba visits Solomon's court.
- **1 Kings 11** King Solomon's sins
- **1 Kings 12** Solomon's kingdom splits into two parts—the Northern and the Southern kingdoms. (This chapter also tells how King Jeroboam set up two golden calves (at Dan in the north and Bethel in the south) to keep his people from going to Jerusalem to worship at the temple. From its beginning, the Northern Kingdom had phony gods, phony priests, phony festivals, and phony sacrifices. They were set up to fall away from the true faith. Satan was trying to destroy God's covenant promise!)
- **1 Kings 17:1–2 Kings 2:14** The prophet Elijah's ministry (God did not give up on the people in the Northern Kingdom. He sent many prophets to call them to repentance. Elijah was one.)
- **2 Kings 2:15–13:25** The prophet Elisha's ministry to the people in the Northern Kingdom after the Lord took Elijah to heaven in a whirlwind and chariot of fire—likely a company of the holy angels (One group of angels is called the "seraphim" in Isaiah 6; their name means "burning ones"!)
- **2 Kings 12** King Jehoash (Joash) repairs the temple and tries to bring his people (the Southern Kingdom) to repentance.
- **2 Kings 17** Assyria attacks and the Northern Kingdom falls; the reasons God allowed it to happen
- **2 Kings 18:1–20:21** King Hezekiah's faithfulness and reforms

- **2 Kings 22:1–23:30** King Josiah's reign and reforms. The prophet Jeremiah was a friend of King Josiah. The people went along with their king's reforms, but after Josiah died, they fell back into their same sins. Jeremiah continued his ministry—mostly alone—proclaiming God's Word.
- **2 Kings 24–25** Waves of invasion by King Nebuchadnezzar and the Babylonian army, ending with the total destruction of Jerusalem and the burning of the temple

Treasures of Solomon's Temple

Even though the Bible gives some details about Solomon's temple, what it actually looked like is not known. Many different drawings and models provide an idea of what it might have looked like.

Inside the temple, in the Holy Place, the stone walls were lined with cedar so that no stone showed. The wood was carved and decorated and then covered with pure gold. The floor was covered with gold. Ten candlestick holders stood in the Holy Place, five on each side. A golden table also

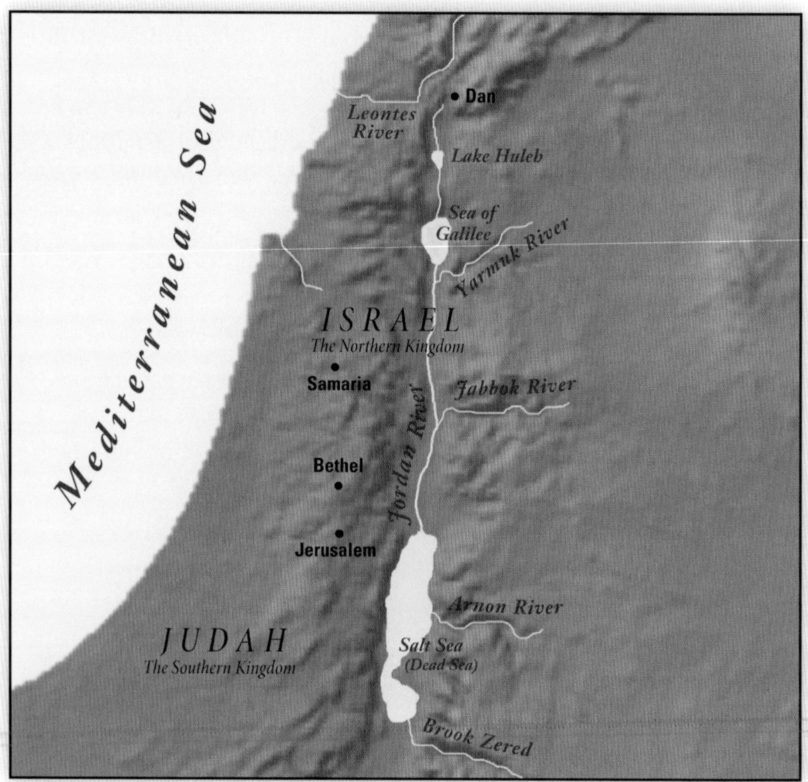

The Kings of Israel and Judah

United Kingdom

Saul	1 Samuel 9:1–31:13; 1 Chronicles 10:1–14
David	2 Samuel; 1 Kings 1:1–2:11; 1 Chronicles 11:1–29:30
Solomon	1 Kings 2:12–11:43; 2 Chronicles 1:1–9:31

Northern Kingdom (Israel)

Jeroboam 1	1 Kings 12:25–14:20
Nadab	1 Kings 15:25–31
Baasha	1 Kings 15:32–16:7
Elah	1 Kings 16:8–14
Zimri	1 Kings 16:15–20
Omri	1 Kings 16:21–28
Ahab	1 Kings 16:29–22:40
Ahaziah	1 Kings 22:51–53; 2 Kings 1:1–18
Joram (Jehoram)	2 Kings 1:17–8:15
Jehu	2 Kings 9:1–10:36
Jehoahaz	2 Kings 13:1–9
Jehoash (Joash)	2 Kings 13:10–25
Jeroboam II	2 Kings 14:23–29
Zechariah	2 Kings 15:8–12
Shallum	2 Kings 15:13–15
Menahem	2 Kings 15:16–22
Pekahiah	2 Kings 15:23–26
Pekah	2 Kings 15:27–31
Hoshea	2 Kings 15:30; 17:1–41

Southern Kingdom (Judah)

Rehoboam	1 Kings 12:1–14:31; 2 Chronicles 10:1–12:16
Abijah (Abijam)	1 Kings 15:1–8; 2 Chronicles 13:1–14:1
Asa	1 Kings 15:9–24; 2 Chronicles 14:1–16:14
Jehoshaphat	1 Kings 22:41–50; 2 Chronicles 17:1–21:1
Joram (Jehoram)	2 Kings 8:16–24; 2 Chronicles 21:1–20
Ahaziah	2 Kings 8:25–29; 2 Chronicles 22:1–9
Athaliah (queen)	2 Kings 11:1–16; 2 Chronicles 22:10–23:21
Joash (Jehoash)	2 Kings 11:17–12:21 2 Chronicles 23:16–24:27
Amaziah	2 Kings 14:1–22; 2 Chronicles 25:1–28
Azariah (Uzziah)	2 Kings 13:10–25
Jotham	2 Kings 15:32–38; 2 Chronicles 27:1–9
Ahaz	2 Kings 16:1–20; 2 Chronicles 28:1–27
Hezekiah	2 Kings 18:1–20:21; 2 Chronicles 29:1–32:33
Manasseh	2 Kings 21:1–18; 2 Chronicles 33:1–20
Amon	2 Kings 21:19–26; 2 Chronicles 33:21–25
Josiah	2 Kings 22:1–23:30; 2 Chronicles 34:1–35:27
Jehoahaz	2 Kings 23:31–33; 2 Chronicles 36:1–4
Jehoiakim	2 Kings 23:34–24:7; 2 Chronicles 36:5–8
Jehoiachin	2 Kings 24:8–16; 25:27–30; 2 Chronicles 36:9–10
Zedekiah	2 Kings 24:17–25:21; 2 Chronicles 36:11–21

stood inside. Loaves of special bread, called "the bread of the Presence," were placed on this table. The altar of incense stood deep inside, just in front of the door to the Most Holy Place.

Many carvings decorated the inside and outside of the temple. The designs included cherubim, palm trees, open flowers, lilies, gourds, lions, oxen, pomegranates, chains, wreathes, and lattice. The woodcarvings were then covered with pure gold.

The priests' work in the temple required many bowls, pots, shovels, tongs, cups, snuffers, dishes for incense, fire pans, and other items. Some of these were made of bronze, but most were made of pure gold. These were stored in the storage chambers surrounding the temple.

The ark of the covenant was kept inside the Most Holy Place. Two cherubim carved from olive wood and covered in gold also stood with the ark. They stood ten cubits (fifteen feet, or five meters) tall. The wingspan of each cherub was also ten cubits, so their wings touched each other and the walls of the Most Holy Place.

The Bible describes the Inner Court that encircled the temple (1 Kings 6:36). It was only for the priests. Outside the Inner Court was the Great Court (2 Chronicles 4:9), where the people gathered. The people and priests entered the courts through doors of bronze.

The Bronze Sea was a large tank for water that sat at the southeast corner of the inner court. It was made of bronze and held about twelve thousand

© Shutterstock, Inc.; iStockphoto.com

gallons (forty-four thousand liters) of water. It rested on the backs of twelve bronze oxen and stood about fourteen feet tall. The priests washed their hands and feet in the bronze sea before making sacrifices and performing other priestly duties.

The Altar of Burnt Offerings was in the southwest corner of the Priests' Court. It was made of bronze, and a ramp led up to the top.

Solomon, Man of God

Scripture records much of the wisdom of Solomon. The Bible credits him with writing three thousand proverbs and more than one thousand songs (1 Kings 4:32). He is also the author or co-author of three books in the Bible—Proverbs, Song of Solomon, and Ecclesiastes. In addition to his literary works, Solomon extended the borders of Jerusalem. He appointed chief officials including secretaries, recorders, priests, personal advisors, and labor managers. He also named twelve governors to help administer the kingdom.

Israel thrived under Solomon's reign. As Solomon's kingdom expanded, so did his wealth. His household alone used 180 bushels of flour, 360 bushels of meal, 10 head of stall-fed cattle, 20 head of pasture-fed cattle, 100 sheep and goats, deer, and other meats each day, all to support his own family and his servants, officials, and their families (1 Kings 4:22–23). He had 40,000 stalls of horses for his chariots, and more than 12,000 horsemen, as well as chariots, fleets of ships, and a huge amount of gold (1 Kings 4:26). In fact, his yearly revenue was more than 666 talents of gold—about 25 tons—as he did business with merchants, kings, and other traders (1 Kings 10:14).

Indeed, Solomon was known throughout the world. His reign was one of peace and prosperity for the kingdom of Israel, as he followed in the footsteps of his father, David.

Where God Dwells

There has never been a time throughout the history of the world when God was not with His people. However, there came a time in Israel's history when God resolved to dwell visibly among His people.

The Tabernacle

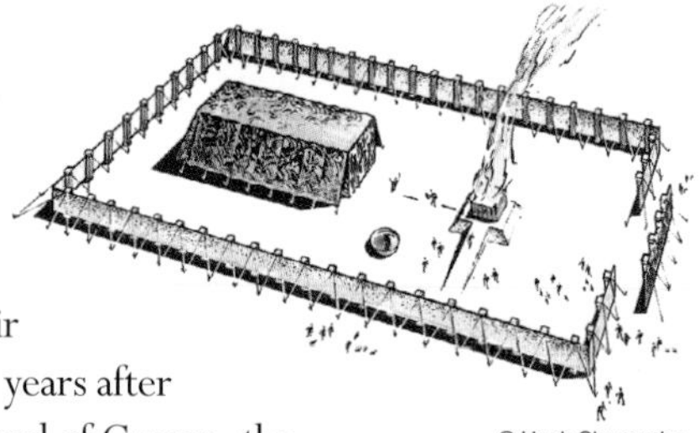

© Hugh Claycombe

At the foot of Mount Sinai, God's people, directed by Moses, created and assembled the first earthly home for God. This was the tabernacle, which would travel with them throughout their forty years in the wilderness. For many years after God's people settled in the Promised Land of Canaan, the tabernacle continued to serve as God's earthly house.

The First Temple

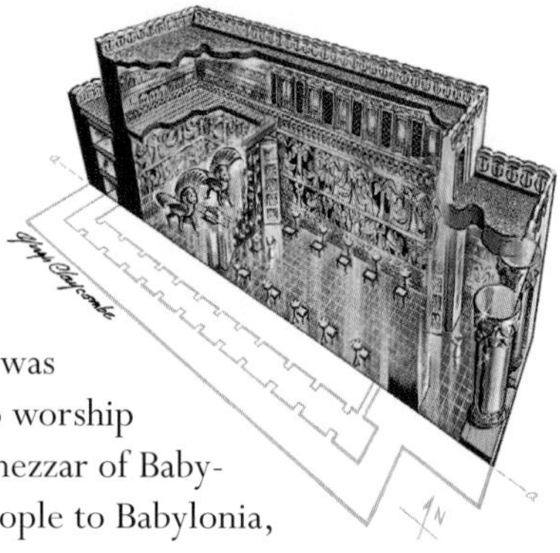

© Hugh Claycombe

The original temple, also known as "Solomon's temple," was built to house the ark of the covenant during Solomon's reign. King David had wanted to construct it, but the Lord said that He had chosen Solomon to build it. It took seven years to build the temple that was to be a permanent place for the people to worship the Lord. Unfortunately, King Nebuchadnezzar of Babylon, who also deported many of God's people to Babylonia, destroyed this first temple.

The Second Temple

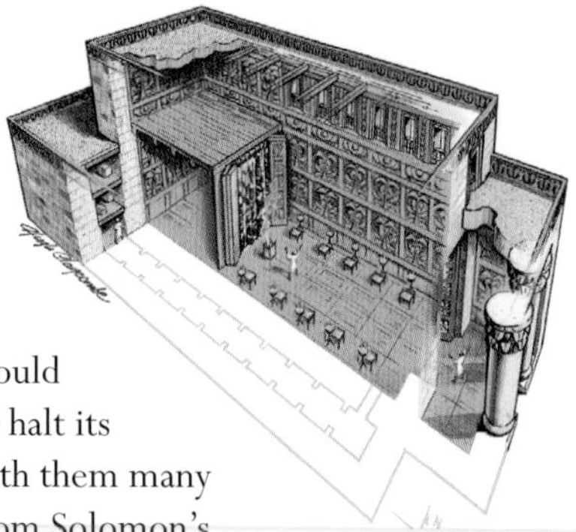

© Hugh Claycombe

When the exiles returned, they set about to rebuild their homes, the walls of Jerusalem, and the temple. Construction of this second temple, known as "Zerubbabel's temple," started in 536 BC and was completed in 516 BC. At times, it seemed as if it would not be finished because enemies tried to halt its construction. The exiles also brought with them many of the original furnishings and vessels from Solomon's temple that had been taken to Babylon. The ark of the covenant, however, had disappeared and may have been destroyed during the Babylonian conquest. A stone slab marked its former location in the Most Holy Place. Although this new temple was not as ornate as the first, it lasted much longer. Throughout the years, Zerubbabel's temple was repaired and reconstructed as necessary.

Ezekiel's Temple Vision

Another temple, "Ezekiel's temple," is mentioned in the Bible, but it was never built. It was described in a vision Ezekiel received from the Lord, recorded in detail in the Book of Ezekiel, chapters 40–44. This temple would have been more ornate than the temple Zerubbabel built.

The Last Temple

© Hugh Claycombe

The temple Jesus knew was a gift to Israel from an unusual source. King Herod the Great was known for his cruelty. He commanded the murder of baby boys in Bethlehem shortly after Jesus' birth. Early in his reign, however, he decided to replace the old temple. Although not ethnically Jewish, Herod enjoyed lavish buildings, and his new temple was fifteen stories high. It took only eighteen months to construct the high sanctuary, but the remainder of the temple complex was not finished until sixty-eight years after Herod's death. This extravagant temple included one stone that was more than thirty-six feet long. Much of the temple was made of the purest white stone or was covered in gold overlay.

© CPH/Greg Copeland

Jesus, Our Temple

A discussion of the temple would be incomplete without referring to the Messiah. Jesus is that temple to which all of the other temples pointed. He is *Immanuel*, "God with us," the glory of the Lord who tabernacles among us through His Word and Sacraments.

© CPH/Greg Copeland

Elijah throughout the Bible

The prophet Elijah appears frequently in the Bible. In fact, no other prophet achieved as much recognition in the New Testament. The name *Elijah* means "the Lord is my God," and his message went hand in hand with this meaning. Elijah's role was to stand against idolatry, especially Baal worship, and to preach repentance to God's people.

Well Traveled

Elijah is first mentioned in 1 Kings 17:1. His hometown is Tishbe in Gilead. Gilead is the region east of the Jordan River. The Bible mentions Tishbe only this one time, and its exact location is not known. Elijah seemed to spend most of his time in the land west of the Jordan River, ranging widely from Zarephath in the far north of Israel to Beersheba, south of Judah.

A "Type" of John the Baptist

During his time as prophet, Elijah displayed characteristics that would be repeated by a future prophet—John the Baptist.

- Elijah prepared the way for the coming of Elisha; John prepared the way for the coming of Jesus. In fact, Jesus said that some biblical prophecy concerning Elijah was fulfilled in John the Baptist. Christ also referred to Elijah's coming when He was speaking about the arrival of John the Baptist.
- Elijah suffered under a brutal ruler; John, too, suffered at the hands of a cruel ruler. After John suffered, Christ would soon suffer and die.

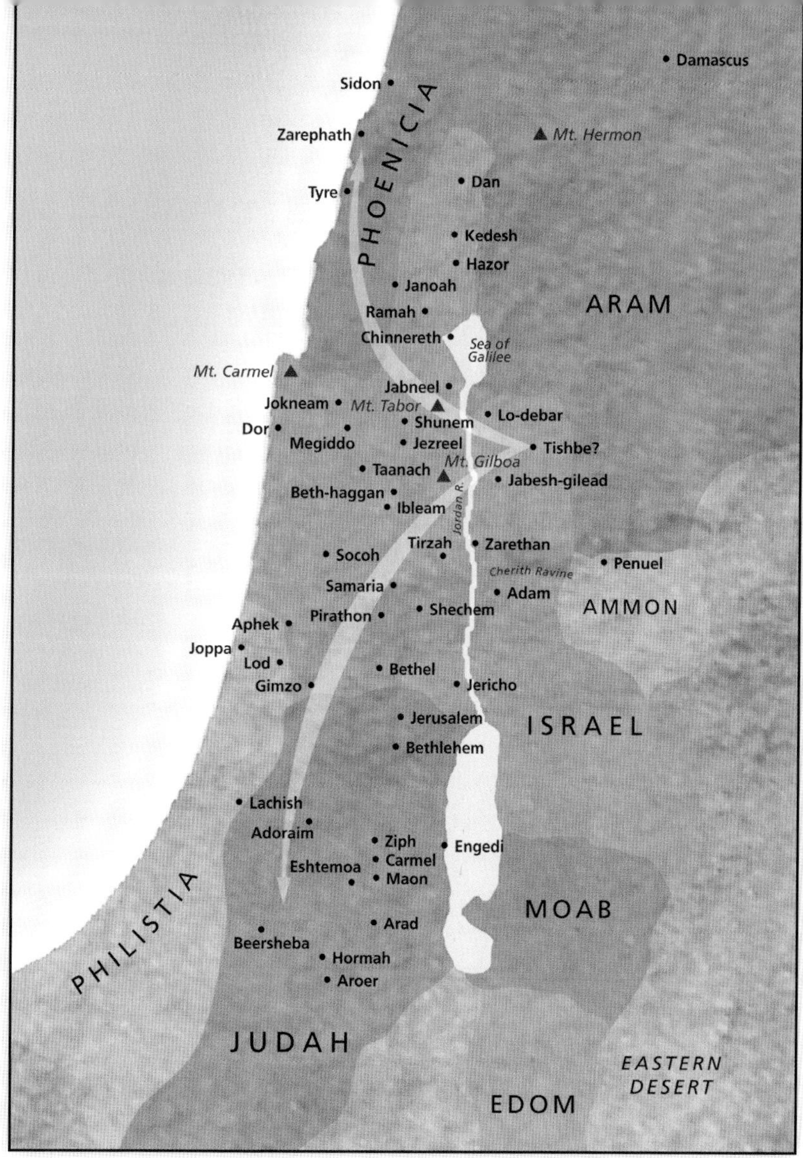

Elijah and Christ

Elijah also foreshadowed Christ. Elijah fasted forty days and nights on his way to Mount Horeb. Before this trip, the Lord provided food and drink in order to prepare him for the days to come. Years later, Jesus fasted forty days in the desert.

The most well-known reference to Elijah in the New Testament is the one that occurs during the transfiguration, when the disciples see Jesus talking with Moses and Elijah, all in glorified bodies. In this revelation, Moses represented the Law, while Elijah stood for the Prophets, reminding the disciples—and us—that the Law and the Prophets all find their fulfillment in Jesus, the Savior, whom God had promised to send to His people.

Children in God's Kindgom

Children are an important part of the kingdom of God. He came to His chosen, helpless, needy, dependent children of all ages and gives His love through Word and Sacrament. Jesus showed great love and respect for children, inviting them to be near Him and blessing them.

© CPH/Corbert Gauthier

Hannah prayed to the Lord for a son. She promised that if she had a son, he would be dedicated to the Lord's service. Samuel was born and served in the temple under Eli the priest. The Lord spoke to **Samuel** when he was a boy (1 Samuel 16:11–13; 3:1–18).

© CPH/Cheri Bladholm

© CPH/Robert Papp

Joseph was the favorite of Jacob's twelve sons (Genesis 37). Joseph's brothers hated him and sold him into slavery. Joseph remained faithful and became a great leader in Egypt, saving the Israelites from starvation.

© CPH/Cheri Bladholm

Moses was born to a Hebrew family in Egypt. To save his life, his mother set him adrift in the Nile River when he was three months old. Pharaoh's daughter raised him as her own son (Exodus 2:1–10). Moses would later see God face-to-face, receive the Law, and lead Israel to the Promised Land.

David, who was only a boy when he was anointed by Samuel (1 Samuel 16:11–13), became the greatest king of Israel and was an ancestor of Jesus (Matthew 1).

© CPH/Sally Schaedler

A young Israelite girl became the servant of the wife of Naaman, the commander of the army of the king of Syria (2 Kings 5:1–3). She told her mistress that the prophet Elisha could cure Naaman of his leprosy. Naaman was cured and worshiped the Lord.

Samuel

Josiah

John the Baptist recognized Jesus as the Christ before either one was born (Luke 1:39–45).

A young boy helped Jesus teach the disciples about greatness and humility. Jesus put him in the middle of the group and said, "Unless you turn and become like children, you will never enter the kingdom of heaven" (Matthew 18:1–4).

Jairus's twelve-year-old daughter died before Jesus arrived, but Jesus raised her from the dead, and people glorified His name (Luke 8:41–42, 49–56).

Games and Toys in Bible Times

Children in Bible times fulfilled important roles in their families. They had to help the family with chores, and their education was very important. However, that is not to say that children in Bible times did not play. Many of their games and toys resemble children's toys of today.

In Matthew 11:16–17, Jesus refers to children copying adult activities of feasts and funerals. So, just like today, children in ancient Israel played house and "pretend," mimicking adult activities.

Children also played with many types of toys. They had game boards that were similar to checkers. They played games with marbles and balls. Children played with dolls and had toy furniture for them. They also had toy tools, such as hammers. Children also played with dice, rattles, and small pieces of pottery, often shaped into animals. Children scratched on the hard, dry ground to play games similar to hopscotch.

Sometimes children turned work into fun. Children rode the ox that was led around in circles as it tramped the grain, separating the grain from the straw and chaff. This was an important job on the farms.

© CPH/Corbert Gauthier

The Bronze Serpent

Bronze

Bronze is an alloy, a mixture of copper and tin, plus traces of other metals. Bronze is easier to work with than pure copper. Because it has a low melting point, it has been used since ancient times for cast statues that are made by pouring liquid bronze into a mold. It also can be worked while it is cold. The finished piece is durable and strong. The colors of bronze vary with the amount of tin and trace metals used and can range from almost silver to a coppery red. By the time of Moses, bronze had been used in the Middle East for more than a thousand years. We don't know what method Moses used to make the bronze snake, but we know that it could have been made quickly.

Idolatry

Snake worship was common in the ancient Near East. We learn from 2 Kings 18:4 that some Israelites had turned the bronze serpent of Moses' time—this gift of healing—into an idol. They burned incense to it during the reign of King Hezekiah. Perhaps they wanted to be like their pagan neighbors, who believed that graven images could help them have a plentiful harvest, strong livestock, and many healthy children. We know that at the time of King Hezekiah, the Israelites had turned away from worshiping the God of their fathers—the true God—and were worshiping the various false gods of their neighbors. Hezekiah sought to do away with idol worship and had the bronze snake destroyed.

Reminders of God's Love

The bronze serpent became an idol for some of the Israelites. Is there a danger that we might make idols of the religious statues, crosses, symbols, and pictures of Jesus or the saints that we display in our church buildings? Visual arts are good when they point us to the truths taught by the triune God. They can help us see that God's grace comes through faith in Jesus, who died in our place on the cross. If we remember that these images intend to point us to God's grace and that they do not have any power to save, we certainly can treat them with respect and thank God for them.

God's Prophets, the Chariots of Israel

As Elijah was transported to heaven by the whirlwind at the end of his ministry, a chariot and horses of fire accompanied him:

And as they still went on and talked, behold, chariots of fire and horses of fire separated the two of them. And Elijah went up by a whirlwind into heaven. And Elisha saw it and he cried, "My father, my father! The chariots of Israel and its horsemen!" And he saw him no more. (2 Kings 2:11–12a)

Weapons of War

More than any other weapon of war, the chariot struck fear into the hearts of enemies. Chariots are emblems of a king's strength. More than six hundred chariots pursued Israel as Moses led them out of Egypt (Exodus 14:7–9).

Chariots of iron thwarted Israel as they sought to take possession of the Promised Land (Judges 1:19). Deborah and Barak faced the Canaanite general, Sisera, and nine hundred chariots in Judges 4, but, with divine help, defeated them. The army of Saul defeated thirty thousand chariots in battle at Michmash (1 Samuel 13). Solomon had fourteen hundred chariots (1 Kings 10:26).

True Strength

The appearance of the fiery chariot and Elisha's passionate cry as Elijah ascended into heaven can then be seen as a tremendous affirmation of Elijah's importance in Israel's history. It was Elijah, God's prophet and Israel's spiritual leader, who was the real strength of the nation, far more than the evil King Ahab.

Elijah's Successor

Some fifty years later, Elisha—Elijah's successor as God's prophet—lay on his deathbed. Jehoash, who was king at that time, went to Elisha in tears and offered the same affirmation, using nearly the same words that Elisha had spoken at Elijah's departure: "My father! My father! The chariots of Israel and its horsemen!" (2 Kings 13:14). God's prophets were truly the chariots of Israel.

Ancient Babylonia

Exiled to Babylon

The Israelites lived in the Promised Land for many years under the rule of judges and prophets. Then God gave the people kings to rule them. Under the rule of King Solomon, the Israelites had peace and prosperity. Solomon oversaw the construction of the temple, and God's people worshiped Him in this permanent structure.

After many years, the kingdom of Israel divided. The northern and southern regions each had their own king. Then, foreign invaders came to the land. The Babylonians conquered the Southern Kingdom, known as Judah, about six hundred years before Jesus was born. Babylonians were from Babylonia, or modern-day Iraq. They destroyed Jerusalem. Some of the

© John Said/Shutterstock, Inc.

conquered Judeans escaped to Egypt or other areas, but many of the Judeans were forced to go to the city of Babylon. Babylon was where the events in the Book of Daniel took place, including God's deliverance of Shadrach, Meshach, and Abednego from the fiery furnace and Daniel from the den of lions.

Babylon, under the rule of King Nebuchadnezzar, became the most important city in the land. It was a center for culture, political strength, and architectural development. The site of ancient Babylon is about fifty miles south of modern-day Baghdad in the country of Iraq.

During the fifteen hundred years since Babylon's downfall, looters have quarried the ancient sites to try to get the excellent baked bricks from the buildings. Left today are the lower-quality bricks, piled in mounds. The government of Iraq has made some effort to restore the structures to their original glory. However, much more work is required.

© CPH/Glenn Myers

Return from Captivity

God told Jeremiah the prophet that the Jews would return to their homeland after seventy years of captivity in Babylon. Their years of weeping in Babylon, while being away from their homeland, were over. However,

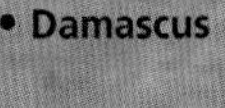
Damascus
Sidon
PHOENICIA
Zarephath
Mt. Hermon
Dan
Tyre
Kedesh
Hazor
Janoah
ARAM
Ramah
Chinnereth
Sea of Galilee
Mt. Carmel
Jabneel
Jokneam
Mt. Tabor
Lo-debar
Dor
Shunem
Megiddo
Jezreel
Tishbe?
Mt. Gilboa
Taanach
Jabesh-gilead
Beth-haggan
Ibleam
Jordan R.
Gath
Tirzah
Zarethan
Socoh
Penuel
Cherith Ravine
Samaria
Adam
AMMON
Shechem
Pirathon
Aphek
Joppa
Lod
Bethel
Gimzo
Jericho
Jerusalem
ISRAEL
Bethlehem
Lachish
Adoraim
Ziph
Engedi
Carmel
Eshtemoa
Maon
PHILISTIA
MOAB
Arad
Beersheba
Hormah
Aroer
JUDAH
EASTERN DESERT
EDOM
© CPH

when they returned to Jerusalem, the Jews were sad to see their glorious temple destroyed and their city in ruins. It took many years to rebuild the city, its wall, and the temple.

However, God had plans for an even more glorious and wonderful temple. In Christ, all the fullness of the Godhead dwelled. Five hundred years later, a baby was born in Bethlehem: the King of kings and Lord of lords—the true Temple.

Prophets in the Divided Kingdom

After the death of King Solomon in 930 BC, the twelve tribes of Israel split into two kingdoms: the Southern Kingdom of Judah, with the capital at Jerusalem, and the Northern Kingdom known as Israel, whose capital city was first Shechem, then Tirzah, and finally Samaria.

Kingdoms

The Northern Kingdom of ten tribes lasted just more than two hundred years before the Assyrians conquered them and took them away into exile in 722 BC, never to return. The Southern Kingdom lasted slightly longer—Jerusalem fell in 587 BC—before the Babylonians conquered them and took them into exile. The powerful Persian Empire later conquered the Babylonians. Unlike the lost tribes of the Northern Kingdom, however, the exiles from the Southern Kingdom received permission from the King of Persia to return to their homeland and resettle Jerusalem. The Jews of today are descendants of the Southern Kingdom of Judah.

Representative Prophets

During a progression of kings—each, it seemed, worse than the last—Israel saw several prophets at work. Elijah, Elisha, Jonah, Amos, and Hosea all prophesied in Israel. Judeans in the Southern Kingdom, both while in Judah and while in exile in Babylon, also heard God's Word from His prophets. Obadiah, Isaiah, and Jeremiah lived and worked before the exile, though Jeremiah wrote two letters to God's people in Babylon early in the years of exile. Daniel and Ezekiel spoke and wrote among the exiled Judeans. Zechariah and Malachi were among the prophets who ministered to those who returned from exile.

God's prophets were not fortune-tellers, though at times their messages revealed future events. The prophets were spokesmen for God, chosen to convey a special message or teaching. Prophets were role models of holiness and closeness to God.

1 and 2 Chronicles

Into 1 and 2 Chronicles

Chronicles means "a chronological record of events, a history."
Theme: Human history = HIS story

Who wrote 1 and 2 Chronicles? When? Why?

Like the books of Samuel and Kings, the books of 1 and 2 Chronicles were originally one book in the Hebrew Bible. At first, this book was called "The Annals of the Days," or "The Things/Events of the Days." It recaps the entire history of God's people from the world's creation to the time the writer lived.

These books were written anonymously, but tradition suggests Ezra authored them. They were written sometime after the exiles in Babylon began to return home in 538 BC. (See 1 Chronicles 9:1–2; 2 Chronicles 36:23.)

The writer intends to comfort the returning exiles with the good news of God's unfailing love for them. Despite their nation's unfaithfulness and idolatry, God had not given up on them. He had not and would not abandon them.

1 and 2 Chronicles detail the history of God's people, beginning with Adam and Eve, but focusing primarily on the reigns of King David, King Solomon, and the history of the Southern Kingdom (Judah)—from about 970 to 538 BC. The books place special emphasis on the worship life of God's people.

How are 1 and 2 Chronicles classified?

These two books are grouped among the Books of History in the Old Testament.

What are the key divisions of 1 and 2 Chronicles?

1 and 2 Chronicles may be divided into four main sections:

- **1 Chronicles 1–9** Creation to exile and restoration; the genealogy of the Messiah
- **1 Chronicles 10–29** The Lord's faithfulness to King David
- **2 Chronicles 1–9** The Lord's faithfulness to King Solomon
- **2 Chronicles 10–36** The Lord's faithfulness to the people of Judah, the Southern Kingdom

How do 1 and 2 Chronicles point to Jesus?

These books record the Lord's faithfulness to the descendants of Abraham, Isaac, Jacob, and Judah as His promise to send a Savior for the world unfolds. (See "How do 1 and 2 Kings point to Jesus?")

Second, both King David and King Solomon are "types," or pictures, of Christ. Their lives and kingdoms reflect in an imperfect way the perfect Kingdom Jesus has established in His Church and will rule forever when He comes again in glory. (See Revelation 19, 21–22.)

Third, the temple that King Solomon built and everything associated with it—its sacrifices, festivals, and even its furniture—point us toward the coming Messiah, the Savior who is our eternal Prophet, Priest, and King.

What are the key chapters in 1 and 2 Chronicles?

- **1 Chronicles 1–9** While these chapters don't make for the most exciting reading, they carefully record the genealogies that allow us to trace the Lord's covenant promise. Generation after generation, He was faithfully at work, preserving the people through whom He would send our Savior.
- **1 Chronicles 11** David ascends to the throne and establishes Jerusalem as his capital city.
- **1 Chronicles 15** God's people worship as King David brings the ark of the covenant into Jerusalem.
- **1 Chronicles 21** David buys Ornan's threshing floor, the site of the future temple.
- **2 Chronicles 1** King Solomon prays for wisdom.
- **2 Chronicles 2–7** The temple is built and dedicated.
- **2 Chronicles 10** Solomon's kingdom splits into two smaller, weaker kingdoms.

- **2 Chronicles 17–20** Jehoshaphat's reign and reforms
- **2 Chronicles 23–24** Joash's reign and reforms
- **2 Chronicles 29–32** Hezekiah's reign and reforms
- **2 Chronicles 34–35** Josiah's reign and reforms
- **2 Chronicles 36** Judah's captivity and the beginning of their return from exile in Babylon

Central Sanctuary

In Holy Scripture, God often makes a big deal out of something we don't see as all that important. At least, not at first. It's worthwhile, though, to dig into topics like that, because there's always spiritual treasure buried there.

Take, for example, the "central sanctuary." In Exodus 20:24; Leviticus 17:1–9; Deuteronomy 12:1–28; 14:23–26; and other Scripture passages, the Lord makes clear His opposition to spontaneous sacrifices that worshipers might want to offer just anywhere. Instead, He commands that the Israelites bring their sacrifices to the location *He* chooses, to the place where He has "put His name" (Deuteronomy 12:5).

For many years, this place was the tabernacle built at Moses' direction. Later, it was the temple built during King Solomon's reign. From the time of Moses, the "central sanctuary" was where God's people gathered to worship Him. There they heard God's Word and celebrated the festivals He had instituted. There they watched the priests slaughter the sacrifices that pointed to the Messiah's final, perfect sacrifice—His sacrifice of Himself.

Why a *central* sanctuary? When travel meant straddling a donkey or making a long trek on foot, what objection could the Lord have had to more convenience? For one thing, the pagans of Canaan sacrificed to their gods on the hills of that land and under certain "sacred" trees. The Lord's prophets in Israel later railed against this practice, which became common despite God's direct prohibition (for instance, see Jeremiah 2:20).

What does this have to do with us New Testament believers? Aren't we free from this law? Yes, absolutely. The Holy Spirit has taken up residence in each of us (1 Corinthians 6:19). That makes *us* the "sanctuary," the dwelling place of our holy God. And that fact gives us a clue about why God's people continue to gather for worship even though the law of the central sanctuary no longer applies to us.

When God's baptized children gather together around Word and Sacrament, *we* are the place He has put His name. God comes among us according to His promise (Matthew 18:19–20; John 4:23). Our worship is no mere memorial service for some dead hero. The living Savior is among us! He forgives sins, giving us His strength, joy, and hope. He touches our hearts and lives so that they reflect His love. Once we grasp this, we run to the altar with the glad hearts the psalmists describe (Psalms 16; 100; 116; 122).

Powerful Prayers

The Bible gives us several examples of how people prayed and the different things they prayed for. The best example of prayer we have is the prayer that Jesus taught us. In the Lord's Prayer (Matthew 6:5–13; Luke 11:2–4), Jesus taught us that we can pray for ourselves and for our neighbors' needs. We can even pray for our enemies. We should also give praise and thanksgiving to God for who He is and what He has done for us. Another example of Jesus praying is found in John 17, called Jesus' "High Priestly Prayer," in which He prays for Himself and us before His Passion.

© Hugh Claycombe

Abraham prayed an intercessory prayer for Sodom, pleading with God not to destroy the city (Genesis 18:22–33). Stephen prayed for his enemies to be forgiven as they were stoning him to death (Acts 7:59–60), just as Jesus prayed for those who had crucified Him (Luke 23:34).

Hannah poured out her heart as she prayed for a son (1 Samuel 1:10–12), then praised God when her prayer was answered (2:1–10). Mary sang a prayer of praise when she learned that she would be the mother of the promised Messiah (Luke 1:46–55).

© CPH/Richard Hook

Solomon prayed for wisdom in his service as Israel's king (2 Chronicles 1:8–12). Daniel prayed to the one God while serving King Darius during the Babylonian exile—even when an order from the king forbade such prayers—risking death in the lions' den (Daniel 6). Later, when, through his study of God's Word,

© Richard Beebe/iStockphoto.com

© Suzanne Tucker/iStockphoto.com

© Jason Stitt/iStockphoto.com

Daniel came to understand the reason for the exile of his people in Babylon and that the time of exile was nearly completed, he prayed a prayer of confession, asking for mercy (Daniel 9).

Jonah prayed from the belly of the fish (Jonah 2:1–9); Elijah prayed from Mount Carmel that God's power might be shown to Israel and against the prophets of Baal (1 Kings 18:20–39).

Some prayed silently; others spoke out loud or sang. From these great examples of praying people, we learn that we can pray anywhere and at any time.

We should also be aware that each of these people of God was a sinful person. God answered their prayers not because of their perfect faith or actions, but because of His great love and compassion. In the same way, it is because of Jesus and the faith God has given us in Him, not our good works or right words, that God listens to and answers our prayers. When we don't know what to pray for or how to pray, the Holy Spirit helps us pray by praying with us and for us.

Abraham, Hannah, Stephen, Mary, and many others prayed with confidence and boldness because of the relationship they had with their heavenly Father. We, too, can bring our requests, or petitions, to God with confidence that He will hear us, for Jesus' sake.

Ezra

Into Ezra

Ezra is named after the main character of the book; his name means "help." In this book, God did help His people—through the priest, Ezra.

Theme: The Lord faithfully brings His exiles home.

Who wrote Ezra? When? Why?

Some scholars think the same author wrote 1 and 2 Chronicles and Ezra. Ezra picks up where 2 Chronicles 36 leaves off. In fact, the first verses of Ezra repeat the concluding verses of 2 Chronicles. Tradition and much internal evidence lead to the conclusion that Ezra himself wrote all three of these books.

After the Babylonians conquered Judah and swept its people into exile, the Babylonian Empire was overrun by the Persian Empire. After seventy years of exile had elapsed (see Jeremiah 25:12–13; Daniel 9:2), the Persians allowed God's people to return to their homeland (537 BC). The Persian rulers Cyrus and, later, Darius encouraged this return and helped to fund it (Ezra 1:5–11; 6:1–12).

Interestingly, the prophet Isaiah had foretold this more than a century earlier—even naming Cyrus as "My shepherd" (Isaiah 44:28).

Together with Nehemiah, the Book of Ezra explains how God's people came back to the Promised Land and, in doing so, set the stage for Messiah—the world's Savior—to be born there, just as God had promised.

How is Ezra classified?

Ezra is one of the Books of History in the Old Testament.

What are the key divisions of Ezra?

Ezra may be divided into four main sections:

- **Ezra 1–2** The first wave of exiles return, led by Sheshbazzar.
- **Ezra 3–6** The temple is rebuilt.
- **Ezra 7–8** The second wave of exiles return, led by Ezra.
- **Ezra 9–10** Repentance and reform

How does Ezra point to Jesus?

Throughout the history recorded here, the Lord was at work, restoring His repentant people to their homeland and preparing them to receive the promised Savior.

The temple courts were the very same place in which Jesus Himself later worshiped. The prophet Haggai told of this in specific detail, and his prophecy in this regard encouraged the people to continue their work, even though they faced many hardships and much opposition. (See Haggai 2:7.)

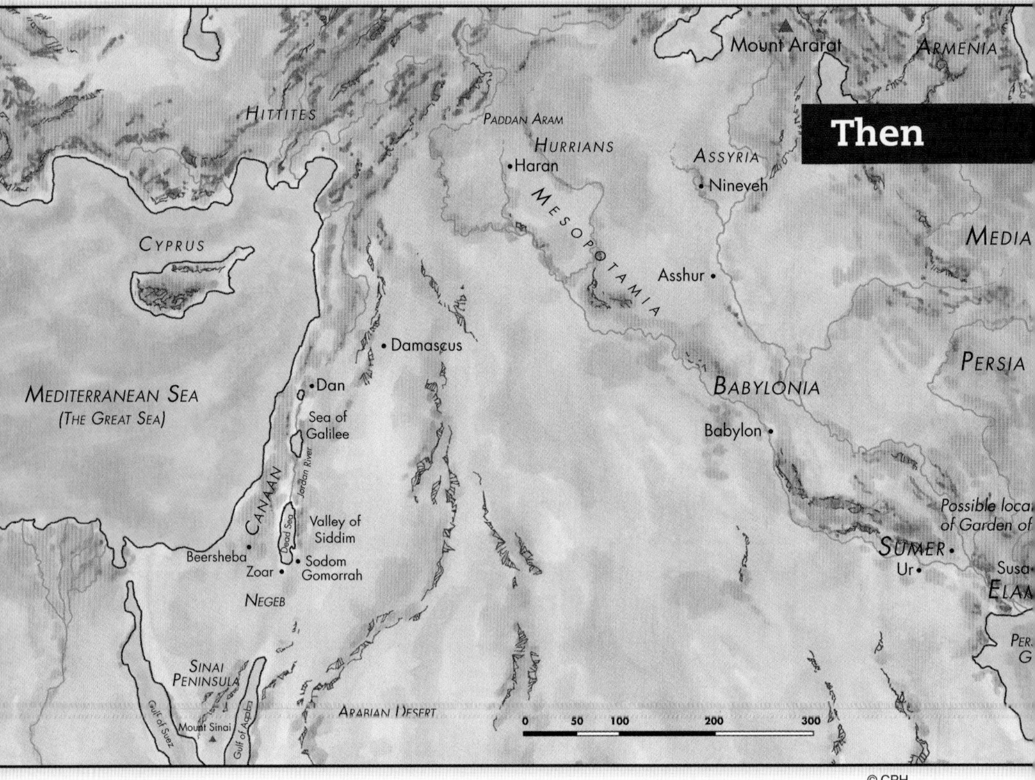

Finally, in Ezra 6:19–23, we read about the first Passover celebration after the Jews' return from exile. Of all the festivals in the worship life of God's people, the Passover most clearly foreshadowed the sacrifice the Lamb of God would one day make to secure our salvation. God had not broken His covenant. The celebration of the Passover underscored that fact.

What are the key chapters in Ezra?

- **Ezra 1** Cyrus's proclamation frees the Jews to return to their homeland.
- **Ezra 2** The return and the census of those who came home with Sheshbazzar
- **Ezra 3** Laying the temple's foundation
- **Ezra 6** The temple is completed and dedicated.
- **Ezra 7** Sixty years later, the second wave of repatriation arrives under the leadership of Ezra.
- **Ezra 9** Ezra's prayer of national repentance

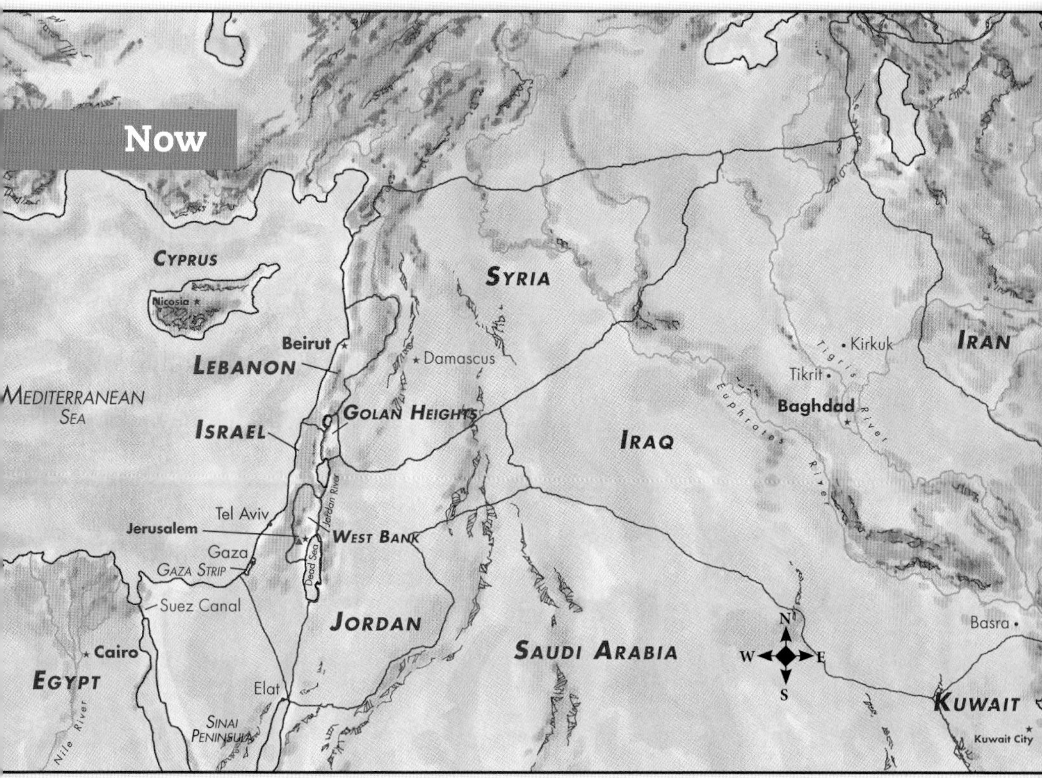

Same Family, Different Names

Hebrews, Israelites, children of Israel, and Jews are all names used to identify Abraham's descendants. Most are variations of the name of a family of origin.

Hebrew

The term Hebrew is used several times in Genesis, but its origin is not clear. Some scholars believe it to be a variation of the name Eber. Eber (Genesis 10:25) was an ancestor of Abraham, who is the first person called a Hebrew in the Bible (Genesis 14:13). However, the word may also be a general term to describe the wandering, tribal people of the ancient Middle East. Joseph was called a Hebrew by Potiphar's wife (Genesis 39:17) and by Pharaoh's cupbearer (Genesis 41:12). The term is used to refer both to a people, the descendants of Abraham, and the language they spoke. It does not refer to a geographical region.

Israel

God changed Jacob's name to "Israel" when He reestablished the covenant with him (Genesis 32:28). Jacob's descendants were thereafter referred to as "Israelites." (In a similar way, descendants of Benjamin might be called "Benjamites" and descendants of Ishmael are often called "Ishmaelites.") Before Jacob died, he gave each of his sons portions of the Promised Land for his clan or tribe.

The clans of Jacob's sons were united as a nation, called "Israel," under three kings—Saul, David, and Solomon—but they split apart after the death of King Solomon. Most of the tribes, in the northern half of Solomon's kingdom, formed the Northern Kingdom. It retained the name Israel and was eventually overrun by the Assyrians. The tribe of Judah and portions of two other tribes formed the kingdom of Judah, or the Southern Kingdom. This kingdom was eventually conquered by Babylon, and many of its residents were taken into exile.

People in both kingdoms, however, thought of themselves as "children of Israel," the descendants of the patriarchs—Abraham, Isaac, and Jacob (whose other name was "Israel").

Jew

The term Jew described citizens of the kingdom of Judah and is a variation of the word Judah. Since New Testament times, the name Jew has been used to identify all descendants of Judah, Jacob's son, who lived in the Promised Land of Canaan. In some places in the New Testament, "Jews" clearly refers to those among the Jewish people who did not believe in Jesus.

Today the term identifies those of the Jewish religion, no matter their country of residence or origin. Today many Jews live in the nation of Israel, part of which is the same Promised Land of Canaan that God promised to Abram.

Priests of God

From the earliest chapters of the Bible, God's people offered sacrifices and burnt offerings to Him as part of their worship, symbolically giving back to Him part of the bounty He provided for them. Cain and Abel gave such offerings, as did Noah, Abraham, and Jacob. Until the time of Moses, the heads of households usually offered such sacrifices on behalf of their families. The Bible mentions only two priests before the exodus—Melchizedek (Genesis 14:18) and Jethro (Exodus 3:1), who became Moses' father-in-law.

At Mount Sinai, after giving the Ten Commandments, God also gave Moses many laws about the worship life of His people, including giving instructions for the building of the tabernacle, creating a system of sacrifices for all kinds of situations, and establishing priests to offer sacrifices for the people in the tabernacle.

Levites

God gave the descendants of Jacob's son Levi charge of the tabernacle. They carried the tabernacle wherever Israel went, set it up, camped around it and guarded it, and took it down when it was time to move again. Levites also became the first musicians in the tabernacle and temple.

Both Moses and Aaron were descendants of Levi. Aaron and his sons became the first priests to serve at the tabernacle.

When Israel entered the Promised Land, the Levites did not settle in a territory of their own. Instead, they lived in cities within the regions of other tribes when they were not serving at the tabernacle and, later, the temple.

Priests

God commanded that Israel consecrate Aaron and his sons to Him for exclusive service in the tabernacle. Descendants of Aaron became the official priesthood for generations to come.

The priests prepared and offered the sacrifices, taught the Law, and met with God on behalf of the people. Only priests could enter the Holy Place of the tabernacle, where incense was burned twice daily during the prayers of the people.

God established special clothing for the priests to wear and special rules of conduct to set them apart for His service. Their clothing consisted of a robe, special coat, turban, and sash. They also wore an ephod, a smock or apronlike garment made of linen.

The High Priest

Aaron was foremost among the priests and was called the high priest. He wore a special ephod and breastplate decorated with twelve precious stones symbolizing the twelve tribes (Exodus 28:15–21). In a pocket in the chest of the high priest's breastplate were two stones, the Urim and Thummim (Exodus 28:30), which in some special way allowed the high priest to consult with God.

After Aaron, his son Eleazar became high priest, and Phinehas, Eleazar's son, succeeded him. At the end of the time of the judges, Eli, a descendant of Ithamar, Eleazar's younger brother, was serving as high priest, and the tabernacle was erected at Shiloh, about twenty-five miles north of Bethlehem.

Jesus, Our High Priest

The Letter to the Hebrews in the New Testament proclaims Jesus to be our High Priest of "the order of Melchizedek" (Hebrews 6:20). He offered the once-for-all sacrifice of Himself on the cross as the final payment for the sins of all people. Through Jesus, we have direct access to God, who loves us, hears our prayers for Jesus' sake, and promises forgiveness, life, and salvation to all who believe in Christ.

Nehemiah

Into Nehemiah

Nehemiah is named after the main character of the book; his name means "the comfort of the Lord." In this book, we read about the comfort God brought to His people as He restored them to their homeland after exile in Babylon.

Theme: The Lord faithfully restores and protects His exiles.

Who wrote Nehemiah? When? Why?

Ezra and Nehemiah were once combined as one book, titled "Ezra." As a result, the Book of Nehemiah was sometimes named after the prophet Ezra in some translations of the Bible (such as the ancient Greek Septuagint and Latin Vulgate translations).

Because much of Nehemiah is told in the first person (i.e., "I did this and that"; see, for example, Nehemiah 1:4–11), it's logical to conclude Nehemiah wrote it. It's possible that Ezra helped Nehemiah organize it.

Nehemiah led the third of three waves of exiles returning to their homeland. Nehemiah also served as governor of the people two different times. King Artaxerxes sent Nehemiah to Jerusalem for the first time in 445 BC, in response to Nehemiah's request to help his distressed and downtrodden people.

Nehemiah held a high position—that of cupbearer—in the court of King Artaxerxes. Cupbearers were trusted advisors who always had the ear of the rulers they served.

Together with the Book of Ezra, Nehemiah explains how God's people came back to the Promised Land and, in doing so, set the stage for Messiah—the world's Savior—to be born there, just as God had promised Abraham centuries earlier.

How is Nehemiah classified?

Nehemiah is one of the Books of History in the Old Testament.

What are the key divisions of Nehemiah?

Nehemiah may be divided into four main sections:

- **Nehemiah 1–2** Nehemiah leads the return of the third wave of exiles to Jerusalem.
- **Nehemiah 3–7** Jerusalem's walls are rebuilt despite opposition and conspiracy.
- **Nehemiah 8–10** The covenant is restored.
- **Nehemiah 11–13** Jerusalem's walls are dedicated; Nehemiah's final reforms

How does Nehemiah point to Jesus?

Just as Nehemiah served God's people as a rebuilder and restorer despite the harassment and ridicule of their enemies, so Jesus is our restorer and rebuilder. Jesus strengthens us to resist the temptations to discouragement Satan throws against us. He leads us to repentance when we break the baptismal covenant our Lord has made with us, just as Nehemiah led his people to repentance when they lapsed into sin (Nehemiah 13).

God's people in Nehemiah's time could count on His forgiveness because of the work the Messiah, the Lord Jesus, would do for them (Romans 3:23–26). We can count on that same forgiveness—for the same reason—today.

What are the key chapters in Nehemiah?

- **Nehemiah 1** Nehemiah's prayer for favor with King Artaxerxes and the Lord's favorable response
- **Nehemiah 6** The wall of Jerusalem is rebuilt in only fifty-two days (v. 15)—almost a miracle, given the opposition from the enemies of God's people!
- **Nehemiah 8–9** The renewal of the covenant
- **Nehemiah 12** The dedication of the wall around Jerusalem

Esther

Into Esther

The Book of **Esther** is named after its main character; her name means "star."

Theme: The Lord preserves His people and His covenant.

Who wrote Esther? When? Why?

No one knows who recorded the events in Esther. Some have suggested that Mordecai, Esther's cousin and also a participant in her story, may have been the author. Others have thought Ezra or Nehemiah may have written this book. But we can't say for certain.

The events documented in Esther took place at about the same time as those in Ezra—around 480 BC. Esther's story was written down some decades after the events occurred, perhaps as early as 460 BC. In any case, internal evidence makes it clear that the book was written before Persia fell to the Greeks in 331 BC.

The book explains how the Judeans came to celebrate the Feast of Purim. It documents their survival and God's faithfulness despite the plotting of the evil Haman and his hatred of God's people.

Many commentators down through history have noted that the Book of Esther does not mention God's name. Nor does it say anything about worship, the temple, or sacrifice. Even so, the Lord is clearly at work, preserving His covenant promises in the events Esther records. The book includes no spectacular miracles, only many small "coincidences"—too many, in fact, to have happened due to "luck" or "chance."

In Esther we see clearly how our Savior-God uses ordinary people and everyday events to accomplish His redemptive purposes.

How is Esther classified?

Esther is one of the Books of History in the Old Testament.

What are the key divisions of Esther?

Esther may be divided into five main sections:

- **Esther 1** Queen Vashti rebels.
- **Esther 2** Queen Esther is crowned.
- **Esther 3–4** Prime Minister Haman plots.
- **Esther 5** Queen Esther defends her people.
- **Esther 6–10** God's people are saved—and safe.

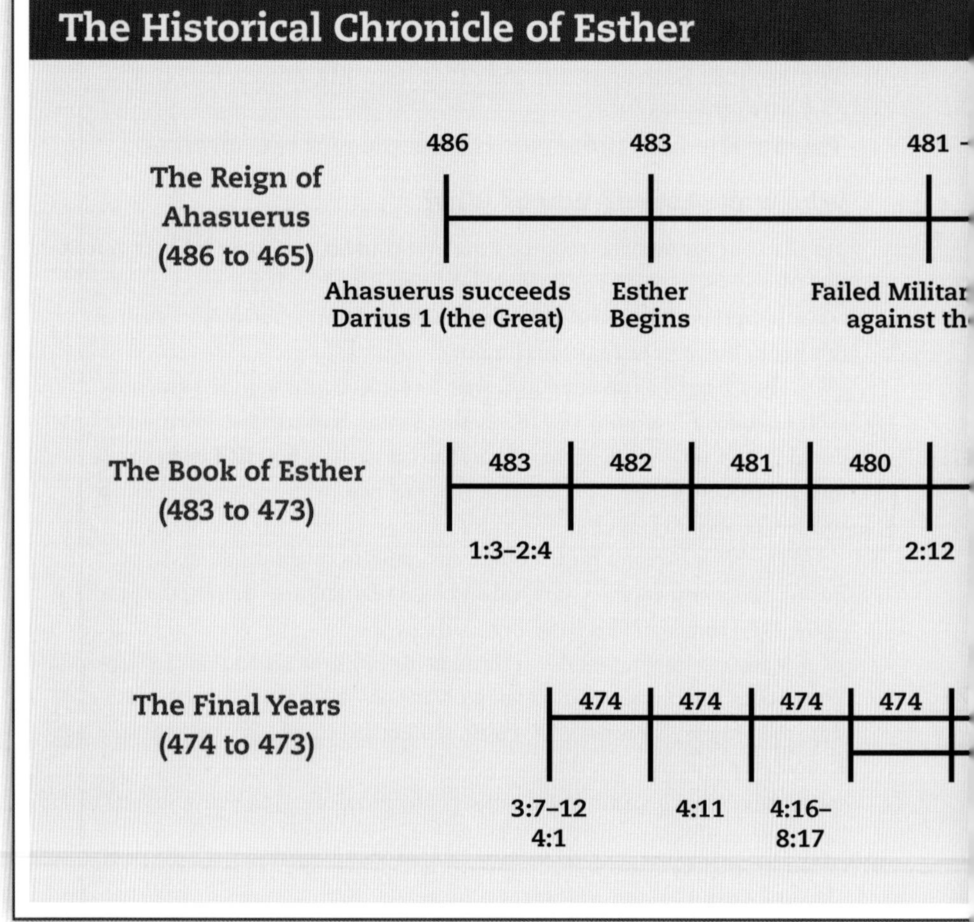

How does Esther point to Jesus?

The story of Esther is an example of how God cared for His people during the most perilous years of their exile. God's providential care in those years, which they celebrated in the Feast of Purim, anticipates how God is ever caring for His people, including His most important care in sending a Savior in the person of His Son, Jesus.

What are the key chapters in Esther?

- **Esther 5 and 7** Queen Esther's courage
- **Esther 9** The first celebration of Purim

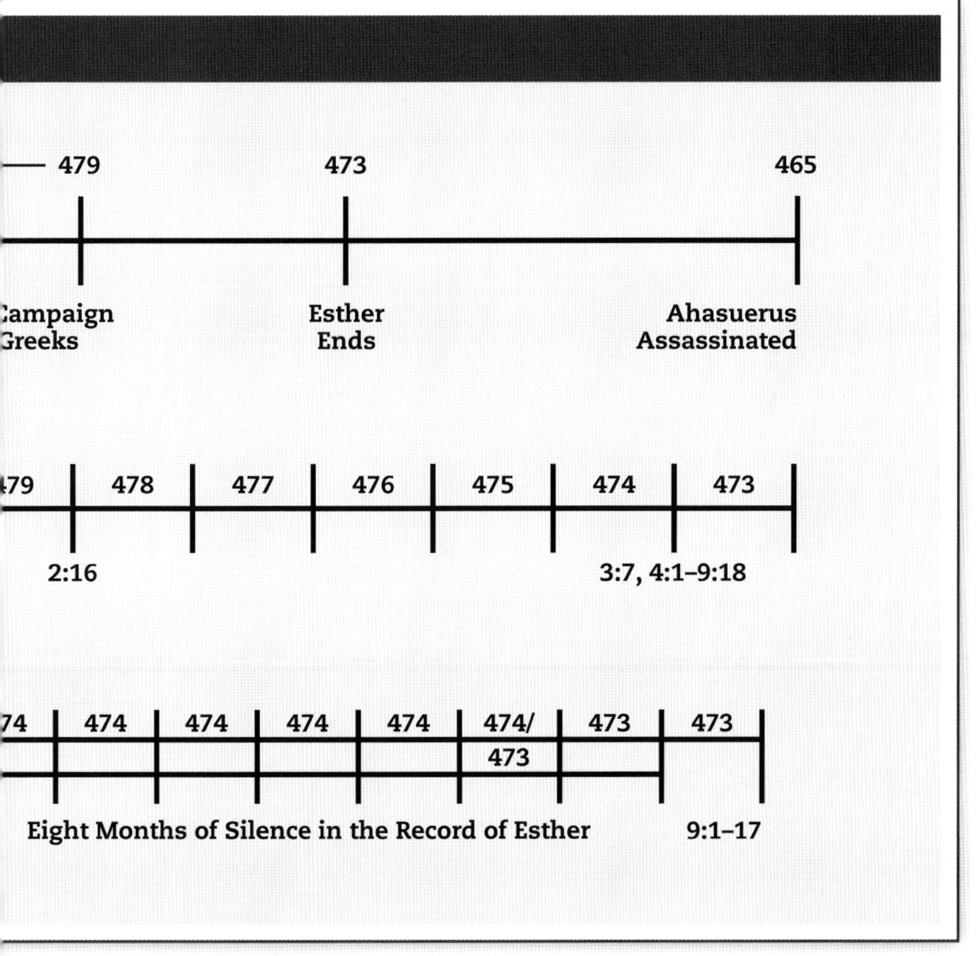

Fasting

Fasting is a spiritual discipline mentioned frequently in both the Old and New Testaments of the Bible. It means to not eat food. Sometimes, it can mean restricting the amount or type of food one eats, such as when Daniel and his friends chose to eat only vegetables and drink only water while in exile (Daniel 1:12–15).

The only fast required in the Old Testament was the fast on the Day of Atonement, from sunset of one day until sunset of the next (Leviticus 16:29; 23:32). Longer fasts are very rare in Scripture, though God gave Moses (Deuteronomy 9:9) and Elijah (1 Kings 19:8) the power to go without food and water for forty days.

Fasting and Sorrow

Fasting is a natural sign of sorrow, an extension of the body's lack of appetite during times of loss. The people fasted, mourned, and wept at the deaths of King Saul and his son, Jonathan (2 Samuel 1:12). The exiles in Persia fasted when they heard of the king's edict allowing their destruction (Esther 4:1–16). David fasted as his first child by Bathsheba lay dying on account of his sin (2 Samuel 12:16).

Fasting and Confession

In Scripture, fasting is most often a sign of sorrow for sin and accompanied confession.

The people of Israel fasted in the time of Samuel when the ark of the covenant, which had been captured by the Philistines, was returned. They confessed their sins of idolatry and asked the Lord's forgiveness (Judges 20:26).

King Ahab fasted as a sign of repentance when he heard God's judgment against him (1 Kings 21:27), and God indeed had mercy on him.

Nehemiah led the exiled people of God in fasting when he heard of the miserable conditions in Jerusalem during the exile. God intervened in history so that Nehemiah could return to Jerusalem to repair the city walls (Nehemiah 1:4; 9:1).

When Jonah finally preached God's Word to them, the people of Nineveh fasted in sorrow for their sins. God spared them (Jonah 3:5).

Fasting and Prayer

The Bible almost always links fasting to prayer, as is likely the case in the story of Esther, who fasted before seeking deliverance for her people (Esther 4:16). The people of God can pray without fasting, but they cannot fast without praying. "You will seek Me and find Me, when you seek Me with all your heart. I will be found by you" (Jeremiah 29:13–14). Fasting is a person's way of showing that he or she wholeheartedly is seeking God, His will, and His leading.

One example is that of Anna, the prophetess mentioned when Jesus was presented at the temple, who "did not depart from the temple, worshiping with fasting and prayer night and day" (Luke 2:37).

Fasting and Jesus

Jesus taught about fasting. He didn't say, "If you fast"; rather, He said, "When you fast." The Pharisees fasted with great show and frequency. Jesus instructed His followers not to tell people and make it obvious, but to do it quietly, because fasting is a private and personal matter between the individual and God (Matthew 6:16–18).

Jesus fasted for forty days in the wilderness after His Baptism (Matthew 4:2), before being tempted by Satan. Jesus was not fasting in confession of His own sins—He was the sinless Son of God. However, He had just been baptized "to fulfill all righteousness" and identify fully with the people whose sins He would carry to the cross at Calvary. His forty-day fast produced that natural human reaction of great hunger, demonstrating His fully human nature. At this early stage of His earthly ministry, and often as it progressed, Jesus spent time in prayer, talking with His Father on behalf of all His children.

The Feast of Purim

Purim brings both a history lesson and some of the most fun of any of the Old Testament feasts celebrated by Jewish people. It marks God's rescue of the Judeans who were still living in Persia in the fifth century BC.

Origin

The origin of Purim is recorded in the Book of Esther. The story takes place around 474 BC. Esther is the heroine of this account because she risked her life and used her position as queen to intercede for her people—the Judeans in exile—to save them from an evil plot. Haman, an administrator for King Ahasuerus, planned to murder all the Judeans in Persia because of his jealousy over honor shown to Mordecai, a Jew. The festival is named Purim, which means "lot," because Haman chose the date on which he planned to massacre the Jews by casting lots (a random-selection process like rolling dice).

Celebration

Purim occurs in late February or early March, one month before Passover, and lasts for one day. One requirement of the celebration is the reading of the entire Book of Esther. During the reading, there is much booing, hissing, and noisemaking whenever the reader mentions the name of Haman, as listeners show what they think about him.

The celebration also includes costumes and plays, and beauty pageants in which girls dress up as Queen Esther. As with any feast, there is a focus on food, such as *hamantaschen*, triangle-shaped sweets usually filled with poppy seeds, apricots, or dates.

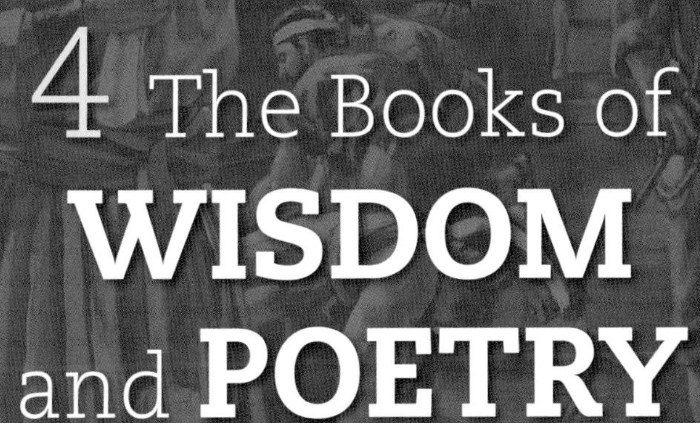

4 The Books of WISDOM and POETRY

Job

Psalms

Proverbs

Ecclesiastes

Song of Solomon

Job

Into Job

The Book of **Job** is named after its main character.

Theme: The Lord is compassionate and merciful. (See James 5:11.)

Who wrote Job? When? Why?

Some scholars have dated the book to 2000 BC, which would make Job the oldest book of the Bible and perhaps one of the oldest pieces of literature still in existence!

The author recorded the dialogues among Job and his three friends. The Holy Spirit alone could have revealed to the book's author the events taking place in heaven between the Lord and Satan while Job suffered here on earth (Job 1, 2).

Whether Job is the oldest book of the Bible or not, it asks one of the world's oldest questions: why do God's people suffer? From chapter 4 through chapter 37, Job and his friends wrestle with that question. The book never fully answers it. Instead, it assures us that we can trust our Savior-God's care for us, even when we don't understand right away (or ever!) what He is up to in our lives.

God is always good—despite the evidence that Satan uses to convince us otherwise. God kept Job in faith through his trials. Even though Job's faith flickered, Satan could not extinguish it. From beginning (Job 1:8) to end (42:8), God calls the book's main character "my servant Job."

James explains the truth that the Holy Spirit intends for us to take away from Job's forty-two chapters:

> *We consider those blessed who remained steadfast. You have heard of the steadfastness of Job, and you have seen the purpose of the Lord, how the Lord is compassionate and merciful. (James 5:11)*

How is Job classified?

Job is counted among the Books of Wisdom and Poetry in the Old Testament. Most of the book is written in poetry. Hebrew poems do not usually rhyme, as English poems often do. Hebrew poems use *parallelism*: repeated, complementary thoughts that unfold different aspects of a subject. Often the first line of a Hebrew poem is repeated with different words in the second line or the second line repeats an aspect of the first while revealing something more about the subject. In this way, the lines of the poem build on one another and hold together.

How is Job organized?

Job may be divided into nine main sections:

- **Job 1–2** Prologue: the dispute between the Lord and Satan
- **Job 3–14** Job's conversations with his "comforters": cycle 1
- **Job 15–21** Job's conversations with his "comforters": cycle 2
- **Job 22–27** Job's conversations with his "comforters": cycle 3
- **Job 28** Job's commentary on wisdom
- **Job 29–31** Job summarizes his case
- **Job 32–37** Elihu's rebuke
- **Job 38:1–42:6** God's response and Job's repentance
- **Job 42:7–17** Epilogue

How does Job point to Jesus?

Throughout the book, Job and his three friends ask unanswerable questions. We don't fully understand why troubles and disasters invade the lives of God's children here on earth. This side of heaven, the answer is not a philosophy, but a Person—Jesus Himself!

Job asks repeatedly for an "umpire," someone to take his side and plead for him (see, for instance, Job 9:33). We New Testament believers know that Umpire's name—Jesus Himself!

Finally, Jesus Himself is the Redeemer to whom Job clings, even in the darkness of doubt and despair:

> *Oh that my words were written! Oh that they were inscribed in a book! Oh that with an iron pen and lead they were engraved in the rock forever! For I know that my Redeemer lives, and at the last He will stand upon the earth. And after my skin has been thus de-*

stroyed, yet in my flesh I shall see God, whom I shall see for myself, and my eyes shall behold, and not another." (Job 19:23–27)

What are the key chapters in Job?

- **Job 1–2** The origin of Job's troubles
- **Job 19** Job's famous statement of faith in his living Redeemer.
- **Job 38–41** The Lord's powerful and poetic answer to Job's accusations of His injustice

Sifted by Satan

Does Job serve God from a heart of love? Or does his praise last only so long as God's blessings flow?

Those questions set the stage for Job's ordeal. Satan tried his best to undermine Job's trust and steal Job's eternal life. But in the end, the Lord vindicated Job. Along the way, the Lord kept Job from losing his faith. The Lord was Job's Redeemer, even when Job himself doubted it (Job 19:25–27).

Do the disciples worship Jesus from pure motives? Or do they follow Him only so long as they anticipate positions of power in His kingdom? Those questions form the background for Jesus' warning in Luke 22:31–32. His use of pronouns is telling, but our English translations can't show that. Paraphrased, the text says, "Simon! Simon! Truly, Satan has asked for all of you, so that he may sift you like wheat. But I have prayed for you personally, Simon, so that your faith fails not. When you have repented, strengthen the others."

How frightening! Satan hates Jesus, and he hates those who follow Jesus. He schemes to destroy us all. This "murderer from the beginning" (John 8:44) petitions for permission to destroy all of us, body and soul. And yet, Jesus intercedes for each of us, as He prayed for Peter.

How comforting! Job's Redeemer gave Peter the gift of repentance and faith. Then He used Peter as His instrument to strengthen the other disciples and, down through history, all of our Lord's followers, who at times fall for Satan's schemes.

This Redeemer serves as our High Priest still today. No matter what Satan tries, he will not snatch us out of our Savior's hand (John 10:28). When the times of "sifting" begin, we can rest in His arms, confident of His promises to protect and keep us.

In the whirlwind, Job comes face-to-face with the reality of his human limitations. Although Job accuses the Lord of being unfair, God responds with a mild yet firm word. The Lord reminds Job that He not only created the world but also continues to care for it. We, too, question God and wonder whether He is actually in charge of the daily events of our lives. Coming face-to-face with our Creator brings us to our knees. Yet the fearsome face of the Creator also smiles on Job and shows him mercy.

Psalms

Into Psalms

The word psalms comes from a Greek root, psalmós, which means roughly "a song sung to the harp." It's related to psállein—"to pluck, pull, play a stringed instrument."

Theme: Songs and prayers for our faithful Savior-God

© Sybille Yates/Shutterstock, Inc.

Who wrote Psalms? When? Why?

The Book of Psalms is a collection of songs and prayers written by many different people over many centuries. The first were likely written fifteen hundred years before Jesus' birth; the last, only three hundred or so years before Jesus was born. This book, sometimes called "the Psalter," was the "hymnal" Jesus and His disciples used. (On the night before Jesus died, He probably sang Psalm 118—and perhaps other psalms too—with His disciples; see Mark 14:26.)

- King David may have written at least seventy-four psalms—more than anyone else; he began composing before he became king and continued throughout his life. See, for example, Psalms 18, 22, 23, and 103.
- Asaph, a Levite and leader in King David's court (1 Chronicles 6:39; 2 Chronicles 29:30), added twelve, including Psalms 50 and 73–83. The Bible mentions Asaph's "sons" as among Israel's worship leaders too (1 Chronicles 25:1; 2 Chronicles 20:14; Ezra 2:41). They may have been Asaph's biological children or, perhaps, students who learned the process of writing and leading worship music from Asaph.

- The "sons of Korah" either wrote or arranged the music for eleven psalms, including 42, 44–49, 84, 85, 87, and 88. (Interestingly, singers from the sons of Korah led Israel into battle during the time of King Jehoshaphat! They sang the refrain of praise from Psalm 136: "Give thanks to the LORD, . . . for His steadfast love endures forever." The enemy armies started fighting—and defeating—each other, and God's people won the battle just standing on the sidelines! (See 2 Chronicles 20.)
- Solomon wrote Psalms 72 and 127. Moses wrote Psalm 90. Ethan penned Psalm 89, and Heman wrote Psalm 88. Forty-eight psalms are anonymous (for instance, 104, 105, 115).

Different psalms have different purposes. All of them, though, like the songs we sing today, express the deep feelings of their composers. All of them "pour out their hearts" to God, counting on Him to hear. (See Psalm 62:8.)

- Some psalms explode in frustration and worry.
- Some psalms shout out thanksgiving and worship.
- Some psalms beg for help.
- Some psalms cry out for forgiveness.
- Some psalms explore God's Word and His wisdom in deep wonder.
- Some psalms burst out in fury at God's enemies.
- Some psalms invite God's people to dance and sing together in praise.

How is Psalms classified?

Psalms is counted among the Books of Wisdom and Poetry in the Old Testament. For more on Hebrew poetry, see "How is Job classified?" (p. 161).

What's the best way to read Psalms?

First, remember it's poetry. The psalmists use metaphors, similes, and other figures of speech to make their point, just like we do today. Psalm 18, for example, pictures God as harnessing a thundercloud and riding to our help. We know the Lord is omnipresent (present everywhere all the time); He doesn't *need* to ride a cumulonimbus cloud like a chariot to come to rescue us when we're in trouble! Still, the picture reassures us at a level deep in our hearts. Our Lord *can* help us, and He *wants* to help us!

Second, don't expect it to rhyme. Hebrew poetry uses word pictures and repeats thoughts and ideas. Here are some common ways Hebrew poets use repetition—"rhyming thoughts" instead of rhyming words:

- Sometimes the second line repeats the main idea of the first line in different words—like Psalm 3:1.
- Sometimes the second line adds ideas to the first line—as in Psalm 33:13.
- Sometimes the second line contrasts with the person, thought, or description in the first line—as in Psalm 44:3.
- Sometimes the first line uses a word picture to illustrate a thought stated in the second line—as in Psalm 52:8.
- Sometimes the second line expands and reinforces the thought of the first line—as in Psalm 61:5.

Third, look for Jesus and how He is at work in your life! Ask yourself, "Is this a psalm Jesus has prayed or sung in my place?" Imagine your Savior standing before God's throne, adding your name, and describing your situation to your heavenly Father—asking for your forgiveness, telling about the help you need with a problem, shouting the praises of your heart. He is doing just that right now!

How is Psalms organized?

There are five divisions, or "books," inside the Book of Psalms. Some close with a verse or two of praise known as a *doxology*. Psalm 1 has been called "the gateway to the Psalms." It introduces the 149 that follow and encourages us to study, believe, and behave according to the truths the Holy Spirit reveals in the rest of the book.

- **Psalm 1** Prologue
- **Psalms 2–41** Book 1
- **Psalms 42–72** Book 2
- **Psalms 73–89** Book 3
- **Psalms 90–106** Book 4
- **Psalms 107–150** Book 5

How does the Book of Psalms point to Jesus?

Many psalms contain explicit predictions of the Messiah's life and work. Psalm 22, for example, describes our Lord's crucifixion in remarkable detail—centuries before crucifixion was even invented! Psalm 23 tells of the Lord, our Shepherd. Jesus called Himself that in John 10.

Other psalms often placed in this category of "Messianic Psalms" include Psalms 24, 45, 61, 72, 110, and 118.

But if we read the Psalms looking only for *direct* prophecies about our Savior, we will miss most of what the Holy Spirit tells us about our Savior in this book!

Don't let that happen to you! Instead, think about it this way. Because we are sinful, we cannot pray any of the Psalms and expect God to hear and help us in the ways He has promised. But Jesus died in our place. He shares His own righteousness with us. Because He has this sacrifice, we can boldly come to God, asking for everything the Psalms promise! In Jesus, we are the "righteous people" the Lord always hears and helps!

What are the key chapters in Psalms?

- **Psalm 3** "Christ, My Shield"
- **Psalm 18** "Christ, My Rock and Fortress"
- **Psalm 22** "Christ, My Rescuer"
- **Psalm 23** "Christ, My Shepherd"
- **Psalm 27** "Christ, My Light and Salvation"
- **Psalm 46** "Christ, My Refuge and Strength"
- **Psalm 100** "Christ, My Joy"
- **Psalm 103** "Blessed in Christ"
- **Psalm 110** "Christ, My High Priest"
- **Psalm 119** "Christ, the Word of God"
- **Psalm 121** "Christ, My Help"
- **Psalm 136** "O Give Thanks!"

The Book of Psalms contains seven prayers of repentance, sometimes called the "Penitential Psalms." These are Psalms 6, 32, 38, 51, 102, 130, and 143. They are helpful at any time, but especially when we as God's people prepare our hearts to receive Holy Communion.

Music has always been important to God's people. It was a part of their daily lives as well as their worship.

Music in Bible Times

© Garo Nalbandian/Israelimages.com

Many of the Israelites were musicians. Miriam, Moses' sister, led the women in song and dance (Exodus 15:20–21); Isaiah composed songs (Isaiah 26:1–6); and Ezekiel was recognized to have a beautiful voice and the ability to play an instrument well (Ezekiel 33:32). David, who began his life as a shepherd boy, played a lyre and probably a shepherd's flute. He later served in Saul's palace, where he played music to soothe King Saul. David also wrote many psalms.

The Israelites had different instruments for different uses. When David led the procession that brought the ark of the covenant to Mount Zion (2 Samuel 6:3–5; 1 Chronicles 13:7–8), the people processed with tambourines, castanets, trumpets, cymbals, harps, and lyres. These instruments, which were also played in the temple, led the singing of psalms. Other instruments were part of everyday life. Simple reed flutes sounded in celebration and in mourning. Shepherds carried flutes to pass the time while tending their flocks. Women used percussion instruments, like the tambourine, while dancing. People also used drums outside of worship.

When the Judeans were exiled in Babylon under the reign of King Nebuchadnezzar, they were to fall down and worship a golden image when they heard horns, pipes, lyres, trigons, harps, and bagpipes (Daniel 3:4–5).

Sometimes the music of the Israelites must have been very loud, as when it was used to call people to worship. It was also joyful, as when the

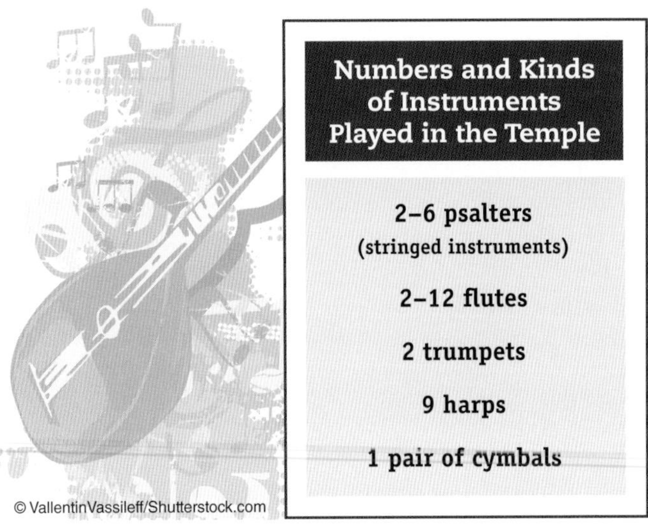

Numbers and Kinds of Instruments Played in the Temple

2–6 psalters (stringed instruments)

2–12 flutes

2 trumpets

9 harps

1 pair of cymbals

© VallentinVassileff/Shutterstock.com

walls of Jerusalem were dedicated (Nehemiah 12:27–43), when a war was won, or during a procession (2 Samuel 6; 1 Chronicles 13). Other times, the music was softer and more beautiful, as when it accompanied the singing of psalms.

The instruments were probably played all together. Sometimes music was played by itself, without singing, to give the people a time to reflect on the words. The word *selah*, found in the Book of Psalms (see Psalm 4 and others), was probably an instruction to the musicians to play for a short time before the words continued. Choirs of men, trained for many years before serving, helped lead worship in Herod's temple.

Bible Songs Sung Today

Some well-known songs in the Bible are part of Christian liturgy today:

- Mary's song, known as the Magnificat (Luke 1:46–55)
- Gloria in Excelsis, "Glory to God in the Highest," the angels' song sung at Jesus' birth (Luke 2:14)
- The Nunc Dimittis, also known as the Song of Simeon (Luke 2:29–32)
- The Benedictus, which is the Song of Zechariah (Luke 1:68–79)
- The Sanctus, which includes the Hosanna hymn of the crowd upon Jesus' entry into Jerusalem (Mark 11:9; based on Psalm 118:26)

Songs in Heaven

In the Book of Revelation, John tells of the heavenly hymns that

- glorify the Creator (Revelation 4:11);
- proclaim the worthiness of the Lamb (Revelation 5:9–10, 12);
- give glory to both the Father and the Son (Revelation 5:13; 7:10, 12);
- celebrate God's triumph over the enemies of His people (Revelation 11:16–18; 12:10–12; 19:1–3, 6–8); and

- proclaim God's justice (Revelation 15:3–4; 16:5–7).

No wonder Christians today joyfully use hymns of praise in worship!

Did Jesus Sing?

At Passover celebrations, Jews sing psalms, in particular Psalms 113–118. Jesus was a Jew who celebrated the Passover (Luke 2:41–42; Mark 14:12–16). After His last Passover meal, He and His disciples sang a hymn before going to Gethsemane, where Jesus prayed for His disciples, for Himself, and for all who would follow Him (Mark 14:26). The hymn might have been Psalms 113–118, which was commonly sung at the end of the Passover meal.

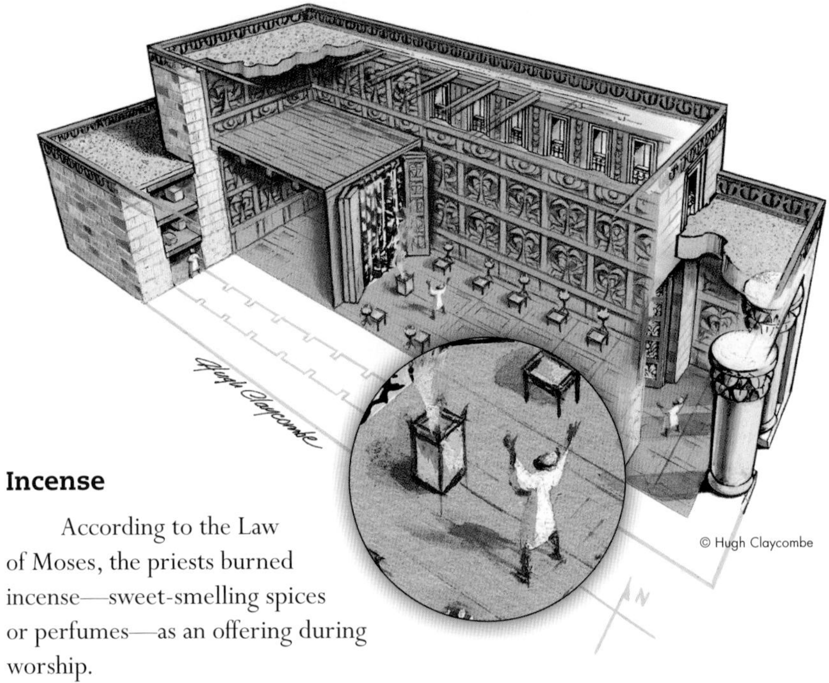

© Hugh Claycombe

Incense

According to the Law of Moses, the priests burned incense—sweet-smelling spices or perfumes—as an offering during worship.

> *"You shall make an altar on which to burn incense; you shall make it of acacia wood. And Aaron shall burn fragrant incense on it. Every morning when he dresses the lamps he shall burn it, and when Aaron sets up the lamps at twilight, he shall burn it, a regular incense offering before the* Lord *throughout your generations."* (Exodus 30:1, 7–8)

The hour of incense was a time of prayer celebrated twice daily, in the morning and in the evening. Jewish law permitted only the priest to enter the Holy Place of the temple to burn the incense at the altar while the people waited outside and prayed. The burning incense served as a fragrant reminder of God's presence, while the rising smoke created an image of the prayers ascending to heaven.

The words of Psalm 141:2, found in the Service of Evening Prayer, paint this image for us of our prayers rising as smoke, reminding us of the ancient worshipers: "Let my prayer rise before You as incense, the lifting up of my hands as the evening sacrifice" (*Lutheran Service Book*, p. 245).

Because Jesus is our High Priest, God invites us to come to Him in prayer freely and at any time. We no longer need a priest to enter the Holy Place for us. Indeed, the Holy Place no longer stands. The Romans destroyed it in AD 70, along with the entire temple complex in Jerusalem.

Shepherds and Their Sheep

Shepherding was a common occupation in Bible times. Because most of the land in the area around the Jordan River was used for farming, sheep were often herded in the more remote wilderness areas away from the villages. These areas were full of rocks and steep slopes that presented many dangers to sheep. A shepherd's tools included a rod, or large stick, used to fight off robbers or wild animals, and a staff, or long walking stick, that the shepherd used to guide the sheep.

Being a shepherd was a dangerous occupation that required alertness and courage. A good shepherd counted his sheep regularly to be certain that none had been stolen or had wandered off. Sheep were easy prey for wild animals. Rescuing a lost sheep might put the shepherd's life in danger.

Patience and gentleness were also required of shepherds. Since domesticated sheep are not intelligent animals, they need help finding clean water and good grass to eat. Sudden noises might cause them to stampede or run away. Knowing the shepherd's voice was important to the sheep when he called them back. Often insects would upset the sheep, causing them to become restless, so a good shepherd would apply oil to the animal's head and nose to keep away irritating flies and parasites and soothe the skin.

During the day, the shepherd led his sheep to calm pools of water or poured well water into troughs for them. The shepherd led the sheep into the sheep pen or sheepfold at night and always slept nearby in order to reassure the sheep of his protecting presence. If a pen was not available, he could have utilized a cave to shelter his sheep at night or built a shelter for them. A sturdy six-foot wall overlaid by thorns or broken glass to ward off wolves or thieves formed a corral at the door of the cave or shelter. As the sheep went through the single entrance, he would call his thirty or forty sheep by name. He might talk quietly to them or play gentle music on a pipe (a flutelike instrument) to soothe and comfort them. While his sheep slept, the shepherd watched over them to protect them from harm. He carried a slingshot and smooth stones as a weapon against predators. The sheep's lives depended on his care and protection. He was willing to die for his sheep.

The Bible contains many references to sheep and shepherds because they were such a common feature of daily life in Israel. The people of Israel understood that God Himself was a shepherd and was their caretaker. Psalm 23 begins, "The Lord is my shepherd." Israel had many false shepherds who led the people into sin. The prophet Ezekiel promised that God would send the true Shepherd, the Messiah, to His people to gather them into one flock (Ezekiel 34).

Jesus chose this image to describe Himself so that we might understand the love and care He gives to us. Like sheep, we often stray; yet Jesus, our Good Shepherd, gently leads us home.

Pilgrim Festivals

Pilgrim festivals are special religious celebrations that commemorate God's great acts of salvation. In the Old Testament, and in accordance with the Law of Moses, there were pilgrim festivals when all Jewish males were required to make a *pilgrimage*, or journey, to the temple in Jerusalem to offer sacrifices and bring offerings from their fields. Women and children usually accompanied their husbands and fathers, making the journey a family event. People traveled in large groups for safety, and the roads became very crowded as the groups neared Jerusalem. Some scholars estimate that when Jesus was a child, hundreds of thousands of pilgrims made the journey to the temple.

The Passover (Exodus 12:17)

The first and most important of the three pilgrim festivals was the Feast of the Passover, remembering God's rescue of the children of Israel from Egypt. It is often referred to as "The Feast of Unleavened Bread" because only unleavened bread (bread made without yeast) was eaten during the seven days immediately following Passover. A lamb was sacrificed and eaten together with bitter herbs and unleavened bread to remind the Jews of the tenth plague, when the angel of death killed the firstborn—both men and animals—of the Egyptian households, but passed over the homes of the Israelites who had obeyed God's command and painted lamb's blood on the doorposts of their homes.

Jesus and His disciples were fulfilling the requirements of this festival when they gathered in the Upper Room on Maundy Thursday to celebrate the Passover. It was during this meal that Jesus instituted the Sacrament of the Altar, Holy Communion.

Pentecost (Leviticus 23:15–21)

Pentecost is the New Testament name for the Festival (or Feast) of the Weeks, the second of the three pilgrim festivals. It was a joyous occasion in late spring or early summer, seven full weeks after Passover, celebrated as a Sabbath Day with rest from work. Pentecost marked the beginning of the wheat harvest. The firstfruits of the harvest were brought to the temple, and two loaves of bread made from the new wheat were offered.

Succoth (Leviticus 23:34)

Succoth, or the Feast of Booths, was a week-long autumn festival of thanksgiving that began five days after Yom Kippur, the Day of Atonement. It reminded the people of Israel of God's protection during their long journey from Egypt to the Promised Land of Canaan and the booths, or temporary homes, they lived in. It also reminded them of the symbol of God's presence among them, the tabernacle. The pilgrims were required to live in booths—temporary shelters—for the seven days of the Feast of Booths and to offer sacrifices of thanksgiving for the harvest. Each family hung samples of their fall crop in their booth to acknowledge God's faithfulness in providing for His people.

These Old Testament pilgrim festivals have great significance in the New Testament. Jesus fulfilled every requirement of the Law of Moses by becoming our sacrificial Passover Lamb and giving us the gift of the Holy Spirit at Pentecost. The Feast of Tabernacles reminds us that God is truly present with us in a new way, revealed to us in His Word and Sacraments.

Proverbs

Into Proverbs

The word **Proverbs** comes from the content of this Bible book. For the most part, it contains short, two-line sentences that describe how God's people can live positive, productive lives.

Theme: Living in true wisdom

Who wrote Proverbs? When? Why?

The Book of Proverbs is a collection of wise sayings that describe how God's people can best deal with life's opportunities and problems. The actions and attitudes of the "wise" contrast sharply with the choices made by "fools."

Most of the book was compiled by King Solomon around 980 BC. Solomon wrote more than 3,000 proverbs in his lifetime (1 Kings 4:32). The Book of Proverbs includes 513 of these. We might think of them as "the best of the best"—the most important proverbs, or those that apply to situations we're most likely to face.

During King Hezekiah's reforms (715–686 BC), God's people took a new interest in this topic. Some of his officials added the material in Proverbs 25 at that point. It's possible that the sayings of Agur (Proverbs 30), the sayings of Lemuel (Proverbs 31:1–9), and the other "sayings of the wise" (Proverbs 22:17–24:34) were added during Hezekiah's reign too.

During the time of the kings, "wise men," or "sages," served as advisors to the ruler and others who served in government. These sages also were expected to instruct the young in practical, productive living. Teaching proverbs was one method they used.

Most of the Proverbs were written so young people could easily memorize them. Most are short—usually just two lines. The second line often uses different language to repeat the idea from the first line. Many proverbs use colorful comparisons; for example, "Like the cold of snow in the time of harvest is a faithful messenger to those who send him; he refreshes the soul of his masters" (Proverbs 25:13).

Martin Luther once wrote, "[Proverbs] may properly be called a book of good works, for in it [Solomon] teaches how to lead a good life before God and the world."

How is Proverbs classified?

Proverbs is counted among the Books of Wisdom and Poetry in the Old Testament. For more on Hebrew poetry, see "How is Job classified?" (p. 161).

What's the best way to read Proverbs?

First, remember that Proverbs does not tell God's people how to find forgiveness for our sins. Instead, it describes the lifestyle we can follow after our Lord brings us to true faith in Him. Proverbs 1:7 sets the stage: "The fear of the Lord is the beginning of knowledge; fools despise wisdom and instruction."

Everything that follows this verse assumes readers are not "fools." Rather, it assumes we already "fear"—trust, honor, and respect—our Savior-God. Since the Lord has put us on that path, the rest of Proverbs talks about where the path leads. It describes how we will want to treat others. It encourages us to study and love God's Word. It outlines the benefits of honesty, honor, and hard work.

Second, remember that Proverbs describes how life usually works here on earth. Its words are not ironclad promises. Instead, the verses explain the benefits we're likely to receive by living wisely. Sometimes, though, things go awry. We live in a sinful world. Those who don't love the Lord sometimes succeed, and we get hurt in the process. That doesn't mean God is lying to us in Proverbs. It just means that the truths in Proverbs aren't always the whole story. We need to read the rest of the Scripture to understand the whole truth about what's happening here on earth.

Third, remember that Proverbs is written as Hebrew poetry—even though it does not rhyme. The writers use pairs of contrasting or complementary thoughts. They also include metaphors, similes, and other figures of speech to make their point, just as we do today. Not everything you will read in Proverbs is meant to be taken literally.

Hint: The Book of Proverbs has thirty-one chapters—one for each day of every month. Some Christians like to read one chapter from Proverbs each day, adding that chapter to their other Bible reading. Try it! And highlight the verses that apply to you as you live with your friends, parents, teachers, and other people throughout the day. You might be surprised at how helpful this book really is!

How is Proverbs organized?

The Book of Proverbs has five main sections:

- **Proverbs 1:1–7** Prologue
- **Proverbs 1:8–9:18** An Introduction to Wisdom
- **Proverbs 10:1–22:16** Solomon's Proverbs
- **Proverbs 22:17–31:9** Additional Proverbs
- **Psalm 31:10–31** Epilogue: the Wise Woman

How does Proverbs point to Jesus?

- Proverbs describes the way Jesus lived from beginning to end during His earthly ministry. It describes the wisdom He wants to work in our hearts, too, as we live with other people here on earth.
- In the New Testament, Jesus is called the "Wisdom of God" (1 Corinthians 1:24–30, Colossians 2:3). John 1:1–3 describes our Savior's role in creating the world. For these reasons, many people see Proverbs 8:22–31 as a picture of Jesus.

What are the key chapters in Proverbs?

- **Proverbs 1:1–7** "Get Wisdom!"
- **Proverbs 8** "Follow Wisdom!"
- **Psalm 31** "A Wise Woman"

Ecclesiastes

Into Ecclesiastes

The English title *Ecclesiastes* comes from the Greek word for "preacher." That's what the author calls himself in Ecclesiastes 1:1.

Theme: Life "under the sun"

Who wrote Ecclesiastes? When? Why?

Both Jewish tradition and the Early Christian Church taught that King Solomon wrote this book. He did so toward the end of his life. When Solomon was a young man, God had given him many gifts—wisdom, wealth, power—and with it all, many opportunities. However, Solomon wasted much of it. He married wives who led him into idol worship, and he disobeyed many direct commands the Lord had set down for Israel's kings. (See Deuteronomy 17:14–20.)

Looking back in old age, Solomon must have had many regrets. This book reflects them.

However, Solomon saw an opportunity to share the wisdom he gained from his mistakes with other people—particularly young people—so they would not make those same mistakes. With this in mind, he repeats a key word and a key phrase again and again:

- The key word is "meaningless," or "vanity." As the king thinks about wisdom, wealth, work, power, prestige, popularity, and pleasure, he shows us that none of these things really matters at life's end. They all evaporate.
- The key phrase is "under the sun." When we try to live as if life here on earth is all there is, life is meaningless. If we trust only what we see and feel and don't take seriously what God tells us in His Word, nothing makes any sense.

But when we live "under the Son"—trusting in Jesus, the Son of God, and following our Savior—then we can see life here on earth as richly meaningful. And we can enjoy God's good gifts to us in the here and now (Ecclesiastes 9:7; 11:8).

How is Ecclesiastes classified?

Ecclesiastes is counted among the Books of Wisdom and Poetry in the Old Testament. For more on Hebrew poetry, see "How is Job classified?" (p. 161.)

What's the best way to read Ecclesiastes?

First, remember that you do not just live "under the sun." You know that life here on earth is not all there is! You are God's baptized, dearly loved child! When life here on earth ends, you will live with God forever in the new heavens and new earth He is preparing for you (John 14:1–3; 2 Peter 3:13). Even when senseless, hurtful things happen, your Savior will always walk through them with you, giving you the courage and hope you need.

Second, remember that Ecclesiastes does not tell God's people how to find forgiveness for their sins. Instead, it talks about the life people live when they don't know and trust in Jesus as their Savior. Because of this, it can be a very discouraging book.

Third, remember that Ecclesiastes describes how life usually works here on earth. Like the Book of Proverbs, the words of Ecclesiastes are not ironclad promises. Instead, the verses explain the benefits we're likely to receive by living wisely, "under the Son" rather than "under the sun." Even when we trust Jesus, though, troubles sometimes come into our lives. We live in a sinful world. The people around us are sinners. Those who live as though God didn't matter sometimes enjoy a wonderful life, while our lives don't seem nearly as good. This is because the truths in Ecclesiastes aren't always the whole story. We need to read the rest of the Scriptures to understand the whole truth about what's happening here on earth.

Fourth, remember that much of Ecclesiastes is written as Hebrew poetry. It doesn't rhyme, but the thoughts from line to line parallel one another. One line balances the next, either by restating the thought, contrasting another thought, or adding a second thought to the first.

Finally, take to heart the wisdom Solomon is sharing with you here. He wrote chapter 12 as the conclusion, and he addresses it to young people. Think about what he's trying to say to you!

How is Ecclesiastes organized?

Ecclesiastes has four main parts:

- **Ecclesiastes 1:1–11** Introduction
- **Ecclesiastes 1:12–11:6** What makes life worth living? (Part 1)
- **Ecclesiastes 11:7–12:8** What makes life worth living? (Part 2)
- **Ecclesiastes 12:9–14** Conclusion: Trust the Good Shepherd, who alone makes life meaningful.

How does Ecclesiastes point to Jesus?

- Many Bible scholars think that Ecclesiastes 12:11 refers to Jesus, our Good Shepherd, the one who gives us a rich, full, eternal life. (See John 10:10.)
- Otherwise, the book makes us think about our Savior because it shows us how meaningless life is for people who don't know His love and care.

What are the key chapters in Ecclesiastes?

- **Ecclesiastes 1** The book's main question: What does life mean?
- **Ecclesiastes 3:1–8** The famous poem, "A Time for Everything"
- **Ecclesiastes 12:1–7** An extended metaphor pictures old age (Even people who don't believe the Bible enjoy reading this poem and trying to figure out what each verse describes.)

Song of Solomon

Into Song of Solomon

A different title, Song of Songs, means something like "the best of the songs."

Theme: authentic love, a gift from the Lord

Who wrote Song of Solomon? When? Why?

King Solomon likely authored this book. In 1 Kings 4:32, we learn that Solomon wrote more than a thousand songs. This one is the only one to survive. The title tells us that either Solomon himself or those around him (or both) considered this the best one—his "greatest hit," as it were.

The author writes to describe God's wonderful gift of love between a man and a woman in marriage. This love is emotional, spiritual, and physical, and our Creator blesses it!

The book also depicts the love between Christ and His people. The Old Testament often describes Israel as a bride (Hosea 2:19–20; 11:1; Isaiah 54:1–8; Ezekiel 16:6–14). The New Testament picks up this picture, calling the Church the "bride of Christ" (Ephesians 5:23, 25; Colossians 1:18; Revelation 19:6–9).

How is Song of Solomon classified?

Song of Solomon is counted among the Books of Wisdom and Poetry in the Old Testament. Song of Solomon is unique in that it is written with the perspectives of three different persons: the bridegroom, the bride, and a chorus. For more on Hebrew poetry, see "How is Job classified?" (p. 161).

What's the best way to read Song of Solomon?

It's helpful to read the book while keeping its two levels in mind:

- On one level, the words describe the beauty and holiness of love between a husband and wife. As we read, we remember and celebrate God's blessing on this kind of love—including sexual love.
- On another level, the words describe Christ's love for His Church. He cherishes us, protects us, and even died to make us His own!

How is Song of Solomon organized?

Song of Solomon uses both Oriental language and images as it describes courtship, the wedding day, and the joys of marriage. In a sense, it's arranged like an opera or even a Broadway musical with three main speaking parts:

- Solomon (the "bridegroom," the "lover")
- The Bride ("the beloved," the "Shulammite," the "shepherdess")
- The Chorus ("friends," "daughters of Jerusalem")

A rough outline of the story, then, goes like this:

- **Song of Solomon 1:1** Authorship
- **Song of Solomon 1:2–2:17** Courtship
- **Song of Solomon 3:1–4:16a** The Wedding Day
- **Song of Solomon 4:16b–8:14** Living Together in Love

How does Song of Solomon point to Jesus?

Throughout the book, the Bridegroom's words and actions symbolize the love of Christ for His Bride, the Church.

What are the key verses in Song of Solomon?

Song of Solomon 3:6–11 describes Solomon's entourage coming for his bride, surrounded by sixty strong warriors and unimaginable wealth and splendor. It's a reminder of Jesus' return on the Last Day to receive us, His Church, to Himself.

Song of Solomon 6:3 sums up one of the main points of the book for New Testament believers: "I am my beloved's and my beloved is mine!"

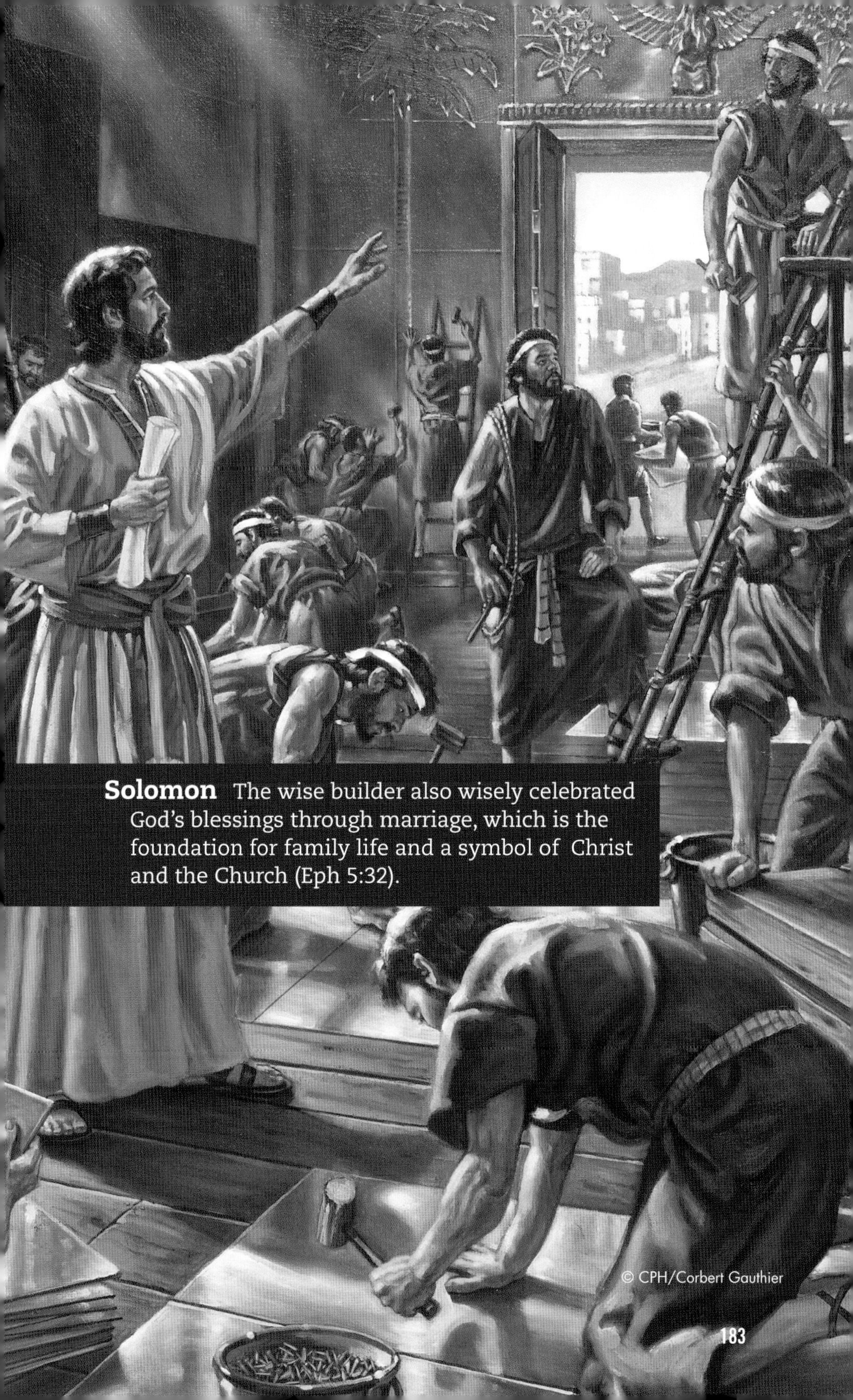

Solomon The wise builder also wisely celebrated God's blessings through marriage, which is the foundation for family life and a symbol of Christ and the Church (Eph 5:32).

Wine and Weddings

Weddings were a joyous occasion in biblical times, just as they are today. The wedding ceremony has changed over the years, yet it likely includes many of the same rituals and traditions.

Wine has a special significance in the Jewish wedding ceremony. As the couple stands under the *chuppah*, or "canopy," the rabbi recites a blessing over wine that praises and thanks God for many things. The blessings are recited over wine because wine is a symbol of life: it begins as grape juice, becomes sour as it ferments, but turns into something wonderful that brings joy and tastes delicious. The full cup of wine also symbolizes God's overflowing love and blessing, as in "my cup overflows" (Psalm 23:5). After the couple exchange rings, seven more blessings are recited, each over a full cup of wine.

Once they are married, the celebration, filled with eating, drinking, dancing, and entertainment, can begin. The meal always begins with a washing of the hands, partly for sanitary reasons and also because it is required by Jewish law. The water needed for this custom may be mentioned in John 2:6: "Now there were six stone water jars there for the Jewish rites of purification, each holding twenty or thirty gallons." The meal ends with the Grace after Meals prayer, and again the seven blessings are recited over wine shared by the bride and groom.

Because large quantities of wine are required for the ceremony and the feast, not having enough was, and still is, considered embarrassing for the host. Jesus showed great care and concern for the wedding couple in John 2 when He performed His first miracle by changing water into wine. What is more important, Jesus demonstrated His power to all who were present, revealing His glory as the promised Messiah.

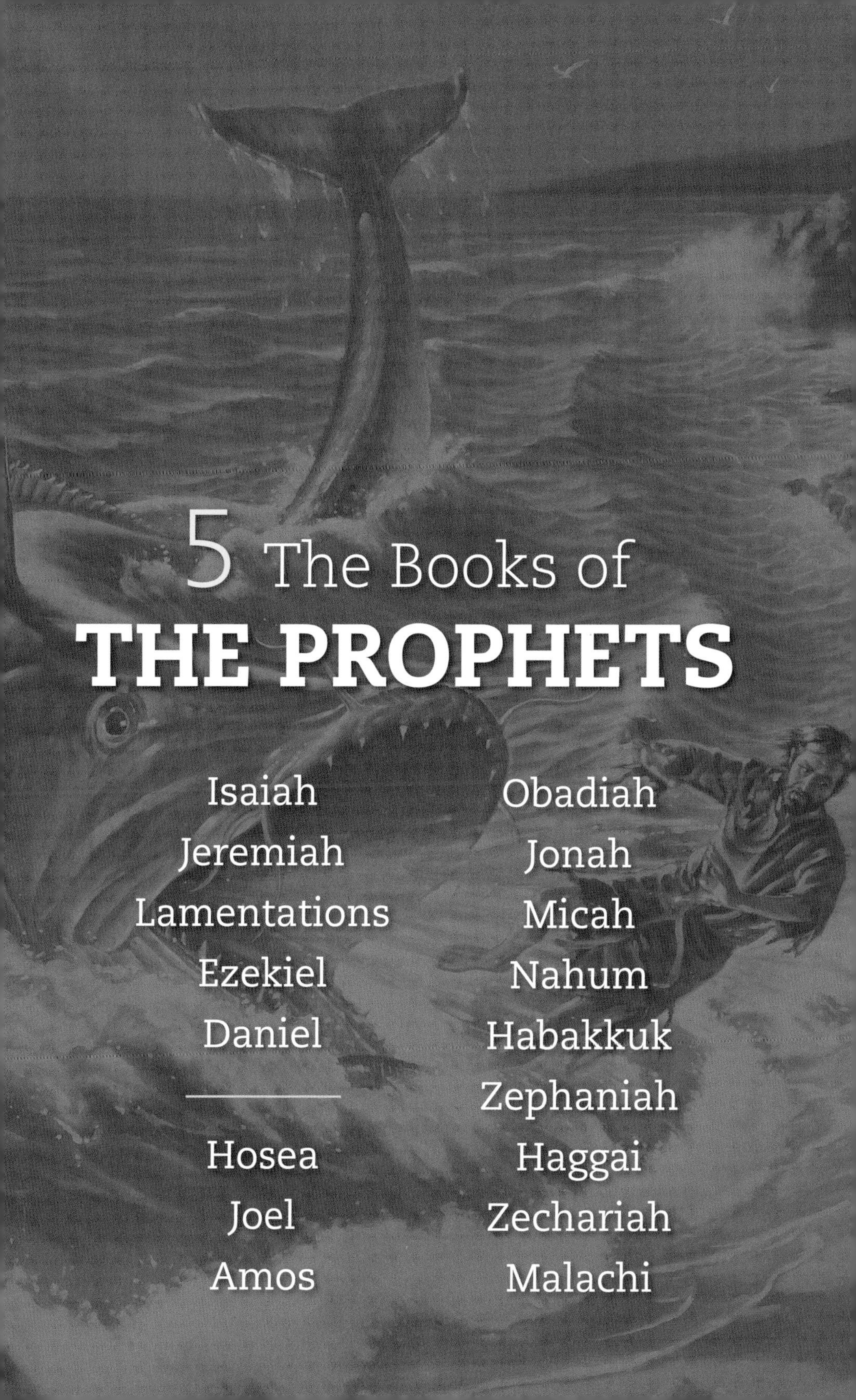

5 The Books of THE PROPHETS

Isaiah
Jeremiah
Lamentations
Ezekiel
Daniel

Hosea
Joel
Amos
Obadiah
Jonah
Micah
Nahum
Habakkuk
Zephaniah
Haggai
Zechariah
Malachi

Prophets

The Prophets of Israel

What is a prophet?

The word *prophet*, in a general sense, refers to a person who takes a message heard and tells it to others. For example, Moses gave God's message to Pharaoh, so Moses could be considered a prophet in the general sense. Prophets spoke for God by proclaiming God's Word and teaching about the coming Savior, a promise fulfilled in the Lord Jesus.

What is the prophetic order?

Although many people in the Bible spoke for God, the prophetic order started with Samuel and continued through the history of the Old Testament, ending with John the Baptist, who was the forerunner of Christ. The ultimate and most perfect Prophet is Jesus, who is the very Word of God made flesh.

What is prophecy?

In Israel, prophecy was much like preaching today, proclaiming and applying God's Word. Prophets sometimes told the people what God planned to do. In the Old Testament, there are many prophecies about the coming of the Messiah. Micah 5:2 told that the Messiah would come out of Bethlehem. Isaiah 53:3–5 foretold that the Messiah would be "wounded for our transgressions" and "crushed for our iniquities" (v. 5). These prophecies helped the people recognize Jesus as the Messiah. Jesus explained this to the disciples on the way to Emmaus: "Beginning with Moses and all the Prophets, He interpreted to them in all the Scriptures the things concerning Himself" (Luke 24:27).

Prophets also pointed out the sins of the people and warned them of God's judgment. For example, Jonah warned the Ninevites of God's judgment for sin and called them to repentance.

Who was Samuel?

The period of the judges came to a close as God raised Samuel to be a prophet. Samuel was dedicated to the Lord as a child and went to live at the tabernacle. The Lord spoke directly to Samuel, giving him a message to pass along to Eli.

Samuel was the transition between the period of the judges and the kings. The prophets gave messages to the people from the Lord, and then became the persons chosen to anoint the kings of Israel. There were many prophets of Israel.

Samuel

Elijah

Elisha

Some Important Prophets

- Samuel brought the Word of God to Israel and anointed Saul, the first king of Israel.
- Elijah challenged the Baal worshipers at Mount Carmel to send fire down on their altar.
- Elisha, who came after Elijah, instructed Naaman to wash in the Jordan seven times for healing.

2 Chronicles 24:19

"Yet He sent prophets among them to bring them back to the LORD. These testified against them, but they would not pay attention."

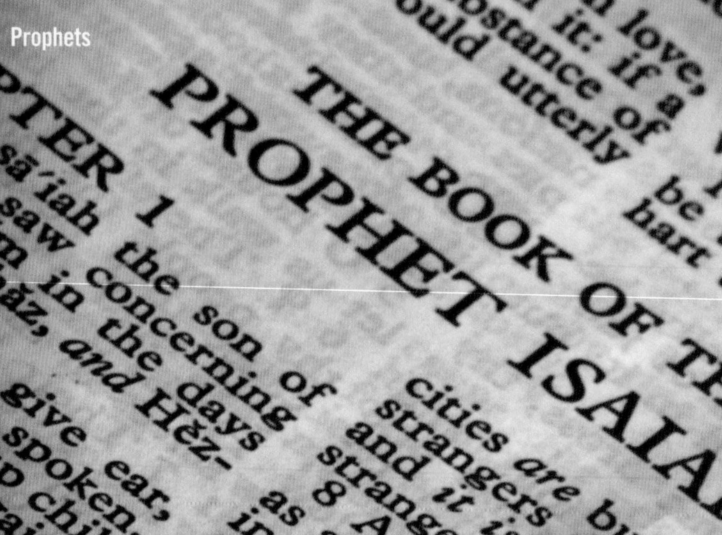

The Prophetic Books of the Bible

Major Prophets (Longer Books)	Minor Prophets (Shorter Books)
Isaiah	Hosea
Jeremiah	Joel
Lamentations	Amos
Ezekiel	Obadiah
Daniel	Jonah
	Micah
	Nahum
	Habakkuk
	Zephaniah
	Haggai
	Zechariah
	Malachi

Isaiah

Into Isaiah

Fast Facts

- Isaiah preached to the Southern Kingdom (Judah) from about 740 to about 681 BC.
- The name *Isaiah* means "the Lord is salvation." His name was a short version of the message Isaiah preached.
- Isaiah is the first of the "major prophets"; his message wasn't more important than that of the minor prophets, but his book is longer. Jeremiah, Ezekiel, and Daniel are the other longer (and thus "major") prophets.
- Isaiah served under at least four kings—Uzziah, Jotham, Ahaz, and Hezekiah.
- Isaiah is famous for his detailed predictions, especially his descriptions of the coming Savior.
- Most of Isaiah's book is written as poetry. This made it beautiful. It also made it easier to memorize for the people of his day, who usually weren't wealthy enough to own a scroll of the prophet's writings. (Because they were handwritten, books were very expensive!)
- Isaiah evidently came from a wealthy, important family. Even so, his authority came from the call God placed upon his life (Isaiah 6) and the Word of God he spoke.
- One of Isaiah's favorite names for God is "the LORD of hosts." The "hosts" of God are His angel armies. The name reminds us He is

supreme and He is able to protect His people. Isaiah uses this name forty-two times in his book.

- Another of Isaiah's favorite names for God is "the Holy One of Israel." He uses it twenty-four times. Isaiah saw God's holiness and majesty in contrast to human sinfulness. Yet the Lord, in mercy, has chosen to identify Himself with His sinful children—believing Israel. We belong to Him through repentant faith! That's Isaiah's message.

How is Isaiah classified?

Isaiah is counted among the Books of the Prophets in the Old Testament. It is the first of the *major* or larger prophetic books. Parts of Isaiah are historical accounts. But much of the book is poetry. The prophets addressed the problems of their day by proclaiming the teachings of the Books of Moses.

What purpose did Isaiah's message serve?

At the time Isaiah began his work, King Uzziah had ruled over God's people for more than fifty years! This long period of peace and stability had brought prosperity to the nation. For this reason, King Uzziah's death brought much worry and many fears. Rumors of Assyria's growing power and the ruthlessness of its army added to these fears.

God's people must have had many questions. What would the new king be like? Could he protect Judah? Would their lives change for the worse? Would taxes go up? Would families be safe?

These worries weren't the people's only problem, and certainly not their biggest problem by far! Their biggest problems were spiritual ones. The nation was simply going through the motions in their worship. The Lord had become a kind of good luck charm. They obeyed and worshiped Him—when it was convenient. But they also worshiped other gods, actually carving figures from wood and fashioning statues from gold and silver—and praying to them!

Isaiah called God's people to repentance. He urged them to prepare their hearts for the coming Savior.

What does Isaiah's message mean to us today?

Like Israel of old, we, too, sometimes look to other "gods" for help in time of need. We obey God's Law—when it's convenient and when we're afraid of getting caught. Our love is halfhearted, and our other sins, many.

The Law thunders from Isaiah's pages as Isaiah reminds us that we can't fool God.

But Isaiah's message doesn't end there. We can't fool God, but we don't have to! God has had mercy on us. From all eternity, He planned to send a

Savior for us! Perhaps more than any other Old Testament prophet, Isaiah brings comfort and hope, especially as he describes the coming Savior.

From the pages of Isaiah, repentant sinners see clearly that "the Lord is salvation"—and it's a beautiful sight!

How does Isaiah point to Jesus?

For one thing, Isaiah is packed with prophecies that are clearly fulfilled in the life and ministry of our Savior. (See the chart "Prophecies of the Savior in Isaiah—An Overview" on the next page.)

Another "don't miss this" feature of Isaiah is his portrait of the Servant. Isaiah composed four Servant Songs to describe the work of the Deliverer whom the Lord would send to defeat sin and Satan, hell and death for us. These appear in Isaiah 42:1–7, Isaiah 49:1–13; Isaiah 50:4–9; and Isaiah 52:13–53:12.

The Servant Songs grow brighter and more detailed with each new chorus. Each in succession adds more depth to the portrait of our Savior that Isaiah paints. We might have expected God's Son to come in pomp—but Jesus came in poverty. We might have expected power—but Jesus endured pain and weakness. We might have looked for a display of authority and demands for respect—but Jesus humbled Himself. He became a servant. He came not to be served but "to serve, and to give His life as a ransom for many" (Matthew 20:28).

What are the key chapters in Isaiah?

In addition to the Servant Songs mentioned above and the chapters that describe the coming Savior, these chapters also form peaks in the mountain range that is Isaiah:

- **Isaiah 6** The Prophet's Call
- **Isaiah 24–27** The "Little Apocalypse"[1]
- **Isaiah 25** Death Destroyed!
- **Isaiah 36–39** The Reign of Hezekiah
- **Isaiah 40** "Comfort My People"
- **Isaiah 43** "You Are Mine!"
- **Isaiah 53** The Coming Messiah, His Death and Victory
- **Isaiah 60** All Nations See the Lord's Salvation
- **Isaiah 65–66** Final Judgment, Eternal Glory

---

[1] *Apocalypse* means "revealing," or "uncovering." In chapters 24–27, Isaiah reveals God's fury at human sin and His coming judgment on the nations. He also reveals the Lord's ultimate victory over sin and death.

Prophecies of the Savior in Isaiah
An Overview

Passage	Prophecy	Fulfillment
9:7	Heir to the Throne	Matthew 1:1
7:14	Born of a Virgin	Matthew 1:18
9:1–2	Ministry in Galilee	Matthew 4:12–16
11:2	Some of His Characteristics	Luke 2:52
50:6	Smitten and Spat Upon	Mark 14:65
53:3	Rejected by His People	John 1:11
53:4	Bore the Infirmities of People	Matthew 8:16–17
53:7	Silent When Accused	Matthew 26:62–63
53:9	Buried with the Rich	Matthew 27:57–60
53:12	Numbered with Sinners	Matthew 27:38; Luke 22:37
53:12	Interceded for Sinners	Matthew 26:28; 10–12 Mark 10:45; John 1:29
53:4–8	Vicariously Sacrificed as the Lamb of God	Mark 10:45; John 1:29
53:10b–12	Rose from the Dead to Enjoy the Fruit of His Victory	Luke 24

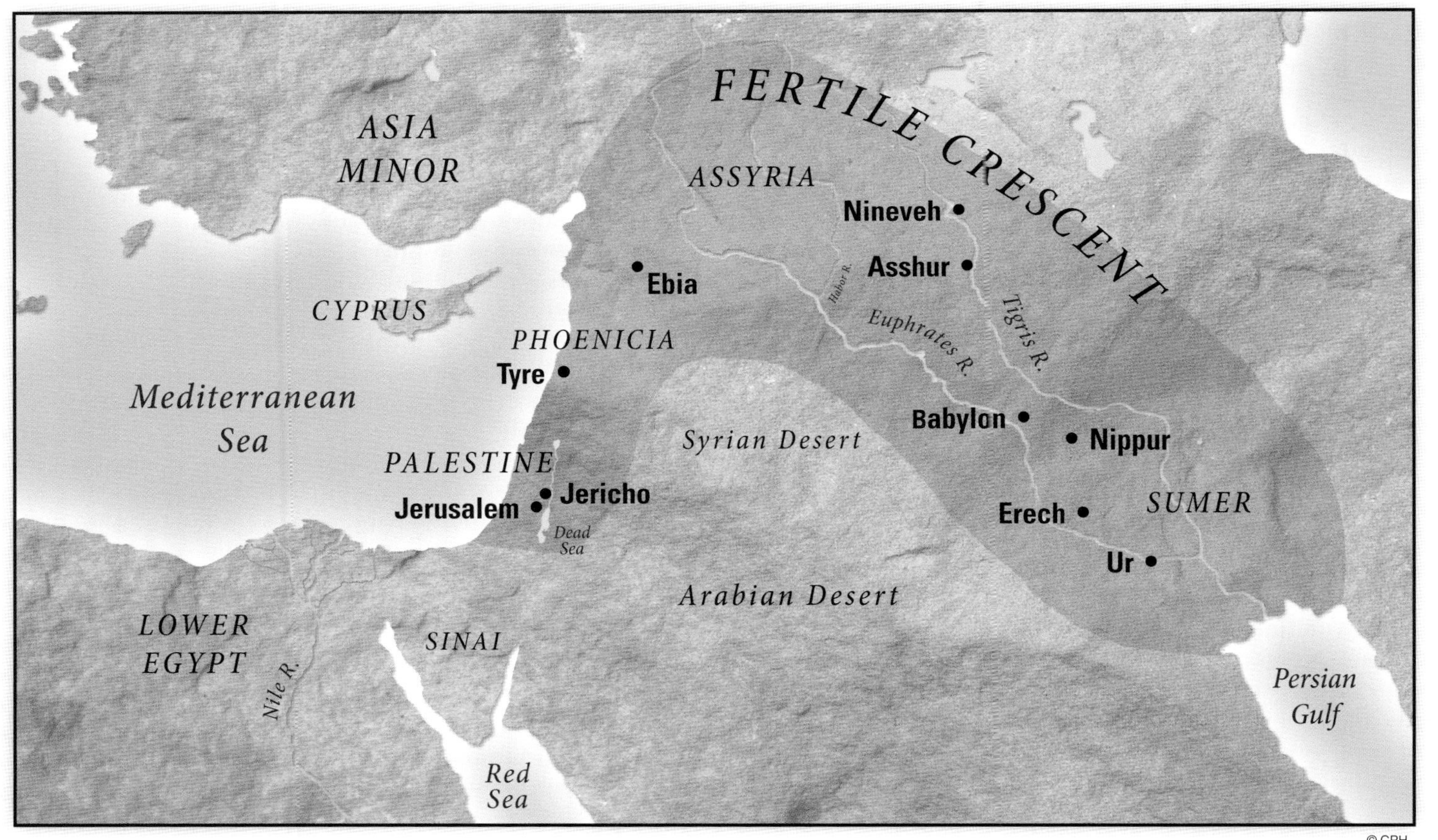
FERTILE CRESCENT
ASIA MINOR
ASSYRIA
Nineveh
Asshur
Ebia
Habor R.
Euphrates R.
Tigris R.
CYPRUS
PHOENICIA
Tyre
Mediterranean Sea
Babylon
Nippur
Syrian Desert
PALESTINE
Jericho
Jerusalem
Dead Sea
Erech
SUMER
Ur
Arabian Desert
LOWER EGYPT
SINAI
Nile R.
Persian Gulf
Red Sea
© CPH

Angels and Archangels

What are angels?

Angels are spiritual beings that are created by God. They are stronger than humans, but not all powerful or omnipotent (Psalm 103:20; 2 Peter 2:11). Matthew 28:3 describes the angel at Jesus' resurrection: "His appearance was like lightning, and his clothing white as snow."

What do angels do?

Angels worship God. In Isaiah 6:3, angels worship and praise God. Their song, the Sanctus, is in the liturgy used in the Divine Service—"Holy, holy, holy Lord God of pow'r and might: Heaven and earth are full of Your glory" (*Lutheran Service Book*, p. 161).

Angels bring messages of God's will to people. Angels delivered the Law to Moses (Acts 7:52–53). They brought messages to Zechariah, Mary, Joseph, the shepherds, and to others in the Bible.

Angels instruct God's people. Angels gave instructions to Joseph about the birth of Jesus (Matthew 1:18–23; 2:13–15, 19–23); to the women at the tomb (Matthew 28:2–8; Mark 16:5–8; Luke 24:1–9; John 20:11–13); to Cornelius (Acts 10:1–8); and to Philip (Acts 8:26).

Angels minister to God's people. Angels brought bread to Elijah (1 Kings 19:5–6). They also ministered to Jesus after His temptation (Matthew 4:11).

Angels guard and protect God's people. They protected Daniel in the lions' den (Daniel 6:19–22). They also guard and protect us (Psalm 91:11).

Angels deliver people from danger once they are in it. Angels released the apostles from prison (Acts 5:17–21) and did the same for Peter (Acts 12:6–11).

Angels carry out God's judgment as soldiers. The Bible refers to angels as "the heavenly host." The word *host* is a military term referring to an army. An angel destroyed 185,000 Assyrians who were enemies of God (2 Kings 19:35–36).

Are there different types of angels?

Cherubim (plural of *cherub*) are a special kind of angel. Cherubim are the angels who, with a flaming sword, guard the tree of life in the Garden of Eden (Genesis 3:24). Cherubim were shown on the mercy seat, the cover of the ark of the covenant. Ezekiel describes cherubim with both human and animal features (1:5–25; 10:1–20).

Seraphim (plural of *seraph*) are a different type of angel. These angels are described in detail in Isaiah 6:1–9. They have six wings and are glorious; their Hebrew name suggests that their appearance is like fire.

Do we know any angels' names?

Gabriel (Luke 1:19) means "man of God" or "God is strong." This angel is sometimes referred to as "the Christmas angel."

Michael, whose name means "Who is like God?" is considered the chief angel (Jude 9). He battled with the dragon, or Satan, in the war in heaven (Revelation 12:7–9).

Myths and truths about angels

Angels are not human beings who have died. According to the Bible, angels are created spiritual beings, but they can appear to people. The angel Gabriel appeared to Zechariah in the temple and to Mary in Nazareth.

Angels often appear as men. At the tomb after Jesus rose from the dead, an angel appeared as a "young man" (Mark 16:5). Hebrews 13:2 reminds us to help strangers, "for thereby some have entertained angels unawares."

Angels are not cute and cuddly infants. Angels appear as fully grown adult men. When people in Bible times saw angels, the first thing the angel told them was "Do not be afraid." Angels are powerful and oftentimes frightening.

Angels do not always fly or have wings for flight. In Scripture, some angels are described as having wings (Ezekiel 1:11; Isaiah 6:2). In other passages, they walk or stand next to people.

The phrase "the angel of the Lord" (Genesis 22:11; Exodus 3:2; Numbers 22:22; Judges 2:1; and others) often does not refer to God's created angels, but rather to the Son of God Himself, Jesus.

Bible Animals

The Bible mentions more than one hundred animals. Adam named the animals, Noah saved the animals, and priests sacrificed animals. Jonah was inside a fish, and ravens took care of Elijah. From creation to Revelation, God's creatures of the animal kingdom have been interesting to God's most treasured visible creatures—humans.

What animals might have kept Jesus company while He was in the wilderness for the forty days of His temptation?

Hyenas

The striped hyena is quite common in Israel. Similar to jackals, they are known for their mournful howls and yelps. They eat carrion, which is dead, putrefying flesh that is unfit food for most creatures (Isaiah 13:22; Jeremiah 12:9).

© Eric Isselee/Shutterstock, Inc.

Scorpions

Scorpions are not insects but arachnids. They are common in the Holy Land. The rock scorpion is found in Israel. It is as thick as a man's finger and about six inches long, with eight eyes and four pairs of legs. Scorpions catch insects and spiders at night. They hold their prey with their upper and lower jaws, called *pincers*, long enough to examine their catch and decide whether it is good to eat. Then they sting the prey with the poison that is in the tip of the tail that curls over their head, paralyze it, and suck out the body juices.

Scorpions don't attack humans, but they will defend themselves if disturbed. Most people in Bible times didn't like the scorpion because its sting is extremely painful and sometimes fatal. A scorpion desires a warm habitat and will often enter houses, especially at night, and hide in beds, blankets, clothing, and shoes.

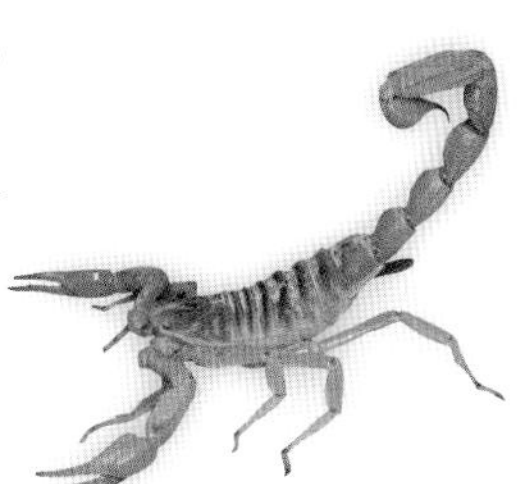

© Casey Bishop/Shutterstock, Inc.

Vultures

There are several varieties of "vultures," including other birds of prey such as hawks and eagles. Usually, vultures find the flesh of dead creatures, called *carrion*. Sometimes, vultures, jackals, and hyenas compete for the carrion.

© Eric Isselee/Shutterstock, Inc.

One type of vulture that lives in Israel today is the griffon vulture, found in the region of the Sea of Galilee. It is light brown with a pale yellow head and neck that are covered with very fine down. It searches for dead animals as it soars high in the air and then swoops down to rip apart the corpse and eat the insides.

© Shutterstock, Inc.

Snakes

Many species of serpents in Israel are poisonous. In ancient times, people thought the tongue was poisonous. Serpents hide themselves and move slyly.

Snakes are mentioned several times throughout the Old Testament Scriptures (Genesis 3:1; 49:17; Numbers 21:6; Proverbs 23:31–32). Most common are the Palestinian viper, also known as an "adder"; the carpet viper, or sand viper, which lives around Jericho; and the cerastes viper.

Images of the Egyptian cobra, or asp, sometimes decorated the headdresses of the Egyptian pharaohs. Their poison is deadly within a half hour.

© Eric Isselee/Shutterstock, Inc.

Lions

Although there are no wild lions in Israel today, the Israelites feared them in Bible times. Most lions attack humans only when they are hungry.

Lions, found in pairs or in large numbers, live in a lair or den. This is a hollow in the ground hidden by shrubbery. In Bible times, they liked the subtropical, junglelike vegetation of the Jordan River Valley.

Lions came out of thickets along the Jordan River to wait for their victims. A blow of the paw to smaller animals or a bite on the throat of larger animals was enough to kill a lion's prey and provide food. Lions also roamed the hilly areas of Judah around Lebanon and Mount Hermon.

The Old Testament mentions the lion about 150 times, more often than most other wild animals. (See Job 4:11; Joel 1:6; Isaiah 5:29; Numbers 23:24; Deuteronomy 33:20.)

Leopards

One of the most dangerous of all hunters, though not as strong as a lion or tiger, the leopard approaches its prey without a sound, pounces upon it, and kills it. It hunts birds, antelopes, monkeys, jackals, and other creatures. Jeremiah 5:6 portrays leopards as deadly predators.

Leopards are difficult animals to track down because they can jump, climb, and even swim. The leopard hides near villages or watering places and waits for prey, sometimes for hours. Sometimes only its tail moves as it is hidden from others.

The leopard was common in the Holy Land in Bible times. "The waters of Nimrim" mentioned in Isaiah 15:6 and Jeremiah 48:34 was a fertile spot southeast of the Dead Sea; leopards still live there.

© Eric Isselee/Shutterstock, Inc.

Lizards

More than forty varieties of lizards live in Israel. The sand lizard, called a skink, is found in desert places, where its yellowish color helps to protect it. It does not climb, but hides under stones or in holes. Geckos are nocturnal hunters that eat insects and spiders. They have suction pads on their feet that enable them to climb smooth surfaces.

© Rhett Olson Photography/ Shutterstock, Inc.

Locusts

© Eric Isselee/Shutterstock, Inc.

As Moses was trying to convince Pharaoh to let the Israelite slaves go, God sent plagues upon Egypt. In one of those plagues, locusts arrived in droves and ate all the vegetation (Exodus 10:1–20).

© Eric Isselee/Shutterstock, Inc.

Foxes and Jackals

The fox and jackal are very much alike, except that the jackal has a broader head, shorter nose and ears, and longer legs. Also, the fox lives alone, whereas jackals stay together in packs and hide during the day in caves.

The jackal feeds on carrion (the flesh of dead creatures), but the fox does not. Foxes do eat almost anything—fruit, plants, mice, beetles, leverets (hares), and birds. They have a well-developed sense of smell, making them cunning, skillful hunters.

Two types of foxes live in Israel. The Egyptian fox, which is smaller than the common red fox, lives in the central and southern parts. Its back is rust colored and its belly is white. The Syrian fox lives in the northern region of the Holy Land and has a shiny golden coat. (See Psalm 63:10.)

Isaiah's Message

The prophet recorded many of the events in the history of God's people during the rise of the Assyrian Empire and the fall of the kingdom of Israel. In 722 BC, Assyria conquered the Northern Kingdom of Israel and captured Samaria, its capital city. King Sennacherib of Assyria, in 701 BC, then threatened Jersualem, the capital of the Southern Kingdom of Judah. God intervened, however, and spared Jerusalem for another hundred years or so.

God spoke to His people many times through the prophet Isaiah, warning of judgment and the captivity that was coming from their new enemy, the Babylonians, and calling them to repentance. Isaiah preached the law to the people of Israel, pointing out to them their sins of idolatry. He also wrote messages of comfort and hope, giving the Israelites a picture of their promised Messiah and the assurance that God would one day redeem His people, even telling them His name: "Behold, the virgin shall conceive and bear a son, and shall call His name Immanuel" (Isaiah 7:14).

The Messiah

Isaiah's prophecies pointed to the coming Messiah who would come as a King to comfort and save His people. "For to us a child is born, to us a son is given; and the government shall be upon His shoulder, and His name shall be called Wonderful Counselor, Mighty God, Everlasting Father, Prince of Peace" (Isaiah 9:6).

Many of Isaiah's other prophecies are also familiar to us, as they describe the Savior as the one who "has borne our griefs and carried our sorrows" (Isaiah 53:4), and by whose "stripes we are healed" (Isaiah 53:5). In 1741, George Frideric Handel set many of Isaiah's prophecies to music in "The Messiah," one of the best-known and most beloved works of music ever written.

Isaiah shared his vision of God sitting on His throne in His holy temple with angels flying and shouting to each other, "Holy, holy, holy is the LORD of hosts" (Isaiah 6:3). His writings give us a glimpse of what life was like for God's people hundreds of years before the Savior was born.

© CPH/Robert Papp

Isaiah Today

One of the biggest archaeological discoveries began in 1947, shortly after World War II, in eleven caves near the northwest shore of the Dead Sea. Over several years, shepherds and archaeologists found portions of more than eight hundred manuscripts, some stored in pottery jars, including several copies of the Book of Isaiah. One of these is a nearly complete text. The scrolls were mostly of sheepskin and tied with linen thread. These caves also contained fragments of other books of the Hebrew Bible. These scrolls, known as the Dead Sea Scrolls, have validated the accuracy of manuscripts of the Book of Isaiah.

© Ella/Shutterstock, Inc.

Jeremiah

Into Jeremiah

Fast Facts

- Jeremiah preached to the Southern Kingdom (Judah) during the reign of its final five kings—Josiah, Jehoahaz, Jehoiakim, Jehoiachin, and Zedekiah (627–586 BC).
- Jeremiah was only a young man when God's call came to him. Some scholars think he may have been in his early teens!
- Jeremiah was both a priest and a prophet. He was among the most unpopular prophets. At one point, people from his hometown, Anathoth, plotted to assassinate him (11:18–23)!
- The name *Jeremiah* means "the Lord will raise up" or "the Lord will set free." Jeremiah's name reflects the promise of his book. Sin had brought Judah very low, but God would raise up His repentant, faithful people.
- Jeremiah is the second of the major prophets; his message wasn't more important than that of the minor prophets, but his book is longer. Isaiah, Ezekiel, and Daniel are the other longer (and thus "major") prophets.
- Jeremiah is often called "the weeping prophet" because of the sad message of judgment he delivered and because so few believed him—or even listened to him.
- The Lord forbade Jeremiah to marry. He had neither wife nor children to give him support. Nor was he allowed to attend funerals or parties. His lifestyle became one long object lesson pointing to the judgment about to overtake Judah.

- Like the Book of Isaiah, most of Jeremiah's book is written as poetry.
- Jeremiah is not organized chronologically, but instead by similarity of subjects.

How is Jeremiah classified?

Jeremiah is counted among the Books of the Prophets in the Old Testament. The book includes both history and poetry. Much of the book expresses sorrow or lament over the sins of Israel.

What purpose did Jeremiah's message serve?

What did Jeremiah's message mean to its original audience? Not much! King Jehoiakim even burned one of the scrolls Jeremiah sent to him! (See Jeremiah 36.)

Still, "the Word of the LORD came," as Jeremiah wrote. In fact, he repeats that phrase forty-two times in his book. That word was a word of warning, a word of doom. God's people didn't listen. Their sin had made their hearts numb. They were drunk on their foolishness. The times were so bad that some people even burned up their children as part of the worship they offered to their idol-god Molech (Jeremiah 7:30–31)!

Jeremiah's message was clear—and he repeated it often. The Hebrew word *shuv* appears seventy-four times in Jeremiah. It means "turn" and often means "repent." Jeremiah begged his people to return to the true God in faith and obedience, but they insisted on following their own path. Their stubbornness is amazing. (In fact, it's a lot like our own at times!)

Still, Jeremiah held out a message of hope for the small group of believers who did listen, who did respect the Lord and want to please Him. To this remnant, Jeremiah described the "righteous Branch" that would grow up from the seemingly dead stump of Judah. This is our Savior, Jesus, who gives us His own righteousness in His cross. (See Jeremiah 23:5; 33:15.)

What does Jeremiah's message mean to us today?

Sin is tricky. It can numb our conscience and put us to sleep, spiritually speaking. It did that to the people of ancient Judah—and it can do that to us too! If we ignore God's warnings long enough, the new life the Holy Spirit has planted in us can shrivel and die.

Jeremiah warns, "The heart is deceitful above all things, and desperately sick; who can understand it?" (Jeremiah 17:9).

That's why it's such a blessing that "the Word of the LORD came" and that it still comes to sinners like you and me. That Word comes to us when we read the Scripture. It came to us when our Savior made us His own in Holy Baptism. It comes as we receive Jesus' very own body and blood in the Lord's Supper.

The Word—Jesus Himself (John 1:14)—came and comes and keeps on coming to warn us of our sin, to urge us to repent, and to remind us of the righteousness He gives to all believers.

Are you listening to that Word?

How does Jeremiah point to Jesus?

Jesus is the "righteous Branch" Jeremiah describes in 23:5 and 33:15. His cross makes the comfort of chapters 30–33 possible for guilty sinners like you and me.

The promises of pardon and peace Jeremiah scatters like precious jewels throughout his book are possible only in the righteousness our Savior has earned for us.

What are the key chapters in Jeremiah?

- **Jeremiah 1** The prophet's call
- **Jeremiah 23:1–6** "The righteous Branch"
- **Jeremiah 25** Seventy years of captivity foretold
- **Jeremiah 29** Jeremiah's letter to the exiles in Babylon
- **Jeremiah 30–32** "The Book of Consolation"
- **Jeremiah 36** Jehoiakim burns Jeremiah's scroll
- **Jeremiah 39 and 52** Jerusalem is sacked and burned

Jeremiah's Object Lessons: No Children's Talks Here

Bible scholars agree that Jeremiah used object lessons to deliver powerful sermons. Scholars differ somewhat as they decide what constitutes an object lesson. Here are the nominees and a brief summary of the prophet's point in each.

The Linen Sash	13:1–11	**Law**—The ruined sash symbolized the filth of Judah's sin and the guilt that clung to the nation.
The Wineskins	13:12–14	**Law**—Every person, including every leader in Jerusalem, would be filled with and broken by God's judgement.
The Potter and Clay	18:1–10	**Law**—The Lord, as Israel's Creator, has the power and the right to destroy the impenitent.
The Broken Vessel	19:1–13	**Law**—The nation of Judah would be shattered by conquest.
Two Baskets of Figs	24:1–10	**Law**—Judah's sin ruined the nation and made it nauseating in God's eyes. Yet— Gospel—a remnant would produce spiritual fruit pleasing to Him. This remnant would return to Jerusalem someday.
Fetters and Yokes	27:1–11	**Law**—All the nations planning alliances with Judah would find themselves led into captivity and serving the ruler of Babylon.
Buying a Field	32:1–15	**Law**— Promised deliverance for the remnant, who would surely return to Judah, and everyday life would return to normal.
The Stones and the Canopy	43:8–13	**Law**—Nebuchadnezzar would set up his throne in Egypt. Those from Judah who disobeyed God by hiding there would die or be taken captive.
The Scroll and Rock	51:59–64	**Law**—The destroyer, Babylon, would be destroyed. It would sink like a stone, never to rise again.

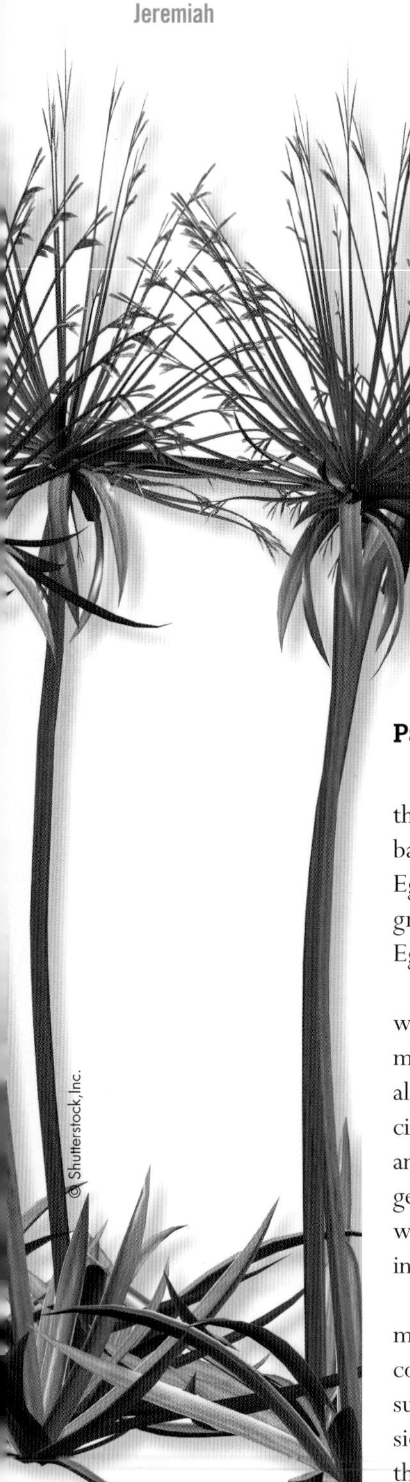
© Shutterstock, Inc.

Papyrus

Papyrus is a tall reed with a triangular stem that grows up to fifteen feet tall. It grows along the banks of the Nile River and was once plentiful in Egypt. Now it is rarely found there, though it still grows along the Nile in Sudan, a country south of Egypt.

The ancient Egyptians used papyrus in many ways. They used it to make sandals; to weave into mats, baskets, and fencing; and to make rope. They also used parts of the plant for food as well as medicine. The reeds were woven together to make boats and were dried to make fuel for fires. Scholars suggest that both the basket in which the infant Moses was placed (Exodus 2:3) and the reeds along the Nile in which the basket was concealed were papyrus.

Papyrus was the most important writing material in the ancient world. Our word *paper* comes from the word *papyrus*. To make a writing surface, the stems were split, flattened, and placed side by side. Additional layers were placed on top of the first layer. The stalks were then pressed, dried, and covered with paste before being beaten flat and

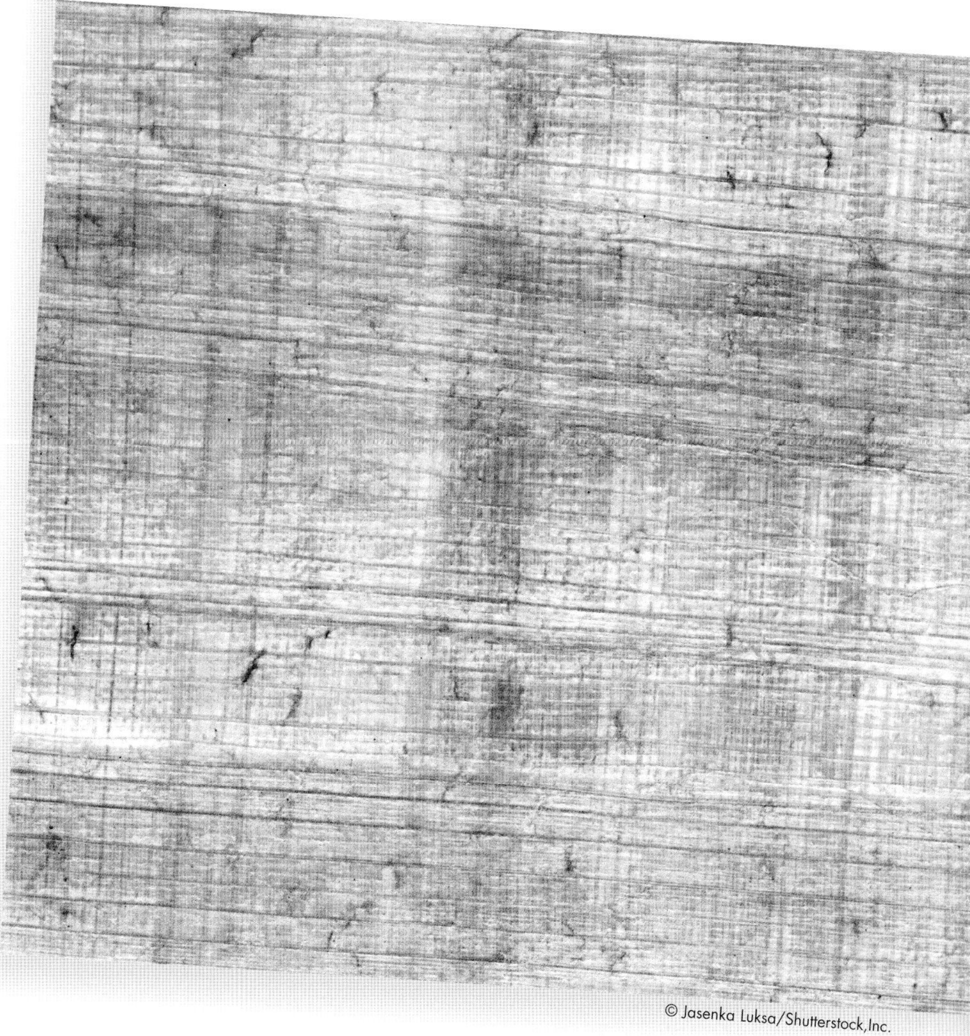

smooth. The papyrus was then ready to use as a writing surface. Sharp reeds were used as pens and a variety of dyes and pigments were used to make ink.

The Egyptians also used papyrus when they mummified their dead. First they prepared the corpses and wrapped them in linen. Then they covered them with several layers of papyrus that were then covered with plaster and painted in bright colors.

Although Egypt exported its writing material to other parts of the ancient world, few *papyri* (the plural of *papyrus*) from outside Egypt survived. Archaeologists have discovered large numbers of ancient papyri in towns south of modern Cairo. These have given modern historians a glimpse of life in ancient Egypt.

© Shutterstock, Inc.

Fig Facts

- The fig tree is a symbol of fertility, abundance, and sweetness. Winners of the Olympic games, which began as early as 776 BC, might have received laurels made of woven fig leaves as their reward.

Figs in the Bible

Figs and fig trees appeared in the Garden of Eden; Adam and Eve sewed the leaves together to make clothing (Genesis 3:7). They were common in Israel during Jesus' lifetime and were so plentiful that they were exported to other nations. Jesus used fig trees several times as examples in His teaching. Once He cursed a fig tree that had beautiful leaves but no fruit (Mark 11:13–14). Jeremiah wrote about figs in chapter 24 of his prophecy.

Fig Foods

Each fig tree generally produces much fruit. Figs are usually harvested in the late summer and early fall, but they are available all year long. Their natural sweetness makes them popular additions to everything from pies and puddings to popovers. Figs add flavor and texture to salads and whole-grain dishes like couscous, and figs are often served with lamb. Whether dried, canned, or fresh, figs also are part of holiday feasts such as Christmas, Hanukkah, Easter, and Passover.

© Shutterstock, Inc.

Lamentations

Into Lamentations

Fast Facts

- Lamentations contains five poems or songs. These are, in fact, like funeral dirges that lament the fall of Jerusalem and the sin of the people that called down God's judgment on the nation of Judah.
- Jeremiah likely wrote Lamentations. (See 2 Chronicles 35:25.) If so, the book was written in 586 BC or after.
- For forty years, Jeremiah had proclaimed a deafening message of judgment to unhearing, uncaring hearts. Then, finally, doom fell. Jeremiah's grief is unimaginable.
- Even though Lamentations is a shorter book, it is grouped with the "major prophets" of the Old Testament because of its association with the Book of Jeremiah.

How is Lamentations classified?

Lamentations is counted among the Books of the Prophets in the Old Testament. In English Bibles, it follows Jeremiah's major book even though it has few chapters. Lamentations is acrostic poetry, in which the letters of the Hebrew alphabet set the order for the first word of each section of poetry. (E.g., 1:1 starts with the first letter of the Hebrew alphabet; 1:2, the second, etc., to the close of the first chapter.) For more on Hebrew poetry, see p. 161.

What purpose did Lamentations serve?

The five "laments" in this book express sorrow over the sins of Judah and the devastation those sins created. The words read like a funeral hymn as the people mourned over the death of their dreams, the death of their nation.

Yet a ray of hope shines through the gloom. At the very center, the very heart of the lament, the mercies of God brings renewed joy (Lamentations 3). Those mercies are "new every morning" (v. 23). The Lord's repentant, faithful people need never despair. Instead, they can return to Him.

What does Lamentations mean to us today?

Like God's Old Testament people, we sometimes find ourselves sitting in the rubble our sins have caused. Even when our misery is our own fault, our Savior-God still loves us. Our misery makes Him impatient (Judges 10:16). He yearns to bring forgiveness, healing, and hope back into our lives.

With that in mind, consider the way Jeremiah arranged Lamentations:

- Chapters 1 and 2 each have twenty-two verses; these chapters recount the sins of God's people and the trouble those sins brought.
- Chapter 3 has sixty-six (three times twenty-two) verses; it describes God's merciful kindness.
- Chapters 4 and 5 each have twenty-two verses; again, these chapters lament Judah's faithlessness and sin's consequences.

Do you see it?! Even the structure of the Book of Lamentations is set up to show that God's grace is much greater than all our sins. That grace lies at the heart, the very center, of our relationship with our Savior.

How does Lamentations point to Jesus?

Sprinkled throughout the Book of Lamentations are verses that point forward—ever so faintly—to our Savior and especially to Calvary's cross. (See, for example, 1:12–13 and 3:19–20.)

Chapter 3 describes the magnificent mercy of God available to all believers in the cross and empty tomb of His Son. (See especially vv. 22–27.)

What is the key chapter in Lamentations?

As we have seen, Lamentations 3 accents the Lord's overwhelming, never-failing mercy—mercy toward sinners who do not deserve it.

Ezekiel

Into Ezekiel

Fast Facts

- Ezekiel was taken into exile with thousands of other Judeans in 597 BC. A few years later (593 BC), the Lord called him as a prophet. Ezekiel's ministry lasted twenty-two years. He never got to return home.
- The other exiles in Babylon kept hoping for an early release from captivity. They listened to false prophets who told them they would soon be headed back to Jerusalem. Ezekiel told them the truth: they would return to their homeland only after they had returned to the Lord in repentance and faith.
- The first thirty-two chapters of Ezekiel speak mostly Law to God's people. These chapters were written before Jerusalem was sacked and burned by King Nebuchadnezzar in 586 BC.
- Once the temple lay in ruins, the people finally began to repent. Ezekiel then wrote chapters 33–48 to comfort God's penitent people.
- Ezekiel's name means "God strengthens." And He did! God gave Ezekiel strength for his ministry, and He gave His people the gifts of repentance and patience in captivity.
- More than any other Old Testament book, Ezekiel describes the work the Holy Spirit does to create faith and to energize the Church for its mission.
- Ezekiel wrote much of his book in a style called *apocalyptic*. That word means "unveiling" or "revealing." John used a

similar style in the Book of Revelation. Both Ezekiel and John reveal powerful truths about our Lord and about the future He has in store for us and all humanity. Writers who use an apocalyptic style want to convey more than facts. They use strange words and pictures to stir up strong feelings in the hearts of readers. These things are not literal but symbolic.

- Some sixty-five times in his book, Ezekiel tells us the goal God had in mind for everything that was happening to His people: "Then they will know that I am the LORD." This "knowing" is more than "knowing about" God. The devil knows about God! This kind of knowing leads to living in a relationship of love and trust with our Savior. That's Ezekiel's message to all God's people of every place and time.

How is Ezekiel classified?

Ezekiel is counted among the Books of the Prophets in the Old Testament. Like Isaiah and Jeremiah, Ezekiel is a mixture of history and poetry. But Ezekiel is written in a visionary style known as *apocalyptic*. (For more on this style, see p. 216.)

What purpose did Ezekiel's message serve?

From Ezekiel, God's sinful people heard words of Law. "Repent!" Ezekiel thundered. False shepherds were making the promises the people wanted to hear and believe. None of these promises would come true. The only road to freedom led through confession and forgiveness.

From Ezekiel, God's repentant people heard words of Gospel. The covenant-making, covenant-keeping Savior-God would lead His people home, just as He had promised. And He would send the true Prophet, the Good Shepherd, just as He had promised Adam, Eve, Abraham, Sarah, Isaac, Rebekah, Jacob, Rachel, Judah, Tamar, Ruth, Obed, David, and all His faithful people throughout history.

What does Ezekiel's message mean to us today?

Ezekiel's message to God's ancient people applies to us today too. These words are for us as well as for the exiles in Babylon: "Then they will know that I am the LORD."

Our Savior-God has adopted us in our Baptism and will never abandon the covenant He has made with us there (see Ezekiel 36:22–28). He wants us to know the truth about His anger at sin, His glory and power in judgment, and the work His Spirit does to call people into His family and keep us there. But He wants that knowledge to go much deeper!

He wants it to live in our hearts and change our lives! He wants us to rely on Jesus, our Good Shepherd, and to flee from false teachers. And He wants us to look forward to the new heaven and new earth where we will live with Him and one another in joy and freedom forever!

How does Ezekiel point to Jesus?

- Even more than Ezekiel, Jesus is our prophet! He speaks to His sinful people, exiled here on earth, calling us to true repentance and faith.
- In addition, we catch other glimpses of our Savior sprinkled throughout Ezekiel. For example:
  - **Ezekiel 34:11–31** paints a beautiful picture of Jesus, our Good Shepherd.
  - **Ezekiel 36:22–28** prophesies the washing of Holy Baptism and gift of the Holy Spirit as fulfilled in the New Testament.
- The holy, restored temple and priesthood of Ezekiel 40–44 reflect our Savior's work for us. He called Himself the "temple" (Mark 14:58; John 2:19) because the fullness of God's glory, grace, and truth filled Him (John 1:14, 16).

What are the key chapters in Ezekiel?

- **Ezekiel 1–3** Ezekiel's Call and the Lord's Glory
- **Ezekiel 8–11** The Glory of God Abandons Jerusalem
- **Ezekiel 16:1–14** God's Faithless Bride
- **Ezekiel 34:1–10** Woe to the False Shepherds!
- **Ezekiel 34:11–31** The One, True Good Shepherd
- **Ezekiel 36** Prophecy of Baptism
- **Ezekiel 37** The Valley of Dry Bones
- **Ezekiel 40–44** A Restored Holy Temple and Priesthood
- **Ezekiel 47:1–12** The River of Life

The Temple That Was Never Built

Infomercials clutter the airwaves, especially late at night and in the early hours of the morning. The best of these work at setting a tone of excitement, anticipation, and, yes, longing. Ideally, the viewer will want what the program offers.

Through the vision Ezekiel records in chapters 37–48, the Lord wants to set a tone, to motivate, to excite, and to stir up longing in His people—the longing to go home to Judah and to worship at the temple once again.

The temple Ezekiel pictures and the details surrounding it are real, but not literal. The prophet Ezekiel sees a vision. In the vision, the Lord shows Ezekiel—and us—realities deeper than the things we can touch with our physical hands. God wants His people to see the beauty of worship, the importance of keeping Him central in their lives, and the eternal victory He wins for us over all the enemies of our Messiah. A cleansed and restored temple. A cleansed and restored priesthood. A cleansed and restored people. These are God's promises to Ezekiel and to us!

Daniel

Into Daniel

Fast Facts

- Daniel was taken into exile in Babylon after Nebuchadnezzar's first invasion in 605 BC. Daniel was likely a teenager at the time. He never went home again.
- The Book of Daniel is the last of the major prophets. It joins Isaiah, Jeremiah, Lamentations, and Ezekiel on the shelf of longer prophetic writings. The message of the minor prophets is no less important—only shorter.
- Daniel served as a high-ranking official in the Babylonian government. When Persia defeated Babylon in 539 BC, the Persians gave Daniel a position of power in the new regime. Altogether, Daniel's career in government likely spanned about seventy years!
- Daniel served as both a government administrator and as a prophet of the Lord. His life shows us that we can serve God and His people in any lawful work. No matter how difficult, joyful, boring, or pleasant our job, we can "Serve the LORD with gladness!" (Psalm 100:2), seeing it as a calling from God, our vocation.
- Daniel likely completed his book around 530 BC, after Babylon fell to Persia.
- Daniel's name means "God is my judge."

How is Daniel classified?

Daniel is counted among the Books of the Prophets in the Old Testament. It is the last of the Major Prophets in English Bibles. Daniel includes history, poetry, and apocalyptic visions. (See p. 216 for more on apocalyptic literature.)

What purpose did Daniel's message serve?

Unlike most of the other Old Testament prophets, Daniel's words did not demand repentance from his readers. Much of the text in chapters 1–6 reads more like the Bible's historical books, books like Joshua or 1 or 2 Chronicles. Daniel 7–12 is, for the most part, apocalyptic in style—similar to much of Ezekiel. Like many music videos, for example, apocalyptic writings use color and dreamlike images to communicate ideas and emotions.

Apocalyptic writing usually tells about the future too. And that's exactly what Daniel did in chapters 7–12. In fact, much of what Daniel predicted took place after Daniel died and before Jesus was born. As God's people watched history unfold just as He had foretold through Daniel, it built faith in their hearts. They could trust the Lord to keep all His other promises to them too! (See "The Time between the Testaments," p. 268.)

Daniel's life and writings show, above all, that the Lord is in charge of events on earth. Because we know He loves us, His power comforts us. Throughout history, He has been at work for the good of His people—especially in making a way to send the Messiah, our Savior!

What does Daniel's message mean to us today?

The reformer Martin Luther wrote this about Daniel:

> *Daniel's life is nothing but a fine, clear mirror. In it we see the conflict and victory of faith, which, by the grace of God, triumphs over all men and devils; we see too the great fruit and use of faith, which it produces through patience and cross-bearing, both before God and the world. (*Luther's Works, American Edition*, vol. 35, pp. 298–99)*

Luther's words are a great summary! Like Daniel, we live by faith—not yet seeing the full victory God has promised us, but trusting that we will receive it. The Holy Spirit continues to work faith in us to believe that when Christ returns, "The saints of the Most High shall receive the kingdom and possess the kingdom forever, forever and ever" (Daniel 7:18).

This certainty keeps us going in good times and bad, in times of trouble and unrest, and in times of peace and prosperity. Our Savior holds us in His hands—and those hands still bear the scars by which He won salvation for us!

How does Daniel point to Jesus?

- In Daniel 2, Nebuchadnezzar dreamed about a stone that would become a mountain, crush all other earthly kingdoms, and fill the whole world. This stone is Christ and His kingdom.

- Daniel 7:9–14 describes Judgment Day and Jesus as judge.
- As He taught about the days before Judgment Day, Jesus quoted Daniel. Compare Daniel 9:27; 11:31; and 12:11 with Matthew 24:15; it deals with the Antichrist and what Jesus called "the abomination of desolation spoken of by the prophet Daniel."

What are the key chapters in Daniel?

- **Daniel 1** Daniel is deported to Babylon with Shadrach, Meshach, and Abednego
- **Daniel 2** Nebuchadnezzar's dream and its meaning
- **Daniel 3** The fiery furnace
- **Daniel 6** The lions' den
- **Daniel 9** Daniel's prayer for his people's release from exile
- **Daniel 7 and 12** The end of the universe as we know it

Daniel

Daniel, Prophet among the Exiles

Daniel was one of the many young Israelites that the Babylonians took away into exile. This event fulfilled Isaiah's prophecy to King Hezekiah one hundred years earlier: the descendants of Judah's king would become servants to the king of Babylon (Isaiah 39:5–7).

Administrator

Daniel would live the rest of his life in exile in Babylon, serving three different kings as a trusted advisor and administrator. Daniel's dedication and trustworthiness made him a favorite of King Nebuchadnezzar, who appointed Daniel as ruler over the whole province of Babylon (Daniel 2:48).

Prophet

God blessed Daniel with the gift of prophecy. A prophet is one who serves as God's spokesperson, revealing His will and plan to God's people. In Old Testament times, prophets such as Elijah and Isaiah were highly regarded as spiritual leaders chosen by God.

Interpreter of Dreams

God also gave Daniel the ability to interpret dreams, and as the king's advisor, Daniel revealed the meaning of several of King Nebuchadnezzar's dreams. With God's help, Daniel interpreted his first dream for Nebuchadnezzar without even knowing what the dream was! This dream revealed that many kingdoms would follow Babylon, including the kingdoms of Persia, Greece, and Rome. Some seventy years later, the Persians conquered Babylon, fulfilling this prophecy.

Daniel also served the Persian king Darius. Daniel refused to pray to the king, however, and was thrown into the lions' den. God used that event to open the eyes of King Darius to the one true God. Darius testified about Daniel's God, "He is the living God, enduring forever; His kingdom shall never be destroyed, and His dominion shall be to the end" (Daniel 6:26).

The Messiah

Daniel also wrote about the coming of the Messiah, whom he called the "son of man" (Daniel 7:14; 8:17) to whom all authority is given by God, the "Ancient of Days" (7:9; 7:22). The people of Israel would have to wait another five hundred years or so to see the fulfillment of that prophecy in the birth of Jesus. According to Daniel's prophecy, at His second coming, the Messiah would rule in righteousness, and His kingdom would be everlasting and not pass away (7:9–14).

Heaven

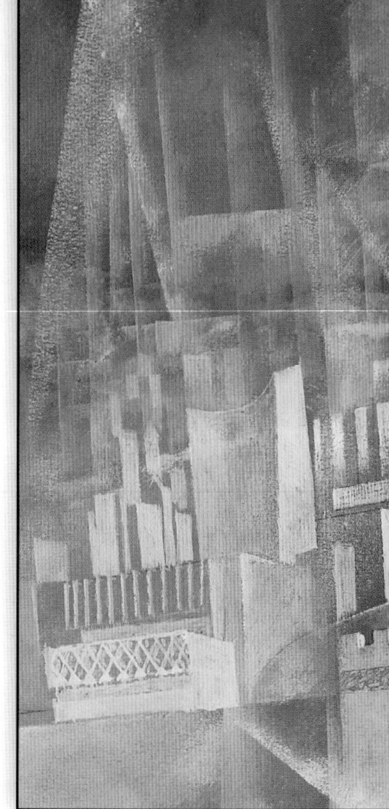

Heaven is (1) the vaulted expanse of the sky with all things in it (Hebrews 1:10); the aerial heavens or sky where clouds and tempests gather (Matthew 16:2); the starry heavens (Hebrews 11:12); (2) the dwelling place of God (Matthew 5:34; 23:22; Acts 7:49) and His holy angels (Matthew 18:10; 24:36) to which Christ ascended (Acts 1:9–11); the eternal home of all believers (Matthew 5:12; 1 Peter 1:4).

When we speak of the heaven to which Jesus ascended and the heaven where we will spend eternity by virtue of our gift of faith, we are of course speaking of the second of these definitions of heaven, the kingdom of God where believers in Christ will spend eternity with Him.

Most of what the Bible tells us about heaven is conveyed to us in symbolic language, and while we can gain some insight about heaven from this, there are many questions that will be answered only by personal experience when we see it for ourselves. For example, the Bible does not tell us anything about the location of heaven. We do know that Jesus promised the repentant thief on the cross that "Today you will be with Me in Paradise" (Luke 23:43), indicating that though our bodies will await the resurrection of the dead on the Last Day, the souls of believers are immediately with Christ in heaven. The Revelation to John speaks of heaven as a "crown of life" (Revelation 2:10); a "marriage supper" (19:9); "a new heaven and a new earth" (21:1); and a place without pain, sorrow, tribulation, hunger, thirst, or death (7:16–17; 21:4). In heaven, the believers will join the angels and other heavenly creatures in singing praises to God (5:9–14). (People, however, do not become angels when they die; angels are separate creations of God.)

Perhaps the most helpful picture of heaven is provided for us at the beginning of God's Word.

In Genesis 3:22–24, we learn that because Adam and Eve had sinned, and because God did not want them to live forever separated from Him by sin, God drove them from the garden of Eden lest they eat the fruit of the tree of life and live forever in sin. Adam and Eve, however, were not left without hope. God revealed to them His plan of salvation. Eve's descendant

© CPH/Arthur Kirchhoff

Jesus would crush Satan and all evil and open again the garden of paradise for all descendants of Adam and Eve who know God by faith. This paradise, the Garden of Eden restored, is heaven.

The descriptions of heaven provided in the Bible make this connection clear with the description of the tree of life as being present both in the Garden of Eden (Genesis 2:8–9) and in heaven (Revelation 2:7; 22:2, 14, 19). In Genesis, it is described as a tree in the garden of Eden from which Adam and Eve were permitted to eat. It was near the tree of the knowledge of good and evil, the tree whose fruit God said they could not eat (Genesis 2:17).

The tree of life is mentioned again in the Revelation to John. Eating from the tree of life is a promise of eternal life in heaven (Revelation 2:7). In heaven, the perfect relationship that was broken by sin is restored. John also tells of his vision of seeing the tree of life near the river of the water of life that flows from the throne of God (22:1–3).

The tree of life is a word picture that gives us a glimpse of what heaven will be like. While we are still on earth, we wait with great anticipation for the joy that will be ours when we spend eternity in the presence of our Lord.

The Babylonian Empire

The Babylonian Empire was the ancient country in the region of Mesopotamia located on the fertile plain between the Tigris and Euphrates rivers. The empire rose to become the most powerful nation in the ancient world in 626 BC, when they defeated Assyria. They remained in power until Persia conquered them in 539 BC.

Babylon

Babylon was the capital of the ancient Babylonian Empire from about 626 to 539 BC. The ruins of Babylon are in present-day Iraq, approximately fifty miles south of Baghdad. Babylon was known for its wealth and splendor and the hundreds of temples and shrines dedicated to the pagan gods that the Babylonian people worshiped. The city named its wide roads after the gods, and a system of canals brought water from the Tigris and Euphrates rivers into the city for irrigation. The famous Hanging Gardens of Babylon were one of the original seven wonders of the ancient world. King Nebuchadnezzar II (who reigned 605–562 BC) supposedly built these gardens as a gift to his wife. Archaeologists have uncovered sections of the eight gates that surrounded the city and parts of the city walls that were remarkably thick.

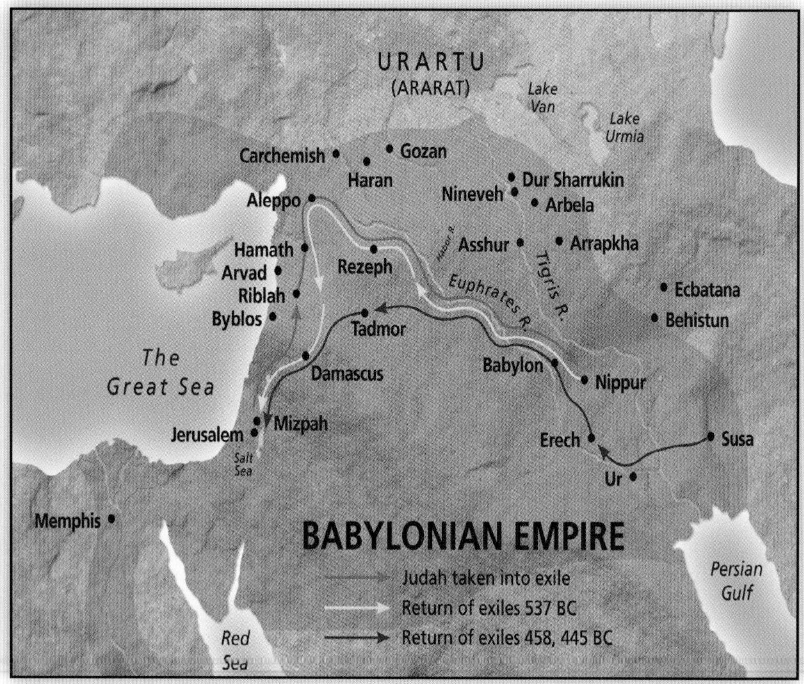

War and Trade

Like the Assyrians, the Babylonians were great warriors and conquerors. Archaeological discoveries have shown that they were also great traders. They traded with Lebanon, Egypt, and Greece. The southern Israelite kingdom of Judah stood in the way of an important trade route to Egypt.

When the Babylonians first attacked Judah in about 605 BC, they took captives back to Babylon as exiles. The healthiest and most gifted of the young Israelite men were taken from Judah to Babylon, where their Hebrew names were changed to those representing the Babylonian gods worshiped by King Nebuchadnezzar. They served their captors in many different positions, and some—like Daniel and his friends Shadrach, Meshach, and Abednego—held powerful and influential government positions in the Babylonian provinces. In 586 BC, Babylon took more Judeans prisoner when Jerusalem was destroyed. The prophet Jeremiah tells of a third deportation (Jeremiah 52:30) in 583 BC.

Defeat and Return

The great Babylonian Empire ended in 539 BC when Persia rose and conquered it, as predicted by Daniel in a prophecy to Nebuchadnezzar. The Persian ruler, Cyrus the Great, gave the Judeans permission to return to Judah to rebuild both the temple and the city walls surrounding Jerusalem. The Old Testament books of Ezra and Nehemiah record the Judeans' return to Judah.

Hosea

Into Hosea

Fast Facts

- Hosea is sometimes called "Israel's deathbed prophet." He served in the Northern Kingdom (Israel) during the reigns of the nation's last seven kings—almost fifty years.
- Hosea's ministry began during a time of great economic prosperity and hope—a golden age, almost like the time of King Solomon. But the people let their material wealth lead them into all kinds of idolatry and disobedience. (See 2 Kings 14–17.)
- As Hosea's career ended, so did Israel as a nation. Toward the end of his life, Hosea saw his warnings of judgment come true. Israel's capital city, Samaria, fell to the fierce Assyrian army (722 BC). Assyria took the people off into an exile from which they never returned.
- Hosea's name means "salvation." This prophet wanted so much for his people to know the saving, forgiving power of the Lord. But very few listened. In the end, most rejected the gift of salvation Hosea—and God!—wanted them to have.

How is Hosea classified?

Hosea is counted among the Books of the Prophets in the Old Testament. It is the first of the *minor* or smaller prophetic books. The last twelve books of the Old Testament were grouped together by Jewish scribes into the "Book of the Twelve," because they fit nicely together on one scroll. Like the major prophetic books, the Minor Prophets usually contain both history and poetry.

What purpose did Hosea's message serve?

Hosea had basically a one-word message: "Repent!" In chapters 1–3, the prophet becomes his own object lesson, illustrating that message, showing the people of Israel their sin and what it meant to the Lord. Here's what I mean.

At God's direction, Hosea married a woman named Gomer. He gave her all his love. Together, they made a home and had a family—two boys and a girl. But then Gomer walked away from it all. She became a prostitute. Hosea tried to win her back, but he failed.

Hosea compares his personal history with that of Israel. God had redeemed His people from slavery in Egypt. He loved them with all His heart. He gave them a home in the Promised Land and prospered them. They had a great life together, but then His people "ran away" from Him, so to speak. They worshiped idols. They even dared to use some of the blessings the Lord had given them as offerings to their idol-gods! No matter what He did to win them back, they refused.

Throughout the rest of his book, Hosea tries to persuade Israel to come to repentance and faith. He assures them that God will forgive them and take them back. But as history shows us, Gomerlike, they wanted no part of it.

What does Hosea's message mean to us today?

Hosea's words describe our relationship with our Savior-God, just as they described Israel's. Jesus has rescued us from slavery to sin and death. He's made us part of His Holy Christian Church—His Bride! He's given us a home with Himself when our life here on earth ends, and He floods our lives here on earth with many blessings.

Still, we are unthankful at times. We sometimes value the gifts more highly than the Giver. We let Satan tempt us into believing our lives would be better if we didn't have to obey the Lord and His commands.

To our sinful hearts, Hosea speaks a one-word message: "Repent!" He demonstrates God's love for us in the story of Gomer, and he describes what will happen when we come back to God in repentance and faith:

> *Return, O Israel, to the LORD your God, for you have stumbled because of your iniquity. Take with you words and return to the LORD; say to Him, "Take away all iniquity. . . ." I will love them freely, for My anger has turned from them. . . . They shall return and dwell beneath My shadow; they shall flourish like the grain; they shall blossom like the vine; their fame shall be like the wine of Lebanon.*
> *(Hosea 14:1, 2, 4, 7)*

How does Hosea point to Jesus?

- Hosea's love for Gomer and what he did to win her love illustrates in a beautiful way Jesus' love for us.
- Matthew (2:15) connects Jesus with the prophetic words of Hosea 11:1.
- Jesus made possible the victory over death Hosea describes in 13:14. (See 1 Corinthians 15:55.)
- Many other verses from Hosea point forward to the saving work the Messiah would do for all God's people. Look for them as you read!

What are the key chapters in Hosea?

- **Hosea 1–3** The Story of Gomer
- **Hosea 11** God's Faithful Love
- **Hosea 13** Israel's Final Judgment
- **Hosea 14** "Return to the LORD!"

Marriage in Bible Times

Were there teenage brides?

Yes. It is important to remember that in times past, most people did not live nearly as long as people do today. Therefore, they started on things like marriage and family at an early age. Most young people married in their midteens. In those days, marrying past the age of 20 was uncommon. If men and women got engaged at a very young age (12 or 13), most often the wedding would be delayed by months or even years, until the future bride and groom were older.

Did young men and women meet at school?

In Bible times, parents arranged marriages for their children. The family, rather than the individuals themselves, decided who would marry whom (compare Genesis 24, especially vv. 50–60). Young men and women were not allowed to be alone together, even with the person they hoped to marry.

Did the bride and groom have any choice about whom they married?

Parents may have taken their children's wishes into account as they made plans for the upcoming marriage, but in the end, the parents made the decision.

How did the young man and woman get engaged?

After both sets of parents made the choice about whom their child would marry, another person made the agreement between the families. The fathers would sign a legal agreement to seal the engagement, also called the betrothal.

What was the engagement like?

During the nine to twelve months of the engagement, the couple still were not allowed to be alone together. The engagement was a legal, binding agreement that could only be broken by signing a divorce document.

Did the bride wear white?

On the wedding day, the bridegroom, dressed in his wedding clothes and escorted by friends, went to the home of the bride. The bride, wearing her best clothes (but most likely not white), came out of her house with her friends to meet the bridegroom. Then everyone went to the bridegroom's home, where the fathers signed the marriage document. Then the couple drank wine from a single cup.

Did they have a big party after the wedding?

The marriage feast followed the wedding. In the months of the engagement, the bridegroom would prepare for this great feast, which could last for several days.

Joel

Into Joel

Fast Facts

- Neither Scripture nor secular history tell us much about Joel. His name means "Yahweh is God," but beyond that, we can say little.
- Joel wrote the book that bears his name sometime after the reign of Jehoshaphat (873–848 BC) or later. A terrible drought and locust plague had just taken place. Since most of the people in that time and place made their living from farms, orchards, vineyards, and raising livestock, the one-two punch of drought and locusts would have caused serious hardship.
- The "day of the LORD" is a central concept in Joel—as it is in Isaiah, Jeremiah, and several other prophets.
- Joel's words confront the comfortable and comfort the penitent in Judah—and they confront us today too!

How is Joel classified?

Joel is counted among the Books of the Prophets in the Old Testament. Joel is mostly poetry.

What purpose did Joel's message serve?

As Joel opens his book, a great disaster has just befallen his people: drought and locust plague. Because such plagues are rare in some parts of the world, not all readers may understand what it could mean for an agricultural society. Literally billions of hungry locusts can make up swarms that eat every edible plant part in sight. Swarms darken the sky, descend, and leave soon after. But the damage is done. Famine follows. Couple that with drought, and both food and water would be scarce. That's the setting in which Joel spoke.

Joel sees in this disaster a shadow of the coming "day of the LORD." In light of that "day," he urges everyone—young and old (1:2, 3), farmers (v. 11), priests (v. 13), and even the town drunks (v. 5)—to repent, to give up their sin and return to the Lord.

What does Joel's message mean to us today?

Joel's words of warning and hope apply to all people of all time—because all are sinners. One day, Jesus will return to "judge the living and the dead," as the Apostles' Creed reminds us. That day will be a day of deliverance and blessing for all who love and trust in Jesus, our Savior.

A centerpiece of Joel's book is his description of the Holy Spirit's coming at Pentecost. The apostle Peter connected Joel's words with that event in his sermon that day:

> *"And it shall come to pass afterward, that I will pour out My Spirit on all flesh; your sons and your daughters shall prophesy, your old men shall dream dreams, and your young men shall see visions. Even on the male and female servants in those days I will pour out My Spirit."* *(Joel 2:28–29)*

How does Joel point to Jesus?

Jesus is the judge of the living and the dead on the "day of the LORD" and the one who will save all believers on that day because of what He did for all people on Good Friday's cross.

What are the key chapters and verses in Joel?

- **Joel 1** The Locust Plague
- **Joel 2:12–14** God invites His sinful children to come home to Him in repentance and faith.
- **Joel 2:28–29** The Holy Spirit's coming is promised.
- **Joel 2:30–32** Christ will come to judge all people.

God Spoke in Dreams

God often used dreams as a way to reveal Himself and His will to people. Sometimes the dream was a warning, as to Abimelech (Genesis 20); to the Wise Men who had come to worship the Christ Child and were instructed not to return to Herod (Matthew 2:12), and to Joseph, who was warned to take the newborn Savior to Egypt for safety (v. 13).

God often revealed His plans to individuals through dreams. Jacob's dream at Bethel reassured him of God's blessing, and in it, God repeated the covenant promise He had given to Abraham and Isaac. Jacob's son Joseph had two dreams in which God revealed that Joseph would eventually rule over his brothers and be in a position of honor one day.

God also gave Joseph the ability to interpret dreams. Joseph's interpretation of the Egyptian pharaoh's dreams made it possible for the country to survive a famine and for Joseph to rise to the position of honor that God had promised. King Solomon also heard from God through a dream (1 Kings 3:5).

Perhaps the most well-known reference to dreams in the Bible is found in the Book of Joel (2:28), which Peter quoted at Pentecost: "I will pour out My Spirit on all flesh; your sons and your daughters shall prophesy, your old men shall dream dreams, and your young men shall see visions." God's promise to each of us is that He will reveal Himself to all believers on Judgment Day.

> *I will show wonders in the heavens and on the earth, blood and fire and columns of smoke. The sun shall be turned to darkness, and the moon to blood, before the great and awesome day of the Lord comes. And it shall come to pass that everyone who calls on the name of the Lord shall be saved. For in Mount Zion and in Jerusalem there shall be those who escape, as the Lord has said, and among the survivors shall be those whom the Lord calls." (Joel 2:30–32)*

Amos

Into Amos

Fast Facts

- Amos was, in a sense, among the world's first foreign missionaries. He grew up about six miles south of Bethlehem in Tekoa. This village was located in Judah, the Southern Kingdom. But God sent him to preach in Israel, the Northern Kingdom.
- During the ministry of Amos, King Uzziah reigned in Judah (792–740 BC) and King Jeroboam II in Israel (793–753 BC). These were especially prosperous times in both kingdoms.
- Amos was not a priest or some other prominent professional. He raised livestock and sycamore figs.
- The book Amos wrote shows that he had a fairly wide knowledge of other nations and world powers at the time. He writes skillfully and organizes his material in a masterful way.
- Most of Amos's ministry took place at Bethel, the site of one of two official places of worship in Israel. (Jeroboam I had set up golden calves in both Dan and Bethel to keep his people from traveling to Jerusalem to worship as God had commanded.)
- Amos is among the first "writing prophets." Along with the work of Hosea and Jonah, Amos's messages were preserved for the nation. (Note: the Major and Minor Prophets of the Old Testament do not appear in chronological order in today's Bibles.)

How is Amos classified?

Amos is counted among the Books of the Prophets in the Old Testament. Amos is mostly poetry.

What purpose did Amos's message serve?

Amos proclaimed God's message to a nation that was outwardly rich but inwardly rotting. Many people lived in luxury, yet they tolerated corruption in the courts, cheated the poor, worshiped idols, and expected the Lord to overlook their self-indulgence.

He did not! Amos spoke out against all these sins—and in no uncertain terms!

We might title the first two chapters of Amos "Zeroing In on the Target" because Amos names a series of nations and condemns their sins. He starts out far away from Israel and gets closer and closer until his words describe Judah and then, finally, Israel itself.

One key verse that summarizes the change God wanted His people to make comes in Amos 5:24: "Let justice roll down like waters, and righteousness like an ever-flowing stream."

What does Amos's message mean to us today?

Of all the Old Testament prophets, Amos's message perhaps fits modern society best. People today often live in luxury, not caring for the poor. We are sometimes selfish and self-indulgent. We care more about our own comfort than about people who go without food or clean water or adequate shelter. We often shrug at God's Word, not caring if we hear it or not (Amos 8:11–12).

The Book of Amos condemns our self-focus in clear words of warning.

But Amos also holds out hope. He describes the Son of David who will give us contrite hearts, pick us up, and restore us to Himself (9:11–15).

How does Amos point to Jesus?

For the most part, the Book of Amos proclaims Law. If we pay attention, his words of warning can make the hairs stand up on the back of our necks in fear.

Amos doesn't end on a note of despair, however. Chapters 9:11–15 describe the restoration and eternal peace Jesus has made possible in His cross. These words are beautiful and filled with comfort.

What are the key chapters and verses in Amos?

Amos uses five visions to picture the coming judgment of the Lord:

- **Amos 7:1–3** The Locust Plague
- **Amos 7:4–6** The Devouring Fire
- **Amos 7:7–11** The Plumb Line of Judgment
- **Amos 8** The Rotten Summer Fruit
- **Amos 9:1–10** The Shattered Altar
- **Amos 9:11–15** The Coming Restorer, the Messiah

Obadiah

Into Obadiah

Fast Facts

- Obadiah wrote the shortest book in the Old Testament—only one chapter, twenty-one verses. It's likely he composed it soon after Jerusalem's destruction by the Babylonians in 586 BC.
- Obadiah's name means "worshiper [or "servant"] of Yahweh," the Lord. He ministered at the same time as the prophet Jeremiah, but we know little else about him.
- Today, the people group known as "Edomites" has completely disappeared, just as Obadiah prophesied.

How is Obadiah classified?

Obadiah is counted among the Books of the Prophets in the Old Testament. It is a short poem.

What purpose did Obadiah's message serve?

In 586 BC, Nebuchadnezzar attacked Jerusalem for the third and final time. He burned the city and left it in ruins. The people of Edom should have helped Judah or at least mourned for them. (The Edomites were descended from Esau, Jacob's brother; see Genesis 27.) Instead, they helped the Babylonian army round up the people who escaped from Jerusalem. Then they looted the city.

This outraged Obadiah. More important, it outraged the Lord! Even though Judah's people deserved the punishment they were receiving, and even though the Lord Himself had allowed the devastation they suffered, God still found Edom's pride and greed disgusting and disgraceful.

The Edomites thought they were safe. They considered their fortresses unconquerable. (See Obadiah 4.) But within five years of Jerusalem's fall, Nebuchadnezzar came back and carried the Edomites into exile.

Obadiah's message no doubt encouraged God's people in exile. The Lord had not forgotten them. He was still on their side, despite their sin. One day, they would return to their homeland, and God would give them the territory of Edom as just payment for the insult and pain Edom had inflicted on them.

What does Obadiah's message mean to us today?

God does not give up on His people. Even when we suffer the consequences of our own sinful attitudes and actions, He's on our side. He takes up our cause, defending us from our enemies—sin and Satan, hell and death. No matter how many our sins or how terrible our disobedience, we never need wonder whether or not He still loves us. In the cross of His Son, we are His children forever.

As the people of Edom learned, external defenses will all eventually fail. True safety comes only from living in a right relationship with the Lord. Everyone will know this on "the day of the LORD," just as Obadiah and the other prophets wrote. On that day, "In Mount Zion [among God's people] there shall be those who escape, and it shall be holy, . . . and the kingdom shall be the LORD's" (Obadiah 1:17, 21).

How does Obadiah point to Jesus?

Many scholars see the closing verse of Obadiah pointing forward to Jesus and His return in glory to live with His people in the new heavens and new earth He is preparing for us even now. Compare Obadiah 1:21 with these words from Revelation 11:15:

> *Then the seventh angel blew his trumpet, and there were loud voices in heaven, saying, "The kingdom of the world has become the kingdom of our Lord and of His Christ, and He shall reign forever and ever."*

What are the key verses in Obadiah?

- **Obadiah 1:10–14** The Lord Rebukes Edom
- **Obadiah 1:15–21** The Day of the Lord

Jonah

Into Jonah

Fast Facts

- Jonah was a prophet during the reign of King Jeroboam II (793–753 BC). His name means "dove," but it may not be a compliment. It may refer to someone who is senseless or silly—a "birdbrain," so to speak. Jonah foolishly refused to see what God clearly wanted to show him.
- The Lord sent Jonah to preach repentance in the city of Nineveh. Nineveh was the capital of Assyria, a wicked, cruel, and powerful enemy of God's people.
- The Book of Jonah is almost all narrative. While the other prophets wrote mostly in poetry, the Book of Jonah focuses on the prophet himself and tells his story.
- Of all the prophets, Jonah is the only one who did not want his message to succeed. He didn't want Nineveh to repent; he wanted them to go on sinning so that God would punish them.

How is Jonah classified?

Jonah is counted among the Books of the Minor Prophets in the Old Testament. Like the major prophetic books, Jonah contains both history and poetry.

What purpose did Jonah's message serve?

Those in both Judah and Israel who read or heard Jonah's story would likely have found it hard to believe. Would the Lord *really* want the wicked Assyrians to repent and come to faith in Him? Would He *really* send a prophet to Nineveh to tell them so?

Yes! God loved the Assyrians. In fact, He loves all the people of every nation on earth!

In a way, Jonah's hatred for Nineveh mirrored the hatred most people in Israel and Judah at the time felt for the people of Nineveh. They saw themselves as God's special—and only!—people. They wanted Assyria destroyed, not saved! But God intended that His stubborn, loveless people hear about the things that had happened to Jonah and then reexamine their attitudes.

What the Lord really wanted was that His people would come to Him in full repentance and true faith. And then, He wanted them to take up the role He had intended for them all along—that they witness of His love to all the nations, telling them about the coming Savior!

The unbelieving sailors, the storm, the fish, the people of Nineveh, the plant, and even the worm obeyed God. Jonah, God's prophet, did not. Would Israel? The Book of Jonah ends with that question unanswered. The Holy Spirit wanted His people to think about it.

What does Jonah's message mean to us today?

Most people today hear the name *Jonah* and think about the three days God's mulish prophet spent sitting in the belly of the great fish. It's an important—and historical—part of the account, but it's not the most important part.

The most important point is the fact that God, in mercy, wants "all people to be saved and to come to the knowledge of the truth" (1 Timothy 2:4). He's sent us with the message of His love in Christ to the people around us. Sometimes, though, we get too busy or too careless or too selfish to share the Good News of His cross and empty tomb with others.

We may be especially reluctant to share that message with those we don't like or those who have hurt us in some way. In patience, God leads us—as He intended to lead Jonah—to repentance. He keeps on forgiving and giving us a new start.

But like Jonah's book, our story is unfinished. Will we take our Savior's love and forgiveness seriously? Will we go with the Gospel into all the world, as Jesus has commanded (Matthew 28:18–20; Mark 16:15–16)?

How does Jonah point to Jesus?

Of all the Old Testament prophets, Jesus compared Himself to only one—Jonah! Listen to the parallels in Jesus' words:

> *Just as Jonah was three days and three nights in the belly of the great fish, so will the Son of Man be three days and three nights in the heart of the earth. The men of Nineveh will rise up at the judgment with this generation and condemn it, for they repented at the preaching of Jonah, and behold, something greater than Jonah is here. (Matthew 12:39–41)*

Jonah's experience inside the fish pictures for us Jesus' own death, burial, and resurrection.

What are the key verses in Jonah?

- **Jonah 2:1–9** is a powerful prayer of repentance and faith

The Lord of All

Ancient religions commonly taught that each of the gods had authority over specific elements of creation. People also thought the gods exercised sovereignty over specific territories or regions. This false theology led the ancients to believe in the existence of many gods, who acted as rivals to one another. Warfare between nations was seen as competition between their respective gods. The victorious nation was believed to have the god who was currently most powerful. Biblical monotheism stands in stark contrast to such false thinking.

Jonah is aboard a ship bound for Tarshish. A great storm comes upon the ship and the sailors deduce that Jonah has brought about divine retribution. Based on standard theology of the time, they might expect that Jonah has offended the god of the sea. They are probably shocked to hear Jonah say that he worships "the LORD, the God of heaven, who made the sea and the dry land" (Jonah 1:9). Jonah is saying that all aspects of creation (heaven, the sea, and the land) are subject to his God, the only God. This point may have astonished the sailors, but we receive great comfort and confidence from the universality of the Lord.

As It Was in the Beginning . . .

Every Sunday, most Christians throughout the world confess the universality of the Lord in the Gloria Patri, "As it was in the beginning, is now, and will be forever." These words deny the notion of rival gods who vie for power. There is only one God whose rule exists at all times. God was there at creation; He was there at the flood; He was there at the exodus from Egypt; He was there with Jonah on the sea; He is with us at all times.

Jonah struggled to appreciate this truth. When he was called by the Lord to preach to the Ninevites, Jonah attempted to flee from Him. Such a move was foolhardy for one who believed in the one God, who is sovereign over all times and places and present in all times and places. Yet it was precisely the universality of the Lord that prompted Jonah to flee. Intellectually, Jonah knew that God had created the Ninevites, but he did not want to embrace the results of the Lord's universality: God was every bit as sovereign over the Ninevites as He was over Jonah, and His love extended to them as well.

Universal Divine Love in Jonah

The Lord left no doubt for Jonah that His love is universal. For one thing, the sailors who were amazed by Jonah's monotheism were moved to faith in the one true God so that they offered a sacrifice to Him upon their deliverance from the raging sea. For another thing, God was not content to allow the Ninevites to perish in their great sin, so He sent His word to them through Jonah. This word led the Ninevites to repent, and God had compassion upon them.

The universality of divine love is seen still more in the animals of Nineveh. It is not merely the men and women of Nineveh who fasted and put on sackcloth as a sign of penitence, but even the animals owned by the Ninevites were brought into these penitential actions. Their inclusion was a confession that all creation, not only humanity, is responsible to the one true God, the Lord, who has authority over all and love for all creation.

Yet the full extent of God's love is most clearly seen in Jonah himself. Jonah was a prophet of the Lord, yet he ran from God. He had been witness to God's love pouring forth from the Jerusalem temple, yet he did not wish to extend that same love to Nineveh. Obstinate and rebellious, Jonah was the least deserving of God's love. Nevertheless, this generous and forgiving love came to him. It is universal.

Scripture is replete with stories of those who rebelled against the Lord's love, but whom God nonetheless sought so He could shower His love upon them. Peter denied Christ three times, then Christ restored him as His apostle to feed His sheep. Paul persecuted the Church violently. Yet God chose to reveal Himself to Paul, not only converting Him to the faith, but calling Him to be the apostle to the Gentiles. No one is beyond the universal love of the Lord given us in Christ.

The Peace of God's Wide Love

Just as Jonah had difficulty in accepting that the Lord's love was intended for the Ninevites, we also sinfully limit the scope of Christ's love in our own lives. Specific individuals may have hurt us so much by their sin that we would rather carry resentment and hatred toward them than communicate Christ's forgiving love to them. There may be a particular class of persons we would rather not see walk into our own church, tempted as we are to see them as remaining beyond the extent of Christ's love. There is grave danger in such thinking. It is biblically inaccurate, to be sure. Moreover, if we begin to place limitations on Christ's love, then we must begin to question whether we also lie beyond its limits.

Thanks be to God that His love is not limited. It is universal! There is no sin so great as to move you beyond the scope of His universal love. The grace earned for us by Christ on the cross is unlimited. All who know the grace of Christ know the universal love of God. That is a source of unending peace! All the sins you have committed in the past, however they assault your conscience, have been forgiven because of Christ. All the sins with which you currently struggle are forgiven because of Christ too. Every sin against which you will ever battle throughout the rest of your life is also covered over by God's grace in Christ. The universality of the Lord's love gives you never-ending peace.

Micah

Into Micah

Fast Facts

- Micah's name means "Who is like Yahweh [the Lord]?" His book describes many ways in which the Lord is truly awesome—unique!
- As is true in the case of many other prophets in Judah and Israel, we know little about Micah. Micah 1:1 tells us he came from the small town of Moresheth in the southern part of Judah.
- Perhaps as Micah grew up, he saw firsthand some of the problems faced by the poor and downtrodden of his area. In any case, he uses the strongest terms as he denounces injustice and his people's lack of care for the needy.
- Micah ministered in Judah (the Southern Kingdom) during the reigns of Kings Jotham, Ahaz, and Hezekiah, sometime between 750 BC and 686 BC. His ministry overlapped those of the prophets Isaiah and Hosea.
- In 722 BC, Samaria, capital city of the Northern Kingdom (Israel) fell, just as Micah had predicted.
- More than seven hundred years before Jesus was born, Micah foretold His coming, adding intriguing and accurate detail! The Messiah would be a royal deliverer, born in the town of Bethlehem, to save God's people from all their enemies. (Compare Micah 5:2 with Matthew 2:5–6.)

How is Micah classified?

Micah is counted among the Books of the Minor Prophets in the Old Testament. Micah is poetry in a style similar to his contemporary, Isaiah.

What did Micah's message mean to the original readers?

Micah's message alternates between gloom and hope. For the most part, God's people live as they please—self-focused, self-indulgent, self-satisfied. Selfish! Micah attacks these ungodly attitudes. The Lord will judge sinners and will punish sin as only He can!

But all is not lost. Just as the Lord is unique in justice, He is also unique in mercy and compassion. He will forgive and rescue His repentant people. Yes, many will perish, but some will be saved. And through this remnant—this small group of faithful believers—the Savior whom God had promised so long ago would come. (See Micah 2:12; 4:7; 5:3, 7, 8; 7:18.)

Throughout his book, Micah speaks of deliverance and peace in words that can't help but remind us of the work Jesus did for us through the cross and empty tomb.

What does Micah's message mean to us today?

"What does God want from me, anyhow?!" People down through history have thought and asked that question. Micha answers it:

> *He has told you, O man, what is good; and what does the LORD require of you but to do justice, and to love kindness, and to walk humbly with your God? (Micah 6:8)*

The problem is we *can't* act in perfect justice, kindness, and humility. Satan tempts us away from that. Our own sinful selves want to refocus attention on ourselves. The society around us tells us that justice, humility, and kindness are simply foolish. And so we fail to meet God's just demands.

In mercy, God sent Jesus to do for us what we could not do. He was perfectly just, kind, and humble in our place. Now, God counts that perfection as our own! In faith and in the obedience that springs from that faith, we find true peace, safety, and joy. And we receive the courage to act with justice, to be kind—even to our enemies—and to live humble, thankful lives.

How does Micah point to Jesus?

Micah refers to Jesus and to His kingdom again and again throughout the book. See, for example, 2:12–13; 4:1–8; and 5:4–5a.

What are the key verses in Micah?

- **Micah 4:1–5** The Mountain of the Lord
- **Micah 5:2** Israel's Royal Deliverer, Born in Bethlehem
- **Micah 6:1–8** The Lord brings a case against His people
- **Micah 7:18–20** The Lord's Faithful Compassion and Love

Who Is a God Like You?

Who is a God like You, pardoning iniquity and passing over transgression? (Micah 7:18).

"All roads lead to heaven." That's what many people say. In fact, however, that is a lie. Jesus says, "I am the way, and the truth, and the life. No one comes to the Father except through Me" (John 14:6).

Consider the world's religions. Confucianism is only concerned with the well-ordered structure of society. Buddhism promises an escape from this life into nothingness. Hinduism knows but one reality, Brahma, and asserts that the material world is only an illusion.

Judaism has the Hebrew Scriptures promising a Savior, but refuses to accept the One who came. Arabia's Islam spread throughout the world like fire. It holds to the worship of one god, Allah, who is supposedly pleased with holy wars and repetitious prayers. Millions of people remain in the grip of philosophies such as atheistic communism, which denies the existence of any god.

All these religions and worldviews look to man and what he can do for himself. They lead where all self-trust leads—to emptiness in this life and condemnation in the life to come.

None of them offers the free forgiveness that Micah speaks of. The true God—the God of the Bible—does not forgive and save partway. He has a just anger against humanity because we are all sinful. Nor can we compromise with God, for we have nothing to offer Him. Yet God gives complete forgiveness anyway. What wonderful pictures He uses to show this forgiveness! He "tread[s] our iniquities underfoot" and hurls them "into the depths of the sea" (Micah 7:19)!

From the time of Adam and Eve until today, God forgives because He promised and sent His Son Jesus to pay for the sins of humankind. In Christ, we have forgiveness and life. So in answer to Micah's rhetorical question, we join believers everywhere and exclaim, "There is no God like You!"

Nahum

Into Nahum

Fast Facts

- Nahum's name means "comfort" or "the comfort of Yahweh [the LORD]."
- This short book communicates one message: the dreaded Assyrian Empire is about to come to an end. Those who fear Assyria need do so no longer. This was very comforting news indeed for God's people in Judah, who had seen the people of Israel carted off into captivity by their cruel conquerors.
- Nahum prophesied about a century after Jonah had delivered his message to Assyria. Like Jonah before him, Nahum warns Assyria and its capital city, Nineveh, to repent. But unlike Jonah, Nahum's message moves no one to repentance.
- Forty or so years after Nahum's warning, judgment fell. Nineveh was totally wiped off the earth (612 BC).
- The prophets Zephaniah, Habakkuk, and a young Jeremiah ministered at the same time as Nahum.

How is Nahum classified?

Nahum is counted among the Books of the Prophets in the Old Testament. Nahum is poetry.

What purpose did Nahum's message serve?

The people of Assyria, notorious for brutality, thought their kingdom would last forever. Their capital, Nineveh, was surrounded by a wall 100 feet high! Its wall was so thick that four chariots could ride on top, side by side. Outside the wall, a moat 140 feet wide and 60 feet deep gave additional protection against invasion.

But no human defenses could stand against the power of God's Word. Nahum predicted a flood that would bring destruction (1:8), followed by an invasion of enemy armies (2:1). That's exactly what happened. The Tigris River flooded, carrying away part of the city wall. The armies of the Medes and Babylonia came pouring in through the breach. They demolished the city and burned it thoroughly.

Nahum's words brought comfort to the people of Judah, who lived in fear of their fierce enemy to the north. Those who feared this cruel nation needed to do so no longer. The Lord would protect and deliver His people.

What does Nahum's message mean to us today?

While we don't fear the Assyrians, we face plenty of other problems and challenges. Some of these are, in the whole scheme of things, minor and temporary. Others, though, loom large in our minds, hearts, and lives.

We find hope and comfort in our Lord, no matter how fiercely Satan shouts his threats and insults to our hearts. Our Savior-God can wipe every fear away in a moment—and one day, He will! His control over earthly powers and events comforts us, because we've seen His love for us on Calvary's cross. If God's own Son died for us, we can know for sure He's there for us, helping in every other need!

How does Nahum point to Jesus?

Nahum 1:1–8 describes our Lord's attributes—both justice and mercy.

What are the key verses in Nahum?

- **Nahum 1:1–8** Justice and mercy in action
- **Nahum 1:15** "Beautiful Feet"

The City of Nineveh

There are not many places mentioned in the Bible that are still in the news today, but the city of Nineveh is one. Nineveh is located on the eastern bank of the Tigris River in present-day Iraq, close to the city of Mosul, the second-largest city in modern Iraq.

Nineveh was the capital city of the Assyrian Empire and flourished from about 800 to 612 BC. Its location on an important trade highway between the Mediterranean Sea and the Persian Gulf made it known as the greatest of all ancient cities.

Nineveh in Scripture

The Bible first mentions Nineveh in the Book of Genesis, naming Nimrod as its founder (Genesis 10:9–12). Nahum foretold Nineveh's ruin (Nahum 1:2–14), as did the prophet Zephaniah (Zephaniah 2:13–15). Zephaniah also foretold the fall of the entire Assyrian Empire. The Book of Jonah describes Nineveh as "an exceedingly great city, three days' journey in breadth" (Jonah 3:3). The evil and wicked ways of the people of Nineveh included witchcraft and worshiping many false gods. Their enemies knew them as cruel people.

In 722 BC, during its time of power, the Assyrian Empire, one of the great enemies of Israel, conquered the Northern Israelite Kingdom and their capital city at Samaria and took the Israelites away into captivity. One hundred years or so later, as God's prophets had foretold, the Assyrian Empire

Nineveh today (reconstructed Ramash Gate at center).

became weak and fell to the Medes, who destroyed the city of Nineveh in 612 BC.

Nineveh Today

Biblical archaeologists have unearthed remains of the royal palace of Sargon, one of the Assyrian kings, and have discovered many wonderful sculptures and items that tell the story of the great city of Nineveh. In modern Nineveh, there is a shrine dedicated to the prophet Jonah (*Nebi Yunus* in Arabic). The bones of a whale hang inside, reminding visitors of the story of Jonah's three days inside the large fish.

Habakkuk

Into Habakkuk

Fast Facts

- Habakkuk's name likely means "embrace"; Habakkuk's message in a nutshell is "hold on to the Lord, even when you don't understand what He is up to."
- Habakkuk probably served as prophet during the last days of King Josiah's reign and the first days of King Jehoiakim's reign in Judah—sometime around 605 BC. The Assyrians had already hauled off Israel, the Northern Kingdom, into captivity.
- Jeremiah and Zephaniah prophesied at the same time as Habakkuk, all of them in Judah.
- Habakkuk is unique among the prophets in that he does not deliver a direct message or "oracle" to his people; instead, he records a dialogue between himself and the Lord. This dialogue wasn't just a private entry in a personal diary, though. Chapter 3 begins with a note that shows Habukkuk's prayer became part of Judah's public worship.

How is Habakkuk classified?

Habakkuk is counted among the Books of the Minor Prophets in the Old Testament. It is poetry.

What purpose did Habakkuk's message serve?

Habakkuk speaks for the faithful in Judah in his day who looked around at all the troubling events in their world and asked, "Why?" Habakkuk begins by asking two questions and receiving two answers from the Lord:

Question 1: Look at how Your people have fallen into sin! Why don't You punish them?

Answer 1: I am about to do that. The Babylonians will invade, and the guilty will receive what they deserve.

Question 2: What?! How can You possibly use the Babylonians—an even more wicked people—to accomplish Your will?

Answer 2: I will use Babylon and then, in turn, punish that nation for their sins. Meanwhile, trust and wait for Me to reward My faithful people.

The Lord's answers satisfied the prophet. In response, he wrote a powerful hymn of praise.

What does Habakkuk's message mean to us today?

Do you ever wish you could ask God some hard questions, questions that really bother you? The Book of Habakkuk and the questions the prophet asked show that we can ask our Lord anything. He's not afraid of our questions, and He's not angry at us when we ask honestly.

Fair warning, though: we may not always understand the answers! And we may not always like what we hear.

Even so, like Habakkuk and the faithful people of Judah, we can trust our Savior-God even when we don't understand the things that are happening around us or to us. One day, our Lord will silence all our questions as we stand in His temple, surrounded by His love and wisdom (Habakkuk 2:20). For now, we live by faith, relying on the grace that sent Jesus all the way to the cross for us.

How does Habakkuk point to Jesus?

The New Testament quotes Habakkuk 2:4 three times (in Romans 1:17; Galatians 3:11; and Hebrews 10:38): "The righteous shall live by his faith."

Each time, the New Testament writer connects this "righteousness" with what our Lord Jesus did for us on Calvary's cross.

Reading from a New Testament perspective, we also see Jesus in the hymn of praise Habakkuk records in chapter 3. Consider, for example, verse 13: "You went out for the salvation of Your people, for the salvation of Your anointed."

What are the key chapters and verses in Habakkuk?

- **Habakkuk 1** Two Difficult Questions
- **Habakkuk 2:4** "The Just Shall Live by Faith"
- **Habakkuk 3** Habakkuk's Hymn of Praise

Complaining to God?

It is a healthy Christian discipline to pray to God on a daily basis. The Lord's Prayer stands as a ready prayer when words escape us. The acronym ACTS can remind us of various aspects of prayer: Adoration (praising God for who He is and what He has done for us), Confession (enumerating those sins which plague our conscience, and then rejoicing in Christ's forgiveness), Thanksgiving (numbering God's many blessings upon us) and Supplication (entrusting our specific troubles to God for His gracious intervention). Both the Lord's Prayer and ACTS are helpful tools for devotional life.

Then there are those times when prayer takes on a different language. We are accustomed to offering our supplications to God, trusting in His mercy to answer. But frustration can set in when God's answer either seems delayed or does not agree with what we fervently desire and expect. At such times, we may find ourselves complaining to God. Words pour forth from our hearts, even if we dare not speak them with our lips: What are You doing, God? Are You ignoring me? Do You not care? Some who have used such words with God are left with a sense of guilt and shame: What kind of Christian am I, to speak to God like that? In truth, such soul-wrenching complaints do not exhibit a faltering faith, but rather a faith that trusts in the Lord and looks to Him for the needed answer.

God accepts, even invites, our complaints

Complaining as the Voice of Faith

The prophet Habakkuk forms a prime example of one whose faith emerged in his complaints to the Lord. His frustration is evident in such words as: "O LORD, how long shall I cry for help, and You will not hear? . . . Why do You idly look at wrong?" (Habakkuk 1:2–3). Habakkuk struggled to wrap his mind around what he saw happening. He knew God. He knew what he could expect from God's faithfulness. Yet the two were not melding in Habakkuk's mind. So he cried out to the Lord, longing for insight into divine reasoning and purposes.

Habakkuk is not alone in bringing his complaints to God. The psalms served as both the hymnbook and prayer book of the faithful. Some of them are perhaps best described as "Complaint Psalms." The most famous of these is Psalm 22, quoted by Christ on the cross: "My God, my God, why have You forsaken me?" This opening verse is but the beginning of the prophetic description of Christ's suffering in Psalm 22. Yet it also reveals a very human sense of abandonment by God.

Psalm 6 speaks words that are reminiscent of Habakkuk's complaint to the Lord as the psalmist complains: "My soul also is greatly troubled. But You, O LORD—how long?" (Psalm 6:3). Likewise, Psalm 69 voices both a complaint and a fervent desire for the Lord's intervention, as in verse 17: "Hide not Your face from Your servant."

While there can be an instinctive reaction of guilt by those who complain to God, their faith is actually seen in their complaints. The complaints illustrate the intimate relationship the Lord has with His people. He is not a capricious God, nor is He unable to accept the honest, heartfelt complaints that arise from His people as they struggle with life's trials. In Christ, God has experienced our every heartache, and He invites us honestly to tell our troubles and anxieties to Him.

Yes, biblical occurrences of the Lord's people offering their complaints to Him illustrate their intimate relationship with Him. These instances also become occasions for bold confession of faith. In each of the "Complaint Psalms," the psalmist is driven back to his confidence in the Lord. Even in the midst of the incredible suffering described in Psalm 22, fervent faith in God's

—when they are offered in faith.

faithfulness is found in the words: "For He has not despised or abhorred the affliction of the afflicted, and He has not hidden His face from him, but has heard, when he cried to Him" (v. 24).

So also, faith pours forth in Psalm 6: "The LORD has heard my plea; the LORD accepts my prayer" (v. 9). In Psalm 69, we hear: "The LORD hears the needy and does not despise His own people who are prisoners. Let heaven and earth praise Him, the seas and everything that moves in them" (vv. 33–34). In each instance where one is faced with the seemingly unexplainable juxtaposition of life's hardships and God's promises, the answer lies in the Lord Himself. The faithful know that His identity as their gracious God will always overcome the difficulties life sets before them.

Finding Answers

We humans are notoriously impatient. When a question stands before us, when troubles confront us, we want a solution right now. Some are so bold as to tell God what He should be doing in the situation. That is not the attitude of faith, but rather a desire to use God as a puppet. Instead of insisting that God do as we say, it is entirely different when we simply ask, why are You doing what You're doing?

God accepts, even invites, our complaints—when they are offered in faith that He knows what He is doing, even if we cannot understand His ways. Questions of why? and how long? demonstrate our trust that God really does listen and He really does answer our supplications. Even more, such questions show our confidence that His ways are better than our ways. For this very reason, we want to know why He has chosen this route.

Approaching the Lord with our complaints does not undermine our faith. Instead, it leads us to fervent trust in the Lord, despite the prevailing circumstances. This is what drove Habakkuk to burst out, "Though the fig tree should not blossom, nor fruit be on the vines, the produce of the olive fail and the fields yield no food, the flock be cut off from the fold and there be no herd in the stalls, yet I will rejoice in the LORD; I will take joy in the God of my salvation. GOD, the Lord, is my strength" (Habakkuk 3:17–19).

Zephaniah

Into Zephaniah

Fast Facts

- Zephaniah's name means "Yahweh [the Lord] hides" or "Yahweh has hidden." He hides His people, keeping us safe, until judgment has passed by.
- Zephaniah prophesied during the early days of Josiah's reign (640–609 BC), perhaps even before King Josiah had begun his reforms. See 2 Kings 22 and 2 Chronicles 34–35 for background.
- Zephaniah was a descendant of King Hezekiah and probably had access to the royal court. He is familiar with then-current political issues.
- The prophets Jeremiah and Nahum were contemporaries of Zephaniah in Judah.

How is Zephaniah classified?

Zephaniah is counted among the Books of the Minor Prophets in the Old Testament. It is poetry.

What purpose did Zephaniah's message serve?

Seven different times, Zephaniah warns of the coming "day of the Lord." That "day" is not a twenty-four-hour event, but instead a period of time in which God will act to judge His enemies and bring justice and peace to His faithful people.

Zephaniah warns the impenitent in Judah that judgment will fall. He urges them to return to the Lord, asking for mercy and trusting in His grace.

For example, consider the warning in Zephaniah 1:12: God promises to "search Jerusalem with lamps." Just as we might use a flashlight to find the spiders and cockroaches that have scurried to hide in the dark corners of the kitchen, so the Lord will search for every single one of His enemies. No one will escape in that day.

But the faithful need not fear. The Lord is "a mighty one who will save" (3:17). He will rescue them and they will rejoice (3:9–20).

What does Zephaniah's message mean to us today?

How easily we shrug off the holiness of God! How eager we are to forget how much He hates sin! How often we discount His promises to punish it! We want to think something like this: "God likes to forgive sin, and I like to sin! So I'll just 'sin it up' and let Him have lots of chances to forgive."

Zephaniah urges us not to do that! We dare not take our Lord's grace for granted!

But when we come to our Savior with hearts broken by our guilt and in true sorrow for the harm our sins have caused, Zephaniah assures us that we can count on our Savior's promise to forgive us and to rescue us.

How does Zephaniah point to Jesus?

Zephaniah clearly points to the fact that the Messiah will fulfill all the promises made in this book.

Jesus Himself alludes to Zephaniah 1:15–16 as He teaches about the final judgment in Matthew 24. (See especially Matthew 24:29.)

What are the key chapters and verses in Zephaniah?

- **Zephaniah 3:1–8** "Woe" (a curse) will befall all who ignore and oppose the Lord.
- **Zephaniah 3:9–20** Blessings await the faithful righteous in the "day of the Lord".

Haggai

Into Haggai

Fast Facts

- Together with Zechariah and Malachi, Haggai is one of the "postexilic" prophets. All three proclaimed God's message after the people of Judah began to return to their homeland from exile. Some seventy years had elapsed, just as Jeremiah the prophet had prophesied (Jeremiah 25:11).
- At the time of Haggai, the Medo-Persian Empire had conquered the Babylonians and begun the process of freeing exiles from the many nations captured by Babylon's army.
- Haggai's name means "festival" or "festival of Yahweh [the Lord]." Haggai wanted God's people to be able to celebrate the dedication of a rebuilt temple—a place where they could gather for worship.
- In 538 BC, the first wave of exiles started out for Jerusalem, and by 536 BC, they had laid the foundation for a rebuilt temple. Shortly after, though, they gave up, discouraged by the opposition posed by their neighbors. (See Ezra 4.)
- God sent Haggai and Zechariah to encourage the people to finish what they had started (520 BC). Four years later, the temple was finished and dedicated (Ezra 6:15–18).

How is Haggai classified?

Haggai is counted among the Books of the Minor Prophets in the Old Testament. Unlike most prophetic books, it is written entirely as history with no poems.

What purpose did Haggai's message serve?

By ignoring the fact that the temple lay in ruins and by focusing instead on rebuilding their own homes and business, the people showed where their real priorities lay. The Lord and worshiping Him didn't matter as much as it should have.

Haggai came, describing the consequences of their disobedience and unbelief (Haggai 1:6–11; 2:16–17). But he also proclaimed the promises of God, the blessings that would follow faithful obedience (2:4–7).

Best of all, the very temple they were building would be the temple that would welcome the Messiah!

> *I will fill this house with glory, says the LORD of hosts. The silver is Mine, and the gold is Mine, declares the LORD of hosts. The latter glory of this house shall be greater than the former, says the LORD of hosts. And in this place I will give peace, declares the LORD of hosts.* (Haggai 2:7–9)

And that's just what happened. Jesus worshiped at the same location of the temple that Zerubbabel and his followers built. By that time, King Herod the Great had begun to renovate and expand it. But the place was the same, which Haggai helped dedicate.

What does Haggai's message mean to us today?

First, Haggai's words remind us of our own misplaced priorities. We often focus on our own comfort or pleasure instead of on serving Jesus by caring for those around us. "But seek first the kingdom of God and His righteousness," Jesus commands His followers; then He goes on to promise, "and all these things [the other necessities of life] will be added to you" (Matthew 6:33). Despite this promise, we often disobey.

Second, Haggai's ministry reminds us that our Savior-God does not leave us alone in our sin. He comes to us with His Word of warning, inviting us to confess our sins and trust our Savior.

Third, Haggai's message encourages us with the truth that our Lord is eager to befriend us. The Lord was eager to see the temple rebuilt because it represented God's presence with His people. God had "tented" with Israel in the wilderness in the tabernacle. Later on, He made Solomon's temple His throne on earth. Still later, Jesus came to our planet to live with us and to die for us. Now, the Holy Spirit dwells in each believer:

> *We are the temple of the living God; as God said, "I will make My dwelling among them and walk among them, and I will be their God, and they shall be My people."* (2 Corinthians 6:16)

We represent the presence of our Savior wherever we go and whatever we do! What an awesome privilege!

How does Haggai point to Jesus?

Haggai 2:7–9 promised the coming of the Messiah to the temple that Governor Zerubbabel and his people were building.

Zerubbabel himself is a picture, or "type," of Christ. He descended from the great King David, just as the Messiah would. Zerubbabel led God's people back to true obedience of His will, just as the Messiah would. In 2:23, Haggai calls Zerubbabel God's "signet ring"—a token or sign that the Lord intended to keep His ancient promise to send a Savior for His people.

What is the key chapter in Haggai?

- **Haggai 2** The Messiah is promised.

The Temple Courts

The first temple was built by King Solomon in 960 BC and was destroyed by the Babylonians in 587 BC. When Israel returned from exile, the temple was rebuilt—though on a smaller scale—by Zerubbabel in 536–516 BC. Another temple was shown to the prophet Ezekiel in a vision (Ezekiel 40–44), but it was never built. Zerubbabel's temple was replaced by King Herod, beginning in 20 BC. The temple building was completed in just eighteen months, but the courts surrounding the temple were still under construction in Jesus' day. The courts were completed in AD 64. The entire temple complex was destroyed by Rome just six years later.

The term "in the temple" in the Bible often refers to the temple courts. Only priests were allowed in the temple building itself. All sacrifices and the worship of the people occurred in the temple courts.

The entire temple area was considered holy, but it became increasingly more holy as one moved from east to west through the temple complex. The temple courts were always crowded, and temple worship and sacrifices happened every morning and evening.

The first court of Herod's temple was a large open space enclosed on three sides by porticos. It was referred to as "the Court of the Gentiles" because those who were not Jews were permitted to walk within it but were forbidden to go any farther. They were excluded from entering into any of the inner courts. Signs in Greek and Latin gave warning that the penalty for trespassing was death.

Next came the Court of Women, where women gathered to pray.

Surrounding the temple building on three sides were two courts. The outer one was the Court of Israel; it was for Israelite men who came to watch the daily services of sacrifices and prayers.

Inside this court was the Court of the Priests. This court incorporated the altar of burnt offerings for sacrifices and a large reservoir ("sea of cast metal" [1 Kings 7:23]) to hold water for the cleansing of the priests.

This courtyard offered access to the temple building, the Holy Place, the largest room in the temple building itself. This room contained lampstands and the altar of incense, where a priest burned incense twice a day during the times of prayer. The holiest spot in the temple was called the Most Holy Place or the Holy of Holies. The ark of the covenant was kept in this room.

All around the Temple Mount were beautiful marble porticos, porches with roofs supported by pillars and stone arches. A wall surrounded the whole area. The entire temple complex was destroyed in AD 70. Only a small portion of it, called "the Wailing Wall" or "Western Wall," remains today. It is a favorite spot of prayer for Jews who visit Jerusalem.

Zechariah

Into Zechariah

Fast Facts

- Like Haggai and Malachi, Zechariah is one of the postexilic prophets. Their ministries took place in and near Jerusalem as God's people returned from exile in Babylon and reestablished their families and lifestyle in the land God had promised to Abraham and his descendants.
- Zechariah was both a priest and a prophet. He was born in Babylon and returned to the Promised Land with Governor Zerubbabel and Joshua, the high priest, in 538 BC.
- Except for Isaiah, no other Old Testament book has as many detailed descriptions of what the Savior's life and work would be like. Zechariah's prophecies are astonishingly precise, and Jesus fulfills them!
- Zechariah tells us a lot about the Savior's first coming, His earthly ministry, and His death. But he also writes about Jesus' second coming—the Last Judgment. Several of his prophecies parallel those in Revelation and other New Testament books.
- The Book of Zechariah includes eight visions—all of them somewhat confusing at first. See the chart "Zechariah's Eight Visions (And What They Meant)" on page 263 for help in interpreting them.
- Zechariah uses an apocalyptic style throughout much of his book. See the comments about this kind of literature in the introduction to Daniel.

How is Zechariah classified?

Zechariah is counted among the Books of the Minor Prophets in the Old Testament. It is a series of apocalyptic visions with some poetry.

What purpose did Zechariah's message serve?

Zechariah urged his people to finish the work of rebuilding the temple. They had made a good start in laying the foundation. But now they needed to make it a priority to build on that foundation.

But Zechariah didn't stop there. He focused on the spiritual renewal needed. Only as God's people lived lives of repentance and faith would they be ready to worship in the temple once it was finally finished.

Zechariah insisted that the exiles treat one another fairly and with compassion. He focused especially on justice for widows, orphans, and foreigners.

Zechariah's message, though, was not only one of Law. His book contains some of the sweetest Gospel in all the Old Testament. Zechariah's name means "Yahweh [the LORD] remembers." The Lord had not forgotten or withdrawn the covenant He had made with Abraham, Isaac, and Jacob. Even though His people had forgotten and rebelled, He brought them back to their homeland. He would continue to work through events to bring the Messiah—the world's Savior—just as He had promised.

What's more, a glorious future awaited the people of God! This promise was fulfilled in part by Jesus in His earthly ministry. It will be fully realized when Christ returns in glory to take us to Himself forever.

What does Zechariah's message mean to us today?

Yahweh remembers! He kept His promises to His ancient people, bringing them back to their homeland and sending the world's Savior through the family of Abraham. In the same way, He keeps His promises to us. This includes the promise of full and final victory over sin and Satan, hell and death. We will one day live in the peaceful kingdom Zechariah describes.

Meanwhile, we come continually to our Savior for forgiveness and renewal. And we ask Him to work in us true concern for those hurt by the injustice around us. We pray and work to right these wrongs.

How does Zechariah point to Jesus?

Here are a few examples:

- The Messiah would come as a lowly Servant, "the Branch" (3:8).
- The Messiah would be both King and Priest for us (6:13).
- The Messiah would ride a donkey and its colt into Jerusalem (9:9; see also Matthew 21:5, John 12:15).

- The Messiah would be rejected and sold for thirty pieces of silver—the price of a slave (11:12–13).
- The Messiah would be pierced, and all Israel would witness it (12:10).
- The Messiah (the "Shepherd") would be struck, and the "sheep" (the disciples) would scatter (13:7).

What are the key chapters and verses in Zechariah?

All of the prophetic texts in Zechariah that describe the Messiah's first and second comings certainly fall into this category, as do the eight prophetic visions.

Perhaps most important of all, Zechariah 3:9 tells us that the Lord "will remove the iniquity of this land in a single day." Surely that "day" was Good Friday!

King Jesus Returns	
Jesus will return visibly—14:4	Acts 1:11
The day will be marked by a great earthquake—14:4–5	Revelation 6:12–14
The sun and moon will dim—14:6	Matthew 24:29
The Lord will be our eternal light—14:7	Revelation 22:5
The river of life will flow through the heavenly Jerusalem—14:8	Revelation 22:1–2

The visions of Zechariah spoke comfort and peace to the postexilic people of God. The first vision seem to introduce the other seven as it summarizes their meaning. These were visions in the night (1:8). Like the vision Daniel saw in the night (Daniel 7), the night visions of Zechariah are highly visual and use an apocalyptic style to communicate the Lord's message.

Zechariah's Eight Visions (and What They Meant)

Zechariah Texts	Vision	Meaning	Related
1:7–17	Introduction; four horses and the myrtle trees	See 1:12–17. God will show mercy to His people and will comfort them.	Isaiah 40:1–11
1:18–21	The four horns and the four craftsmen	The enemies of the Lord who scattered God's people will be destroyed.	Psalm 73
2:1–13	Measuring Jerusalem	God will preserve and protect His people. He will be a "wall of fire" (2:5) around Jerusalem and will be her glory.	Isaiah 26:1–9
3:1–10	Joshua forgiven	God will cleanse His people of their sins, silencing Satan's accusations.	2 Corinthians 5:21 1 John 1:7–2 :2
4:1–14	A golden lampstand and two olive trees	As God's people completed their work on the temple they would be His lights in the world.	Matthew 5:14–16
5:1–4	The flying scroll	God will keep His Word of Law to judge the wicked.	Isaiah 11:1–5
5:5–11	The woman	The Lord will remove evil and those who bring it from among His covenant people.	Revelation 18:1–8
6:1–8	Four chariots	God's angels will swiftly deliver His judgment on the nations who destroyed His people.	Revelation 16:1–21
6:9–15	Climax; Joshua's coronation	The Messiah to come will serve as King and High Priest, forever bringing peace.	Revelation 5:1–14

Malachi

Into Malachi

Fast Facts

- Together with Haggai and Zechariah, Malachi is one of the postexilic prophets. All served God's people after their return from exile in Babylon.
- Malachi was the last prophet in Old Testament times. Between Malachi's work and that of John the Baptist lay four hundred years of silence when no prophetic voice was heard in Israel.
- Malachi may have worked with Nehemiah in leading God's people to repentance. The two condemned similar sins—worshiping idols and intermarriage with idol worshipers.
- Malachi wrote about Jesus' first coming as the world's Savior and His second coming as the world's judge.
- Malachi's name means "My messenger" or "Messenger of Yahweh [the LORD]."

How is Malachi classified?

Malachi is counted among the Books of the Prophets in the Old Testament. It is the last of the Minor Prophets and the last book of the Old Testament. It narrates a series of warnings from God to His people.

What purpose did Malachi's message serve?

In 516 BC, God's people finished building the temple and began worshiping there. Many thought that the blessings Haggai and Zechariah had promised would come right away. When struggles, dangers, and troubles continued instead, the people became discouraged. Had God lied to them? Some wondered about that. Malachi wrote to reassure them of the Lord's enduring love. He would be faithful to keep His promises.

But Malachi also wrote to confront some of the people with their faithlessness. Zechariah had called for inward repentance and a renewed commitment to the Lord. What God wanted most was that His people live in love for Him and for one another. Only then would their worship in the new temple mean anything! The almighty, all-glorious God of the universe didn't need human beings to build a hut in the desert for Him!

Malachi called out several specific sins:

- The priests were corrupt and greedy. They took bribes and looked for ways to enrich themselves by cheating the people.
- The people were going through the motions in worship, not really caring about God, and shrugging off His Law and His love. They brought the fewest offerings they could get away with and thought God should be satisfied. They were robbing Him (Malachi 3:8)!
- Many husbands and wives were quarreling and getting divorced. They were hurting themselves and their children. The Lord wanted it stopped.
- Some of the people were cheating one another whenever they could get away with it. They let the poor go hungry. They neglected widows and orphans.

Malachi called everyone to repent of these sins—not just to feel sorry, but to change their ways of thinking and living.

What does Malachi's message mean to us today?

If we didn't already know that Malachi wrote his book almost twenty-five hundred years ago, we might think he wrote yesterday! Look back at the list of sins in the preceding section. Do any look familiar?

Malachi's message rings as true today as when he first proclaimed it:

- Make your worship heartfelt, not an empty ritual!
- Stop robbing God! Bring to Him the offerings He rightly deserves as an act of worship from the heart!
- Care for those in need—and show your compassion by really helping them!
- Live in love—for those in your families, your church, your community, your world!

All of this is Law, isn't it? It shows us how far short we come, even when we try our hardest to obey God. If we pay attention, it frightens us. It frightened some of Malachi's first readers too. Malachi's words brought them to repentance and true faith. They talked to one another about it (Malachi 3:16–17) and remembered God's love to His people from the beginning of time.

Malachi reminded them—and us!—that our Father is faithful:

> *Behold, the day is coming, burning like an oven, when all the arrogant and all evildoers will be stubble. The day that is coming shall set them ablaze, says the LORD of hosts, so that it will leave them neither root nor branch. But for you who fear My name, the sun of righteousness shall rise with healing in its wings.*
>
> *(Malachi 4:1–2)*

How does Malachi point to Jesus?

Malachi foretold the coming of John the Baptist, who would be the forerunner of the Messiah (Malachi 4:5–6).

Malachi also foretold the coming of the Messiah Himself as the "messenger of the covenant"; you can read the description of Jesus as judge in Malachi 3:1–4.

What are the key chapters and verses in Malachi?

- **Malachi 3:1–4** The Messenger Who Would Come Suddenly in Judgment
- **Malachi 3:8–12** God's people are accused of robbing Him; blessings are promised when they "bring the full tithe into the storehouse" (v. 10).
- **Malachi 4** Terror and Joy on "the Day of the Lord"

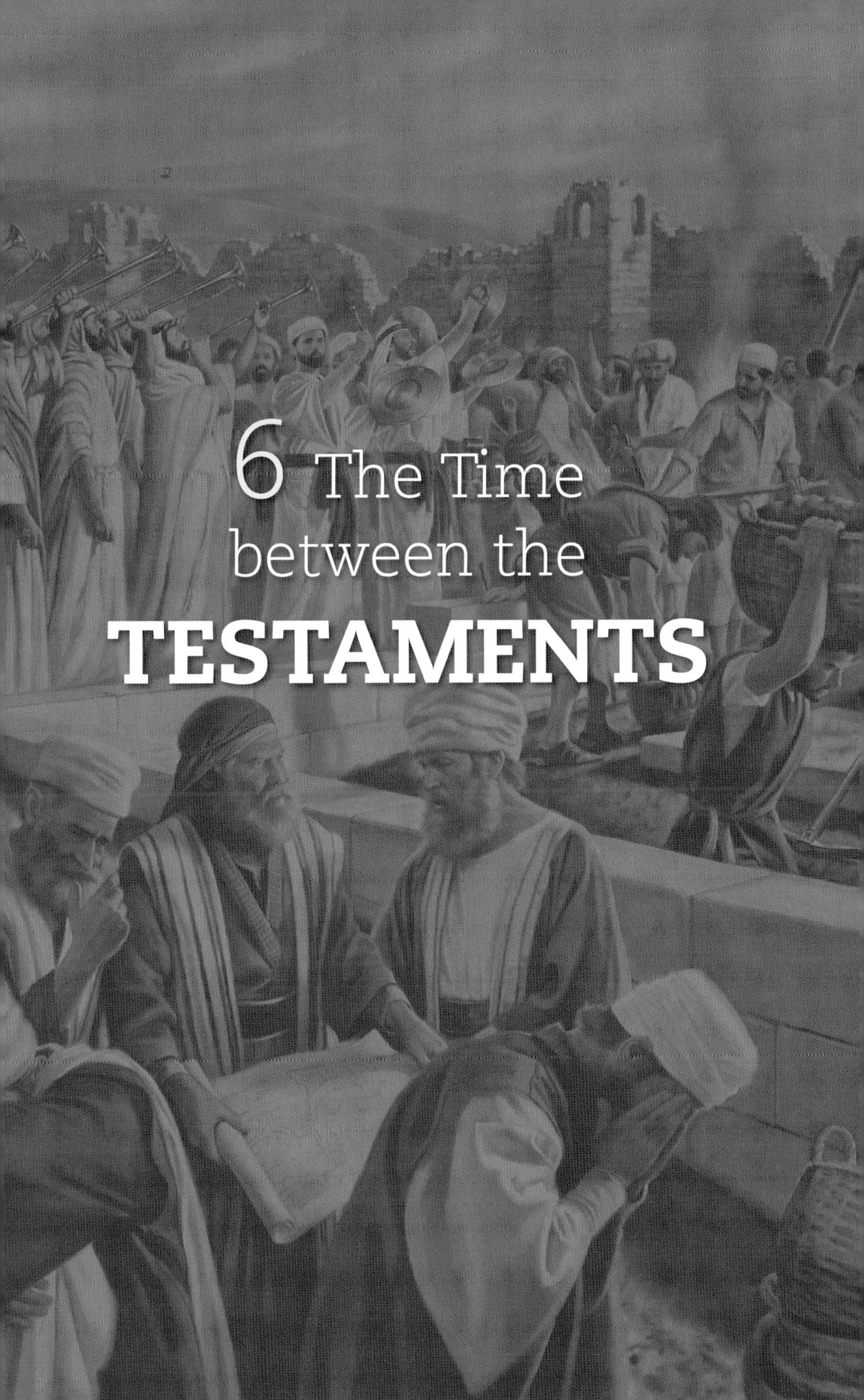

6 The Time between the TESTAMENTS

The Time between the Testaments

The four hundred years between the Old and New Testaments have often been called "the silent years." In one sense, those years were silent. Following the prophet Malachi, there were no new revelations from God. The prophets had ceased to speak (1 Maccabees 4:46; 9:27; 14:41).

Yet the Lord did continue to speak through the inspired Old Testament Scriptures. And God used these years to continue setting the stage for the coming of our Savior, Jesus.

The prophet Daniel had described four great kingdoms to come. These would be replaced by an eternal, universal kingdom. That kingdom would include people from every nation, tribe, tongue, and people—the kingdom of God, in which Jesus rules and reigns forever. (See Daniel 2.) More about that kingdom in a moment.

Let's consider the four earthly, temporary kingdoms Daniel described:

- *Babylon*. After their arrival on the scene, Babylon's armies defeated the Assyrians and several other major world powers in a very short time. Babylon didn't last long, but it was glorious while it lasted. Law, astronomy, architecture, and other disciplines flourished in Babylon. The Hanging Gardens of Babylon were once numbered among the seven wonders of the ancient world. Babylon took the Judeans into captivity and kept them there for seventy years. The Babylonian Empire was overthrown by the Medo-Persians in 538 BC.

- *Persia*. This world power, led by Cyrus, allowed the Jews to return to their homeland. Cyrus and the rulers who followed him sent many of the temple treasures back home with the Judeans and encouraged them to resume temple worship. (Isaiah had foretold all this more than a century before it happened, even naming Cyrus as the ruler who would do it! See Isaiah 45:1–13.)

- *Greece*. Around 330 BC, Alexander the Great marched through the region and conquered the Persians. Alexander spread Greek culture and the Greek language throughout the Middle East. This language would become the language in which the New Testament was originally written. During this time, the Judeans managed to establish nearly a century of national independence. Under the leadership of the Maccabees, they also got rid of the pagan worship practices that the prophets had condemned for centuries. By the time Jesus was born, no Jew was bowing down to a statue of gold or silver, stone or wood.

- *Rome*. Jewish independence came to an end with the rise of the Roman Empire. In 63 BC, the Roman general Pompey invaded and subdued the Jewish nation. Greek culture continued, but Roman laws prevailed. The Roman armies brought a time of relative peace and stability. This allowed safe travel throughout the empire. Along with the widespread use of the Greek language, this peace—the *Pax Romana*—became an important factor in the spread of the Gospel.

During the time between the Testaments—the intertestamental period—a number of Jewish sects arose. The New Testament mentions several of these. Understanding some of their beliefs and practices helps us better understand the New Testament.

- *Sadducees*. These were the ruling leaders; many were scribes and/or priests. Sadducees were religious skeptics who denied the existence of angels and demons. They didn't believe in a final judgment or even in the resurrection. They accepted only the five Books of Moses (Genesis–Deuteronomy) as genuine Scriptures. The Sadducees made up the majority of the Sanhedrin, the Jewish ruling council at the time of Christ. This Sanhedrin opposed Jesus' teachings and eventually condemned Him to death. However, Joseph of Arimathea, the believer who courageously helped bury Jesus, was a member of the Sanhedrin (Matthew 27:57–68; Mark 15:42–46).

- *Pharisees*. The Pharisees were lay leaders, mostly from the middle class. They accepted the entire Old Testament and added many traditional rules and man-made laws to it. This was the largest sect at the time of our Lord's earthly ministry. While Jesus often pointed out their hypocrisy, some early Christians came out of this group—the apostle Paul among them (Acts 23:6). Nicodemus, too, was a Pharisee (John 3:1).

- *Zealots*. These persons were named for political rather than religious beliefs. They hated the oppression the Roman armies had imposed on their nation. One of Jesus' disciples, Simon the Zealot, came from this group.

- *Essenes*. Some members of this group withdrew into the desert so that they could follow God's laws more fully—at least, that's what they hoped. They refused to marry. Members of the group owned everything in common. They may have been influenced by Greek philosophy as well as the Old Testament. The Dead Sea Scrolls, the oldest known copies of the Old Testament, may have come down to us from the Essenes. Some scholars think John the Baptist grew up among this sect.

Were these years really silent? In some ways, yes. But in other ways, God was making final preparations to send the Savior into the world. As these years came to an end, the stage was set for the birth of Jesus. God preserved the Holy Scriptures during this time, despite all the turmoil and the march of armies back and forth across the Middle East. And during the time between the Testaments, the Old Testament was translated into another language—Greek—for the first time. This translation, the Septuagint, is the text that the New Testament writers most often used when they quoted from the Old Testament. For more about other books written at this time, see "Apocrypha" in the Bible Dictionary.

With the coming of Jesus, life on our planet changed forever. Jesus came to announce the coming of Daniel's fifth kingdom—the eternal kingdom that Daniel had foretold (Daniel 2:44). But more than just announcing it, Jesus came to bring that kingdom—the kingdom of God—into its fullness.

All true believers enjoy that kingdom right now; we live in the kingdom of grace—the Holy Christian Church on earth. One day, we will join our Savior in the kingdom of glory—the "new heaven and new earth" the Scriptures describe as the eternal home of God's faithful people (Revelation 21). Jesus came to make our citizenship in both these kingdoms possible.

As the New Testament begins, the silence is about to break. God is about to speak through His last Prophet, Priest, and King—the Word, our Lord Jesus. The stage is set, and a new chapter in the story of God's covenant love is about to open!

Roman Rule

Living under foreign rule was nothing new to the Jewish people. Israel had been held captive in Egypt and in Babylon. In their own land, they were subject to rulers from Persia, Greece, and Egypt. Under some of these rulers, the Jewish people prospered. For example, the Hebrew Old Testament was translated into Greek, the language of commerce and culture of the times.

Syrian Rule

About two hundred years before the birth of Jesus, Syria took control of the Jewish state. Under the leadership of one of the Syrian kings, Antiochus IV Epiphanes, the Jewish people suffered greatly. He hated their religion and severely punished anyone who tried to worship the true God. He defiled the temple and introduced idol worship.

Brief Independence

A leading Jewish family, the Maccabees, led a revolt. The Jewish people won their freedom from Syria against great odds. Unfortunately, after a short time of national glory and freedom, the country fell into internal arguments among the tribes. They divided into factions that were bitterly angry toward one another; when one faction asked Rome for assistance, the Romans were happy to enter the conflict. Then, in 63 BC, General Pompey captured Jerusalem for Rome—not for the feuding Jewish faction. The country remained under Roman rule for many years.

Herod Rules for Rome

Public Domain

King Herod the Great

Herod the Great, king of Judea, Galilee, Iturea, and Trachonitis, was appointed by the Roman emperor to govern the region, and he did so from 39 BC until his death in 1 BC. He was a cruel, ruthless, evil king who murdered his wife, three sons, his mother-in-law, and many others when he suspected they were plotting against him. The Jewish people also resented him deeply because he was not a Jew, even though he was related to them as a descendant of Esau.

This wicked king also tried to kill baby Jesus. When the Wise Men followed the star to Jerusalem, looking for the newborn King, they asked Herod, "Where is He who has been born king of the Jews?" (Matthew 2:2). The Roman senate had named Herod as the "king of the Jews," but now he was worried that a new king had been born to replace him. To make sure there would be no competition for his throne, and to ensure that no other child would become king, he gave orders to kill all of the baby boys two years old and younger who had been born in and around Bethlehem. Those baby boys were the very first martyrs of the New Testament era. The Church commemorates them on the fourth day of Christmas, December 28, as the Holy Innocents.

Herod's evil plot failed, as an angel warned Joseph in a dream to escape to Egypt with the baby Jesus and Mary.

While he ruled Judea, Herod the Great built cities, theaters, monuments, and roads. He also built many altars to pagan gods. Among his building projects was the restoration and expansion of the temple in Jerusalem. Herod wanted to be remembered as the builder of the largest, greatest temple of the Jews. Herod's temple was larger and taller than the temple Zerubbabel had built in the sixth century BC (Ezra 3:8–13; 6:13–15); he wanted it to be seen from a greater distance than the temple it replaced.

The project began in 19 BC, but the work was not finished until long after his death. The Romans destroyed Herod's temple in AD 70. Only a portion of the retaining wall that surrounded the Temple Mount remains today. It is known as "the Western Wall," or "Wailing Wall," and it is a popular site for pilgrims who visit Jerusalem.Herod died not long after Jesus was born. His son Herod Archelaus ruled Judah for a relatively short time before being removed by Rome (see "The House of Herod," p. 275). After that, Judea was ruled directly through Roman governors. Pontius Pilate was the governor at the time of Jesus' crucifixion.

Pontius Pilate

© CPH/Keith Neeley

Little is known about Pontius Pilate's ten-year governorship of Judea. Tacitus, an ancient Roman historian, writes that Christ was crucified under Pilate's rule. The Roman governor was the one who had to order executions; the Jewish leaders had no power to do so. Josephus, a Jewish historian of the times, writes that Pilate later sent Roman soldiers into the streets of the Holy City of Jerusalem, carrying figures of the Roman emperor. This act angered the Jews, who considered this idol worship. When he tried to make improvements to Jerusalem's water supply with money earmarked for the temple, people revolted. Pilate had these rebels killed. The Roman emperor was not entirely pleased with Pilate's actions, and he was ordered back to Rome to face investigation. He is believed to have been exiled to France, where he died.

The King of the Jews

Even though the Jews were allowed to practice their religion under Roman rule, many wanted to be free. Some extremely patriotic men, called zealots, stirred up opposition to Rome. Perhaps Barabbas, the prisoner whose release the people demanded instead of Jesus', was one of these zealots. Many Jews were longing for a messiah who would deliver them from Roman rule. As shown by Jesus' triumphal entry into Jerusalem, many looked to Him as the one who would bring back the glory days of David and Solomon. But the Jewish rulers did not see Jesus as one to fulfill their hopes for their people. They feared that Jesus and His followers would make matters worse between the Jews and their Roman oppressors. Though they did not understand God's plan, He allowed their fear to drive Jesus to the cross and grave. There, Jesus paid the penalty for the sins of all people, including those who feared Him. Jesus' resurrection showed that He was, in fact, the divinely appointed Savior, for the Jews and for all people.

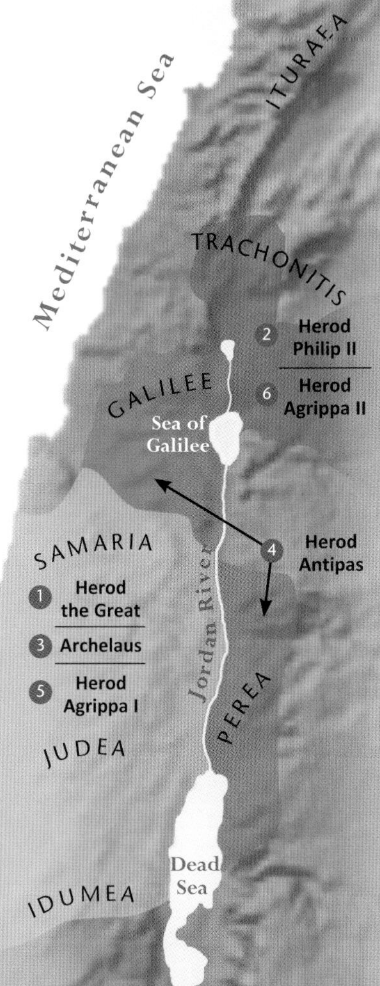

The House of Herod

When Herod the Great died shortly after Jesus was born (see "Herod Rules for Rome," p. 271), his kingdom was divided among his sons.

Herod Philip II ruled as tetrarch (a term designating a ruler of one quarter of a kingdom) of Iturea and Trachonitis, north of Galilee, from 1 BC to AD 34. He is mentioned only once in the Bible, in Luke 3:1.

Herod Archelaus ruled as tetrarch and governor of Judea, Idumea, and Samaria from 1 BC to AD 6. Mary, Joseph, and Jesus avoided him by settling in Galilee when they returned from Egypt (Matthew 2:19–23). Rome eventually stripped him of his throne because there were many complaints about him.

Herod Antipas ruled as tetrarch of Galilee and Perea from 1 BC to AD 39. It was Antipas who imprisoned and killed John the Baptist (Matthew 14:1–12) and interviewed Jesus before His crucifixion (Luke 23:7–12).

Herod Agrippa I ruled as king of Judea from AD 41 to 44. Agrippa was the grandson of Herod the Great through another of Herod's sons, Aristobulus (who is not mentioned in the

The Herod Family Tree

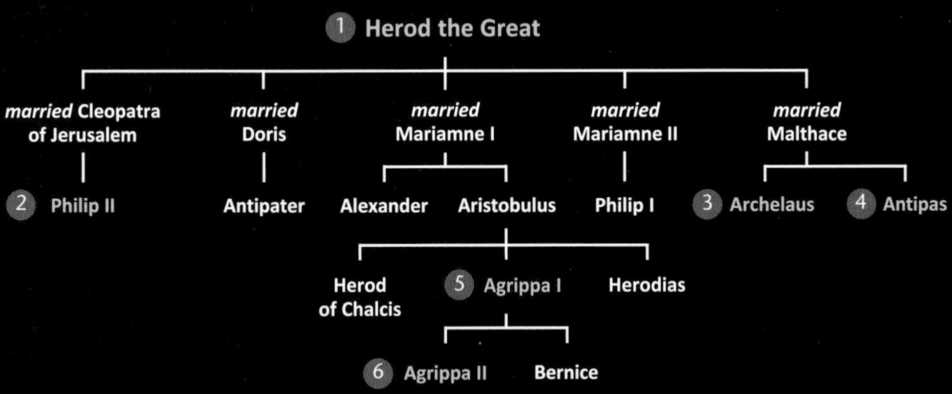

Bible). This Herod killed James and imprisoned Peter (Acts 12). He ruled a region equal to that of his grandfather.

Herod Agrippa II was only seventeen when his father, Agrippa I, died. Most of his father's kingdom was ruled directly from Rome through procurators (a kind of governor). Beginning in about AD 50, Agrippa II was given control of territory around the Sea of Galilee. Although he had the title "King of Judea," he never actually ruled Judea. The apostle Paul appeared before him (Acts 25:13–26:32) before being transferred as a prisoner to Rome. Agrippa II was the last of the Herods to rule.

Herod the Great, King of Judea

Herod the Great, the governor of Galilee, was ruler over Judea at the time of Jesus' birth. He ruled from 39 B.C. until his death in 1 B.C. He was a cruel, ruthless, evil king who murdered his wife, his three sons, his mother-in-law, and many others when he suspected they were plotting against him. The Jewish people also resented him deeply because he was not a Jew.

This wicked king also tried to kill baby Jesus. When the Wise Men followed the star to Jerusalem looking for the newborn king, they asked Herod, "Where is he who has been born king of the Jews?" (Matthew 2:2). Because the Roman Senate had named Herod as the "king of the Jews," he was worried that a new king had been born to replace him. To make sure there would be no competition for his throne, and to ensure that no other child would become king, he gave orders to kill all of the baby boys two years old and younger who had been born in and around Bethlehem. The church commemorates these baby boys on the fourth day of Christmas, December 28 as the Holy Innocents—the very first martyrs of the New Testament era. An angel warned Joseph to escape to Egypt with the baby Jesus and Mary.

While he ruled Judea, Herod the Great built cities, theaters, monuments, and roads. He also built many altars to pagan gods. Among his building projects was the restoration and expansion of the temple in Jerusalem. The project began in 19 B.C., but the work was not finished until long after his death. Herod was to be remembered as the builder of the largest, greatest temple of the Jews. Herod's temple was larger and taller than the temple built by Zerubbabel in the sixth century B.C. (Ezra 6:13–15) so that it could be seen from a greater distance than the temple it replaced.

The Romans destroyed Herod's temple in A.D. 70. Only a portion of the retaining wall that surrounded the Temple Mount remains today. It is known as the Western Wall or Wailing Wall and is a popular site for pilgrims who visit Jerusalem.

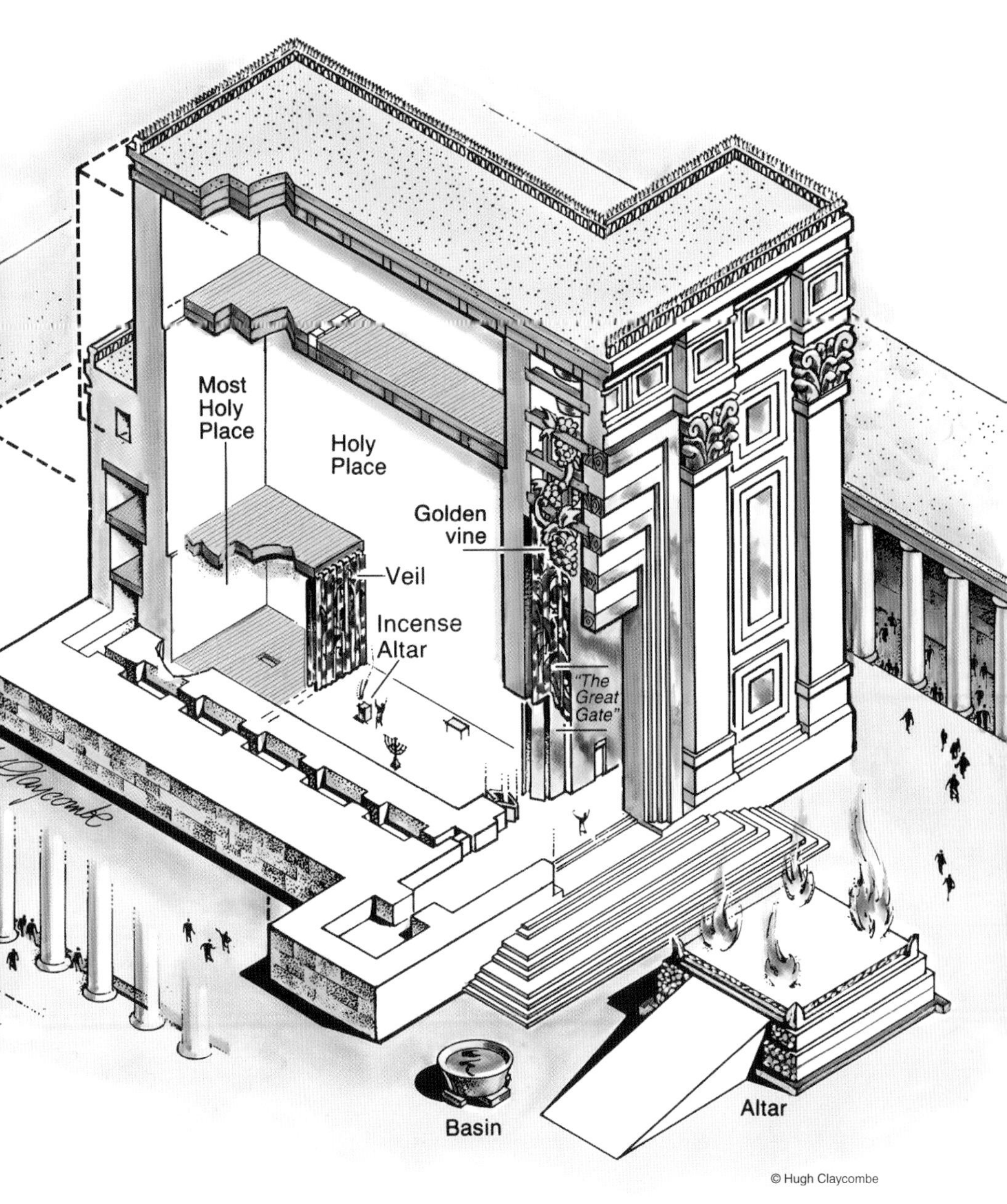
Most Holy Place
Holy Place
Golden vine
Veil
Incense Altar
"The Great Gate"
Basin
Altar
Claycombe
© Hugh Claycombe

At the time of his death in B.C., shortly after Jesus was born, Herod's kingdom was divided among his sons. One of them, Herod Antipas, imprisoned and then murdered John the Bptist and, later, interviewed Jesus before His crucifixion. Another son, Herod Archelaus, ruled Judea briefly from 4 B.C. to A.D. 6; he was the Herod whom Joseph and Mary sought to avoid by settling in Nazareth after their escape to Egypt. A grandson and great-grandson of Herod also figured into biblical history. The first, Herod Agrippa I, murdered James and imprisoned Peter in Acts 12. The other, Herod Agrippa II, interviewed Paul after his "arrest" and prior to Paul's long journey to Rome (Acts 25:23–26:32).

7 The NEW TESTAMENT

"He taught in their synagogues. . . . But He said to them, 'I must preach the good news of the kingdom of God to other towns as well; for I was sent for this purpose.'" (Luke 4:15, 43)

More than fifteen hundred years ago, St. Augustine described the relationship between the Old and New Testaments. Modern writers have worded Augustine's comment this way: "*The New is in the Old concealed, the Old is in the New revealed*."

The two biblical testaments complement and explain one another. The New Testament picks up where the Old Testament leaves off. The four-hundred-year gap between Malachi and Matthew changes God's message not at all. All sixty-six books of the Bible agree: *Repent! The kingdom of God is near!*

Each of the Gospel writers—Matthew, Mark, Luke, and John—makes the connection between the Old and New Testaments clear. Take Mark, for example. For Mark, the Gospel of Jesus Christ, the Son of God, began in the Old Testament. Mark 1:1–3 shows us the tight connection the holy writer saw:

> *The beginning of the gospel of Jesus Christ, the Son of God. As it is written in Isaiah the prophet, "Behold, I send My messenger before your face, who will prepare your way, the voice of one crying in the wilderness: 'Prepare the way of the Lord, make His paths straight. . . .'"*

Seven centuries before Mark, Isaiah had written about the Messiah and His forerunner, John the Baptist. Then John came, proclaiming Isaiah's message. Jesus of Nazareth preached the message when John could no longer do so (Mark 1:14–15).

God's Word to the human race has never changed, and it never will! We are sinners and we face the consequences of our sin, but the Lord is merciful and has provided a Savior from sin and its consequences. As He works in us, we are to turn from sin and live lives of repentance and faith.

Each day we need to hear that message! When the reformer Martin Luther urged Christians to remember their Baptism each day, that's what he meant. Each day, we recall again the fact that in Christ, God has changed our direction and our destination:

- We used to run *from* our Father as fast as our feet would carry us. Now we run *to* Him with our sin, confident of His compassion and pardon.
- We once lived a hopeless, hellish existence—alone, and without a purpose, headed for eternal death. Now we live in the sunshine of God's smile, looking forward with joy to life with our Savior in heaven when our life on this earth ends.

In Jesus and His cross, we have new life and a new reason to live. That's the message of the Holy Scriptures from beginning to end. That's the new life God has revealed to us!

© Israelimages.com

Coins from Bible Times

The Prutah (PROO-tah) or Mite

These tiny copper coins were the smallest unit of currency. Archaeologists have found thousands of these little coins, showing that they were extremely common at the time of Jesus. They were used until the fourth century. The mite is referred to in Luke 21:2.

The Silver Dinar (DEE-nahr) or Denarius

The silver dinar was another common coin used at the time of Jesus. On one side of the coin was the name of Caesar Tiberius (a Roman ruler), and on the other side was a picture of a female figure. The Good Samaritan gave the innkeeper two denarii to take care of the wounded man he cared for (Luke 10:35). The dinar is also referred to in Luke 20:24.

The Tyrian Shekel (TIR-ee-uhn SHEH-kuhl)

The Tyrian shekel contained about 14.2 grams of silver.
192 prutahs or mites=1 dinar
4 dinars=1 Tyrian shekel
26 silver dinars=1 gold dinar

What Money Could Buy in Bible Times

Wages

Vineyard worker's daily wage	1 dinar
Scribe's weekly wage	12 dinars
Roman soldier's yearly wage	50 dinars

Clothing

Cloak of a rich man	100–200 dinars
Woman's yearly clothing allowance	50 dinars

Food

Pomegranate	1 prutah
A cluster of grapes	1 prutah
Large meal	1 dinar
1 seah (about 2 gallons) of flour	1 dinar
12 loaves of bread	1 dinar
Jar of olive oil	1 dinar

Animals

Donkey foal	2–4 dinars
Lamb	4 dinars
Ram	8 dinars
Calf	20 dinars
Ox	100–200 dinars

Housing

Rental of house for a month	4 dinars

The Land of Jesus

© Hanan Isachar/0Israelimages.com

The Synagogue in Nazareth

THE GREAT SEA
(Mediterranean Sea)

© Hanan Isachar/0Israelimages.com

Mount Tabor is another possible site for the Transfiguration of Jesus.

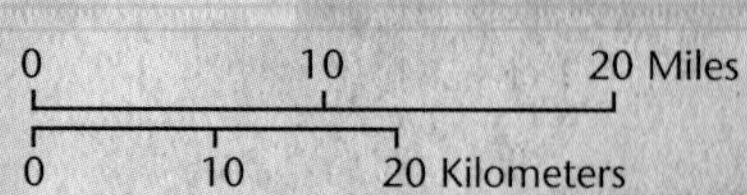

N
W
E
S

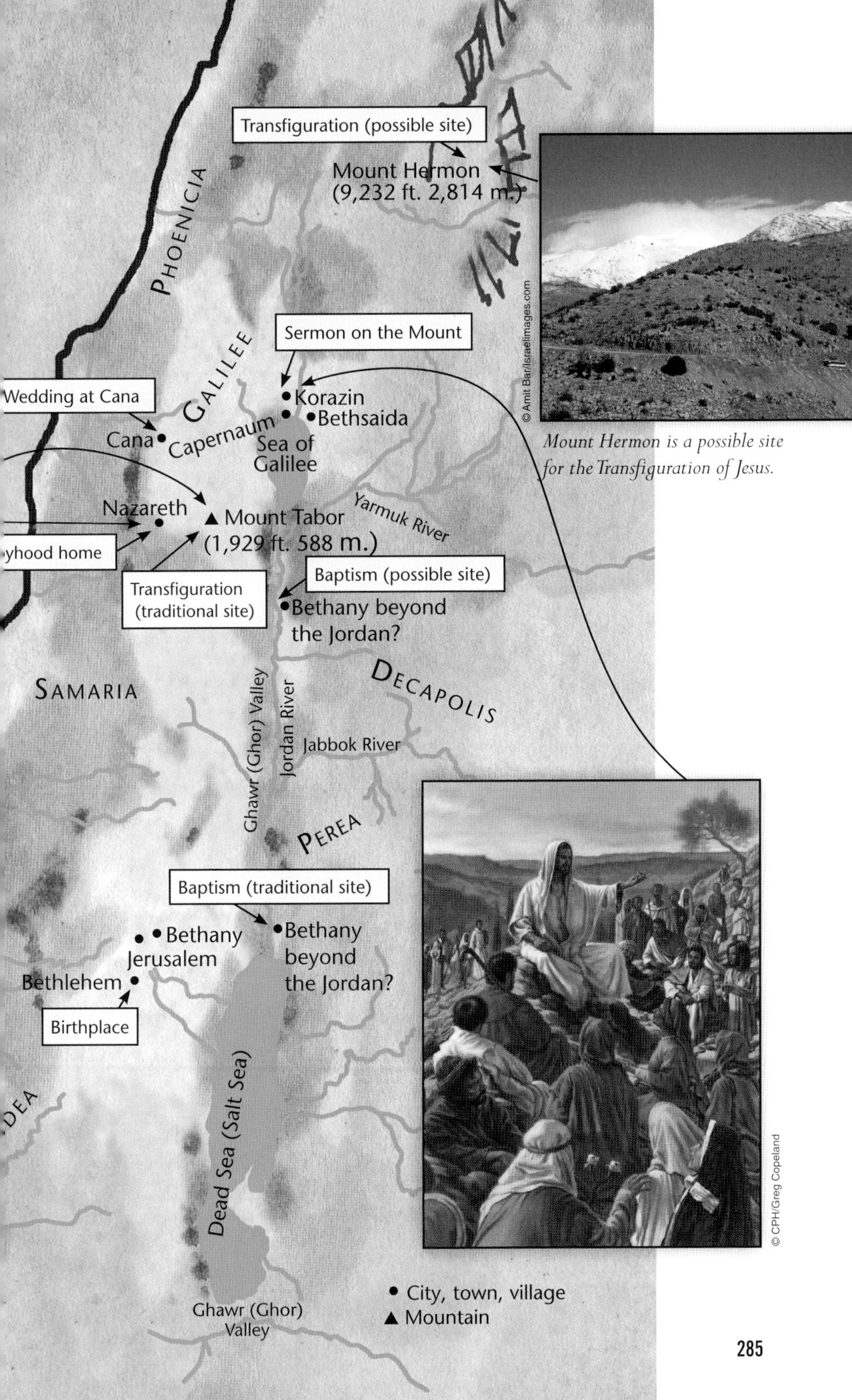

Mount Hermon is a possible site for the Transfiguration of Jesus.

Disciples of Jesus

Andrew

- Name means "manly."
- Brother of Simon Peter.
- Fishing partner of James and John, the sons of Zebedee.
- Tradition holds that he was crucified on an X-shaped cross because Andrew did not want to die on a cross that was the same shape as Jesus' cross.

Matthew

- Names means "gift of the Lord."
- Also known as Levi, son of Alphcus.
- First man to write down the teachings of Jesus.
- Symbol is three moneybags or a winged man representing the genealogy of Jesus.

Bartholomew

- Name means "son of Talmai."
- Also known as "Nathanael" (or "Nathaniel").
- Tradition holds that he brought the Gospel to India.
- Thought to have been flayed alive.
- His symbol is a flaying knife and a book, or sometimes three parallel knives.

Peter

- Name means "the rock."
- Known as Simon until Jesus called him Peter.
- Tradition holds that he was martyred on a cross, requesting to be crucified head downward because of his unworthiness.

James

- Sometimes known as "St. James the Greater."
- The first disciple to be martyred, about fifteen years after Jesus' death.
- Three scallop shells refers to his pilgrimage by the sea.

Phillip

- Name means "lover of horses."
- Friend of Andrew, Peter, and Bartholomew.
- Sometimes shown with two loaves and a cross because of his part in the feeding of the five thousand and his role in stressing the cross as a sign of Christianity and victory.

James the Less

- Name means "supplanter."
- Known as "the Less" because he was small.
- Tradition tells us that he died as a martyr at age 96; his dead body was sawed into pieces.

Simon the Zealot

- Name means "he hears" or "hearing."
- Had a strong love for Jesus and the rest of the disciples.
- His symbol is a fish lying on a Bible, indicating he had been a fisherman who became a fisher of men through preaching.

John

- Name means "the Lord has been gracious."
- Known as "the beloved disciple."
- Died a natural death at an old age.
- His symbol is a cup and serpent because it is thought that God spared him from being poisoned.

Thaddaeus

- Name means "large-hearted" or "courageous."
- Killed with arrows at Ararat.
- His symbol shows a ship because he was a missionary thought to have traveled far.

Judas Iscariot

- Came from Judah, near Jericho.
- Took care of the money for Jesus and the disciples.
- Betrayed Jesus for thirty pieces of silver.
- Hanged himself.
- His symbols are a moneybag and thirty pieces of silver, or a hangman's noose.

Thomas

- Name means "the twin."
- Also called "Didymus," a Greek name.
- Best remembered as "doubting Thomas."
- Killed by a spear.
- His symbol is a spear with a carpenter's square.

Disciple, Apostle, Missionary

Disciple: a follower. In the Bible, this term describes a person who follows Jesus. We are Jesus' disciples through God's gift of faith in Jesus, which comes through His Word and Sacraments.

Apostle: messenger or "sent one"; applied most frequently to the twelve disciples whom Jesus selected during His early ministry "whom He also named apostles" (Mark 3:14).

Missionary: one chosen to share the Good News with those of another country or culture. This is not a biblical term; it is generally used to designate those selected by a church body or mission society for this purpose.

Disciples

Jesus chose twelve men to be His first followers, or disciples. Even though Jesus was a carpenter, many of the men He chose were fishermen from Galilee who were used to hard work. Fishermen experienced many treacherous storms and disappointing catches on the Sea of Galilee. They were often courageous and persistent—just the qualities that "fishers of men" would need. Matthew records this list of disciples: "Simon, who is called Peter, and Andrew his brother; James the son of Zebedee, and John his brother; Philip and Bartholomew; Thomas and Matthew the tax collector; James the son of Alphaeus, and Thaddaeus; Simon the Cananaean, and Judas Iscariot, who betrayed Him" (Matthew 10:2–4).

The word *disciple* is also used in Scripture to identify all the people who followed Jesus and His teachings, including many references in the Book of Acts that apply to people who probably never saw Jesus personally. In this sense, we, too, are disciples of Jesus. People other than Jesus may have followers called "disciples," but there are only a few such references in the Bible: in Isaiah 8:16, Isaiah refers to "my disciples," and the Gospels refer occasionally to the disciples of John (Matthew 9:14; Mark 6:29).

When His twelve disciples were ready, Jesus sent them out on their own, two by two, to preach the Gospel and heal the sick in the areas around Galilee, as He had been doing (Mark 6:7–13). He gave them very specific instructions: they were to carry no bag, no bread, no money, not even an extra tunic—things that every traveler in Bible times considered basic essentials for safety. Jesus wanted them to be totally dependent on Him and on the hospitality of others and to stay completely focused on the mission.

Soon, as word about Jesus spread, He chose seventy-two more disciples (some ancient manuscripts say seventy) and sent them out as apostles on an urgent mission to the villages and towns in Judea near Jerusalem. They traveled ahead of Jesus to preach the Gospel and heal the sick. Jesus gave them the same instructions as He had given the Twelve. He told them they were being sent out "as lambs in the midst of wolves" (Luke 10:3) with the message that the "kingdom of God" in the person of Jesus Christ was near (v. 9). Because the "harvest is plentiful" (v. 3), meaning that many people still needed to hear the message that the Messiah had come, these disciples were to pray for even more workers to be sent out. It is believed that the number seventy or seventy-two represents "all nations" ("Go therefore and make disciples of all nations" [Matthew 28:19]) and reminds us that Jesus' message of salvation was first for the Jews and then for the Gentiles of all nations of the world.

Caesarea

Great Sea

(Mediterranean Sea)

At Home in Capernaum

Capernaum

Capernaum was a busy fishing and commercial center on the northwest shore of the Sea of Galilee. This was Jesus' home territory. His hometown, Nazareth, was about twenty miles to the southwest. You may recognize other towns in the region of Galilee on the map.

Jesus called some of His disciples from their fishing occupation along the Sea of Galilee, including two brothers, Peter and Andrew. No one really knows whose house Jesus was teaching in when he healed the paralytic, but some scholars say it may have been Peter's home. It would have been a logical place for Jesus to stay when He was in Capernaum.

The House

A Galilean village home had rooms situated around a center courtyard that often had its own well. There were workrooms for weaving, cooking, and other daily tasks. Inhabitants lived and worked right next-door to their animals, which actually lived in one of the rooms of the house. Often, there was a large room for family meals and entertaining guests.

The Roof

Each house was usually home to many people, members of an extended family. Both young and old spent much of their day outdoors in the courtyard and on the flat, sun-baked clay roof. It was easy to get up to the roof; all you had to do was take the stairs. Heavy wooden roof beams held up a layer of long sticks covered with straw and topped by packed clay.

Miracles

A miracle is something that only God can do. It is an extraordinary event that cannot be explained in human terms and that shows God at work. The four Gospel accounts of Jesus' life record about thirty-five separate miracles that Jesus performed during His earthly ministry. Only one miracle—the feeding of five thousand men—appears in all four Gospels, unless you count the miracle of Jesus' own resurrection from the dead.

Jesus performed most of His recorded miracles in the regions around the Sea of Galilee. He also healed a woman's daughter in Tyre (Matthew 15:21–28), a woman in Judea (Luke 13:11–13), a man in Perea, east of the Jordan (Luke 14:1–4), and blind men on at least two occasions in Jericho (Matthew 20:29–34; John 9:1–7). He raised Lazarus back to life in Bethany (John 11:1–44). Only two miracles took place in Jerusalem, both during Jesus' last week on earth—withering a fig tree (Matthew 21:18–22) and healing the severed ear of the high priest's servant (Luke 22:50–51).

The Purpose of Jesus' Miracles

Jesus performed His miracles publicly and for a specific reason: to show that He was true God—the promised, long-awaited Messiah—and that He had all authority and power in heaven and on earth. Jesus showed His divine power and authority over nature when He fed five thousand men with just five small loaves of bread and two fish. His amazed disciples later watched as He calmed a storm and walked on the water.

Miracles by the Disciples

After His resurrection, Jesus gave His disciples authority to perform miraculous signs and wonders in His name (Acts 5:12, 15–16). Peter healed a man who was lame (3:1–10). Philip healed many sick and demon-possessed people in Samaria (8:4–8). Peter healed paralyzed Aeneas in Lydda and raised Tabitha (also called Dorcas) from the dead in Joppa (9:32–42). Paul raised Eutychus from death in Troas (20:7–12).

The Greatest Miracle

Miracles are God's way of introducing Himself and demonstrating His power and His love. Perhaps the greatest miracle of all is God's intervention in our lives, saving us from eternal damnation by sending Jesus into the world. Through Christ's sacrificial death on the cross and His miraculous resurrection on the third day, our sins are paid for and our eternal life in heaven is guaranteed.

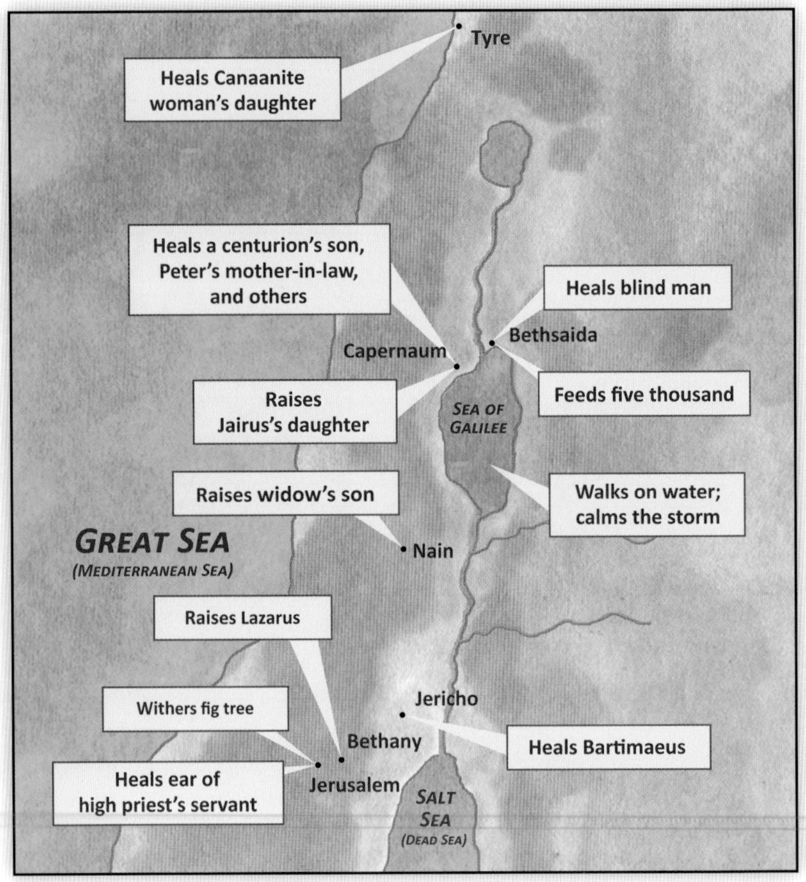

Miracles of Jesus

	Matthew	Mark	Luke	John
Healing				
Man with leprosy	8:2–4	1:40–42	5:12–13	
Roman centurion's servant	8:5–13		7:1–10	
Peter's mother-in-law	8:14–15	1:30–31	4:38–39	
Two men from Gadara	8:28–34	5:1–15	8:27–35	
Paralyzed man	9:2–7	2:3–12	5:18–25	
Woman with bleeding	9:20–22	5:25–29	8:43–48	
Two blind men	9:27–31			
Man mute and possessed	9:32–33			
Man with a shriveled hand	12:10–13	3:1–5	6:6–10	
Man blind, mute, and possessed	12:22		11:14	
Canaanite woman's daughter	15:21–28	7:24–30		
Boy with a demon	17:14–18	9:17–29	9:38–43	
Two blind men (one named)	20:29–34	10:46–52	18:35–43	
Deaf mute		7:31–37		
Man possessed, synagogue		1:23–26	4:33–35	
Blind man at Bethsaida		8:22–26		
Crippled woman			13:11–13	
Man with dropsy			14:1–4	
Ten men with leprosy			17:11–19	
The high priest's servant			22:50–51	
Official's son at Capernaum				4:46–54
Sick man, pool of Bethesda				5:1–9
Man born blind				9:1–7
Command over the forces of nature				
Calming the storm		4:37–41		
Walking on the water		6:48–51		6:19–21
Five thousand people fed		6:35–44		6:5–13
Four thousand people fed		8:1–9		
Coin in the fish's mouth				
Fig tree withered		11:12–14, 20–25		
Catch of fish				
Water turned into wine				2:1–11
Another catch of fish				21:1–11
Bringing the dead back to life				
Jairus's daughter	9:18–19, 23–25	5:22–24, 38–42	8:41–42, 49–56	
Widow's son at Nain			7:11–15	
Lazarus				11:1–44

From Concordia Self-Study Bible, New International Version, p. 1606

True God and True Man

As Christians, we believe and confess that Jesus is both true God and true man. This dual nature of Jesus Christ is a mystery that we accept by faith. For example, in Martin Luther's explanation of the Second Article of the Apostles' Creed, we confess, "I believe that Jesus Christ, true God, begotten of the Father from eternity, and also true man, born of the Virgin Mary, is my Lord."

© CPH/Corbert Gauthier

Controversy in Church History

In the Early Christian Church, hundreds of years before Martin Luther lived, there were false teachers who claimed that Jesus was only similar to God but was not truly God Himself. Others taught that Jesus was a good man and a great teacher, but He was not God—only the Father was truly eternal and truly God. There were many questions about Jesus. Was He sometimes God and sometimes man?

The Council of Nicaea

To decide the matter, the Church leaders came together in AD 325 at the Council of Nicaea, where they debated—and ultimately rejected—the false teachings about Jesus. The result was the Nicene Creed, a statement of belief that the Church adopted and updated. It is still used in the Divine Service today. It states that Jesus was "begotten, not made, being of one substance with the Father, by whom all things were made" (*LSB*, p. 158). Jesus was affirmed as the Second Person of the Trinity, different from the Father and the Spirit in some ways, but equally God.

© CPH/Phil Howe

© CPH/Robert Papp

In His nativity, Jesus took on a human nature so that He could dwell among us as one of us, fulfill the Law for us, suffer all of our temptations, and die on the cross as the full sacrifice for the sins of all humankind. He retained His divine nature so that He might resist all temptation to sin, redeem all people through a sufficient sacrifice on the cross, and conquer sin and death through the resurrection on Easter.

Rejected by the Jews

Many Jews did not believe that Jesus was the Son of God, the promised Messiah. Some even refused to believe that He was a real human being! Some false teachers taught that Jesus just "appeared" to be human but was not truly flesh and blood.

The Truth of God's Word

We know that Jesus had human ancestors (Luke 3:23–38). He was born of a human mother (Luke 2:6–7). The Bible tells us that Jesus was a flesh-and-blood man who was hungry and thirsty, and who ate, drank, slept, and cried. We believe and confess that He is also true God.

© CPH/Corbert Gauthier

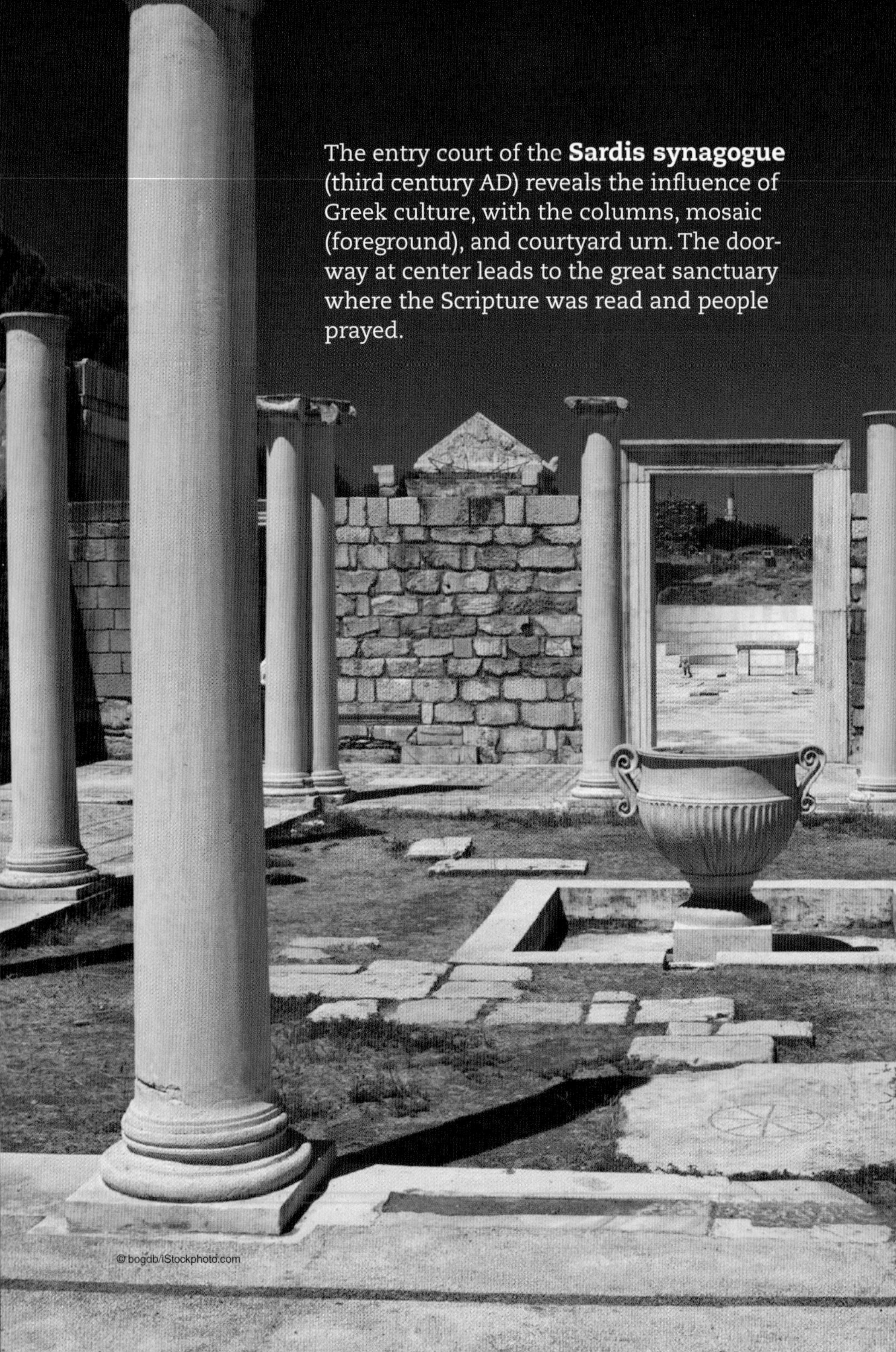

The entry court of the **Sardis synagogue** (third century AD) reveals the influence of Greek culture, with the columns, mosaic (foreground), and courtyard urn. The doorway at center leads to the great sanctuary where the Scripture was read and people prayed.

Synagogues and Rabbis

Synagogues are houses of prayer established in Jewish communities to support religious life. Though some scholars claim that early forms of synagogue worship date from the time of Moses, synagogues seem to have developed during the exile after the destruction of Solomon's temple. Most large Jewish communities established a synagogue for the purposes of prayer and religious study. Synagogues continued to be centers for Scripture reading and prayer through Jesus' lifetime, and they became the sole location for Jewish worship after the destruction of Herod's temple in AD 70. Sacrifices were never performed in the synagogue, but, as prescribed in the Books of the Law, only in the temple.

There is no set architecture for a synagogue. Traditionally, its furniture includes an ark (a box, cabinet, or shrine for the storage of sacred scrolls) and a platform from which Scripture is read. In some cases, an area is set aside for women as was also done at the temple in Jerusalem.

The Hebrew word *rabbi* was used as a sign of respect by the Israelites when addressing their teachers and religious instructors. The term eventually developed into three words, denoting the teacher's position: *rab* indicated the lowest level; *rabbi* was the next level; and *rabboni* was the highest level. The words mean "great one," "my great one," and, less literally, "my lord, my master," respectively.

In Jesus' day, there appeared to be no automatic connection between rabbis and synagogues, although, as houses of prayer and study, synagogues were natural places for rabbis to spend time, just as Jesus did during His ministry, particularly on the Sabbath.

Similarly, there is no exclusive connection between rabbis, synagogues, and education in the Jewish community. Although the religious instruction of their children was among parents' most important duties, such instruction was not the primary role of a rabbi. During the time of Christ's appearance on earth, the average Jewish child began school around age 5 or 6. The children were taught moral lessons as well as intellectual ones. Religious training consisted of questions and answers in a catechetical format. The teacher lectured on a topic; afterward, the students asked questions concerning the theme. The teacher usually responded with parables or more questions. Jesus often used this method when teaching His disciples.

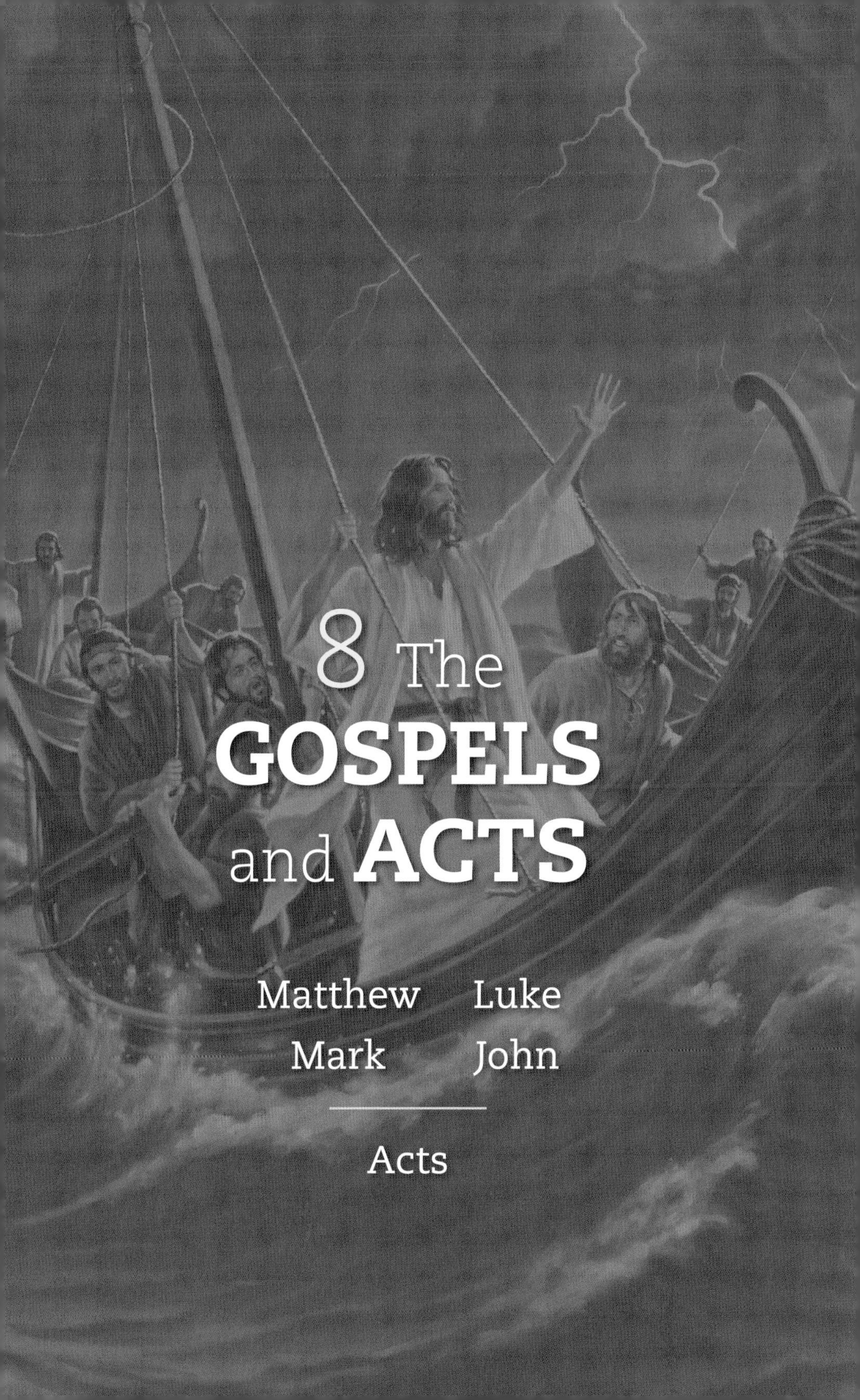

8 The GOSPELS and ACTS

Matthew
Mark
Luke
John

Acts

Matthew

Into Matthew

This Gospel at a Glance

- The four Gospels—Matthew, Mark, Luke, and John—present biographies of Jesus. They tell the story of His earthly life and ministry.
- Matthew is one of the three Synoptic Gospels; Mark and Luke are the others. The term *synoptic* means "seeing together," or "seeing alike." The picture of Jesus' life and ministry presented in each of these three Gospels is quite similar, while John's content differs quite a lot from that found in Matthew, Mark, and Luke. They don't contradict one another; rather, they simply add another viewpoint.
- Matthew was an eyewitness to much that he recorded. He was one of Jesus' twelve disciples, the tax collector who walked away from his tax booth to follow Jesus (Matthew 9:9–13).
- Matthew's name means "gift of the Lord." He likely wrote the Gospel that carries his name sometime around AD 50.
- Matthew's first readers were Jewish. Matthew's Gospel highlights Jesus as the Son of David, the messianic King sent by God as the Savior. Matthew refers again and again to Jesus' kingship and includes many "kingdom parables."
- Matthew concentrates on Jesus' power and authority, often using the Greek word that combines these concepts (Gr: exousia).
- The turning point in Matthew's Gospel comes in chapter 12, when the official representatives of Israel reject Jesus' claims to be their King. (See especially vv. 23–24.)

- In his resurrection chapter, Matthew shows Jesus vindicated by His Father despite the rejection of the Jewish leaders. The risen and reigning King Jesus then shares His mission and His authority with His people, His Church (28:18–20).

How is the Book of Matthew classified?

Matthew is a Gospel, which presents the life of Jesus while also teaching how Jesus' life fulfilled the Old Testament promises about salvation. Matthew is called a "Synoptic Gospel" because his outline is very similar to that of Mark and Luke.

Matthew's Portrait of Jesus

Matthew focuses on showing his first Jewish readers that Jesus is their Messiah and King.

Matthew clearly intends to portray Jesus as Messiah. He carefully traces Jesus' genealogy from Abraham (Matthew 1:1–16) to show that Jesus fulfilled the covenant the Lord cut with Abraham (Genesis 15, 17).

In addition, Matthew testifies to Jesus' identity as Messiah by setting His birth and early ministry in the context of the Old Testament prophecies. He links Jesus to the Old Testament prophetic texts seven times in his first three chapters alone. Again and again, we read phrases like "All this took place to fulfill what the Lord had spoken by the prophet."

Matthew also shows Jesus as the King of Israel. The Wise Men call Jesus the "king of the Jews" (Matthew 2:2). John the Baptist announces the coming of the Kingdom (3:1–3), and Jesus Himself picks up that message (4:17, 23). The Lord teaches about His kingdom, the "kingdom of heaven," using that phrase thirty-one times in Matthew's Gospel. Israel's leaders reject this claim, accusing Jesus of being allied with "Beelzebul, the prince of demons" (12:24). From this point on, they grow more hardened in their unbelief, and Jesus begins to warn that their rejection of Him will end in His death.

Matthew gives a full account of Jesus' entry into Jerusalem as King—but not the kind of king God's people expected. Matthew makes two key Old Testament connections (21:1–11):

- Like King Solomon, Jesus comes to His people as a lowly servant. Solomon rode the mule of his father, the great King David (1 Kings 1:38). So, too, King Jesus comes—not on a war-horse, encouraging rebellion against Roman oppressors, but humbly, on a donkey, as the King of peace, about to die so we can be forgiven.
- Matthew tells us this humble approach fulfilled the words of the prophet Zechariah. The King of Israel would come to His people

> "mounted on a donkey, and on a colt, the foal of a beast of burden" (Matthew 21:5; see also Zechariah 9:9).

How Can I Best Grow in Grace as I Read Matthew?

As you read Matthew, look for the way he moves back and forth between Jesus' teachings and His miracles. Each of the "discourses," or teaching sections, sums up the point of the events that come before it. These discourses come in chapters 5–7 (the Sermon on the Mount); chapter 10; chapter 13; chapter 18; and chapters 24–25.

Bethlehem Today

© Garo Nalbandian/Israelimages

Many people visit Bethlehem in Palestine every year. It is still a holy city for Jews and Christians. The town is about six miles south of Jerusalem on an ancient route once taken by caravans. Visitors can see vineyards, olive trees, tiny villages, and the mountain range near the Jordan River beyond the Dead Sea.

© Yasha Mazur/Israelimages.com

The region of Bethlehem is divided into three ancient small towns. They are called Beit Lahm (Bethlehem), Beit Jala, and Beit Sahour. The busy markets sell daily needs for residents as well as handcrafted items that tourists enjoy. This region is famous for carvings from olive wood, jewelry made from mother-of-pearl, and embroidered items.

© Yasha Mazur/Israelimages.com

The climate in the area from April to October is hot, sunny, and dry, with temperatures averaging between 75–80 degrees Fahrenheit. Winter temperatures, from November to March, are 45–60 degrees Fahrenheit.

© Yasha Mazur/Israelimages.com

Over the centuries, Bethlehem has been influenced by many different cultures. One can hear many languages spoken there, including Arabic, English, Spanish, Italian, German, and French. Much of the written language is in Fusha, which is classic Arabic. Businesses in Bethlehem accept U.S. dollars, Jordanian dinars, and New Israeli shekels.

© CPH

© Hanan Isachar/Israelimages

The Jordan River

Jesus was baptized in the Jordan River. The Jordan River is still important today. It supplies water for the people to use as well as for irrigating crops such as olives, tomatoes, and apples. Since the population in the region is increasing, less water flows in the river.

The Jordan River flows through the Ghawr (Ghor) Valley, part of the Rift Valley. This valley is the border between Jordan on the east and Israel and Palestine on the west. The Jordan River begins at the base of Mount Hermon.

The Jordan River system includes the Sea of Galilee and two rivers, the Yarmuk and the Jabbok, that flow into the Jordan from the east below the Sea of Galilee. The Jordan River flows a total of about two hundred miles and ends at the Dead Sea.

Joseph—Mystery Man

If you ask people to name the people in the Bible's account of Christmas, they'll usually say Mary, Joseph, and the baby Jesus. Further discussion will reveal that few people know very much about Joseph. What do we know about Jesus' earthly father?

Scripture tells us that Joseph was descended from the line of David, which is why he and Mary went to Bethlehem to register for the census that Caesar Augustus had ordered. The Bible describes him as a carpenter (Matthew 13:55). At the time they married, Mary was probably quite young. Joseph, however, may have been older, since the Bible does not mention him after Jesus visited the temple at age 12. Matthew 13:55–56 reveals that Jesus had at least four brothers—James, Joseph, Simon, and Judas—and some sisters.

Joseph was a kind man. Under Jewish law, he and Mary were promised to each other in marriage. Betrothal was a binding contract in Joseph's day, requiring a divorce decree to end it, just like marriage. Because of this law, they referred to each other as husband and wife; therefore, when Mary told him she was expecting a baby, he decided it might be best to divorce her (Matthew 1:18–25). Though he no doubt felt hurt and betrayed, Joseph showed his concern for Mary. The typical punishment for being pregnant outside of marriage would have been stoning, but Joseph wanted to spare Mary from such an act. He set out to divorce her quietly.

It is at this point that we see that Joseph was also a righteous man of faith. After the angel appeared to him in his dream, Joseph took Mary as his wife. He believed the words the angel spoke to him and prepared to become the earthly father of the Christ Child. We also see this when he had Jesus circumcised (Luke 2:21) and brought Him to the temple for redemption as the firstborn (vv. 22–24) according to Jewish law. Later, he quickly moved to protect his family from death when an angel warned him of Herod's plot to kill the child (Matthew 2:13–15).

As Jesus grew, Joseph evidently taught Him his trade; thus, the Bible also calls Jesus a carpenter (Mark 6:3).

Joseph observed the Jewish customs, bringing his family to Jerusalem for the Feast of the Passover (Luke 2:41–42). After this, however, Joseph's role as Jesus' earthly father disappears from Scripture. The Bible mentions Jesus' mother and siblings, but not Joseph. This omission seems to indicate that Joseph probably had died. The man who was Jesus' earthly father had joined his Father in heaven.

Taxes and Tax Collectors

In Jesus' time, the Roman government ruled in Judea. Like our government today, the Romans collected taxes to pay for roads, aqueducts (structures for carrying large quantities of flowing water), the military, and other things needed to run a country. The taxes were quite high. The Jews hated the Romans, who were harsh rulers, and they hated to pay taxes because the taxes reminded them that the Romans were in control.

The Romans hired Jews to collect their taxes. Like the Romans they served, these tax collectors were hated. Their fellow Jews considered them traitors who had turned against their own people. Often, tax officials collected taxes unfairly. They contracted with the Roman government to collect a certain amount of money, and any extra money they collected was theirs to keep. As a result, they became very wealthy men, even though many Jews rejected them. The Bible says that Zacchaeus "was a chief tax collector and was rich" (Luke 19:2). He may have been in charge of many tax collectors, and perhaps he had become wealthy by cheating many people.

One of the Roman taxes was a customs tax charged on goods transported through their vast empire. The Romans erected tax offices or booths near city gates and ports to collect the customs tax. The tax collector's booth where Jesus found Matthew (who was also called "Levi") was probably a toll booth near Capernaum on the Via Maris (Way of the Sea), a major

© Shutterstock, Inc.

road from Damascus that went through Capernaum, then west to the Great Sea (the Mediterranean Sea), and then along the coast to Egypt. Many traders passed by on their way to and from Egypt. No doubt Matthew's job was to collect a toll on any goods transported past him as they entered the region.

The Jews often shunned or avoided tax collectors because of their constant contact with Gentiles and foreigners. This and their reputation as cheaters caused tax collectors to be considered as sinners, ceremonially unclean. Tax collectors could not serve as witnesses in legal matters. Their money was considered unclean because it had been obtained by taking advantage of others. The religious leaders considered tax collectors to be unrepentant sinners, and they were not allowed to participate in religious activities in the temple or the synagogue.

To the Jews, there was no hope for a tax collector. Even a house that a tax collector entered was considered unclean. They and their families were social outcasts. Gentiles and other sinners, whom the religious leaders also considered unrighteous, were the only friends Jewish tax collectors had.

Like Zacchaeus, Matthew was a tax collector. Each day, he dealt with people who hated him for what he was and who considered anything he touched to be unclean. Imagine Matthew's joy when Jesus called him to be a disciple! Matthew learned the true joy of receiving forgiveness.

Sinners

The term *sinner* often identified individuals who didn't follow the strict rules of purity and righteous behavior set by the Pharisees. To Pharisees, nearly everyone else was a sinner. Eating with a Gentile or tax collector was especially wrong

© Jens Stolt/Shutterstock, Inc.

by Pharisees' standards, because eating with a person was a sign of friendship. To eat with sinners was to be contaminated and ceremonially unclean. It meant the person could not enter a synagogue or the temple. When the Pharisees saw Jesus eating at Matthew's house, it's no wonder, then, that they asked, "Why does He eat with tax collectors and sinners?" (Mark 2:16).

Mark

Into Mark

This Gospel at a Glance

- Like Matthew and Luke, Mark is one of the three Synoptic Gospels. (For the meaning of *synoptic*, see "This Gospel at a Glance," p. 302) These three biographies of our Savior take a similar approach as they tell our Savior's life story.
- Mark's Gospel is the shortest. Mark's earliest readers were likely Gentiles and probably Romans. Among other clues leading to this conclusion is the fact that Mark often explains Jewish customs, and he seldom quotes directly from the Old Testament.
- Mark was likely the John Mark (Acts 12:12, 25) who accompanied Paul on his first missionary journey. He was not one of the twelve disciples, and thus he was likely not an eyewitness to the events he records. Instead, he interviewed various eyewitnesses as he composed his manuscript.
- Many scholars think Mark interviewed Peter extensively and used Peter's eyewitness testimony as he put his account together. Of course, this in no way takes away from the divine inspiration of Mark's Gospel. (See "Who Wrote the Bible?" on p. xvi)
- Mark uses a crisp, fast-paced style of writing; he uses the words "immediately" and "at once" more than forty times in his book. In doing so, he communicates his urgency to proclaim the Good News. Chapter 1 plunges us into the midst of the story; Mark says nothing about Jesus' birth or boyhood.
- Mark pictures Jesus as powerful and decisive, but also as a humble servant.

- Like Matthew, Mark focuses on the coming kingdom of God, but Mark accents the forces opposing that kingdom—both human and demonic. Unbelieving people and Satan himself clash with Jesus throughout Mark's Gospel.
- Mark's Gospel falls roughly into two main sections, each focusing on a different aspect of what Jesus came to do: to serve (chapters 1–10) and to sacrifice (chapters 11–16).
- Many scholars believe Mark was the first Gospel written, perhaps between AD 50 and the early 60s.

How is the Book of Mark classified?

Mark is a Gospel, which presents the life of Jesus while also teaching how Jesus' life fulfilled the Old Testament promises about salvation. Mark is called a "Synoptic Gospel" because its outline is very similar to that of Matthew and Luke.

Mark's Portrait of Jesus

Mark pictures Jesus as the Suffering Servant. In doing so, he echoes the Servant Songs composed by the prophet Isaiah some seven hundred years before Jesus' birth. (See "Into Isaiah," p. 189.)

In painting this portrait, Mark invites his readers to see Jesus as the Servant who calls His followers to serve also.

How Can I Best Grow in Grace as I Read Mark?

Mark writes to draw us in. One way he does this is to use four overlapping cycles in narrating his account:

- John the Baptist comes onto the scene, preaches the coming kingdom of God, faces opposition, and is killed.
- Jesus comes onto the scene, preaches the coming kingdom of God, faces opposition, and is killed, but rises from the dead.
- The twelve disciples come onto the scene and begin to preach the coming kingdom of God. Mark's early readers had likely heard about the persecution and death that faced the Twelve and other followers who had begun to witness about Jesus and His kingdom.
- Now we readers have come onto the scene, simply by reading this Gospel! Will we "take up [the] cross" Jesus talks about (Mark 8:34–37)? Or will we join the religious leaders and demons who oppose Him? What's our answer to Jesus' question, "Who do you say that I am?" (Mark 8:29)?

As you read, ask the Holy Spirit to help you answer this question: where am I in this book?

What are the key chapters and verses in Mark?

- **Mark 1:1–7** John the Baptist appears and serves.
- **Mark 1:9–14** Jesus appears and serves.
- **Mark 3:13–21** Jesus calls the Twelve to serve.
- **Mark 4:1–20** The parable of the sower explains what faithful servants can expect.
- **Mark 6:1–6** Jesus is rejected.
- **Mark 6:14–29** John the Baptist is killed.
- **Mark 8:27–30** Peter confesses Jesus as the Messiah.
- **Mark 8:31–38** Jesus warns Peter and the other disciples to expect the cross.
- **Mark 14–15** Jesus suffers and dies.
- **Mark 16:1–13** Jesus rises; some believe and some doubt.
- **Mark 16:14–20** Jesus sends the Eleven, knowing what awaits them. As readers, we are left with the question, how will we respond?

Disease and Medicine in Bible Times

Many diseases and health problems are mentioned in the Bible. People suffered from tumors, fevers, seizures, blindness, paralysis, and a wide variety of skin diseases. These included leprosy, boils, and other sores and infections. The Bible describes demons that caused illness, so casting out demons was a form of healing.

© Hanan Isachar/Israelimages

Doctors and physicians are mentioned in the Bible, but they were unable to help many people. Some of their practices actually increased their patients' suffering.

Antibiotics—the type of medicine we use today to cure infections—did not exist in Bible times. Instead, people used certain plants, oils, wine, and other natural substances as medicines. The Good Samaritan used oil and wine on the wounds of the man who had been badly beaten (Luke 10:30–34).

Soothing ointments were prepared from various herbs. Some of these worked, but often these "medicines" could not heal the injury or cure the illness or disease.

People with arthritis, rheumatism, or other aches and pains found relief in warm springs near the Dead Sea, which was rich in minerals.

© Mili Koren/Israelimages

© CPH/Glenn Myers

Gethsemane

© CPH/Robert Hook

You might be familiar with the name Gethsemane as that of a garden that Jesus frequented. It was in this garden that He went to pray just before he was arrested, tried, and crucified. The Savior went to this garden to pray for strength to undo what Adam had done in another garden. It was to Gethsemane that Jesus came to pray to His Father, and it was from there that He went forward to complete the promise made so long ago—to become the Savior of all humankind.

Gethsemane is a Hebrew word that means "oil press," no doubt referring to the pressing of oil from the olive trees in the area. In Jesus' time, the garden was probably an orchard containing various fruit trees.

Religious tradition gives two sites for Gethsemane. Representatives of the Roman Catholic Church claim that the original garden is now a small, fenced piece of land located at the base of the Mount of Olives; it measures only about seventy paces around, and it contains old olive trees. Representatives from the Greek Orthodox Church, however, insist that the actual spot of Gethsemane is farther up the Mount of Olives.

© Israelimages.com

The Sea of Galilee

Much of Jesus' ministry took place along the shores of the Sea of Galilee. In fact, Nazareth, Jesus' hometown, was only about twenty miles from Capernaum, which is near the Sea of Galilee. Close to the Sea of Galilee, Jesus called His first disciples, and on the waters of Galilee, Jesus calmed the storm. The Sea of Galilee is also called the Sea of Tiberias (John 6:1) and the lake of Gennesaret (Luke 5:1).

Capernaum—*Jesus preached and performed many miracles in this town and the surrounding area.*

Magdala—*Mary Magdalene, one of the women who followed Jesus, was from the town of Magdala, which is on the Sea of Galilee.*

This boat, known as the "Jesus Boat," is believed to be about 2,000 years old and is typical of the boats used in Bible times. It was found buried in deep mud on the shores of the Sea of Galilee. It is called the "Jesus Boat" because archaeologists believe it was being used during the time Jesus performed His ministry around the Sea of Galilee.

Tabgha—*We believe this is where Jesus multiplied the two fish and five loaves of bread. Today, a church called the Church of the Multiplication of the Loaves and Fishes stands at Tabgha.*

This mosaic in the Church of the Multiplication of the Loaves and Fishes is believed to be about 1,500 years old. Some Christians believe this is the spot where Jesus fed thousands of people, using only five barley loaves and two fish.

Washing, Bathing, and Anointing

In Bible times, bathing or washing was important, and not just for physical cleanliness. It also served as a religious ceremony, as washing symbolized being purified from sin.

Did the disciples take showers?

In ancient times, almost no one had running water for bathing in their homes. Most people bathed in a river or drew water into a bucket and bathed themselves with that—what we might call a "sponge bath." Without a bathtub or shower as we know it, they simply used a cloth and water to clean themselves.

In Jesus' day, Jews built ritual washing pools or tanks (*miqwaoth* in Hebrew) that held about sixty gallons of water. The Romans built large, luxurious public baths. Their bathhouses served the wealthy. They might have steam rooms or pools, and bathers could sit in the warm steam or get a soothing massage. Water was often brought into the public bath from a river or lake by aqueduct. Often, men used the public baths in the afternoons, and women went during the morning hours.

Most wells were small, like this first-century AD example. Others were so large that they included a staircase so villagers could walk down to the water.

Did the disciples use perfume?

Because the climate was warm, and because bathing was somewhat difficult, Middle Eastern men and women used fragrant oils and perfumes after bathing. They were made with spices and resins that were added to olive oil. The most expensive of these perfumes is known as nard or spikenard. It cost about 300 denarii. (The approximate value of a denarius is 16 cents, so 300 denarii would be equal to $48.)

Why was hand washing important?

In the Middle East, utensils such as knives and forks were not used for eating. Before eating a meal, therefore, it was necessary to wash at least one hand to ensure cleanliness.

Why are people always washing feet in the Bible?

There are several stories of foot washing in the Bible. This was a common practice among the people of Jesus' day because most people wore sandals. The climate created very dusty conditions, so most of the time, feet were dusty and dirty. Foot washing was a task performed by slaves or servants. Poor people usually washed their own feet.

In Luke 7, the woman who comes to Jesus cries on His feet, wipes them with her hair, and applies expensive ointment to them. When Jesus' host, Simon the Pharisee, objects, Jesus scolds him and says that Simon failed to even provide water for Jesus to wash His own feet. Hosts were expected to provide water for their guests for foot washing or have a slave perform the task.

Coins in the Roman World

Coins tell a story. They provide a snapshot of the history and values of a country. For example, famous places, like the Lincoln Memorial in Washington DC, and the faces of past presidents appear on coins in the United States along with symbols of freedom, victory, and strength. Biblical coins tell of ancient Jewish governments and leaders and give us information about events during Jesus' lifetime. The faces of pagan gods and goddesses and rulers all appeared on coins used in biblical times.

© Jens Stolt/Shutterstock, Inc.

Coins in Bible Times

Before coins were minted, lumps of silver were used for money. Early coins—even those of similar design—often varied in shape, size, and value. This created opportunities for dishonesty and cheating, especially by the money changers whose job it was to exchange foreign coins for Roman and Jewish money.

Most of the coins referred to in the New Testament were coins of the Roman government. The most common was the silver denarius, which bore the likeness of Caesar Tiberius and was used for paying taxes to the Roman government. One denarius could buy twelve loaves of bread. Four could purchase a lamb.

Mites

It is believed that the two coins offered by the widow in Mark 12:41–44 were the only small copper Jewish coins that were available at that time—the common prutahs. They were first issued approximately a hundred years before the day Jesus watched the woman drop them into the temple treasury. Coins often stayed in circulation for hundreds of years in ancient times, so it is not surprising that archaeologists have discovered tens of thousands of prutahs. They were the most common coin in circulation then, and they were still in use four centuries later.

Mark 12:42 reads, "And a poor widow came and put in two small copper coins, which make a penny." In some other translations of the Bible—the King James Version, for example—the term *copper coins* is translated as "mites," and the word *penny* is translated as "farthing," using common terms for money in the seventeenth century, when the King James Version of the Bible was created. *Mites* remains a popular term for the widow's offering to this day.

Miracles of Jesus

What is a miracle?

The word *miracle* comes from a Latin word that means "to wonder." Miracles are occurrences that cause wonder because they are unusual and out of the ordinary. But they are more than just remarkable events, like a fantastic last-minute basketball shot that surprises everyone by going in. Miracles are times when God intervenes directly in history to change the way things normally work so that He can reveal His glory and His mercy.

Jesus performed miracles that caused witnesses to wonder and marvel at the amazing things they saw.

Why did Jesus perform miracles?

The accounts of Jesus' miracles help us to know and believe that He is the Son of God, who came to earth to save us from sin, death, and the devil, and to give us eternal life. Jesus is the compassionate Creator and Redeemer of the world.

What kinds of miracles did Jesus do?

Jesus performed many miracles that showed His power over creation, sickness, the devil, and death.

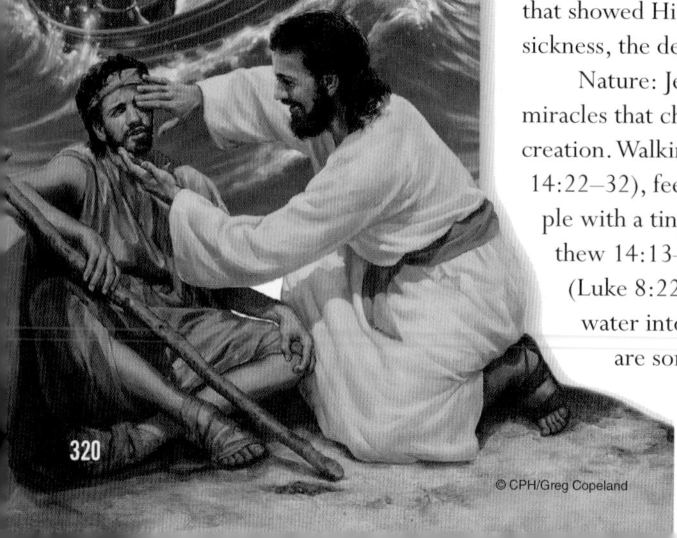

Nature: Jesus performed many miracles that changed the natural creation. Walking on water (Matthew 14:22–32), feeding five thousand people with a tiny amount of food (Matthew 14:13–18), calming the storm (Luke 8:22–25), and changing water into wine (John 2:1–11) are some of Jesus' miracles involving nature. These miracles show Jesus' divine power over all creation.

Healing: Many of Jesus' miracles involved healing people from illness, injury, or disability. During His ministry, Jesus restored sight to the blind (Matthew 9:26–28; 12:21–23), healed people from leprosy and other diseases (Luke 17:11–19; Mark 5:25–34), and made the lame walk again (Matthew 15:29–31; 21:14; John 5:2–17). These miracles show Jesus' power over sin.

Exorcism: An exorcism is the process by which a demon is cast out of a body it has possessed. Jesus cast out many demons during His ministry (for instance, see Matthew 8:28–34; Mark 1:33–35; Mark 5:1–20). Jesus' miracles of exorcism directly show the power He has over the devil.

Resurrection: The Gospels present three resurrection miracles of Jesus: the widow's son at Nain (Luke 7:11–17), the daughter of Jairus (Luke 8:40–56), and Lazarus (John 11:1–44). These miracles show Jesus' power over death itself, and they foreshadow His own resurrection.

Fishing Boats on Galilee

Fishing was a common occupation in ancient Galilee. Normally, fishermen dropped huge nets into the water from the side of a boat. These boats were large, usually about twenty-five feet long and seven feet across. They were big enough to have two or three seats that stretched from side to side and a space near the middle for casting nets. There was room for several fishermen, because it took lots of muscle to haul a heavy catch of fish aboard.

At the stern (the back of the boat), there was a raised platform that also served as a seat. Cushions were stored underneath the platform and were used for resting during a long night of fishing. Jesus was resting on one of these cushions the night of the big storm that frightened the disciples (Matthew 8:23–27; Mark 4:35–41; Luke 8:22–25).

The fishing boats were often made of cypress and cedar, wood that was readily available in the region. A carpenter or boat maker first constructed the shell using a type of joint called mortise and tenon, in which a lip on one piece of wood fit into a groove on the adjoining piece of wood. It is similar to what we refer to as a "tongue-in-groove" joint. This formed a tight fit so that the boat would not leak.

The boat was equipped with a simple sail to catch the wind and move the boat over the water.

The boats were not deep and could have taken on water easily during a storm. The great storm in the Bible account certainly would have sunk the boat if it were not for Jesus' command to the wind and sea to be calm.

Luke

Into Luke

This Gospel at a Glance

- Luke is the third of the Synoptic Gospels. With Matthew and Mark, Luke describes Jesus' earthly life and ministry in a similar way, though each of the synoptic writers accents different themes. (See p. 302.)
- Luke was a physician—a doctor—by profession, and it's therefore not surprising that he emphasizes Jesus' healing miracles. He also pays special attention to our Lord's teachings about prayer, His interest in the poor, and His welcoming attitudes toward women, Gentiles, and those in society called "sinners."
- Like Mark, Luke likely interviewed the apostle Peter as he organized his manuscript. His rich descriptions of Jesus' birth and His experience in the temple at age 12 have led many scholars to believe that Mary served as a primary source for Luke as he wrote. If not for Luke, we would know little about Jesus' birth. Many of Jesus' parables are unique to Luke's Gospel too.
- Also like Mark, Luke writes primarily for a non-Jewish audience. Some think Luke might have been a Gentile himself. If so, his Gospel is probably the only Bible book written by an author who was not an Israelite.

- Luke traveled with the apostle Paul on his missionary journeys and Luke was probably in Rome when he composed his Gospel, sometime between AD 59 and 63.
- Luke also wrote the Book of Acts; it forms a kind of "volume 2" to the "volume 1" of his Gospel. In both books, Luke uses a polished style and rich vocabulary. His command of the Greek language is outstanding.
- Luke dedicates his Gospel to Theophilus. This name means "lover of God." It's thought that Theophilus may have been an important government official.
- One theme permeates Luke's pages: the mission of our Lord, as He Himself put it: "*The Son of Man came to seek and to save the lost*" (Luke 19:10).

How is the Book of Luke classified?

Luke is a Gospel, which presents the life of Jesus while also teaching how Jesus' life fulfilled the Old Testament promises about salvation. Luke is called a "Synoptic Gospel" because his outline is very similar to that of Matthew and Mark.

Luke's Portrait of Jesus

Luke pictures Jesus as "the Son of Man" (see, for instance, Luke 5:24; 6:22; 9:58; 12:10). While not denying Jesus' divinity in any way, Luke nevertheless focuses on our Lord's humanity. He came to earth to be one of us! From the straw of Bethlehem's manger, to the hunger pangs after forty days of fasting in the wilderness, to the fatigue that kept Him fast asleep despite the storm on Galilee, to the hot tears that stung His eyes as He wept over Jerusalem's stubborn unbelief, to the whips that tore His flesh and the nails that pierced His hands, we see in Luke's Gospel Jesus' oneness with His people.

When we cry, Jesus truly does know how we feel. When we laugh with joy, He knows what that's like too. When we enjoy a delicious meal with friends and family or find ourselves sweaty and exhausted at the end of a hard day's work, our Savior understands.

But the term "Son of Man" means more. The title connects Jesus to the Old Testament prophets who foretold the Messiah's coming. The prophet Daniel, especially, used this title for the promised Savior (Daniel 7:13–14). In picking it up, Luke affirms Jesus' identity as the fulfillment of God's ancient promises.

How Can I Best Grow in Grace as I Read Luke?

Luke includes many details and describes events perhaps more fully than any of the other Gospel writers. Therefore, as you read Luke's Gospel, you may want to put yourself in the picture. Imagine standing in the crowd or sitting in the boat or reaching across the table for a piece of the bread Jesus and His disciples are sharing.

Ask yourself, what would I have seen? heard? thought? And how will the things I'm witnessing impact what I believe and do?

What are the key chapters and verses in Luke?

- **Luke 1–2** Jesus' Birth and Early Life
- **Luke 4** Jesus and Satan in the Wilderness
- **Luke 10:38–42** Mary and Martha
- **Luke 14–18** Parables and Teachings
- **Luke 19:1–10** Jesus and Zacchaeus
- **Luke 22–23** Jesus' Suffering and Death
- **Luke 24** Jesus' Resurrection and Ascension

Synagogue and Temple

At the time of Jesus, Jews built synagogues where they lived. Jews gathered in synagogues to worship, to study Scripture, and to govern the community. Their worship services then were different from ours today. Before, after, and maybe even during the readings and explanation of God's Word, the people in attendance would make comments and discuss the teaching.

Life in the Temple

In Jesus' time, the temple in Jerusalem was the most important place to worship. It was where sacrifices were made to atone for sins and where teachers gathered to teach and discuss God's Word. People could buy animals for sacrifices there or pay the tax that was required.

Jews who lived far away would travel to the temple to worship at least three times a year. These travelers were called pilgrims, and their journey was called a pilgrimage. Tens of thousands of pilgrims would fill Jerusalem during special religious celebrations and holidays. A pilgrimage was a joyful occasion. Jesus and His family made the pilgrimage during Passover every year.

The temple itself had many porches, gates, and courts.

Parts of a Synagogue

Raised Wooden Platform

The religious leader for the day stood on a platform. He read from the scrolls of the Law and the Prophets. There was no altar in a synagogue. Reading God's Word and praying took the place of offering sacrifices.

Portable Ark

The scrolls of the Law and the Prophets (the Old Testament books of the Bible) were kept in a portable ark. On special days, the ark was carried in a procession.

Moses Seat

After reading from the scrolls, the teacher sat down in the Moses Seat to explain the Scripture readings. Some of those gathered at the synagogue sat on benches that lined the walls. Others sat on mats on the floor.

Courts of the Temple

Many Israelite men dedicated their lives to professions in the temple. To be a priest, a man had to be a descendant of Levi. It was the priest's job to offer sacrifices on behalf of the people of Israel.

Rabbis were teachers, and they spent their time reading, discussing, and teaching the Scriptures. Ordinary people would gather to hear the teachings of the rabbis and to ask questions.

The Birth of the Savior

A Look at the Historical Facts of Jesus' Birth

Was Jesus born in a stable?

Luke 2:7 gives a few details about the actual birth of Jesus: Mary gave birth to Jesus, "wrapped Him in swaddling cloths and laid Him in a manger, because there was no place for them in the inn." Although this text does not say that He was born in a stable, many people assume this was so because Jesus was placed in a manger, a humble place where animals ate their dinner. Where are mangers usually found? Since a manger is a feeding trough, mangers will be found where there are animals. However, it is not known for sure that Jesus was born among animals.

Many caves dotted the hills around the city of Bethlehem. Caves were often used to house animals. Some historians say that animals were even sometimes kept in the same buildings where people lived.

A cave near Bethlehem.

What is the star that was seen by the Wise Men?

In the Church season of Epiphany, we celebrate the Wise Men, or Magi, coming to visit Jesus. How were they led to Jesus? They saw His star when it rose, and they followed the star to come worship Him.

What is this star? Some have speculated that the star was a comet. Others think it could have been an alignment of certain planets. Could it have been a supernova—a star that exploded? The Bible doesn't tell us. What is known is that God provided a miraculous sign because He wanted the

Gentile Magi to find the Christ Child and thus show that Jesus came for all people—not just Israelites, but all other nations as well.

Were there three kings who visited Jesus?

© CPH/Keith Neeley

A popular Christmas carol, "We Three Kings," causes many people to think that the Wise Men who visited Jesus were kings and that there were three of them. But the Bible does not specify that the Wise Men were kings, nor does it tell us how many came from the East to worship Him. Matthew 2:11 tells us that the Wise Men visited Jesus and presented three gifts to Him—gold, frankincense, and myrrh—so it is sometimes assumed that there were three givers of the three gifts. Martin Luther explained that these Wise Men were probably experts in the sciences, perhaps like professors in a university. They might have been stargazers or astrologers, men who studied the stars, since they noticed the unusual phenomenon of the star in the East.

Was Jesus in His manger when the Wise Men visited?

Two clues in the Bible lead most people to believe that the Wise Men visited Jesus when He was a little older. Matthew 2:11 relates how the Wise Men found Jesus: "And going into the house they saw the child with Mary His mother, and they fell down and worshiped Him." According to this text, Jesus was living in a house.

© CPH/Cheri Bladholm

Matthew 2:16 helps determine Jesus' age at the time of the Wise Men's visit. When Herod realized that he had been tricked by the Wise Men, in anger, he had all the boys killed that were two years old and younger. It is possible that Jesus could have been nearly two years old by the time the Magi visited.

Gabriel and Mary

© CPH/Cheri Bladholm

One of the most famous scenes depicted in classical art is that of the angel Gabriel greeting the Virgin Mary (Luke 1:26–38). Artists have painted countless portraits of that meeting, seeking to capture the wonder and awe that Mary must have felt, while at the same time conveying the sense of peace and comfort Gabriel sought to bring to the young woman. The two characters are key instruments in the nativity story.

Gabriel is one of two angels named in Scripture. (The other is Michael [Daniel 12:1; Revelation 12:7; and others].) Gabriel's name can mean "mighty man of God" or "God is strong." He was the angel who appeared to Zechariah, telling him that he and Elizabeth would become parents (Luke 1:19). Gabriel also appeared in the Old Testament, delivering God's message to Daniel (Daniel 8:16; 9:21).

Mary was a young Jewish girl whom God chose to be the mother of the Christ Child. She was descended from the house of David, and because she was no doubt older than twelve, she was required to register in Bethlehem. This registration took place around the time that her child, Jesus, was to be born. Mary knew that the child she was carrying was her Savior.

Later, we see that she had some understanding of His ministry when she told workers at a wedding to listen to Him and follow His instructions. When Jesus was crucified, Mary was there, crying as only a mother can for the loss of her child. Even on the cross, Jesus cared for His mother, appointing His disciple John to watch over her. From that time forward, Mary is said to have stayed in John's home.

Mary's willingness to serve God as the mother of His only Son is an example of faith, which only God can give. We, too, serve God as His children, though imperfectly and from wrong motives. Like Mary, we are saved not by the actions God inspires in us, but through His gift of faith through Word and Sacrament.

Old Testament Rituals for Jesus

Jesus began fulfilling the Law for us very early during His life on earth. These events are important parts of the Gospels of Matthew and Luke.

Naming of Jesus

The angel announced to Mary and later to Joseph what the child would be named. Eight days after Jesus was born, He was circumcised and given the name "Jesus" (Luke 2:21).

Presentation in the Temple

An important ritual in Israel at the time of Jesus was the presentation of the firstborn son in the temple forty days after his birth. The presentation recalled the Passover, when the angel of the Lord passed over, or spared, the firstborn of the Israelites from death, but destroyed the firstborn of the Egyptians.

As faithful Israelites, Mary and Joseph brought Jesus, their firstborn son, to the temple for presentation to consecrate Him to the service of the Lord as the Law required. Jesus' presentation is important because He came to fulfill every part of the Law.

The Law of God required that a firstborn male be consecrated to the Lord (Exodus 13:2), or dedicated for a sacred purpose. If the child was not given into the service of the Lord, the parents needed to redeem him, or buy him back, by paying five shekels (Numbers 3:46–47). Mary and Joseph may not have made this payment since Jesus was consecrated to the Lord in the fullest possible way.

At the time of presentation in the temple, Mary also would have undergone a ritual purification. After a woman bore a son, she was considered unclean for forty days. That meant she could not touch anything holy or come into the sanctuary. After the forty days, a woman went to the temple for cleansing, bringing to the priest a year-old lamb for a burnt offering and either a pigeon or a turtledove for a sin offering. A poor person, however, was required to bring only two turtledoves or two pigeons.

For nearly two thousand years, the Church has celebrated both of these events—the Purification of Mary and the Presentation of Our Lord—on February 2, forty days after Christmas. The presentation marks the meeting between Jesus and the elderly Simeon and Anna. Simeon's song, called the Nunc Dimittis, is an important part of the Divine Service (*LSB*, pp. 165, 182, 199, 211, 258).

The Passion of Christ

The word *passion* today is often understood in terms of an intense feeling, such as saying, "His passion is soccer." However, in the history of the Church, we refer to the suffering, crucifixion, and death of Jesus as "the Passion of Christ" because the common meaning for the word *passion* referred to Jesus' suffering and death. In older times, the word meant "suffering much pain and death" and referred to the suffering one endured at the hands of others. Jesus' Passion was the trial, the mocking, the spitting, the crown of thorns placed on His head, the whipping, having to carry the cross, being nailed to the cross, the sour vinegar He was given to drink, and the spear piercing His side. This suffering He endured obediently to take away the sins of the world.

© Nola Rin/Shutterstock, Inc.

Crucifix

A crucifix depicts Jesus dying on the cross. Jesus endured His Passion so that we can be redeemed. Seeing a crucifix reminds Christians of the great love of our Savior, whose death on the cross prevents us from being lost in sin and separated from God. Because of Jesus' death for us, we are beloved children of God, and we will someday go to heaven.

Sanhedrin

After Jesus was betrayed by Judas, He went with the soldiers from the Garden of Gethsemane to stand before "Caiaphas the high priest, where the scribes and elders had gathered" (Matthew 26:57). This group of Jewish leaders, the ruling council, was also known as "the Sanhedrin." Although they did not have the authority to put Jesus to death, they could decide whether Jesus was guilty of doing something wrong according to the Jewish laws. If they found Him guilty, then they could send Him to the Roman governor, Pontius Pilate, who would decide His punishment.

On the night of Jesus' trial, the Sanhedrin declared that Jesus was guilty of blasphemy because He claimed to be God. Blasphemy means "speaking evil about God." However, they were so wrong! Jesus, both God and man, was not blaspheming. They were! He was speaking the truth. Jesus is God. After making their false ruling, the Sanhedrin sent Jesus to Pilate to decide His punishment.

Pontius Pilate

The Roman governor, Pontius Pilate, who was in charge of Jesus' trial,

© Jamam Isachar/Israelimages.com

thought Jesus was innocent and wanted to release Him. His wife had had a dream, and afterward, she told Pilate to have nothing to do with Jesus, "that righteous man" (Matthew 27:19). So Pilate tried to talk to Jesus and to convince the crowd that they should release Him. In the end, though, he decided to have Jesus scourged and crucified (v. 26).

Releasing One Prisoner at the Passover

The Bible tells us that it was a custom at the time of Passover for the governor to release a prisoner to the people. Pilate told the crowd to choose between Jesus and a criminal named Barabbas. Barabbas was a known "bad guy" in Jerusalem at the time of Jesus. In Luke 23:19, we learn that he was part of a mob that committed murder; and in Matthew 27:16, we learn that he was a well-known robber. The crowd chose Barabbas; Jesus was punished.

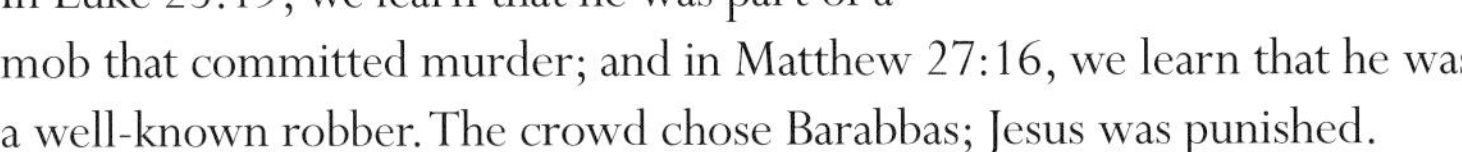
© CPH

© CPH

Flogging

In Jesus' time, convicted criminals were often punished by flogging. This meant that the prisoner's bare back was whipped with a cat-o'-nine-tails, which was made of leather straps with small bits of rock or bone attached. This made the whipping all the more painful. The prisoner bled a great deal, and some even died.

Crown of Thorns and Robe

After Jesus was flogged, the soldiers mocked Him by twisting together a "crown" of thorny stems and pushing it down onto his head. If you've ever been poked by a thorn on a rose bush or some other plant, you have some idea of how much this would hurt. The soldiers then placed a purple (some translations say "scarlet") robe on Jesus' shoulders. Purple (or scarlet) signified royalty, but by using this royal color for the robe, the soldiers were actually mocking Jesus rather than worshiping Him as the King.

Carrying His Cross

After the trial, the scourging, and the mocking—all of His suffering—Jesus was paraded through the streets of Jerusalem. He even had to carry His own cross to the place outside the city limits where He was to be crucified. However, His body was so weak that He could not manage it alone. So they pulled someone out of the crowd—a man named Simon—to help carry the cross. Simon was from Cyrene (Luke 23:26), which is in northern Africa in an area that is in modern-day Libya.

Crucifixion was a horrible yet common punishment for criminals. The criminal would be nailed by his hands and feet to the beams of the cross. Then he was left hanging there to die.

Death usually came because the person could not breathe any longer. The body's position, hanging from the cross, led to suffocation.

Golgotha

The place outside Jerusalem where Jesus was crucified was called "Golgotha," which means "the place of the skull." Scholars think it was referred to by this name because of the rocky formations on the hillside of the site. The Latin name for this place is "Calvary." Although that word does not appear in English translations of the Bible, it has been used in the Church to refer to the place where Jesus was crucified.

Took, Blessed, Broke, Gave

The First Passover

The Passover feast is full of symbolism for Jewish people. It is celebrated once a year as a reminder of how God saved the children of Israel and helped them leave Egypt and return to the Promised Land.

The Egyptian pharaoh refused to let the children of Israel leave, so God promised to send an angel to kill the oldest child in every home in Egypt. The children of Israel were told to kill lambs and paint the blood of the lambs on their doorposts and lintel (the beam at the top of the door). When the angel saw the blood on the doorposts and lintel, he would "pass over" those homes.

The Last Supper

Jesus and His disciples were celebrating the Passover on the night before His crucifixion and death. The Passover meal includes lamb as a reminder of the lambs that were sacrificed, as well as other foods—unleavened bread, bitter herbs, and wine—that help Jewish people remember other aspects of their lives in Egypt and how God delivered them from slavery. (See p. 37) Jesus did something very unusual at this Passover dinner, though. "And He took bread, and when He had given thanks, He broke it and gave it to them, saying, 'This is My body, which is given for you. Do this in remembrance of Me' " (Luke 22:19).

Jesus then did the same thing with the wine. After the Passover meal was over, traditionally an additional cup of wine was drunk. It is referred to as the "cup of blessing" because it comes after the blessing at the end of the meal. It is also called the "cup of redemption" because it represents the blood of the sacrificed lamb. Imagine the disciples' surprise when Jesus announced that the cup of redemption was His blood, and that they were to drink it to remember Him (v. 20)!

An Easter Supper

© Christ Evangelical Lutheran Church, Saginaw, Michigan

The two disciples on the road to Emmaus recognized Jesus in "the breaking of the bread" after they had invited Him to stay and eat with them. Jesus was a guest in their home, yet He acted as the host: "When He was at table with them, He took the bread and blessed and broke it and gave it to them" (Luke 24:30).

No wonder their eyes were opened! This was not a sacramental meal, not the Lord's Supper. However, the words used in the Bible to describe it clearly suggest the Last Supper where Jesus instituted the Sacrament of the Altar and our celebration of it. By the power of the Holy Spirit and through Jesus' words and actions, these disciples recognized Jesus as the risen Lord. In the Word and Sacrament at the Lord's Supper, God allows us to do the same—recognize the body and blood of the risen Lord, given and shed for us.

Why were Moses and Elijah at Jesus' transfiguration?

© CPH/Robert Hunt

Why did God send Moses, to whom God gave the Law, and Elijah, the prophet, to appear with Jesus on the mountain? What connection do these men have with Jesus' ministry? In important ways, they confirm Jesus' identity as the Savior of the world, for all of Scripture points to Jesus Christ.

God's Law

God gave His people the Ten Commandments through Moses to serve as a curb to bad behavior and to keep order in this world. God's Law guides us in our daily living, showing us how God wants us to treat our neighbors. Most importantly, it leads us to see that we are unable to live up to its demands, and thus, we are sinners in need of a Savior. From the time of Adam and Eve's fall into sin, God has promised to redeem and save His beloved people through the Seed of the woman. That Seed is Jesus, true God and true man.

God's Word

As God's messengers, prophets did not just foretell future events. They proclaimed many kinds of messages from God, including commands, instructions, and history. God sent His prophets to call people to repent of their sins.

The great prophet Elijah, whose name means "the Lord is my God," was sent to show that Baal was a worthless idol and to turn the people back to the true God. (Read about it in 1 Kings 18:16–46.) Malachi, another prophet of God, foretold that an Elijah would appear again before the Savior came. John the Baptist fulfilled that role. Now the time had come for Jesus to carry out God's plan of salvation.

Witnesses to the Truth

In Bible times, it took two or three witnesses to settle a dispute. The witnesses' testimony established the truth to the satisfaction of the courts. Moses and Elijah witnessed to the truth about Jesus on the Mount of Transfiguration. Jesus is the perfect lawkeeper in our place. He is the Savior of whom the prophets foretold. By appearing with Jesus, these ancient fathers, Moses and Elijah, showed and confirmed that Jesus was the long-awaited Savior.

Jesus' Exodus

The Bible reports that Jesus, Moses, and Elijah spoke together on the mount at Jesus' transfiguration. Luke reports that they talked about Jesus' "departure, which He was about to accomplish at Jerusalem" (Luke 9:31). Jesus, in His suffering, death, and resurrection, would fulfill all that Moses, Elijah, and all God's Old Testament people hoped for—forgiveness of sins, life, and salvation for all who believe.

John

Into John

This Gospel at a Glance

- Like Matthew, Mark, and Luke, John also wrote the history of Jesus' earthly life and ministry. His Gospel differs from the Synoptic Gospels written by the other three authors in several significant ways.
- The Gospel of John was written sometime after the Synoptic Gospels, perhaps as late as AD 90. Because the facts of Jesus' life had already been recorded by Matthew, Mark, and Luke, John takes a more theological, doctrinal approach as he writes.
- Except for the accounts of Jesus' Baptism, the feeding of the five thousand, and Jesus' suffering and death, John repeats little of the material included in the Synoptic Gospels. John focuses much more on what Jesus taught than on what He did. When John does record a miracle, he uses it to introduce or to illustrate a specific teaching.
- John was an eyewitness to the events he records, one of the "inner circle" of Jesus' disciples. He is not John the Baptist.
- Tradition tells us that the apostle John became the pastor of the Church in Ephesus and that he was the only one of Jesus' original twelve disciples to die a natural death.
- John also wrote the three letters that bear his name (1 John, 2 John, 3 John) and the Book of Revelation.
- John uses deceptively simple words to convey powerful truths. As you read, look for words like *light, life, word, truth, hour, bread, believe,* and *love*.

- In the entire Gospel, John never refers to himself by name. He speaks of himself a half dozen times as "the disciple whom Jesus loved." This is not a prideful claim, but an expression of wonder. "Think of it!" he says, almost to himself; "Jesus loves me!"

How is the Book of John classified?

John is a Gospel, which presents the life of Jesus while also teaching how Jesus' life fulfilled the Old Testament promises about salvation. John is different from the Synoptic Gospels of Matthew, Mark, and Luke since John presented a unique outline and collection of sayings from Jesus.

John's Portrait of Jesus

Just as Luke focuses on Jesus' humanity, John focuses on our Lord's divinity. He portrays Jesus as the eternal Son of God who took on human flesh and blood to save us.

John records seven "signs"—miraculous evidence chosen because it points the reader to Jesus' true identity as the Son of God and our eternal Savior. John also records seven "I am" sayings of Jesus. In these sayings, Jesus clearly claims to be divine, connecting Himself to the great "I am" of Moses' burning bush in Exodus 3. (See the charts "Seven Signs in John's Gospel" and "Seven 'I am' Sayings of Jesus" on pages 340 and 350–351.)

John uses the word *believe* or a variation of it more than fifty times in his Gospel. And he spells out his distinct purpose in writing the Gospel that carries his name:

> *Jesus did many other signs in the presence of the disciples, which are not written in this book; but* these are written so that you may believe *that Jesus is the Christ, the Son of God, and that by believing you may have life in His name.*
>
> *(John 20:30–31; emphasis added)*

How Can I Best Grow in Grace as I Read John?

We might divide John's Gospel into roughly two parts:

- **John 1–11** The Book of Signs
- **John 12–21** The Book of the Passion

As you read John's Gospel, prepare to slow down and savor the words. John's vocabulary makes his book seem simple. In reality, it's deep and powerful! Let the truth of Jesus' love wash over you and create wonder in your heart. You, too, are a disciple "Jesus loves"!

Key Chapters in John

- **John 1** The Word of God, the Lamb of God
- **John 3** God So Loved the World
- **John 6** The Bread of Life
- **John 8** The Light of the World
- **John 10** The Good Shepherd
- **John 11** Lazarus Raised
- **John 13** Jesus Washes the Disciples' Feet
- **John 14–16** Jesus' Final Teachings
- **John 17** Jesus' High Priestly Prayer
- **John 18–19** Jesus' Suffering and Death
- **John 20–21** Jesus' Resurrection Appearances

Seven Signs in John's Gospel	
John 2:1–11	**Changing water into wine**
John 4:46–54	**Healing the nobleman's son**
John 5:1–15	**Healing a lame man**
John 6:1–15	**Feeding five thousand**
John 6:16–22	**Stilling the storm**
John 9:1–41	**Healing the man born blind**
John 11:1–45	**Raising Lazarus from the dead**

John attaches the term *sign* to only four of these miracles (see 2:11; 4:54; 6:14; 12:18). But the structure of the book and the selective way John chooses the miracles he includes lead some scholars to conclude that John intended each of the seven to be signs that pointed to Jesus as the Messiah (see also 2:23; 3:2; 6:2; 7:31; 20:30).

The most convincing sign of all was, of course, Jesus' own resurrection. The final miracle recorded by John (21:1–14) took place outside the view of the multitudes and serves as a kind of appendix to John's Gospel.

Marriage

At the time Jesus lived on earth, most young men and women were married by the time they were seventeen years old. Some were married as young as thirteen or fourteen. If you lived in Bible times, your parents would choose the person you would marry.

The Marriage Feast

Many guests were invited to the marriage feast. The feast itself could last as long as a week. The groom was expected to provide a feast worthy of his social standing. Guests, including relatives, neighbors, and visitors who were with the family at the time, were seated according to their rank or according to the honor the groom wished to show to them.

The Wedding Ceremony

On the day of the wedding, the bridegroom and his friends dressed in their finest clothes and walked to the bride's home. The bride's friends also dressed in fine clothing and veils. They carried lamps and went out to meet the groom and his friends. The bride, perfumed and beautifully dressed, would greet the groom at the door. The whole festive procession would then walk to the groom's house for the marriage feast.

Isaac and Rebekah

Abraham's trusted servant arranged the marriage between Abraham's son, Isaac, and Rebekah. But God was their matchmaker too. Read about it in Genesis 24.

The Well at Sychar

No faucets. No running water.

In Bible times, all the water needed by the family had to be carried from a river, lake, stream, or well. A woman usually carried water in a large clay pot on her head or shoulder. Women of the village met at the well in the cool of the morning and the evening.

© Hanan Isachar/Israelimages.com

© Israel Talby/Israelimages.com

Jacob's Well

Jacob's well still exists today, and the water is cool and sweet. The location of the city of Sychar mentioned in John 4:5 is not known, but the modern village of Askar is close to the well. Jacob's Well was cleaned out in 1935. At that time, it was 138 feet deep. Water is usually abundant in this region, so it is rather odd that the well was dug so deep.

© Richard Nowitz/Israelimages.com

Cisterns

If no springs or brooks or underground streams were in the area, the people would dig a hole, maybe at the base of a hill, plaster it so that it could hold water, then collect the rainwater that ran down the hill into the hole. They also used clay pots to collect rainwater.

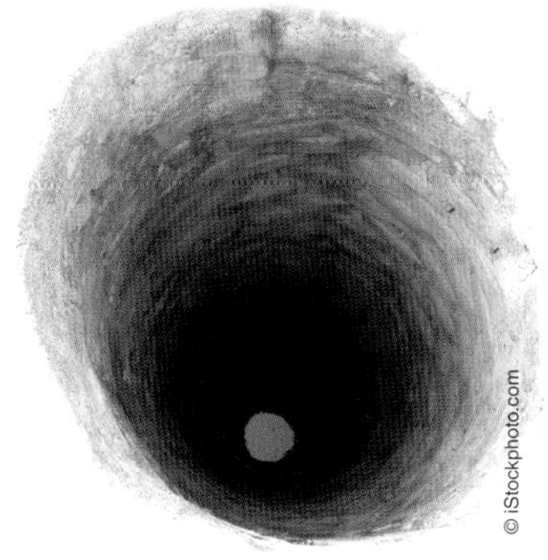

© iStockphoto.com

© Corel

Where did the Samaritans come from?

When the Assyrians destroyed the Northern Kingdom of Israel, most of the Israelites who lived there were moved to other countries. The Israelites who remained in the land lived with and married people brought from other countries. The children born to these marriages were of mixed race and were not full-blooded Israelites. These children and their descendants lived in the region of Samaria and became the people known as "Samaritans."

© Johan Swanepoel/Shutterstock, Inc.

Lion Attacks

The people the Assyrians brought from the other countries worshiped all kinds of different gods. God wanted them to repent of their idolatry, so He sent lions to kill some of the people (2 Kings 17:25). The people told the king of Assyria that lions were attacking them because they didn't know what the God of Samaria required. The king sent an Israelite priest who taught the people how to worship the true God.

Samaritan Worship and Beliefs

The Samaritans' Bible consisted only of the five books written by Moses. Samaritans didn't use nor know much about the other Old Testament books. The Samaritans also built their own temple on Mount Gerizim instead of worshiping in Jerusalem.

Why did the Jews look down on the Samaritans?

- The Jews thought they were superior to the Samaritans. Why?
- The Jewish Bible contained all the books of the Old Testament.
- For the most part, the Jews had followed God's command not to marry people from other countries.
- The Jews worshiped at the temple in the Holy City of Jerusalem.

Because of their religious beliefs and their animosity toward the Samaritans, Jews avoided traveling through Samaria. They crossed the Jordan and traveled on the east side to get where they wanted to go. Since the Samaritans were regarded as unclean, Jews would not drink from a cup handled by a Samaritan. Many Jews would not even speak the word *Samaritan*.

Did Jesus look down on the Samaritans?

Jesus was a Jew, but His attitude toward the Samaritans was very different from the attitude of His fellow Jews. Jesus willingly traveled through Samaria. Jesus spoke to the Samaritan woman, and He was willing to drink out of her vessel. Jesus stayed with the Samaritans for two days in order to give them the gift of faith (John 4:1–42). Jesus loved the Samaritans just as He loved His fellow Jews—just as He loves us!

The Good Shepherd

In John 10:1–18, Jesus tells the Pharisees that He is the Good Shepherd. He uses this picture so that His people can understand His tremendous love for them.

How do I know the Good Shepherd?

- A shepherd knows his sheep and calls each one by name. The Good Shepherd calls me by name at my Baptism, where the Holy Spirit gives me faith to be His child.

- A shepherd leads his sheep to green grass to eat and to pure water to drink. The Good Shepherd feeds me with His own body and blood in the Sacrament of the Altar so that my faith is strengthened and so that I may know the forgiveness of sins.

- A shepherd directs his flock so they stay on safe ground. The Good Shepherd has fulfilled the Law so that I may walk in righteousness.

- A shepherd watches his sheep to keep them safe. The Good Shepherd sets His holy angels over me, so I may be safe from the power of sin and the devil.

- A shepherd keeps harmful animals away from his sheep. The Good Shepherd protects me from the evil that the devil would do to me.

- A shepherd seeks out a lost sheep, no matter how often it wanders. The Good Shepherd seeks me while I am lost in sin, and He forgives me continually.

- A shepherd purchases his flock with money. The Good Shepherd has purchased me with His holy, precious blood.

© CPH/ Donald Kueker

Roman Execution

Have you ever stopped to think that the most popular piece of Christian jewelry is actually a symbol of an instrument of torture and execution? Crucifixion, suspending the condemned person from a wooden cross, was originally a Persian method of execution that was incredibly brutal. It was one of the worst forms of execution, involving an enormous amount of suffering. In fact, Romans decided to reserve crucifixion for the lowest members of society—slaves and those who were not Roman citizens.

Preparation

Before crucifixion, the victim was often flogged with a whip. Although the Jewish people limited the number of stripes—strokes of the whip—to no more than forty, the Romans placed no limits on their flogging.

Afterward, they took the condemned person to the cross, where they hammered large iron nails through the bones of the wrists and heels. In a supposed act of mercy, the soldiers sometimes offered the victim wine/vinegar mixed with myrrh to dull the pain. Jesus refused such wine.

Crucifixion

Once raised on the cross, it could take several days before the victim died. The weight of the body on the outstretched arms gradually compressed the chest, making it increasingly difficult for the person to breathe. Fluid might fill the victim's lungs, hastening death. Late in the afternoon on the day of Jesus' crucifixion, the two criminals beside Him had their legs broken to hasten their death. Jesus, however, was already dead, so there was no need to break His bones. Even so, the soldiers pierced His side to make sure that He was dead.

Completion

After execution, the condemned person's body often remained unburied, or it was discarded. Joseph of Arimathea, however, requested permission from Pilate to bury Jesus' body properly. Before sundown on Good Friday, which would be the beginning of the Sabbath, the soldiers took Jesus' body from the cross, and Joseph buried Him in a nearby tomb.

Through this suffering and death, Jesus fulfilled for us what we could not do ourselves. He paid the price for the sins of all humankind. His resurrection on the third day would complete His triumph on our behalf.

Fishing in Bible Times

© Hanan Isachar/Israelimages.com

Jesus' first disciples were fishermen. Jesus told them they would be fishing for men. Their fishing skills may have had some application to their new calling. Fishermen needed patience, perseverance, courage, and knowledge of their craft. These qualities would prove helpful in their new line of fishing.

The fishermen during Jesus' time used three different kinds of nets: the trammel net, the dragnet, and the cast net. Each was used for a different type of fishing.

The trammel net was probably the net used when Jesus called Simon, Andrew, James, and John to be disciples. This net consisted of two outer nets and one inner net. The outer nets were about five feet tall and were made of a large mesh, while the inner net was finer mesh. After dropping one end of the net into the water, the fishermen would let out the rest as they formed a circle in the water. Once the net had been arranged in a barrel shape in the water, the fish would be caught. Struggling against the inner net only resulted in being caught by the outer one as well. The nets had to be cleaned and mended after each throw and again at the end of the day.

Because the dragnet, the longest and heaviest net, was about a hundred feet long and twelve feet high, it needed sinkers to give it weight to drop it to the floor of the sea. One boat held the rope that stretched from the bottom to the top at one end of the net while the other boat sailed until the net was stretched out. The second boat then grabbed the rope at the other end of the net, and both boats dragged the net to the shore.

The round cast net was small enough to be thrown into the water from the shore or a boat. Small weights were tied around the edges of the net. After it parachuted into the water, the fisherman would dive underneath and gather the edges together, trapping fish inside.

The Sea of Galilee supports thirty types of freshwater fish. The musht, or comb fish, is most plentiful, and was probably the type of fish the disciples were catching when Jesus "caught" them. Musht are often fried because their flat shape lends itself well to a skillet. Eventually, this fish was given the nickname "St. Peter's fish."

The Significance of "I Am"

Numerous times in the Gospel of John, Jesus refers to Himself using a metaphor beginning with the words "I am":

"I am the bread of life."
(John 6:35)

© Magda Zurawska/Shutterstock, Inc.

© Vladimir Daragan/Shutterstock, Inc.

"I am the light of the world."
(John 8:12)

© CPH/ Keith Neeley

"I am the door of the sheep."
(John 10:7)

© CPH/ Robert Hook

"I am the good shepherd."
(John 10:11, 14)

Jesus could have described Himself and His ministry in other ways, but He knew that using the words "I am" would have special meaning for Jewish believers. In Exodus 3:14, God said to Moses, "I am who I am. . . . Say this to the people of Israel, 'I am has sent me to you.' "

"I am the resurrection and the life."
(John 11:25)

"I am the true vine."
(John 11:25)

"I am the way, and the truth, and the life."
(John 14:6)

Jesus could have said "I am like a good shepherd" or "I am like the door of the sheep" to describe His nature and His ministry. Simply using the words "I am" was His way of saying to the Jewish people that He was God Himself, the promised Messiah. Though He used common metaphors—things like bread, light, shepherds, and vines—that were familiar to all people at that time, Jesus declared Himself to be the Savior of the world, who would bring God's sheep into His sheepfold.

Acts

Into Acts

This Book at a Glance

Acts is sometimes called "The Acts of the Apostles." However, a better name might be "The Acts of Jesus Christ through the Apostles" or "The Acts of the Holy Spirit through His Church." Throughout this historical book, we see God at work to preserve and extend His kingdom.

Theme verse: [Jesus said,] "You will receive power when the Holy Spirit has come upon you, and you will be My witnesses in Jerusalem and in all Judea and Samaria, and to the end of the earth" (Acts 1:8).

How is the Book of Acts classified?

Acts is a book of history, which speaks most often about the lives of Peter and Paul.

Who wrote Acts? When? Why?

Together, the books of Luke and Acts form a two-volume history. Volume 1 records Jesus' birth, ministry, death, and resurrection. Volume 2 describes the way in which He continued His work on earth through His followers after His ascension.

Luke, the "beloved physician" (Colossians 4:14) and traveling companion of the apostle Paul, wrote both volumes. He completed Acts sometime between AD 60 and 62. Luke was an eyewitness of some of the events he records. He no doubt interviewed eyewitnesses as he wrote other sections of this book.

Acts forms a bridge, connecting the Gospels and their accounts of Jesus' life and ministry with the Epistles (letters) that form the last half or so of the New Testament. Acts gives us some of the background information we need in order to understand those letters and the people to whom they were addressed.

Where is Jesus in Acts?

It's hard to read Acts and not see Jesus! This book describes the transition of the Holy Christian Church from a tiny, mostly Jewish group with its headquarters in Jerusalem to a worldwide faith community made up of mostly Gentiles. This transition took place by the beginning of the second century! How did Christ's Church make that astonishing leap?

God was at work! Jesus had promised His followers, "I will build My church, and the gates of hell shall not prevail against it" (Matthew 16:18). Our Lord kept that promise—and in a dramatic way! Acts records the adventure as it happened. Acts portrays Jesus as the ever-present, ever-living Lord of the Church.

What are the key chapters and verses in Acts?

- **Acts 1–12** The Expansion of the Church (This expansion, from Jerusalem to Judea and on into Samaria, happened just as Jesus had promised before He ascended into heaven [Acts 1:8].)
- **Acts 9** The Conversion of "Saul the Persecutor" to "Paul the Missionary"
- **Acts 13–14** Paul's First Missionary Journey
- **Acts 15** The Council of Jerusalem (At this famous council, the Church affirmed that salvation comes by grace alone through faith alone to both Jews and Gentiles alike.)
- **Acts 16–18:22** Paul's Second Missionary Journey.
- **Acts 18:23–21:16** Paul's Third Missionary Journey.
- **Acts 21:17–28:31** Paul Travels to Rome to Testify before Caesar.

How can I best grow in grace as I read Acts?

Acts ends awkwardly. It doesn't tell us what happened to the apostle Paul in Rome. To readers, it feels like an unfinished story. Luke likely did this on purpose. The story hasn't ended! Jesus is still at work through His Church. You and I are still His witnesses to those in an unbelieving world who don't yet know Him! As Jesus' disciples today, we get to help finish the story as we live and witness in love.

Life in the Early Christian Church

At the time when Christianity was just beginning to spread, Christians used Jewish synagogues as meeting places for worship. Later, Christians gathered in homes. Special church buildings weren't built until the third century AD. Christians not only worshiped together, but also supported each other physically with food and clothing and by providing for other needs. They especially helped the poor, the widows, and the orphans.

The Worship Service

Sunday was the day for group worship in the Early Church. Worship included singing, prayer, Scripture readings, and participation in the Lord's Supper. The offerings gathered were often food and other items needed for the poor. Sometimes worship included the sharing of a meal.

The Church in Rome

Because of persecution, Christians in Rome sometimes gathered for worship in caves called catacombs. Christians had buried their dead in these underground caves. There were hundreds of miles of catacombs under the city of Rome.

The walls in the catacombs were covered with drawings of scenes from the Old and New Testaments, including the stories of Jonah, Noah, Daniel in the lions' den, the raising of Lazarus from the dead, and the Good Shepherd. There were also pictures in the catacombs that showed church leaders using a seashell to pour water over people being baptized.

© Shutterstock, Inc.

Persecution in the Early Church

The Roman people worshiped many different false gods. Many did not like the Christians. The Roman emperor Nero blamed the Christians for a fire that destroyed much of Rome in AD 64. Angry Romans arrested Christians. Christians were expected to curse Jesus Christ and offer praise and sacrifices to Roman gods. If they refused, they were killed. Some were torn to death by animals. Some were crucified. Some were beheaded. Some were burned alive. These executions took place in front of large audiences who cheered and celebrated, as if they were watching a sporting event. Peter and Paul were probably martyred during this time of persecution.

Even during these days when persecution was common, the Christian Church grew. Many early Christians considered it a great blessing to die for the Christian faith.

Prisons

Prisons in Bible times were different from prisons today. A prison or jail was a place to keep prisoners until trial or until they were punished in other ways. Sometimes people were in prison for months or even years before they had a trial. If a prisoner was found guilty during a trial, prison was not usually given as punishment. Punishments could include fines, flogging or beating, exile (being forced to leave their home or being told where to live), or death.

Conditions were difficult in ancient prisons. Often there were dark chambers with only small amounts of light coming in through very small openings in the walls. The prisoners often were mistreated. Prisoners were commonly chained during the day and put into stocks at night (Acts 16:23–24).

Prisoners in Bible Times

Joseph	Genesis 39:11–23; 41:14
Joseph's Brothers	Genesis 42:15–20
Samson	Judges 16:21–26
Jeremiah	Jeremiah 37:1–21
Unforgiving Serant	Matthew 18:21–35
John the Baptist	Matthew 4:12; 11:2–3; 14:3–10; Mark 6:17–29; Luke 3:19–20
Barabbas	Matthew 27:15–23; Mark 15:6–15
Peter and John	Acts 4:1–4
Early Christians	Acts 8:3; Hebrews 13:3
Peter	Acts 12:1–18
Paul and Silas	Acts 16:16–40
Paul	Acts 24:24–27; Ephesians 3:1; 6:20; Philemon 1

The prison didn't provide daily necessities for the prisoners. Family members and friends brought food, blankets, medicine, and other items to the prisoners. Without help from family and friends, prisoners might starve or die of illness. This may be why Jesus commended those who visited prisoners (Matthew 25:36). Such a visit was more than social; it provided some of the prisoners' daily needs.

Guards were held personally responsible for prisoners. If a prisoner escaped, a guard might be punished or even killed for neglecting his duty (Acts 12:19; 16:27).

The Ethiopian

Cliff dwellings on the shore of the Nile River

The Ethiopian that Philip met on the road between Jerusalem and Gaza was an important man. He was the royal treasurer for Candace, the queen of the Ethiopians.

Candace, the Queen of the Ethiopians

Candace was not her name, though. Actually, it was her title, just like the title pharaoh. The queen of the Ethiopians at this time was Amantitere (c. AD 25–41), who is mentioned by Roman authors. Candace had to take care of all the secular, or nonreligious, duties of the kingdom. The king was thought to be much too sacred for such work.

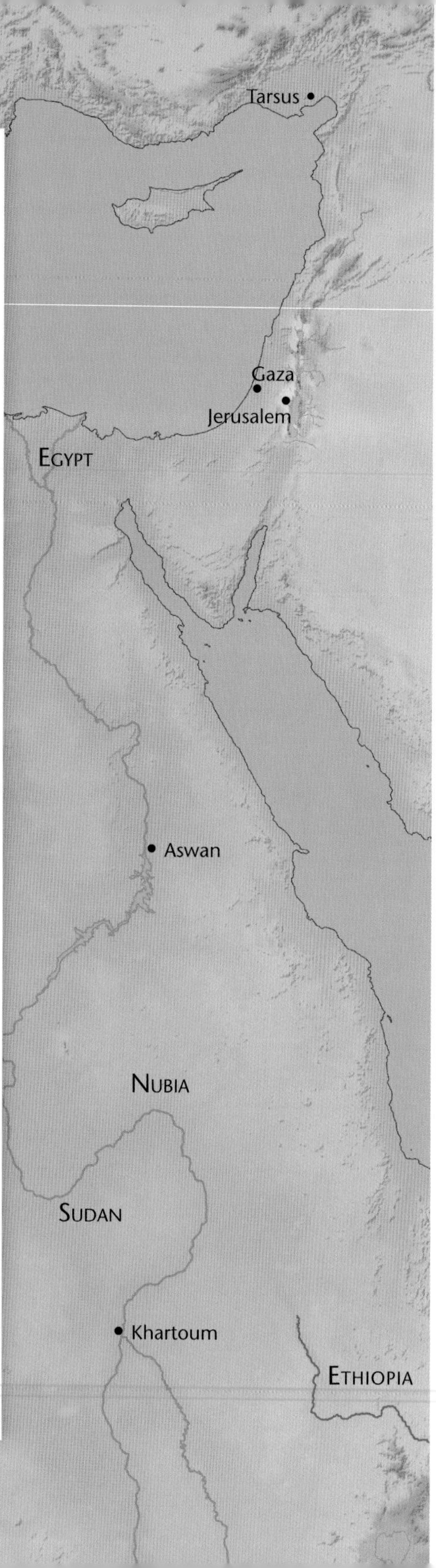

Where was the Ethiopian born?

The Ethiopian was not from the area we know as Ethiopia today. He was actually from Nubia, a land that stretched from the Upper Nile region at Aswan, Egypt, to modern-day Khartoum, Sudan. The people from Nubia were much darker skinned than Egyptians. The Greeks called them "Aithiopes," which means "burnt-faced ones," and their land was called "Aithiopia" ("Land of the Burnt Faces"). In New Testament Greek, Nubia is called "Aithiopia," or "Ethiopia."

Why had the Ethiopian made the long trip to Jerusalem?

The Ethiopian was a Gentile who believed in the God of Israel. He probably went to worship in Jerusalem for one of the Jewish religious festivals.

He might have heard about Jesus before Philip talked to

Ethiopian church in Jerusalem

him, but the Bible doesn't tell us if he had or not. He definitely didn't know that Jesus was his Savior.

Why was the Ethiopian reading out loud?

People at that time almost always read aloud, being trained to do so. Ancient handwriting and ancient books were sometimes very difficult to read because a manuscript might have no spaces between words, and vowels might be left out.

How did Philip and the Ethiopian find water in the desert?

There were natural pools, springs, and brooks in this desert area of Judea. Some believe the Ethiopian was baptized in the Wadi el Hasi just north of Gaza.

Paul's Missionary Journeys

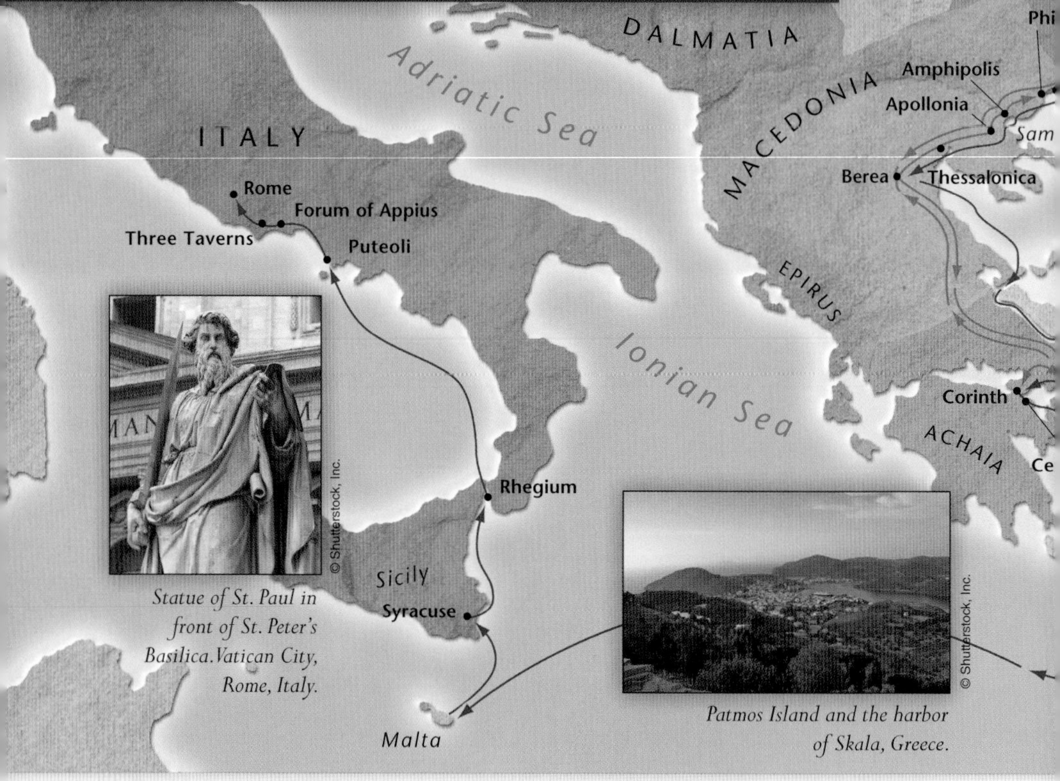

Statue of St. Paul in front of St. Peter's Basilica.Vatican City, Rome, Italy.

Patmos Island and the harbor of Skala, Greece.

Paul's First Missionary Journey AD 47–48 (Acts 13:1–14:28)

Who: Paul, Barnabas, John Mark (the latter leaves them in Perga to return to Jerusalem).

Where: Antioch in Syria, Seleucia, Salamis, Paphos, Perga, Antioch in Pisidia, Iconium, Lystra, Derbe. Retraced their route to Pisidian Antioch, then to Attalia and Syrian Antioch.

What: Preached to Jews first in the synagogues, then to Gentiles.

Paul's Second Missionary Journey AD 49–51 (Acts 15:39–18:22)

Who: Paul and Silas; Timothy joins them in Lystra; Luke joins them in Troas; Aquila and Priscilla travel with Paul to Ephesus

Where: Syrian Antioch, through Syria and Cilicia, Derbe, Lystra, Galatia and Phrygia, Troas, via the island Samothrace to Macedonia, Neapolis, Philippi, Amphipolis, Apollonia, Thessalonica, Berea, Athens, Corinth; then via Cenchreae and Ephesus to Caesarea Maritima, Jerusalem, and Syrian Antioch.

What: Preached to Jews and Gentiles. Paul wrote 1 and 2 Thessalonians from Corinth; he wrote the Epistle to the Galatians from Antioch.

250 BC†AD 1 36 37 38 39 40 41 42 43 44 45 46 48 4

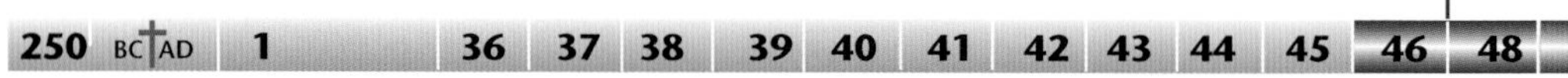

Jerusalem Council AD 49 (Acts 15:1–35)

Who: Paul, Barnabas, James, Peter, Silas

Where: Jerusalem

What: Met with leaders of the entire Church, who then wrote a letter to Gentile Christians in Antioch.

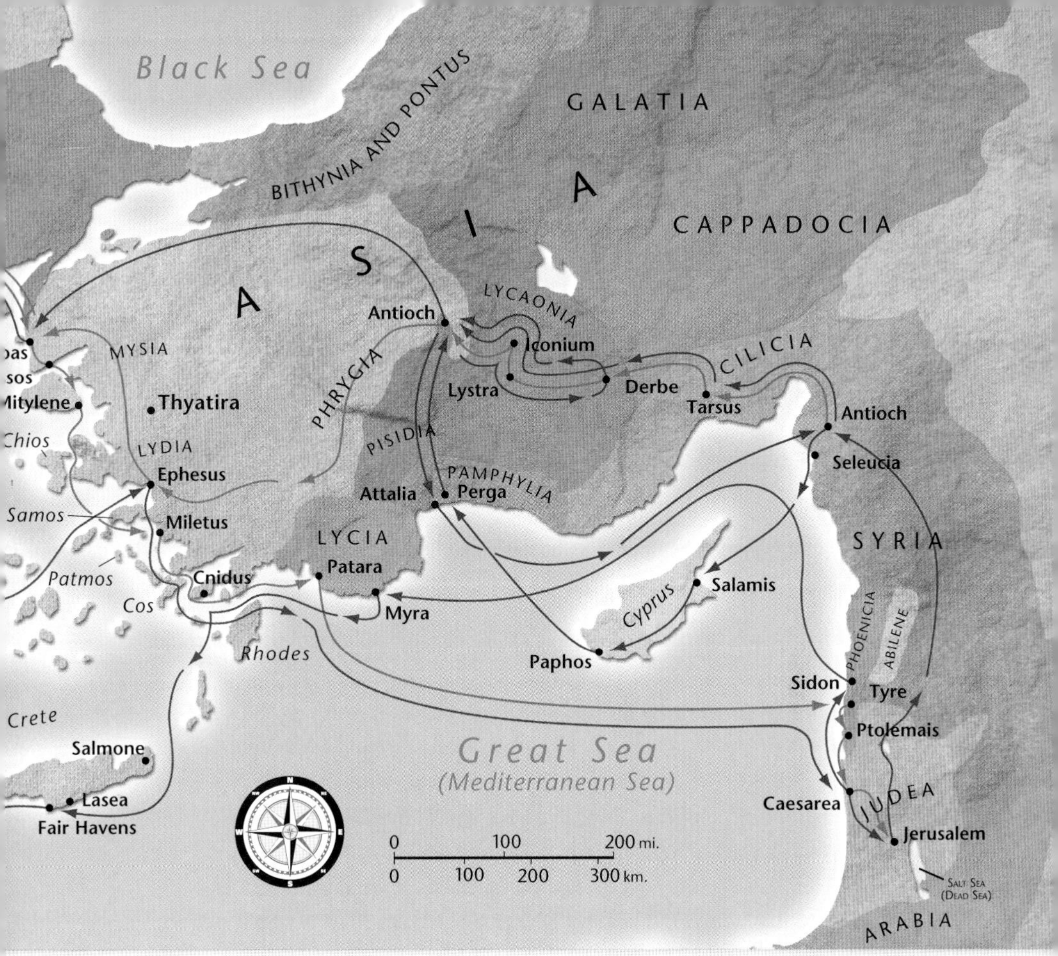

Paul's Third Missionary Journey AD 52–55 (Acts 18:23–21:17)

Who: Paul, Timothy, and Luke later join Paul

Where: Inland route from Syrian Antioch to Ephesus, Macedonia, Achaia, Philippi, Troas, Assos, Mitylene, Miletus, Rhodes, Patara, Tyre, Ptolemais, Caesarea Maritima, Jerusalem

What: Preached to Jews and Gentiles. Paul wrote 1 and 2 Corinthians and the Epistle to the Romans.

Paul's Trip to Rome AD 57–58 (Acts 27:1–28:16)

Who: Paul, as a prisoner of a centurion named Julius, and Luke

Where: Caesarea Maritima, Sidon, Myra, Cnidus, Fair Havens, Cauda, Malta, Syracuse, Rhegium, Puteoli, Forum of Appius, Three Taverns, Rome

What: Preached to Jews and Gentiles. Paul wrote his epistles to the Ephesians, Philippians, Colossians, and Philemon from Rome. Paul later wrote the books of 1 Timothy, Titus, and 2 Timothy.

1 | 52 | 53 | 54 | 55 | 56 | 57 | 58 | 59 | 60 | 61 | 62 | 63 | 65 | 100

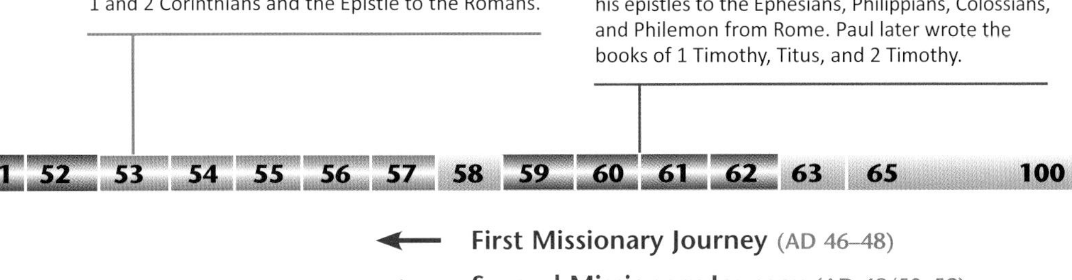

← **First Missionary Journey** (AD 46–48)

← **Second Missionary Journey** (AD 49/50–52)

← **Third Missionary Journey** (AD 52/53–57)

← **Trip to Rome** (AD 59–61/62)

Pentecost

The word *Pentecost* means "fiftieth." Jews celebrated the Feast of the Pentecost on the fiftieth day after the Sabbath of Passover week. It was also called "the Feast of Weeks" or "the Feast of Harvest" and marked the completion of the harvest season, a period of seven weeks that followed the Passover. Like the American holiday of Thanksgiving, Pentecost was a thanksgiving festival, at which God's people joined in giving thanks for the goodness of God the Creator. It was celebrated by taking time off from work to worship.

The Feast of Weeks was as important an occasion as Passover because God commanded the Jewish people, through Moses in the Old Testament Book of Leviticus, to observe this day "forever in all your dwelling places throughout your generations" (Leviticus 23:21). God instructed them to count off seven full weeks after Passover and then present an offering of new grain to the Lord. They were told to bring two loaves of bread baked with yeast as a firstfruits offering and animals for a burnt offering to the Lord. They were to do no regular work, and they were expected to be part of the sacred assembly. Jews from all over the world came to the temple in Jerusalem for the annual celebrations of Passover and Pentecost.

Pentecost was the feast being celebrated ten days after Jesus' ascension. The eleven apostles who were present at Jesus' ascension had remained in Jerusalem as instructed (Acts 1:4). Also present were Matthias and many unnamed disciples. On this festival day, God fulfilled His promise to send the Holy Spirit to His people (Acts 2:1–6).

The coming of the Holy Spirit was evident in at least three ways. The Spirit came with the sound of "a mighty rushing wind" (2:2). "Divided tongues as of fire" appeared and rested on the disciples (v. 3), and they began to "speak in other tongues as the Spirit gave them utterance" (v. 4). Jews from all over the world

were present in the temple for the festival, and the disciples were able to share God's Word with many through this special gift of language. These foreign visitors were then able to take news of this mighty sign of God back to others in their home countries. This gift of languages also reversed the results of God's judgment during the building of the great tower of Babel (Genesis 11:1–9), when God confused the languages of the world.

© CPH/Donald Kueker

As a result of the gift of the Holy Spirit that day and the preaching of the Gospel that took place, "about three thousand souls" (Acts 2:41) were added to God's kingdom.

Christians today celebrate Pentecost fifty days after Easter, remembering that Jesus, our victorious Lamb, kept His promise to send the Holy Spirit, the Comforter, on that day. We give thanks for the gifts that the Spirit continues to bring through God's Word and Sacraments—faith, forgiveness, new life, and salvation. We continue to share this Good News with people of many languages and cultures around the world as the Holy Spirit "calls, gathers, enlightens, and sanctifies the whole Christian church on earth" (Luther's Small Catechism: explanation of the Third Article).

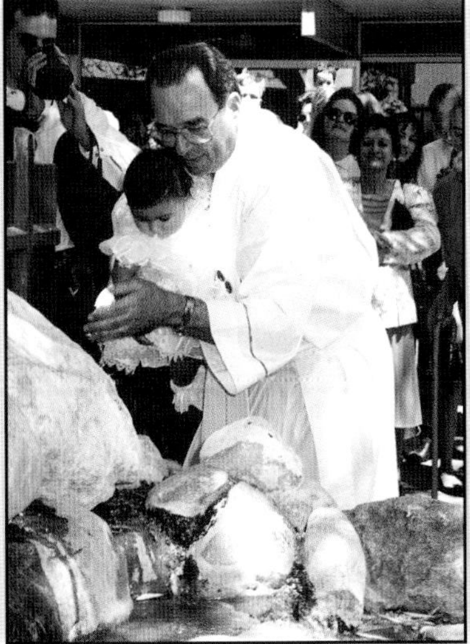

© CPH

The Beautiful Gate and Solomon's Portico

The account of Peter and John healing the lame man (Acts 3) mentions two specific locations within the grounds of the temple in Jerusalem: "the Beautiful Gate" (v. 2) and "the portico called Solomon's" (v. 11). If you envision the temple as a series of structures built in expanding circles, it would look like this:

- The center is the temple itself.
- Around the temple was the Court of Priests, which encompassed the Altar of Sacrifice.
- Around this was the Court of Israel, from which Jewish men were able to observe the sacrifices and prayers of the priests.
- In front of this court was the Court of Women. The two were separated by a large archway called the Nicanor Gate.
- The entire structure was surrounded by a much larger area called the Court of Gentiles.

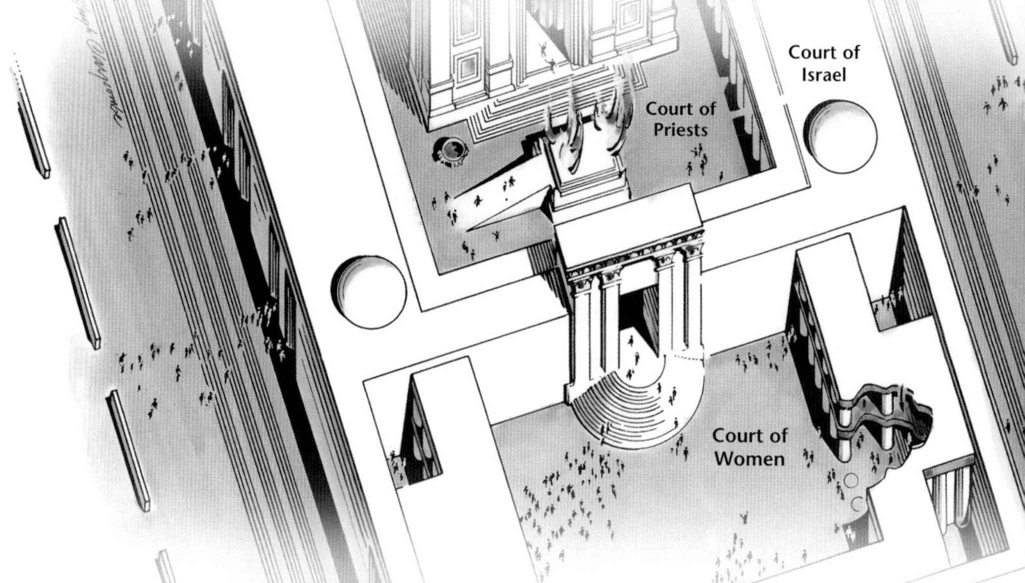

The Beautiful Gate

The gate that led from the Court of Women into the Court of Israel was called "the Beautiful Gate." This was a large opening that also allowed those in the Court of Women to observe the temple sacrifices.

Solomon's Portico.

Solomon's Portico Surrounding the entire temple complex was a large wall. Along the walls, facing into the Court of Gentiles, was a continuous covered porch, or colonnade. The cedar roof of this porch was supported by twenty-seven-foot pillars; this area apparently became a gathering spot for Jewish believers in Christ. These colonnades may have been the site of the booths for the selling of animals and exchanging of foreign currency that Jesus disrupted (Matthew 21:12–13; Mark 11:15–18; John 2:14–22).

The colonnade along the east wall of the temple courts was called "Solomon's Colonnade" or "Solomon's Portico." It was here that people gathered after Peter healed the lame man. Jesus had taught here as well (John 10:22–30).

Although most of the renovations of the temple that were begun by Herod the Great had been completed during his lifetime, the reconstruction of the colonnades was not completed until AD 66, just a few years before the entire city of Jerusalem and the temple were destroyed in AD 70.

© Bill Grove/iStockphoto.com

True God, Not Myth

Paul and Barnabas attracted crowds whenever they preached. The message of salvation that they delivered had great impact on those who heard it. In the lands that they visited, they encountered many who worshiped false gods. The Greek and Roman gods that we hear of only in literature classes were the gods of many, including those living in the area of Lystra.

Many Gods

Greek and Roman mythology stated that Zeus (Jupiter was his Roman name) was one of the three main gods, with his domain consisting of the earth and sky. The other two heads were his brothers. Poseidon (Neptune to the Romans) ruled the waters, and Hades (to the Romans, Pluto) controlled the underworld. There were many other lesser gods. Among them was Hermes (whom the Romans called Mercury). Hermes was the messenger of the gods. He is often pictured wearing boots with wings attached to them.

Gods on Earth?

Today we read mythology as a source of entertainment and to better understand ancient civilizations. Many Greek and Roman citizens living during New Testament times, however, accepted these stories as truth. This mythology portrays the gods as a temperamental group who used humans for their amusement. They watched the world from their home on Olympus, entering into men's lives whenever they wanted. At these times, they would help or harm people, often in response to another god's actions. The people

Zeus Trevi Fountain, Rome, Italy

of Lystra believed in these unpredictable gods. When they saw Paul and Barnabas heal a crippled man, they thought that their gods had appeared in human form. They set out to offer sacrifices to them.

One God

The reaction of the two disciples was to tear their clothes and declare forcefully that they were human. Tearing clothes was a sign of great distress, usually in response to something blasphemous. The disciples rightly pointed the people to Jesus and His sacrifice on their behalf. They declared all other gods to be false gods, and Jesus to be true God.

Hermes Sculpture in the Vatican Museum, Rome, Italy

The Jerusalem Council

Luke records the first missionary journey of Paul in Acts 13–14. Throughout that journey, in each community he visited, Paul adhered to a pattern of preaching first to the Jews. Though some responded to Paul's message of salvation through Christ, more often the Jews became angry at Paul's message. He then turned his efforts to preaching to the Gentiles—the non-Jews—in those places, often with positive results. Paul's role as the apostle to the Gentiles became well-known, and many Gentiles came to faith in Christ because of the Holy Spirit's influence through the Word and Sacraments.

There was a problem in Antioch, however. Some men came down from Judea and began preaching in the church there. These men, called "Judaizers," were preaching a doctrine contrary to the pure Gospel of Jesus Christ. They falsely taught that the only way to faith and salvation was to keep the ceremonial law of Moses as well as believe in Jesus. Paul and Barnabas were sent to Jerusalem to seek a resolution to this problem.

Why Jerusalem?

Even though the Early Church in Jerusalem was under attack by leaders of the Jewish faith, this city remained the center of Christianity. Among the faithful Christian leaders in that city were the apostle Peter and James, the brother of Jesus. The Jerusalem leaders were the respected authority in doctrinal matters in the rapidly spreading Church. The year was probably about AD 49. St. Paul had been an apostle for almost fifteen years. He had just ended his first missionary journey.

The Result

The apostles and elders of the Christian Church met as a council in Jerusalem to discuss this issue and determine the teaching of God's Word. They decided the matter—not by human reasoning, but through the Scripture and through the power of the Holy Spirit at work in the leaders of the council. Their decision: Gentile converts were not to be burdened with the entire Jewish law.

The council sent a letter to clarify and teach the Gospel. It is likely that copies of this letter were carried to the many congregations outside Jerusalem. Pastors used this letter and others to catechize new Christians in the faith, so that the people would hear the true Word of God and believe. Faith comes through hearing the Word.

Other Councils

While there were later councils in the Early Church, there is no evidence that these occurred on a regular basis. Rather, when false teachings arose, the Church came together to resolve matters. These assemblies, using Scripture as their standard, preserved the purity of the Gospel.

Martin Luther later wrote that the Holy Spirit dwells in the hearts of believers, and if council members are selected from the people of God, the council is true and ruled by the Spirit. Such a true council is a gathering of pious people for the preservation among them of the pure Word.

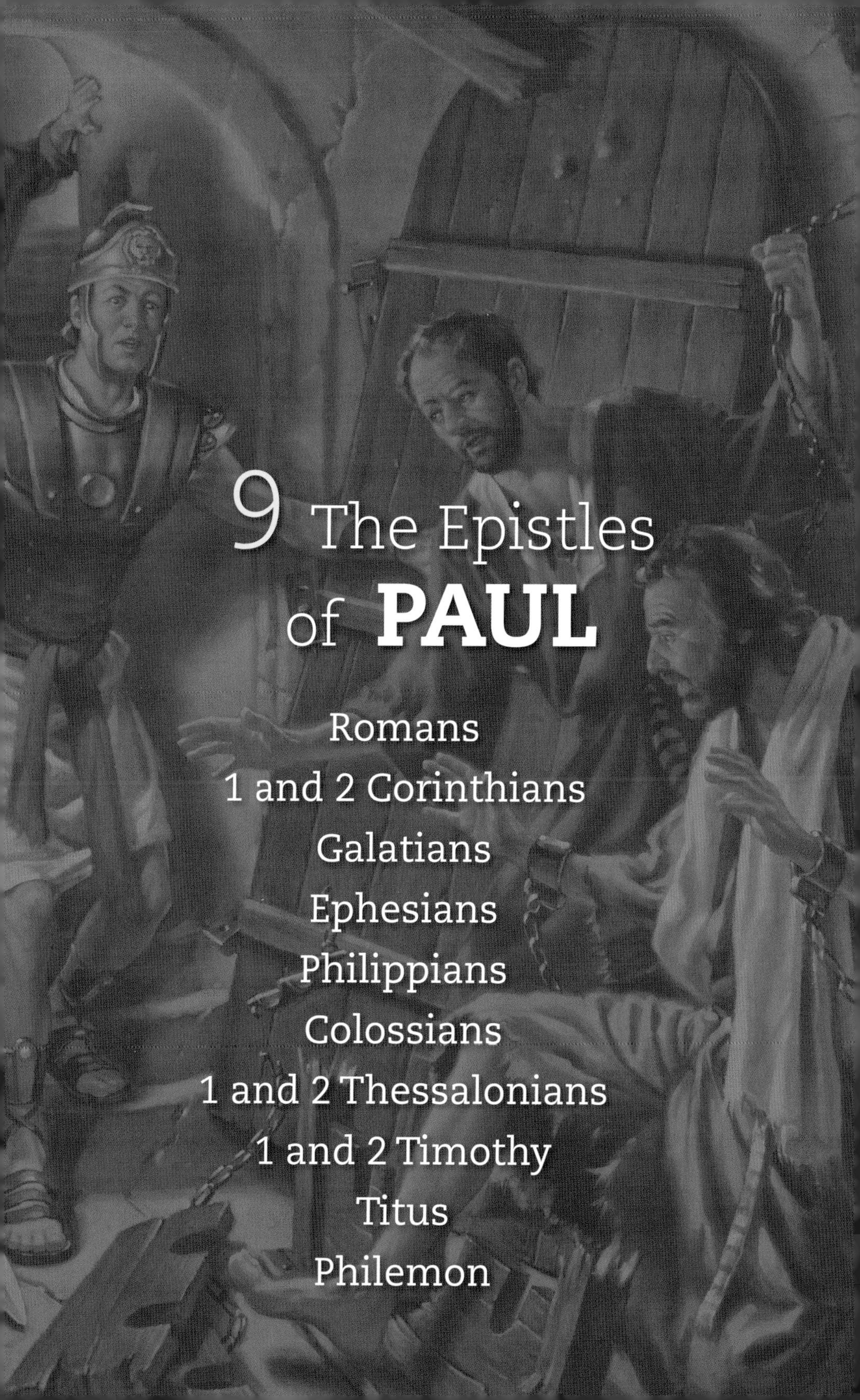

9 The Epistles of PAUL

Romans

1 and 2 Corinthians

Galatians

Ephesians

Philippians

Colossians

1 and 2 Thessalonians

1 and 2 Timothy

Titus

Philemon

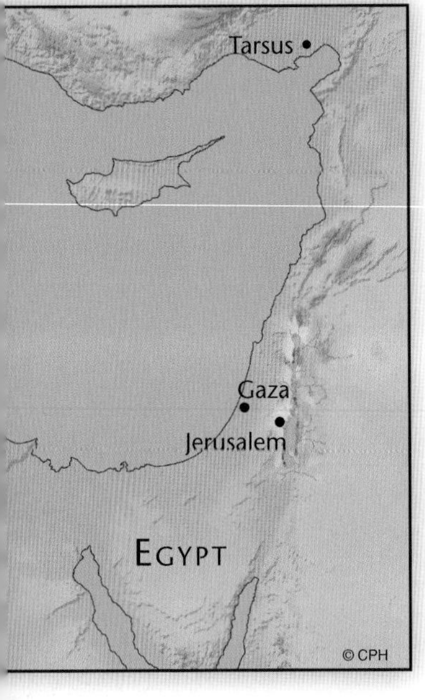

Paul's Hebrew name was Saul. He was born in Tarsus, a Greek city in what is now eastern Turkey. Saul was from a Jewish family, descendants of the tribe of Benjamin (Romans 11:1). He was also born a Roman citizen (Acts 22:28). Saul went to school in Jerusalem and studied Jewish law. He became a Pharisee and was an expert in Jewish laws and traditions. He was a tentmaker by trade (Acts 18:3).

Because Saul was such a faithful Jew, he hated those who didn't uphold the Jewish faith. That meant he hated members of the Way, which is how early Christians identified themselves. He did whatever he could to keep Christians from spreading their faith. Saul was present when the first Christian martyr, Stephen, was stoned to death in Jerusalem. In fact, Saul looked after the coats and cloaks of those who were throwing the stones (Acts 7:58), and he approved of Stephen's execution (Acts 8:1).

Saul hated Christians so much that he got permission from the Jews in Jerusalem to arrest and imprison any Jews that he found who followed the Way. When he experienced his conversion, Saul was on his way to Damascus, the biggest city in ancient Syria, to arrest Christians. A blinding light from heaven knocked Saul to the ground, and Jesus Himself spoke to Saul from heaven. Jesus asked, "Saul, Saul, why are you persecuting me?" (Acts 9:4). Saul's traveling companions took him to Damascus, where he neither ate nor drank for three days. He remained blind and prayed often. God sent Ananias to lay hands on Saul so he could be healed of his blindness and receive the Holy Spirit.

Saul, also known as Paul, became the greatest missionary and teacher the Christian faith has ever known. Paul traveled on at least three missionary journeys to take the Gospel into places that had not yet heard of Jesus. Along the way, many people heard Paul preach, and they became believers in Jesus. Yet, other people rejected Paul and his

Paul's Epistles or Letters

- Romans
- 1 Corinthians
- 2 Corinthians
- Galatians
- Ephesians
- Philippians
- Colossians
- 1 Thessalonians
- 2 Thessalonians
- 1 Timothy
- 2 Timothy
- Titus
- Philemon

[Saul] said, "Who are you, Lord?" And He said, "I am Jesus, whom you are persecuting. But rise and enter the city, and you will be told what you are to do." (Acts 9:5–6)

message. Paul was often mistreated and chased out of town. His journeys are recorded in the Book of Acts.

Paul wrote many books of the Bible known as Epistles. These Epistles are letters, which were sometimes written to different congregations and sometimes written to specific people. These Epistles were written to encourage and to teach the people who read them.

Historians don't know everything about Paul. In 2 Corinthians 12:7, Paul writes, "a thorn was given me in the flesh, a messenger of Satan to harass me, to keep me from being too elated." It is not known exactly what this thorn was, but some believe it may have been a disability of some kind. Details about Paul's death are not known, but tradition taught that Paul died as a martyr, at Rome. Paul is called an apostle because he was a witness to the risen Christ; he is known as a saint because he died in the Christian faith.

In 2 Corinthians 11:24–28, Paul listed his many misadventures:

> *Five times I received at the hands of the Jews the forty lashes less one. Three times I was beaten with rods. Once I was stoned. Three times I was shipwrecked; a night and a day I was adrift at sea; on frequent journeys, in danger from rivers, danger from robbers, danger from my own people, danger from Gentiles, danger in the city, danger in the wilderness, danger at sea, danger from false brothers; in toil and hardship, through many a sleepless night, in hunger and thirst, often without food, in cold and exposure. And, apart from other things, there is the daily pressure on me of my anxiety for all the churches.*

Yet, Paul also writes:

> *I count everything as loss because of the surpassing worth of knowing Christ Jesus my Lord. For His sake I have suffered the loss of all things and count them as rubbish, in order that I may gain Christ."(Philippians 3:8)*

Paul treasured his Lord Jesus and gladly dedicated his life to spreading the Gospel.

Paul's Second Missionary Journey

Paul and Silas set out on Paul's second missionary journey right after the council met in Jerusalem, and Timothy joined them in Lystra. The year was about AD 49. Acts 16:6–10 says that the Holy Spirit, referred to in this passage as "the Spirit of Jesus" (v. 7), directed them away from Asia and toward Europe. The writer of Acts, Luke the physician, who also wrote the Gospel of Luke, joined them.

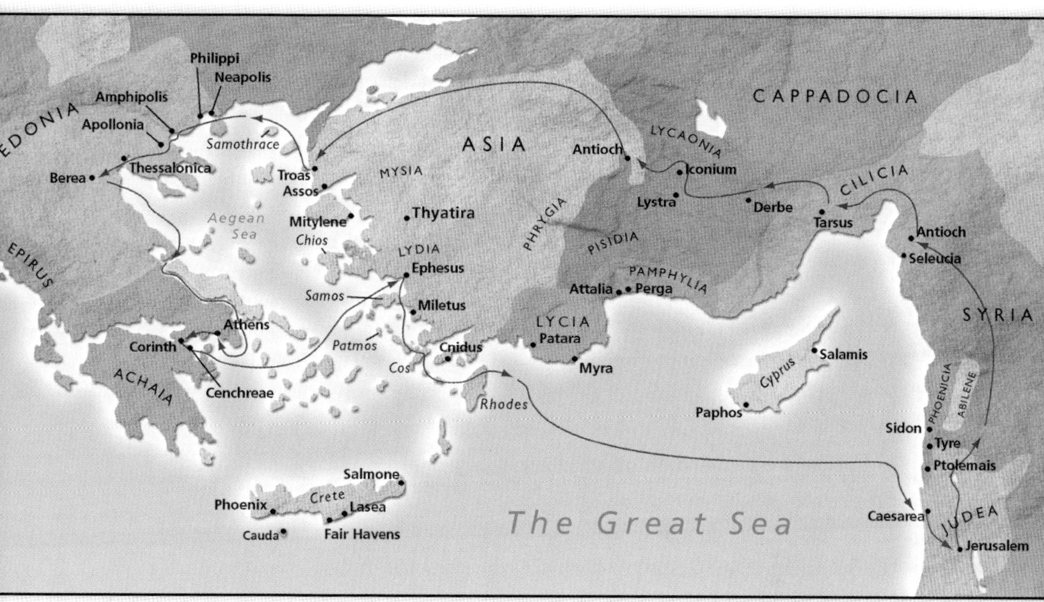

Paul's Second Missionary Journey

The Journey Begins

The group began its journey traveling on land north and then west out of Antioch in Syria. Twenty miles a day would have been an aggressive pace for such a trip, and the distance from Antioch to Philippi was nearly one thousand miles. It likely took months. Trace this part of their journey on the map; note the cities and districts of Phrygia, Galatia, Mysia, Bithynia (which the Holy Spirit would not let them enter), Macedonia, Samothrace, Neapolis, and Philippi.

Jesus' Great Commission to go and make disciples of all nations (Matthew 28:19–20) was happening! Paul and his companions taught and baptized in the name of the triune God at Philippi in accord with Jesus' command.

In Philippi

Philippi, in Macedonia, was named for Philip II, the father of Alexander the Great. This self-governing Roman colony was a retirement city for many

Roman soldiers. It was a well-known city in the ancient world because it was a gateway between the East and West, between Europe and Asia. There were so few Jews living there that Philippi did not have a synagogue. The few Jews who lived there came to the Gangites River to worship. This is not surprising either when we think of times water played a great part in the history of the Jews—the flood and the crossing of the Red Sea, for example. Also, Jewish law required ceremonial washing as part of their ritual. This was closely connected to their worship of God. Gentiles who worshiped God met there with the Jews.

Lydia

Lydia was one of the Gentiles who waited for God's promise of a Savior to be fulfilled. Lydia, whose name was associated with her home province of Thyatira, was a businesswoman who was in Philippi to trade her beautiful, rich, purple cloth.

Athens and Corinth

Paul and his companions were forced to leave Philippi after their encounter with a demon-possessed slave girl and brief imprisonment (see "Roman Justice," p. 399).

They continued west into Macedonia and south into Greece. In Athens, Paul preached to the men of Athens in the Areopagus, a council of scholars and theologians, converting some.

Continuing on to Corinth, Paul met fellow tentmakers Priscilla and Aquila, with whom he stayed and worked. Paul continued his pattern of preaching to the Jews first, but when they rejected his message of salvation through Jesus Christ, Paul turned to preaching to the Gentiles, the non-Jews, who were more receptive.

Paul stayed in Corinth for more than a year and a half, preaching and teaching. It was to this group of believers that Paul wrote the two letters that have become part of the Bible. He then sailed for home. (You can read the details of this journey in Acts 15:39–18:22.)

Paul's Third Missionary Journey and Journey to Rome

After his second missionary journey, Paul stayed briefly in Antioch in Syria, but he took to the road again the following year (AD 52/53) to revisit the many places he had preached in his first two mission trips.

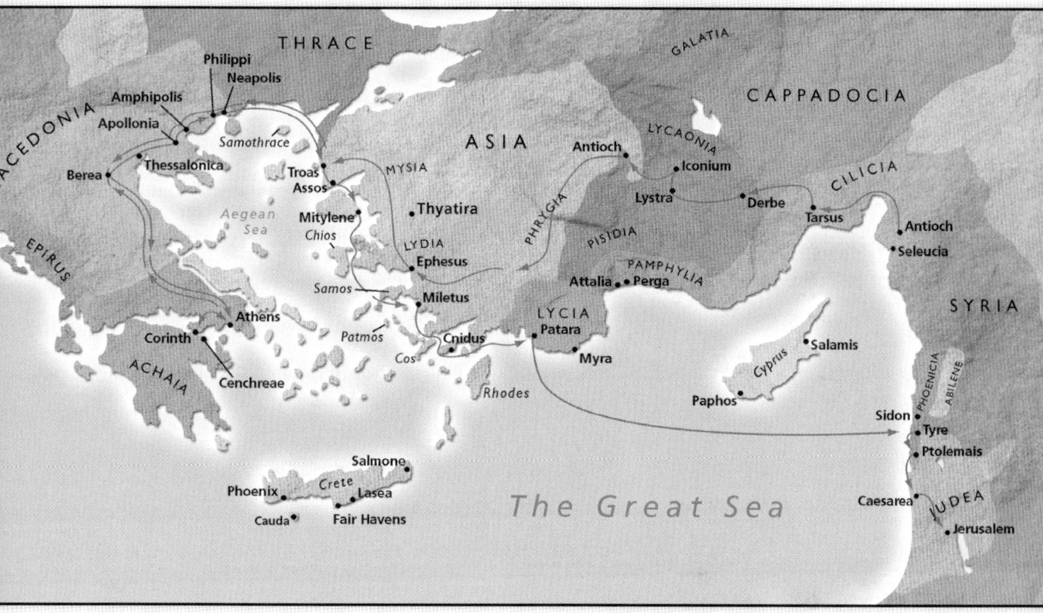

Paul's Third Missionary Journey

The Third Journey

He first traveled from Antioch and made Ephesus the center of his mission work, staying there for two or three years. While he was there, he offended the silversmith workers because the Gospel had reached so many people that they were giving up their silver idols. He barely escaped a riot in that city, and he spent a winter in Corinth. The Bible relates the details of this journey in Acts 18:23–21:17.

In the spring of AD 56, he traveled to Jerusalem to bring the Christian Church there money donated by the outlying churches. A famine in the land at this time caused the Church to be in great need.

The Journey to Rome

While Paul was in Jerusalem, a mob of Jews, angered by Paul's preaching of the Gospel of Jesus Christ, accused him of defiling the temple. He escaped with the help of Roman soldiers. The resulting commotion, however, caused the Roman centurion to hold Paul in a kind of protective custody, eventually transferring him to Caesarea.

In Caesarea, Paul appeared before the Roman governor, Felix, who was a devious man. Felix kept Paul in prison in Caesarea, hoping to get bribe money from him. After two years, Felix was removed from power, and his replacement, Festus, made an offer to Paul. He proposed to take Paul to Jerusalem again for a court hearing where Paul could face his accusers. Festus was certain Paul would be acquitted. Instead, Paul, a Roman citizen, appealed to the emperor of Rome, and Festus granted his appeal. He had to go to Rome for trial. The remainder of the Book of Acts records the rest of his journey.

Paul's journey to Rome and his time there was in a sense another missionary journey. Though in this journey Paul was not sent by the Church, all along the way, during shipwreck and danger, he witnessed to the power of the Gospel of Jesus Christ. In Rome, he was given freedom (under the guard of a Roman soldier) to receive visitors and talk with them as he pleased. He preached ceaselessly in Rome to anyone who would listen.

Paul's Journey to Rome

Romans

Into Romans

This letter was addressed to the Church (believers) in Rome.

It was written by Paul in AD 55.

It pictures Jesus as "Christ, Our Righteousness."

This Epistle at a Glance

- No one knows who planted the Church in Rome. It wasn't Paul; he had never been there. But he cared deeply about the believers there. Many were Gentiles, but there were likely a large number of Jews too.
- Paul wrote Romans to communicate the basic teachings of the Christian faith. He also wrote to prepare the people in Rome for a visit he planned to make there soon.
- Most scholars think Paul wrote Romans toward the end of his third missionary journey.
- The book is arranged a lot like a legal brief. Paul uses a logical arrangement and many proof texts and examples from the Old Testament to make his points.
- Romans includes many quotes from the Old Testament.
- The reformer Martin Luther thought so highly of Romans that he recommended all Christians memorize the entire book!

How can I best grow in grace as I read Romans?

It's easier to read and understand Romans if you begin with a rough idea of the outline Paul had in mind. He writes like an attorney, making a case.

First, he acts as the prosecutor (Romans 1:1–3:20). He presents evidence that everybody sins and that God will judge sin. Everybody needs a Savior—Jews, Gentiles, religious people, skeptics, common people, leaders—everybody!

Next, Paul becomes the defense attorney (3:21–5:11). He shows that Jesus already took our punishment. From all eternity, God had a wonderful plan in mind to make sinners right with Himself. Jesus died for our sin, and now we receive Jesus' righteousness—free!

Third, Paul answers the question, how does the righteousness God give me help me when I feel guilty, trapped in habit sins, or overwhelmed by life's problems (6–8)?

Finally, he gives practical guidelines for how God's righteous people live (12–16).

You'll note that three chapters are left out of this outline. That's because Romans 9–11 are a kind of parentheses, a long footnote. They answer the question, what about the Jews, God's chosen people? Are they saved in the same way as Gentiles or are they saved simply because they carry Abraham's genes?

Romans is more doctrinal, more theological, than it is devotional. But many passages in Romans are deeply devotional. For example, many Christians consider Romans 8 their favorite chapter in all the Scriptures!

As you read this book, ask the Holy Spirit to open your heart to understand more fully and appreciate more deeply the sacrifice Jesus made—for you!

What are the key chapters and verses in Romans?

Romans 1:16 is the theme verse for the entire book:

> *I am not ashamed of the gospel, for it is the power of God for salvation to everyone who believes, to the Jew first and also to the Greek.*

In this verse, Paul uses exaggerated understatement to make his point when he says, "I am not ashamed of the gospel." In reality, the Gospel was Paul's boast! He was so very proud and glad about what God had done in sending Jesus to live, suffer, die, and rise again for us!

Romans 8 is a favorite chapter of many Christians, especially verses 18–39. This chapter concludes with a shout of triumph:

> *I am sure that neither death nor life, nor angels nor rulers, nor things present nor things to come, nor powers, nor height nor depth, nor anything else in all creation, will be able to separate us from the love of God in Christ Jesus our Lord. (vv. 38–39)*

Romans 11:33–36 records one of the most beautiful hymns of praise in all of Scripture. Romans 13:1–7 outlines the duties Christian citizens owe to their leaders in the government.

Ancient Rome

When Paul arrived in Rome as a prisoner, he may have seen some of these important places, which are ruins today:

The ***Appian Way*** was the common name of Rome's most important road. It was paved by Appius Claudius in 312 BC. Paul came from Puteoli to Rome (170 miles) on the Appian Way (Acts 28:15–16; v. 15 mentions the Forum of Appius, which was part of the Appian Way).

Building along the Appian Way.

The ***Roman Forum*** was the center of town. All the major roads radiated out of this town center, and all important business was conducted in the Forum. Though the forces of nature took their toll over the centuries, the Forum can be seen much as it appeared in Paul's day.

Rome, Italy

The ***Curia*** is where Roman senators met and made decisions for the people of Rome. It would be similar to the meeting place of the United States Senate in the Capitol in Washington DC. Over the centuries, the Curia was burned down four times.

Curia

© Alister G. Jupp/Shutterstock, Inc

Trimuphal Arch

The ***triumphal Arch*** of Septimius Severus commemorated a great victory in battle. Rome commanded a skilled and highly organized military. This arch was not built until almost two hundred years after Peter and Paul were in Rome, but it is a dominant feature in the ruins of the Forum.

A ***basilica*** is a building of a specific architectural type. Today, we hear mostly of large cathedrals built in this design. In Paul's time in Rome, basilicas were similar to shopping malls. Markets were set up under the cooling roofs of the basilica. The Basilica Julia was also used as a courtroom. On the floor of the porch, diagrams of games scratched into the white marble can be seen today.

The ***Temple of Saturn*** honored the Roman god of the harvest and was one of many temples to the gods that the ancient Romans believed in. The Roman national treasure was kept there. The festival honoring Saturn, known as Saturnalia, was celebrated on December 17.

© Pippa West/Shutterstock, Inc

Temple of Saturn

Tabularium

The ***Tabularium*** housed the Roman public record office. The Roman government kept specific records that have taught historians much about life in ancient Rome. The Tabularium foundation is original, but in the 1500s, Rome built a new building on top of the second floor to house the city's town hall. The tower was added in AD 1300.

The ***Tullianum***, or ***Mamertine Prison,*** was the Roman state prison. Historians believe it is where Paul was imprisoned. Today, a church above the ancient jail marks the place.

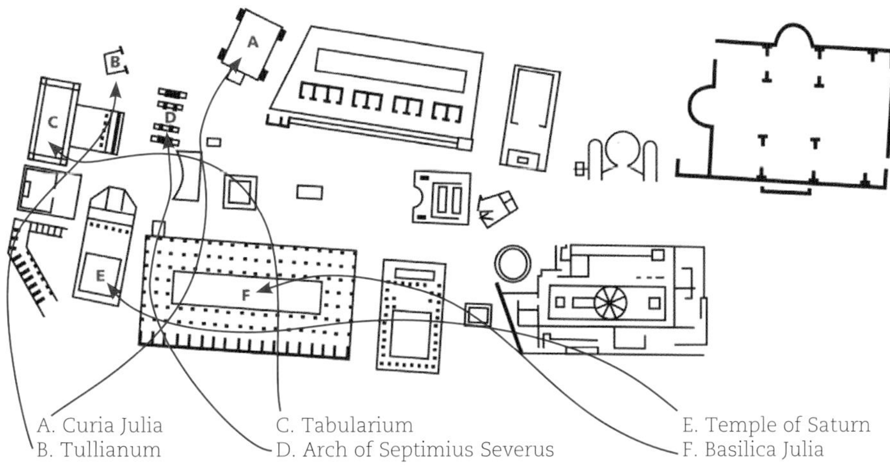

1 and 2 Corinthians

Into 1 and 2 Corinthians

These two letters were addressed to the Church (believers) in Corinth, a seaport in Greece.

They were written by Paul in AD 55.

They picture Jesus as "Christ Our Glorious Lord, Our Comfort in Life and Death."

These Epistles at a Glance

- Corinth was a seaport with not one but two harbors! Like many seaports, Corinth became known for its sexual immorality, its many different religions, and its corruption.
- Corinth was more immoral than most ports of its kind. The Greeks even invented a word that, in English, is translated "to corinthian-ize," and it means "to engage in drunken parties and gross sexual immorality."
- At the time Paul ministered in Corinth, the city had more than a million inhabitants. Perhaps as many as 400,000 of them were slaves.
- Paul wrote 1 Corinthians in response to reports he had received about immorality in the Church there. (A man had married his stepmother and was living in open sin with her.) Paul had also heard reports about arguments and divisions among the believers. In addition, the believers in Corinth had written to Paul with a list of questions, and Paul wanted to answer them.

- After the Corinthian Church received Paul's letter, they repented of the sins Paul had pointed out to them. But a new problem had arisen. New teachers in the church were saying that Paul wasn't a real apostle and that people couldn't rely on everything Paul taught. In response, Paul wrote 2 Corinthians to commend them for the changes they had made and to defend his ministry.

How can I best grow in grace as I read 1 and 2 Corinthians?

As each year passes, our society grows more and more like Corinth. Sexual immorality has invaded the Church. Christians quarrel with one another. Believers fail to respect the spiritual leaders God has given us. Few people consider drunkenness a sin. Even Christians who attend church every week sometimes take the Lord's Supper for granted; we fail to prepare our hearts to receive the amazing and powerful gift Jesus has given us in the Sacrament of the Altar.

As you read 1 and 2 Corinthians, compare the problems of first-century Corinth with what you see in your own life, your own church, your own city. Ask the Holy Spirit to help you see events and people through His eyes. Ask Him to teach you to hate sin and the hurt it causes and to trust Jesus more and more deeply. Let your Savior both confront and comfort you!

What are the key chapters in 1 and 2 Corinthians?

- **1 Corinthians 11** The Lord's Supper and how Jesus wants to use it in the lives of His people.
- **1 Corinthians 12** Spiritual gifts and how we can each use the gifts God has given us for the good of other believers and to honor our Savior.
- **1 Corinthians 13** True love—the love of our Savior *for* us and the love that His love works in us. (People often choose to have this chapter read as they take their wedding vows.)
- **1 Corinthians 15** Jesus' resurrection and what it means for us. (This chapter provides great comfort for Christians, especially as we grieve the death of a loved one.)
- **2 Corinthians 1** The comfort the Holy Spirit brings to our hearts when we're hurting.
- **2 Corinthians 8** The blessings of having a generous heart.
- **2 Corinthians 12** Paul's famous "thorn in the flesh" chapter (He concludes, "When I am weak, then I am strong," v. 10).

Hospitality in Bible Times

The Middle East has a tradition of hospitality toward guests that, for the most part, is carried on today. In Jesus' time, a guest was welcomed with a kiss, given a meal, and protected while in the host's home. As a sign of acceptance, welcome, and honor, the host provided water to wash the guest's feet. It was the least a host could do for a guest with dusty, tired feet. A servant might have the job of washing the guest's feet. Failure by a host to provide such hospitality could be considered an insult or seen as a sign of hostility.

To eat a meal with someone showed friendship and commitment. People who ate together, who had "bread and salt between them," were no longer strangers but friends and had an obligation to each other. One would not betray a friend, but protect and serve him.

It was common for men to greet each other with a hearty welcoming hug, a kiss on each cheek, and a greeting such as "Peace to you" or "The Lord bless you." Likewise, a good-bye was drawn out, with many hugs, kisses, and blessings. This again was seen as a sign of friendship and acceptance. Without these gestures, there would be feelings of uneasiness and hostility.

In Luke 7:36–50, Jesus criticizes Simon, a Pharisee in whose home He is a guest, for a lack of hospitality, while He commends the sinful woman who showed Jesus the hospitality that He might reasonably have expected from His host. On Maundy Thursday, Jesus displays true hospitality and humility to His disciples, hosting the Passover meal for them and washing their feet Himself.

Before His ascension to the Father, Jesus leaves this farewell to the disciples and to all believers: "Peace I leave with you; My peace I give to you. Not as the world gives do I give to you. Let not your hearts be troubled, neither let them be afraid" (John 14:27). This blessing as Jesus departs from His disciples is His farewell greeting to us as well.

The Real Presence

Now, what is the Sacrament of the Altar? "It is the true body and blood of our Lord Jesus Christ under the bread and wine, instituted by Christ Himself for us Christians to eat and to drink" (Luther's Small Catechism: The Sacrament of the Altar).

> *Just as we have said that Baptism is not simple water, so here also we say that though the Sacrament is bread and wine, it is not mere bread and wine, such as are ordinarily served at the table [1 Corinthians 10:16–17]. But this is bread and wine included in, and connected with, God's Word.*
>
> *(Luther's Large Catechism: The Sacrament of the Altar)*

God's Word makes this Sacrament what it is: the body and blood of Christ, and not just ordinary bread and wine. It is Christ's body and blood because He said so. Jesus cannot lie or deceive us. We do not try to explain how Jesus is present under the bread and wine, but we rely on His own words to tell us that it is His body and blood. At the Last Supper, Jesus said, "This is My body, which is given for you. . . . This cup is the new testament in My blood, which is shed for you for the forgiveness of sins." These are the Words of Our Lord (*LSB*, p. 162), drawn from Matthew 26:26–29; Mark 14:22–25; Luke 22:14–20; and 1 Corinthians 11:23–25.

It is a mystery, hidden from our eyes and comprehension, how the body and blood of Christ are present. We simply rest on the words of Jesus and believe them through faith.

> *What is the benefit of this eating and drinking? These words, "Given and shed for you for the forgiveness of sins," show us that in the Sacrament forgiveness of sins, life, and salvation are given us through these words. For where there is forgiveness of sins, there is also life and salvation.*
>
> *(Luther's Small Catechism: The Sacrament of the Altar)*

Occupations and Professions

By the time Jesus lived on earth, Jerusalem and the surrounding area had grown into a large population center, supporting people with all kinds of occupations. Through the writings of Jewish historians and the discovery of old manuscripts, we know much about the most common professions of the people who lived in and around Jerusalem. Most of the people had jobs related to four categories: food gathering or production, providing goods or services in the marketplace, working for the Roman government, and serving in or around the temple.

Food Production

Fishermen, hunters, farmers, shepherds, and herdsmen worked to provide most of the food for the village or town. Shepherds and herdsmen were different only in the animals they kept—shepherds cared for sheep, while herdsmen kept cattle.

The Marketplace

The marketplace was busy with artists, who sold souvenirs to the many pilgrims visiting Jerusalem, as well as skilled workers, such as carpenters, potters, silversmiths, and metalworkers. Masons cut stones for building, while tentmakers sold their tents, and tanners prepared skins for clothing and use as containers.

Government Workers

Because the Jewish people hated the Roman conquerors who had taken over their government, anyone working for the government was unpopular and considered unclean because of their contact with non-Jews. Some Jews who followed Jewish law strictly avoided such people, especially tax collectors, known as publicans. These workers had a reputation for cheating, overcharging, and becoming rich at the expense of the other Jews.

Temple Workers

One of the most respected persons was the rabbi, or teacher, who taught in the local synagogue or at the temple. Other temple workers included musicians, such as harpists and trumpeters, and scribes, who did the difficult work of copying the Old Testament scrolls.

Unpopular Occupations

Many occupations were looked down upon. Donkey and camel driving were jobs no self-respecting Jew wanted. People suspected butchers of violating Jewish law by selling the meat of unclean animals. Even bankers, or moneychangers, were suspect, because Jewish law forbade lending money for interest. Doctors, too, were held in contempt because they often gave special treatment to the rich while ignoring the poor.

Jesus did not share the common prejudices of the Jewish people. He called Matthew, a tax collector, to be one of the twelve disciples. He also sought out another tax collector, Zacchaeus of Jericho, in order to honor him by dining at his house. Jesus made it clear that He "came to seek and to save the lost" (Luke 19:10).

Death and Resurrection

Death is an unavoidable reality for everyone. Yet it is a complex subject, one that we might sometimes avoid talking about and one about which even knowledgeable Christians don't always speak clearly.

Death points us to our Savior, Jesus, who conquered death for us. We can remember some significant things the Bible teaches about death and what comes after death by remembering what Jesus experienced on our behalf.

Life

In His life, Jesus fulfilled all righteousness, living without sin to fulfill the Law on our behalf. He lived a perfect life because we who are sinful from birth cannot. Life for human beings is a struggle with sin and all that sin brings into the world—sickness, violence, hardship, and eventually death.

But sin is not the only reality in life for the Christian. Because of our Baptism, we share even now in the eternal life that Jesus won for us on the cross. The Bible is clear that eternal life begins with faith and comes to Christians through God's Word and His Sacraments.

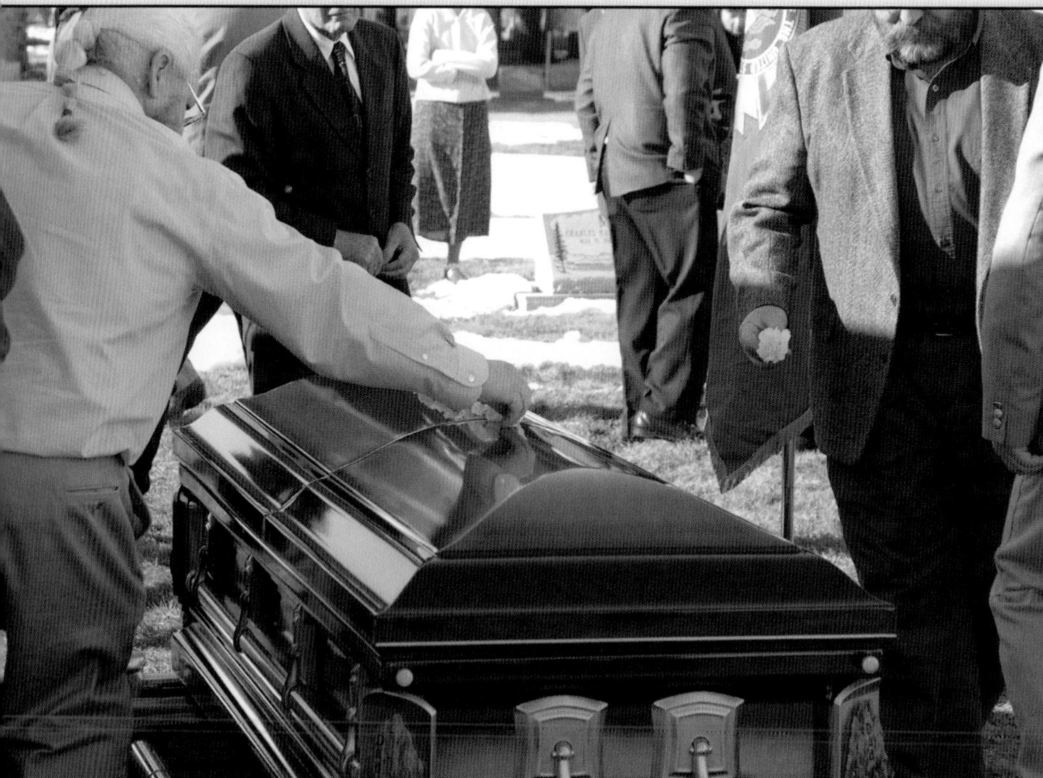

© Trista Weibell/iStockphoto.com

Death

Death is the end of earthly life. Death is the result of sin; it entered the world when Adam and Eve were forced from the Garden of Eden, away from the tree of life. Death is a reminder of our sinful nature. Death is the separation for a time of the soul from the body. At death, the body is committed to the grave. But the grave is not the Christian's final resting place.

For those left behind, the death of a loved one is an occasion for grief, for we are separated for the rest of this life from those who die. We miss them.

Death is release from the troubles of this earthly existence. Those who have suffered weakness and pain because of sickness and old age suffer no more.

Jesus experienced death. After suffering on the cross for the sins of humankind, He "gave up His spirit" (John 19:30). It was God's plan that, through Jesus' death, our death might become just a doorway to life with Him.

Rest

Death brings about a kind of interim state—the Bible refers to it as being asleep (Matthew 27:52), in paradise (Luke 23:43), and at rest (Revelation 14:13). While the soul is at rest with Jesus, the body remains in the grave, but only for a time.

The Bible reports that Jesus' body rested in the tomb for three days—from the afternoon of Friday through the early morning hours of Sunday, the first Easter Sunday. Though our bodies may rest in the grave for more than three days, the Bible promises that for all Christians, the sleep of death will be temporary.

Resurrection

The victory—for Jesus and for us—is the resurrection from the dead. That is the hope and promise that will bring comfort at a funeral service—that our loved one will, by God's promise, celebrate with us on the Last Day. This resurrection of the dead, which is the heart and core of God's promise, will occur for most at the Last Day.

This resurrection, not death itself, is the victory for the Christian that Paul proclaims in 1 Corinthians 15:50–57. When God raises our bodies, in a changed and immortal condition, then sin and death will be defeated.

This victory will take place on the Last Day, the day when Jesus comes to judge the living and the dead. Some believers—those who are still alive on that day—will not sleep in the grave, but apparently will be changed without experiencing death (1 Corinthians 15:51–52).

God will fulfill many other promises on that day. In 2 Timothy 4:8, Paul writes that the crown of righteousness is "laid up" for the Christian to be awarded on the Last Day, at the end of time. It will be given to all Christians simultaneously.

So, too, God's Words "Well done, good and faithful servant" (Matthew 25:21) are spoken in the context of a parable about the Final Judgment.

A Reminder

Jesus is a wonderful reminder of what we can expect—life, death, rest, and resurrection. A favorite hymn also stands out as a helpful reminder of how we Christians can think about death: "For All the Saints" (*LSB* 677), a meditation on the Church Triumphant. Here on earth, God's saints (all who follow their "captain," stanza 2) "feebly struggle" (stanza 4), but are encouraged in the fight against sin and all sin brings by the "distant triumph song" of the saints in heaven (stanza 5). Death, "the golden evening" (stanza 6), brings rest from the struggle, a sleep in "paradise." "But, lo, there breaks a yet more glorious day" (stanza 7), the resurrection of the dead on the Last Day.

Galatians

Into Galatians

This letter was addressed to the Church (believers) in the region of Galatia.
It was written by Paul sometime between AD 51 and 53.
It pictures Jesus as "Christ, Our Freedom Fighter."

This Epistle at a Glance

- Paul wrote thirteen of the epistles, or letters, of the New Testament. Many scholars believe Galatians was the first of those. If so, he likely wrote it just before the famous Council of Jerusalem (Acts 15).
- The region of Galatia included cities like Antioch, Iconium, Lystra, and Derbe. This area is part of central Turkey today. Paul visited this region on his first missionary journey (Acts 13:13–14:23) and then returned to encourage the believers there on his second and third missionary journeys.
- After Paul left Galatia for the first time, people called "Judaizers" came in. Paul had preached salvation by grace through faith in Jesus alone. Knowing this, the Judaizers wanted to add many "but yah gottas" to Paul's teaching. They said, in essence, "Yes, Jesus is our Savior—but yah gotta follow the Law of Moses about your diet—no ham in those sandwiches! And yah gotta be circumcised. And yah gotta observe all the festivals of Judaism. . . ." On and on it went. Paul wrote Galatians to say, "No way! In Jesus Christ, we are free from the condemnation of the Law of Moses. Live in that freedom!"
- Like no other Bible book, Galatians stands as a mighty fortress, guarding the heart of the Gospel. It was one of the reformer Martin Luther's favorite books, maybe because Luther fought the same kind of battle against legalism that Galatians fights.

How can I best grow in grace as I read Galatians?

Galatians lays out in clear and certain terms the freedom all believers—Jews and Gentiles alike—share in Christ. Still today, people often try to hang all kinds of conditions on the Gospel. Usually these things are religious things. Sometimes they are good things! Legalists today might say things like these:

- "Sure, Jesus died for your sins. But yah gotta go to church twice a week."
- "Yes, you're saved by grace. But yah gotta give 10 percent of your income to church."
- "You bet, Jesus saves us. But yah gotta fast [go without eating] before Holy Communion."

God's people want to worship with other believers. We want to support the work of missionaries, pastors, and others who help us grow in grace. Fasting before the Lord's Supper is a helpful practice. But none of these things saves us. Nothing we can do will remove our sins or make up for them. Jesus' death and resurrection alone make us right with God. The Holy Spirit joins us to the benefits Jesus won for us by creating faith in our hearts.

We don't "gotta" do anything to earn God's gifts! Galatians 1–4 emphasizes this—and in powerful terms!

But once we're saved, we *get to* do all kinds of exciting, challenging, adventurous things. Galatians 5–6 explains this and gives some examples. In Jesus, we are free to be like Jesus in the lives of others. We get to live in a way different from anyone else in the world as we travel, step-by-step, the exciting path God sets out before us. We even get to invite others to know Jesus and the freedom He gives all believers.

As you read Galatians, ask the Holy Spirit to show you where any legalism lurks in your heart. Ask yourself, "When do the 'but yah gottas' begin whispering their lies and try to shame me into doing something that seems 'holy' or might impress someone around me?" Then ask Jesus to forgive you and wash that out of your heart. Ask Him to replace it with genuine excitement about the "but I get tos" He will show you.

What are the key chapters and verses in Galatians?

- **Galatians 1:1–2:14** Paul's Authority as an Apostle.
- **Galatians 2:15–5:12** Our Freedom in the Gospel.
- **Galatians 5:13–6:18** The Life of a Free Christian

Key verse: *For freedom Christ has set us free; stand firm therefore, and do not submit again to a yoke of slavery. (Galatians 5:1)*

Ephesians

Into Ephesians

This letter was addressed to the Church (believers) in the city of Ephesus and the surrounding region.

It was written by Paul, probably around AD 60.

It pictures Jesus as "Christ, the Head of the Church."

This Epistle at a Glance

- While in custody in Rome, Paul wrote Ephesians, Philemon, Philippians, and Colossians. His confinement must have seemed frustrating at times, and Paul must have yearned to be released so he could go on proclaiming the Gospel. But how thankful we can be for this "detour" in his plans! Each of the letters he wrote during this time is a treasure!
- Paul founded the Church in Ephesus and served as its pastor for nearly three years. Acts 20:17–38 describes a touching event that illustrates the affection Pastor Paul and his people shared for one another.
- From Ephesus, the Gospel of Christ spread into the whole region of what is today eastern Turkey. The Church in Ephesus was influential and managed to avoid the doctrinal problems and gross outward sins that plagued some of the other first-century churches.
- Many of the letters Paul wrote address controversies or correct errors. In contrast, Ephesians simply encourages the Church, reminding us of the blessings we inherit in Christ and urging us to live out our faith in the strength He provides.
- In the original Greek Paul used as he wrote, Ephesians 1:1–14 is one long sentence! It's as though Paul got so excited about what God has done for us in Christ that he didn't want to pause even to

take a breath. Count the times "in Christ" appears in these verses. What do you think it means?

How can I best grow in grace as I read Ephesians?

One can argue that Ephesians is a book of superlatives. Among the New Testament letters, Ephesians paints one of the

- most glorious pictures of the believer's inheritance in Christ (1:3–22);
- clearest contrasts of life before and after the Holy Spirit brings us to faith (2:1–10);
- most beautiful pictures of the unity Jesus creates in His Church (3:1–4:16); and
- most graphic descriptions of our battle with sin and Satan (6:10–20).

Do you need encouragement as you walk with Jesus? Then Ephesians is for you! As you read it, ask the Holy Spirit to make the realities you don't see (heaven, hell, angels, demons, sin, grace) as real to you as the realities you do see. Let God work in you a deep, deep trust in His love at work in you!

What are the key chapters and verses in Ephesians?

- **Ephesians 1:3–14** Our Riches in Christ
- **Ephesians 2:1–10** Life Before and After Christ
- **Ephesians 4:1–16** One Body in Christ
- **Ephesians 6:6–20** Stand Strong in Christ

Key verses:

> *For by grace you have been saved through faith. And this is not your own doing; it is the gift of God, not a result of works, so that no one may boast. For we are His workmanship, created in Christ Jesus for good works, which God prepared beforehand, that we should walk in them. (Ephesians 2:8–10)*

Philippians

Into Philippians

This letter was addressed to the Church (believers) in the city of Philippi and the surrounding region.

It was written by Paul, probably around AD 60.

It pictures Jesus as "Christ Our Joy."

This Epistle at a Glance

- The city of Philippi took its name from King Philip II of Greece. He was the father of Alexander the Great. During Paul's time, Philippi was a thriving Roman colony.
- Paul wrote Philippians while in prison. Like Ephesians, Philemon, and Colossians, Philippians is considered one of the "prison epistles." Unless you know this fact already, though, it would be hard to discover it just by reading these letters, especially Philippians; this letter overflows with joy, despite the frustration and other hardships Paul was enduring as he wrote.
- It's possible that Paul was not in a dungeon as he wrote the "prison epistles." Acts 28:30 indicates that he rented a house in Rome and was under "house arrest" there.
- Paul's optimism and joy grew from the security of knowing our Savior and trusting that he belonged to Jesus—in life and in death. Paul writes to build up this same confidence in the hearts of his readers.
- Paul had a second reason for writing. Philippians is a thank-you note of sorts. The believers in Philippi had supported Paul's ministry in several ways. They had even sent a fellow worker,

Epaphroditus, to minister to Paul in prison. Epaphroditus had become ill and had almost died. He had recovered, and now Paul was sending him back to Philippi to encourage the saints there. (See Philippians 4:14–20.)

- Third, Paul wrote Philippians to urge his readers toward the true unity found only in Christ. He links that unity with Christlike humility in chapter 2.

How can I best grow in grace as I read Philippians?

Philippians describes in very practical terms what it means to live as a forgiven, humble, joyful child of God. Paul is no "armchair Christian," writing about how things should work in theory. No, he's writing from the heat of battle. He knows what it means to stand alone. He knows what it's like to have his friends turn against him. He knows how it feels to be cold and hungry. He understands how convincing Satan's lies sometimes sound.

Still, he lives in joy. This is not a "paste a smile on your face and pretend to be happy" joy. And it's not an "I always feel good" joy. It's a joy that keeps on going despite outward circumstances and inward feelings. It's a joy that explodes in hearts that trust our Savior's promise that nothing can separate us from the love of God in Jesus and His cross.

As you read Philippians, ask the Holy Spirit to teach you how to access that joy—no matter what's going on around you. Ask Him to show you how to live in the kind of confident faith Paul describes. And then notice as He begins to do that—minute by minute, wherever you are, and whoever you're with.

What are the key chapters and verses in Philippians?

- **Philippians 1:3–11** Abounding in Love
- **Philippians 2:3–11** Living in Humility
- **Philippians 3:7–16** Knowing Christ, My Lord
- **Philippians 4:10–20** Rejoicing in God's Abundant Supply

Key verses:

> *Rejoice in the Lord always; again I will say, Rejoice. Let your reasonableness be known to everyone. The Lord is at hand; do not be anxious about anything, but in everything by prayer and supplication with thanksgiving let your requests be made known to God. And the peace of God, which surpasses all understanding, will guard your hearts and your minds in Christ Jesus. (Philippians 4:4–7)*

© iStockphoto.com

Roman Justice

The Roman system of government granted certain privileges to Roman citizens. In all of its colonies, citizens were entitled to a hearing in a court of law, where they were permitted to defend themselves against their accusers. Roman citizens could not be punished with imprisonment, torture, or beating without what we would call "due process" today.

During the first century AD, Claudius, emperor of the Roman Empire, expelled Jews from Rome because he considered them troublemakers. However, as it expanded through the known world, the Roman Empire exhibited great religious tolerance and recognized the Jewish faith as one of many legal religions.

Trouble in Philippi

In Philippi, which was a Roman colony, Paul and Silas were arrested for preaching the Gospel of Jesus Christ after driving a demon out of a slave girl (Acts 16:16–24). At the time, Rome still considered the Christian Church to be a branch, or sect, of the Jewish faith. Therefore, even though Jews—and Christians—were not highly regarded, what Paul preached was probably not against the law. The owners of the slave girl Paul had healed were angry about their loss of income from the girl's fortune-telling. The magistrates were concerned with keeping order and maintaining the flow of commerce. None of them knew that Paul and Silas, though Jews by heritage and Christians in practice, were also Roman citizens.

Paul was born a Roman citizen (Acts 22:28), but Scripture does not tell us how Silas became a Roman citizen. In addition to being born into a Roman family, one could receive citizenship as a reward for service to the state, or one could purchase Roman citizenship for a large sum of money. Many Jews in Tarsus, Paul's hometown, were apparently Roman citizens.

Injustice

So troublemakers Paul and Silas were brutally beaten, thrown into prison, and tortured with chains that held them in an intolerable, painful position—and all without benefit of a trial. There were no witnesses to testify for Paul and Silas and there was no legally proclaimed sentence. There were only the accusers, the crowd in the marketplace, and the magistrates, who acted unlawfully. Because Paul and Silas were Roman citizens, their arrest, flogging, and imprisonment without trial were serious offenses against Roman law.

Opportunity for Escape

There surely were prisoners in the jail with Paul and Silas who were hardened criminals. Some may have been murderers facing execution. The jailer had a huge responsibility. If one of these condemned men escaped, the jailer was subject to the same punishment—death. No wonder he was prepared to fall on his own sword when the doors to the jail opened. Imagine his relief to learn that no one had left!

Luke does not explain why the magistrates decided to release Paul and Silas, even before learning that they were citizens. When they did learn of it, however, they agreed to escort the men from prison, requesting that they leave Philippi—probably to avoid further trouble in the marketplace.

Colossians

Into Colossians

This letter was addressed to the Church (believers) in the city of Colossae.
It was written by Paul, probably around AD 60.
It pictures Jesus as "The True God, Our Eternal Hope."

This Epistle at a Glance

- Colossians is classified as one of Paul's "prison epistles." Scholars believe he wrote it (and Ephesians, Philippians, and Philemon) all from Rome during his imprisonment there. Rather than writing from a prison cell, it's likely Paul was under a kind of "house arrest" and that he wrote from a house he was renting. (See Acts 28.)
- Paul did not plant the Church in Colossae, nor had he ever been there (Colossians 2:1). It's possible that Epaphras (1:7–8) began the congregation shortly after his own conversion, but no one knows for sure.
- This letter corrects false teaching that had begun to root itself among the Colossian Christians. Some leaders had begun to teach the people to worship angels. They encouraged "mystical experiences" and insisted on the celebration of certain religious festivals. They also imposed strict rules about what Christians should eat and drink.
- The false teachers in Colossae rejected physical things (including the human body) as unimportant or even harmful to one's faith; instead, they stressed the "spiritual." It led them to deny that Jesus even had a human body! This was perhaps an early form of a heresy known as Gnosticism. The word means "knowing." Gnostics formed secret groups to share "secret knowledge"—things that supposedly only they knew.

- Every so often today, someone will grab headlines by claiming to have found a lost book or manuscript that explains what Christianity was "really like" in the first century. They sometimes even try to make it seem as though what Christians believe today is a corrupt version of what Jesus taught. Quite often, their "new discoveries" are books written by Gnostics, books that the Early Church knew about, but rejected as not faithful to the true faith. Colossians is an example of how Paul defended true Christianity.

How can I best grow in grace as I read Colossians?

People in our world today who don't know and believe the Bible still argue about who Jesus was—and is! Some say He was just a good man who taught the world about love. Some say that if He was God, He couldn't also be a true human being. Islam teaches that Jesus couldn't have been the Son of God; it also denies that He died on the cross. God saved Him from that and took Him to heaven, they say, because His enemies were confused about who He was.

Colossians addresses all such confusion directly. The reformer Martin Luther might have had Colossians in mind when he wrote:

> *I believe that Jesus Christ, true God, begotten of the Father from eternity, and also true man, born of the Virgin Mary, is my Lord. (Luther's Small Catechism: The Apostles' Creed, explanation of the Second Article)*

In explaining the truth about Jesus, Colossians speaks both to our heads (our intellect and understanding) and to our hearts (our feelings and need for assurance). Colossians tells who Jesus is—and who He is for us! Colossians tells what Jesus did—and what that means for us!

Colossians is a great book to read when we're feeling weak and uncertain, confused or guilty. It shouts out the truth in clear and encouraging words. And it invites us to keep on following the Savior whose death and resurrection have brought us peace. As you read, ask the Holy Spirit to work all this in you!

What are the key chapters and verses in Colossians?

- **Colossians 1:15–20** The Powerful, Eternal Christ
- **Colossians 2:11–14** Baptized into Christ
- **Colossians 3:12–17** Accessories for the New You!

Key verses:

> *[Christ] is the image of the invisible God, the firstborn of all creation. For by Him all things were created, in heaven and on earth, visible and invisible, whether thrones or dominions or rulers or authorities—all things were created through Him and for Him. And He is before all things, and in Him all things hold together. And He is the head of the body, the church. He is the beginning, the firstborn from the dead, that in everything He might be preeminent. For in Him all the fullness of God was pleased to dwell. (Colossians 1:15–19)*

1 and 2 Thessalonians

Into 1 and 2 Thessalonians

These letters were addressed to the Church (believers) in the city of Thessalonica.

They were written by Paul, the first in around AD 51, the second around AD 52.

They picture Jesus as "Our Returning Savior."

These Epistles at a Glance

- At the time Paul visited Thessalonica, it was a thriving seaport with a population of about 200,000. It lay at the intersection of two major trade routes and was the largest city in Macedonia.
- Paul stopped in Thessalonica while on his second missionary journey. You can read about it Acts 17:1–10.
- A few weeks after Paul arrived in Thessalonica, serious persecution arose. The believers hurried Paul and Silas away to safety. The two went on to Berea, Athens, and Corinth.
- Later, Paul sent Timothy back to Thessalonica to see how the new believers were doing. Paul wrote 1 Thessalonians soon after Timothy came back to Corinth to report on what was happening in Thessalonica.
- Timothy's report about these new believers had two main points. First, persecution continued and it was serious. (See Acts 17:10–13.) Second, the new believers had many questions about Jesus' return, His second coming.
- Paul wrote 1 Thessalonians to encourage the believers in Thessalonica to stay close to Jesus despite the persecution, and he wrote it to answer their questions.

- About six months later, Paul heard about yet more questions among the believers in Thessalonica. And he heard rumors that some in the church had quit working; they were sitting around, waiting for Jesus to come back and take them to heaven. So Paul wrote a second letter to address these issues.
- Together, the two Thessalonian letters contain more about Jesus' second coming than any of Paul's other writings.
- 2 Thessalonians 2:7–12 describes the "Man of Lawlessness." In other places, the New Testament calls this person "the Antichrist."

How can I best grow in grace as I read 1 and 2 Thessalonians?

As we think about Jesus' return, we can make one of two errors. We can ignore it, living as though we believe it will never happen. Or, like the Thessalonian Christians, we can focus on it so intently that it crowds out everything else our Lord would want us to be doing.

There are many Christians today who live as though Jesus will never keep His promise to return. And there are Christians today who construct elaborate charts and timelines, trying to predict the exact day or week in which Gabriel will blow his trumpet and God will part the sky.

Jesus wants us to avoid these two extremes and, instead, to live with joy as we look forward to seeing Him and as we serve Him by serving others.

As you read the two Thessalonian letters, ask the Holy Spirit to flood your heart with excitement over the truth that one day, you will see Jesus face-to-face—and it could be today! But also pray that He will keep you faithful to the work He's given you to do while He delays.

Also as you read these letters, pray for believers all around the world who are enduring persecution because they worship Jesus as Savior and Lord. Ask that God will keep them faithful and that He will encourage them with the good news of His certain return.

What are the key chapters and verses in 1 and 2 Thessalonians?

- **1 Thessalonians 4:13–5:11** The Coming Day of the Lord
- **2 Thessalonians 1:5–12** The Coming Judgment and Justice
- **2 Thessalonians 2:1–12** The "Man of Lawlessness"

Key verses:

> *But we do not want you to be uninformed, brothers, about those who are asleep, that you may not grieve as others do who have no hope.*

For since we believe that Jesus died and rose again, even so, through Jesus, God will bring with Him those who have fallen asleep. For this we declare to you by a word from the Lord, that we who are alive, who are left until the coming of the Lord, will not precede those who have fallen asleep. For the Lord Himself will descend from heaven with a cry of command, with the voice of an archangel, and with the sound of the trumpet of God. And the dead in Christ will rise first. Then we who are alive, who are left, will be caught up together with them in the clouds to meet the Lord in the air, and so we will always be with the Lord. Therefore encourage one another with these words. (1 Thessalonians 4:13–18)

1 and 2 Timothy

Into 1 and 2 Timothy

These letters were addressed to Timothy, a young pastor in the Church at Ephesus.

They were written by Paul, the first in AD 65, the second in AD 68.

They picture Jesus as "Our Savior and Faithful Witness."

These Epistles at a Glance

- The Early Church had no schools that resemble our seminaries today. So Paul mentored several young men, teaching and encouraging them as shepherds, or pastors, of God's people.
- Timothy and Titus were the most prominent of Paul's protégés. When Paul couldn't be with them in person, he wrote letters of advice and encouragement. When we read the books of 1 and 2 Timothy and Titus today, we're literally reading someone else's mail!
- Paul met Timothy in Lystra (Acts 16:1–5) and may have led him to faith. Timothy became Paul's traveling companion and, eventually, his trusted assistant. Paul considered Timothy his spiritual son.
- We know for sure that Paul made three missionary journeys; it's likely he made a fourth after the events recorded in Acts 28. At this time, Timothy was in Ephesus, serving as pastor of the believers there. Piecing the evidence together, we can deduce that Paul saw he probably wouldn't make it back to Ephesus anytime soon. So he wrote to Timothy to give counsel and direction. This letter is 1 Timothy.
- Different circumstances led Paul to write 2 Timothy. As the letter itself indicates, Paul was in prison for the last time, awaiting execution. Acts 28 describes Paul's first Roman imprisonment; then, he

stayed in a house he had rented. This time, he is in a dungeon. It's cold and lonely. He knows he will die soon. He writes to encourage Timothy. He also writes to outline and celebrate Christ's victories over a lifetime of faith and service.

- Both letters also address issues of congregational organization, leadership, and worship. Both also discuss false doctrine and the ways in which both pastor and people in the Church will want to live out their Christian faith.

How can I best grow in grace as I read 1 and 2 Timothy?

Every New Testament book reminds readers in one way or another of the persecution that lurked in the background throughout the first century. Some books bring this fact of daily life more to the foreground. Take Acts, for example, or 2 Thessalonians.

Paul's two letters to Timothy are vivid reminders that the early Christians faced trouble and even the threat of death for their faith. And yet, the joy that stirred and encouraged their hearts is unmistakable! Paul was not a sour old man, bemoaning his life and fearing his death—just the opposite, in fact!

As you read Paul's letters to Timothy, ask that the Holy Spirit will work in you the same confident trust in your Savior. Ask that He stir up in your heart a deep hunger for the inspired Word that so encouraged the early Christians. And pray for courage to keep on obeying Jesus, no matter what kind of opposition you face.

What are the key chapters and verses in 1 and 2 Timothy?

- **1 Timothy 1:12–17** The Gospel Message: Christ Died to Save Sinners.
- **1 Timothy 3:1–13** Qualifications for Overseers ("elders") and Deacons.
- **1 Timothy 6:11–16** To Timothy: "Fight the Good Fight of Faith."
- **1 Timothy 2:1–7** Living as Witnesses: the Qualities We Need (This is of special note for pastors; Paul uses the illustrations of a soldier, an athlete, and a farmer.)
- **2 Timothy 3:10–17** The Inspiration of the Holy Scriptures Confirmed: "God-breathed."
- **2 Timothy 4:1–4** To Timothy and All Pastors: "Preach God's Word—When It's Convenient and When It's Not."

Key verses:

> *But as for you, continue in what you have learned and have firmly believed, knowing from whom you learned it and how from childhood you have been acquainted with the sacred writings, which are able to make you wise for salvation through faith in Christ Jesus. All Scripture is breathed out by God and profitable for teaching, for reproof, for correction, and for training in righteousness, that the man of God may be competent, equipped for every good work. (2 Timothy 3:14–17)*

Women in the First Century

God created Adam, and then saw that Adam was lonely. So, out of Adam's rib, God created Eve. Both were created in God's image. Women of Israel in the New Testament attended worship in the tabernacle and temple and brought offerings for sacrifice.

Scripture mentions women assisting Jesus in His ministry. Most notably, Jesus' own mother, Mary, was given the honor of being the mother of God. Mary and Martha were devoted followers of Christ throughout His ministry. The widow mentioned in Mark 12:41–44 was commended by Jesus for her generosity. Lydia, another New Testament woman, sold purple goods and, through her trade, helped to support the apostles. But what was life like for these New Testament women?

Marriage and Motherhood

Most women married at age 15 or 16. The youngest for girls to marry was perhaps age 12; a twenty-year-old woman who was not married would be considered a disgrace. Once married, the women hoped to have children. Mothers were happy to have daughters, but they had higher hopes for having sons. Some of the saddest women in the Bible are those who, like Hannah, were childless.

Mothers took care of the household and provided for the education of the young children. Faithful mothers in Scripture taught their children God's Word. After the boys were sent to school or to serve as an apprentice at work each day, the mothers continued with the training of their daughters, teaching them to sew, knit, spin, weave, grind grain, prepare bread and other foods, sweep and clean the house, and take care of the younger children.

Cosmetics

Wealthy women used oils to care for their skin and hair. Some women in Bible times used cosmetics. They painted their eyebrows and eyelashes. They used a dark blue eye shadow called kohl.

Wealthier women used mirrors of polished bronze. They did not have the more reflective mirrors that are available today.

© Hanan Isachar/Israelimages.com

Working in a vineyard at Nazareth Village.

Widows

In Bible times, widows—women whose husbands had died—often relied on the generosity of their families and on charity for their food and shelter. If a widow's husband had been wealthy, she had money for her care, but these women could be in danger of losing their money if they were unprotected. Women could not easily get a job to help pay the expenses of daily life, but they were not forgotten by God. The Word of God clearly states that believers are to take care of the poor and widows (Psalm 68:5; James 1:27). This is at least part of the reason why the gift of the widow in Mark 12 is so remarkable. She had so little to give, and yet she gave it freely.

© Hanan Isachar/Israelimages.com

Replica of a first-century house in Nazareth Village.

Clothing and Jewelry

Ring

Women often wore long, flowing robes that reached to their ankles. Wealthier women also wore a long coat, which was like an outer dress, made of finely woven wool, fine linen, or silk. Such women also wore clothing that was dyed with scarlet or other colors that were more expensive to use. Their clothing was embroidered with gold and costly needlework. Women could also wear a veil as protection from the sun or as wedding attire.

Women in ancient times wore jewelry, such as pendants, nose rings, bracelets, anklets, and earrings made from gold with precious stones. They also wore pins, necklaces, rings, and robe fasteners.

Bracelet

The Laying On of Hands

> *And the twelve summoned the full number of the disciples and said, "It is not right that we should give up preaching the word of God to serve tables. Therefore, brothers, pick out from among you seven men of good repute, full of the Spirit and of wisdom, whom we will appoint to this duty. But we will devote ourselves to prayer and to the ministry of the word." And what they said pleased the whole gathering, and they chose Stephen, a man full of faith and of the Holy Spirit, and Philip, and Prochorus, and Nicanor, and Timon, and Parmenas, and Nicolaus, a proselyte of Antioch. These they set before the apostles, and they prayed and laid their hands on them.* (Acts 6:2–6)

The laying on of hands has great significance in the Bible as the method used to bestow a special blessing. In the Old Testament, there are many references to the laying on of hands as it confirmed the giving of the birthright, as Isaac did with Jacob. It was also used to give special recognition or transfer authority from one person to another. It was usually donc in a formal ceremony, as when Moses laid hands on Joshua, making him the new leader of the nation of Israel (Numbers 27:18–23).

In the New Testament, the laying on of hands was also performed on newly baptized persons to convey peace and recognize them as new members of the Body of Christ. Leaders of the young Church were commissioned to service by this rite (Acts 6:6).

Today, this practice is used as both a symbolic and formal method of invoking the Holy Spirit during Baptism, confirmation, and the ordination and commissioning of ministers, elders, deacons, and other church officers. In many cases, it is accompanied by anointing with oil, which symbolizes consecrating or setting someone or something apart for a special purpose.

Titus

Into Titus

This letter was addressed to Titus, a young pastor on the island of Crete.
It was written by Paul in AD 68.
It pictures Jesus as "Our Great God and Savior."

This Epistle at a Glance

- We read in the Old Testament about the "sons of the prophets" and the "company of the prophets." (See, for example, 2 Kings 6:1–7.) Evidently, they provided training opportunities for young men who wanted to serve God by proclaiming His Word. The New Testament mentions nothing like this. Instead, experienced leaders mentored younger leaders. That's how Paul came to work with Titus.
- Titus and Timothy were the most prominent of Paul's students. When Paul couldn't be with them in person, he wrote letters of advice and encouragement. The books of Titus and Timothy fall into this category.
- Titus was Greek, not Jewish. Perhaps not as well-known as Timothy, his name nevertheless appears some dozen times in the New Testament. He was an important leader of God's first-century Church.
- After accompanying Paul and Barnabas as they shared the Gospel, Titus served in the city of Corinth for a while at Paul's request.
- Later, Titus and Paul went to the island of Crete together. Once the work was started there, Paul left Titus in Crete to finish organizing the Church and help people live Christ-honoring lives.
- Later still, Titus served in Dalmatia—present-day Croatia and Montenegro (2 Timothy 4:10).

- Together with 1 and 2 Timothy, Titus is one of the "pastoral letters"—letters Paul wrote to help young pastors in their work.

How can I best grow in grace as I read Titus?

In several places, this short book makes it clear that holy living and pure teaching are two sides of the same coin. What we believe affects what we do, and what we do grows out of what we believe. Paul starts his letter by referring to this truth, then comes back around and underscores it in a more lengthy passage later; most of chapter 2 focuses on this idea. Here's the introduction from chapter 1:

> *Paul, a servant of God and an apostle of Jesus Christ, for the sake of the faith of God's elect and* their knowledge of the truth, which accords with godliness . . . *(v. 1; emphasis added)*

Are we saved by being good? No. Absolutely not. Jesus died and rose again for us to make us God's children. It's all about what Jesus did and not about what we do. Paul makes that clear in every letter he writes. But once we know and believe the truth about God's love for us in Christ, we can't keep on living as "liars, evil beasts, [and] lazy gluttons" (v. 12)! We're God's baptized children! Eternal life is growing in our hearts! It *will* change us!

As you read the Book of Titus, think about that. Notice God's goodness to you as Paul describes it. Think about your Baptism and the enormous change our Savior worked in you through it. Then ask the Holy Spirit to point out any attitudes or habits He wants to change in you. Invite Him to do just that!

What are the key chapters and verses in Titus?

- **Titus 1:5–9** Qualifications for Spiritual Leaders
- **Titus 2:1–15** Sound Doctrine and Holy Living Go Together
- **Titus 3:4–7** Baptism: a Beautiful Description (These verses are sometimes read at Christmastime.)

Key verses:

> *When the goodness and loving kindness of God our Savior appeared, He saved us, not because of works done by us in righteousness, but according to His own mercy, by the washing of regeneration and renewal of the Holy Spirit, whom He poured out on us richly through Jesus Christ our Savior, so that being justified by His grace we might become heirs according to the hope of eternal life. (Titus 3:4–7)*

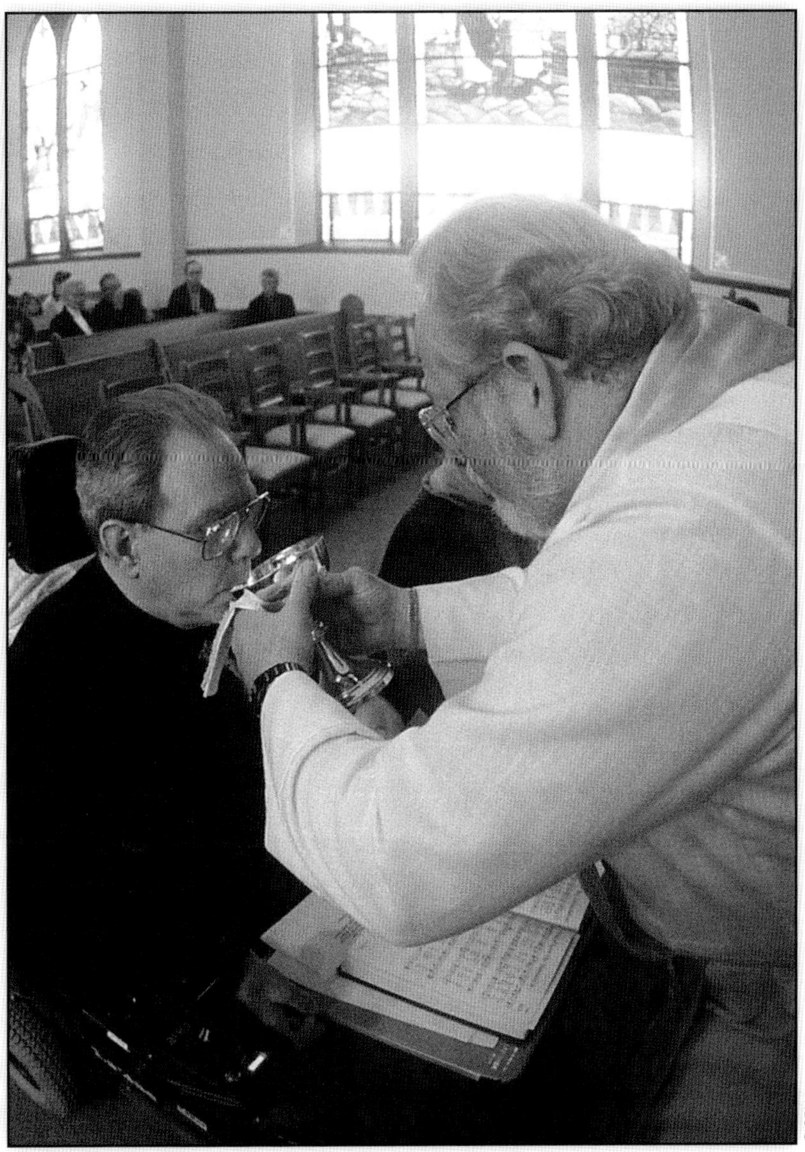

The Pastoral Office

Where do pastors come from?

Jesus did not ascend into heaven and leave us alone. He calls men to be pastors (Latin for "shepherds") to preach His Word and to administer the Sacraments to us, His flock. Pastors are Christ's servants who care for the people of God with these gifts of forgiveness, life, and salvation.

In the years immediately after Jesus' resurrection and the giving of the Holy Spirit at Pentecost, Jesus' disciples served as leaders, preachers, and teachers for followers of "the Way," as the early Christians were called (see Acts 9:2; 19:23). These men also trained others to be elders to "shepherd the flock of God" (1 Peter 5:2), as Paul trained Titus and Timothy. The word *pastor* has its roots in this shepherding ministry of the Early Christian Church.

The Office of the Ministry is a God-given institution. Pastors do not represent themselves, but the person of Christ. When God's servants deal with us, it is as if Christ our dear Lord deals with us Himself. (See "What is confession?" in Luther's Small Catechism.)

This gift of pastors was given to the Church for the building up of the Body of Christ (believers). Not all men are called to be ministers.

When a man desires to become a pastor, he receives training often at a seminary, is certified by the Church, and is then called to serve a congregation. Many churches teach that nobody should preach publicly in the Church or administer the Sacraments unless he is regularly called. In this case, *call* means that God issues an invitation through a congregation of the Church to a specific public ministry. When he accepts his first call to serve a congregation, the candidate is ordained. Ordination is a public rite of confirmation of his call into ministry. Through Word and prayer, he is set apart for service to Christ and the Church.

Our pastors preach, catechize (teach the faith), administer the Sacraments, hear the confessions of penitent sinners, pronounce absolution, and comfort the sick.

People support their pastor by regarding him highly, praying for his ministry, and understanding that his authority comes from God, so that as he cares for them, his work is a joy.

Philemon

Into Philemon

This letter was addressed to Philemon, a slaveholder.

It was written by Paul, probably during his first imprisonment in Rome, around AD 60.

It pictures Jesus as "Our Lord and Master."

This Epistle at a Glance

- From this short letter itself, we can piece together the reasons Paul wrote and the result he wanted to see.
- Philemon was a Christian and a friend of Paul. Perhaps Paul had even led Philemon to faith.
- Onesimus had been Philemon's slave, but he had escaped. In the process, he robbed Philemon. Somehow, Onesimus came under Paul's influence and had become a believer. Now, Paul was sending him back to Philemon.
- Ancient Roman society considered slaves to be property. Masters could punish and even execute slaves who escaped.
- Paul wanted Philemon to forgive Onesimus. The Book of Philemon is a kind of "postcard"—it's not long enough to be a real letter—asking Philemon to do just that. But Paul also hints that he'd like to see Philemon go further and free Onesimus. He doesn't want to demand it, though. Paul wants Philemon to act willingly.
- Onesimus carried Paul's "postcard" with him as he traveled back to Philemon's estate. Paul intended that it introduce Philemon to his new brother, Onesimus.
- The name *Onesimus* means "useful." Paul suggests that Onesimus is much more useful to Philemon now that he's more than a slave; he's a brother in Christ!

- Philemon is one of Paul's "prison epistles." Paul probably wrote Philemon, Philippians, Ephesians, and Colossians during his first imprisonment in Rome. See Acts 28 and the Bible book introductions on pages 395, 397, 401, and 417 for more background information.

How can I best grow in grace as I read Philemon?

Many slaves became followers of Jesus in the first century. Although slavery posed a deep moral problem in Roman society, the New Testament never calls for a slave uprising. Instead, God's people trusted that the Gospel would do its work.

Jesus once compared His kingdom to yeast (Luke 13:20–21). That kingdom grows one heart at a time, one life at a time, as the Holy Spirit brings people to faith and teaches them what it means to love one another as Christ Jesus has loved us.

Eventually, the "whole loaf"—the society—experiences the results. When Christian slaveholders in Rome came to see their slaves as brothers and sisters in Christ, they freed them. And, in general, that's how it worked in Christian regions around the world as the Gospel spread.

Did some Christians keep on holding slaves—sometimes for decades? Yes. It was sinful, and it damaged their walk with the Lord—just as our own sins damage us still today! But that doesn't mean that Christ condones slavery. Wherever Christianity has spread, slavery has eventually disappeared. Many of the emancipators who fought against slavery in the United States before and during the Civil War relied on the Book of Philemon for inspiration.

You probably don't own slaves or ever intend to do that, though! So what does the Book of Philemon say to you? At its core, this little book is about forgiveness. What do we do with those who hurt us?

Knowing we *should* forgive and *wanting* to forgive are two different things. God knows this. As you read Philemon, notice that Paul never uses the word *should*. Instead, he points Philemon back to the Gospel, back to God's love in Jesus Christ. That's where Philemon's ability to forgive—and ours too—begins.

As you read this book, talk with Jesus about the person or the people you have trouble forgiving. Let Him continue His work in you as you soak up His love and rely on His strength.

What is the key verse in Philemon?

> *I pray that the sharing of your faith may become effective for the full knowledge of every good thing that is in us for the sake of Christ. (Philemon 1:6)*

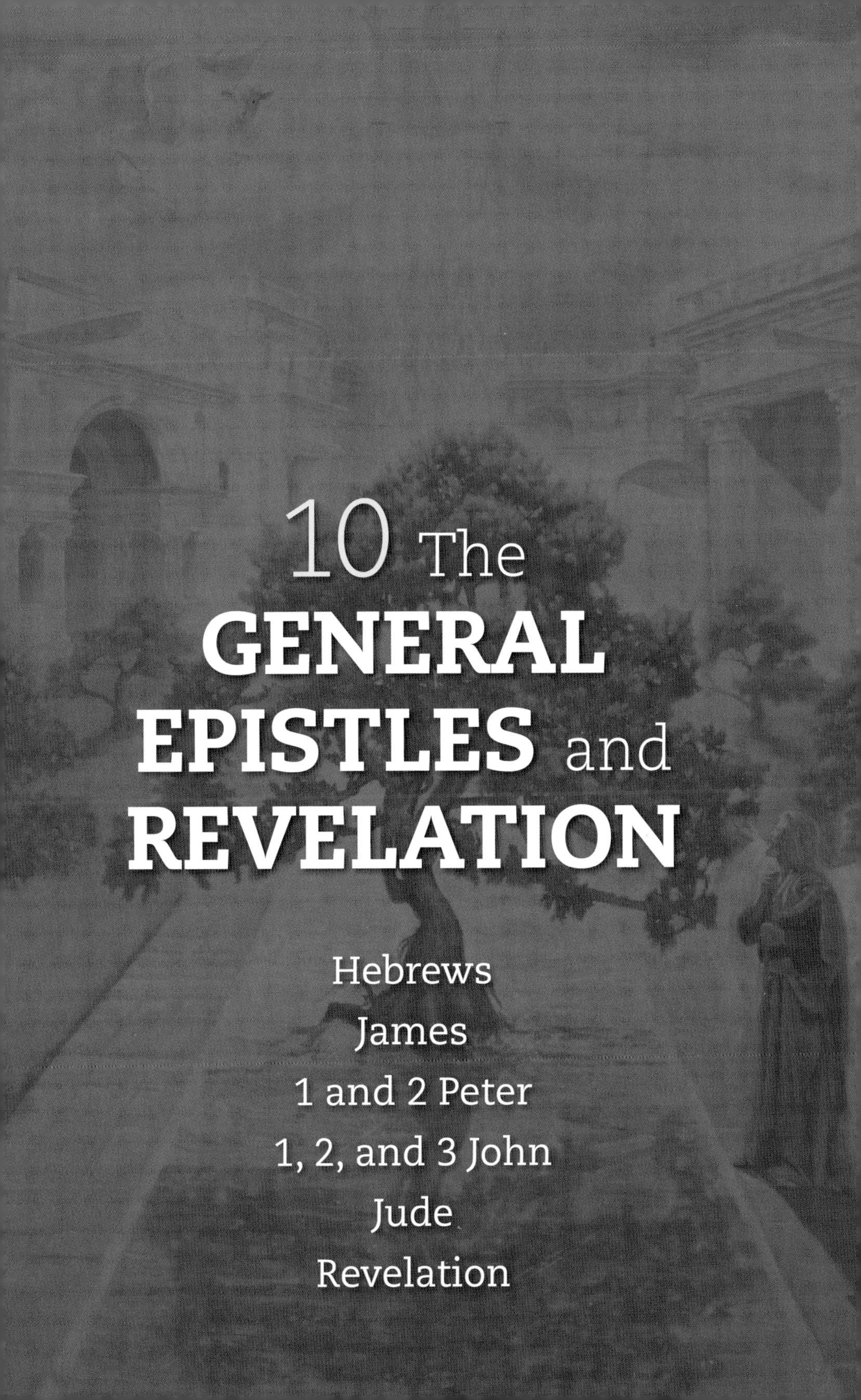

10 The GENERAL EPISTLES and REVELATION

Hebrews

James

1 and 2 Peter

1, 2, and 3 John

Jude

Revelation

Introduction

Unlike the thirteen Epistles of Paul, which were all written by the same author, this group of letters was written by various authors. The eight General Epistles are: Hebrews, James, 1 Peter, 2 Peter, 1 John, 2 John, 3 John, and Jude. Paul wrote his letters to specific congregations in specific cities or to specific persons. In contrast, most of the General Epistles were written to persons or congregations in a more general way, though some may have been written to specific persons or congregations (e.g., Hebrews, 2 John, and 3 John).

Hebrews

Into Hebrews

This letter was addressed to a group of Jewish Christians during a time of persecution. Perhaps they lived in Rome under Emperor Nero, but no one knows for sure.

No one knows who wrote Hebrews. Suggestions have included Paul, Barnabas, Silas, Apollos, and Priscilla. The book does not identify its author, and the witness of the Early Church about authorship is unclear. Some passages in Hebrews lead to the conclusion that the temple was still standing in Jerusalem when the author wrote. That means it must date to before AD 70, when the Roman general Titus besieged and destroyed Jerusalem.

Hebrews pictures Jesus as "The Final, Perfect Sacrifice for Our Sin."

This Epistle at a Glance

- Hebrews is the first of the "general epistles," letters that are not clearly addressed to a specific congregation or individual. The letters penned by James, Peter, John, and Jude also fall into this category.
- The first readers of Hebrews were new converts from Judaism to Christianity. But they were tempted to go back to Judaism because of the persecution they faced. It is likely that Christianity was illegal in the Roman Empire at this time; Judaism was allowed.
- The author of Hebrews argues that Jesus is superior to Judaism in every respect:
- He's greater than the Old Testament prophets (Hebrews 1:1–2).
- He's greater than the angels (1:4–9).
- He's greater than Moses and Joshua (3:1–4:13).
- He's greater than all the Old Testament priests—even Melchizedek (4:14–7:20).

- His covenant is a greater covenant than the covenant of the Law given at Sinai (7:22–8:13).
- His sacrifice of Himself accomplished what all the Old Testament sacrifices put together could not do—remove sin forever (9:1–10:39).
- Hebrews assumes its readers are familiar with Old Testament customs, laws, sacrifices, festivals, and temple customs. The book contains many quotes from the Old Testament, particularly the five Books of Moses (Genesis–Deuteronomy) and Jeremiah.
- In most of Paul's letters, the first several chapters focus on doctrine and the last chapters on how it applies in our lives. In Hebrews, the applications are scattered throughout the book.
- One primary application is crystal clear: don't abandon your relationship with Jesus! In a way, the Book of Hebrews is a repetition of the dialogue Jesus once had with Peter and the other disciples:

  Jesus said to the Twelve, "Do you want to go away as well?" Simon Peter answered Him, "Lord, to whom shall we go? You have the words of eternal life." (John 6:67–68)

How can I best grow in grace as I read Hebrews?

Sometimes it's tempting to think that there's got to be an better way to go through life than relying on Jesus. We like to think we're smart enough or friendly enough or persistent enough or *something* enough to make our lives run more smoothly. If we were in control, things would be better.

Or we want to believe that our troubles would be over if we could just focus on being popular or athletic instead of thinking about how to act like a Christian.

When our friends (or even our teachers!) laugh at our faith, it hurts. When we decide not to see certain movies or watch certain TV programs or play certain video games because of our faith, it can feel lonely. We can feel left out—and maybe it seems there's no good reason for missing out on the fun.

Do you see yourself in any of the descriptions above? Even if not, there's something in your life that sometimes makes you want to turn down the volume on your faith, even if you don't want to walk away from it altogether.

The Book of Hebrews talks about that temptation. As you read it, ask the Holy Spirit to use His Word to help you face it head-on. Ask that He work in you a deeper confidence in God's love and the courage to stand up against the pressures you face—whether those pressures come from other people or from right inside your own heart. He wants to help! He inspired the writer of this book for that very reason!

What are the key chapters and verses in Hebrews?

- **Hebrews 1:1–4** Christ Jesus: a Glorious Picture.
- **Hebrews 2:14–15** Jesus: Death's Destroyer.
- **Hebrews 4:12** God's Living, Active Word: Powerfully at Work in Us.
- **Hebrews 4:14–16** Come to Our Savior in Prayer: He Will Hear and Help.
- **Hebrews 11:1–39** Sometimes called the Bible's "Hall of Fame," but more properly called the "Hall of Faith," this describes what God has done for, in, and with His people. (Surprisingly, this "family album" contains no hint of the sins committed by the individuals pictured here. Jesus' blood has washed away all their guilt.)
- **Hebrews 12:1–2** Run the Race of Faith with Patience: Jesus Has Won for Us!

That Mysterious Melchizedek

The shadowy figure of Melchizedek passes across the pages of Genesis 14, only to disappear into the mists of time. He would be largely forgotten if the writer to the Hebrews had not made such stunning comparisons between Melchizedek and the Messiah.

Some have thought the Melchizedek of Genesis was the actual person of Christ before His incarnation. What's more likely, though, is that Melchizedek was a human being, a sinner like you and me, and at the same time a "type," or picture, of Christ. Melchizedek and Jesus are alike in these ways:

- The name *Melchizedek* means "king of righteousness"; Jesus is our righteous King who bestows on us the righteousness He won for us.
- Melchizedek was the king of Salem (Genesis 14:18). *Salem* means "peace." In Jesus, we have peace with God.
- Born decades before Levi, Melchizedek could not have belonged to the tribe of Levi. Jesus was born into the tribe of Judah. Under the covenant of Sinai, all priests had to come from the tribe of Levi. Both Jesus and Melchizedek thus served "God Most High" (Genesis 14:18) under God's direct authorization, not under the old covenant.
- In all history, only two priests served in "the order of Melchizedek"—Melchizedek and Jesus. Jesus still serves as High Priest of that order and will serve forever in that order because "He always lives to make intercession for [us]" (Hebrews 7:25).

Sabbath vs. Sunday

What is the best day to worship? Why do some religions worship on Saturday and some on Sunday?

The Sabbath

The Sabbath was a special day for the nation of Israel. From the very beginning of time, God's people recognized the uniqueness of this day:

> *And on the seventh day God finished His work that He had done, and He rested on the seventh day from all His work that He had done. So God blessed the seventh day and made it holy, because on it God rested from all His work that He had done in creation.*
> *(Genesis 2:2–3)*

The first mention of a Sabbath Day for God's people comes during the exodus, when God began to feed His people with manna and quail (Exodus 16). Moses relayed this command from God about the manna: "This is what the Lord has commanded: 'Tomorrow is a day of solemn rest, a holy Sabbath to the Lord; bake what you will bake and boil what you will boil, and all that is left over lay aside to be kept till the morning' " (v. 23).

A short time later, the Sabbath rest was included in the Ten Commandments that God gave His people at Sinai: "Remember the Sabbath day, to keep it holy" (Exodus 20:8). Special Sabbath sacrifices were specified (Leviticus 24:8; Numbers 28:9–10). It was a day of leisure by which the Israelites remembered their delivery from slavery (Deuteronomy 5:14–15). Later, it became a custom for Jewish men to assemble in the synagogue on the Sabbath for the reading of God's Word.

Sunday

The first Easter introduced a new practice. Jesus was crucified on the sixth day of the week, our Friday—Good Friday. He lay in the tomb through the Sabbath, the seventh day, the day of rest. On Sunday, "the first day of the week" (Matthew 28:1), Jesus' tomb was found empty. He had risen from the dead. Throughout the day, Jesus appeared to His followers many times: to the women (Matthew 28:9), to the two disciples on the Emmaus Road (Luke 24:13–35), and to the disciples minus Thomas in the Upper Room (John 20:19–23).

Public Domain

From the earliest days of the Christian Church, Sunday became a special day. It was the day on which the Holy Spirit was given during the Feast of Pentecost. It quickly became the day when the Christians ate the Lord's Supper (Acts 20:7) according to His command.

Although Jews continue to mark the Sabbath, and some denominations such as the Seventh-day Adventists worship on Saturday, the tradition of weekly celebration of the Divine Service on Sunday has its roots in the Early Christian Church and has been the Church's continuous practice for nearly two thousand years.

James

Into James

This letter was addressed to "the twelve tribes in the Dispersion" (James 1:1). They were Jewish Christians who had been scattered into many different territories by persecution.

It was probably written by James, Jesus' half-brother, after Jesus ascended to heaven, sometime around AD 50.

It pictures Jesus as "the Lord of glory" (2:1).

This Epistle at a Glance

- James is counted among the "general epistles," letters that are not clearly addressed to a specific congregation or individual. Hebrews is also a general epistle, as are the two letters written by Peter, the three by John, and the letter written by Jude.
- The first readers of this book were on the run. Some had their homes taken away. Others had been threatened with physical harm or even death. They had to escape. And so they found themselves in strange territory, away from family and friends—and all because of their faith in Jesus. James writes to encourage and comfort them.
- James assumes his readers are familiar with the Old Testament. He quotes from it or refers to passages from it more than forty times.
- In some ways, James is a lot like the Old Testament Book of Proverbs. It focuses on the "how-tos" of the faith rather than on doctrines like the Trinity or Baptism or how God saves us. In fact, it's been called "the Proverbs of the New Testament" because of its practical tone.
- James has also been called "the Amos of the New Testament" because James—like the prophet Amos before him—cared so much about the poor.

- James focuses on wisdom and on living wisely. In Scripture, wisdom has little to do with having a brain like a supercomputer. Instead, those with godly wisdom have the skills and practical knowledge for living day by day as God's people.
- Like a novel with several subplots or a symphony with repeating themes, the Book of James cycles back around to several topics several times. For instance, James touches on patience several times. Each time he returns to that topic, he adds deeper insights.
- James focuses on perseverance, controlling the tongue, justice, submitting to God's will, caring for the poor, and living with patience because Jesus is returning soon. He addresses other practical issues too. Watch for these as you read!

How can I best grow in grace as I read James?

One challenge of the Christian faith is sorting out the relationship between our faith in Christ and how we act. Those who concentrate on just one Bible verse or even one Bible book can easily get off track. We say, "Scripture interprets Scripture." This means, in part, that if we want to be sure what's true, we need to take everything the Bible says about it into account.

Some people have thought that the Book of James contradicts Paul's writings, especially Galatians and Romans. If we're saved by God's grace alone though faith, as Paul writes, then why does James focus so much on behavior, on "works"? How can James write, "Faith by itself, if it does not have works, is dead" (2:17)?!

James can write it because it's true. But there is more to understand. To get at the complete truth, we need to add Galatians and Romans to the mix. James here uses the word *faith* differently than Paul does. By "faith," James means bare knowledge and belief, whereas Paul means a sincere trust when he writes about faith. Christian leaders in the past have come up with this sentence to summarize how faith and works fit together: Faith (trust) alone saves, but faith is never alone.

When we know and trust Jesus, when we realize more and more His love for us and the amazing things He's done for us on the cross, we want to do kind, helpful things for others. We just can't help it! The reformer Martin Luther put it this way:

> *Faith, however, is a divine work in us which changes us and makes us to be born anew of God, John 1[:12–13]. It kills the old Adam and makes us altogether different men, in heart and spirit and mind and powers; and it brings with it the Holy Spirit. O it is a living, busy, active, mighty thing, this faith. It is impossible for*

> *it not to be doing good works incessantly. It does not ask whether good works are to be done, but before the question is asked, it has already done them, and is constantly doing them. Whoever does not do such works, however, is an unbeliever. He gropes and looks around for faith and good works, but knows neither what faith is nor what good works are. Yet he talks and talks, with many words, about faith and good works.*
>
> *Faith is a living, daring confidence in God's grace, so sure and certain that the believer would stake his life on it a thousand times. This knowledge of and confidence in God's grace makes men glad and bold and happy in dealing with God and with all creatures. And this is the work which the Holy Spirit performs in faith. Because of it, without compulsion, a person is ready and glad to do good to everyone, to serve everyone, to suffer everything, out of love and praise to God who has shown him this grace. Thus it is impossible to separate works from faith, quite as impossible as to separate heat and light from fire. Beware, therefore, of your own false notions and of the idle talkers who imagine themselves wise enough to make decisions about faith and good works, and yet are the greatest fools. Pray God that he may work faith in you. Otherwise you will surely remain forever without faith, regardless of what you may think or do. (Luther's Works, American Edition, vol. 35, pp. 370–71)*

As you read James, look for practical suggestions for how to live out the faith God has given you. Ask the Holy Spirit to help you make connections between what James writes and your everyday life in your family, with your friends, in your neighborhood. Then, get ready for an adventure! A life of faith is that for sure!

What are the key chapters and verses in James?

- **James 1:2–18** How to Grow through Hardships
- **James 2:1–13** How to Love Your Neighbors—All of Them
- **James 4:1–12** How to Live in Peace with Others
- **James 5:7–18** How to Get through Hard Times

Key verse: *Be doers of the word, and not hearers only, deceiving yourselves. (James 1:22)*

1 and 2 Peter

Into 1 and 2 Peter

The first letter Peter wrote is addressed to the "elect exiles of the dispersion in Pontus, Galatia, Cappadocia, Asia, and Bithynia" (1 Peter 1:1). These were Jewish Christians who had been scattered into many different territories by persecution.

Peter addressed his second letter "To those who have obtained a faith of equal standing with ours by the righteousness of our God and Savior Jesus Christ" (2 Peter 1:1).

Both letters were written by Peter, one of Jesus' twelve disciples; the first was written before AD 67 and the second around AD 68.

Peter pictures Jesus as "Our Soon-Coming Savior."

These Epistles at a Glance

- 1 and 2 Peter are counted among the "general epistles," letters that are not clearly addressed to a specific congregation or individual. Hebrews, James, Jude, and John's letters all also fall into this category.
- Like the first readers of Hebrews and James, Peter's first readers faced persecution. Nero was emperor, and he was making life very, very difficult for Christians. Shortly after Peter wrote his second letter, he would be executed for his faith. Tradition tells us that Peter and his wife were crucified together, Peter asking to be nailed upside down because he didn't consider himself worthy to die in the same way as his Lord. Tradition also tells us that Peter comforted his wife with these words: "Remember the Lord."
- Whether these traditions are true or not, no one can doubt that the Peter who denied Jesus and then hid on the day Jesus died is a very different person from the apostle who wrote the two letters that bear his name. The bold hope he expresses makes it clear that Jesus made a dramatic change in Peter's life!

- 1 Peter focuses mainly on issues of faith, hope, submission to authority, and encouragement for those who suffer.
- 2 Peter focuses on the danger posed by false teachers and encouragement to grow up in the faith.
- Peter also defends the inspiration of Scripture (2 Peter 1:16–21), describes the Day of Judgment (2 Peter 3:7–10), and hints at Jesus' descent into hell after His crucifixion (1 Peter 3:18–22).

How can I best grow in grace as I read 1 and 2 Peter?

Do you ever wish you were more secure, more confident, more steady, more faithful in your witness about Jesus? Do you ever wonder what it might be like to stand rock solid in hope, no matter what's happening around you?

Jesus changed Peter in remarkable ways. First, Jesus changed his name to "Peter"—"Rock." And then He changed Peter's life so that Peter became a "rock" others could look to and rely on for comfort and hope. In his letters, Peter shares some remarkable insights about that process. And he helps us as readers fit those insights into our own faith walk.

As you read Peter's letters, notice the powerful ways Peter describes all God has done for us in Jesus and the new identity He has, in grace, given us. Notice, too, how much Jesus' return in glory energized and encouraged Peter. Remember the terrible persecutions Peter and his readers were experiencing, and notice how the Holy Spirit buoyed them up in hope despite their troubles.

Then ask the Holy Spirit to continue working the same hope, confidence, boldness, and peace He worked in Peter. Ask that you become more and more the person He's created you to be as His inspired (and inspiring!) Word works in you.

What are the key chapters and verses in 1 and 2 Peter?

- **1 Peter 1:3–5** Born Again to a Living Hope!
- **1 Peter 2:19–10** "You Are a Holy Nation, a Royal Priesthood"
- **1 Peter 3:21–22** Remember Your Baptism
- **1 Peter 5:6–11** Stand Firm against Satan's Attacks
- **2 Peter 3:1–13** The Coming Day of the Lord

Key verses:

> *We have something more sure, the prophetic word, to which you will do well to pay attention as to a lamp shining in a dark place, until the day dawns and the morning star rises in your hearts,*

knowing this first of all, that no prophecy of Scripture comes from someone's own interpretation. For no prophecy was ever produced by the will of man, but men spoke from God as they were carried along by the Holy Spirit. (2 Peter 1:19–21)

Peter

Many churches bear the names of apostles. St. Peter is often used in honor of the fisherman God chose to be a leader in the Early Christian Church on earth. Peter, though respected by Christians throughout the centuries, was every bit as much a sinner as you and I. One moment, he told Jesus that he would die with Him. The next moment, he denied even knowing the Savior.

Disciple

Simon Peter was from Bethsaida. He was among the first disciples Jesus called to follow Him. The evangelists consistently list him first among the twelve disciples. When Christ called Simon to be a disciple, Jesus gave him a new name—Peter (in Greek), or Cephas (in Aramaic). Both *Peter* and *Cephas* mean "rock." We do not know much about Peter's personal life, but we do know he was married, for Scripture records Jesus' healing of Peter's mother-in-law (Matthew 8:14–15).

After Jesus' resurrection, He reaffirmed Peter's call as a disciple (John 21:19), and Peter became a leader of the Christian Church in Jerusalem. He led the apostles in replacing Judas Iscariot, and he went on to teach and preach with boldness and clarity. On the day of Pentecost, when God sent the Holy Spirit to Jesus' followers, Peter spoke the message of life and salvation for the other eleven.

Missionary

In the years following Jesus' ascension, Peter traveled, often with John, to various places, spreading the Gospel message. He performed miracles in Jesus' name. He even spoke to the Sanhedrin—the council of Jewish leaders—telling them that the same Jesus they crucified was alive and was indeed the Messiah (Acts 4:5–12). Though he and the other apostles were commanded to stop saying such things, Peter replied that he was unable to keep silent; he was compelled to tell others of the Christ (vv. 18–20). In the course of his ministry, the Jewish leaders imprisoned and persecuted Peter, but Scripture records no other time when Peter failed to proclaim Jesus as the Savior of both Jews and Gentiles.

Peter heals the lame man.

Peter and John discover the empty tomb.

An Author of Scripture

In the midst of his travels, Peter wrote two letters that are in the Bible—1 and 2 Peter. The first letter focuses on God's grace, given to us especially in times of persecution by those outside the Church. The second discusses God's grace in the face of false teaching within the Church. Peter's pastoral care for his fellow Christians is evident in these books, which also encourage us as we encounter daily trials and adversities.

Tradition

Church historians teach that Peter, like Jesus, died by crucifixion, probably around AD 68. Tradition holds that Peter did not consider himself worthy to die in the same manner as his Lord, so he requested to be crucified upside down. Peter died a martyr for the Christian faith. His apostolic symbol is a set of keys, for, in Matthew 16:19, Christ gave Peter the keys to the kingdom. Though he was not very rocklike in the Gospels—he was often impulsive and impatient—Peter indeed became a rock in the Early Christian Church. Jesus named Peter not for what he was, but for what by God's grace he would become.

Transfiguration Facts —The Five Ws

Three of the Gospel writers—Matthew, Mark, and Luke—record the account of the transfiguration (Matthew 17:1–8; Mark 9:2–8; Luke 9:28–36). Peter, himself a witness to the transfiguration, wrote:

> *For we did not follow cleverly devised myths when we made known to you the power and coming of our Lord Jesus Christ, but we were eyewitnesses of His majesty. For when He received honor and glory from God the Father, and the voice was borne to Him by the Majestic Glory, "This is My beloved Son, with whom I am well pleased," we ourselves heard this very voice borne from heaven, for we were with Him on the holy mountain. (2 Peter 1:16–18)*

Who witnessed the transfiguration?

Peter, James, and John, the three closest disciples of Jesus, witnessed the transfiguration.

What does this event show about the two natures of Christ?

The Bible teaches that Jesus is true God and true man, as Martin Luther explains in the Second Article of the Apostles' Creed in his Small Catechism: "I believe that Jesus Christ, true God, begotten of the Father from eternity, and also true man, born of the Virgin Mary, is my Lord." Jesus has both a divine and a human nature. He is at all times divine and at all times human. For a moment during the transfiguration, He revealed His divine nature to His disciples, showing them a glimpse of His full divine glory.

Where did the transfiguration occur?

Although the precise mountain cannot be identified, many think that it was probably on Mount Hermon, which measures a height of 9,232 feet (2,814 meters) above sea level. Another possible site is Mount Tabor, which is about 1,850 feet (588 meters) above sea level.

Events of the transfiguration

- On the mountain, Jesus was transformed, and His garments shone with heavenly brightness.
- Moses and Elijah appeared and talked to Jesus.
- Perhaps wanting to preserve the moment, Peter suggested making three tents for Jesus, Moses, and Elijah.
- A voice from a cloud declared that Jesus is the Son of God, thus showing Jesus' divine authority.

Why did Moses and Elijah appear with Jesus?

When speaking about His own death and resurrection at the end of the Book of Luke (24:44), Jesus stated, "These are My words that I spoke to you while I was still with you, that everything written about Me in the Law of Moses and the Prophets and the Psalms must be fulfilled." Everything written in the Old Testament, in the Books of the Law and the Prophets, would be fulfilled in Jesus.

What do Moses and Elijah have to do with that? Moses was the Old Testament leader who received the Ten Commandments, the Law, from God. He wrote the first five books of the Bible, which are sometimes referred to as "the Law."

God's Old Testament prophets spoke His Word to the people. Elijah was the prophet when God sent fire to Mount Carmel to miraculously burn a sacrifice (1 Kings 18:20–40).

Moses and Elijah symbolize the Law and the Prophets. Christ fulfilled the teaching of the Law and the Prophets. Moses and Elijah appeared with Jesus in order to show that all the fullness of the deity (Godhead) dwells in bodily form in Christ, and that He fulfilled everything in the Old Testament.

When did the event happen?

The transfiguration occurred a week after Peter's great confession that Jesus is the Messiah.

1, 2, and 3 John

Into 1, 2, and 3 John

The letters of 1, 2, and 3 John are among the "general epistles." They are not addressed to a specific known person or church. Hebrews, James, Jude, and Peter's letters all also fall into this category.

All three letters were written by the apostle John, one of Jesus' twelve disciples. All date to the late first century.

John pictures Jesus as "Our Eternal Advocate."

These Epistles at a Glance

- John was one of the disciples closest to Jesus during our Savior's earthly ministry. He wrote the Gospel that bears his name, the Book of Revelation, and three short letters.
- John does not name his first readers; however, at various points in 1 John, the apostle calls his readers "little children." This is likely a general term for his Christian readers.
- He writes as "the elder to the elect lady" in 2 John 1:1. The "elect lady" may be a specific person, but the phrase may also refer to a church; remember, the Holy Christian Church is also sometimes called "the Bride of Christ."
- In 3 John 1:1, the address reads "the elder to the beloved Gaius." Gaius was likely a real person, perhaps a friend of John.
- In 1 John, we read arguments against Gnosticism, an early Christian heresy that denied Jesus' humanity; taught that the spiritual is good and that matter is evil; and encouraged immoral living (see p. 401).
- In 2 John, the apostle speaks against false teachers and warns his readers not to compromise the truth.

- In 3 John, we see a warning against an individual named Diotrephes, a bully and gossip who refuses to extend hospitality to Christian teachers that traveled from place to place, sharing the Gospel.
- In all three letters, John uses the same kinds of simple words we read in his Gospel: *life, light, love, sin, world,* and the like. While the words are simple, John's message is not. He writes as a mature believer and pastor at the end of his life, and his wisdom is much deeper than it might appear at first glance!

How can I best grow in grace as I read 1, 2, and 3 John?

Tradition says that the apostle John lived to be a very old man—the only one of the original twelve disciples who did not die a martyr's death. He spent his last years at the Church in Ephesus. One story says that the congregation asked John to say a few words to them. By then, the aged apostle could not put many words together, but he would say repeatedly, "Little children, love one another" (Jerome *Commentary on Galatians* III:VI; notes on Gal 6:10; PL 26:433).

As we study the three letters of John preserved for us in the New Testament, that story seems more and more likely. Real love—the love that gives to give and not to get, the love that does what's best for the other person, no matter what—that kind of love is hard!

Actually, it's impossible for us sinners to do on their own. So as you read John's letters, ask the Holy Spirit to do something impossible. Ask that He plant and water that kind of love in you. Ask that it will make a difference in you and in the people around you.

What are the key chapters and verses in 1, 2, and 3 John?

- **1 John 1:1–4** Jesus Christ, God and Man
- **1 John 3:1–3** We Will Be Like Him!
- **2 John 1:5–6** Love One Another
- **3 John 1:4** Walk in the Truth

Key verses:

> *If we say we have no sin, we deceive ourselves, and the truth is not in us. If we confess our sins, [God] is faithful and just to forgive us our sins and to cleanse us from all unrighteousness.*
>
> *(1 John 1:8–9)*

Jude

Into Jude

This letter was addressed to "those who are called, beloved in God the Father and kept for Jesus Christ" (Jude 1:1).

It was written by Jude, likely Jesus' half-brother and the brother of James, around AD 68.

It pictures Jesus as "Our Keeper."

This Epistle at a Glance

- Jude is considered as one of the "general epistles," letters that are not addressed to a specific congregation or individual. Hebrews and James are both general epistles, as are the two letters written by Peter and the three by John.
- Jude writes to warn of intruders in the Church who have introduced dangerous errors. He cites several examples from the Old Testament of people who ignored the truth and fell into gross sin.
- The Book of Jude is similar in thought and focus to 2 Peter. Also, like Titus and several other New Testament letters, Jude makes it clear that holy living and pure teaching are two sides of the same coin. What we believe affects what we do, and what we do grows out of what we believe.

How can I best grow in grace as I read Jude?

It's easy to think we are different from the ungodly people Jude observed. We could never fall into the kinds of errors and disobedience he describes!

Or could we? Again and again, the Bible warns God's people to be on guard against false teaching and an immoral lifestyle. Our Lord knows us much better than we know ourselves. We're all vulnerable to the lies and subtle temptations of Satan.

As you read Jude, ask the Holy Spirit to make you always hungry and thirsty for the truths of God's Word. Set aside time every day to read the Scriptures and to talk with Jesus about what you're reading. Immerse yourself so deeply in the truth that you'll be able to spot errors and their dangers immediately—and avoid them.

What are the key verses in Jude?

Jude's "doxology"—his closing hymn of praise—is one of the key passages:

> *Now to Him who is able to keep you from stumbling and to present you blameless before the presence of His glory with great joy, to the only God, our Savior, through Jesus Christ our Lord, be glory, majesty, dominion, and authority, before all time and now and forever. Amen. (vv. 24–25)*

Revelation

Into Revelation

This Book at a Glance

- Revelation was written by the apostle John from the island of Patmos in AD 95. John had been exiled there because of his faith in Jesus.
- At the time Revelation was written, Christians were enduring terrible persecution under the Roman emperor Domitian.
- Like some other New Testament books—James, for example—Revelation moves forward in a series of repeating cycles. It is not organized topically or chronologically. Failing to realize this, some people have tried to read Revelation like some kind of horoscope or as the key to unlocking future world events and assigning dates to those events. This has led to some unfortunate misunderstandings down through the centuries.
- John wrote Revelation using an approach called "apocalyptic" style. The word *apocalypse* means "unveiling" or "revealing." The Book of Revelation reveals Jesus in all His majesty and glorious victory. Its pictures and descriptions are true, but not literal.
- Writers who use an apocalyptic style want to convey more than facts. They use strange words and pictures to stir up strong feelings in the hearts of these readers. These things are not literal, but symbolic.
- The book's pictures of Jesus' victory and its symbolic descriptions of His purposes and His second coming brought deep comfort to Christians experiencing persecution.
- Ezekiel, Daniel, and Zechariah also used an apocalyptic style; parts of all three of these books make an impact similar to that of Revelation. Together, all four books reveal powerful truths about our Lord

and about the future He has in store, especially for His Church, when He returns.

How is the Book of Revelation classified?

Revelation contains a series of letters and descriptions of visions. Writings like this are known as apocalyptic (see p. 216).

What did Revelation's message mean to the original readers?

Many early Christians endured unimaginable pain simply because they refused to give up their faith in Jesus. They were thrown to lions and other wild beasts while onlookers cheered. They were set on fire, hurled down cliffs, skinned alive, and reportedly even boiled in oil. The cruelty was off the charts!

As these believers watched friends and family members being tortured, it would have been easy to give up hope. It would have been easy to deny their faith.

The Book of Revelation helped God's people stand firm despite the storms that roared all around them. The book has one focused message: *Jesus is victorious, and He is coming soon*!

Using that message of hope, the Holy Spirit worked patience and endurance in the hearts of our first-century brothers and sisters. By His grace, they did stand firm. They did receive the "crown of life" Jesus promised them (Revelation 2:10). And their witness speaks to us through the centuries still today.

What does Revelation's message mean to us today?

Believers in many places around the world still face persecution as cruel as anything Emperor Domitian thought up. Add up the number of Christians killed for their faith during the twentieth century, and that number totals more than all the martyrs of all the previous nineteen centuries combined! Persecution has not slowed. In fact, it seems to be increasing.

Satan has not suddenly stopped hating the Church! He will not suddenly stop hounding the Bride of Christ in the twenty-first century.

Despite all this hatred, despite all the misery God's people have endured for the name of Jesus, the victory is already His. And because it is His, it is also ours! He gives it to us freely. We are His forgiven, dearly loved sisters and brothers.

The persecution you face probably doesn't involve lions or dungeons. At least, not yet. But you may be called to stand up for Jesus. You may face ridicule or the laughter of friends or the loss of a job or a scholarship. When that happens, remember that you're in good company—the company of your Savior, the company of the saints and martyrs. Someday soon, you'll join the company of the angels around the throne in endless joy.

As our planet lurches through its last, troubled days, our Lord does not promise to make things easy for us. Quite the opposite, in fact. We will endure hardship. But we can trust both sides of Jesus' promise:

> *In the world you will have tribulation. But take heart; I have overcome the world. (John 16:33)*

Where is Jesus in Revelation?

It's hard to read Revelation and not see Jesus. He is at the very center of every event described. John wrote this book to reveal Christ in His glory. For example:

- In Revelation 1:9–20, John describes his vision of the Son of Man, the Lord of the Church.
- In Revelation 2–3, each letter to each Church describes Jesus in His relationships to His people on earth.
- In Revelation 5 and 7:9–17, we catch a glimpse of the Lamb of God and the worship He is receiving in heaven even now.
- In Revelation 19:11–21, John describes Christ arriving to rescue His own, riding a white horse. He is King Jesus, the "Faithful and True"!
- In Revelation 22, we can read about the city of Christ and of His Bride, the Church.

What are the key chapters in Revelation?

- **Revelation 2–3** The Letters to the Seven Churches
- **Revelation 6–7** True Believers Sealed as Christ's Own
- **Revelation 12** World History in Seventeen Verses
- **Revelation 18** The Fall of "Babylon" (the wicked world system that opposes Christ)
- **Revelation 20:1–10** Satan Judged, His Power Destroyed
- **Revelation 21–22** The New Heaven and New Earth

The New Jerusalem:
Frequently Asked Questions about Heaven

© CPH/Robert Papp

What descriptions of heaven name other things that the Bible teaches about?

Revelation includes picture-language about heaven that sounds like other teachings in the Bible. For example, Jesus identified Himself as the living water (John 4:7–26). The river of the water of life flows from the throne of God and of the Lamb, who is Jesus (Revelation 22:1). Water with God's Word in Baptism gives us eternal life (1 Peter 3:21–22).

The tree of life is one of the two special trees in Eden (Genesis 2:9). When sin entered the world, God sent an angel to guard the tree of life to protect humans from eating from it, so that they would not live forever in sin. In heaven, the tree of life grows on either side of the river and bears fruit. The saints of God will no longer be barred from the tree. Its leaves provide healing to the people, to keep them forever happy and contented in true heavenly bliss (Revelation 22:2).

Jesus is the light of the world (John 1:4–5; 8:12). There will be no need for the sun or moon in heaven because there is no night. The Lord God is the light in heaven (Revelation 22:5).

The teachings of the apostles became the foundation of the Christian Church (Ephesians 2:19–22). The wall of the new Jerusalem has twelve foundations, each bearing the name of one of the twelve apostles (Revelation 21:14). The twelve tribes of Israel represent all those who trusted in God's promise of a Savior (Exodus 6:6–8). The gates to the new Jerusalem also bear the names of the tribes of Israel (Revelation 21:12–13).

What will the new Jerusalem look like?

John describes a magnificent scene in Revelation 21 and 22. Because it is in prophetic language, it is difficult to picture exactly what heaven looks like. The most important detail that John shares is that God Himself is present in heaven, dwelling among His people (Revelation 21:3). God's people see Him face-to-face (Revelation 22:4). There will be no more sorrow, tears, mourning, or pain (Revelation 21:4). God's presence is comfort and joy for His people.

The prophet Ezekiel also had a vision of heaven (Ezekiel 47:1–12). He described heaven in more detail than John did. John's vision is a continuation of Ezekiel's vision. Ezekiel 48:35 also names the place "The Lord Is There."

Why don't we have more details?

The Bible is written for our salvation. It doesn't tell us everything, but it tells us everything we need to know most—that Jesus Christ is our Savior.

Why is heaven called "the new Jerusalem"?

God's Old Testament people looked to the earthly city of Jerusalem as a center for worship. God's presence filled the temple at Jerusalem (1 Kings 8:11). In heaven, called the new Jerusalem, God's people will dwell in His presence and worship forever.

Who is the Bride?

The Bride of the Lamb (Revelation 21:9) is the Church, the body of all believers. The Bride wears the most splendid of garments—a robe of righteousness—given to her by the Groom, Jesus Christ (Isaiah 61:10). The Church is righteous because Jesus died for the sins of all people. Those who trust in Jesus Christ for salvation are part of the Church, the Bride of Christ.

Isn't God with us now on earth?

There are different ways to speak of God's presence. Heaven is called God's "dwelling place" (2 Chronicles 6:21). Yet God, speaking through His Son, promises to be with us always (Matthew 28:20). What's more, God is truly present in His Word and Sacraments. We receive faith in Jesus Christ through Baptism, which is water connected to God's Word. We receive Jesus' body and blood in the bread and wine at Holy Communion. God's Word gives us faith and strengthens us until He takes us to heaven to see Him face-to-face.

The seven churches of Revelation.

What style of writing is used in the Book of Revelation?

Revelation is written in a prophetic, apocalyptic language. God's prophecies of heaven are described in pictures or visions. The ideas are true, but the details may be symbolic. For instance, if something is described as being made of jewels, it may not be made of jewels as we know them, but it is certainly very precious and beautiful indeed.

Did John imagine everything in the Book of Revelation?

All Scripture is inspired by God (2 Timothy 3:16–17) and given for our instruction. God told the writers of Scripture what to write. Scripture is God's truth. John did not imagine what he described in the Book of Revelation, but he wrote down what God showed him in a vision (Revelation 1:1–3, 9–11). A vision is a dream that is specifically given by God, and all of its details are controlled by God. John's vision was a prophecy of the end of time.

What Is The Kingdom of God?

The kingdom of God is a New Testament phrase describing the rule of God through the Holy Spirit in the hearts of people. It is this kingdom that Jesus came to bring, and Jesus refers to it frequently, often calling it "the good news of the kingdom" (Luke 4;43 and other places)

The meaning of this phrase—"kingdom of God"—is identical to "kingdom of heaven." Mark, Luke, John, and Paul use "kingdom of God" exclusively. In his writings, Matthew more often uses the phrase "kingdom of heaven," even when quoting the words of Jesus.

What more does the Bible say about the kingdom?

What we know about the kingdom we glean from the way Jesus and New Testament writers talk about it.

- John the Baptist first announced the kingdom of heaven (Matthew 3:2).
- Jesus preached about it frequently (Matthew 4:17; 5:3; 6:33; and many other places). The kingdom was the subject of many of Jesus' parables.
- In Matthew 13, the kingdom is like good seed (v. 24), a grain of mustard seed (v. 31), leaven (v. 33), treasure hidden in a field (v. 44), a merchant searching for pearls (v. 45), and a net (v. 47). Elsewhere in Matthew, it is likened to a king settling accounts with his servants (18:23), a master hiring laborers throughout the day (20:1–16), a wedding feast (22:2), and ten virgins meeting the bridegroom (25:1).
- We enter the kingdom of God through rebirth by water and the Spirit (John 3:3–5).
- The kingdom of God belongs to those who recognize their own inability to come to the kingdom by their own strength, but are brought like children—Luke says "infants"—through the mercy of God (Mark 10:13–16).

It is clear that the Bible is not pointing to an external kingdom like that of David or one of the Herods, but a spiritual one, a kingdom that results from the fulfillment of God's plan of salvation through Jesus Christ.

Three Kingdoms

It can be helpful to think of the kingdom of God, the kingdom where Christ rules, in three ways.

1. Christ rules a kingdom of power. As the divine Creator, He rules over all creation and all creatures by His almighty power. This kingdom includes all people—believers and unbelievers alike. Those who do not see and acknowledge His rule will be judged along with believers at the end of time.
2. Christ rules a kingdom of grace. This kingdom is His Church on earth, all believers who serve Him because of God's gift of faith—the Church Militant.
3. Christ rules a kingdom of glory. This is the Church Triumphant—the saints and angels in heaven.

The Tree of Life, the Cross of Jesus

In Eden

God placed the tree of life in Eden to nourish our first parents. He told them to eat its fruit and live forever in perfect peace with Him. It was the source of eternal life. Adam and Eve were without sin, disease, or death. God called this heavenly garden "very good." However, Adam and Eve, out of their God-given free will, chose to follow their own desires into sin instead of faith. They ate the fruit of the tree of knowledge of good and evil and fell from God's grace. The entire creation fell into sin and chaos. God barred the way to the tree of life out of love for Adam and Eve because if they had eaten from it in their fallen state, they would have lived forever in a world of sinful disaster. That is not how God wants His beloved children to spend eternity.

On the Cross

Our Savior, Jesus Christ, by whom all things were made, who was in the beginning, is the source of eternal life. He died on the tree of the cross to reconcile us to the Father. He gives us His living body and blood for the forgiveness of sins in Holy Communion while we still live in this world. It is for our health and salvation.

In Heaven

Christians have long recognized the connection between the tree of life in the Garden of Eden, the cross of Jesus, and the tree of life in the new Jerusalem. This tree of the new heaven and new earth bears fruit every month to feed the faithful. Its leaves heal the nations. The living water flows by it to refresh us unto eternal life.

Jesus Christ, the First and Last, the Beginning and the End, the Alpha and the Omega, is the true Lamb of God, crucified for our sake so that we may at last live in heaven in perfect peace with God. At last, we will eat of the tree of eternal life in heaven.

DICTIONARY

Abbreviations

Scripture

Gn	Genesis
Ex	Exodus
Lv	Leviticus
Nu	Numbers
Dt	Deuteronomy
Jsh	Joshua
Jgs	Judges
Ru	Ruth
1Sm	1 Samuel
2Sm	2 Samuel
1Ki	1 Kings
2Ki	2 Kings
1Ch	1 Chronicles
2Ch	2 Chronicles
Ezr	Ezra
Ne	Nehemiah
Est	Esther
Jb	Job
Ps	Psalms
Pr	Proverbs
Ec	Ecclesiastes
Sg	Song of Solomon
Is	Isaiah
Jer	Jeremiah
Lm	Lamentations
Ezk	Ezekiel
Dn	Daniel
Hos	Hosea
Jl	Joel
Am	Amos
Ob	Obadiah
Jnh	Jonah
Mi	Micah
Na	Nahum
Hab	Habakkuk
Zep	Zephaniah
Hg	Haggai
Zec	Zechariah
Mal	Malachi
Mt	Matthew
Mk	Mark
Lk	Luke
Jn	John
Ac	Acts
Rm	Romans
1Co	1 Corinthians
2Co	2 Corinthians
Gal	Galatians
Eph	Ephesians
Php	Philippians
Col	Colossians
1Th	1 Thessalonians
2Th	2 Thessalonians
1Tm	1 Timothy
2Tm	2 Timothy
Ti	Titus
Phm	Philemon
Heb	Hebrews
Jas	James
1Pt	1 Peter
2Pt	2 Peter
1Jn	1 John
2Jn	2 John
3Jn	3 John
Jude	Jude
Rv	Revelation

A

AARON (AIR-uhn; of uncertain meaning). Moses' assistant, the first high priest (Ex 4:14–17; 7). Aaron was born in Egypt. His family was from the tribe of Levi, the descendants of one of the twelve sons of Jacob (Ex 6:19–20). Miriam was his older sister, and Moses was his younger brother (Nu 26:59).

Aaron was praised because he spoke well in public (Ex 4:14). At God's command, Aaron spoke to the people for Moses because Moses did not believe himself to be a good public speaker.

During a battle in the wilderness between the children of Israel and the Amalekites, Aaron helped Hur hold up Moses' hands (Ex 17:12). While Moses was on Mount Sinai receiving the Ten Commandments, the people became impatient, so Aaron made a golden calf for an idol (Ex 32). Aaron and Miriam criticized Moses because of the foreign woman he had married (Nu 12:1).

Moses anointed Aaron and Aaron's sons to the priesthood (Nu 3:1–3). The Lord confirmed Aaron as His high priest when the staff with Aaron's name on it blossomed (Nu 17). Because Aaron and Moses doubted God at Meribah, they were not allowed to enter the Promised Land (Nu 20:12–13). Aaron's son Eleazar followed him as high priest. Aaron died at age 123 and was buried on Mount Hor (Nu 20:22–29). See pp. 39, 149–50.

AARON'S STAFF. When Aaron's staff swallowed the staffs of the magicians and sorcerers summoned by Pharaoh, God demonstrated His supremacy over the gods of Egypt (Ex 7:8–13). Later, by making the staff with Aaron's name on it blossom, God proved Aaron's authority. This staff was placed before the ark of the covenant (Nu 17; Heb 9:4). See pp. 34, 65.

ABASE. To humble or make low. The proud and wicked are to be abased (Jb 40:11). God abases the priests who fail to preach His Word (Mal 2:9).

ABBA (AB-ah; Aramaic "father"). Conveys childlike intimacy and confidence (Mk 14:36; Rm 8:15; Gal 4:6). Expresses the deep, loving relationship Jesus had with the Father and which believers now share. *Ab* and *abi* are also used to form proper names, e.g., Abraham.

ABEDNEGO (ah-BED-ne-go; servant of Nego). The Babylonian name given to Azariah, one of Daniel's friends (Dn 1:7). Abednego was thrown into the fiery furnace for not worshiping the golden idol set up by King Nebuchadnezzar (Dn 3). See pp. 121, 137, 217, 224.

ABEL 1. (AY-buhl; perhaps meaning "son" or "vapor"). The second son of Adam and Eve. Abel was a keeper of sheep. When God was pleased with Abel's sacrifice, Abel's brother, Cain, became jealous and murdered him (Gn 4:1–8). In the New Testament, Abel is described as a righteous man because, by faith, he offered God "a more acceptable sacrifice than Cain" (Heb 11:4). See pp. 12, 149.

2. (AY-buhl; meadow). A prefix for the names of towns and places (Gn 50:11; Jgs 7:22).

ABHORRENCE (ab-HAWR-uhns). Aversion or loathing; shrinking or withdrawing from someone or something that is disgusting. Believers abhor wicked, unholy things and sins (Dt 7:26; Ps 119:163). The wicked abhor both God's Law and the person who speaks God's truth (Lv 26:43; Am 5:10). God abhors those who worship false gods and break His Law (Lv 26:30).

ABIATHAR (ah-BIGH-ah-thahr; father of abundance). The son of the high priest Ahimelech. When Saul put Abiathar's father and 84 other priests to death, Abiathar escaped and fled to David's camp for protection (1Sm 22:20–23). He became David's counselor and with Zadok brought the ark of the covenant to Jerusalem (1Ch 15:11–14; 27:34). Toward the close of David's reign, Abiathar joined with Joab in supporting David's son Adonijah as the next king. Solomon became the new king, however, and expelled Abiathar from office (1Ki 1:7, 19, 25, 41–42; 2:26–27).

ABIJAH (ah-BIGH-jah; the Lord is father). 1. A descendant of Aaron's son Eleazar. When David organized the priests into 24 divisions, the eighth division was named after Abijah (1Ch 24:10; Ne 12:17). Zechariah, the father of John the Baptist, belonged to this division (Lk 1:5).

2. The second son of Samuel. Because Abijah was a wicked judge, the elders asked for a king (1Sm 8:1–5). See p. 88.

3. The son of Jeroboam I (1Ki 14:1–18).

4. The son of Rehoboam and Maacah. Abijah was also known as Abijam. After his father died, Abijah became the next king of Judah. In an effort to regain the ten northern tribes, he made war on Jeroboam I. Abijah reigned three years, following in the wicked ways of his father, and then he died (1Ki 15:1–8; 2Ch 12:16; 13). See p. 125.

5. The wife of Ahaz and mother of Hezekiah (2Ch 29:1).

ABIMELECH (ah-BIM-uh-lek; my father is king). 1. The king of Gerar who made a covenant with Abraham (Gn 20; 21:22–34).

2. The king of Gerar who made a covenant with Isaac (Gn 26:1–33). He may have been the same person as the king who made the covenant with Abraham.

3. Gideon's son by his concubine (Jgs 8:31). See p. 88.

4. The son of Abiathar and grandson of Ahimelech the priest. Abimelech, who is sometimes referred to as Ahimelech, was a priest during David's reign (1Ch 18:16).

5. The name given to the Philistine king (probably King Achish, 1Sm 21:10) in the title of Psalm 34. It is thought that Abimelech was the throne name or title of Philistine kings.

ABNER (AB-nur; father is light). The son of Ner and commander of his cousin Saul's army (1Sm 14:50–51; 17:55; 26:5–14). When Saul died, Abner brought Ish-bosheth, Saul's son, to Mahanaim and made him king over Israel (2Sm 2:8–9). Then Abner and his men met David's army in combat at the pool of Gibeon and were defeated (2Sm 2:12–17). Later, Abner quarreled with Ish-bosheth and left his camp to join with David. Although David received him in peace, David's commander, Joab, and Joab's brother Abishai murdered Abner because he had killed their brother in the battle at Gibeon (2Sm 3:6–30). David mourned for Abner and described him as a prince and great man (2Sm 3:31–39).

ABOMINATION (ah-bahm-i-NAY-shuhn). That which is disgusting, loathsome, detestable, particularly in a religious context. The term is applied to animals the

Israelites were not allowed to eat, pagan practices, and idolatry (1Ki 11:5). Cf. "tainted" and "detestable" in Lv 7:18, 21; Dt 29:17; Hos 9:10. See p. 217.

ABOMINATION OF DESOLATION. This is mentioned in Dn 9:27; 11:31; 12:11, and may refer to the time when Antiochus IV Epiphanes desecrated the sanctuary by putting an idol to Zeus on the altar where sacrifices were offered. Ultimately, Daniel's prophecy concerning the abomination of desolation finds its fulfillment in messianic times.

Christ also referred to the abomination of desolation (Mt 24:15–16; Mk 13:14). Here Jesus announced a new desolation and destruction of the Jerusalem temple, which would be carried out by the Romans in AD 70. This event would end all temple worship and sacrifice. However, these desolations are but a taste of what lies in the future (cf. 2Th 2:3–4). In a figurative sense, this term is applied to the neglect of the Gospel in the Church. See p. 217.

ABRAHAM (AY-brah-ham; father of a multitude). The son of Terah and founder of the Hebrew nation. Abraham's name, before God changed it, was Abram. Abram and his family descended from Shem and lived in Ur of the Chaldeans. Abram had two brothers, Nahor and Haran. After Haran died, Terah, Abram, Abram's wife, Sarai, and Haran's son, Lot, left Ur for Canaan. But when they arrived in Haran, a city in Mesopotamia, they settled there instead. When Terah was 205 years old, he died in Haran (Gn 11:27–32).

After Terah's death the Lord told Abram to leave his country, his family, and his father's house for a land the Lord would show him. He also promised to make Abram a great nation and bless him and all the families of the earth in him. So Abram, now 75 years old, left Haran with Sarai, Lot, and all their possessions and began the journey to Canaan. In Canaan Abram pitched his tent by Shechem's holy place, the oak of Moreh. The Lord appeared to him there and promised to give the land to Abram's descendants. Then Abram built an altar to the Lord both there and, a little later, east of Bethel. When a famine came to the land, Abram went to Egypt. In order to be well received by Pharaoh, Abram told Sarai to say she was only his sister. Not realizing she was also Abram's wife, Pharaoh decided to marry Sarai because her beauty pleased him. When plagues fell on his household, however, Pharaoh found out that Abram had deceived him. He told Abram to take his family and many possessions and leave (Gn 12).

Abram and his family returned with Lot to the altar near Bethel. Because of bickering and fighting between their herdsmen, Abram and Lot decided to part ways. Lot, given his choice of the land, chose the Jordan Valley and pitched his tent as far as Sodom. The Lord repeated his promise to bless Abram, who moved to the oaks of Mamre at Hebron (Gn 13).

When four kings defeated five other kings in the territory where Lot lived and took Lot captive, Abram chased after the enemies, recovered the goods they had stolen, and rescued Lot. After this Abram received a blessing from Melchizedek, the priest and king of Salem (Gn 14).

Then God made a covenant with Abram, sealing His promise to make of Abram a great nation by giving him and his descendants the land of Canaan (Gn 15). But when Sarai did not become pregnant, she thought she could not have children of her own, so she gave her maid, Hagar, to Abram. He and Hagar had a son whom they named Ishmael (Gn 16). Then God changed Abram's name to Abraham and promised that His everlasting covenant would be fulfilled in Isaac, his son with Sarai. He made circumcision the sign of the covenant (Gn 17). God also changed Sarai's name to Sarah.

While Abraham was sitting at the door to his tent by the oaks of Mamre, the Lord appeared to him and told him that Sarah would bear him a son within the year. When Sarah heard this, she laughed because she thought she was too old to have a baby. The Lord rebuked her for laughing and told her nothing was too difficult for Him (Gn 18). When Abraham was 100 years old, Isaac was born. Soon after that Hagar and Ishmael were cast out (Gn 21).

Then the Lord tested Abraham's faith in His promise by commanding Abraham to sacrifice his son Isaac. At the last minute the angel of the Lord stopped Abraham from doing this. He told Abraham not to harm Isaac and provided a ram for sacrifice instead (Gn 22).

Because Abraham did not want Isaac to marry a Canaanite woman, he sent his servant back to his homeland to get a wife for Isaac. The servant returned with Rebekah, Abraham's great-niece. She became Isaac's wife (Gn 24). When Abraham was 175 years old, he died and was buried in the cave of Machpelah (Gn 25).

God called Abraham, who is later described as the friend of God, from a family that served idols (Jsh 24:2). God took the first step in making the covenant with Abraham, a covenant in which He bound Himself to give without receiving anything in return. Circumcision is a sign of His covenant (Rm 4:11).

By faith Abraham was just, as God wanted him to be, and thus became the father of all believers (Rm 4; Gal 3). This faith showed itself in works (Jas 2:21). In Christ, Abraham's offspring from all nations of the earth are blessed (Gal 3:16). Believers are the spiritual sons and heirs of Abraham (Rm 4:13–14; Gal 3:29). See pp. 11–13, 15–16, 18, 24.

ABRAHAM'S SIDE. A term for everlasting life (Lk 16:22). Perhaps the place of honor at the heavenly banquet (cf. Mt 8:11).

ABRAM (AY-bruhm; exalted father). *See* ABRAHAM.

ABSALOM (AB-sah-luhm; father is peace). The handsome son of David and Maacah (2Sm 3:3). When Amnon, his half-brother, raped Absalom's sister, Absalom killed him. Then Absalom fled to Geshur, where he stayed for three years (2Sm 13–14).

Four years after his return to Jerusalem, Absalom made plans to seize the throne from his father, David. To this end, he gathered people around him who were unhappy with David's rule. Ahithophel advised Absalom to attack David before the king had time to regroup his followers, but Hushai cautioned Absalom to wait. He told Absalom that he would need a big army to defeat David's able warriors (2Sm 17).

The two armies met in the forest of Ephraim, where Absalom's men were defeated by David's. When Absalom was fleeing, his hair became tangled in an oak branch. While he was hanging from the tree, Joab killed him with three spears. When David heard that Absalom died, he grieved for his son (2Sm 18). See p. 103.

ABSTINENCE (AB-stuh-nuhns). The act of abstaining from or not partaking of something. There are various examples of abstinence in the Old Testament. The Israelites were to abstain from eating fat and blood, certain kinds of meats, parts of the offering sacred to the altar, and meats consecrated to idols (Ex 34:13–15;

Lv 3:9–17; 11). Abstinence also was commanded under some special circumstances (Jgs 13:14; Nu 6:3; Jer 35:6; Lk 1:15). See p. 111.

In matters that are neither commanded nor forbidden, the New Testament does not command abstinence. It allows one freedom to decide for oneself as long as the decision is made in love and does not go against one's conscience (Ac 15; Rm 14:1–3; 1Co 8). The New Testament opposes sects that live by the Law (Col 2:16; 1Tm 4:1–4).

ABYSS (ah-BIS). When the New Testament speaks of "abyss," it refers to Satan's domain, hell (Lk 8:31; Rm 10:7). It is the source of all evil (cf. "bottomless pit" in Rv 9:1–11; 11:7; 17:8; 20:1, 3).

ACHAN (AY-kan; trouble). A descendant of Judah who went against God's command and stole spoils of war at Jericho. For this sin Achan was stoned to death in the Valley of Achor (Jsh 7; 22:20).

ACHOR (AY-kawr; trouble). The valley south of Jericho where Achan was stoned to death (Jsh 7:24–26; 15:7; Is 65:10; Hos 2:15). Today this valley is identified with el-Buqei'a, which is about 10 miles south of Jericho.

ACTS, BOOK OF. The fifth book of the New Testament. According to tradition, Luke, the beloved physician, wrote both the Gospel named for him and the Book of Acts. Acts traces the growth of the Early Christian Church and credits this growth to the work of the Holy Spirit. It describes the mission activity first of Peter and then of Paul. See pp. 352–53.

ADAM (AD-uhm; human being, man). The first human being. God created Adam in His own image. He placed him in the Garden of Eden and gave him dominion over animals and all other creatures. God made Eve from one of Adam's ribs so that Adam would have a helpmate. God told Adam and Eve to have children and rule over the earth. When Adam and Eve broke God's commandment by eating the fruit of the tree in the middle of the garden, God drove them out of Eden. Adam died when he was 930 years old (Gn 1–5).

Paul says that the first man, Adam, is the source of sin and death, and the second man, Christ, is the source of life and righteousness (Rm 5:12–21; 1Co 15:22, 45; cf. Eph 4:22–24; Col 3:9–10). See pp. 11–12, 15, 220.

ADIAPHORA (ad-i-AF-o-rah). A term the Church uses to refer to matters that are neither commanded nor forbidden by Scripture. In these matters individuals have freedom to make their own decisions or choices as long as they act in love and do not violate their consciences (Rm 14:3; 1Co 6:12; 8; 10:23; Col 2:16–17). *See also* LIBERTY.

ADONAI (AD-o-nigh; my lord). The Hebrews spoke this word whenever they saw the consonants YHWH, which spell *Yahweh*, a word commonly translated "Lord" (see LORD). When the vowels of the word *adonai* are placed with the consonants of YHWH, this results in the word *Jehovah*.

ADONIJAH (ad-o-NIGH-jah; Lord is my lord). The fourth son of David. Encouraged and supported by Joab and Abiathar, Adonijah proclaimed himself king. David, however, appointed Solomon as the new king (1Ch 23:1; 28:5). Solomon first pardoned Adonijah but later had him executed (1Ki 1–2). See p. 118.

ADOPTION. A Greco-Roman legal term signifying the granting of the full rights and privileges of sonship in a family to which one does not belong by birth (Ex 2:10; Est 2:7; Acts 7:21). Paul says believers are adopted children of God. They have become members of God's family, the true Israel (the Church), by the work of the Holy Spirit, who brought them to faith in Christ (Rm 8:14–17; 9; Gal 3:26–28). That Christians have the Holy Spirit in their hearts as witness to the fact that they are children and heirs of God (Gal 4:4–7). See p. 212.

ADULTERY. In the Old Testament, adultery refers to sexual intercourse between a man and another man's wife (Dt 22:22–24). Under the Law of Moses, the two people who had committed adultery were punished by death (Lv 20:10; Jn 8:3–5). Symbolically, adultery expressed the sins of God's people Israel when they worshiped idols (Jer 3:9; Ezk 23:36–49).

Jesus interprets the Sixth Commandment as forbidding all kinds of sexual indecency in both deed and thought (Ex 20:14, Mt 5:28). The New Testament lists adultery, or sexual immorality, among the sins of the flesh (Gal 5:19).

ADVENT OF CHRIST. This term refers to Christ's coming in three ways: (1) The coming of Christ in the flesh—as the baby born in Bethlehem, the one who lived on earth, who died, and who rose again (Zec 9:9; Mt 21:1–5; Lk 2). (2) The spiritual coming of Christ in the hearts of people through faith and His presence in the Church (Jn 14:18, 23). (3) Christ's return for judgment at the end times (Mt 24:30). *See also* PAROUSIA.

ADVERSARY (AD-vur-ser-ee). 1. A political or personal enemy (1Ki 11:9–43).

2. An enemy of God and His people. The devil especially is an adversary of God and His people (1Tm 5:14; 1Pt 5:8).

ADVOCATE (AD-vo-kayt). Someone who pleads the cause of another (1Jn 2:1). Often this word refers to the Holy Spirit and is translated as *comforter*, *counselor*, or *helper* (Jn 14:16). See p. 437.

AENEAS (i-NEE-uhs). A paralyzed man at Lydda who was healed by Peter (Ac 9:32–35). See p. 294.

AGABUS (AG-ah-buhs). A prophet who came to the church at Antioch while Paul and Barnabas were there and prophesied worldwide famine. Later Agabus warned Paul that he would be arrested in Jerusalem (Ac 11:28; 21:10–11).

AGAPE (Ah-GAH-pay). *See* LOVE; LOVE FEAST.

AGED. Old age was regarded as a token of God's favor, and the elderly were respected for their wisdom (Jb 5:26; 15:10; 32:4; Zec 8:4). Young people were commanded to honor them (Lv 19:32). See p. 180.

AGRAPHA (AG-rah-fah; unwritten). Sayings ascribed to Jesus that are not recorded in the Gospels (Jn 21:25; Ac 20:35).

AGRICULTURE. After the conquest of Canaan, Joshua allotted the conquered territory to nine and one-half tribes. The tribes of Reuben and Gad and the half-tribe of Manasseh had already received their allotment under Moses (Jsh 13–14; Nu 32). Joshua also gave each household a small section of land to be its inheritance forever. These family plots were improved over the years by the generations that followed. The people removed boulders, cultivated the ground carefully, and built terraces (Is 5:1–2).

After the first rainfall, the ground was cultivated. They cultivated either by hand with a shovel and mattock or else by a plow drawn by a donkey, cow, or ox. Sometimes a heavy, forked branch of a tree was used as a plow. At other times branches were bound and pegged together so that one long end became the tongue, a shorter end became the plowshare (which might be shod with stone or iron), and a third end became the handle to steer the plow.

After the plow had torn up the ground, large lumps were broken up with a mattock and then raked fine with a harrow, a bundle of brushwood, or a wooden platform shod with stones or iron spikes.

The farmer sowed the grain by hand, taking it from a basket or from folds in his garment. After sowing the ground, he harrowed it again or drove his animals back and forth over the ground to trample in the seed.

Ripe grain was cut with a sickle. Some early sickles were made from the lower jawbone of donkeys or cows. Other people at this time used more advanced sickles of bronze or iron set in wooden handles. These instruments eventually replaced the more primitive ones.

After the reaper cut the grain, he raked it up and tied it into bunches with its own straw. Fallen or missed grain was left for poor gleaners (Ru 2:2–3). The grain was transported from the field to the threshing floor on a rack fixed to a cart or bound to the back of a donkey. Sometimes this rack was carried on a litter-like frame by two women.

The threshing floor was a roughly circular plot of clay or a limestone rock carefully patched and leveled. Workers opened the bundles of grain and spread them about a foot deep over this area. Then unmuzzled cows, calves, sheep, and donkeys trampled the grain out of the straw (cf. Dt 25:4). A primitive threshing sled or wooden flails were also used. Grain was winnowed by tossing the straw and grain into the air with a wooden shovel or fork. Then it was cleansed with a sieve. After this the grain was washed, dried, and stored in insect-proof jars.

In Scripture, the processes of agriculture are often applied to the spiritual realm (Mt 3:12; 9:37–38; 13:18, 39; Jn 4:35; Gal 6:7). See pp. 95–96.

AHAB (AY-hab, father's brother). After his father, Omri, died, Ahab became the seventh king of Israel (1Ki 16:29). He ruled for 22 years and was more evil in God's eyes than all the kings who had gone before him. Ahab married Jezebel, a princess from Tyre who worshiped the pagan idols Baal and Astarte. Ahab began to worship these gods with his wife. He built an altar to Baal and killed the prophets of the Lord. On Mount Carmel, the prophet Elijah demonstrated to Ahab and all the people that Baal and his prophets were false.

Later Ahab had his eye on Naboth's vineyard and sulked when Naboth refused to sell it to him. So Jezebel arranged to have Naboth killed. Then Ahab claimed the vineyard as his own. Because of this wicked act, God sent Elijah to tell Ahab that dogs would lick Ahab's blood in the same place where Naboth had been killed (1Ki 21:1–19). This prophecy came true when Ahab died in battle from an arrow wound and his chariot was taken to the pool of Samaria, where dogs licked the blood off it (1Ki 22:33–38). See pp. 125, 136, 156.

AHASUERUS (ah-haz-yoo-EE-ruhs). 1. The father of Darius the Mede (Dn 9:1).

2. The Persian king who married Esther (Est 1:2, 19; 2:16–17). The Hebrew name in the Book of Esther corresponds to the Aramaic and Babylonian spelling of Xerxes, who reigned from 486 to 465 BC. For this reason it is believed that

Ahasuerus and Xerxes were the same man. See pp. 154–55, 157.

AHAZ (AY-haz; possessor). 1. The idolatrous son of Jotham. When his father died, Ahaz became the twelfth king of Judah. During his reign, Judah became a vassal of Assyria. Ahaz turned his back on God and built altars to worship false gods. When he died, he was buried in Jerusalem (2Ch 28:22–27). Isaiah, Hosea, and Micah prophesied during the reign of Ahaz. See pp. 125, 189, 242.

2. The son of Micah and great-great-grandson of King Saul (1Ch 8:35–36; 9:42).

AHAZIAH (ay-ha-ZIGH-ah; the Lord took). 1. The son of Ahab and Jezebel. When his father died, Ahaziah became the eighth king of Israel. He was wicked and worshiped the idol Baal-zebub. When Ahaziah became sick, Elijah delivered a message to him from God: he was going to die since he did not worship the true God (1Ki 22; 2Ki 1; 2Ch 20). See pp. 77, 125.

2. The son of Jehoram and sixth king of Judah. He was also known as Jehoahaz and Azariah (2Ch 21:17; 25:23). His rule was wicked in the eyes of the Lord (2Ki 8:25–9:28; 2Ch 22). See p. 125.

AHIJAH (a-HI-ja; brother of the Lord). 1. The son of Ahitub and great-grandson of Eli, the priest. Ahijah was the high priest at Gibeah (1Sm 14:3, 18).

2. A scribe or secretary of King Solomon (1Ki 4:3).

3. A prophet at Shiloh. He told Jeroboam that the kingdom of Israel was going to split at Solomon's death and that Jeroboam would rule over the ten northern tribes (1Ki 11:29–39). Later, when Jeroboam's son became sick, Jeroboam sent his wife to the prophet. Ahijah told her that the child would die because of Jeroboam's wickedness (1Ki 14:6–16). A record of events in the "prophecy of Ahijah the Shilonite" is referred to in 2Ch 9:29.

AHIMELECH (ah-HIM-uh-lek; brother of Melek). 1. A priest at Nob who helped David by giving him holy bread and a sword. When Saul heard this, he ordered his soldiers to kill Ahimelech and the priests with him (1Sm 21:1–9; 22:9–19).

2. *See* ABIMELECH 4.

AHITHOPHEL (ah-HITH-o-fel; brother is folly). One of David's counselors. Although Ahithophel's counsel was wise, he was untrustworthy. When Absalom decided to overthrow his father, Ahithophel joined forces with Absalom, advising him how to go about the task. However, when Absalom took Hushai's advice instead, Ahithophel went home and hanged himself (2Sm 15:12, 31; 16:23; 17:1–23; 1Ch 27:33).

AI (AY-igh; ruin). A city about 1 1/2 miles from Bethel. In the conquest of Palestine, Joshua and the Israelites attacked Ai twice, the second time successfully. Ai is mentioned numerous times in Scripture (Gn 12:8; 13:3; Jsh 7; 8; 9:3; 10:1–2; 12:9; Ezr 2:28; Ne 7:32; Jer 49:3).

AIJALON (AY-jah-lahn; deer field). A town in Dan (Jsh 19:42; 21:24; Jgs 1:35; 1Sm 14:31; 1Ch 6:69; 8:13; 2Ch 11:10; 28:18). During a battle, Joshua told the sun to stand still in Gibeon and the moon in the Valley of Aijalon (Jsh 10:12).

ALABASTER. Carbonate of lime, a white or cream-colored mineral that is easy to carve. It resembles marble and was popular for making perfume vases (Sg 5:15; Mt 26:7; Mk 14:3; Lk 7:37).

ALEXANDER (al-eg-ZAN-dur). 1. Alexander the Great, king of Macedonia. He was born in Macedonia (now Greece) in 356 BC and died in Babylon (now Iraq) in 323 BC. One of the greatest generals of all time, Alexander was responsible for the spread of Greek culture in Asia and Egypt. See p. 269.

2. The son of Simon of Cyrene (Mk 15:21).

3. A person who tried to quiet the riot of the silversmiths at Ephesus (Ac 19:33).

4. The coppersmith who did Paul "great harm" (2Tm 4:14). He may be the same Alexander whom Paul speaks against in 1Tm 1:20.

ALEXANDRIA (al-eg-ZAN-dri-ah). The Egyptian city founded by Alexander the Great in 332 BC. It was a center for Greek culture and was noted for its libraries, architecture, and commerce. Because many Greek-speaking Jews lived in Alexandria, a translation of the Hebrew text of the Bible into Greek was undertaken. This text, the Septuagint, was begun in the third century BC and completed before 132 BC. Later Alexandria became a Christian center noted for its scholarship and textual criticism (Ac 6:9; 27:6; 28:11). See pp. xx, xxix.

ALLEGIANCE (uh-lee-JUHNS). The act of being loyal to kings and to God (1Ch 12:29; Is 19:18).

ALLEGORY. A figure of speech that represents a deeper spiritual reality. The word *allegorically* is used only once in the Bible (Gal 4:24), but as a figure of speech it is used frequently, for example, "vine" in Jn 15.

ALMS (AHMZ). Gifts, freely given, to the needy. In the Old Testament, almsgiving was a duty that God commanded His people to perform (Dt 15:11; Lv 19:9). Later it became an important religious duty (Ps 112:9). Christ and the apostles encouraged the giving of alms (Mt 25:35–36; Mk 9:41; Ac 24:17; Rm 15:25–27; 1Co 16:1–4; 2Co 9:7–9). Containers for receiving alms stood in the temple (Mk 12:41).

ALPHA (AL-pha). The first letter of the Greek alphabet. When *alpha* is used with *omega* (the last letter of the alphabet), it means the beginning and the end (Rv 1:8; 21:6; 22:13; cf. Is 41:4; 44:6). See p. 449.

ALPHABET. Letters used in writing and printing. Picture writing known as pictograms have been found in Palestine from the fourth millennium BC, and hieroglyphics from the end of the third millennium. The Serabic alphabet, for example, which was found at Sarabit al-Khadim in the Sinai Peninsula, dates from between 1850 and 1500 BC. It is an early example of Semitic writing. The KJV records the letters of the Hebrew alphabet in Psalm 119. The alphabet found on the Moabite stone closely resembles Old Testament Hebrew. *See also* WRITING. See pp. 5, 209.

ALPHAEUS (al-FEE-uhs). 1. The father of James (the Less) and Joses (Mt 10:3; Mk 3:18).

2. The father of Matthew the tax collector (Mt 9:9; Mk 2:14).

ALTAR (high). An elevation made usually of earth or stone, though other materials were sometimes used (Ex 20:24–26). According to an ancient Old Testament custom, an altar was erected wherever the Lord showed Himself (Gn 8:20; 12:7; 26:25; 35:1). The tabernacle had two altars. The first was the altar of burnt offering (Ex 27:1–2). All sacrifices were offered at this altar. These sacrifices were to remind Israel that it had access to God only through atonement. The second altar was the altar of incense (Ex 30:1–10). It symbolized adoration. See pp. 24, 39–40, 49–50.

AMALEKITES (AM-ah-lek-ights). An ancient group of nomads who descended from Esau (Gn 36:12). They were called first of the nations (Nu 24:20) and lived south of Canaan in the Sinai Peninsula, penetrating north into the Arabah. Traditionally they were enemies of Israel (Ps 83:7). The Amalekites were defeated by Gideon, Saul, and David (Jgs 7; 1Sm 15; 30:18). See pp. 79, 117.

AMASA (AM-ah-sah; burden). David's nephew and Joab's cousin (2Sm 17:25; 1Ch 2:17). Although Amasa was the captain of the rebel forces under Absalom, David forgave him and made him the commander-in-chief of his army in place of Joab (2Sm 19:13). Later, Joab, pretending to greet Amasa with a kiss, struck him with a sword and killed him (2Sm 20:4–13).

AMAZIAH (am-a-ZIGH-ah; Lord is mighty). The son of Joash and ninth king of Judah. Amaziah became king after his father was murdered. Once he was firmly in power, Amaziah had his father's murderers put to death. He led an army against the Edomites, defeated them, and captured their capital. Later, he fought against Jehoash, king of Israel, but was defeated and taken prisoner. Some years later, Amaziah was murdered at Lachish (2Ki 12:21; 14–15; 2Ch 24:27; 25–26). See p. 125.

AMBASSADOR. An envoy or messenger of great power (Is 18:2; Ezk 17:15). Paul called himself an ambassador of Christ (2Co 5:20; Eph 6:20).

AMEN (AY-MEN; true). 1. Amen is a name for Jesus. It emphasizes that He is the truth (Rv 3:14).

2. The word *Amen* is spoken when one wants to express "so be it." It indicates confirmation or agreement (Nu 5:22; Dt 27:15–26; Mt 6:13; 1Co 14:16). God's promises are described as "Yes" or "Amen" (2Co 1:20). See pp. xxi, 440.

AMMONITES (AM-un-ights). The people who lived east of the Dead Sea and the Jordan River. Their capital city was Rabbah (Dt 3:11), which is modern day 'Amman. Saul defeated the Ammonites in battle, and David took their capital (1Sm 11; 2Sm 12:26–31). The Ammonites worshiped idols and were fierce enemies of Israel (Dt 23:3–6; Jgs 3:13; 1Sm 11:1–11; Ne 4:3–9; Jer 49:1–6; Ezk 25:1–7; Am 1:13). The Moabites and Ammonites were descendants of Lot, Abraham's nephew (Gn 19:36–38). See p. 117.

AMON (A-mun; skilled workman). 1. The fifteenth king of Judah. He was the son and successor of King Manasseh and the father of King Josiah. Amon worshiped idols. He was murdered by his servants (2Ki 21:19–26; 2Ch 33:21–25).

2. The ancient Egyptian city of Thebes. It was a center for the worship of the sun-god Amon (Jer 46:25; cf. Na 3:8). See p. 125.

AMORITES (AM-o-rights). A powerful nation in Canaan that occupied both sides of the Jordan River (Gn 10:16; 14:7; Nu 21:26–31; Jsh 5:1; 13:15–21). When Samuel judged Israel, Israel had peace with the Amorites (1Sm 7:14). Solomon made the Amorites his slaves (1Ki 9:20, 21). See p. 79.

AMOS (AY-mus; burden). A shepherd of Tekoa who became a prophet to Israel during the reigns of Uzziah and Jeroboam II. His prophecy is recorded in the Book of Amos. See pp. 139, 188, 233.

AMOS, BOOK OF. The third book of the Minor Prophets as they appear in the Old Testament. It was written by the prophet Amos and emphasizes the judgment of God. See pp. 233–35.

AMOZ (AY-mahz; strong). Isaiah's father (Is 1:1).

AMPLIATUS (am-pli-AY-tuhs; enlarger). Paul's friend at Rome to whom he sent a greeting (Rm 16:8).

AMULETS (AM-yuh-lets). Charms people wore to protect themselves against sickness, accident, sorcery, and evil spirits (Is 3:20).

ANALOGY OF FAITH. A term that means there is agreement or harmony among scriptural teachings. According to this rule, the interpretation of each Bible passage should harmonize, not conflict, with the totality of scriptural teachings (Rm 12:6).

ANANIAS (an-ah-NIGH-uhs; the Lord has covered). 1. A member of the church in Jerusalem. Ananias died suddenly after he and his wife tried to deceive and cheat the church (Ac 5:1–6).

2. The disciple at Damascus who was sent to restore Paul's sight (Ac 9:10–20; 22:12). See p. 372.

3. A high priest before whom Paul was tried (Ac 23:1–5; 24:1).

ANATHEMA (ah-NATH-i-mah). In the Old Testament, anathema is a vow by which persons or things were devoted to God. Nonliving things devoted to God were given to the priests (Nu 18:12–14); living things were killed (Lv 27:28–29). Later, anathema removed a person from the community of faith (Ezr 10:8). In the New Testament, anathema is a solemn curse that implies separation (Rm 9:3; 1Co 12:3).

ANATHEMA MARANATHA (ah-NATH-i-mah mar-ah-NATH-ah). This is a term that means accursed person (1Co 16:22), lit, "the Lord comes to curse" that person. *See also* MARANATHA.

ANATHOTH (AN-ah-thahth; answers). A Levitical city in Benjamin, noted as the birthplace of Jeremiah (Jsh 21:18; Jer 1:1; 11:21–23; 29:27). Today it is identified with 'Anata. See p. 202.

ANCESTOR. Cf. Jsh 19:47; Jgs 18:29; Heb 7:10. *See also* FATHER 1.

ANCIENT OF DAYS. A name Daniel applies to the Lord to inspire awe and reverence for Him and to convey His majesty (Dn 7:9–22). See p. 219.

ANDREW (AN-droo; manly). The brother of Simon Peter (Mt 4:18; Mk 1:16–18). Andrew came from Bethsaida and was a fisherman by trade (Jn 1:44). He was a disciple of John the Baptist but was directed by John to Jesus as the Lamb of God. Convinced that Jesus was the Messiah, Andrew brought his brother Peter to Jesus (Jn 1:35–42).

Later, Andrew became a permanent disciple of Jesus and was appointed an apostle (Mt 4:18–19; 10:2; Mk 1:16–17; 3:18; Lk 6:14; Ac 1:13). When Jesus asked how He could feed a great number of people, Andrew called Jesus' attention to a boy with five loaves and two fish (Jn 6:8–9). Andrew and Philip told Jesus about some Greek people who wished to see Him (Jn 12:20–22). Andrew was also one of the disciples who asked Jesus about the destruction of the temple (Mk 13:3–4). According to tradition, Andrew was crucified on November 30 in Achaia on a cross shaped like an *X*. See p. 286.

ANGELS (messengers). 1. Unseen, spiritual, holy, heavenly beings who continually do God's bidding (Ps 89:5, 7; 104:4; Mt 4:6; 22:30; Heb 1:14; 2:7). Angels protect and serve those who fear God (Gn 48:16; Ps 34:7; Is 63:9). They differ in rank and dignity (cf. "prince" in Dn 10:13, 21; see also Lk 1:19, 26; Rm 8:38; Eph 1:21). See pp. 194–196.

2. An "angel of the Lord" may refer to an angel who carries out God's will (1Ki 19:5, 7). Frequently, however, when the angel of the Lord is mentioned in the Bible, it refers to a distinct person and yet a being who is of the essence of the Lord, who reveals God, and who has the Lord's name and presence (Gn 16:10, 13; 18:2–4, 13–14, 22:11; Ex 3:2; 23:20–21; 32:14). For these reasons the angel of the Lord is often identified with the Second Person of the Trinity, the preincarnate Son of God. See p. 196.

3. Evil angels are fallen spirits (2Pt 2:4). *See also* DEMONS; SATAN.

4. The "angels of the seven churches" are representatives of the churches mentioned in the Book of Revelation. John may be referring to the pastors of those churches (Rv 1:20; 2:1, 8, 12, 18; 3:1, 7, 14).

5. John the Baptist is called a messenger (or angel) who was sent to prepare the way for Christ (Mt 11:10; Mk 1:2; Lk 7:27).

ANGER. Reaction of people against unfavorable situations (Gn 30:2; 1Sm 17:28). It may be evil or a reaction to evil (1Sm 20:34; Jn 2:15; 2Co 12:20). Human anger is described as a work of the flesh (Gal 5:20). *See also* WRATH.

ANKLET. An ornamental metallic or glass ring that was worn around the ankle (Is 3:18). See p. 411.

ANNA (AN-ah; grace). The prophetess who thanked God when she saw the infant Jesus in the temple (Lk 2:36–38). See p. 331.

ANNAS (AN-uhs; merciful). The high priest at Jerusalem from AD 6–c AD 15 (Lk 3:2). He was appointed by Quirinius and deposed by Valerius Gratus. Annas was the father-in-law of Caiaphas, the high priest before whom Jesus was tried (Jn 18:13). Five of Annas's sons were also high priests. During the time when they and Caiaphas held office, Annas was also regarded practically as high priest, perhaps because he was the head of the family and therefore the most influential member (Ac 4:6).

ANOINT. To apply oil to a person or thing. A common custom among Egyptians, Hebrews, Greeks, and Romans, anointing was done for several reasons.

1. Sometimes it was simply a part of grooming. After washing or bathing, people anointed themselves (Ru 3:3). Anointing was also an expression of joy (Ps 23:5; 45:7). See p. 318.

2. Hosts anointed their guests as an act of courtesy or respect (Lk 7:46). See pp. 110, 317–18.

3. Anointing was also done as an act of consecration and at a person's induction to the office of priest or king (Gn 28:18; Ex 30:23–26; 40:15; 1Sm 9:16). See pp. 101–02, 187, 412.

4. The sick were anointed as an act of healing (Jas 5:14).

5. Christ was anointed with the Holy Spirit (Lk 4:18; Ac 4:27; 10:38; cf. Ps 45:7; Is 61:1). See p. 102.

ANOINTED ONE. *See* MESSIAH.

ANT. The ant is held up as an example of diligence and wisdom (Pr 6:6–8; 30:24–25).

ANTELOPE. This is one of the animals God's people in the Old Testament were allowed to eat because it was ceremonially fit for food (Dt 14:5; Is 51:20). See p. 33.

ANTICHRIST (AN-ti-krighst; against Christ). One who is both an enemy of Christ and a usurper of His rights and names. In the New Testament, John alone uses the word *antichrist* (1Jn 2:18, 22; 4:3; 2Jn 1:7). The other passages in Scriptures that speak about an antichrist were applied early in the history of the Church to the Antichrist (Dn 7–8; 2Th 2:3–12; Rv 13; 17–18). See pp. 217, 405.

ANTILEGOMENA (an-ti-lee-GAHM-i-nah; spoken against, questioned). Those books of the New Testament that were not received as canonical by the Church everywhere until the latter part of the fourth century. They include James, Jude, 2 and 3 John, 2 Peter, Hebrews, and Revelation.

ANTIOCH (AN-ti-ahk; from Antiochus, Syrian king). 1. A city in Syria on the south bank of the Orontes. It was founded around 300 BC by Seleucus Nicator. In 64 BC, Pompey made Antioch the seat of the legate of Syria and a free city. Both Barnabas and Paul worked in Antioch, and it was in Antioch that the followers of Jesus were first called Christians (Ac 11:19–26; 13:1–3; 14:26; 15; 18:22; Gal 2:11). Today Antioch is called Antakya and is located in Turkey. See pp. 360–61, 368, 393.

2. A city in Pisidia, Asia Minor, which was also founded by Seleucus Nicator (Ac 13:14–52; 14:21). See pp. 360–61.

ANTIOCHUS (an-TIGH-o-kus; opponent). 1. Antiochus III, called the Great, was the king of Syria from 223 to 187 BC. He was the sixth ruler of the Seleucid dynasty ("king of the north," Dn 11:14–19).

2. Antiochus IV, whose given name was Epiphanes, was the son of Antiochus III. He was the eighth ruler of the Seleucid dynasty, reigning from 175 to 164 BC. He was both an intolerant and energetic ruler. See p. 271.

3. Antiochus V, whose name was Eupator, was the son of Epiphanes. He ruled only two years, 164–163 BC, before he was slain.

ANTIPAS (AN-ti-pas; like father). 1. A Christian who suffered martyrdom at Pergamos (Rv 2:13). According to tradition, he was a bishop who was burned in a brazen bull under Domitian.

2. Herod Antipas, the son of Herod the Great. See pp. 275, 278.

ANTIPATER (an-TIP-ah-tur; like father). The father of Herod the Great.

ANTIPATRIS (an-TIP-ah-tris). A city Herod the Great built between Caesarea and Jerusalem. Herod named the city after his father. Paul was a prisoner there (Ac 23:31).

ANTITYPE. A perfect thing that is represented or prefigured by a type (1Pt 3:21). For example, Christ is the antitype of the paschal lamb (type).

ANTONIA (an-TO-ni-ah). A fortress on the northwest side of the temple. It was rebuilt by Herod the Great and named by him in honor of Mark Antony. Roman soldiers who watched over the temple area were housed there (cf. "barracks" in Ac 21:31–40; 22–23).

APOCALYPSE (ah-PAHK-ah-lips; uncover). Another name for the Book of Revelation.

APOCALYPTIC LITERATURE. There are two types of apocalyptic literature: canonical and uncanonical. The first includes Daniel and Revelation. These books reveal events of the end times, judgment, and the hereafter.

The uncanonical apocalyptic literature appeared during the period of late Judaism and early Christianity. It includes works such as *1 and 2 Enoch*, the *Apocalypse of Peter*, the *Ascension of Isaiah*, the *Assumption of Moses*, the *Book of Jubilees*, and the *Shepherd of Hermas*. See pp. xvii, 191, 211, 216, 260, 441–42, 446.

APOCRYPHA (ah-PAHK-ri-fah; hidden). A term the Church Fathers used for writings that were either difficult to understand or obscure and for books whose authorship was unknown. Gradually the term came to be used for those books that were outside the Old Testament canon. During the time of the Reformation, the books that appeared in the Vulgate (the Latin translation of the Bible by Jerome), but did not appear in the Hebrew Old Testament, were classed as apocryphal. They included Judith, the Wisdom of Solomon, Tobit, Ecclesiasticus, Baruch, the Letter of Jeremiah, 1 and 2 Maccabees, Old Greek Esther, Susanna, Bel and the Dragon, the Prayer of Azariah, the Song of the Three Holy Children, the Prayer of Manasseh, 1 and 2 Esdras, 3 and 4 Maccabees, and Psalm 151.

APOLLOS (ah-PAHL-us; belonging to Apollo). A well-educated Jewish man from Alexandria. John baptized him, and Aquila and Priscilla instructed him more accurately in the Christian faith (Ac 18:24–28). Apollos then became an eloquent preacher and a friend of Paul (1Co 1:12; 3:4–22; 4:6; 16:12; Ti 3:13). See p. 421.

APOSTASY (ah-PAHS-tah-see). Forsaking the Lord or departing from the faith (Jer 2:19; 5:6; Heb 6:6). The Scriptures contain many warnings against apostasy (Heb 6:1–8; 10:26–29; 2Pt 2:15–21). An apostate, one who forsakes the Lord, should not be confused with an errorist or a heretic. A heretic, unlike an apostate, still professes faith, even though he or she rejects a particular teaching or teachings of the Church.

APOSTLE (one sent forth). 1. In one sense the New Testament uses the word *apostle* as the official name for Jesus' twelve disciples: Simon Peter, Andrew, James, John, Philip, Bartholomew (perhaps another name for Nathanael), Thomas, Matthew (Levi), James the son of Alphaeus, Thaddeus, Simon, and Judas Iscariot (Mt 10:1–4). Judas Iscariot's place was taken by Matthias (Ac 1:15–26). Later, on his way to Damascus, Paul also was called to be an apostle (Ac 9; 1Co 1:1; 2Co 10–12).

The apostles were eyewitnesses to Jesus' ministry and miracles (Ac 1:21–22). Through them, Christ established His Church (Mk 16:20; Acts), and through their written and spoken testimony, Christ laid the foundation of the Church (Eph 2:20). The apostles went with the full authority of Christ, their sender, to proclaim the Gospel. See pp. 286–89, 445.

2. In a general sense, the New Testament uses the word *apostle* to refer to anyone commissioned to preach the Gospel (cf. Rm 10:13–15; "messenger" in 2Co 8:23; Php 2:25). See p. 288.

3. Christ is referred to as an apostle (Heb 3:1).

APPEAL. In ancient Israel appeals were made to the head of the tribe. At Moses' time, Moses himself first handled all appeals. But when this became too burdensome for him, he appointed judges for this purpose (Ex 18:13, 26). Later, difficult decisions were made at the sanctuaries (Dt 17:8–11).

Both judges and kings handled appeals (Jgs 4:5; 2Sm 15:3). Jehoshaphat established courts and delegated his authority of appeal to judges (2Ch 19:8). These courts were reestablished by Ezra (Ezr 7:25). After the Sanhedrin was instituted, it became the highest court of appeal for the Jews. Roman citizens could appeal to the emperor (Ac 25:11–12).

AQUILA (AK-wi-lah; eagle). A Jewish man who was born in Pontus. He was a tentmaker by trade (Ac 18:1–3). With his wife, Priscilla, Aquila was a prominent co-worker of Paul (Ac 18:18–19, 26; Rm 16:3; 1Co 16:19; 2Tm 4:19). See p. 376.

ARABAH (AR-ah-bah; desert). The name of the valley between the Dead Sea and the Gulf of Aqaba (Dt 1:1, 7; 11:30; Jsh 3:16; 1Sm 23:24, 2Sm 2:29; 2Ki 14:25; Jer 39:4; Ezk 47:8).

ARABIA (ah-RAY-bi-ah; desert). Originally, the northern part of the peninsula between the Red Sea and the Persian Gulf (Is 21:13; Jer 25:24) but later the entire peninsula (Ne 2:19; 6:1 Ac 2:11; Gal 1:17; 4:25).

ARAM (AY-ram). 1. A son of Shem (Gn 10:22, 23; 1Ch 1:17).

2. The area where the Aramean people (Syrians) lived. It extended from the Lebanon Mountains to beyond the Euphrates River and from the Taurus Mountains to south of Damascus. Several divisions of the Aramean people are mentioned in the Old Testament (Gn 31:20, 24; Dt 26:5; 1Ch 7:14).

ARAMAIC (ar-ah-MAY-ik). A Semitic language in Aram that spread to all of southwest Asia. It was incorrectly called Chaldee on the basis of Dn 2:4–7:28. Aramaic inscriptions from as early as 850 BC still exist today. Parts of the Old Testament are in Aramaic (Dn 2:4–7:28; Ezr 4:8–6:18; 7:12–26; Jer 10:11). Jesus also spoke Aramaic.

ARARAT (AR-ah-rat). A name for Armenia and its mountain range, especially its two peaks, which are 14,000 and 10,000 feet high (Gn 8:4; Jer 51:27). Armenia is a mountainous country north of Assyria, between the Black Sea and the Caspian Sea, and extends from the Caucasus Mountains to the Taurus Mountains.

ARCHAEOLOGY (ahr-kee-AHL-o-jee). A study of the material remains of the past. Biblical archaeology is concerned with Palestine and the ancient countries with which the Hebrews and early Christians came into contact.

Modern archaeology is usually traced to Napoleon's 1798 expedition to Egypt. About 100 scholars went with him on this trip to study the Egyptian monuments. C. J. Rich, of the East India Company in Bagdad, made the first excavations in Mesopotamia, and in 1838 and 1852, Edward Robinson of Union Theological Seminary made observations in Palestine.

From these beginnings biblical archaeology developed. Although earlier excavations (1800–1890) were mainly concerned with finding objects of interest, the scientific aspects of archaeology soon developed (1890–1915). The results of biblical archaeology often are used in Bible dictionaries. See pp. 80–81, 84–85, 201.

ARCHANGEL (ARK-AYN-juhl). Chief angel (1Th 4:16; Jude 9). *See also* ANGELS 1. See pp. 194–96.

ARCHELAUS. *See* HEROD 2.

ARCHERY. The art or practice of shooting with a bow and arrow, the weapons used in ancient times. Some famous archers were the Philistines, the Benjaminites, the Medes, and the Elamites (1Sm 31:3; 1Ch 8:40, Is 13:18; Jer 49:35). The word *arrow* is used figuratively for deep trouble, danger, power, and a wicked tongue (Jb 6:4; Ps 91:5; 127:4; Jer 9:8). *Bow* is also used figuratively (Ps 78:56–57). A *quiver* is a case for carrying arrows (Gn 27:3).

ARCHITECTURE (AHR-kuh-tek-chur). The art or science of building. Hebrew architecture, in the proper sense of the word, came into being around the time of the kings. David built a house trimmed with cedar, and Solomon built palaces and a harem (2Sm 7:2; 1Ki 7). The palaces of later kings were showier, often decorated with ivory (cf. Am 3:15). The temple, city gates, pillars, and the like offered further opportunity for architectural development and achievement.

Jesus' disciples admired the splendor of Jerusalem under Herod (Mk 13:1). For examples of early architecture, *see also* HOMES.

ARCHIVES. A place for storing official papers (Ezr 5:17; 6:1).

AREOPAGITE (ar-i-AHP-ah-jight). A member of the court that met at the Areopagus or Mars Hill in Athens (Ac 17:34).

AREOPAGUS (ar-i-AHP-ah-guhs). Hill of Ares or Mars, the Greek god of war. The Areopagus was also a council during Paul's day (Ac 17:19–34). Its chief concern was with education and religion.

ARIEL (AIR-i-el; lion of God). 1. A leader whom Ezra sent to obtain ministers for the house of God (Ezr 8:16).

2. A poetic name for Jerusalem (Is 29:1–10).

ARIELS. Although sometimes translated as "heroes" or "sons of Ariel," the meaning of this word is unknown (2Sm 23:20; cf. 1Ch 11:22).

ARIMATHEA (ar-i-mah-THEE-ah; height). The home of the Joseph who buried Jesus in his own new tomb (Mt 27:57; Lk 23:50).

ARIOCH (AR-i-ahk; servant of moon-god). The captain of Nebuchadnezzar's guard (Dn 2:14).

ARISTOBULUS (ah-ris-to-BYOO-luhs; best counselor). A Christian at Rome. Paul sent greetings to his household (Rm 16:10).

ARK (chest). The name given to three vessels in the Bible: 1. The floating home God commanded Noah to make in order to save himself, his family, and certain animals from the flood. The ark was made of gopher wood and was about 450 feet long, 75 feet wide, and 45 feet high (Gn 6–8). See pp. 13–14.

2. The basket into which baby Moses was placed (Ex 2:3–10 KJV). See p. 13.

3. The ark of the covenant, a chest about 3 3/4 feet long and 2 1/4 feet wide. It was made of acacia wood and lined and covered with gold. The solid gold lid of this chest was called the mercy seat. It had two cherubs on it, one on each end. Poles passed through two golden rings at the bottom of the ark so that the

ark could be carried (Ex 25:10–22). The ark held manna, the stone tablets of the Law, Aaron's staff, and the Book of the Law (Ex 16:33; 25:21; 31:18; Nu 17:10; Dt 31:26; Heb 9:4).

The ark went before Israel in its wilderness journeys "to seek out a resting place for them" (Nu 10:33). Priests carried it into the Jordan River, where it halted the waters so that the people could cross over on dry land into Palestine (Jsh 3:11–17). In the days of Eli and Samuel, the ark was kept in the temple at Shiloh (1Sm 3:3).

Once the Israelites carried the ark into battle for good luck, but the Philistines defeated them and captured the ark (1Sm 4). Convinced by ill fortune, however, that the ark was too dangerous to keep, the Philistines soon returned the ark to the Israelites at Beth-shemesh (1Sm 6:12–20). When 70 of the men there died because they had looked into the ark, the people at Beth-shemesh asked the people of Kiriath-jearim to come and take it (1Sm 7:1–2).

David brought the ark to Jerusalem (2Sm 6:12–23). Later it was placed into the Most Holy Place in Solomon's temple (1Ki 8:1–9).

The ark is also called the "ark of testimony" and the "ark of God" (Ex 25:16, 22; 1Sm 3:3). See pp. 40, 64–65, 126, 128–129, 259.

ARMAGEDDON (ahr-mah-GED-on; hill of Megiddo). The name the New Testament gives to the final battlefield for the forces of good and evil (Rv 16:16).

Har-Magedon in Aramaic, the name may be derived from the hill on the southern rim of Esdraelon where many battles were fought. It was on this plain that Barak defeated the Canaanites and Gideon defeated the Midianites (Jgs 5:19; 7). Both Ahaziah and Josiah were killed there (2Ki 9:27; 23:29).

ARMENIA (ahr-MEE-ni-ah). *See* ARARAT.

ARMLET; BRACELET. A piece of jewelry usually worn on the upper arm (2Sm 1:10).

ARMOR; ARMS. Weapons used in battle. The offensive weapons, or arms, of the Hebrews included swords, javelins, spears, bows and arrows, slings, engines, darts, hammers, battle axes, and battering rams (1Sm 13:19; 17:6; 2Sm 2:23; 2Ki 3:25; 2Ch 26:15; Jb 41:26; Jer 51:20; Ezk 4:2). See p. 108.

The defensive weapons, or armor, that the Hebrews used included coats of mail, greaves and war boots, helmets, bucklers, shields, girdles, and breastplates (1Sm 17:5–6, 38; 1Ch 5:18; 12:24; Is 9:5; 59:17). See pp. 107–08.

ARMOR-BEARER. Someone who carried an officer's armor, guarded him, and helped him in whatever way he could. Abimelech, Jonathan, and Saul each had an armor-bearer (Jgs 9:54; 1Sm 14:7; 31:4)

ARMORY. A place where weapons were kept (Ne 3:19; Is 39:2; Jer 50:25; cf. Sg 4:4).

ARMY. In order for the children of Israel to defend themselves against hostile attacks, they organized themselves into armies. In the wilderness they marched according to tribes. All males, except for the Levites, could be called into the army at age 20 (Nu 1–2). In time of war, the number of fighting men were gathered for war by inspectors (Dt 20:1–9; 2Ki 25:19). Army divisions were subdivided into companies of thousands and hundreds under their respective captains and still further into families (Nu 2:34; 31:14). The kings also had bodyguards (1Sm 13:2).

The first standing army in Israel was organized during the reign of Saul (1Sm 13:1–2). A captain of the host, or commander, was in charge of this army (1Sm 14:50). The army first consisted of infantry or foot soldiers (1Sm 4:10), but in time horsemen and chariots were added (2Sm 8:4; 1Ki 10:26, 28–29).

The Roman army consisted of legions, which were divided into cohorts (Ac 10:1; 21:31). Cohorts were further divided into three maniples, and each maniple into two centuries (Mt 8:5; 27:54).

ARNON (AHR-nahn). The river flowing east of the Jordan into the Dead Sea. The Arnon formed a natural boundary, first between the Amorites and Moabites (Nu 21:13; Jgs 11:18) and later between Israel and the Moabites (Dt 2:24; Jsh 12:1).

AROD (AY-rahd). A son of Gad and the forefather of the Arodites (Nu 26:17). He is referred to as Arodi in Gn 46:16.

AROER (ah-RO-ur; naked). 1. A Reubenite town on the Arnon (Dt 2:36). During Jehu's time King Hazael of Syria took Aroer from Israel, but later it fell back to Moab (2Ki 10:33; Jer 48:19–20). Today it is called 'Ara'ir.

2. A town 12 miles southeast of Beersheba in the southern part of Judah (1Sm 30:26–28).

ARPACHSHAD (ahr-PAK-shad). The son of Shem and an ancestor of Abraham (Gn 11:10–13).

ARPAD (AHR-pad). A city in the northern part of Syria near Hamath (Jer 49:23).

ARROWS. *See* ARCHERY.

ARSENAL. *See* ARMORY.

ARTAXERXES (ahr-tugh-ZURK-seez). 1. The Persian king who stopped the rebuilding of the temple (Ezr 4:7, 23–24). His other name was probably Smerdis.

2. Longimanus, the Persian king who reigned from 464 to 424 BC. He sent Ezra to Jerusalem and was also a friend to Nehemiah (Ezr 7; Ne 2:1–8). See pp. 151–52.

ARTEMIS (AHR-ti-mis). The Greek goddess of the moon, woods, and fields corresponding to the Roman Diana. She was a hunter and a symbol of chastity. The Artemis worshiped in Ephesus was a combination of Artemis and Ashtoreth (Ac 19:24–28).

ARUBBOTH (ah-RUB-uth). A district assigned to Ben-hesed to provide food for Solomon's court (1Ki 4:10).

ARUMAH (ah-ROO-mah; height). A place near Shechem where Abimelech lived (Jgs 9:41).

ASA (ay-SAH; physician). The son of Abijah and the third king of Judah. Asa was the first of the five kings of Judah who did "what was good and right in the eyes of the Lord" (2Ch 14:2). Asa began his reign with 10 years of peace, during which time he made many religious reforms (2Ch 14:1, 3–5; 15:1–17).

Then Zerah, the Ethiopian, waged war upon Judah, but with the Lord's help Asa and his armies defeated them (2Ch 14:9–15). Later in his reign Asa purchased the help of Ben-hadad of Damascus against Baasha of Israel (1Ki 15:16–22; 2Ch 16:1–10). In his later years, Asa was not as true to the Lord as he had once been. He died in the forty-first year of his reign.

ASAHEL (AS-ah-hel; God had made). 1. The nephew of David and a brother of Joab. Asahel was killed by Abner (2Sm 2:18–23).

2. A Levite and teacher of the Law under Jehoshaphat (2Ch 17:8).

3. An overseer of the temple in Hezekiah's reign (2Ch 31:13).

ASAIAH (ah-SAY-yah; Lord had made). An officer who was sent by Josiah to ask Huldah the prophetess about the Law (2Ki 22:12, 14; 2Ch 34:20).

ASAPH (AY-saf; collector). 1. A Levite, the son of Berechiah. Asaph sounded the cymbals before the ark when it was brought to the city of David (1Ch 15:16–19). He was then given the permanent job of sounding the cymbals for religious functions (1Ch 16:4–5, 7). See p. 164.

Asaph's family, with him as the head, was one of the families in charge of music and song (1Ch 25:1–9). Like the other chief singers, Asaph was called a seer (2Ch 29:30; Ne 12:46). Psalms 50 and 73–83 are called Psalms of Asaph.

2. The father of Joah, Hezekiah's recorder (2Ki 18:18; Is 36:3, 22).

3. A keeper of the royal forest in Palestine under Artaxerxes Longimanus, king of Persia (Ne 2:8).

ASCENSION. Forty days after His resurrection Christ returned to His Father in heaven. The ascension marks the end of Christ's bodily ministry on earth (Mk 16:19; Ac 1:1–12; Eph 4:8–10; 1Pt 3:22).

ASCENTS, SONG OF. The title given to Psalms 120–134. Some scholars think these psalms were named this because they may have been sung on the 15 steps that led from the court of women to the court of men. Others think that the word *degrees*, or *ascents*, refers to the way the poetic thought of the music advanced.

ASENATH (AS-i-nath; devotee of Neith, Egyptian goddess). The daughter of Potiphera, priest of On. Pharaoh gave her to Joseph to be his wife (Gn 41:45, 50). They had two children, Manasseh and Ephraim (Gn 46:20).

ASHAN (AY-shuhn; smoke). A town assigned to the tribe of Judah that was later transferred to Simeon (Jsh 15:42; 19:7; 1Ch 4:32). It was made a city of refuge and given to the Levites (1Ch 6:59).

ASHARELAH (ash-ah-REE-lah). A son of Asaph. Asharelah was in charge of temple music (1Ch 25:2).

ASHBEL (ASH-bel; man of lord). The second son of Benjamin (1Ch 8:1).

ASHDOD (ASH-dahd). One of the five chief cities of the Philistines. It was situated between Gaza and Joppa, and was the center of worship for the god Dagon (Jsh 13:3; 1Sm 5). Although assigned to Judah, it was never taken by that tribe (Jsh 15:46–47). When the Philistines captured the ark at Ebenezer, they carried it to Ashdod but soon returned it (1Sm 5–6). Uzziah, king of Judah, broke down the wall of Ashdod, and a number of years later it was captured by Sargon II of Assyria (2Ch 26:6; Is 20:1). In 630 BC, Ashdod was partially destroyed by Psammetichus of Egypt. In New Testament times it was called Azotus (Ac 8:40) See p. 104.

ASHDODITES (ASH-dahd-ights). The people who lived in Ashdod (Ne 4:7).

ASHER (ASH-ur; happiness). 1. The eighth son of Jacob (Gn 30:12–13; 35:26). See pp. 17, 21.

2. The territory along the seashore north of Carmel that was given to the

tribe that descended from Asher (Jsh 19:24–31).

ASHERAH (ah-SHER-rah). A Canaanite goddess of sex and war. She was the wife or sister of El. *Asherah* means goddess or wooden image. Cf. Dt 16:21; 1Ki 15:13; 16:33.

ASHERIM (ah-SHER-rim). The plural form of Asherah.

ASHERITES (ASH-ur-ights). The people from the tribe of Asher (Jgs 1:32).

ASHEROTH (ah-SHER-rahth). The feminine plural form of Asherah.

ASHES. People in Bible times sat in or sprinkled themselves with ashes to show humiliation, grief, or penitence (2Sm 13:19; Est 4:3; Jb 2:8; Jer 6:26; Mt 11:21). When people felt depressed, they were described as eating ashes (Ps 102:9). Because of the ageless custom of burning captured cities, the expression "to reduce to ashes" implied complete destruction (Ezk 28:18; 2Pt 2:6). The ashes of a red heifer were used for cleansing the unclean (Nu 19:17–22).

ASHKELON (ASH-kuh-lahn; migration). One of the five chief cities of the Philistines. It was located about 12 miles north of Gaza. During the time of the judges, the tribe of Judah captured Ashkelon, but the Philistines soon got it back (Jgs 1:18; 14:19; 1Sm 6:17). Ashkelon's destruction is foretold in both Zep 2:4 and Zec 9:5. In AD 1270, the Bibars destroyed it. See p. 104.

ASHKENAZ (ASH-kuh-naz). Noah's great-grandson (Gn 10:3). His descendants lived near Ararat.

ASHPENAZ (ASH-pi-naz). The chief of the eunuchs in Babylon during Nebuchadnezzar's time. Ashpenaz gave Daniel and his friends their new names (Dn 1:3, 7).

ASHTORETH (ASH-to-reth). A Canaanite goddess who was worshiped particularly at Sidon (1Ki 11:5, 33; 2Ki 23:13). During the time of the judges the people of Israel periodically stopped worshiping the Lord and served Ashtoreth instead (Ashtaroth, Jgs 2:13; 10:6). Toward the end of his reign Solomon built altars in Israel for the worship of Ashtoreth (1Ki 11:5; 2Ki 23:13).

Ashtoreth has been equated with Ishtar of the Babylonians, Astarte of the Greeks, and Venus of the Romans. The plural form of her name is Ashtaroth. Her male partner was Baal. See p. 77. *See also* ARTEMIS.

ASIA (AY-zhah). When the New Testament speaks of Asia, it may be referring to either Asia Minor (Ac 19:26), Proconsular Asia (Ac 20:4; 1Co 16:19), or more restricted areas (Ac 2:9).

ASP. A poisonous snake (Dt 32:33; Rm 3:13; cf. Is 11:8). See p. 198. *See also* SERPENT.

ASRIEL (AS-ri-el; vow of God). A descendant of Manasseh and founder of a family (Nu 26:31).

ASSHUR (AHS-shoor). The second-named son of Shem (Gn 10:22). The people who descended from Asshur settled in Assyria. *See also* ASSYRIA.

ASSHURIM (uh-SHOO-rim). A tribe that descended from Abraham (Gn 25:3).

ASSOS (AS-ahs). A seaport of Mysia in Asia Minor (Ac 20:13–14).

ASSYRIA (uh-SIR-i-ah). The country that dominated the biblical world from the ninth to the seventh century BC. At its height, Assyria encompassed the land between the Black Sea, the Caspian Sea, the Persian Gulf, and the Mediterranean Sea (including Egypt). Its capital city was Nineveh. Semitic in origin, it appears that the people of Assyria were originally colonists from Babylonia (Gn 10:11). They wrote with ideograms and syllabic signs. Chief among their gods were Asshur, Anu, Bel, and Ea.

The kings of Assyria often invaded Israel (2Ki 15:19, 29; 16:7–9; 2Ch 28:20). In 722 BC, the Assyrians finally carried the Israelites into captivity (2Ki 17:6; 18:11).

In 612 BC, Nineveh fell to the Medes, and after the battle of Carchemish in 605 BC, the Assyrians as a nation ceased to exist. See pp. 117, 122–23, 225, 238, 245.

ASTROLOGERS (as-TRAHL-o-jurs). People who tried to predict the future by studying the stars (Dn 2:27; 4:7; 5:7, 11). See p. 329.

ATHALIAH (ath-ah-LIGH-ah; affected of the Lord). The wicked daughter of Ahab and Jezebel. Under Athaliah's influence, her husband, King Jehoram, introduced Baal worship to Judah. Later, when her son King Ahaziah was killed, Athaliah seized the throne and reigned for six years. While trying to stop a rebellion, she was killed by her guard (2Ki 11; 2Ch 22–24).

ATHARIM (ATH-ah-rim). The route the Israelites followed when approaching Canaan (Nu 21:1).

ATHENS (ATH-enz; city of Athena). In ancient times Athens was the capital of Attica; today it is the capital of Greece. Located near the Gulf of Aegina, Athens grew up around the 512-foot-high rocky hill known as the Acropolis. It was connected to the harbor Piraeus by 5-mile-long walls. Athens was a center for both learning and civilization. During his second missionary journey, Paul visited the city and spoke to a group of people on the Areopagus (Ac 17:19–22). See p. 376.

ATONEMENT (ah-TON-muhnt; ransom, reconciliation). "At-one-ment." Moses closely relates atonement to the idea of redemption, where an innocent life is offered as a substitute for a guilty life (e.g., the transfer of guilt to the sacrificial animal in Lv 1:4; 4:4; 16:21). See pp. 15, 49–50, 63, 65.

Atonement is the removal of the separation that exists between God and people because of sin. It is accomplished by the life and death of Jesus in humanity's place. Cf. "reconciliation" in Rm 5:11. See pp. 44–45, 63.

ATONEMENT, DAY OF. A Hebrew festival held on the tenth day of the seventh month. It was observed with fasting, humiliation, and sacrifice for sin (Ex 30:16; Lv 16; 23:27–32). See pp. 44–47, 63.

ATTAI (AT-ay-igh; ready). A son of Rehoboam and Maacah (2Ch 11:20).

ATTALIA (At-ah-LIGH-ah). A seaport on the coast of Pamphylia (Ac 14:25).

AUGURY. Using signs or omens to predict the future. This practice was forbidden (2Ki 21:6; 2Ch 33:6). *See also* ENCHANTMENT; MAGIC.

AUGUSTUS (aw-GUS-tuhs; venerable). The title of Gaius Julius Caesar Octavianus, the first Roman Emperor, who reigned from 27 BC to AD 14. Christ was born during his rule (Lk 2:1).

AVENGER OF BLOOD. When a person was murdered, it was the duty of the person's nearest relative to pursue the murderer and obtain satisfaction for the relative's death, generally by killing the murderer (Dt 19:6). The person who made satisfaction for a relative's death in this way was known as the avenger of blood.

AVVA (Av-ah). A city of the Assyrian Empire. People from Avva helped colonize Samaria (2Ki 17:24).

AVVIM, AVVITES (AV-im, AV-vights). 1. Indigenous people who lived in Gaza before the time of Moses (Dt 2:23).

2. A town probably named after the Avvites (Jsh 18:23).

AZARIAH (az-ah-RIGH-ah; help by the Lord). 1. The prophet who met King Asa on his return from victory over Zerah. Asa followed Azariah's advice by putting away idolatry and restoring the altar of God. A national reformation followed (2Ch 15:1–8).

2. A son of Obed and another of Joash's captains. He also helped restore the throne to Joash (2Ch 23:1).

3. A son of Jeroham and one of Joash's captains. He helped place Joash on the throne (2Ch 23:1).

4. The son and successor of Amaziah. Azariah was the tenth king of Judah (2Ki 14:21; 15:1–7; 1Ch 3:12). He is also referred to as Uzziah.

5. The Hebrew name of Abednego, one of Daniel's friends (Dn 1:7; 2:17). Azariah was thrown into the fiery furnace for not worshiping the golden idol set up by King Nebuchadnezzar (Dn 3).

AZAZEL (ah-ZAH-zel). The word occurs only in Leviticus 16, where its meaning is unknown, though several have been suggested: (1) a solitary place; (2) a scapegoat, or goat that was allowed to run away (see p. 63); (3) a devil or demon of the wilderness; (4) dismissal or removal.

AZGAD (AZ-gad; strong of fortune). The head of a family of Israelites, a large number of whom returned from Babylon with Zerubbabel (Ezr 2:12; 8:12; Ne 7:17).

AZMAVETH (az-MAY-veth; death is strong). 1. One of David's warriors (2Sm 23:31). His sons joined David's army at Ziklag (1Ch 12:3).

2. David's treasurer (1Ch 27:25). Perhaps the same as 1.

3. A village of Judah or Benjamin situated between Geba and Anathoth (Ezr 2:24; Ne 12:29).

AZOTUS (ah-ZO-tuhs). *See* ASHDOD.

AZUBAH (ah-ZYOO-bah; forsaken). King Jehoshaphat's mother (1Ki 22:42; 2Ch 20:31).

AZZUR (AZ-ur; helpful). The father of the false prophet Hananiah (Jer 28:1).

B

BAAL (BAY-uhl; lord, possessor). 1. A common name for "god" among the Phoenicians. It was also a name used for the master of the house and a person who owned land or cattle (cf. "owner"; Ex 21:28; Jb 31:39).

2. The storm god of the Phoenicians and Canaanites. Baal was said to give increase to families, crops, fields, and flocks. He was worshiped on high places

with self-torture and human sacrifices (Jer 19:5). Often he was associated with the goddess Ashtoreth (Jgs 2:13; 6:30; 1Ki 16:32–33).

Early in their history, the Hebrews were attracted to Baal worship (cf. Nu 22:41; Dt 4:16; Jgs 2:13; 6:28–32). Altars to Baal were built in Palestine. Jezebel in Israel and Athaliah in Judah championed Baal worship (1Ki 16:31–32; 18:17–40; 2Ki 11:18; 2Ch 17:3; 21:6; 22:2). Numerous times the altars and images of Baal were torn down and destroyed, and the people of Israel returned to the Lord; yet Baal worship persisted in Judah and Israel (2Ki 21:3; 23:4–5; 2Ch 28:2; Jer 19:4–5; Hos 2:8). See p. 77.

3. Often *Baal* is combined with other words or syllables in the names of people and places, e.g., Baal-hazor.

BAAL-BERITH (BAY-uhl-BEE-rith; Baal of the covenant). The god worshiped at Shechem (Jgs 8:33; 9:4).

BAAL-HAZOR (BAY-uhl-HAY-zawr; Baal of a village). A place near Ephraim, where Absalom had a sheep farm. It is here that he had his half-brother Amnon murdered (2Sm 13:23).

BAALIS (BAY-ah-lis). A king of the Ammonites (Jer 40:14).

BAAL-PERAZIM (BAY-uhl-pi-RAY-zim; Baal of openings). A place where David defeated the Philistines (2Sm 5:20; 1Ch 14:11).

BAAL-ZEBUB (BAY-uhl-ZEE-bub; Baal of flies). The name by which Baal was worshiped in Ekron (2Ki 1:2–6). See p. 77. *See also* BEELZEBUL.

BAAL-ZEPHON (BAY-uhl-ZEE-fahn). A place near which the Israelites camped before crossing the Red Sea (Ex 14:2, 9; Nu 33:7).

BAANAH (BAY-ah-nah; son of affliction). An officer in the army of Ish-bosheth, Saul's son. Baanah and his brother killed Ish-bosheth (2Sm 4:2–12).

BAASHA (BAY-ah-shah). The son of Ahijah of the tribe of Issachar. Baasha became the third king of Israel while Asa was king of Judah. Baasha began a long war with Asa. He built Ramah to block the flow of traffic in and out of Judah (1Ki 15:16–17). Baasha ruled Israel for 24 years (1Ki 15:27–34; 16:7).

BABEL (BAY-buhl; gate of God). 1. A city in the Plain of Shinar (Gn 10:10).

2. The Tower of Babel was a brick structure built on the Plain of Shinar. As a result of this building project, God confused people's language and scattered the people over the face of the earth (Gn 11:4–9). See p. 15.

BABYLON (BAB-i-lahn; Greek form of Babel). An ancient city-state on the Plain of Shinar; first mentioned as "Babel" in Gn 10:8–10.

Babylon began its rise to power in the nineteenth century BC. The great Hammurabi became its ruler in the eighteenth century BC, but it did not reach the height of its power until Nebuchadnezzar II, who reigned from 605 to 562 BC. Then in 538 BC, Babylon was conquered by Cyrus of Persia.

Babylon was noted for its temple of Bel (or Marduk) and the Ishtar Gate, as well as for its ziggurats, hanging gardens, bridges, palace, and overall strength and splendor. The prophets often spoke about it (Is 13–14; 21; 46–47; Jer 50–51). In the New Testament, Babylon is used figuratively for that which opposes God both within and without the Church (1Pt 5:13; Rv 14:8; 16:19; 17:5; 18:2, 10, 21). See pp. 136–39, 193, 222–24, 268.

BABYLONIA (Bab-i-LO-ni-ah). A region of West Asia, the capital of which was Babylon. Babylonia was also called Shinar (Gn 10:10; 11:2; Is 11:11) and the land of the Chaldeans (Jer 24:5; Ezk 12:13). See pp. 136–39, 193, 222–24.

BACA (BA-kah; weeping or balsam tree). An unidentified valley in Palestine that was named for its balsam trees, which produced a tearlike gum. Some people identify Baca with Rephaim because of the balsam trees there (2Sm 5:22–24). It is usually interpreted figuratively, however, to describe any vale of tears (Ps 84:6).

BACKBITE. To speak evil of someone (Pr 25:23; cf. "slander" in Ps 15:3).

BACKSLIDING. Describes a person turning away from the Lord to follow his own way (Is 57:17; Ezk 37:23). *See also* APOSTASY.

BAG. Used for carrying weights, stones, and money (Dt 25:13; 1Sm 17:49; 2Ki 5:23). Judas's "moneybag" was probably a chest (Jn 12:6; 13:29).

BAKER. Some people in Israel earned their living by baking (Jer 37:21). Often rulers had their own bakers (Gn 40; 1Sm 8:13).

BALAAM (BAY-lahm). The son of Beor, probably a Midianite (Nu 31:8; Dt 23:4). Balaam was the diviner hired by King Balak of Moab to curse Israel. God, however, used Balaam to bless Israel instead (Nu 22–24).

Before leaving the king of Moab, Balaam told him that the Lord would surely curse the Israelites if Balak could get them to worship false gods (Nu 31:15–16; Rv 2:14). Balak did this. To avenge themselves, the Israelites warred against the Midianites, killing their kings and Balaam (Nu 31:8). See pp. 58–59.

BALAK (BAY-lak; destroyer). The king of Moab. He hired Balaam to curse Israel (Nu 22–24; Jsh 24:9; Jgs 11:25; Rv 2:14).

BALANCE. An instrument for weighing (Lv 19:36; Ezk 45:10; Am 8:5). In a figurative sense, the word *balance* is used for measuring the worth or trouble of people (Jb 6:2; Ps 62:9; Dn 5:27). It is also a symbol of fair dealing (Jb 31:6; Pr 11:1).

BALDNESS. Natural baldness is not mentioned often in the Bible. Sometimes it was connected with leprosy or misery (Lv 13:40–43; Is 3:24).

Shaving the head was a sign of mourning (Jer 16:6; Ezk 7:18). The Israelites were forbidden from doing this because they were a holy people (Dt 14:1–2). However, it was sometimes a punishment used for captives (Dt 21:12). When a Nazirite shaved his head, it marked the end of his vow (Nu 6:9, 18).

"Baldhead" was a term of ridicule (2Ki 2:23).

BALM. The resin or gum of trees that at one time grew in Gilead (Gn 37:25; Jer 8:22; 46:11). This balm or ointment was used to heal wounds (Jer 51:8). It made up part of the export trade of Palestine (Gn 37:25; Ezk 27:17).

BALSAM TREE. An unidentified plant in Israel (2Sm 5:22–24; 1Ch 14:14–15).

BAMAH (BAH-mah; high place). A place where idols were worshiped (Ezk 20:29).

BAMOTH (BAY-mahth; heights). A camp of the Israelites located in the land of the Moabites (Nu 21:19–20).

BAND. The tenth part of a Roman legion, a cohort or battalion (2Sm 23:13, 1Ch 12:21; Ezr 8:22). *See* ARMY, COHORT.

BAPTISM (bap-tiz'm). When the word *baptism* (Greek) appears in Greek translations of the Old Testament, it often means to dip, bathe, or wash (cf. Ex 30:17–21; 2Ki 5:14). Ezekiel prophesied the coming of Baptism to Israel (36:22–29). The Jews baptized proselytes; ceremonial washings were also common (cf. Mk 7:3–4; Heb 9:10).

John's Baptism was connected with repentance so that those baptized might be spiritually prepared to recognize and receive the Messiah. It worked the forgiveness of sins (Mt 3; Mk 1:4–8; cf. Ezk 36:25) but was distinguished from the Baptism Jesus instituted (Lk 3:16; Jn 1:26; Ac 1:5; 11:16; 19:4–6).

The Baptism Jesus received from John was unique because Jesus was without sin and therefore had no reason to repent. It signified His public entrance into His work of saving the world from sin (Mt 3:13–15; Mk 10:38; Lk 12:50).

In Christian Baptism an individual participates in the death and resurrection of Christ (Rm 6:3–11; Col 2:12) and is made a member of Christ (1Co 1:13; Gal 3:27; Eph 4:5). Baptism works the forgiveness of sins, delivers one from spiritual death and the devil, and it gives eternal salvation to all who believe in Christ (Ac 2:38; 22:16; 1Pt 3:21). Baptism also makes an individual a member of the Body of Christ, the Church (1Co 12:13; Gal 3:27–28; Eph 5:26) and bestows the Holy Spirit (Ac 3:28; 1Co 12:13). The blessings of Baptism are received by faith (Rm 6:1–11).

Christian Baptism must include the application of water in the name of the triune God—the Father, Son, and Holy Spirit (Mt 28:19) as Jesus instituted it. The practice by which the water is applied to the individual, however, can vary (Jn 3:23; Ac 2:38; 8:12, 36; 10:47–48; 16:15, 33; cf. Ezk 36:25; Heb 10:22). The New Testament does not restrict Baptism on the basis of age or mental ability but commands Baptism for all nations (Mt 28:19).

BARABBAS (bah-RAB-bas; son of Abba). The prisoner that the mob in Jerusalem asked Pilate to free instead of Jesus (Mt 27:16–26; Mk 15:7–15; Lk 23:18–25; Jn 18:40). See p. 274.

BARACHEL (BAR-ah-kel; blessed of God). The father of Job's friend Elihu (Jb 32:2, 6).

BARAK (BAIR-uhk; lightning). The Israelite whom Deborah, the prophetess and judge, summoned to lead an army against Sisera, commander-in-chief of the king of Canaan. Under Barak's leadership the Israelites defeated the Canaanites and killed Sisera (Jgs 4; 5:1, 12; Heb 11:32). See pp. 88, 136.

BARBARIAN (rude). At first, anyone who did not speak Greek was called a barbarian. The name was used to imply vulgarity and lack of culture. Later, barbarians were those people outside the Greco-Roman culture. When the New Testament talks about barbarians, no insult is intended (Rm 1:14; Col 3:11; cf. Ac 28:4; 1Co 14:11).

BAREFOOT. To go barefoot was a sign of either distress or of reverence for a holy place (Ex 3:5; 2Sm 15:30; Is 20:2–4).

BAR-JESUS. A Jewish magician and false prophet in the court of Sergius Paulus, also known as Elymas. When Bar-Jesus tried to hinder the conversion of Sergius Paulus by interfering with Paul's work, he was struck blind for awhile (Ac 13:6–12).

BAR-JONAH (bahr-JO-nah; son of Jonah or son of John). A kinship name for the apostle Peter (Mt 16:17).

BARLEY. A cereal grain grown in Palestine and neighboring areas (Lv 27:16; Ru 1:22). The Hebrews called it the hairy, bristling thing. It was made into cakes or loaves and was often eaten by the poor (Jgs 7:13; 2Ki 4:42; Jn 6:9).

BARNABAS (BAHR-nah-buhs; son of exhortation). A Levite from Cyprus who was also called Joseph (Ac 4:36–37). Barnabas was Paul's friend and co-worker (Ac 9:27). He helped Paul at Tarsus and went with him on his first missionary journey and to the council at Jerusalem (Ac 11–15). Because of a disagreement he had with Paul over John Mark, Barnabas separated from Paul before the second missionary journey (Ac 15:36–41). However, in his epistles Paul speaks highly of Barnabas (1Co 9:6; Gal 2:1, 9, 13; Col 4:10). See pp. 366–67, 421.

BARSABBAS (BAR-sab-uhss; son of Sabas). 1. The kinship name of Joseph, one of the men nominated by the apostles to take the place of Judas Iscariot (Ac 1:23).

2. The kinship name of Judas, a member of the church at Jerusalem. He was sent on their behalf to Antioch with Silas, Paul, and Barnabas (Ac 15:22). Judas and Joseph Barsabbas may have been brothers.

BARTHOLOMEW (bahr-THAL-o-myoo; son of Tolmai). One of the 12 apostles (Mt 10:3; Mk 3:18; Lk 6:14; Ac 1:13). Bartholomew may have been the kinship name of Nathanael (Jn 1:45). See p. 286.

BARTIMAEUS (bahr-ti-MEE-uhs; son of Timaeus). A blind beggar at Jericho (Mk 10:46–52).

BARUCH (BAIR-uhk; blessed). 1. Jeremiah's friend, scribe, and fellow prisoner (Jer 32:12; 36:4–32; 43:3–6). Other apocryphal books are attributed to Baruch as well.

2. One of Nehemiah's co-workers. He helped in rebuilding the wall of Jerusalem (Ne 3:20; 10:6).

BASEMATH (BAS-i-math; fragrance). 1. A Hittite wife of Esau (Gn 26:34). She is referred to as Adah in Gn 36:2.

2. Ishmael's daughter. She was Esau's last wife (Gn 36:3–4, 13, 17). She is also referred to as Mahalath (Gn 28:9).

3. One of Solomon's daughters (1Ki 4:15).

BASIN. A type of bowl used in the Old Testament for various rituals in worship (Ex 30:17–21; 40:30). Some basins were very large (1Ki 7:38). See p. 39.

BAT. This animal is classed among the fowls in the Old Testament and is considered unclean (Lv 11:19; Dt 14:18).

BATH. *See* MEASURES 3c.

BATHE. Bathing and cleanliness were practiced by the Hebrew people from earliest times (Ex 2:5; Sg 5:3, 12; cf. Ru 3:3; 2Sm 12:20). They associated bathing with cleanliness before God. It held a chief place in their rituals (Lv 13–16; 17:15–16). See p. 317. *See also* WASHING.

BATHSHEBA (bath-SHEE-bah; daughter of oak). The wife of Uriah the Hittite, an officer in David's army (2Sm 11:3–4). As a consequence of David's adulterous relationship with Bathsheba, she conceived a child (2Sm 11:1–5). So David arranged Uriah's death on the battlefield in order that Bathsheba might become David's wife (2Sm 11:6–27). Four sons, including Solomon, were born to David and Bathsheba (2Sm 5:14; 1Ch 3:5). See pp. 103, 118.

BDELLIUM (DEL-i-uhm). The name the Greeks gave to a fragrant gum resin. The Old Testament lists it with precious stones (Gn 2:12; Nu 11:7).

BEARD. A badge of manly dignity. Tearing, cutting, or neglecting one's beard was a sign of mental abnormality, affliction, or mourning (1Sm 21:13; 2Sm 19:24; Jer 41:4–5). When greeting another person, it may have been customary to take hold of his beard (2Sm 20:9). Men also swore oaths by their beards (cf. Mt 5:36). Lepers were not allowed to have beards (Lv 14:9). The Egyptians shaved their beards (Gn 41:14). Shaving the corners of the beard, a practice followed by some nationalities but forbidden to the Israelites, was probably part of a heathen religious act (Lv 19:27; Jer 9:26).

BEAST. 1. A mammal, not man, distinguished from birds and other land animals (Gn 1:29–30).

2. Wild animals (cf. Is 13:21; Mk 1:13).

3. Animals, including birds and reptiles (cf. Ec 3;18; Ac 28:5).

4. A destructive power that is an enemy of God's kingdom and people (Dn 7; Rv 13:1–10; 17:3–18). *See also* LEVIATHAN.

5. In Rv 13:2–18, a beast identified with the Antichrist fights Christians and persuades people to worship the first beast.

BEATITUDES (bee-AT-uh-toods). Declarations of blessedness (Mt 5:3–11; Lk 6:20–22). Isolated beatitudes appear throughout the New Testament (cf. Mt 11:6; 13:16; Lk 7:23; Jn 20:29; Jas 1:12; 1Pt 3:14; Rv 1:3; 14:13). *See also* BLESSING.

BECHER (BEE-kur; young camel). The second son of Benjamin (Gn 46:21).

BED. Poor people and travelers often slept on the ground or a mat (Gn 28:11; Mt 9:6). Early beds were made of wood, iron, and even ivory (Dt 3:11; 2Ki 1:4, 6; Am 6:4). They had mattresses, pillows, and coverings (1Sm 19:13; Is 28:20). At times, beds had ornamental trimmings and canopies (Est 1:6; Am 6:4). *See also* HOMES; LITTER.

BEE. Many Bible passages speak of bees (Dt 1:44; cf. Ex 3:8; 1Ki 14:3; Ezk 27:17). These insects are plentiful in Palestine, where they nest in rocks, woods, and the remains of dead animals (Jgs 14:8; cf. 1Sm 14:25; Ps 81:16).

BEELZEBUL (bee-EL-zee-bul). The prince of the demons (Mt 10:25; 12:24; Mk 3:22; Lk 11:15, 18–19). Jesus identified him with Satan (Lk 11:18). See p. 77. *See also* BAAL-ZEBUB.

BEER (BEE-ur; well). 1. A place where Israel set up camp (Nu 21:16–18).

2. A place to which Jotham fled (Jgs 9:21).

BEER-LAHAI-ROI (BEE-uhr-lah-high-roy; well of living one who sees me). The well where the Lord appeared to Sarah's handmaid, Hagar, and where Isaac lived for awhile (Gn 16:6–14; 24:62; 25:11).

BEERSHEBA (BEE-uhr-SHEE-bah; well of oath, or of seven). A town in southern Judah. The expression "from Dan to Beersheba" is used to designate the northern and southern extremities of Israel (2Sm 3:10). Abraham made a covenant with Abimelech there, and Isaac's servants dug a well there (Gn 21:31; 26:33).

BEHEMOTH (bi-HEE-mahth). From common Hbr word for "animal" or "beast." Scholars often suggest that the animal being described is a hippopotamus. Cf. Jb 40:15–24.

BEKA (BEE-kah). Half a shekel (Ex 38:26).

BEL (BEHL; lord). The patron god of Babylon (Is 46:1). The Hebrews called him Merodach (Jer 50:2).

BELIAL (BEE-li-uhl). In the Old Testament, the word *Belial* is not a proper noun but one that means worthlessness, wickedness, or restlessness (cf. Dt 13:13; Jgs 19:22; 1Sm 2:12). Belial is personified in 2Co 6:15.

BELL. Bells of gold were attached to the priests' robes (Ex 28:33–35; 39:25). People also wore bells on their ankles and put them on horses (Zec 14:20; cf. Is 3:16–18).

BELLOWS. A device made of skins and used for blowing the fire of a furnace (Jer 6:29).

BELSHAZZAR (bel-SHAZ-ur; Bel protect the king). The son of Nabonidus, the grandson of Nebuchadnezzar, and the last ruler of the Neo-Babylonian Empire (Dn 5).

BELTESHAZZAR (bel-ti-SHAZ-ur; protected by Bel). The name Nebuchadnezzar gave to Daniel (Dn 1:7).

BENAIAH (bi-NAY-yah; son of the Lord). The son of Jehoiada, the priest (1Ch 27:5). Benaiah was known for his brave deeds (2Sm 23:20–21; 1Ch 11:22–23). He was captain of David's bodyguard and, later, commander-in-chief of Solomon's army (2Sm 8:18; 1Ki 2:34–46).

BEN-AMMI (ben-AM-ee; son of my kindred). Lot's son, the ancestor of the Ammonites (Gn 19:38).

BENE-JAAKAN (BEE-ni-JAY-ah-kuhn; sons of Jaakan). A place in the wilderness where the Israelites camped (Nu 33:31–32).

BEN-HADAD (ben-HAY-dad; son of Hadad). The name of two or three Syrian rulers. 1. Ben-hadad I was king of Damascus at the same time as Asa ruled Judah. Ben-hadad helped Asa oppose Baasha, king of Israel (1Ki 15:18–21; 2Ch 16:1–6).

2. Another king named Ben-hadad defeated King Ahab of Israel (1Ki 20:1–34). Then in the days of Jehoram he again attacked Israel (2Ki 6:24–7:20; 8:28). He was killed by Hazael, who took over his throne (2Ki 8:7–15). Some people identify him with Ben-hadad I.

3. Ben-hadad II, son of Hazael. When Jehoahaz ruled Israel, first Hazael and then his son Ben-hadad II attacked the 10 tribes (2Ki 13:3–13). On three different occasions, however, Josiah was able to defeat Ben-hadad II and recover the cities of Israel (2Ki 13:22–25).

BENJAMIN (BEN-jah-muhn; son of right hand). 1. The youngest son of Jacob and Rachel. Just before she died, Rachel named him Ben-oni (son of my sorrow), but Jacob renamed him Benjamin (Gn 35:16–20). Jacob loved Benjamin very much (Gn 42). See p. 21.

2. The tribe that descended from Benjamin (Gn 49:27). When Joshua divided the land among the 12 tribes, the tribe of Benjamin received territory be-

tween Judah and Ephraim (Jsh 18:11–28). Saul, the first king of Israel, and Paul, the apostle, were Benjaminites (1Sm 9:1–2; Php 3:5).

BENJAMIN, GATE OF. A gate in Jerusalem (Jer 20:2).

BEN-ONI (ben-O-nigh; son of my sorrow). *See* BENJAMIN 1.

BEOR (BEE-awr; torch). Balaam's father (Nu 22:5; 2Pt 2:15).

BERA (BEE-rah). The king of Sodom in the days of Abraham (Gn 14:2).

BERACAH (BER-ah-kah; blessing). 1. A Benjaminite who helped David at Ziklag when David was fleeing from Saul (1Ch 12:3).

2. A valley in Judah near Tekoa. Jehoshaphat celebrated his victory over the Ammonites and Moabites there (2Ch 20:26).

BEREA (bi-REE-ah). A city in Macedonia (Ac 17:10–14; 20:4). On his second missionary journey Paul started a church there. See pp. 360, 404.

BERNICE (BUR-NEE-si; bringing victory). The oldest daughter of Herod Agrippa. She and her brother Agrippa listened to Paul's defense at Caesarea (Ac 25:23; 26:30).

BERYL (BER-il). One of the precious stones in the high priest's breastpiece (Ex 28:20; 39:13).

BETHANY (BETH-ah-ni; house of affliction). A village on the Mount of Olives about two miles from Jerusalem (Mt 21:17; Lk 19:29). Bethany was the home of Mary, Martha, and Lazarus (Jn 11:1). Today it is el-'Azariyeh. See pp. 293–94.

BETH-AVEN (beth-AY-ven; house of wickedness). 1. A town east of Bethel, near Ai (Jsh 7:2).

2. Ironic pun on the name Bethel, "house of God" (Hos 4:15).

BETH-CAR (BETH-kahr; house of the lamb). A place to which the Israelites pursued the Philistines (1Sm 7:11).

BETHEL (BETH-uhl; house of God). A town about 10 miles north of Jerusalem (Gn 28:19). Abraham camped near it (Gn 12:8). Originally it was called Luz by the Canaanites, but after his vision Jacob renamed it Bethel and built an altar there (Gn 28:11–19). See pp. 24, 233.

In the division of territories, Bethel was assigned to Benjamin (Jsh 18:13). Later the tribe of Ephraim captured it (Jgs 1:22–26). The ark was brought to Bethel from Shiloh (Jgs 20:26– 27). When Jeroboam was king, he set up a golden calf in Bethel and made it a center of idolatry (1Ki 12:25–13:32). The children of Bethel mocked Elisha (2Ki 2:23–24). Its ruins are called Beitin.

BETHESDA (bi-THEZ-dah; house of grace or house of mercy). A spring-fed pool at Jerusalem that had five porches (Jn 5:2). In 1888, such a pool, probably Bethesda, was found near St. Anne's Church in Jerusalem.

BETHLEHEM (BETH-li-hem; house of bread). A town 5 miles south of Jerusalem. Originally it was called Ephrath or Ephrathah, but after the conquest of Canaan, it was renamed Bethlehem in Judah to distinguish it from Bethlehem of Zebulun (Jgs 17:7). In Mi 5:2 it is referred to as Bethlehem Ephrathah. Bethlehem was the burial place of Rachel, the home of Ruth, and the birthplace of David and Jesus (Gn 35:19; Ru 1:19; 1Sm 17:12; Mt 2:1–2). See pp. 112–13, 304–05, 328.

2. A town in Zebulun (Jsh 19:15).

BETH-PEOR (beth-PEE-awr; house of Peor). A place in Moab where Israel camped while fighting Sihon and Og (Dt 3:29; 4:46; Jsh 13:20). Moses was buried in the valley opposite Beth-peor (Dt 34:6).

BETHPHAGE (BETH-fah-jee; house of figs). A village near Bethany not far from the descent of the Mount of Olives (Mt 21:1; Mk 11:1; Lk 19:29).

BETHSAIDA (beth-SAY-i-dah; house of fishing). 1. A city on the Sea of Galilee, probably near Capernaum (Jn 1:44; 12:21). Bethsaida was the home of Peter, Andrew, and Philip. Along with Chorazin and Capernaum, Bethsaida was rebuked by Jesus for not receiving His teachings (Mt 11:21; Lk 10:13).

2. Another Bethsaida on the east side of the Sea of Galilee where Jesus fed 5,000 people (Lk 9:10–17). Also where He restored sight to a blind man (Mk 8:22–26).

BETH-SHAN, BETH-SHEAN (beth-SHAN, beth-SHEE-uhn; house of security, or house of Shahan). A fortress city strategically located at the junction of the Jezreel and Jordan valleys. Dating to the early part of the third millenium BC, Beth-shan was under Egyptian rule for three centuries. Under Joshua, Beth-shan was allotted to the tribe of Manasseh. The tribe found the city too formidable to conquer, however, because of the Philistines who held the city with their chariots of iron (Jsh 17:11–16). After Saul died on Mount Gilboa, the Philistines hung his body on the wall of Beth-shan, put his armor in the temple of Ashtoreth, and placed his head in the temple of Dagon (1Sm 31:10–13; 1Ch 10:10).

BETH-SHEMESH (beth-SHEE-mesh; house of sun). A city in northern Judah set aside for priests (Jsh 15:10; 21:16). There Jehoash, king of Israel, defeated Amaziah of Judah and took him prisoner (2Ki 14:11, 13). While Ahaz was king, Beth-shemesh was occupied by the Philistines (2Ch 28:18). During one battle the Philistines captured the ark of the covenant, but a plague convinced them to return it. They put the ark on a cart pulled by cattle and headed it toward Beth-shemesh (1Sm 6:1–21).

BETHUEL (bi-THYOO-uhl; house of God). The nephew of Abraham and father of Laban and Rebekah (Gn 22:20–24; 28:5).

BETROTHAL (bi-TROTH-uhl). *See* MARRIAGE.

BIBLE (book). The name given to the collection of 39 Old Testament and 27 New Testament books. See pp. xiii–xxvii. *See also* CANON.

BIDKAR (BID-kahr). Jehu's aide (2Ki 9:25).

BIER (BEER). A stretcher used to carry the dead to their graves (2Sm 3:31; 2Ch 16:14; Lk 7:14).

BILDAD (BIL-dad; Bel has loved). A Shuhite who was one of Job's three friends (Jb 2:11). Bildad made three speeches (Jb 8; 18; 25).

BILGAH (BIL-gah; cheerful). The head of the fifteenth division of priests during David's time (1Ch 24:14).

BILHAH (BIL-hah). Rachel's handmaid and Jacob's concubine. Bilhah was the mother of two of Jacob's sons, Dan and Naphtali (Gn 29:29). See pp. 17, 19.

BINDING AND LOOSING. *See* KEY.

BIRD. The Bible mentions a number of birds, classifying them as clean and unclean (Lv 11:13–19; Dt 14:11–19). It particularly describes the characteristics of the eagle, hawk, and ostrich (Jb 39:13–30). Cf. Mt 6:26. People in Bible times ate bird's eggs (Is 10:14; Lk 11:12).

BISHLAM (BISH-lam). A Persian officer who complained to Artaxerxes about the rebuilding of Jerusalem (Ezr 4:7).

BITHYNIA (bi-THIN-i-ah). A country in northwest Asia Minor whose capital was Nicaea. Although Paul and his companions wanted to bring the Gospel to Bithynia, they did not, because the Holy Spirit was leading them to Europe instead (Ac 16:6–10). Nevertheless, there were Christians in Bithynia in the first century. Peter greets them in his letter (1Pt 1:1).

BITTER, BITTERNESS. 1. The opposite of sweet (Ex 15:23).
2. Sorrow, trouble (Ex 1:14; Jb 7:11). See p. 37.
3. Inner displeasure (Eph 4:31).
4. Evil (2Sm 2:26).
5. Hostile wickedness (Ac 8:23).
6. Wickedness that corrupts (Heb 12:15).

BITTER HERBS. Plants such as lettuce, endive, horseradish, and watercress. The Israelites ate bitter herbs in the Passover feast to remind themselves of their slavery in Egypt (Ex 12:8; Nu 9:11). See p. 37.

BITUMEN (bi-TYOO-muhn; slime). A mineral pitch or asphalt used for sealing together wood, bricks, and the like (Gn 11:3; 14:10; Ex 2:3). Bitumen pits were located along the Euphrates and Dead Sea.

BLASPHEMY (BLAS-fi-mee). Speaking evil of God (cf. Ps 74:10; Rv 16:9). Blasphemy was punished by stoning (Lv 24:16). False charges of blasphemy were brought against Naboth, Stephen, and Jesus (1Ki 21:10–13; Mt 26:65–66; Ac 6:11). See pp. 332, 367.

BLASPHEMY AGAINST THE HOLY SPIRIT. *See* SIN, UNPARDONABLE.

BLEMISH. Any spot or deformity (Lv 21:18–20; 22:20–24).

BLESSING. Something that makes one happy. 1. God blesses (Gn 12:1–3; 2Sm 6:11).

2. Godly people can give blessings by asking God to bestow His favor on an object or person (Gn 12:2; 27:28–29; Nu 23–24). See pp. 13, 21, 24, 184.

3. God's blessing can also be a direct application of His grace through the Word (Gn 48:17–19; Nu 6:22–27; cf. Mt 19:13). See p. 386.

4. Well-known blessings include the Aaronic blessing and the apostolic blessing (Nu 6:22–27; 2Co 13:14). See pp. 50, 58.

BLINDNESS. Since blindness was common in Bible times, blind beggars are often mentioned in the Scriptures (Mt 9:27; 12:22). Some ancient tribes blinded the people they captured (Jgs 16:21; 1Sm 11:2). God told the Israelites to be kind to blind people (Lv 19:14; Dt 27:18). See pp. 295, 314.

BLOOD. Because blood contains the essence of human and animal life and is necessary for that life, the two were often thought of as the same thing (Gn 9:4; Lv 17:11, 14; Dt 12:23). The Israelites were forbidden to eat blood or the flesh of animals from which the blood had not been carefully removed (Gn 9:4; Ac 15:20, 29).

Under Mosaic Law the blood of animals was used in all offerings for sin, for "without the shedding of blood there is no forgiveness of sins" (Heb 9:22). These Old Testament offerings pointed forward to Christ's supreme sacrifice on Calvary that took away the sins of the world. The expression "the blood of Christ" refers to His atoning death (1Co 10:16; Eph 2:13; 1Pt 1:2, 19). See pp. 49, 347, 423.

BLOODGUILT. The guilt of murder (Ex 22:2–3; 1Sm 25:33; Hos 12:14).

BLOT. To destroy or abolish. To blot out sin is to fully remove it (Is 44:22). To blot people out of God's book is to cut them off from fellowship with God and His people and to give them over to eternal death (Ex 32:32; Ps 69:28).

BOANERGES (bo-ah-NUR-jeez; sons of thunder). A name Christ gave to James and John (Mk 3:17).

BOATS. Biblical references to boats within Palestine are not numerous because the Hebrew people were mostly farmers, not seagoers. There were small fishing and passenger boats on the Sea of Galilee, however, and perhaps small boats or ferryboats on the Jordan River (2Sm 19:18; Mt 4:21; 9:1; Mk 1:19; Jn 6:17). See pp. 316, 322, 349.

Solomon built a fleet of ships at Ezion-geber on the Red Sea (1Ki 9:26). His fleet sailed the Mediterranean with the Phoenician navy of King Hiram (1Ki 10:22, 2Ch 9:21). Later Jehoshaphat and Ahaziah also built ships at Ezion-geber (2Ch 20:35–37).

The Bible frequently refers to the ships of other nations (Pr 31:14; Ps 107:23). Luke's account of Paul's voyage to Rome is a good picture of the adventures at sea during New Testament times (Ac 27–28).

BOAZ (BO-az). 1. A wealthy Bethlehemite who was a relative of Elimelech, Ruth's father-in-law. Boaz married Ruth. They had a son, Obed, who became David's grandfather. Obed was an ancestor of Jesus (Mt 1:5). See pp. 93–94, 97–99.

2. The left pillar in the porch of Solomon's temple (1Ki 7:21; 2Ch 3:17).

BOIL. An inflamed, open sore (Ex 9:8–11). Boils were a common symptom of leprosy (Lv 13:18–20). Hezekiah and Job suffered from boils (2Ki 20:7; cf. Jb 2:7). See pp. 35, 314.

BONE. Often used figuratively to show a close relationship (Gn 2:23; Jgs 9:2; 2Sm 19:12).

BOOK. *See* WRITING.

BOOK OF THE LAW. Used at the close of Deuteronomy, referring to all or part of that book (Dt 29:21). However, in later Scripture, it may refer to the five books written by Moses. See p. 27.

BOOTH. A temporary hut or shelter, usually made of tree branches (Gn 33:17; Lv 23:34, 42; Jb 27:18; Is 1:8). *See also* HOMES; BOOTHS, FEAST OF.

BOOTHS, FEAST OF. The third yearly festival of the Jewish people, commemorating the tent life of Israel. The people celebrated this festival by building booths or huts from the branches of fruit and palm trees (Ex 23:16; Lv 23:34–43; Dt 16:13–15; 31:10–13; Ne 8). Other names for this festival are the Feast of Ingathering, the Feast of the Lord, and the Feast of Tabernacles (Ex 23:16; Lv 23:34, 39). See pp. 46–47, 171.

BOOTY. Spoils of war. It consisted of everything of value in a conquered town. At the conquest of Canaan the Israelites were told to kill all living things and destroy all idols and the places where idols were worshiped (Nu 33:52). Often the army took the spoils and divided them among themselves, the rest of the people, and the Levites (Nu 31:26–47). David made a law that the troops who guarded the baggage should share in the spoils of war equally with those who did the fighting (1Sm 30:21–25).

BOTTLE. *See* FLASK.

BOTTOMLESS PIT. *See* ABYSS.

BOW. 1. *See* ARCHERY.

2. A bodily posture which demonstrates respect or obedience to God, an idol, an earthly ruler, or another person (Gn 43:28; Ex 18:7; 2Sm 1:2; 2Ki 5:18, Mi 6:6). See pp.17, 87.

BOWING. A combination of bending the knee and moving the head forward. Bowing was a respectful way to greet someone (Gn 23:7; Php 2:10).

BOX. 1. A flask or jar for holding oil or perfume (Is 3:20). *See also* FLASK.

2. A box for giving offering (Mk 12:41, 43; Lk 21:1).

3. A box fastened to the cart on which the Philistines returned the ark (1Sm 6:8, 11, 15).

BOZRAH (BOZ-rah). A city in Edom (1Ch 1:43–44). Both Amos and Jeremiah predicted its destruction (Jer 49:13, 22; Am 1:12). Today it is called Buseirah.

BRAMBLE. *See* THORNS AND THISTLES.

BRANCH. A title applied to the Messiah as David's offspring (Jer 23:5; 33:15; Zec 3:8; 6:12). A branch is also a symbol of prosperity (Gn 49:22). See p. 204.

BREASTPIECE, BREASTPLATE. 1. A sacred article of dress worn by the high priest (Ex 28; 29:5).

2. Armor designed to protect the body in battle (1Ki 22:34; Is 59:17; Rv 9:9). See p. 108.

BRIMSTONE. *See* SULFUR.

BRONZE SERPENT. When the children of Israel complained in the wilderness against God and Moses, God sent fiery serpents against them. Many of the people died. Then God told Moses to make a serpent of bronze (or copper) and set it on a pole. Whenever a person who had been bitten by a snake looked at this bronze serpent, he or she lived (Nu 21:5–9). This bronze serpent was a type of Christ (Jn 3:14). See pp. 134–35.

BROOK. A small stream that usually flows only during the rainy season (Dt 2:13). The Kishon and Kidron were brooks (1Ki 18:40; 2Sm 15:23).

BROOM. A bush with many, almost leafless, branches and pinkish white flowers (1Ki 19:4–5; Jb 30:4; Ps 120:4).

BROTHER. 1. A male who shares the same parents or the same mother or father as his siblings (Gn 27:6; 38:1; Jgs 8:19).

2. A male relative, such as a nephew or cousin (Mt 12:46).

3. Someone from the same tribe (Nu 8:26; Ne 3:1).

4. Someone from the same country (Mt 5:47).
5. A friend or companion (Jb 6:15; Ne 5:10).
6. Someone who is greatly loved (2Sm 1:26).
7. A peer (Mt 23:8).
8. All men (Mt 5:22; 18:35).

BROTHERS OF THE LORD. James, Joseph, Simon, and Judas are referred to as the Lord's brothers (Mt 13:55). Sisters of Jesus are also mentioned in Mt 13:56. There are differences of opinion as to whether these are full brothers and sisters, cousins, or children of Joseph by a former marriage. See p. 308.

BUCKLER. *See* ARMOR, ARMS.

BULL. A male ox or cow (Ps 22:12; Ezk 43:19). Oxen were used for plowing, threshing, pulling wagons, and bearing burdens (Nu 7:3; Dt 22:10; 25:4; 1Ch 12:40). People also ate them and sacrificed them (Dt 14:4; 1Ki 1:9).

BULRUSH. A marsh plant, such as the papyrus, or a swamp plant, such as the reed or rush (Ex 2:3; cf. Is 18:2; 19:15).

BURIAL. The people of Israel nearly always buried their dead, usually within 24 hours. When a person died, his or her body was washed, wrapped in a cloth or closely bound in bands, and, if the person had been wealthy, anointed with spices and perfumes (Jer 34:5; Mt 27:59; Jn 11:44; 12:7; Ac 9:37). The body was then carried on a bier to the grave (2Sm 3:31; Lk 7:14). Although holes in the ground were sometimes used as places of burial, often the grave was a cave or hole cut out of rock (Gn 25:9–10; Mt 27:60).

When a person died, friends expressed their grief by loudly weeping and wailing (Mk 5:38). Often professional mourners were hired (Jer 9:17).

BURNT OFFERING. *See* SACRIFICE.

BUSHEL. *See* MEASURES 2d.

BYWAY. Paths off the main roads. Byways were traveled to escape danger (Jgs 5:6). Figuratively, byways or side roads describe departure from the way of God (cf. Jer 18:15).

C

CAESAR (SEE-zur). A title given to all the Roman emperors after Julius Caesar (Mt 22:17; Jn 19:15; Ac 17:7). The New Testament mentions by name Caesars Augustus, Tiberius, and Claudius (Lk 2:1; 3:1; Ac 11:28). Nero, the Caesar under whom Peter and Paul were martyred, is also referred to in Ac 25:8. See pp. 308, 319.

CAESAREA (Ses-ah-REE-ah; for Caesar). A city built between 25 to 13 BC by Herod the Great. Located about 23 miles south of Mount Carmel, Caesarea was the Roman capital of Palestine. It was the home of Cornelius, in whose house Peter preached to the Gentiles (Ac 10:1, 24; 11:11). Philip also stopped in Caesarea at the end of his preaching tour (Ac 8:40).

Paul visited Caesarea a number of times (Ac 9:30; 18:22; 21:8, 16). The Roman commander at Jerusalem also sent Paul to Caesarea to be heard by Felix. From there Paul was sent to Rome (Ac 23:23, 33; 25). Today Caesarea is known as Kayseri. See pp. 290, 360–61, 378.

CAESAREA PHILIPPI (Ses-ah-REE-ah fi-LIP-igh). A city at the foot of Mount Hermon. Philip the Tetrarch, Herod's son, enlarged the city and called it Caesarea Philippi to distinguish it from the other Caesarea. Peter made his well-known confession, "You are the Christ, the Son of the living God," in Caesarea Philippi (Mt 16:13–20).

CAIAPHAS (KAY-yah-fahs). The son-in-law of Annas. Caiaphas was the high priest during Jesus' public ministry and crucifixion (Mt 26:3, 57; Lk 3:2). After Jesus raised Lazarus from the dead, Caiaphas advocated putting Jesus to death. Caiaphas was afraid that the people would believe in Jesus, which would lead to the destruction of their holy place and nation by the Romans (Jn 11:45–50). So he and the chief priest planned Jesus' death (Mt 26:3–5). After Jesus' arrest, He was brought before Caiaphas. Caiaphas declared Jesus guilty of blasphemy and sent Him to the Roman governor Pilate with the recommendation that Jesus be put to death (Mt 26:57; Jn 18:28).

Caiaphas also took part in the trial of Peter and John (Ac 4:6–22). See p. 332.

CAIN (KAYN; acquisition, spear). The oldest son of Adam and Eve. He made his living by farming. Cain killed his brother Abel (Gn 4). *See also* ABEL 1.

CALEB (KAY-luhb; dog). The son of Jephunneh and one of the twelve spies whom Moses sent into Canaan (Nu 32:12). When the spies returned, only Caleb and Joshua encouraged the people to take the land (Nu 13:6–14:9). Because of his faithfulness, Caleb was allowed to enter the Holy Land. When the land was distributed, Caleb received Hebron (Jsh 14). See pp. 66, 78.

CALENDAR. *See* TIME.

CALF. A young bull or cow. The Hebrews considered a "fattened calf" to be the best possible food (Gn 18:7; 1Sm 28:24; Lk 15:23).

While Moses was receiving the tablets of the Law on Mount Sinai, Aaron made an image of a calf out of gold and set it up in the wilderness for the people to worship (Ex 32:4).

Jeroboam also set up two golden calves, one at Bethel and one at Dan (1Ki 12:28–29). At first these images were viewed as symbols of God, but soon they came to be worshiped as common idols. Calf worship was denounced (Hos 8; 10; 13).

CALVARY (KAL-vah-ree). *See* GOLGOTHA.

CAMEL. In Bible times, one-humped Arabian camels or dromedaries were valued animals. Some were used as pack animals and were frequently found in caravans, carrying heavy loads of goods across the hot, sandy land (2Ki 8:9). Others were bred for riding, often traveling 60 to 75 miles per day (Is 66:20).

Camels were considered a source of wealth (Jgs 7:12; 2Ch 14:15; Is 30:6). Abraham had camels among his livestock (Gn 12:16). Job had 3,000 camels before he lost everything and 6,000 after God restored his fortune (Jb 1:3; 42:12).

Because camels were unclean, the Israelites were not allowed to eat them

(Lv 11:4). They did make clothing, however, from the camels' hair (2Ki 1:8; Zec 13:4; Mt 3:4).

CAMP, ENCAMPMENT (place of pitching a tent). The place where an army or other body of transient people set up their tents (Ex 14:9; 1Sm 4:1, 5; 2Ki 7:7). Camps were erected both for short periods of time and as temporary dwellings.

When the Israelites were in the wilderness, they kept clean and orderly camps. They patterned their camps after a square, with the tabernacle and Levites in the center and an equal number of tribes on each side (Nu 1:47–2:34; 3:14–39). See pp. 57–59.

CANA (KAY-nah). A town in Galilee near Nazareth. Jesus performed two miracles here (Jn 2:1–11; 4:46). See pp. 285, 290–91, 341.

CANAAN (KAY-nuhn). 1. One of Ham's sons (Gn 10:6). His descendants occupied Canaan and took their name from that country (Gn 10:15–19).

2. Canaan, one of the old names for Palestine, was the country between the Jordan and Mediterranean (Ex 6:4; Nu 34:3–12). After the people of Israel captured the land, it was referred to as the Holy Land (Zec 2:12). See pp. 78, 116–17, 128, 148.

CANAANITE (KAY-nahn-ight). A person who lived in Canaan (Gn 10:18–20; Nu 13:29; Jsh 11:3). The Canaanites were talented people who early developed arts and sciences. Their languages included Phoenician and Ugaritic. Their religion, however, was immoral, centering around war gods and fertility goddesses. They worshiped such well-known deities as El, Baal, Astarte, and Asherah. See pp. 78, 117.

CANDACE. A queen of Ethiopia mentioned in Acts 8:27. See p. 357.

CANON. The collection of books of the Bible accepted by the Church as genuine and inspired. By New Testament times the 39 books of the Old Testament were already recognized as canonical (cf. Rm 3:2). Although a few of the 27 New Testament books were questioned for awhile, they gradually found their way into the canon. See ANTILEGOMENA.

CAPERNAUM (kah-PUR-nay-uhm; town of Nahum). A city on the northwest coast of the Sea of Galilee (Mt 4:13; Jn 6:24). Capernaum had its own customs station and synagogue (Mt 9:9; Lk 7:5). It was the headquarters of Jesus and the apostles, and the scene of many miracles (Mt 9:1; Mk 2:1). See pp. 290–91.

CAPPADOCIA (Kap-ah-DO-shi-ah). A province in the eastern part of Asia Minor. People from Cappadocia were present when the Holy Spirit descended upon the disciples at the Feast of Pentecost (Ac 2:9). Later Peter wrote a letter to the exiles of the Dispersion that included those who lived in Cappadocia (1Pt 1:1).

CAPTAIN. As a military title, *captain* was applied broadly to any officer who held a leadership position, from a commander-in-chief to a commander of the guard (Gn 37:36). The captain of the temple was not a military officer but a priest who was in charge of the temple guard (Ac 4:1).

CAPTIVITY. In the Old Testament, it mainly refers to the subjection of God's people to their enemies, especially in a foreign land. Over a period of years the 10 tribes of the Northern Kingdom (Israel) were taken prisoner by the Assyrian kings Tiglath-pileser, Shalmaneser, Sargon II, and Esarhaddon (2Ki 15:29; 17:3, 6; 19:37;

Is 20:1). The Southern Kingdom (Judah) was taken captive in stages by King Nebuchadnezzar of Babylon (2Ki 24:10–17; 25:8–11; 2Ch 36:17–21). The prophets Ezra and Nehemiah describe the return of God's captive people to their homeland. See pp. 120–22. See pp. 120–22, 136–39, 219.

In the New Testament, unbelievers are described as captives of the devil and his kingdom (Gal 4:3, 8). But Jesus announced that He came to set people free from the devil and sin (Lk 4:18). By His death and resurrection Jesus captured sin, death, and the devil (Eph 4:8).

CARAVAN (KAR-ah-van). A group of traveling merchants, pilgrims, or others who joined together for a mutual purpose or for protection. These people often used camels, donkeys, and horses to carry their goods (Gn 37:25). They followed regular routes, such as the one leading from Damascus across the Jezreel Valley to the Mediterranean Sea (Jgs 8:11; Jb 6:18–19).

CARBUNCLE (KAHR-bung-k'l). A precious gem in the high priest's breastpiece (Ex 28:17; Ezk 28:13; Is 54:12).

CARCHEMISH (KAHR-kuh-mish). A Hittite city on the west bank of the Euphrates River (2Ch 35:20; Is 10:9). In 605 BC, Nebuchadnezzar of Babylon defeated Egypt in a battle at Carchemish (Jer 46:2).

CARMEL (KAHR-mel; garden). 1. A mountainous range of hills in the territory of Asher in Israel. It averages 1,500 feet in height and runs 12 to 15 miles in length. This range forms the southwest boundary of the Jezreel Valley, and on its northwestern end, it juts into the Mediterranean Sea (Jsh 19:26; 2Ki 2:25; Jer 50:19). Elijah defeated 850 heathen prophets on Mount Carmel (1Ki 18). See pp. 144, 187.

2. A town in Judah about 7 miles southeast of Hebron (Jsh 15:55). It was the home of Nabal, the first husband of David's wife Abigail (1Sm 25:2–44).

CARPENTER. A general term for a builder who worked in wood, stone, and metal (2Sm 5:11; 2Ch 24:12; Is 44:13). Joseph, Mary's husband, was a carpenter (Mt 13:55; Mk 6:3). *See also* TRADE.

CART. A two-wheeled vehicle for carrying people or freight. Carts were pulled usually by oxen (1Sm 6:7–16; Am 2:13).

CASSIA. (KASH-i-ah). An aromatic wood used in anointing oil. It probably tasted like cinnamon (Ex 30:24; Ps 45:8; Ezk 27:19).

CASTLE. A fortified building or stronghold (Ne 7:2; cf. 1Sm 22:4–5).

CATTLE. A term broadly used in the Old Testament to include large or small domestic animals, such as horned cattle, horses, donkeys, camels, sheep, and goats (Lv 19:19; Nu 32:26; Ps 50:10; Jb 1:3). Cf. "livestock" in Gn 1:24–25; Ex 12:29; Nu 20:19.

CAVE. A hollow place or cavern in the side of a hill or cliff. Caves are often found in areas of limestone, of which Palestine has a great deal. The people in Bible times used caves as dwellings, as places of refuge, and for burials (Gn 19:30; 23:1–20; 49:29; Jgs 6:2; cf. 1Sm 14:11; Mt 27:60). See p. 354. *See also* HOMES.

CEDAR. Most often the cedar referred to in Scriptures is the tall tree found in Lebanon. The wood of this tree was prized for its use in palaces, temples, idols, and ship masts (2Sm 5:11; 1Ki 5:5–6; Is 44:14–15; Ezk 27:5). See p. 124.

CENCHREAE (SEN-kri-ee). A harbor of Corinth visited by Paul (Ac 18:18). Phoebe was a deaconess or servant of the Christian church there (Rm 16:1).

CENSER. A container for burning incense. Censers for the tabernacle were made of copper; those for the temple were made of gold (Lv 16:12; Nu 16:39; Ezr 1:9).

CENSUS. A numbering and registration of people. The Old Testament records several censuses (Ex 30:12–14; Nu 1:2–3; 26:51; 1Ki 5:15; 1Ch 21:1–6; 27:24; 2Ch 2:17–18). The New Testament mentions the Roman censuses in Lk 2:1 and Ac 5:37.

CENTURION (sen-TYOO-ri-ahn; hundred). A Roman officer in command of 100 soldiers (Mk 15:39; Lk 7:1–10; Ac 10:1). See pp. 294–95, 361, 378.

CEPHAS (SEE-fuhs; rock). The Aramaic name Jesus gave to Peter (Jn 1:42; 1Co 1:12).

CHAFF (CHAF). The leftover part of winnowed grain (Jb 21:18; Ps 1:4; Zep 2:2); also straw or dry grass (cf. Is 5:24; Jer 23:28). Figuratively, the word *chaff* often refers to something that has no value or is bad (Mt 3:12).

CHALDEA (kal-DEE-ah). Originally the southern part of Babylonia on the Persian Gulf; later, nearly all of Babylonia (Is 48:20; Jer 50:10; Ezk 11:24).

CHALDEANS (kal-DEE-ahnz). People who came from or lived in Chaldea. Their roots can be traced beyond 1000 BC. In the eighth century BC, Chaldean kings conquered and ruled Babylon and began to extend their rule over the then-known world (2Ki 24:2; 25; Is 13:19–22; Jer 21:4–14; Dn 1:4). Chaldeans were noted astronomers (Dn 2:2; 4:7). *See also* BABYLONIA.

CHALKSTONE. Limestone rock used to make mortar (Is 27:9). *See also* LIME.

CHAMBERLAIN (CHAYM-bur-lin). An important officer, good at keeping secrets, who served a ruler (2Ki 23:11; Ac 12:20). The chamberlain looked after the private chambers or rooms of the ruler's palace.

CHARIOT. A two-wheeled vehicle for travel and war (Gn 41:43; 46:29; 2Ki 5:9; Ac 8:28). Israel's enemies used chariots (Ex 14:7; Jsh 11:4; Jgs 4:3; 1Sm 13:5). Beginning with the time of David, Israel also used them (2Sm 8:4; 1Ki 9:19; Is 31:1). See pp. 135–36.

CHARMER. *See* MAGIC.

CHASTISEMENT (CHAS-tiz-muhnt). Refers to the punishment endured by Christ for sin (Is 53:5) as well as the suffering endured by Israel at God's hand (Lm 4:6).

CHEBAR (KEE-bahr). A river of Chaldea on whose banks Ezekiel had visions (Ezk 1:1, 3).

CHEDORLAOMER (ked-or-la-O-mer; servant of god Lagamar). The king of Elam against whom Abraham fought (Gn 14).

CHEMOSH (KEE-mahsh; subduer). The god of Moab who was worshiped with child sacrifices (Nu 21:29; 2Ki 3:27). To please one of his foreign wives, Solomon built a place to worship Chemosh (1Ki 11:7). Later King Josiah destroyed this place of idol worship (2Ki 23:13). See p. 77.

CHERETHITES (KER-i-thights). A Philistine tribe that lived in southwest Canaan (1Sm 30:14; Ezk 25:16). Some were members of David's guard (2Sm 8:18; 15:18).

CHERITH (KEE-rith). A brook east of the Jordan where Elijah hid during the first part of the famine he had predicted (1Ki 17:3, 5).

CHERUB (CHER-uhb). The plural form of this word is cherubim (CHER-ah-bim). The Bible pictures cherubim as winged, heavenly beings with the faces of men and the bodies of lions. Ezekiel describes them as four-winged and four-faced (Ezk 1:5–12; 10:1–22).

When God drove Adam and Eve out of the Garden of Eden, He put cherubim at the entrance of Eden to guard it (Gn 3:24). To adorn the ark of the covenant, craftsmen made two golden cherubim and placed them on top of it (Ex 25:18–22; 37:7–9; Heb 9:5). Cherubim were also embroidered on the curtain and veil of the tabernacle (Ex 26:1, 31). Solomon placed two cherubim in the Most Holy Place in the temple (1Ki 6:23–28; 8:7).

The Bible pictures the Lord as living between cherubim and as riding on them (Nu 7:89; 2Sm 22:11; Ps 18:10; 80:1). See pp. 40, 65, 126, 195–96.

CHIEF PRIEST. *See* PRIEST.

CHILEAB (KIL-i-ab). A son of King David and Abigail (2Sm 3:3).

CHILION (KIL-i-on; pining). A son of Elimelech and Naomi (Ru 1:2).

CHINNERETH, CHINNEROTH (KIN-i-reth, KIN-i-rahth; harp). 1. A fortified city of Naphtali on the northwest shore of the Sea of Galilee (Jsh 19:35).

2. The region around the city of Chinnereth. It is often identified with the Plain of Gennesaret (1Ki 15:20; Mt 14:34).

3. An old name for the Sea of Galilee (Nu 34:11; Jsh 11:2). *See also* GALILEE, SEA OF.

CHLOE (KLO-ee; green grass). A Christian woman well-known to the Christians at Corinth (1Co 1:11).

CHOSEN. Key New Testament description of Christians (1Th 1:4; 2Th 2:13; 1Pt 1:1–2; Rv 17:14). Although God chose us "before the foundation of the world" (Eph 1:4), His choice was not arbitrary. He chose us to be saved by Christ and in union with Christ, who Himself is God's "Chosen One" (Lk 9:35; 1Pt 2:4–6). God chose us in love, not anger or judgment; Paul speaks only of a choosing for redemption. Cf. Rm 8:29–33; 11:5; Jn 15:16.

CHRIST (KRIGHST). *See* JESUS CHRIST; MESSIAH.

CHRISTIAN (KRIS-chuhn). A follower of Christ. The disciples were first called Christians at Antioch, Syria (Ac 11:26; 26:28; 1Pt 4:16).

CHRONICLES, FIRST AND SECOND BOOK OF (KRAHN-i-k'lz). Two historical books in the Old Testament. Bible scholars generally believe they were written by one person (perhaps Ezra) and originally formed one book. The books speak of the history of the priests from the death of Saul to the end of the captivity. See pp. 140–42.

CHRONOLOGY (kro-NAHL-o-jee). The science of dating biblical events. To arrive at these dates, scholars use statements in the Bible, for instance, Lk 3:1–2, as well as historical events and dates. The chronology of a man named Ussher is one well-known system of dating biblical events. However, many scholars do not agree with all of his dates.

Dates often given for key events are approximately 2100 to 1800 BC for the time of the Patriarchs, 1446 (or sometimes 1290) BC for the Exodus, 1048 to 587 BC for the period of the kings, around 740 to 600 BC for the captivity of Israel, 587 to 538 BC for the captivity of Judah, and 2 BC for the birth of Christ. *See also* TIME.

CHURCH. The Church is the collected gathering of God's people. In the Old Testament, the word used for church means assembly or congregation (Dt 23:2; Ezr 10:8; Ps 149:1). The New Testament speaks of the Church both as the Christians gathered in a specific place and as all Christians everywhere of all time (Mt 16:18; Ac 5:11; 8:1; 1Co 10:32).

The Church, the Body of Christ, draws its life and nourishment from the Gospel in the Word and Sacraments. It passes on its life by preaching and sharing the Sacraments (Mt 28:19, 20; Ac 20:28; 1Co 4:17; 2Co 8:18).

According to the New Testament, the Church belongs to God in Christ (Ac 20:28; 1Co 1:2; Gal 1:22; 1Th 2:14). It is described as the fellowship of God's people, the Bride of Christ, the Body of Christ, and a building of which Jesus Christ is the chief Cornerstone (Rm 12:5; Eph 2:20–22; 4:4; 5:25–33; 1Pt 2:9). See p. 445. *See also* FELLOWSHIP.

CIRCUMCISION (sur-kuhm-SIZH-uhn; cutting around). Removal of the foreskin of the penis. God instituted the rite of circumcision upon Abraham and his descendants (Gn 17:10). It showed that He would be their God and that they were to belong to Him, worshiping and obeying only Him. While in the wilderness, Moses made circumcision a legal institution (Lv 12:3; Jn 7:22–23). The Hebrew people looked down upon those who were not circumcised (Jgs 14:3; 15:18; 1Sm 14:6). Some other nations, such as the Egyptians, also practiced circumcision. See pp. 16, 41.

Christians in the New Testament era refused to force Gentiles to submit to circumcision (Ac 15:1–5; Gal 5:2).

God circumcises the heart by purifying it so that it will be able and willing to love God (Dt 10:16; 30:6).

CISTERN. A hole dug in the earth or rock to hold rainwater or water from a spring (Pr 5:15; Ec 12:6; Is 36:16; Jer 2:13). Empty cisterns were sometimes used as prisons (cf. Gn 37:22–24). See p. 62.

CITIZEN, CITIZENSHIP. 1. An inhabitant of a city or country (Lk 15:15).

2. A Roman citizen had special rights, including the right to appeal to the emperor. The rights of Roman citizenship belonged to those who were born Roman citizens, who purchased citizenship, or who received citizenship through special service or favor (Ac 16:37–39; 22:25–29; 23:27). See pp. 348, 372, 378, 399–400.

3. Christians are citizens of heaven, together with the saints (Eph 2:19; Php 3:20). See p. 270.

CITY OF GOD. *See* JERUSALEM, THE NEW.

CITY OF REFUGE. *See* REFUGE, CITIES OF.

CLAUDIUS (KLAW-di-uhs). The Roman emperor from AD 41 to 54. Claudius took over after Caligula. He banished all the Jews from Rome (Ac 18:2). See p. 399.

CLAUDIUS LYSIAS (KLAW-di-uhs-LIS-i-uhs). *See* LYSIAS, CLAUDIUS.

CLEOPAS (KLEE-o-pas; of renowned father). One of the two disciples to whom Christ appeared on the way to Emmaus (Lk 24:18).

CLOPAS (KLO-pahs). Another name for Alphaeus. He was the husband of one of the Marys who stood beside the cross (Jn 19:25).

CLOUD. Many times when the Bible refers to clouds, it is speaking figuratively. Clouds show God's power and wisdom (Ps 135:7; Na 1:3). Sometimes they stand for a great number or for great trouble or danger (Is 44:22; 60:8; Ezk 30:3; Heb 12:1). Clouds are also a sign of God's presence (Is 19:1).

COAT. *See* DRESS.

COCK. A male chicken. Cockcrowing is mentioned in Mt 26:34, Mk 13:35, and Lk 22:34. It refers to the time between midnight and 3 a.m.

COHORT. Roman military unit (Ac 10:1; 21:31; 27:1). *See* ARMY; BAND.

COL-HOZEH (kahl-HO-ze; all-seeing). Baruch's father (Ne 11:5).

COLONY. A settlement of Roman citizens in a conquered territory (Ac 16:12). Often the colonists were retired Roman soldiers who settled in places where they could keep the enemies of the empire in check.

COLOSSAE (ko-LAHS-ee). An old city of Phrygia. Paul began a church at Colossae on his third missionary trip (Col 1:2). See p. 401.

COLOSSIANS, LETTER OF PAUL TO (ko-LAHSH-ahnz). Paul wrote this letter to the Church at Colossae probably while he was a prisoner at Rome for the first time. (Some scholars think Paul may have been jailed in Caesarea or Ephesus when he wrote this letter rather than in Rome.)

In his letter, Paul warned the Colossians against false teachers who taught such things as angel worship and severe self-denial. These people were making Christianity a religion based on the Law and said that Jesus was only a lesser god. See pp. 401–03.

COMMANDMENTS. *See* DECALOGUE.

COMMONWEALTH. *See* CITIZEN, CITIZENSHIP.

COMMUNION. *See* FELLOWSHIP; LORD'S SUPPER.

COMPASSION. *See* MERCY.

CONANIAH (kahn-ah-NIGH-ah; Lord has established). A Levite who was in charge of the offerings and tithes during King Hezekiah's reign (2Ch 31:12–13).

CONCUBINE (KAHNG-kyoo-bighn). A lesser wife who was often taken from among the purchased slaves or captives (Gn 16:1; Jgs 8:31). Although her status was lower, her rights were protected by the law (cf. Ex 21:7–9; Dt 21:10–14). See p. 18.

CONDUIT. A channel cut in the rock or made underground for the purpose of moving water from one place to another (2Ki 18:17; 20:20; Is 7:3; 36:2).

CONFESS. 1. To acknowledge publicly or make known as one's own. One confesses Christ by acknowledging one's faith in Him and His Gospel and by obeying Him (Mt 10:32; Lk 12:8; Rm 10:9). One confesses one's sins by admitting them, either publicly or privately, to God or another person (Ps 32:5; Jas 5:16; 1Jn 1:9). See p. xxii–xxiii, 416, 439.

2. To acknowledge, praise, and thank God (Is 48:1; Dn 9:4).

3. To declare openly one's faith (Heb 3:1; 4:14). See pp. xxix, 296–97, 313, 436.

CONGREGATION. The Hebrew people viewed as one holy, religious group (Nu 16:3). Sometimes the word *congregation* refers to an assembly of all the people (Ex 12:6; 35:1); sometimes it refers to the people even when they are not assembled (Ex 12:3; Lv 4:13). The leader of the congregation often represented it (Jgs 21:10–20). *See also* CHURCH.

CONSCIENCE (KAHN-shuhns). A sense of right and wrong with an inner urge to do right and a guilty feeling if one goes against one's own standard of right and wrong (Ac 23:1; 1Tm 1:5; 1Pt 3:16). A "weak" conscience has a faulty norm (1Co 8:10–13).

CONSECRATE (KAHN-si-kraht). To set someone or something aside for God. The firstborn, whether man or beast, were set apart for the priesthood (Ex 13:2). Precious metals, persons, nations, fields, and cattle were consecrated to God (Nu 6:2–13; Jsh 6:19; 2Ch 29:33; cf. "devoted" in Lv 27:28). See pp. 41, 56, 149, 331.

All Christians are consecrated or set aside for God (1Pt 2:9). There are also special consecrations. For example, Barnabas and Paul were set aside for the work of the ministry (Ac 13:2). *See also* ORDINATION.

CONTRITION (kun-TRISH-uhn). A sure knowledge of one's sin, grief because of it, and fear of God's punishment (Ps 51:17; Is 57:15; Lk 15:18; Ac 2:37). Contrition comes before forgiveness (Ps 34:18; Is 66:2).

CONVERSION (kun-VUR-shuhn). An act of God's grace by which a sinful person is turned around and brought into Christ's kingdom (cf. Col 1:13). Conversion is accomplished by the Holy Spirit, who brings the person to faith in Christ through the Word (Ps 51:13; Is 55; Jn 3:16; Ac 3:19; 11:21; 15:3; 26:18; Rm 1:16; 2Co 3:16; 1Pt 2:25). See pp. 353, 376, 421.

CONVOCATION. A meeting of the people that was called for the purpose of worshiping God (Lv 23:2–8; Nu 28:18–25).

CORAL. The Hebrews highly valued coral, ranking it with precious stones (Jb 28:18; Lm 4:7).

CORBAN (KAWR-ban). An offering or sacrifice to God (cf. Lv 1:2–3; 2:1; 3:1; Nu 7:12–17). In Mk 7:11, corban refers to money or service dedicated to God.

CORD. Cord was made of flax, animal hides, date tree fibers, or camel hair. It was used for holding together tents, binding prisoners, scourging, and making ship ropes (Ex 35:18; Jn 2:15; cf. Jgs 15:13; Ac 27:32).

CORINTH (KAHR-inth). A wealthy, worldly Greek city on the isthmus connecting Peloponnesus and the mainland. Corinth was destroyed by the Romans in 146 BC and rebuilt by Caesar in 46 BC. Paul began a church there (Ac 18:1). See pp. 376, 384–85.

CORINTHIANS, FIRST LETTER OF PAUL TO (KO-RIN-thi-ahnz). While in Ephesus on his third missionary journey, Paul wrote this letter to correct the abuses in the Church at Corinth and to strengthen the faith of the people there. See pp. 384–85.

CORINTHIANS, SECOND LETTER OF PAUL TO (KO-RIN-thi-ahnz). While in Macedonia on his third missionary journey, Paul wrote this Letter to the Corinthians to praise them for their repentance and to speak well of the ministry. See pp. 384–85.

CORNELIUS (kawr-NEEL-yuhs; of a horn). A Roman centurion and the first Gentile convert (Ac 10).

CORNERSTONE. The foundation stone laid at the corner of a building as its starting point (Jb 38:6; Is 28:16). Christ is the Cornerstone of the Church (Mt 21:42; Eph 2:20; 1Pt 2:5–7).

COS (KAHS). An island in the Aegean Sea mentioned in connection with Paul's third missionary journey (Ac 21:1).

COUNCIL. 1. A group of people gathered for discussion and decision-making (Gn 49:6; Ac 25:12).

2. The Sanhedrin and lesser courts (Mt 26:59; Mk 13:9; Ac 5:34). The Sanhedrin was the highest Jewish court during the Greek and Roman periods for enforcing Mosaic Law. It was made up of the high priest, elders, and scribes—the maximum number being 71. The high priest was in charge of this council. During Jesus' time, this council had jurisdiction over Palestine (Mt 5:22; 26:59; Mk 14:55; 15:1; Lk 22:66; Jn 11:47; Ac 4:15; 6:12). See pp. 332, 368–69. *See also* APPEAL.

COURIER. A messenger (Est 8:10, 14).

COURT, COURTYARD. The enclosed yard of a house, palace, or prison (2Sm 17:18; Jer 32:2), or the outer area of the tabernacle and temple (Ex 27:9; 1Ki 6:36). *See also* HOMES. See pp. 326–27, 364–65.

COURTS OF THE LORD. In the Old Testament, the various courtyards that surrounded the tabernacle and temple were restricted by the various standards of holiness. To enter these holy places was to enter God's presence (2Ki 21:5; Ps 84:2).

COVENANT (KUHV-i-nahnt). A mutual agreement between two or more tribes, nations, or individuals to do or refrain from doing something. People called upon God to witness the pacts they made with others (Gn 21:27; 31:50; Jsh 9:6; 1Sm 20:8).

The covenants God made with Noah and Abraham were pledges of His grace (Gn 9:9–16; 15:7–21). In the covenant God made with Israel, He promised to continue being their God and to care for them. They in turn promised to be His people and keep His commandments (Ex 24). The prophets spoke of a new covenant that would center in a person (Is 42:6; 49:8; Jer 31:31–34).

In the New Testament covenant, one is placed into a right relationship to God through the work of Christ (2Co 3:6–18; Heb 7:22; 8:6–13). The New Covenant stresses the forgiveness of sins accomplished through the shedding of Christ's blood (Mt 26:28; Rm 11:26–27). This leads to a new, holy life (Gal 5:22–26; Heb 8–10). See pp. 26–27, 303, 423. *See also* BAPTISM; CIRCUMCISION; LORD'S SUPPER; PASSOVER.

CREATION. An act of God by which He calls something into being (Gn 1–2). God is the one who does the creating (subject); the object of His creation is an entirely new thing. God creates by His Word (Jn 1:3; Eph 3:9; Heb 1:2). See pp. 11, 15–16.

CRETANS, CRETE (KREE-tahns). Crete is an island in the Mediterranean Sea about 165 miles long and 6 to 35 miles wide. Paul began a church there (Ac 27:7–13; Ti 1:5–14). It also is called Caphtor (Jer 47:4). See p. 413.

The people of Crete were referred to as Cretans. They were known for being good sailors and skillful archers. According to Paul they were also untruthful (Ti 1:12). Some Cretans were present in Jerusalem on the Day of Pentecost (Ac 2:11).

CRISPUS (KRIS-puhs; curled). A ruler of the synagogue at Corinth who was brought to the Christian faith by Paul (Ac 18:8; 1Co 1:14).

CROCUS. *See* ROSE.

CROSS. The cross commonly was found in four forms: (1) The simple upright beam; (2) St. Anthony's cross, which was in the form of the letter T; (3) St. Andrew's cross, which was in the shape of an X; and (4) the Latin cross, with the crossbeam near the upper part of the upright beam ✝. The Greek cross ✝ and the double and triple crosses were additional forms. The cross upon which Christ died may have been of the Latin type (Mt 27:32–35).

The word *cross* is often used figuratively for the Gospel, for Christ's sufferings, and for that which is suffered as, and as a result of being, a disciple (Mt 16:24; Gal 6:14; Eph 2:16). See pp. 332, 334, 348, 449.

CRUCIFIXION (kroo-sah-FIK-shuhn). A method of killing a person by hanging the person on a cross. Crucifixion was practiced by the Egyptians, the Persians, the Greeks, the Romans, and other old civilizations (Gn 40:19). Jesus was crucified by the Romans (Mt 27; Mk 15; Lk 23; Jn 19). See pp. 334, 348.

CUBIT (KYOO-bit). *See* MEASURES 1d.

CUP. A small drinking vessel made from a horn or of clay or metal (Gn 44:2; 1Sm 16:13; Mt 26:27). Figuratively, the word *cup* is used to express one's lot in life (Ps 11:6; Mt 26:39; Mk 10:38). *See also* HOMES.

CUPBEARER. An officer who was in charge of wines and drinking vessels in a royal household (Gn 40; 41:9; 1Ki 10:5; 2Ch 9:4). Nehemiah was the cupbearer of King Artaxerxes (Ne 1:11). See pp. 148, 151.

CURDS. *See* FOOD.

CURSE (KURS). The opposite of bless. On the human level, to curse means to wish evil, harm, or suffering on someone (Gn 9:25; 49:7); on the divine level, it implies judgment.

All ancient people used curses (cf. 1Sm 17:43) but typically regarded them as magic formulas that, if pronounced properly, would obligate the gods to harm someone. The Lord uses curses especially to describe applications of His Law and its penalties.

God cursed the serpent and the earth after Adam and Eve's fall into sin (Gn 3:14, 17). God's curse was also spoken on various sins (Dt 27:15–26). Under the Mosaic Law, a person who cursed his or her parents was put to death (Lv 20:9). Christians are told to bless, not curse, those who curse them (Mt 5:11; Lk 6:28; Rm 12:14). See pp. 27, 68–69, 208, 255.

CUSH (KUSH). 1. A son of Ham and grandson of Noah. Cush was the father of Nimrod (Gn 10:8; 1Ch 1:10).

2. The territory in the region of the Tigris and Euphrates Rivers (Gn 2:13).

CUSHITE (KUSH-ight). A person from Ethiopia (Nu 12:1).

CUTH, CUTHAH (KUTH, KYOO-thah). A city of Babylonia whose people worshiped Nergal. Sargon, king of Assyria, brought people from Cuth to colonize the area of Samaria that he had sacked in 722 BC (2Ki 17:24, 30).

CYPRESS. A tall fir tree (1Ki 5:8; Is 14:8). See p. 322.

CYPRUS (SIGH-pruhs). An island about 148 miles long and 50 miles wide in the Mediterranean Sea off the coast of Syria. It was famous for its copper.

Cyprus was the home of many Jewish people. Barnabas came from Cyprus, and Stephen preached there (Ac 4:36; 11:19–20). Paul, Barnabas, and Mark visited there on the first missionary journey (Ac 13:4; 15:39). See p. 361.

CYRENE (sigh-REE-ni). The capital city of Cyrenaica (Tripoli) in northern Africa. It was colonized by Greeks (Mt 27:32; Mk 15:21; Ac 2:10). See p. 334.

CYRUS (SIGH-ruhs). Founder of the Persian Empire. Cyrus was a humane king. In 538 BC he captured Babylon and issued a decree allowing the captive Hebrews to go back to their native land and rebuild their temple (2Ch 36:22–23; Ezr 1:1–14; Is 44:28). Cyrus died in battle in 530 BC. See pp. 145, 224. *See also* DANIEL; EZRA.

D

DAGON (DA-gahn; may mean grain or fish). A pagan god with the body of a fish and the head and hands of a man. He was the god of natural powers, especially of grain. The Canaanites in Mesopotamia worshiped Dagon, and he was the national god of the Philistines. Temples were built to him at Ashdod and Gaza and in Israel (Jgs 16:21–30; 1Sm 5:1–7; 1Ch 10:10). Samson destroyed a temple to Dagon at Gaza (Jgs 16:30). See p. 77.

DAMASCUS (Dah-MAS-kuhs). An old Syrian city situated on a plateau watered by the Abana and Pharpar Rivers (Gn 14:15; 2Ki 5:12). The plateau is about 2,300 feet above sea level and is at the eastern foot of the Anti-Lebanon Mountains. Damascus played an important part in biblical history. Both David and Jeroboam II captured it (2Sm 8:6; 2Ki 14:28). The rulers of Damascus who played a prominent role in the history of Israel and Judah were Rezon (1Ki 11:23–25), Benhadad (1Ki 15:19–20; 22:15–37; 2Ki 8:15; 2Ch 16:3), Hazael (2Ki 8:15; 13:22–

25), and Rezin (2Ki 16:5, 7–8). Paul was converted to Christianity near Damascus (Ac 9:1–18). See pp. 307, 372.

DAMNATION. Those who do not believe in Christ will be separated from God eternally and will receive awful punishment (Mt 23:33; Mk 16:16; 2Th 1:9). This punishment is described as imprisonment, outer darkness, and fire (Mt 5:25–26; 8:12; Mk 9:47–48).

DAN (DAN; judge). 1. The fifth son of Jacob by Bilhah (Gn 30:5–6). See p. 17.

2. The tribe that descended from Dan and the territory allotted to it in Canaan (Nu 1:12, 38–39; Jgs 1:34–35).

3. A city, formerly named Laish, which was in the extreme north of Palestine. Members of the tribe of Dan captured and renamed it (Jsh 19:47; Jgs 18).

DAN TO BEERSHEBA. An expression used to refer to the length of Palestine (Jgs 20:1; 1Ch 21:2). Dan was in the extreme north of Palestine, and Beersheba was in the south.

DANCE. When people wanted to express joy or celebrate victory, they often danced (Jgs 11:34; Jb 21:11; Lk 15:25). Dancing as part of a religious ceremony or as an act of worship was common among the Hebrews (Ps 149:3). The women were usually the ones who danced, but occasionally men did as well (Ex 15:20; Jgs 21:21, 23). David, for instance, danced before the ark (2Sm 6:14–23). Dancing was also used for bad purposes (Ex 32:19; Mk 6:22). See p. 165.

DANIEL (DAN-yuhl; God is my judge). A prophet who was born into a princely family of Judah around the time of Josiah's reformation. In 605 BC, when Daniel was just a young man, King Nebuchadnezzar's soldiers took him captive to Babylon (Dn 1:1, 3). Nebuchadnezzar's chief servant gave Daniel the Babylonian name Belteshazzar and trained him in the wisdom of the Chaldeans (Dn 1:4–5). Although he was in a foreign land, Daniel continued to have faith in the Lord.

God blessed Daniel with great learning and the ability to interpret dreams (Dn 1:17). Because of these abilities, Daniel held a high, powerful position in the Babylonian court under Kings Nebuchadnezzar, Belshazzar, Darius, and Cyrus. Throughout his life, Daniel showed concern for his people. See pp. 137, 139, 143–44, 215, 219.

DANIEL, BOOK OF. Though Daniel had the gift of prophecy, he was a not a prophet by vocation but a government official.

The Book is written in both Hebrew and Aramaic. Because it is apocalyptic in character, it is full of symbolic and picture language. For this reason Bible scholars have interpreted it in a number of ways.

The title "Son of Man," which Jesus often used of Himself, is found in Dn 7:13–14. The New Testament refers to the Book of Daniel in a number of places (Mt 24:15; Lk 1:19; Heb 11:33–34). See pp. 215–17.

DARIC (DAR-ik). A Persian gold coin that had the picture of a king with a bow and javelin on one side and a square figure on the other side (1Ch 29:7; Ezr 2:69; 8:27; Ne 7:70–72).

DARIUS (Dah-REE-uhs). A common name for the Medo-Persian rulers. 1. Darius the Mede. He was the son of Ahasuerus and the governor of Babylon under Cyrus (Dn 5:31; 9:1). He is mentioned often in the Book of Daniel (6:1, 6, 9, 25, 28; 11:1). Darius was tricked into writing a law that required everyone in the land to worship only him for 30 days. When Daniel broke this law by worshiping the Lord, he was thrown into a lions' den (Dn 6:4–24). See pp. 143, 219.

2. Darius Hystaspes. He ruled from 522 to 486 BC and was the fourth and greatest king of the Persian Empire. He renewed the decree of Cyrus that allowed the Hebrews to return to their native land, and he helped them in rebuilding their temple (Ezr 4:5, 24; 5:5–7; Zec 1:1, 7; 7:1). See p. 145.

3. Darius the Persian. The last king of Persia, he reigned from 423 to 405 BC. He was defeated by Alexander the Great (Ne 12:22).

DAVID (DAY-vid; beloved). The second king of Israel. He was from the tribe of Judah and was the youngest son of Jesse of Bethlehem (1Sm 16:1–13; 1Ch 2:13–15). After God rejected Saul as king, He sent the prophet Samuel to Bethlehem to anoint David as the next king (1Sm 16:13).

When Saul became troubled by evil spirits and bad moods, his servants told him to find a lyre player to soothe him. So Saul sent for David because he had heard that David had great musical gifts. David came and played the harp for Saul (1Sm 16:14–23). Later David killed Goliath, the Philistine warrior, when everyone else was afraid to fight him (1Sm 17).

David was loved by Jonathan, Saul's son, but feared and envied by Saul (1Sm 18). When Saul tried to take David's life, David fled to Gath, where he pretended to be mad (1Sm 18:1–3; 19–21; Ps 34 title). Living in a cave, David gathered 400 men around him who were unhappy with Saul's rule (1Sm 22). Among them was Abiathar the priest. With this group of men David protected the Israelites from the Philistines and bands of robbers. In return for this, the Israelites gave David and his men food (1Sm 23–25).

Informed of David's activities, Saul led his men in pursuit of David (1Sm 26). Eventually David left Judah and lived in Ziklag. Some time later the Philistines went to war with Saul. When David heard that Jonathan had been killed and that Saul had killed himself, he was sad (1Sm 27–30).

Then the tribe of Judah, to which David belonged, elected him king (2Sm 2–4). Ish-bosheth, Saul's son, was made king of the rest of the tribes. When Ish-bosheth was killed two years later, David was elected king over all of the tribes (2Sm 5). David set to work to unite the tribes into one kingdom. He took Jerusalem from the Jebusites and made it his capital. Then he defeated the Philistines (2Sm 5:17–25; 21:15–22; 1Ch 14:8–17). After this he brought the ark to Jerusalem, organized worship, and planned a beautiful temple (2Sm 6–7; 1Ch 13; 15–17; 22:7–10).

To ensure the safety of the nation of Israel and to keep it from being polluted by the idolatry of the surrounding countries, David waged war on and subdued the Moabites, Aramaeans, Ammonites, Edomites, and Amalekites (2Sm 8; 10; 12:26–31).

David was a great king and a man of devout faith in God. Yet he was also a sinful human being. He committed a great sin when, after committing adultery with Bathsheba, he had her husband, Uriah, killed so that he could marry Bathsheba himself (2Sm 11:1; 12:23; 24; 1Ch 21; Ps 51). David also had many family problems (2Sm 12–19; 1Ki 1).

David reigned 40 years (2Sm 2:11; 5:4–5; 1Ch 29:27). Before he died, he said that Solomon should be the next king (1Ki 1–2).

David is referred to as the sweet psalmist of Israel (2Sm 23:1). Over 73 psalms are said to have been written by him. He was a man after God's own heart and an ancestor of Jesus (1Sm 13:14; Mt 22:41–45; Ac 13:36). See pp. 101–03, 112–113, 141, 164.

DAVID, CITY OF. 1. A part of Jerusalem that David captured. He called it the city of David and made it his capital. It stood on the ridge south of the temple area (2Sm 5:6–9).

2. Bethlehem, the birthplace or home of David (Lk 2:4).

DAY. *See* TIME.

DAY OF ATONEMENT. *See* ATONEMENT, DAY OF.

DAY OF THE LORD. 1. In the Old Testament, the day of the LORD refers to a day of victory for the kingdom of God, the day upon which evil is defeated. It is that day when God reveals Himself as the Lord, judges evil, and completes His work of redemption among people (Is 13:6, 9; Ezk 13:5; Zep 1:14). See pp. 231, 254.

2. In the New Testament, the day of the Lord refers to the day when Christ comes in the glory of the Father, the Day of Judgment. To those who do not trust in Christ, that day will be a day of terror (Mt 10:15; Rm 2:5–6; 2Pt 3:7, 12); to believers, it will be a day of great joy (Mt 16:27; 24:30; Jn 6:39; 2Co 1:14; Php 1:6, 10). See pp. 405, 430. *See also* PAROUSIA.

DAY'S JOURNEY. *See* MEASURES 1h.

DEACON (DEE-k'n; minister or servant). Someone who serves (cf. Lk 22:25–27; Mk 10:45). In the Early Church, deacons were chosen to relieve the apostles of caring for the physical needs of widows and other poor people (Ac 6:1–6). Qualifications for the office of deacon are given in Php 1:1 and 1Tm 3:8–13. See pp. 408, 412.

DEACONESS (DEE-k'n-es). A female helper in the church (Rm 16:1).

DEAD. 1. A lifeless body (Gn 23). *See also* BURIAL; DEATH.

2. People who do not have faith in Christ are spiritually dead (Eph 2:1).

3. Believers are dead to the Law (Col 2:20).

4. Faith that produces no works is dead (Jas 2:17).

DEAD SEA. *See* SALT SEA.

DEATH. When life ceases. The Bible describes death as departure or separation from the body (Ec 12:7; 2Tm 4:6; cf. 2Co 5:1–5). Death is a result of sin (Gn 2:17; Rm 5:12–14). Because all human beings are sinful, all will die (Heb 9:27). For those who believe in Christ, death is the beginning of eternal bliss (2Co 5:1; Php 1:23; 2Tm 4:6–8; Jas 1:12). See p. 391.

DEBORAH (DEB-o-rah; bee). 1. Rebekah's nurse (Gn 24:59; 35:8).

2. A prophetess and judge of the Israelites who urged Barak to fight Sisera (Jgs 4:4–14). After the battle Deborah wrote a song of triumph for the victory (Jgs 5). See pp. 88, 136.

DEBT. That which is owed to another person. Within certain limits, people who were unable to pay their debts could have their property, family, and even their own persons seized as payment (Lv 25:25–41; Dt 15:1–15; 24:6–13).

DECALOGUE (DEK-ah-log). The Ten Commandments, which God wrote on tables of stone and gave to Moses on Mount Sinai (Ex 20; 31:18; 32:15–19; Dt 10:1–5). The Ten Commandments form the basis of God's Law. In the Old Testament they are also referred to as the "words" or "the covenant" (Ex 20:1; 34:28; Dt 4:13; 5:22).

In the New Testament they are called commandments (Mt 19:17; Eph 6:2). Jesus' interpretation of the commandments is found in Mt 5:17–48; 19:16–22; Mk 2:24–27; Lk 6:1–10; 13:10–16. Perfect love is the fulfillment of the commandments (Mt 22:35–40). See p. 70.

DEDICATION. The act of devoting something to a holy use. For example, the people dedicated the tabernacle, the altar, and the temple, as well as other things to God (Ex 40; Nu 7; Dt 20:5; 2Ch 24:7; Ezr 6:16–17). See pp. 111, 141, 147, 152, 256.

The Feast of Dedication, an annual festival of the Jewish people, was the occasion when they remembered the cleansing of the temple (Jn 10:22). See p. 47.

DEEP. 1. The sea or its deepest part (Gn 7:11; Jb 38:30).

2. *See* ABYSS.

DELILAH (De-LIGH-lah; coquette). A Philistine woman from Sorek whom Samson loved. The Philistines bribed Delilah to discover the secret of Samson's strength (Jgs 16:4–20). See p. 112.

DEMAS (DEE-mas). One of Paul's co-workers. Demas left Paul and went to Thessalonica (Col 4:14; 2Tm 4:10; Phm 24).

DEMETRIUS (De-MEE-tri-uhs; belonging to Demeter). A silversmith at Ephesus (Ac 19:23–30).

DEMONS. Evil spirits who are against God and His work. Jesus called them unclean spirits (Mk 5:8). They form a hierarchy under Satan and take possession of persons in peculiar ways (Mt 8:16; Mk 1:32; Lk 8:36). See pp. 77, 314, 321, 376, 396.

DENARIUS (de-NAIR-i-uhs). A silver coin that looked like a dime. In New Testament times it was equal to a day's wage for people who worked on the land (Mt 20:2). The plural is *denarii* (Mt 18:28; Mk 6:37; Lk 7:41; Jn 6:7). See pp. 282, 318–19.

DESTRUCTION, SON OF. Found in the New Testament, this phrase refers to someone who spreads destruction and will ultimately be destroyed himself. Jesus calls Judas Iscariot by this title (Jn 17:12). Paul uses the same title to refer to the "man of lawlessness" (2Th 2:3).

DEUTERONOMY (dyoo-tur-ON-o-mi). The fifth book of the Pentateuch. It is named "Words" in the Hebrew Scriptures because of its opening sentence: "These are the words that Moses spoke to all Israel . . ." (1:1).

The book contains Moses' three farewell addresses and a renewal of Israel's covenant with God. Mosaic authorship is claimed in Deuteronomy 31:9, 24, 26. See pp. 67–69.

DEVIL. *See* DEMONS; SATAN.

DEW. A heavy dew was considered a great blessing. It refreshed the earth and helped make it fertile (Gn 27:28; Jgs 6:37–40). The absence of dew was looked upon as evil (2Sm 1:21; 1Ki 17:1). Dew was considered a symbol of silent blessing (Dt 32:2; Ps 110:3).

DIADEM. A headdress worn by men, women, high priests, and kings (Is 28:5). The diadems of olden times were often made of silk and covered with gems. Cf. "turban" in Jb 29:14; Is 3:23; Ezk 21:26.

DIAL. *See* TIME.

DIAMOND. 1. A precious stone (Ex 28:18; Ezk 28:13).
2. A symbol of hardness (Zec 7:12).

DIANA. *See* ARTEMIS.

DIDYMUS (DID-i-muhs; twin). A Greek name or nickname of the disciple Thomas (Jn 11:16; 20:24; 21:2). See p. 287.

DINAH (DIGH-nah; judged). Jacob and Leah's daughter. Shechem, the prince, raped her (Gn 30:21; 34). See pp. 17, 19.

DIONYSIUS (digh-o-NISH-uhs; devotee of Dionysus). A member of the Areopagus, the supreme court at Athens. Dionysius was converted by Paul (Ac 17:34).

DISCIPLE (learner). A pupil. The prophets, Jesus, John the Baptist, and the Pharisees all had followers or disciples (Is 8:16; Mt 5:1; 9:14; 22:16). The word is used especially of Jesus' twelve disciples (Mt 10:1; 11:1; 20:17). See pp. 286–89. *See also* APOSTLE.

DISCIPLINE. Action taken for instruction and correction (Dt 8:5; Pr 13:24; 19:18; 1Co 11:32; Eph 6:4). Discipline is not merely punishment for sin, but for the purpose of building up and edification. *See also* EDUCATION.

DISEASE. The physical diseases and ailments mentioned in the Bible were generally the same as the ones existing today. They include fever (Mt 8:14), boils (Dt 28:27; Jb 2:7), gangrene (2Tm 2:17), dropsy (Lk 14:2), tumors (1Sm 5:6), dysentery (Ac 28:8), itch (Dt 28:27), scabs (Dt 28:27), leprosy (Ex 4:6), insanity (1Sm 21:15), plague (Ex 9:3), paralysis (Mt 9:2), worms (Ac 12:23), fractures (Lv 21:19), bruises (Is 1:6), lameness (Lk 14:21), illness (Jn 5:5), inflammation (Lv 13:28), discharge (Lv 15:2), sores (Is 1:6), and wounds (Lk 10:34).

Doctors are rarely mentioned in the Old Testament (Gn 50:2; Jb 13:4). By New Testament times, however, medicine was a regular profession (Mt 9:12; Lk 4:23; Col 4:14). Figuratively, sin is described as a great disease (Is 1). See pp. 51, 314, 321, 323.

DISPERSION. The body of Israelites scattered about in lands other than their own. Through Moses, God warned the people that they would be scattered in other lands if they departed from the Mosaic Law (Dt 4:27; 28:64–68). These prophecies were largely fulfilled in the Assyrian and Babylonian captivities. Some scattering also took place due to smaller captivities or to migration and traveling.

In New Testament times, groups of Jewish people could be found in nearly all parts of the civilized world (Jn 7:35; Jas 1:1; 1Pt 1:1). See pp. 136–139, 151, 219, 426, 429.

DISTINGUISHING BETWEEN SPIRITS. The ability some Christians have that enables them to decide whether others speak by God's Spirit or by false spirits. This ability is given to them by the Holy Spirit (1Co 12:10).

DIVINATION (div-uh-NAY-shuhn). The practice of foretelling future events or discovering hidden knowledge (1Sm 6:2; Ezk 21:21; Dn 2:2). Divination was often practiced by heathen nations, but it was forbidden to Israel (Lv 19:26; Dt 18:10; Is 19:3; Ac 16:16). Rods, arrows, cups, a liver, dreams, and oracles were among the means used for divination (Gn 44:5; Dt 13:3; Is 41:21–24; Ezk 21:21; Hos 4:12).

DOCTRINE. Something that is taught; instruction or teaching (Dt 32:2; Pr 4:2; Mt 15:9; 1Tm 1:3; 4:13; 2Tm 3:10; Ti 2:1). See pp. xvi, xx, 414, 426.

DOG. An unclean animal that ran wild in the streets and was generally despised (Ex 11:7; 22:31; 2Sm 3:8; Mt 7:6). Sometimes dogs were looked upon more favorably (Lk 16:21). To call someone a dog was an insult. Enemies, lustful people, those who did not appreciate holy things, teachers of false doctrine, Gentiles, and wicked people are referred to as dogs (Dt 23:18; Ps 22:16; Mt 7:6; 15:26; Php 3:2; Rv 22:15).

DOOR. Biblical writers often use the word *door* figuratively. Christ says, "I am the door," that is, the way of salvation (Jn 10:9). The word *door* is also used to picture the entrance or way into a sinner's heart, the way to God's grace, and the entrance into heaven (Lk 13:25; Rv 3:20; 4:1). The picture of God opening a door is a way of saying that He provides the opportunity to preach the Gospel (Ac 14:27; Col 4:3). See pp. 350, 391. *See also* HOMES.

DOORKEEPER. Someone who watches the gate of a city, temple, palace, house, or other private entrance to make sure that no unauthorized person goes through (Ps 84:10; Mk 13:34). Cf. "gatekeeper" in 1Ch 9:21; Jn 10:3.

DOORPOST. The framework around the doorway. Following an Egyptian custom, the Israelites often wrote important matters on their doorposts (Dt 6:9).

DORCAS (DAWR-kuhs; gazelle). The Greek name for Tabitha, a Christian woman who lived at Joppa and was well-known for her deeds of love. Peter raised her from the dead (Ac 9:36–42).

DOT. A small line or dot used to tell one Hebrew letter from another (Mt 5:18; Lk 16:17).

DOTHAN (DO-thuhn; two wells). A place near Shechem and Samaria where Joseph was sold to the Ishmaelite traders and where Elisha had a vision (Gn 37:17–28; 2Ki 6:13–23).

DOVE. A gentle, timid bird that nests in holes in the sides of cliffs (Sg 2:14; Jer 48:28; Ezk 7:16; Hos 11:11).

Noah released a dove from the ark to see if the waters had subsided after the flood (Gn 8). At Jesus' Baptism the Holy Spirit appeared in the form of a dove (Mt 3:16). Poor people often sacrificed turtledoves (Lv 12:6–8; Lk 2:24).

DOXOLOGY (doks-AHL-o-jee). Words or songs of praise to God (cf. Ps 96:6; Lk 2:14; Rm 11:36; Eph 3:21; 1Tm 1:17). See pp. 166, 440.

DRAGON. 1. A sea monster (Is 27:1; cf. Ps 74:13). *See also* LEVIATHAN.

2. A mythical monster used to picture Satan (Rv 12:3).

3. Egypt (Ezk 32:2).

DRAM. *See* DARIC.

DREAM. Thoughts and ideas one has while sleeping. There are a number of times in the Bible when God revealed something to people, particularly His prophets, through a dream (Gn 20:3; 28:12; 37:5–11; 40:5; Dn 2; 4; Mt 1:20). The ability to interpret dreams was a special gift (Gn 40:5–23; Dn 4:19–27). See pp. 16, 24, 216, 232, 272, 447.

DREGS. The sediment or thick portion of wine that falls to the bottom (Ps 75:8; Is 51:17). "To settle on the dregs" is an expression for a lazy, luxurious, unhampered, stupid life (Jer 48:11).

DRESS. Adam and Eve made clothing out of leaves (Gn 3:7). Later, people made clothing out of animal skins, hair, wool, linen, and cotton (Gn 3:21; 38:12; Pr 31:13; Is 19:9; Mt 3:4; 7:15).

Men wore an inner tunic (Ex 28:4), an outer tunic (Lk 3:11), a mantle or cloak (Ex 12:34), breeches, a girdle or belt (cf. 2Ki 4:29; Ac 12:8), a cap (Ex 28:40), and sandals (Mt 3:11). Women wore similar clothing. Theirs, however, was longer and made of finer material. Women also wore veils and ornaments (Gn 38:14; Is 3:18–23).

DRINK. The Hebrew people drank water, milk, vinegar, wine, and strong drink (Gn 14:18; 24:11–18; Lv 10:9; Nu 6:3; Jgs 4:19; Ru 2:14; Jn 2:3). Strong drink was anything of an alcoholic nature, such as barley beer, cider, honey wine, date wine, and raisin wine.

Strong drink is frequently mentioned in the Bible, and abuse of it is warned against (Gn 9:21; Pr 20:1; Is 5:11; 24:20; Jn 2:1–11). See p. 62.

DRINK OFFERING. Pouring wine or some other liquid as an act of worship (Ex 29:40–41; Jer 44:17–25).

DROPSY. *See* DISEASE.

DROUGHT. A period of dryness due to lack of rain (Jb 24:19; Jer 51:43; cf. Ps 32:4). Little rain falls in Palestine from May to October.

DRUSILLA (droo-SIL-ah). The daughter of Herod Agrippa I. She was first the wife of Azizus, king of Edessa, and later of Felix, the governor of Judea. Paul preached before Drusilla and Felix about judgment and righteousness (Ac 24:24–25).

DUMAH (DU-mah). 1. The son of Ishmael. The descendants of Dumah lived in the northwestern part of the Arabian peninsula (Gn 25:14; 1Ch 1:30; Is 21:11–12).

2. A town in Judah, 10 miles southwest of Hebron (Jsh 15:52).

DURA (DYOO-rah). A plain of Babylon. King Nebuchadnezzar set up an image made of gold on this plain (Dn 3:1).

DYSENTERY. A disease caused by the inflammation and ulceration of the large intestine (Ac 28:8).

E

EAR. When priests were consecrated or lepers cleansed, blood was put on their ears (Ex 29:20; Lv 14:14). The Bible describes a disobedient person as having an uncircumcised or heavy ear; and an obedient person, an open ear (Is 50:5; Ac 7:51).

EARTH. 1. The world where we live (Gn 1:1).

2. Dry land (Gn 1:10).
3. The people who live in the world (Gn 6:11).
4. Soil (Ex 20:24).
5. Carnal or unspiritual things (Jn 3:31; Col 3:2).

EAST. The direction toward the sunrise. The Hebrews faced toward the rising sun to determine direction (Gn 2:8; 3:24; Jsh 12:3). Traditionally, Christian churches (and graves) have been oriented toward the east because Christ, the sun of righteousness (Mal 4:2), rose at dawn in the east. Cf. Ezk 8:16.

EAST COUNTRY. The region east of Palestine, especially Syria and Arabia (Gn 25:6).

EAST WIND. A hot, dry wind from the east (Gn 41:23, 27; Ezk 17:7–10).

EASTER (Possibly derived from "Eostre," Teutonic goddess of light and spring). The Christian celebration of Passover (Pascha), focused on the resurrection of Jesus. By the eighth century the name Easter was likely used in England because the celebration coincided with the spring Teutonic festival. See pp. 336, 363, 425.

EASTERN SEA. *See* SALT SEA.

EBAL (EE-buhl). A mountain about 2,700 feet above the sea. It was separated from Mount Gerizim by the Valley of Shechem. Mount Ebal was the mount of cursing; Mount Gerizim was the mount of blessing (Dt 11:29; 27:12–26; 28; Jsh 8:30–35). See p. 69.

EBED-MELECH (EE-bed-MEE-lek; king's servant). An Ethiopian who heard that Jeremiah had been thrown into a dungeon. Ebed-melech obtained the king's permission to draw Jeremiah out (Jer 38:7–13; 39:15–18).

EBENEZER (eb-uhn-EE-zur; stone of help). A memorial stone that Samuel set up between Mizpeh and Shen to show the place where the Israelites had defeated the Philistines (1Sm 7:12).

EBER (EE-bur; beyond). A descendant of Shem. The Hebrews, the Joktanide Arabs, and the Arameans descended from Eber (Gn 10:21–30; 11:14–17; Lk 3:35). See pp. 12, 148.

EBONY. A heavy, hard, dark wood used for ornamental work (Ezk 27:15).

ECCLESIASTES (e-klee-zi-AS-teez; preacher). The name of this Old Testament book means "one who sits and speaks in the assembly or church." The author of the book reflects on the value of life. He points out that, in theory, there can be no gain in everyday life since the same fate comes to everyone (1:9). Therefore, a person's source of satisfaction lies within, in the way the person uses his or her mind and body for work and for pleasure at the proper time (2:24; 3:1–9, 13; 5:18).

The writer also notes that enjoyment of the good things in life is a gift of God (2:24; 25; 3:13; 5:19). In everything a person does, he or she should remember God, the Creator. Since no one can keep the commandments or fear God perfectly, the author's final thought—that one's chief duty is to do these very things (12:13)—prepares the reader for recognizing his or her need for the Gospel. See pp. 178–80.

EDEN, GARDEN OF (EE-d'n; delight). The garden in which God put Adam and Eve was in the region of Eden (Gn 2:15).

EDOM (EE-duhm; red). 1. The name given to Esau because he sold his birthright for a dish of red stew (Gn 25:30).

2. The people who descended from Esau and their country, located in the southeastern part of Palestine (Jgs 11:17; Nu 34:3; Ps 83:6). Later, the Greeks renamed this country Idumaea. See pp. 117, 236–37.

EDOMITES (EE-duhm-ights). The descendants of Esau (Dt 23:7). They lived in the land of Edom, which they had taken from the Horites (Dt 2:12). When the Israelites were on their way to Canaan, they asked permission of the Edomites to pass through their country, but the Edomites said no (Nu 20:18–21). Saul fought against the Edomites, and David defeated them (1Ki 11:15–16; 1Sm 14:47; 2Sm 8:13–14). The Edomites were constant enemies of Israel (1Ki 11:14–22; 2Ch 21; 25; Is 34:5–8; 63:1–4; Jer 49:17). See pp. 19, 79, 117, 236–37.

EDUCATION. In early times, Hebrew children were taught about God and their nation by their parents. Later, the Book of Deuteronomy was used as a textbook (Dt 4:9; 6:6–7). Moses and the prophets were also leaders in education. Before the exile, those who were considered wise became teachers. The Book of Proverbs contains ideas about the education of that period. See pp. 105, 132–33, 300, 409–10.

After the exile, Ezra added to the number of teachers (Ezr 8:16). He also encouraged people to read, something which only a few people had been able to do before (cf. 2Ki 5:7; 22:8–10; 23:2). People who made their living at teaching taught in synagogue schools.

Around 75 BC, compulsory education was begun. Students learned their work by memorizing what their teacher said.

EGLON (EG-lahn; calflike). 1. A city in Canaan whose king, Debir, encamped against Gibeon. Joshua, through the Lord's help, routed the city's troops and executed the king (Jsh 10:1–28).

2. A king of Moab who captured Jericho and made Israel serve him for 18 years. Eglon was killed by Ehud, a judge of Israel (Jgs 3:12–30).

EGYPT (EE-jipt). A country largely in northeast Africa with a small part in the Sinai Peninsula. It is also called the country of Ham (Ps 105:23, 27; cf. Gn 10:6). Egypt is watered by the Nile River, the longest river in the world. The river is divided into a narrow valley and delta, both of which are surrounded by desert. Egypt's rulers were called pharaohs. Its religion was polytheistic, that is, the people believed in many gods. Some of the well-known gods were Ptah, Ra, Thum, and Amon.

Egypt was a powerful kingdom during Old Testament times. For many years the Hebrew people were slaves there until God sent Moses to free them (Ex 1–14). In New Testament times Egypt was a center of culture. See pp. 32–33.

EKRON (EK-rahn). One of five chief Philistine cities. After the Philistines captured the ark of God, they brought it to Ekron (Jsh 13:3; 15:11, 45–46; Jgs 1:18; 1Sm 5:10; 2Ki 1:2–16; Jer 25:20; Am 1:8). Today this location is identified as Tel Miqne. It is located about 11 miles from Gath. See p. 104.

EL (EL; God, divine being). An ancient name for God that can be traced to the Canaanites. It is often used in forming other words, e.g., El-bethel (Gn 35:7). Elohim, the plural form of El, is the more common word for God in the Old Testament.

ELAH (EE-lah; terebinth). 1. The son of Baasha and fourth king of Israel. Elah was killed by Zimri (1Ki 16:8–10).

2. The father of Hoshea, the last king of Israel (2Ki 15:30; 17:1; 18:1).

3. A valley southwest of Jerusalem where David killed Goliath (1Sm 17:2, 19; 21:9).

ELAM (EE-luhm). A son of Shem (Gn 10:22; 1Ch 1:17). Elam's descendants lived east of Babylonia and ruled it during Abraham's time. At that time the capital of Babylonia was Shushan (Ezr 4:9; Is 21:2; 22:6; Jer 49:34–39; Ezk 32:24; Ac 2:9).

EL-BETHEL (el-BETH-el; God of Bethel). The name Jacob gave to the altar he built at Bethel (Gn 35:7).

ELDAD (EL-dad; God has loved). One of 70 elders whom Moses appointed to help him (Nu 11:16, 26–29).

ELDER. In biblical times, the elderly were treated with great respect because of their wisdom and experience (Lv 19:32; Dt 32:7; Jb 32:6). An elder was one of the older men in his family or tribe who, by right of being firstborn, became its head (cf. Ex 3:16; 19:7). The elder made all the major decisions for his family or tribe and was the leader in various activities (Gn 24:2; 2Sm 12:17; Ezk 27:9). Each city also had an elder who was called the elder of the city (Dt 21:3; 22:18). The elders became rulers of the synagogue.

In the New Testament, the terms *elder* and *overseer* are used to mean the same thing. The elder or presbyter was a man the apostles appointed in each Christian church to be its pastor (Ac 20:17, 28; 1Tm 5:17; Ti 1:5–9; 1Th 5:12; 1Pt 5:1–3). See pp. 332, 368, 408, 416, 437.

ELEAZAR (el-i-AY-zur; God has helped). The third son of Aaron. Because Aaron's two older sons had died, Eleazar took over the job of chief priest from Aaron (Ex 6:23; Nu 20:25–28). He helped Joshua divide the Promised Land among the tribes (Jsh 14:1). See p. 150.

ELECT, ELECTION. Election is the eternal act of God by which, out of His grace and for Christ's sake, He chooses from sinful people those whom He will save (the elect). God chose the people of Israel not because of the peoples' own goodness but because of His divine love (Dt 4:37; 7:7–8; 9:4–6; 10:15; 23:5). Although many of the people lost their faith and fell away from God, those who remained faithful to Him and trusted in Him received the blessings of election (Is 4:3; 37:31–32). The Old Testament also talks about God choosing individuals (Ne 9:7; Ps 78:70; 105:26).

The Gospels speak of Christ choosing disciples (Lk 6:13). They also note that the elect are the messianic community, those who have faith in Christ as the promised Messiah and Savior (Mt 24:22, 24; Mk 13:20–27).

The New Testament letters explain the doctrine of election. No one deserves to be saved. God, however, chooses from eternity those whom He will save. Those whom He will save are brought to faith in Christ Jesus by the Holy Spirit and are kept in faith by Him. They are placed in the company of other elect

(Rm 9–11; 1Co 1:27–31; Eph 1:4–14; 1Pt 1:2). Election should not make the elect feel like they have "made it"; rather, their response will be thankfulness to God for His love and grace in choosing them (2Pt 1:10). Those who are of the elect are described as members of God's Church (Rm 8:33; 16:13; Col 3:12; Ti 1:1; 1Pt 1:1; 2Jn 13).

EL-ELOHE-ISRAEL (el-e-LO-he-IZ-rah-el; God, the God of Israel). The name of Jacob's altar near Shechem (Gn 33:20).

ELEVEN, THE. After Judas betrayed Christ and then killed himself, the remaining disciples were called the Eleven (Mt 28:16; Mk 16:14; Lk 24:9, 33; Ac 1:26). See p. 313.

ELI (EE-ligh; high). A descendant of Aaron (Lv 10:12). Eli lived at Shiloh and was both a devoted high priest and judge of Israel (1Sm 1:17; 2:20–30; 4:18). Eli's sons, who were also priests, acted shamefully; they had no regard for the Lord or His work. When Eli failed to discipline them, divine judgment was spoken against him and his household (1Sm 2:12–3:13).

In a battle between the Israelites and the Philistines, Eli's sons were killed, and the ark of the covenant was captured. When Eli heard the news, he fell backward, broke his neck, and died (1Sm 4). The priesthood passed from Eli's family to Zadok's (1Ki 2:27). See p. 150.

ELI, ELI, LEMA SABACHTHANI (AY-lee, AY-lee, LEH-mah sah-bahk-TAH-nee). *See* ELOI, ELOI, LAMA SABACHTHANI.

ELIAB (i-LIGH-ab; God is Father). David's oldest brother (1Sm 17:13–14, 28; 2Ch 11:18).

ELIADA (i-LIGH-ah-dah; whom God notices). One of David's sons (2Sm 5:16). He is referred to as Beeliada in 1Ch 14:7.

ELIAKIM (i-LIGH-ah-kim; whom God sets up). 1. The master of Hezekiah's household (2Ki 18:18, 19:2; Is 22:20). When Jerusalem closed its gates against the Assyrians, Eliakim was one of the men sent to receive a message from the leader of the invading army (2Ki 18:18, 26–27). After reporting to Hezekiah what the Assyrian leader had said, Eliakim was then sent to the prophet Isaiah for advice (2Ki 19:2; Is 37:1–7). Isaiah highly praised him (Is 22:20–25).

2. One of Josiah's sons. When he became king, he changed his name to Jehoiakim (2Ki 23:34; 2Ch 36:4).

ELIDAD (i-LIGH-dad; God has loved). A leader of the tribe of Benjamin who helped divide the land of Canaan among the tribes (Nu 34:21).

ELIEZER (el-i-EE-zur; God is help). 1. Abraham's steward (Gn 15:2–3).

2. Moses' younger son (Ex 18:2–4; 1Ch 23:15–17; 26:25).

3. A chief whom Ezra sent to ask the Levites to return to Israel (Ezr 8:16).

ELIHU (i-LEE-hyoo; my God is He). One of Job's three friends (Jb 32–37).

ELIJAH (i-LIGH-jah; my God is Lord). A Tishbite and great prophet. When King Ahab, influenced by his wife Jezebel, made Baal worship the court religion, Elijah predicted a drought as punishment for forsaking the Lord. During the three years of dry weather, Elijah was fed by ravens at the brook Cherith. Later he lived in the house of the widow of Zarephath (1Ki 16:29–17:24). Then God told Elijah to go and show himself to Ahab.

Elijah proposed a test to Ahab to see whether Baal or the Lord was the true God (1Ki 18:1–19). On Mount Carmel two altars were prepared: one to Baal by his prophets, and the other to the Lord by Elijah. Only the altar of the Lord was consumed by fire. In this way God proved He was the only true God; Baal was a false one. Then Elijah put to death the 450 prophets of Baal (1Ki 18:20–40).

After this Jezebel plotted against Elijah's life. So Elijah fled to Horeb, where he heard the still, small voice of the Lord. Then Elijah was sent to anoint Hazael as king over Syria, Jehu as king over Israel, and Elisha as prophet in Elijah's place (1Ki 19). Elijah pronounced God's judgment on Ahab for the murder of Naboth (1Ki 21:17–29). At the end of his life, Elijah was taken to heaven in a whirlwind (2Ki 2:1–12).

In the New Testament, John the Baptist is referred to as Elijah (Mt 11:14; 17:10–13; Lk 1:17). See pp. 130–31, 135–36, 139, 187.

ELIM (EE-lim; large trees). An oasis in the desert where the Israelites camped during the exodus (Ex 15:27; 16:1; Nu 33:9). There were 12 wells and 70 palms there. Today it is the site of Wadi Gharandel.

ELIMELECH (i-LIM-uh-lek; my God is king). Naomi's husband (Ru 1:1–3).

ELIPHAZ (EL-i-faz; God is gold). 1. The son of Esau and Adah (Gn 36:4; 1Ch 1:35–36).

2. The chief of Job's three friends. In his talks with Job, Eliphaz traced all suffering and distress to sin and told Job to make his peace with God (Jb 3–8; 15:22–24). God rebuked Eliphaz for saying this and told him to make a sacrifice (Jb 42:7–9).

ELISHA (i-LIGH-shah; God is salvation). The prophet who took Elijah's place as prophet to the Northern Kingdom. Elisha was the son of Shaphat and came from the tribe of Issachar. He prophesied during the reigns of Jehoram, Jehu, Jehoahaz, and Joash. During this time Elisha performed many miracles (2Ki 2–9; 13). See pp. 123, 135–36, 139, 187.

ELISHAMA (i-LISH-ah-mah; God has heard). 1. The captain of the tribe of Ephraim at the exodus and an ancestor of Joshua (Nu 1:10; 2:18; 7:48, 53; 1Ch 7:26).

2. Jehoiakim's scribe (Jer 36:12, 20–21).

ELISHEBA (i-LISH-i-bah; God of oath). Aaron's wife (Ex 6:23).

ELIZABETH (i-LIZ-ah-beth; God is oath). The wife of Zechariah and the mother of John the Baptist (Lk 1).

ELIZAPHAN (el-i-ZAY-fan; God has protected). The chief of the Kohathites when the Israelites were in the wilderness (Ex 6:22; Nu 3:30). He and his brother Mishael removed the bodies of Nadab and Abihu from the camp (Lv 10:4).

ELKANAH (el-KAY-nah; God has acquired). Samuel's father (1Sm 1:1–2:21).

ELKOSH (EL-kahsh). The place of Nahum's birth (Na 1:1).

ELNATHAN (el-NAY-ahn; gift of God). 1. The grandfather of Jehoiachin (2Ki 24:8; Jer 26:22).

2. One of the "men of insight" Ezra sent to Iddo to obtain priests for the house of God (Ezr 8:16).

ELOHIM (e-LO-heem). *See* EL.

ELOI, ELOI, LEMA SABACHTHANI (i-LO-igh, i-LO-igh, LAY-mah, say-BAK-thah-nigh; My God, my God, why have You forsaken Me?). Jesus' fourth cry from the cross (Ps 22:1; Mt 27:46; Mk 15:34).

ELYMAS (EL-i-mas; wise). *See* BAR-JESUS.

ELZAPHAN. *See* ELIZAPHAN.

EMBALM. To prepare a dead body with spices so that it will be preserved from decay. The Egyptians were noted for embalming. When Jacob died, Joseph had the Egyptians embalm Jacob. Joseph was also embalmed when he died (Gn 50:2, 26).

EMBROIDERY. The Hebrews and their neighbors did weaving, sewing, and artistic needlework (Ex 38:23; Jgs 5:30; Ps 45:13–14). They embroidered the hangings of the temple and the priests' clothing (Ex 26:36; 27:16; 28:33, 39; 39:29). See p. 40.

EMMAUS (e-MAY-uhs; hot springs). The village where two of Jesus' disciples were going on the day of Jesus' resurrection. It was near Jerusalem, though its exact location is unknown (Lk 24:13–33). See pp. 336, 425.

EMMER. An inferior type of wheat (Ex 9:32; Is 28:25; Ezk 4:9). *See also* FOOD 1.

ENCAMPMENT. *See* CAMP, ENCAMPMENT.

ENCHANTMENT. The use of magic arts, spells, or charms. Balaam's omens, sorcery, and serpent charming are some examples of enchantment (Nu 24:1; cf. 2Ki 9:22; Ec 10:11; Is 47:9–12). The Egyptians practiced enchantment, but it was forbidden to God's people (Ex 7:11–22; 8:7; Dt 18:10–14).

EN-DOR (EN-dawr; fountain of Dor). A village near Mount Tabor (Jsh 17:11; 1Sm 28:7; Ps 83:10). King Saul consulted with a medium from this village (1Sm 28).

ENGEDI (en-GEE-digh; fountain of wild goat). A town on an oasis on the western shore of the Dead Sea about 15 miles southeast of Hebron. It is fed by warm spring water (Jsh 15:62; 1Sm 24:1–7; Sg 1:14; Ezk 47:10).

ENGRAVING. To cut or etch letters or a design on a surface. This was a well-known practice in Israel and neighboring regions (2Ch 2:14). Examples of engraved articles include the Ten Commandments, stones and signets, and idols (Ex 20:4; 28:11, 36; 32:4, 16).

ENOCH (EE-nuhk; dedicated). 1. The first son of Cain (Gn 4:17).

2. The father of Methuselah. After the birth of Methuselah, Enoch walked with God for 300 years, and then God took him to heaven (Gn 5:18–24; 1Ch 1:3; Heb 11:5; Jude 14).

3. A city built by Cain (Gn 4:17).

ENOS, ENOSH (EE-nahs, EE-nash). The son of Seth and grandson of Adam (Gn 4:26; 5:6–11; Lk 3:38).

EPAPHRAS (EP-ah-fras; lovely). A Christian at Colossae who visited Paul when he was in prison (Col 1:7–8; 4:12; Phm 23). See p. 401.

EPAPHRODITUS (I-paf-ro-DIGH-tuhs; lovely). A Christian who carried the gifts of the church at Philippi to Paul while Paul was in prison at Rome (Php 2:25–30; 4:18). See p. 398.

EPHAH (EE-fah). *See* MEASURES 2d.

EPHES-DAMMIM (EE-fes-DAM-im; end of Dammim). A place in Judah between Socoh and Azekah. David fought Goliath there (1Sm 17:1). It is also referred to as Pas-dammim (1Ch 11:13).

EPHESIANS, LETTER OF PAUL TO THE (i-FEE-zhuhns). This letter is commonly regarded as a circular letter that Paul wrote to the churches in Asia, the chief of which was Ephesus (1:1; 3:1; 4:1). In this letter Paul speaks about what the Church is and its relationship to the Lord of the Church. Eph 2:10 is a good summary of the entire book: "We are His workmanship, created in Christ Jesus for good works . . . that we should walk in them." See pp. 395–96.

EPHESUS (EF-uh-suhs). A city situated on the Cayster River about three miles from the Aegean Sea. Ephesus was the capital of the Roman province of Asia. It was a commercial city and melting pot of different people, languages, and backgrounds. The city was dedicated to the worship of the Phoenician goddess Astarte, associated with Artemis or Diana.

Many Jewish people who had Roman citizenship lived in Ephesus and had a synagogue there (Ac 18:19). On one of his missionary journeys Paul began a Christian church there (Ac 19:20; 1Co 16:8). See pp. 338, 360–61, 377, 395, 407, 438.

EPHOD (EF-od; covering). An apronlike garment with shoulder straps and a belt. Made of gold, blue, scarlet, and fine-twined linen and beautifully adorned, it was one of the many garments worn by the high priests for worship (Ex 29). Later, others also wore ephods (1Sm 2:18; 2Sm 6:14; 1Ch 15:27). See pp. 44, 150.

EPHPHATHA (EF-ah-tha; be opened). Jesus spoke this when he healed a deaf man (Mk 7:34).

EPHRAIM (EE-fray-im). 1. The second son of Joseph and Asenath (Gn 46:20). Jacob, Ephraim's grandfather, adopted both Ephraim and his brother, Manasseh, as his own sons. When the two sons were brought to Jacob on his sickbed, Jacob gave Ephraim the greater blessing, bestowing on him the birthright of the firstborn son (Gn 48:8–20). Ephraim's descendants were numerous (Nu 1:33; 26:37). See pp. 19, 21.

2. The tribe of Ephraim was given land west of the Jordan between Manasseh on the north and Dan and Benjamin on the south (Jsh 16). It became the heart of the Northern Kingdom (1Ki 12; Is 7:2; 11:13; Ezk 37:15–22).

3. A city near Absalom's sheep farm (2Sm 13:23).

4. A gate in Jerusalem (2Ki 14:13; 2Ch 25:23).

EPHRAIM, MOUNT. The central range of mountains in Samaria (Jer 4:15; cf. Jsh 19:50; 1Sm 1:1).

EPHRATH (EF-rath; fruitful). An old name for Bethlehem (Gn 35:16, 19; 48:7).

EPHRATHAH (EF-rah-tha). The wife of Caleb and mother of Hur (1Ch 2:24, 50; 4:4).

EPHRATHITE (EF-rah-thight). An inhabitant of Bethlehem (Ru 1:2).

EPICUREANS (ep-i-kyoo-REE-uhnz). The followers of Epicurus, a Greek philosopher who died in 270 BC. Epicurus taught that the chief purpose of human beings is to achieve happiness. He denied life after death (Ac 17:16–32).

EPIPHANES (e-PIF-ah-neez). *See* ANTIOCHUS 2.

EPISTLE (i-PIS'l). A formal letter that contains Christian doctrine and instruction (Ac 15:30; Rm 16:22). The term refers particularly to the 21 New Testament books. These epistles are divided into Pauline and Catholic, or General, Epistles. The New Testament books are also called letters.

Paul refers to Christians as epistles written by the Holy Spirit (2Co 3:2–3).

ERASTUS (i-RAS-tuhs; beloved). A convert of Paul. Erastus, who lived in Corinth, was with Paul at Ephesus (Ac 19:22; Rm 16:23; 2Tm 4:20).

ESARHADDON (ez-ur-HAD'n; Asshur has given a brother). A son of Sennacherib and ruler of Assyria from 681 to 669 BC (2Ki 19:37; Is 37:38). Esarhaddon was one of Assyria's greatest conquerors. He rebuilt the city of Babylon, defeated Egypt and made it pay tribute, and took captive Manasseh, the fourteenth king of Judah (2Ch 33:11).

ESAU (EE-saw; hairy). The firstborn of Isaac and Rebekah's twin sons (Gn 25:25). Esau sold his birthright to his brother, Jacob, for a bowl of lentil stew (Gn 25:29–34; 27:28–29, 36; Heb 12:16–17). Since lentil stew is red, Esau was referred to as Edom, which means "red."

Esau married two Canaanite women and an Ishmaelite woman (Gn 26:34; 28:9; 36:2). He tried to kill Jacob for tricking him out of Isaac's blessing (Gn 27:41–45). Later he forgave his brother and warmly welcomed him back to Canaan (Gn 33). The country of Esau's descendants is called Edom (Gn 36). See pp. 12, 19, 79, 117.

ESCHATOLOGY (es-kah-TOL-o-ji; doctrine of last things). A study of the last things, such as death, resurrection, life after death, the second coming of Christ, Judgment Day, and heaven.

The Old Testament emphasizes the destiny of God's chosen people and the Day of the Lord (Is 13:6, 9; Jl 3:14; Am 9:11–15; Zep 1:7). The resurrection of the body and life after death is talked about in Is 26:19–21 and Dn 12:2. See also Jb 19:25–26; Is 53:10. See p. 262.

The New Testament emphasizes Christ's return to judge the world (Mt 24:25–27; *see also* PAROUSIA). It also talks about the resurrection of the body and the end times, when the wicked shall be thrown into hell and those who believe in Christ shall enter the joy of the Father (Mt 5:29–30; 25:31–46; Rm 8:11; 1Co 15).

ESHTAOL (ESH-tay-ol). A town 13 miles northwest of Jerusalem that was allotted to the tribe of Dan (Jsh 15:33; 19:41). Samson carried out his work in this area (Jgs 13:24–25; 16:31).

ESHTEMOA (esh-ti-MO-ah). A village 9 miles south of Hebron. It was given to the priests (Jsh 21:14; 1Ch 6:57).

ESSENE (e-SEEN). A Jewish sect in existence from the second century BC to the second century AD. They had settlements in Jerusalem, Judea, and around the Dead Sea.

Although the Bible does not speak of the Essenes by name, Josephus, Philo, and the Dead Sea Scrolls do talk about this group. The Essenes lived a simple life of sharing everything among one another. They believed that people should remain unmarried. While against slavery and animal sacrifice, they practiced cleanliness and tried to keep the Law. The Essenes also believed in life after death. Some scholars believe the Qumran community was an Essene settlement. See p. 270.

ESTHER (ES-tur; Ishtar, Babylonian goddess, star). A Jewish orphan maiden who was the cousin of Mordecai, a minor official of King Ahasuerus (Xerxes I). Ahasuerus ruled Persia from 486–465 BC. Esther became his wife, and when her people were going to be put to death, Esther saved them. Esther's Hebrew name was Hadassah, which means "myrtle" (Est 2:7). See pp. 153–55.

ESTHER, BOOK OF. This book is the last of the historical books in the English Bible. The author of Esther was familiar with Persian government and the palace of Shushan. The book explains the origin of the Feast of Purim, or day of Mordecai (Est 9:21–32). See pp. 153–55.

ETAM (EE-tam; hawkground). Rock Etam was a place where Samson lived (Jgs 15:8, 11).

ETERNAL LIFE. Eternal life begins when the Holy Spirit by grace brings a person to faith in Jesus Christ, the Son of God and Savior of the world (Jn 1:4; 10:10; 17:3; Rm 6:23). Although the Christian already has eternal life, he or she will not experience it fully until the resurrection of the body and the life of the age to come (Mt 25:46; Jn 6:54; Rm 2:7; Ti 3:7). See pp. 414, 422, 444, 449.

ETERNITY. Without beginning or end. Eternity is described as "forever" or "from everlasting to everlasting" (Ps 90:2). Only God is before and after all things (cf. Jer 1:5; Ps 90; Rv 1:8; 21:6). His reign, power, and glory are eternal (Ps 29:10; Is 44:6; 57:15). See pp. 296, 434.

ETHAM (EE-tham). The second place where Israel set up camp after leaving Egypt (Ex 13:20; Nu 33:6).

ETHBAAL (eth-BAY-uhl; with Baal). A king of Sidon who was the father of Jezebel (1Ki 16:31).

ETHIOPIA (ee-thi-O-pi-ah; from Greek, possibly describing the dark complextions of African people). A country in eastern Africa, south of Egypt. Both Cush, the Hebrew name for this country, and Ethiopia refer to the same country (Gn 10:6–8; 1Ch 1:8; 2Ch 12:3; 14:9; Ezk 30:9; Ac 8:27). The people of Ethiopia were merchants (Is 45:14). They were also a strong military power (2Ch 14:9–12). See p. 358. *See also* CUSH.

EUCHARIST. *See* LORD'S SUPPER.

EUNICE (YOO-nuhs; victorious). Timothy's mother (Ac 16:1; 2Tm 1:5).

EUNUCH (YOO-nuhk; bedkeeper). A castrated man. Eunuchs were court officials and guardians of women and children (2Ki 20:18; Est 1:10–15; Dn 1:3; Ac 8:27). The Hebrews did not practice castration, nor did they permit eunuchs to enter the congregation (Dt 23:1). Philip baptized an Ethiopian eunuch after explaining what the eunuch was reading from Isaiah (Ac 8:26–40).

EUPHRATES (yoo-FRAY-teez). A great river, 1,780 miles long, flowing from Armenia to the Persian Gulf. The Euphrates is one of the rivers that ran through Eden (Gn 2:14). In the Old Testament it is frequently called the great river or the River (Gn 15:18; Dt 11:24). It was regarded as an ideal boundary of Palestine and of David's conquests (Dt 11:24; Jsh 1:4; 2Sm 8:3; 1Ch 18:3). See pp. 193, 222.

EUTYCHUS (YOO-ti-kuhs; fortunate). A young man who went to sleep while Paul was preaching and fell from a third story window to his death. Paul brought him back to life (Ac 20:9–10). See p. 294.

EVANGELIST (i-VAN-juh-list; publisher of good tidings). Someone who preaches the Gospel (Ac 8:4–40; 21:8; 2Tm 4:5). The office of evangelist is mentioned in Eph 4:11. At a later date, the name evangelist was given to the writers of the four Gospels.

EVE (EEV; life). The first woman. God formed her out of Adam's side. She is the mother of all living beings (Gn 2:18–25; 3–4). See pp. 11, 12, 39.

EVIL. 1. Anything not in harmony with the divine order; that which creates disorder in the universe (Gn 3; Jb 2:10; Ps 23:4; Pr 15:15; cf. Lk 16:25).
2. *See* SIN, II.

EVIL-MERODACH (EE-vil-mi-RO-dak; man of Marduk). The king of Babylon from 562 to 560 BC. He reigned after Nebuchadnezzar (2Ki 25:27; Jer 52:31).

EXILE. *See* CAPTIVITY; DISPERSION.

EXODUS (EK-so-duhs; a going out). The departure of Israel from Egypt (Ex; Heb 11:22). See pp. 26, 424.

EXODUS, BOOK OF. The second book of the Pentateuch. The Israelites referred to it as "and these are the names" because of its opening words in Hebrew. The name Exodus comes from a Greek word that means going out. The Book of Exodus describes the way God brought His people Israel out of Egypt and made of them a nation. It also speaks of the covenant God made with Israel, the giving of the Law, and the establishment of the priesthood and system of sacrifice. See pp. 26–31.

EXORCISM (EK-sawr-siz'm). The driving out of demons and evil spirits by the use of God's Word, though some wrongly attempted it by magical spells and charms (cf. Mt 12:27; Mk 9:38; Ac 19:13). See p. 321.

EXPANSE. The span of sky dividing the primeval waters so that part were above it and part were below it (Gn 1:6–7; Ps 19:1; Ezk 1:22–26).

EZEKIEL (i-ZEEK-yuhl; God strengthens). One of the Old Testament prophets. He was a son of Buzi and from a priestly family (Ezk 1:3). Ezekiel was taken into captivity to Babylon in 597 BC with Jehoiachin (Ezk 33:21; 40:1; 2Ki 24:11–16). In Babylon, Ezekiel lived on the Chebar Canal, where he began his prophecies (Ezk 1:1, 3; 3:15). See pp. 121, 139, 211–12, 445.

EZEKIEL, BOOK OF. The prophet Ezekiel wrote this book while he was a captive in Babylon. His purpose was to show God's hand in punishing Israel for worshiping idols, but also to comfort the house of Israel and to reassure them that they had not been forsaken. The last part of the book emphasizes the New Covenant. The book is full of imagery—for example, the sections about the valley of bones, the Good Shepherd, and the showers of blessings. See pp. 211–13.

EZION-GEBER (EE-zi-on-GEE-bur; backbone of giant). A place on the north end of the Gulf of Aqaba where the Israelites camped on their journey in the wilderness (Nu 33:35–36; Dt 2:8). Later, Ezion-geber was a naval port and copper refining center of King Solomon (1Ki 9:26; 22:48; 2Ch 8:17). Today it is identified with Tell el-Khel-eifeh.

EZRA (EZ-rah; help). A Jewish priest, scribe, and prophet (Ezr 7:6–12). With the help of Artaxerxes, Ezra led a group of exiles back to Jerusalem c 458 BC. Ezra reformed Jewish life, worship, and government. He read the Law in public and rebuilt the temple (Ezr; Ne). See pp. 140, 145–47.

EZRA, BOOK OF. The fifteenth book of the Old Testament. It describes the activities of Ezra, the scribe, and records the Israelites' return to their home country and their separation from foreign customs and idolatry. See pp. 145–47.

F

FABLE. 1. A story in which animals and other objects in nature are made to act and speak as if they were human beings (Jgs 9:8–15; 2Ki 14:9).

2. A myth or fictitious story (1Tm 1:4; 4:7; 2Tm 4:4; Ti 1:14; 2Pt 1:16).

FACE. 1. Used both literally and figuratively. To fall on the face was an act of reverence, petition, or sorrow (Gn 17:3; Nu 14:5; Jsh 7:6).

2. The face of God is God in His active presence (Nu 6:25–26). No one can see God's face and live (Ex 33:20). To seek God's face means to worship Him (Ps 27:8).

FAITH. That belief and trust in the promise of God in Christ Jesus, worked by the Holy Spirit, through which a person is declared just, brought into a right relationship with God, saved (Rm 5:1; 1Co 2:10–13). A gift of God's grace (Eph 2:8–9), not a natural human power that we are to offer to God. Faith can be pictured as the hand that receives the blessings of salvation that God, out of grace, has provided in Christ Jesus.

In the Old Testament, faith is described by the words *believe* (Ex 14:31), *trust in* (Ps 28:7), and *take refuge* in (2Sm 22:3). In the New Testament, the word *faith* occurs on nearly every page. It is described as belief and trust in Jesus Christ as the Lord, the one who paid for the sins of the world with His blood and His innocent suffering and death (Lk 24:46–48; Jn 3:16; 20:31; Ac 2:36; 16:31; Rm 10:6–15; Gal 2:20; 1Jn 1:7).

The Holy Spirit works faith in Christ in the individual through the Gospel and the Means of Grace, the Word and Sacraments (Rm 1:16; 10:17). Through faith in Christ, the individual dies, is buried, is raised, and lives with Christ (Rm 6:4, 8; Col 2:12; 3:3). See p. 92.

FAITHFULNESS. From Hbr *'aman*, "to be steady, faithful, true," from which our term "Amen" comes.

FALL. The fall of humanity into sin is described in Gn 3. It was that act by which Adam and Eve turned away from God, yielded to temptation, and broke God's commandments. The fall involved not only Adam, but all of humanity, in sin, misery, and death (Rm 5:12–21).

As one man's fall affects all of humanity, so Christ's death and resurrection for the sins of the world brings God's grace to all (Rm 5:18). See pp. 15, 39.

FALSE PROPHET. A person, not sent by or responsible to God, who performs signs and wonders to lead people astray (Jer 29:9; Ezk 13). *See also* PROPHET. See p. 211.

FAMINE. 1. A lack of food and drink caused by war or the absence of rain (Gn 12:10; 26:1; 1Ki 17:1–2; 2Ki 6:25). See pp. 21, 99, 231–32.

2. A lack of God's Word (Am 8:11–12).

FASTING. Partially or totally abstaining from food. Moses fasted on Sinai for 40 days and nights (Ex 34:28). In the Old Testament, fasting was a sign of religious humiliation. At first, fasting was supposed to be done only on the Day of Atonement (cf. "afflict yourselves" in Lv 16:29; 23:27–32). Later, days of national disaster and the like were added.

The disciples of John fasted, but not those of Jesus (Mt 9:14–15; Lk 5:33–35). Jesus fasted 40 days and nights in the desert (Mt 4:2). He approved of fasting, but not if it were done for show (Mt 6:16–18). See pp. 52–53, 156–57.

FATHER. This word has several meanings in the Bible. 1. It can mean one's own father (Gn 19:31), an ancestor (1Ki 5:1; Nu 18:2; Mt 3:9), or the founder of a community, tribe, or nation (Gn 10:21; 17:4–5; 1Ch 2:51; 4:14). See p. 24.

2. God as creator (Mal 2:10; Is 63:16) or Savior (Rm 8:15; Gal 4:6). God is the Father of Jesus (Mt 11:26; Mk 14:36). See p. 296.

3. A man who acts with fatherly kindness toward another person (Jb 29:16; Is 22:21); or a teacher (2Ki 2:12).

4. A father in the faith (1Co 4:15). See pp. 135–36.

FEAR. This word can mean reverence, terror, dread, trembling, or fright (Gn 9:2; Jb 41:33; Pr 29:25; Ac 10:2, 22). The "fear of the Lord," however, generally means to show awe and respect for His holiness (Ps 34:11; Pr 1:7; Ec 12:13; cf. Gn 20:11) and to trust in Him. See p. 176.

FEAST. 1. A lavish and costly meal that people attended with great joyfulness (Dn 5:1; Lk 5:29; Jn 2:1–8).

2. A time when the Jewish people celebrate their religious festivals. Their major feasts included (a) the Passover, or Feast of Unleavened Bread (Lv 23:5–8; Nu 28:17–25); (b) the Feast of Weeks, Pentecost, Harvest, or Firstfruits (Ex 23:16; Nu 28:26–31); and (c) the Feast of Booths (Lv 23:34–36; Dt 16:13–17).

Lesser festivals included (a) the Feast of Dedication, or Lights (Jn 10:22); (b) Purim (Est 9:21–28); (c) the Feast of Wood Offering (Ne 10:34); and (d) Sheep-Shearing (1Sm 25:4–11). See pp. 46–47, 56, 173–74, 362–63.

FELIX (FEE-liks; happy). A Roman procurator of Judea (Ac 23:26). See p. 378.

FELLOWSHIP. The basic idea of fellowship is that of sharing something in common. Christian fellowship shares the common bond of the Gospel, faith in Christ, and various spiritual gifts (1Co 12; Php 1:5–7; Phm). Fellowship is created by God, who calls Christians into participation in Christ so that they share in His work, blessing, and glory (Rm 6:3–8; 14:8; 1Co 1:9; 1Jn 1:3, 6–7). Through the work of the Holy Spirit believers have a oneness in Christ (Jn 17:11, 21–22; 2Co 13:14; Gal 3:28; 1Jn 1:7). The mark of fellowship is love (1Co 13:1–3; 1Pt 1:22).

FESTIVAL. *See* FEAST.

FESTUS, PORCIUS (FES-tuhs, PAWR-shi-uhs). The Roman governor of Judea who came after Felix (Ac 24:27). See p. 378.

FETTERS. Chains for binding the feet of prisoners (Ps 105:18). Cf. "shackles" in Jgs 16:21; 2Ch 33:11; Mk 5:4.

FIRE. A symbol of God's presence and a means of His judgment (Ex 3:2; 19:18; 2Pt 3:7). God's anger burns like fire (Ps 79:5). Christ will appear in fire (2Th 1:7–8).

Fire was used for cooking, for warmth, and to burn up sacrifices (Is 44:16; Jer 36:22). It was to burn continuously on the altar (Lv 6:9–13).

FIRSTBORN The first one born of a mother's offspring (Ex 12:12). 1. The firstborn son was privileged to receive a double portion of inheritance (Dt 21:17) and leadership over the family (Gn 35:23; 43:33; 2Ch 21:3). Sometimes the birthright was given to a younger son (Gn 25:23; 49:3–4).

2. The firstborn of human beings and of animals belonged to God (Ex 13:2, 15). The firstborn of man was given to God as a priest. When the Aaronic priesthood was established, the Levites took the place of the Israelites' firstborn (Nu 3:12–13; 18:15–17). See p. 41.

The firstborn of animals were given to the sanctuary. The clean were sacrificed; the unclean were either replaced by suitable sacrifices or killed (Ex 13:2, 13; 22:30; 34:19–20; Lv 27:26–29).

FIRSTFRUITS. The first ripe fruits, whether raw as in grain or fruit, or prepared as in wine, oil, or flour. The first produce harvested each year was offered to the Lord with thanksgiving (Ex 23:19; 34:26; Lv 2:12; 23:10; Nu 18:12). See pp. 46–47, 174, 362.

FISH. 1. The Sea of Galilee, filled with a great variety of fish, was the chief source of fishing for the people of Israel (Mt 4:18–22). Once the fish were caught, they were sold in Jerusalem (2Ch 33:14; Ne 13:16).

The word *fish* is used figuratively for the Egyptians, the Church, and captives (Ezk 29:4–5; Hab 1:14; Mt 13:47–48). The letters of the Greek word for fish became a symbol for "Jesus Christ, God's Son, Savior." *See also* FOOD 3.

The disciples were called "fishers of men" because they "caught" people with the Gospel (Mt 4:19; Mk 1:17). See pp. 322, 349.

2. The name of a number of larger sea creatures might also be translated as fish (cf. Gn 1:21; Ezk 32:3). The Greek word used in Mt 12:40 means any large fish or sea creature. The word is also translated as great fish (Jnh 1:17).

FISH GATE. A gate of Jerusalem near the fish market (2Ch 33:14).

FLAGON (skin). A bottle or pitcher made of skin or earthenware (Is 22:24).

FLASK. An object or jar for holding oil or perfume (2Ki 9:1, 3; Mk 14:3). May also be a type of bottle (Jer 19:10–11).

FLESH. 1. The muscles or softer parts of any living thing (Jb 33:21; Lk 24:39).

2. All beings have flesh (Gn 6:13, 19; Ac 2:17; cf. Rm 3:20).

3. Meat (Ex 16:12; Lv 7:19).

4. Flesh as opposed to spirit (Jn 6:52; 1Co 5:5).

5. Our ordinary human physical condition (Gn 2:23; Mt 19:5–6; 1Co 6:16).

6. Human nature deprived of the Spirit of God and corrupted by sin (Rm 7:5; 8:5–8; 2Co 7:1; Gal 5:16–20; 2Pt 2:9–10).

FLOCK. 1. Sheep (Lk 2:8).

2. Israel as a covenant nation (Is 40:11).

3. The New Testament church (Mt 26:31; Ac 20:28–29; 1Pt 5:2–3).

FLOOD. 1. Water, especially a river or the sea (Ex 15:8; Jsh 24:2; Ps 66:6). A flood is also anything overflowing, e.g., the overflowing of a body of water (Na 1:8; Lk 6:48).

2. The deluge in the time of Noah is referred to as "the flood." It is that event when God destroyed all living things on earth by water except the creatures in Noah's ark (Gn 6:9–9:17). See pp. 15–16.

FLUX. *See* DYSENTERY.

FOOD. The people in Bible times ate various kinds of food. 1. Bread and water were the "support and supply" of life (Is 3:1). Bread was made mainly from wheat. Sometimes barley, beans, lentils, millet, and emmer were also ground for bread or were eaten by the poor (Ezk 4:9).

Crushing the grain between two stones was one ancient method for grinding flour. The Canaanites used a rotary-type mill in which the cone of the upper millstone fit into a hollowed out spot in the lower millstone.

Once the grain was carefully sifted, it was ready to make into bread. Yeast, salt, olive oil, and water or milk were added to the flour to make the bread.

The people used different types of ovens to bake the bread. The simplest type was a slightly curved, circular sheet of iron that was heated over the fire. Then a thin layer of dough was placed on it to bake. Another type of oven was a dome of clay. The dough was placed under it, and then it was covered with fire. Community ovens were also used.

2. Wheat, barley, flour, parched grains, beans, and lentils were an important part of the Hebrew diet (Gn 25:34; 2Sm 17:28). The people also freely ate fish, melons, cucumbers, onions, garlic, and leeks (Nu 11:5; Is 1:8). Dill, mustard, and coriander seed provided strong flavoring for their foods (Ex 16:31; Is 28:25, 27; Mt 13:31). Cinnamon, mint, cumin, and saffron flavored both food and wine (Ex 30:23; Sg 4:14; Mt 23:23). In addition to these items, parsley, celery, lettuce, and cabbage were grown.

One of the favorite dishes of the Israelites, which used many of the above items, was vegetable stew. Since good quality meat was scarce in Palestine, the people ate it only on special occasions (Lk 15:23–24; Ex 12:3–10). At these times they might barbecue and serve whole animals (Gn 18:7; Lk 15:23). Poorer quality meats were stewed or used to flavor vegetable stew.

3. Fish were taken mainly from the Sea of Galilee (Mt 4:18), the Jordan River, and the Mediterranean Sea. They were roasted over charcoal (Jn 21:9) or salted and dried for later use (cf. Mk 8:7–8). Wild or domestic birds and their eggs also provided a good source of protein (Ex 16:13).

4. Milk and milk products supplied the Israelites with protein, calcium, and fat. At mealtime the people, particularly the children, drank cow's, sheep's, or goat's milk (Gn 18:8; Dt 32:14; 1Sm 6:7; Heb 5:12–13). They ate curds of milk and cheese made from sour milk (Gn 18:8; 1Sm 17:17–18; Pr 30:33). Cream skimmed from the top of sour milk was churned inside a goatskin to make butter.

See pp. 61–62, 208.

FOOL. A person who has no wisdom or understanding, or one who is lacking in morals or religion (Ps 14:1; 92:6; Pr 12:15; Jer 17:11; Lk 12:20). See pp. 175–76.

FOOTMAN. A soldier who fights and marches on foot (2Ki 13:7). Cf. "guard" in 1Sm 22:17.

FOREIGNER. Among the Israelites, anyone who was not part of their nation was a foreigner or stranger (Ex 12:45; Eph 2:12). The New Testament describes those who are not citizens of God's kingdom as foreigners or strangers (Eph 2:19; 1Pt 2:11).

FOREKNOWLEDGE. God's eternal knowledge or foresight of all future events (Ac 2:23; 1Pt 1:2). *See also* ELECT, ELECTION.

FORERUNNER. Someone who prepares the way (Heb 6:19–20).

FORGIVENESS. God's act whereby He ends the separation caused by peoples' sins and puts them back into a proper relationship with Himself. No one deserves to be forgiven, nor can anyone earn forgiveness (Mt 18:23–25; Eph 2:8). Rather, forgiveness is a gift of God, given out of grace for Christ's sake (Mk 2:5, 7, 10; Lk 24:47; Jn 20:23; Eph 1:7; 1Jn 2:12). As a result of Christ's forgiveness, we are to forgive our neighbor (Mt 6:12–14; Eph 4:32). Recognizing and being sorry for our sins precedes forgiveness (Ps 51; Is 57:15; Jer 14:20). See pp. 337, 347, 363, 415, 418. *See also* REPENTANCE.

FORK. *See* WINNOWING FORK.

FORTIFICATION, FORTRESS. Cities in ancient times were fortified with walls built of brick and stone. Jerusalem, Samaria, and Damascus were well-known fortified towns. God's protection is often pictured as a strong fortress (2Sm 22:2; Ps 31:3). See pp. 78, 82, 167, 237, 393.

FOUNTAIN. Springs of water were of great importance in Palestine (Gn 16:7; Dt 8:7; 33:28; 1Sm 29:1). God, the source of grace, is described as having or being the fountain of life (Ps 36:9; Jer 17:13). Jesus told the woman at the well that the water He gives becomes a "spring of water welling up to eternal life" (Jn 4:14).

FOWLER. A person who catches birds with a net or cords (Ps 91:3; 124:7).

FRANKINCENSE (FRANGK-in-sens). A fragrant gum resin from certain types of trees. It was an ingredient in meal offerings and in the oil used to anoint priests to their offices (Ex 30:34; Lv 2:1). Frankincense was also burned and poured on showbread (Lv 6:15; 24:7). *See also* SHOWBREAD.

FRINGE. Tassels made of twisted blue thread that were fastened on to each corner of a garment. The Israelites wore these to remind themselves of the Law and their loyalty to the Lord (cf. Nu 15:37–40; Dt 22:12). In the Gospels, the people seek to touch the fringe of Jesus' garments for healing (Mt 9:20; 14:36; Mk 6:56; Lk 8:44).

FRONTLET. Anything bound on the forehead. The Jewish people bound jewels or amulets between their eyes. Later they wore phylacteries (prayer bands) around their foreheads or on their left arms (Ex 13:9, 16; Dt 6:8; 11:18; Mt 23:5).

FULLER. A person who bleaches, cleans, thickens, or dyes cloth (Mal 3:2; cf. Mk 9:3). A fuller's field, the place where this work was done, lay outside the east wall of Jerusalem (cf. "Washer's Field" in 2Ki 18:17; Is 7:3; 36:2).

FURNACE. People smelted iron, burned bricks, and melted silver and gold in furnaces or kilns (Dt 4:20; Pr 17:3; Ezk 22:20; cf. "kiln" in Ex 9:8, 10; 19:18). The New Testament pictures everlasting punishment as a furnace of fire (Mt 13:42; cf. Mt 25:41).

FUTURE LIFE. *See* ESCHATOLOGY; ETERNAL LIFE; ETERNITY.

G

GABBATHA (GAB-ah-thah). The place where Pilate held court and where Jesus was tried (Jn 19:13).

GABRIEL (GA-bri-uhl; man of God). The angel who interpreted visions to Daniel (Dn 8:16–27; 9:20–27) and announced the births of John the Baptist (Lk 1:11–22) and Jesus (Lk 1:26–38). See pp. 196, 330.

GAD (GAD; good fortune). 1. Jacob's seventh son (Gn 30:9–11; 49:19). See p. 19.

2. The name of a tribe of Israel that descended from Jacob's seventh son (Nu 1:24–25; 26:15–18). This tribe settled east of the Jordan River (Nu 32). In 722 BC, Tiglath-pileser, king of Assyria, took this tribe into captivity along with the other nine northern tribes (1 Ch 5:26).

3. The name of a prophet who helped and wrote about David (1Sm 22:5; 2Sm 24:11–24; 1Ch 29:29).

GADARENES (gad-ah-REENZ). The people who lived in the city of Gadara, about 6 miles southeast of the Sea of Galilee, or in the town of Gerasa on the east coast of the Sea of Galilee (Mt 8:28; cf. Mk 5:1; Lk 8:26, 37).

GAIUS (GAY-yuhs). 1. A man of Macedonia who helped Paul at Ephesus (Ac 19:29).

2. A man from Derbe who helped Paul (Ac 20:4).

3. A Christian at Corinth who was baptized by Paul (1Co 1:14).

4. The person to whom the Third Letter of John was sent (3Jn 1). Some scholars believe that some of these men may have been the same person. See p. 437.

GALATIA (gah-LAY-shi-ah). A region of central Asia Minor (modern-day Turkey) named after the Gauls, who settled there about the third century BC. After the Romans captured the area in 64 BC, a Roman province called Galatia was formed. It included the region Paul visited on his first missionary journey (Ac 16:6; 18:23; Gal 1:2). See p. 393.

GALATIANS, LETTER OF PAUL TO. Paul wrote this letter probably to the churches that started on his first missionary journey (Ac 13–14) and soon after that journey was over. He stresses that one is saved by grace through faith and not by works. See pp. 393–94.

GALILEAN (GAL-uh-lee-uhn). A person from Galilee. *See also* GALILEE.

GALILEE (GAL-uh-lee; circle). The name of the northernmost province of the three provinces of Palestine. This name was already used in Old Testament times (Jsh 20:7; 1Ki 9:11). Galilee was given to the tribes of Zebulun, Asher, and Naphtali

(Jsh 19:10–16, 24–39). The land was fertile, and a number of important trade routes crossed the area (Is 9:1).

At the time of Christ, Galilee extended from Mount Hermon on the north to Mount Carmel on the south, and from the Jordan River on the east to the Mediterranean Sea on the west. Herod Antipas was its ruler. Jesus performed the major part of His ministry there. The twelve disciples, except Judas Iscariot, were all from Galilee (Mk 14:70). The leaders of Judea hated Galileans, who were known by the way they talked. See pp. 290–91.

GALILEE, SEA OF. A freshwater lake fed by the Jordan River, which flows in at the north end and out at the south end. It is 13 miles long, 7 miles wide, and 160 feet deep at its deepest point. Its blue, fresh water is full of fish.

The Sea of Galilee is also referred to as the Sea of Chinnereth (Jsh 13:27) or Chinneroth (Jsh 12:3), the Lake of Gennesaret (Lk 5:1), and the Sea of Tiberias (Jn 6:1; 21:1). See pp. 290–91, 316, 322.

GALL. 1. A bitter material produced by the liver (Jb 16:13).

2. People thought that the poison of snakes was gall (cf. Jb 20:14).

3. A poisonous, bitter-tasting plant (cf. Hos 10:4).

4. Part of the drink the soldiers offered to Christ to lessen His suffering on the cross (Mt 27:34).

5. A symbol for a bitter, painful experience (Ac 8:23; cf. "poisoned water" in Jer 8:14).

GALLEY. A low, flat-looking ship with a row of oars along each side. It was often rowed by slaves (Is 33:21).

GALLIO (GAL-i-o). The Roman proconsul (governor) of Achaia from AD 51 to 52. He was the brother of the philosopher Seneca. Gallio refused to hear the Jews' case against Paul in Corinth (Ac 18:12–17).

GALLOWS. An instrument used to hang people. Gallows (lit. "tree") are mentioned nine times in the Book of Esther as a means of execution. The word translated as gallows may refer to a pale or stake.

GAMALIEL (gah-MAY-li-uhl; reward of God). The grandson of Hillel, the great Jewish teacher, and one of Paul's most influential teachers (Ac 22:3). Gamaliel was a Pharisee and a member of the Sanhedrin (Ac 5:34). He gave wise advice to the other leaders at the trial of Peter and the other apostles (Ac 5:38–40).

Gamaliel is considered one of the greatest Jewish rabbis. He is referred to as "rabban" (our teacher).

GAMES. Children often played in the streets (Zec 8:5). They played make-believe and kept birds (Jb 41:5; Mt 11:16–17).

Adult "games" included reveling (Jer 15:17), telling riddles (Jgs 14:12–19), playing music, dancing (Lk 15:25), racing (Ps 19:5), and using the bow and sling (1Sm 20:20; Jgs 20:16). Paul references Greek sports contests (1Co 9:24–27; 2Tm 2:5; 4:7–8). A board for an ancient game was found at Saul's castle in Gibeah. *See also* DANCE; MUSIC.

GATE. The door or entrance to the tabernacle, the camp of the Israelites, the temple, cities, houses, and prisons (Gn 19:1; Ex 27:16; 32:26; 2Ch 8:14; Ac 10:17; 12:10). Markets and courts, or places of judgment, were often near gates because many people walked past or met to talk or do business there (Dt 17:5; Ru 4:1–12; 2Sm 15:2; 2Ki 7:1). See pp. 364–65.

A gate is a symbol of power (Gn 22:17; Mt 16:18). It also describes the beginning of something or the way to have access to something, for example, the gate of heaven (Gn 28:17), the gate of righteousness (Ps 118:19–20), the gates of the New Jerusalem (Rv 21:12, 21), the gates of death (Jb 38:17).

GATH (GATH; wine press). One of the five great Philistine cities (Jsh 13:3), though its site is unknown. Gath was the home of Goliath (1Sm 17:4) and one of the places where David hid from Saul (1Sm 21:10). David later captured Gath (1Ch 18:1). See p. 104.

GAZA (GAY-zah). The capital city of Philistia (Gn 10:19). It was given to Judah when Canaan was divided (Jgs 1:18). Gaza was the scene of Samson's death (Jgs 16) and the place near which Philip converted the treasurer of Ethiopia (Ac 8:26). See p. 104.

GAZELLE (gah-ZEL). The smallest of the antelopes in Israel. This animal was considered ceremonially clean, i.e., one of the animals the Israelites were allowed to eat (Dt 12:15, 22).

GEHENNA. *See* HELL.

GENEALOGY (jen-ee-AL-o-jee; birth record). The tracing forward or backward of the ancestral relationships of tribes and families (Gn 35:22–26; Ne 7:5; Mt 1:1–16; Lk 3:23–38). Genealogies often contain gaps (cf. Ex 6:16–24). See pp. 12, 94, 97, 122, 141.

GENERATION. 1. Creating or procreating (Gn 2:4).

2. Offspring or successions of offspring (Gn 5:1).

3. Age as a period of time (Gn 15:16; Dt 32:7; Ps 45:17).

4. People of a specific historical period (Lv 3:17; Mt 11:16; 17:17).

GENESIS (JEN-i-sis; beginning). The first book of the Pentateuch. As the book of beginnings, Genesis describes the origins of the physical universe, plants, animals, human life, and human institutions. See pp. 10–16.

GENNESARET (ge-NES-ah-ret). 1. The plain northwest of the Sea of Galilee (Mt 14:34; Mk 6:53).

2. *See* GALILEE, SEA OF.

GENTILES. Used primarily in the New Testament to refer to non-Jewish people (Mt 4:15; 10:5). It also may refer to non-Jewish people who worship false gods (Mt 6:7; 10:18). Now, in Christ, there is no distinction between Jew and Gentile (Ac 10:34–48; Rom 3:29; 9; 11). All are members of God's house through faith. *See also* NATIONS. See pp. 353, 360–61, 365, 368, 374, 376.

GERASENES (GER-ah-seenz). *See* GADARENES.

GERIZIM (GER-i-zim). A mountain about 2,850 feet high that stands opposite Mount Ebal. The blessings were read from Mount Gerizim; the curses, from Mount Ebal (Dt 11:29; 27:12). The Samaritans built a temple for themselves on Mount Gerizim (cf. Jn 4:20). See pp. 290–91, 345.

GETHSEMANE (geth-SEM-ah-nee; oil press). An olive yard east of Jerusalem. It was the place of Jesus' agony and arrest (Mt 26:36–56; Mk 14:26–50; Lk 22:39–54; Jn 18:1–13). See p. 315.

GIANTS. People who are unusually tall and powerful. The Nephilim are the first giants mentioned in the Bible. They were on the earth in the days before the flood and in Canaan when the spies went through the land (Gn 6:4; Nu 13:33).

Giants known as the Rephaim (Gn 14:5; 15:20) lived in Canaan, Edom, Moab, and Ammon. At the time of the conquest, Og, king of Bashan, was the only one left of this race. His iron bedstead was about 13 1/2 feet long (Dt 3:11; Jsh 12:4). The Anakim, another race of giants, were connected with the Rephaim because of their size (Nu 13:22; Dt 2:10–12). When the Hebrews captured Hebron, the Anakim who escaped destruction found refuge in Philistine cities. Goliath of Gath was probably one of these remaining Anakim (1Sm 17:4). See p. 78.

GIBEAH (GIB-i-ah; hill). 1. A city of Benjamin a few miles north of Jerusalem (Jgs 19:13–14). It was the birthplace of Saul and the place where he lived after becoming king (1Sm 10:26; 15:34). Its modern-day site is Tell el-Ful. Excavation there has uncovered Saul's fortress-palace.

2. Gibeah at Kiriath-jearim. It was the place where the ark was kept after the Philistines returned it (1Sm 6:21).

GIBEON (GIB-ee-uhn; hill city). A city in Benjamin that was given to the Levites (Jsh 18:20–28; 21:13–19). Originally it was a Hivite city. At the time of the conquest, the people of Gibeon made a treaty with Joshua under false pretenses. By doing this, they saved their city but brought slavery upon themselves (Jsh 9–10; 2Sm 21:1–9).

GIDEON (GID-ee-uhn; cutting down). The son of Joash of the tribe of Manasseh (Jgs 6:11). While threshing wheat, the angel of the Lord called Gideon to deliver his people. That night Gideon tore down his father's altar to Baal and built one to the Lord. The townspeople wanted to kill Gideon for doing this, but his father told them to let Baal defend himself if he were a god. Because of this incident Gideon was known as Jerubbaal, which means "let Baal contend against him" (Jgs 6:32).

Gideon defeated the Midianites and destroyed Succoth. When his people wanted to make him king, Gideon refused (Jgs 6–8; Heb 11:32–34). He was also called Jerubbesheth, meaning contender with shame (2Sm 11:21). Because of his work Gideon is regarded as one of the judges of Israel, even though he is not specifically called by that title. See pp. 88, 91–92.

GIHON (GIGH-hon; gushing forth). 1. One of the four rivers of Eden (Gn 2:13).

2. A spring in the Kidron Valley near Jerusalem that supplied some of the water to that city. Hezekiah built the Siloam Tunnel to carry water from the Gihon to the pool of Siloam within the city walls of Jerusalem (2Ki 20:20; 2Ch 32:30).

GILBOA (gil-BO-ah). A mountain range overlooking the Valley of Jezreel. Saul and Jonathan died there while fighting the Philistines (1Sm 31).

GILEAD (GIL-i-and; to be rough). The name given to the land east of the Jordan River. It extended from the Sea of Galilee on the north to the Dead Sea on the south (Gn 31:21–25; Dt 3:12–17). See p. 130.

GILGAL (GIL-gal; circle). The place near Jericho that became Israel's base camp after the Israelites crossed the Jordan (Jsh 4:19–24; 9:6). Saul was crowned king of Israel at Gilgal (1Sm 11:15) and also had his kingship taken away there (13:4–15).

GLASS. By 1500 BC opaque glass was widely used by the Egyptians and Phoenicians (Jb 28:17). Clear glass was made in Roman times (Rv 21:18, 21).

GLEANING. The gathering of grain left in the fields or grapes left on the vines after harvest. According to Old Testament law, owners of fields and vineyards were to leave leftover grain, grapes, and fallen fruit for the poor (Dt 24:19–21; Ru 2:2–3). See pp. 95, 99.

GLORY. 1. That which shows the greatness of someone or something. The glory of God is shown in and by His great miracles, His eternal perfection, His creation, and all His works (Ps 8; Mt 17:2; Jn 2:11). Most important, it is shown by His Son, our Lord Jesus Christ (Jn 1:14; 2Co 4:6). The glory of people is truly shown only by their relationship to God (2Co 3:18). See pp. 44, 184, 434.

2. That which is itself the greatness of someone or something. Here glory is spoken of as a possession of, or even part of, someone or something. Scripture speaks of God's glory and of the glory awaiting believers in the life to come (Is 42:8; Lk 2:9; Rm 8:18; Php 3:20–21). See pp. 129, 212, 434.

GNOSTICISM (NOS-tuh-siz'm). A system of belief that reached its peak in the second to third century AD. According to Gnostics, salvation came by hating the world and everything physical and by escaping to the spirit world. Gnostics said Jesus came not to save people from sin but to show them how to escape to a spiritual world.

Gnosticism was a problem for Christians during the first few centuries after Christ. Some of the books of the New Testament seem to have been written in part to fight against it (Jn; Col; Ti; 2Pt; 1, 2, 3Jn; Jude; Rv). See p. 401.

GOAT. A valued animal that is mentioned many times in the Bible. Its hair was woven into cloth (Ex 35:26); its flesh and milk provided food (Dt 14:4); and the whole animal was used for sacrifice (Lv 3:12; 4:24; 9:15). *See also* AZAZEL.

Jesus used the goat as a symbol for those going to hell (Mt 25:32–33).

GOD. The Being who is not limited in any way or by anything, who is not held by time or space, who possesses all power, knowledge, and wisdom, and who created the world and all people. God shows Himself through His creation, but because all people have fallen into sin, they exchange their knowledge of the true God for a lie and worship false gods (Rm 1:18–32; Ac 14:15–17; 17:22–31). Because of this, God chose to show Himself and His will to people through Jesus Christ so that they might know and believe in Him and be saved (Jn 1:14, 18; 2Co 4:6; 5:18–20).

The chief names for God in the Old Testament are Elohim and Yahweh (*see* JEHOVAH). God is all-powerful; He is a spiritual being. Yet, the Bible describes Him as though He were a human person so that people can somewhat understand Him and talk about Him. For instance, Ps 145:16 speaks of God's "hand," even though God does not have hands as people do. Although Scripture often describes God as though He has a human body and human feelings or as acting in a human way (Gn 3:8; Ps 2:4; Zep 3:17), the only way He is truly like people is in Jesus Christ (Is 55:8–9; Jn 1:14).

The name God can rightly be used to refer to the entire Trinity or to any one of the three Persons of the Trinity (Eph 1:3; Jn 1:1; Ac 5:3–4). *See also* GODS, FALSE; HOLY SPIRIT; JESUS CHRIST; TRINITY.

GOD-FEARERS. *See* PROSELYTE.

GOD MOST HIGH. *See* HIGH, MOST.

GODS, FALSE. *See* ARTEMIS; ASHERAH; ASHTORETH; BAAL; BAAL-ZEBUB; CHEMOSH; HADAD 1; MERODACH; MILCOM; MOLECH; NEHUSHTAN; RIMMON; SAKKUTH; ZEUS.

GOG. The prince of Rosh, Meshech, and Tubal. The prophet Ezekiel described him as invading Israel in the Last Days (Ezk 38–39; cf. Rv 20:7–10).

GOLD. A precious metal Israel obtained from foreign lands (1Ki 10:2; 22:48). The Israelites made ornaments, money, and temple furnishings out of gold (Gn 24:22; Ex 36:34–38; 1Ki 10:2; 22:48). Gold was a symbol of purity and perfection (Jb 23:10; Rv 21:15, 21).

GOLGOTHA (GOL-go-thah). A place outside the city gate of Jerusalem where Christ was crucified and near where He was buried (cf. Mt 28:11; Jn 19:17–18, 41; Heb 13:11–13).

Another common word, *Calvary*, is the Latin rendering of the Greek word for skull. The Hebrew word for skull, *Golgotha*, also refers to this place (Mt 27:33; Mk 15:22; Jn 19:17). Its name may be due to the shape of the hill or to the number of executions carried out there. See p. 334.

GOLIATH (go-LIGH-uth). The Philistine giant whom David killed (1Sm 17). See pp. 78, 102, 104, 107–09.

GOMER (GO-mur). The unfaithful wife of the prophet Hosea (Hos 1:3). See p. 226.

GOMORRAH (go-MAHR-ah; submersion). A city that was destroyed by fire (Gn 19:24, 28). It was on a plain that is now under the Dead Sea. *See also* SODOM.

GOOD. That which is right, helpful, or better than others of its kind. The only true good is from God; in fact, God is good, and everything He does is good (Gn 1:31; Ex 18:9; Ps 118:1; Jer 32:40; Mk 10:18; Rm 7:12). Especially His plan of salvation is good. If a person wants to "do good," then he or she must have faith in and live for Jesus Christ (Rm 6; Gal 5:24–26). See pp. 15, 160, 396, 414, 427–28, 449.

GOPHER WOOD. The type of wood Noah used to build the ark. Bible scholars are not certain what kind of wood this was, but some think it may have been something like cypress (Gn 6:14). See p. 13.

GOSHEN (GO-shuhn). 1. The area in northeastern Egypt assigned to the Israelites (Gn 46:28). See pp. 35–36.

2. An area in southern Palestine, possibly named after the town of Goshen in the hills of Judah (Jsh 10:41; 15:51).

GOSPEL (good news). The Good News that God has forgiven all people because Jesus Christ has fulfilled the Law in their place and paid the penalty for their sin (Jn 3:16; Rm 1:16–17; 1Co 15:1–15; 2Co 5:18–20; Eph 2:8–9). See pp. xxiii, 380, 408.

GOSPELS. The first four books of the New Testament. Matthew, Mark, Luke, and John each wrote one of the books. They are called Gospels because they tell the Good News of how salvation was won for all people by Jesus Christ. The first three Gospels are referred to as the Synoptic Gospels because they can be placed side by side for comparison. The writers of all four of the Gospels are often referred to as evangelists. See pp. 10, 281.

GOVERNOR. Although this title is used for many officials in the Bible, it usually refers to someone who ruled a city or province and reported to the ruler above him (Gn 42:6; Ezr 5:14; Lk 3:1). See pp. 272, 275–76, 332, 378.

GRACE. God's generous mercy toward undeserving people (Rm 5:12–21; Jn 3:16;Ti 3:3–7). God's free and underserved favor toward sinful humanity is demonstrated in Christ's work of redemption. It is an unearned and undeserved gift. The word *grace* is sometimes used of a gift, quality, or virtue; saving grace, however, is none of these things. It is a quality within God. It is also referred to as God's steadfast love or faithfulness (2Sm 7:15; Ne 9:17; Ps 31:21; 42:8). See pp. xxiii, 4, 353, 428, 443.

GRAPE. *See* VINEYARD.

GRASS. Used in the Bible as the general name for all small green plants (Mt 6:30). Grass is also a symbol for the shortness of life (Ps 90:5–6; Jas 1:10–11).

GREECE (GREES). The name for the area in Bible times that included Macedonia, Achaia, and the islands of the Aegean Sea (Acts 20:2). Today Greece is the name of a modern country in southeastern Europe that is almost identical in location to the Greece of Bible times. See p. 269.

GREEK (GREEK). 1. The language of Greece, from which the original language of the written New Testament came.

2. A person who was born in or lived in Greece (Acts 17:12). When Jews and Greeks are contrasted in the New Testament, the term Greek is used for a foreigner in general (Rm 1:16). Greek-speaking Jews were referred to as Hellenists. See p. 380.

GUILT. *See* CONSCIENCE, SIN, II.

H

HABAKKUK (hah-BAK-uhk; embrace). A prophet of Judah whose message of hope in God's grace is recorded in the Book of Habakkuk. Habakkuk prophesied about 605 BC while the temple was still standing (cf. 2:20). See p. 249.

HABAKKUK, BOOK OF. The eighth book of the Minor Prophets. Written by the prophet Habakkuk, the book contains a message of hope in God's grace despite the harshness of His judgment. See pp. 249–50.

HADAD (HAY-dad; thunderer?). 1. The name of the Aramean god of storm and thunder (like the Canaanite god Baal).

2. Possibly also a title, since several kings and princes of Edom had this name

(1Ki 11:14–25; 1Ch 1:46, 50).

HADES (HAY-deez). In classical Greek this word refers first to a person and then to the place in the depths of the earth where the spirits of the dead go. The Hebrew word *Sheol* has a similar meaning. In the New Testament, Hades refers to the place of the dead (Lk 10:15; Ac 2:27; Rv 6:8). See p. 366. *See also* HELL; SHEOL.

HAGAR (HAY-gahr; flight). Sarah's Egyptian servant. Hagar took Sarah's place and had a son, Ishmael, for Abraham (Gn 16; 21:1–21). Hagar represents slavery under the Law (Gal 4:24–25). See pp. 18–19, 89.

HAGGAI (HAG-ay-igh; festive). A prophet c 520 BC during the days of Darius (Hg 1:1). Haggai was a leader in rebuilding the temple (Ezr 5:1). His prophecy is recorded in the Book of Haggai. See pp. 146, 256.

HAGGAI, BOOK OF. The tenth book of the Minor Prophets. The book contains four prophetic sermons concerning the rebuilding of the temple. See pp. 256–58.

HAGIOGRAPHA (hag-i-OG-rah-fah; sacred writings). The third main division of the Jewish Old Testament. Its Hebrew name is *Kethubim*, which means writings. The Hagiographa include Ruth, Chronicles, Ezra, Nehemiah, Esther, Job, Psalms, Proverbs, Ecclesiastes, Song of Solomon, Lamentations, and Daniel.

HAIL. 1. A word of greeting or respect for a superior. The soldiers who mocked Jesus addressed Him with this word (Mt 27:29).

2. Pellets of ice that fall from clouds like rain. God sent a plague of hail on Egypt (Ex 9:18–29). People feared hail because it destroyed their crops and hurt or damaged other things (Ps 78:47–48). See p. 35.

3. A symbol of God's judgment (Is 28:2).

HAIR. In Old Testament times both men and women had long hair (2Sm 14:26). Nazirites, people who had made a special promise to God, were not supposed to cut their hair (Nu 6:1–5). *See also* NAZIRITE. See pp. 110–12.

Baldness was disliked and was used as a symbol for God's anger or judgment (Is 3:24; Jer 47:5). In New Testament times long hair was for women only (1Co 11:14–15).

Scripture forbids or warns against certain ways of wearing one's hair (Lv 19:27; 1Pt 3:3). It also mentions barbers and describes how hair was trimmed (Ezk 5:1; 44:20).

HALLEL (ha-LAYL; praise). The name given to certain psalms that played a special part in Israel's worship, e.g., Psalms 113–118. Jesus and His disciples probably sang the Hallel at the Last Supper.

HALLELUJAH (HAL-i-LOO-yah; praise the Lord). A call or command to praise God and His name. This word became an important part of the language of Israel's worship. It is found in the Book of Revelation (Rv 19:1, 3, 4, 6).

HALLOW. To set apart as holy, for special use for or by God (Lk 11:2; cf. Ex 20:11). See p. 46.

HAM (HAM; black; also the Egyptian name for Egypt). 1. The third son of Noah (Gn 5:32). When Ham uncovered his father's nakedness, Noah spoke a curse on Canaan (Gn 9:21–27). Ham's sons were Cush, Egypt, Put, and Canaan (1Ch 1:8). Their descendants lived in South Arabia, Egypt, Ethiopia, and Canaan. See p. 78.

2. The poetic name for Egypt (Ps 105:23, 27).

HAMAN (HAY-muhn). The wicked prime minister of Ahasuerus. Haman tried to have all the Jews in Persia killed (Est 3:1). See pp. 153–54, 157–58.

HAMMER. 1. A tool used, much like today, for many tasks that required forceful blows, e.g., driving tent pins, tearing down buildings, shaping gold or other metals, and breaking rock (Jgs 4:21; 1Ki 6:7; Ps 74:6; Is 41:7).

2. A symbol of power or strength (Jer 50:23).

HAMMURABI (ham-uh-RAH-bi). A king of Babylon who ruled during the eighteenth century BC. He is known for the battles he fought, the cities he built, and the Code of Hammurabi, which was a set of laws he put together.

HANAMEL (HAN-ah-mel; God has pitied). The prophet Jeremiah's cousin. Before the siege of Jerusalem, Jeremiah bought a field from him (Jer 32:6–12).

HANANIAH (han-ah-NIGH-ah; Lord has favored). 1. The false prophet who opposed Jeremiah (Jer 28:1–17).

2. The Hebrew name of Shadrach, one of the three men thrown into the fiery furnace because he would not worship the golden image King Nebuchadnezzar set up (Dn 1:3–19; 3).

HAND. 1. Figurative for power, strength, or control (Ex 13:3, 14, 16; 1Sm 23:20; Ps 76:5). The phrase "hand of God" refers to God's actions or presence (1Sm 5:11; Ezr 8:22; 1Pt 5:6). The open hand stands for generous giving (Dt 15:8; Ps 145:16).

2. People gave directions by using their right hand for the south and their left hand for the north (Jb 23:9).

3. The Bible speaks of the right hand as the place of honor and authority (1Ki 2:19; Mt 25:33; Ac 2:33).

4. Hands were used to give a blessing (Mk 10:16; 2Tm 1:6).

HANNAH (HAN-ah; grace). Samuel's mother (1Sm 1–2). See pp. 105, 132, 143–44.

HARAN (HAY-rahn; road). 1. Abraham's brother (Gn 11:26–31).

2. A city in upper Mesopotamia where Abraham went after leaving Ur (Gn 11:31–32). See pp. 12, 18.

HARDNESS OF HEART. A condition of stubbornness and disobedience in which a person refuses to listen or change his or her mind (cf. Pharaoh in Ex 7–10). Hardness of heart can prevent understanding and belief (cf. Ac 19:9). People may harden their hearts against God or other people (Ex 8:32; Dt 15:7). God sometimes confirms their hardness of heart as punishment (Ex 10:1; Rm 9:18).

HARLOT. *See* PROSTITUTE.

HAROD (HAY-rod; fear). The spring or well where Gideon camped with his men (Jgs 7:1).

HARP. *See* MUSIC.

HARROW. A farming tool. The harrow was a toothed instrument that animals dragged along the ground to break up clods of earth after plowing (Is 28:24–25). *See also* AGRICULTURE.

HARVEST. *See* AGRICULTURE; ORCHARD; VINEYARD.

HARVEST, FEAST OF. *See* PENTECOST 1.

HASMONEANS (haz-mo-NEE-ahnz). From Gk *Hasmonaios*, which likely refers to a place-name associated with the priest Mattathias, who led his family in revolt (AD 167) against Antiochus IV Epiphanes. Mattathias's son, Judas Maccabeus ("the hammer"), became the leader of the movement and established the Hasmonean dynasty (167 BC–AD 63) over Judea. *See* MACCABEES.

HATE. 1. To dislike or regard as ugly or wrong; to have feelings toward someone or something that are the opposite of love (Ps 45:7; Mt 24:10).

2. To withdraw from or avoid someone or something so that a proper relationship with God can be kept (Am 5:15; Lk 14:26; cf. Mt 10:37–39).

HAZAEL (HAZ-ay-el; God sees). A great king of Syria whom God used to bring judgment upon Israel (1Ki 19:15–18). Hazael followed Ben-Hadad II, ruling Damascus from about 840 to 800 BC. Hazael captured Israel's land east of the Jordan, continually troubled Jehoahaz, and once even planned to attack Jerusalem (2Ki 10:32–33; 12:17–18; 13:3–7, 22–25).

HAZOR (HAY-zawr; enclosure). A city of northern Galilee near the headwaters of the Jordan River. Jabin was the ruler of Hazor when Joshua captured it (Jsh 11:1–14). Later it was given to the tribe of Naphtali (Jsh 19:36, 39). Another King Jabin of Hazor was defeated by Deborah and Barak (Jgs 4).

HEAD. 1. A part of the body.

2. A whole person (Pr 10:6).

3. The capital of a country or region (Is 7:8–9).

4. A leader in society (Is 9:14–15).

5. The name for one who has authority over others (Eph 5:23).

6. The expression "upon the head" refers to guilt, responsibility, or duty (Jsh 2:19; Ezk 9:10).

7. The expression "lift up the head" or the action of lifting up the head means to restore or renew favor, life, strength, etc. (Gn 40:20–21; Ps 83:2).

HEAD OF THE CHURCH. Christ, who gives life, strength, and direction to every believer and who rules as the head of the Body, the Church (Eph 1:20–23; 4:15–16).

HEADBAND. Probably a sash or other piece of cloth worn around the head (Is 3:18).

HEAL. *See* DISEASE.

HEAR. 1. To receive sound by means of the ear (2Sm 15:10).

2. To listen to God's Word and will (Mt 13:18).

3. To understand and follow God's Word and will (Jn 8:47; 10:27).

4. To listen to and approve as right (cf. 1Jn 4:5).

5. God's "hearing" describes His action of answering prayer (Ps 116:1).

HEART. 1. A symbol for the life of the whole body (Jgs 19:5).

2. A word for describing the center of thought, understanding, decision-making, emotion, will, and conscience (Dt 29:4; Ne 7:5; Is 44:18; 65:14; 1Co 7:37). Some Bible translations use the word *mind* instead of *heart* to describe these things.

3. The place within us where Christ and the Spirit live (Eph 3:17; 2Co 1:22).

HEARTH (HAHRTH). 1. A portable fireplace (cf. "fire pot" in Jer 36:22–23).

2. A fireplace on an altar (Ezk 43:15–16).

HEATHEN. *See* BARBARIAN; GENTILES.

HEAVEN (HEV-uhn). 1. The layer of air surrounding the earth and everything in it (Dn 7:13; Mk 14:62).

2. The upper or outer part of the universe and all that is in it; the firmament, especially the "waters above" (Ps 148:4; Is 40:22).

3. The invisible world or universe from which God rules (Ezr 1:2; Ps 115:3); the home of angels (1Ki 22:19; Mk 12:25). Christ rules from heaven and receives believers there (Heb 8:1; cf. Jn 14:1–3; Ac 7:55). See pp. 220–21, 444–449. *See also* PARADISE.

HEBREW (HEE-broo). The language in which most of the Old Testament was written. Scripture refers to it both as the language of Canaan (Is 19:18) and as the language of Judah (2Ki 18:26, 28). The language is closely related to ancient languages from the region of Israel and is probably based on a Canaanite dialect adopted by the patriarchs.

The Hebrew alphabet, consisting only of consonants, came from the writing of the Phoenicians and was in existence by the fifteenth century BC. About AD 600 to 800, scribes known as the Masoretes added vowel sounds to the Hebrew text of the Old Testament. See pp. xviii, xix, xxv, 3, 5.

HEBREWS (HEE-broos). Abram is the first person in the Old Testament to be referred to as a Hebrew (Gn 14:13). From that point on the name is given to his descendants in both the Old and the New Testaments. Hebrew is another name for an Israelite (e.g., a person who lives in the United States is referred to as an American).

The word *Hebrew* may come from a word that means to pass over, referring back to Abram's crossing of the Euphrates River after he had left home, or it may come from the name Eber, an ancestor of the Israelites (Gn 10:21). In ancient writings from Bible times the Hebrew people are sometimes linked with people known as the Habiru. See p. 148.

HEBREWS, LETTER TO THE. Scholars are uncertain about who wrote this book. They think it could have been Paul, Barnabas, or Apollos. It is certain, however, that the letter was written to Christians, especially Hebrew Christians, who were in danger of falling from the faith (10:19–39). See pp. 421–23.

HEBRON (HEE-brun; union). A city about 20 miles southwest of Jerusalem. It was originally called Kiriath-arba (Gn 23:2). Hebron played a large part in Abraham's life (Gn 13:18). The spies visited this place (Nu 13:21–22), Joshua conquered it (Jsh 10:36–37), and David was anointed as king and ruled Judah from Hebron for more than seven years (2Sm 2:1–4, 11).

HEDGE. A kind of fence or enclosure made of plants, often thorns (Is 5:5; Hos 2:6).

HEIFER. A young cow that has not produced a calf (Dt 21:3). A heifer is often used in metaphors (Jgs 14:18; Jer 46:20; 50:11). The Israelites used a red heifer for purification ceremonies and as a sin offering (Nu 19:1–10).

HEIR. The individual to whom another person's wealth or possessions, the person's inheritance, is given after the person dies. When a man died, his inheritance was first divided among the sons of his legal wives (Gn 21:10; 24:36; 25:5). The oldest son usually received a double share and became the head of the family (Dt 21:15–17). *See also* FIRSTBORN. If the man had no sons, the inheritance was divided, in order, among his daughters, brothers, paternal uncles, or other relatives (Nu 27:8–11).

In the New Testament, it describes the relationship of believers to the heavenly Father, based on grace (Rm 8:16–17). See p. 414.

HELL. Either the place of eternal punishment or the punishment itself. It is called Sheol in the Old Testament, and it is the translation of the Greek word *Gehenna* in the New Testament. Hell is described as eternal punishment (Mt 25:46), a fire that cannot be put out (Mk 9:48), a place where worms continually eat and fires continually burn the damned (Is 66:24), a lake of fire (Rv 20:14), the outer darkness (Mt 25:30), and the furnace of fire where people cry out and grind their teeth (Matthew 13:42, 50). Unbelievers are put in hell because they are under the wrath of God (John 3:36). *See also* HADES.

HELLENIST (HEL-en-ist). Jews who accepted the Greek language and culture following the rule of Alexander the Great (356–323 BC). When the Ptolemies ruled Judea (323–198 BC), they encouraged Greek ways but did not force their religion on the people. After the Seleucids took over Judea (198 BC), they forced Greek ways on the people under threat of torture and death. This sharply divided the Jewish community. Acts reports that Hellenists readily converted to Christianity (Ac 6:1; 9:29), though the cultural conflict that divided Judaism likewise affected the Early Church. The Hellenist Christians actively spread the Gospel to Gentiles (cf. Ac 11:19–20).

HELMET. *See* ARMOR, ARMS.

HELPER. Sometimes Paraclete. One who is called to one's side or pleads one's cause before a judge. In 1Jn 2:1, the term is used of Christ. He is the believer's advocate with the Father; He pleads for the Christian before God. Elsewhere the word often refers to the Holy Spirit, who is the believer's Helper on earth (Jn 14:16, 26; 15:26; 16:7). It is He who indwells the Christian, bringing Christ and His work of salvation to remembrance; it is He who guides the believer into all truth.

HEM. The edge, fringe, or border of a piece of clothing (Ex 28:33–34; Mt 9:20). The Pharisees wore especially long fringes because they wanted to show off their obedience to the command in Nu 15:38–39 (cf. Mt 23:5).

HEMLOCK. *See* GALL 3; WORMWOOD.

HEPHZIBAH (HEF-zi-bah; my delight is in her). 1. The wife of Hezekiah (2Ki 21:1).

2. The symbolic name God gave to Israel to show His love and mercy for the covenant people (Is 62:4).

HERALD. 1. A messenger or someone who publicly announces decrees of the government or other news (Is 41:27; Dn 3:4).

2. Someone who spreads the Gospel, especially someone who preaches it (2Pt 2:5).

HERD. *See* CATTLE.

HERDSMAN. A person in charge of cattle or pigs (Gn 13:7; Mt 8:30–33). The Israelites viewed this job favorably, but the Egyptians looked down on it (cf. "shepherd" in Gn 46:34; 47:6).

HERESY (HER-uh-see; choice). In the New Testament world various schools of thought or belief were called heresies, that is, sects or parties within a larger system of belief. For instance, Sadducees, Pharisees, and Christians were all regarded as heresies, that is, sects or parties within Judaism (cf. Ac 5:17; 15:5; 24:5, 14).

2. The word can describe differences of opinion, goals, or belief that cause divisions within the Church (cf. 1Co 1:10; 11:18–19).

3. The word is used as a name for false, harmful teachings (2Pt 2:1). See pp. 401, 437.

HERMON (HUR-mun; holy mountain). A mountain about 9,100 feet high that stands approximately 30 miles southwest of Damascus and about the same distance northeast of the Sea of Galilee. Water runoff from the rain and snow on its slopes feeds the Jordan River.

Mount Hermon marked the northern extent of Israel's conquests east of the Jordan River (Dt 3:8). Some think it may be the mountain where the transfiguration of Christ took place (Mk 9:2). It is called Baal-hermon in Jgs 3:3 because it was a major center of worship of the false god Baal.

HEROD (HER-uhd; heroic). The family name of a line of rulers from Idumea (south of Israel) who ruled in Israel during New Testament times (55 BC–AD 93). 1. Although the line was begun by Herod Antipater, it was his son who was known as Herod the Great. Herod the Great was the Roman procurator of Judea in 47 BC and was king of the Jews for more than 30 years, from 36 to 1 BC (or 37–4 BC; there are different conclusions about the dating). To stay on the good side of Rome and of the people in Israel, Herod rebuilt cities and temples, most importantly the temple at Jerusalem (Jn 2:20). To maintain his power he did many wicked things, often deceiving or killing people. He was the king who spoke to the Wise Men and had all the baby boys in Bethlehem killed (Mt 2:1–18). See pp. 271–72, 276–78.

2. Herod Archelaus, the son of Herod the Great, was the ruler of Judea, Idumea, and Samaria from 1 BC to AD 6 (Mt 2:22; or 4 BC to AD 1). See pp. 275, 278.

3. Herod Antipas, another son of Herod the Great, ruled Galilee and Perea from 1 BC to AD 39 (Lk 3:1, 19; or 4 BC to AD 39). He was the ruler during Jesus' lifetime. Herod was rich and sly. Jesus referred to him as "that fox" (Lk 13:31–32). See pp. 275, 278.

4. Herod Philip, yet another son of Herod the Great, is known only as the husband of Herodias. His brother Herod Antipas took Herodias from Herod Philip and married her himself (Mt 14:3–4). See p. 275.

5. Herod Philip II was not the son of Herod Philip but of Herod the Great. Herod Philip was his half-brother. Herod Philip II ruled Ituraea and other regions (Lk 3:1). See p. 275.

6. Herod Agrippa I, a grandson of Herod the Great, ruled different areas of the region of Israel from AD 41 to 44. He persecuted Christians. An angel of the Lord killed him because of his pride and wickedness (Ac 12:1–23). See pp. 275–76, 278.

7. Herod Agrippa II was a son of Agrippa I and a great-grandson of Herod the Great. He was king of the territory east of Galilee from about AD 50 to 70. Paul was brought before him (Ac 25:13–26:32). See pp. 276, 278.

HERODIANS (hi-RO-di-ahnz). The dynasty of Herod the Great and its political supporters. Descendants of Herod ruled the region of Israel on behalf of the Romans (63 BC–AD 100). Cf. Mk 3:6. See pp. 271–72, 276–78.

HERODIAS (hi-RO-di-as). Herod the Great's granddaughter. She left her first husband, Herod Philip, to marry her brother-in-law Herod Antipas (Mt 14:3–4). Herodias caused the death of John the Baptist (Mt 14:6–12). See p. 275.

HEZEKIAH (hez-i-KIGH-ah; strength is the Lord). The thirteenth king of Judah. Hezekiah was the son of Ahaz and the father of Manasseh. He returned Judah to the worship of the true God after a long period of idolatry (2Ch 29–31). Under his direction many of the godly teachings of Solomon were written down (Pr 25:1). Judah prospered during his rule. Then Hezekiah became mixed up in a power struggle among Egypt, Assyria, and other nations.

Hezekiah strengthened the defenses of Jerusalem (2Ch 32:5–8). He also supervised the building of the Siloam Tunnel to bring water into the city (2Ki 20:20). When Sennacherib attacked, Hezekiah and the prophet Isaiah prayed to God for help, and God destroyed the attacking army (Is 36–39). See pp. 123, 125, 142, 189, 242.

HIEROGLYPHIC (high-ur-o-GLIF-ik; sacred carving). A system of picture writing used in Egypt and other ancient nations. It is one of the earliest forms of writing.

HIGH, MOST. A name for God (Ps 9:2; 21:7; Lk 8:28). Melchizedek served God Most High (Gn 14:18–20). See pp. 101, 216, 423.

HIGH PLACES. 1. Places of worship located on high ground. They usually had some type of altar and often one or more buildings (1Ki 12:31–32). Because the Canaanite high places brought the threat of idolatry and immorality, God commanded the Israelites to destroy them (Nu 33:52). But the kings of Israel, beginning already with Solomon, rebuilt the high places, sometimes to worship the true God but more often to worship false gods (1Ki 3:2, 4; 11:7; 2Ki 17:7–20).

2. The term *high place* eventually became a general name for any place of worship, even one in a valley (Jer 7:31). The place was considered high because of the lordship of the deity.

HIGH PRIEST. *See* PRIEST.

HILKIAH (hil-KIGH-ah; portion is the Lord). One of Ezra's ancestors who was the high priest in the days of King Josiah (Ezr 7:1). Hilkiah found the Book of the Law in the temple (2Ki 22:4–14).

HINNOM (HIN-um). A valley south of Jerusalem where the Hebrews offered their children to the false god Moloch (Jsh 15:8; 2Ki 23:10; Jer 7:31; 19:2–6). It was also called Gehenna. Later this place became a dump for unclean matter; fires burned in it continually. For this reason the New Testament writers used the word *Gehenna* to name the place of the eternal destiny of unbelievers (cf. "hell" in Mt 5:22, 29–30; 10:28; 18:9; 23:15, 33; Mk 9:43, 45, 47; Lk 12:5). *See also* HELL.

HIRAM (HIGH-ram; brother of exalted one). 1. The king of Tyre who sent cedar and workmen to David for his house, and lumber and gold to Solomon for use in building the temple (2Sm 5:11; 1Ki 9:11–14).

2. The workman who made all the bronze items in or around the temple (1Ki 7:13–46). Both of these men were sometimes referred to as Huram.

HISS. A way of showing surprise or contempt (1Ki 9:8; Jb 27:23; Jer 19:8). It is sometimes translated as "scoff."

HITTITES (HIT-ights). The descendants of Heth (Gn 10:15). The Hittites were a great nation that at one time ruled a large portion of the ancient Near East. They are frequently mentioned in the Old Testament (Gn 26:34). Archaeologists have discovered remains of the Hittite civilization and have learned their language. See p. 79.

HOLY. That which is set apart to be used for or by God, or that which is recognized as partaking in God's holiness. God's very name is "holy" because He is perfect in every way and is "high above," or set apart from, all things (Is 57:15). God demands that His people be holy or set apart for Him (Lv 19:2; Nu 15:40). The holiness of God is imparted to people through His act of choosing them in grace and through His other mighty acts (Dt 26:18–19). It culminates in the saving work of Jesus Christ (Jn 17:19; 1Pt 2:1–10). Jesus is called the Holy One of God (Mk 1:24). See pp. 42–43.

HOLY LAND. *See* CANAAN 2.

HOLY SPIRIT. The Third Person of the Trinity (Mt 28:19; 2Co 13:14). The Holy Spirit works through and is sent by God the Father and God the Son (Jn 15:26; Ac 1:8). The Holy Spirit is God and performs the works of God (Gn 1:2; Rm 8:9). He creates and sustains the universe and the Church (Gn 1:2; Jb 33:4; Ac 2). Moreover, each individual believer is created, or born again, through the Spirit, who works through water and the Word (Jn 3:3–8; 6:63; 1Co 12:13).

The Holy Spirit lives in the hearts of believers, strengthening and encouraging them in the faith and building them up in the unity of the Spirit and in the unity of the body of believers, the Church (Eph 4:1–6; 1Co 12; 2Co 1:22). The Holy Spirit also unites believers to God the Father and to Jesus Christ (Rm 8:14–17).

The Holy Spirit gave a special measure of understanding to the prophets, worked in a special way in certain leaders of God's people, and was given without measure to Jesus Christ (Jgs 3:10; Is 61:1; Lk 4:1; Col 1:19; 1Pt 1:10–12; 2Pt 1:21). The Holy Spirit dwells in believers (2Tm 1:14). He continues to give understanding of God and His will to believers and gives them all spiritual blessings (Jn 14:26; 16:13–15). See pp. 362–63.

HOLY SPIRIT, SIN AGAINST. *See* SIN, UNPARDONABLE.

HOMES. Shepherds, exiles, outcasts, and lepers often lived in caves found throughout the limestone ridges of Israel (1Ki 18:4; 19:9). People built temporary shelters, or booths (Is 1:8), by covering four upright poles with a network of sticks and leaves. Sometimes they made these shelters out of woven river reeds that they plastered with mud.

Nomadic people lived in tents (Gn 4:20), which were often woven from dark-colored goat or camel hair. These tents were usually very large. They had several supporting poles, sloping sides that were held in place by cords anchored in the ground with stakes, and curtains to divide up the living space inside (Is 54:2; Jer 10:20).

In sections of Israel where building stone was readily available, people built homes out of blocks of limestone. Mortar made from lime and sand held these blocks together. In some areas of the ancient world people built homes made from clay bricks (Gn 11:3). They constructed doors from planks of wood or slabs of stone. The windows of their homes were usually very narrow; they were placed high up in the wall and fitted with wooden latticework (Pr 7:6). To make roofs for their homes, people laid beams across the tops of the walls. Then they covered these beams with a layer of branches laid crosswise, a layer of rushes and straw, and a layer of clay. More alternating layers of rushes and straw were added, and the roof was finished with a solid layer of clay. The walls extended about three feet above the roofline (Dt 22:8). The people often worked or stored things on their rooftops or went there to be alone or to enjoy cool breezes (Jsh 2:6; Ac 10:9). A stairway on the outside of the house led from street level up to the roof. Sometimes people built an upstairs room, or upper room, on one side of the building (2Ki 4:10; Mk 14:15; Ac 1:13). They also might make the one main room into two levels, the upper level for living quarters and the lower one for sheep and goats.

The furnishings of a typical house included mats or rugs woven from wool, grass, or straw. These were used for mattresses at night and in place of chairs during the day. A stove or fireplace for heating and cooking was located in the middle of the house. Sometimes it was only a hole in the earthen floor. Spoons, forks, and other utensils and pots and pans were made of copper. Knives were made of bronze or iron and had wooden handles. Plates, cups, bowls, jugs, and other containers were made of pottery. People stored wheat in large, pottery jars. Other things were stored by hanging them from the roof beams.

Wealthier homes had furniture—couches, beds, chairs—more like today's furniture. Often these homes had walled courtyards or consisted of a series of rooms built around an open court. As the nation of Israel grew richer, the wealthy and powerful people built big, beautiful mansions and palaces (1Ki 7:1–8; Am 6:4–8).

See pp. 22–23, 292.

HONEY. Wild honey, which was plentiful in Canaan, was eaten in various ways (Ex 16:31; 1Sm 14:25). It was often a symbol of wealth and plenty (Nu 14:8).

HOOKS. Hooks were used for fishing (Jb 41:1), hanging curtains (Ex 26:37), leading animals or prisoners (2Ch 33:11; Ezk 19:4), pruning and trimming (Jl 3:10), and hanging meat (Ezk 40:43).

HOPE. A feeling of peace and joy; confident trust in what is not seen. The Christian's hope is centered in Jesus Christ (1Tm 1:1). It flows from the new, loving relationship a Christian has with God through faith in Jesus Christ (Rm 5:1–11). Faith, hope, and love are often linked in Scripture (1Co 13:7, 13; Heb 11:1; 1Th 1:3; 5:8). Christian hope looks beyond this life to the glory of heaven (cf. 2Co 4:16–18). It takes Christ's resurrection as the promise of God that the Christian will also be raised to life eternal (cf. 1Co 6:14). Christians who live in such hope are comforted in times of trouble and are motivated to live lives pleasing to God (Ps 43:5; 1Jn 3:1–3).

HOR (HAWR; mountain). 1. A mountain on the edge of Edom where Aaron died (Nu 20:22–29).

2. A mountain north of Israel, probably in Lebanon, that was used to mark the northern boundary of Canaan (Nu 34:7–8).

HOREB (HO-reb; dryness). The mountain where the Law was given to Israel (1Ki 8:9). Also called Mount Sinai.

HORN. At first people blew on animal horns to give signals. They also made containers out of animal horns (Jsh 6:5; 1Sm 16:1). Later they made horns out of metal (cf. Nu 10:2). The projecting corners of the altar in the tabernacle and the temple were called horns (1Ki 1:50). The horn was a symbol of honor and strength (Dn 7:7; Lk 1:69).

HORSE. The Hebrew people during Jacob's time were familiar with horses (Gn 49:17). The Egyptians used horses, mainly for war (Ex 14:9). The Israelites were ordered not to keep any horses captured in battle, and the rulers of Israel were directed not to keep large numbers of horses (Dt 17:16; Jsh 11:6). Later kings, however, did keep horses (1Ki 1:5; 4:26).

HOSANNA (ho-ZAN-ah; save now). At Jesus' triumphant entry into Jerusalem the crowds chanted this as they waved palm branches (Mt 21:9–15). Usage of the word may have originated with Ps 118:25–26.

HOSEA (ho-ZAY-ah; salvation). A prophet at the time of Kings Uzziah, Jotham, Ahaz, Hezekiah of Judah, and Jeroboam II of Israel (Hos 1:1). Isaiah, Amos, and Micah were other prophets at the same time as Hosea. Hosea's prophecy is recorded in the Book of Hosea. See pp. 139, 225.

HOSEA, BOOK OF. The first of the Minor Prophets as they appear in the Old Testament. The first three chapters are the key to the whole book. By discussing Hosea's marriage to the unfaithful Gomer, these chapters provide a clear picture of Israel's unfaithfulness and God's forgiveness. The rest of the book is a collection of largely unconnected sayings and prophecies. See pp. 225–27.

HOSHEA (HO-SHEE-ah; salvation; same as Hosea). The last king of Israel. Hoshea gained the throne by joining with a foreign king to assassinate Pekah, who was then king of Israel (2Ki 15:30). Hoshea placed himself under the control of Assyria by paying tribute to the king of Assyria, Shalmaneser V (2Ki 17:3). When Hoshea stopped paying tribute, the Assyrians conquered Israel and took the people captive. Apparently Hoshea was not as wicked as other kings of Israel (2Ki 17:2). See p. 125.

HOSPITALITY (hos-puh-TAL-uh-tee). The readiness to help strangers by giving them food, clothing, shelter, or whatever else they might need. Hospitality is commanded in the Levitical law and is encouraged elsewhere in the Old and New Testaments (Heb 13:2; cf. Gn 18:1–8; Lv 19:34; Jb 31:32). See p. 386.

HOST. 1. A great number. The host of heaven refers either to the numerous stars and other heavenly bodies that people often wrongfully worshiped or to the angels and the company of saints in heaven (Dt 4:19; 1Ki 22:19; Lk 2:13).

2. One of God's names is Sabaoth, or Lord of hosts. He is named this because He rules over the angels, the stars, and all things (Is 40:26; cf. Gn 28:12; Jb 37–39).

3. Someone who shows hospitality.

HOUSE. 1. The name for a family line (Ex 2:1; Lk 2:4). See pp. 101–102, 113.

2. The name for the place where God makes His presence known, for instance, at Bethel, which means house of God, in the tabernacle, and in the temple (Gn 28:17; Ex 34:26; 1Ki 6:1).

3. *See* HOMES.

HULDAH (HUL-dah; weasel). A prophetess in the Old Testament. She was the wife of Shallum (2Ki 22:14–20; 2Ch 34:22–28).

HUMILITY. The opposite of pride; not thinking more of oneself than one should. Someone who is humble puts God and others ahead of self (Pr 15:33; Rm 12:3; cf. Lk 18:9–14).

HUNTING. The Israelites hunted many types of wild deer, sheep, and birds (Dt 14:5; 1Sm 26:20). They used bows and arrows, slingstones, spears, nets, pits, and traps (Gn 27:3; Jb 41:28–29; Ps 9:15).

HUR. 1. The man who helped Aaron hold up Moses' hands at Rephidim so that Joshua was able to defeat the Amalekites (Ex 17:8–16).

2. A king of Midian (Nu 31:8).

HYMN. A song telling about God and praising Him (Ex 15:1–18; Dt 32:1–43; Jgs 5; 1Sm 2:1–10; Lk 1:46–55, 68–79). Christians are encouraged to worship God by using psalms, hymns, and spiritual songs (Col 3:16). See p. 169.

HYPOCRISY (hi-PAHK-ru-see). To play a part; to pretend to be what one is not. In the Bible hypocrisy usually describes a condition of pretending to have faith when no faith is present in the heart at all (Mt 23:28). It also refers to any type of trickery, lying, or falsehood (Mk 12:15).

HYSSOP (HIS-uhp). Although the Bible mentions this plant numerous times, it apparently is not always referring to the same type of plant. Ex 12:22 seems to speak of a bushy plant that the Israelites used to sprinkle blood on the doorposts at the first Passover. Jn 19:29 mentions a long stalk or stem as part of the hyssop plant that was used to put the bitter drink to Jesus' lips while He hung on the cross. The plant was used in certain religious ceremonies and also as a symbol of purification, correction, and forgiveness (Lv 14:4, 6, 49; Nu 19:6; Ps 51:7).

I

IBEX (IGH-beks). Probably a large, light-colored antelope. Since the ibex was classed among the clean animals, the Israelites were allowed to eat it (Dt 14:5).

ICE. Snow and ice can be found on the higher mountains of Palestine (Jer 18:14). Otherwise, snow and ice are rare except in the extreme north of the country (Jb 6:16; 37:6, 10).

ICHABOD (IK-ah-bod; there is no glory). The son of Phineas and grandson of Eli. Ichabod was born after his father was killed in a battle with the Philistines, a battle in which the Philistines captured the ark of the covenant. Ichabod's mother named him as she did because she felt the glory had departed from Israel (1Sm 4:19–22).

ICONIUM (igh-KO-ni-uhm). A city on the southwestern edge of the central plain of Asia Minor (modern-day Turkey). Paul visited this city on his missionary journeys (Ac 13:51; 14:1–22; 16:2). See p. 393.

IDDO (ID-o). 1. The name of a wise man who wrote down the events of the reigns of Solomon, Rehoboam, Jeroboam, and Abijah (2Ch 9:29; 12:15).

2. The grandfather of the prophet Zechariah (Zec 1:1, 7).

IDOL, IDOLATRY (IGH-dol, igh-DOL-ah-tree). A false god or anything that is placed ahead of the true God is an idol. Worshiping a false God or placing a thing or person ahead of God is called idolatry. Often idols had names and were represented by pictures or some type of statue or figurine made of various materials and in varying sizes (Gn 31:34; Is 40:19–20; Dn 3:1). Idols and idolatry are forbidden and are spoken of as foolish, hateful, and horrible in Scripture (Ex 20:4–5, 23; Is 44:9–20; Ezk 37:23). Paul describes idols and idolatry as exchanging the truth about God for a lie (Rm 1:21–23, 25). See pp. 76–77, 134–35.

IDUMEA (id-yoo-MEE-ah). The Greek name for Edom, the area south of Judah (Mk 3:8).

IGNORANCE. A lack of knowledge. In the Bible ignorance is especially a lack of knowledge concerning the true God and His will. It is sometimes described as excusable and at other times as inexcusable (Ezk 45:20; Eph 4:18).

ILLYRICUM (i-LIR-i-kuhm). The name of a Roman province on the east coast of the Adriatic Sea, northwest of Greece. It was later called Dalmatia (2Tm 4:10). As far as we know, it is the northernmost part of Europe into which Paul traveled on his missionary journeys (Rm 15:19). Today Illyricum is part of the country of Yugoslavia.

IMAGE. *See* IDOL, IDOLATRY.

IMAGE OF GOD. God created people in His image (Gn 1:26–27). Because God is a spiritual being and no person or thing can equal Him in any way, the likeness of people to God is spiritual, not physical, and is always "less than," not "equal to."

In the most proper sense, being created in the image of God means that people were created without sin. But this image was lost in the fall into sin. In the broader sense, the image of God refers to humanity's rationality and will, and still remains in people, though the presence of original sin has also corrupted that likeness (Gn 9:6; Jas 3:9). Christ is the image of God, and in Him we can see God (Jn 1:1, 14, 18; Col 1:15). Through Christ people regain the likeness to God (Rm 8:29).

IMMANUEL (i-MAN-yoo-uhl; God is with us). The name of the child whom the prophet Isaiah predicted would be born of a virgin (Is 7:14; Mt 1:22–23). This is an important prophecy predicting the birth of the Savior, Jesus Christ, the Promised One spoken of in many Old Testament prophecies (Gn 3:15; Is 9:6–7; 11:1; Mi 5:2–3). See p. 129.

IMMORTALITY (im-awr-TAL-uh-tee). *See* ESCHATOLOGY; ETERNAL LIFE.

IMPERIAL GUARD. The bodyguard and household of the emperor in Rome (Php 1:13).

IMPUTATION (im-pyoo-TAY-shuhn). Placing the blame for something bad or the credit for something good on someone else. When Adam and Eve fell into sin, that sin was imputed to all, that is, the blame for it was placed upon all people. In the same way, when Christ paid the price for sin by His death and resurrection, that payment was imputed or credited to all who believe in Christ (Rm 5:12–21; 2Co 5:19–21).

INCARNATION (in-kahr-NA-shuhn). The term for what took place when the Son of God took on a human body and soul. The word itself does not occur in the Bible, but it is used properly in the Nicene Creed to describe Jesus' birth. *See also* JESUS CHRIST.

INCENSE. Any substance that gives off a sweet smell when burned. Incense played an important part in Israel's worship. It was burned on the altar of incense morning and evening, carried into the Most Holy Place on the Day of Atonement, and used at other times as well. The incense the Israelites used is described in Ex 30:34–35. People also burned incense to worship false gods (Lv 26:30).

Incense is a symbol for prayer or worship (Ps 141:2; Rv 5:8). See pp. 170–71.

INCEST. Having sexual relations with members of one's own family. Incest is forbidden in Scripture (Lv 20:11–17, 19–21; 1Co 5:1).

INDIA (IN-di-ah). The country on the east of the Persian Empire (Est 1:1).

INHERITANCE. *See* HEIR.

INIQUITY (i-NIK-wi-tee). *See* SIN, II.

INK. A substance used for writing. Ink was made by mixing charcoal or lampblack (a fine black powder) with water and plant gum (Jer 36:18; 2Jn 12).

INN. Places where travelers can sleep at night. Hebrew hospitality made inns and hotels in our sense practically unnecessary. The inns in Lk 2:7 and 10:34 were probably more like private homes than places of business.

INSPIRATION (in-spuh-RAY-shuhn). The special way the Holy Spirit worked in certain people that caused them to act out, speak, or write God's Word (Mi 3:8; 1Co 2:13; 1Pt 1:10–11). When the Holy Spirit did this, the person who was inspired or motivated to act, speak, or write was certainly under the direction of God's power, but he or she was not a robot (Luke 1:1–4). See pp. xvi, xxi, xxv.

INTERCESSION. *See* PRAYER.

IOTA (igh-O-tah). The smallest letter of the Greek alphabet, particularly as a subscript (Mt 5:18; Lk 16:17).

IRON. Iron is mentioned already in Gn 4:22. The Hittite people passed the knowledge of ironworking to the Philistines. When David conquered the Philistines, the Israelites learned about ironworking as well. Tools, weapons, chariots, chains and shackles, and writing tools were all made from iron (Nu 35:16; Jsh 6:19, 24; 17:16; 1Sm 17:7; Jb 19:24; Ps 105:18). Iron is also a symbol of strength.

ISAAC (IGH sahk; laughter). Abraham's only son by Sarah (Gn 17:19). Isaac was the son of the promise, the one through whom God continued to work out His plan of salvation (Gn 21:12). Isaac showed himself to be a faithful, obedient son when God ordered Abraham to sacrifice him (Gn 22:1–18). Isaac married Rebekah and had two sons: Jacob and Esau. Rebekah and Jacob plotted together to trick Isaac into giving Jacob the blessing of the firstborn son (Gn 24–27). Isaac died at Mamre (Gn 35:27–29). See pp. 12, 15, 39, 60.

ISAIAH (igh-ZAY-yah; the LORD is salvation). A prophet of Judah during the reigns of Uzziah, Jotham, Ahaz, and Hezekiah (Is 1:1). The year that Uzziah died, Isaiah saw a vision in the temple (Is 6). This is sometimes referred to as Isaiah's call to be

God's prophet. Isaiah, who lived in Jerusalem, married and had two sons (Is 7:3; 8:3). Hezekiah sought the help of Isaiah when the Assyrians were about to attack Jerusalem (2Ki 19:1–7). See pp. 139, 145, 189–90, 200–01.

ISAIAH, BOOK OF. This is the longest of all the prophetic books. It is about God's judgment and grace and contains many passages about the promised Savior, much beautiful poetry, and history. See pp. 189–92.

ISCARIOT (is-KAR-i-ut). *See* JUDAS 2.

ISH-BOSHETH (ish-BO-sheth; man of shame). One of Saul's sons. He was originally called Eshbaal (1Ch 8:33). Ish-bosheth ruled two years at Mahanaim but was defeated by David's men. Later he was assassinated (2Sm 2:8–16; 3:6–15; 4:5–12).

ISHMAEL (ISH-may-uhl; God hears). 1. The son of Abraham and Sarah's maidservant, Hagar (Gn 16:3, 15; 17:25). Sarah became jealous of her stepson and demanded that Abraham send him and his mother away. Abraham was disturbed by this, but trusting God's word to him, he sent them away (Gn 21:8–20; cf. Gal 4:21–31). Ishmael's descendants became a great nation (Gn 17:20; 25:12–16). See p. 89.

2. The man who assassinated Gedaliah and caused Jeremiah to flee to Egypt (Jer 40:7–41:18).

ISHMAELITES (ISH-may-ul-ights). Descendants of Ishmael. The Ishmaelites were mostly traveling desert merchants and traders (Gn 37:25–28). See p. 89.

ISLAND (IGH-lahnd). 1. Dry land surrounded by water (Ac 13:6).

2. Habitable land that once was water (Is 42:15).

3. Symbolic for faraway lands, whether islands or not. It often describes the majesty of God and the broad scope of messianic prophecy (cf. "coastland" in Ps 97:1; Is 49:1).

ISRAEL (IZ-ray-el; God strives; he strives with God). 1. The name given to Jacob at Penuel after he wrestled with an stranger (Gn 32:28).

2. The name of the nation composed of the descendants of Jacob and his 12 sons. Jacob and his sons founded the 12 tribes of Israel (Ex 3:16). The name Israel is used more than 2,000 times in Scripture to refer to the children, or nation, of Israel. See pp. 90, 148.

3. The name given to the 10 northern tribes of Israel after Solomon's death when they revolted under Rehoboam and the kingdom split into two. The Northern Kingdom was called Israel to distinguish it from the Southern Kingdom, which was called Judah (1Sm 11:8). The capital of Israel was first Shechem (1Ki 12:25) and later Samaria (1Ki 16:24). When a remnant of the people returned to Palestine after the Babylonian exile, the name Israel was used again of all the descendants of Jacob and his sons (Ezr 10:10). See p. 148.

4. In the New Testament, Israel became a name for the Church, which constitutes believers from all nations (Ps 73:1; Rm 9:6–8; 11:25–36; Gal 3:26–29; 6:16).

ISRAELITES (IZ-ray-uhl-ights). *See* ISRAEL.

ISSACHAR (IS-a-kahr; hired laborer). 1. The ninth son of Jacob, the fifth by his wife Leah (Gn 30:14–18). A tribe of Israel was made up of Issachar's descendants. Jacob prophesied that Issachar's descendants would become slaves (Gn 49:14–15). See pp. 19, 21.

2. The area southwest of the Sea of Galilee that was assigned to the tribe of Issachar (Jsh 19:17–23). It included the Plain of Esdraelon, also called the Valley of Jezreel (Jgs 6:33).

ITALY (IT-ahl-ee). The name of the whole peninsula of land that begins with the Alps on the north and juts southeastward into the Mediterranean Sea. The city of Rome is on the western shore of this peninsula (Ac 18:2).

ITHAMAR (ITH-ah-mahr; palm coast). The youngest son of Aaron (Ex 6:23). Ithamar was consecrated as a priest and directed the construction of the tabernacle (Ex 28:1; 28:40–29:9; 38:21).

ITTAI (IT-ay-igh). A powerful man from Gath who was loyal to David and led 600 of his men against Absalom (2Sm 15:18–22).

ITUREA (i-tyoo-REE-ah). A hilly area in the mountains of Lebanon, north of Palestine. At one time war-like descendants of Ishmael lived there. Iturea was later also the name of a small Roman province (Lk 3:1).

IVORY. Both a symbol and a source of wealth, ivory was imported into Palestine and used to decorate houses and furniture (1Ki 10:18, 22; Am 3:15). People also made many objects and implements out of ivory and decorated with it.

J

JABBOK (JAB-uk; effusion). An eastern tributary of the Jordan River that runs through Gilead. Cf. Gn 32:22. It rises near Amman and flows through a deep canyon to join the Jordan about 23 miles north of the Dead Sea (cf. Jgs 11:13). See p. 24.

JABESH-GILEAD (JAY-besh-GIL-i-uhd). A city east of the Jordan River and about 10 miles southeast of Beth-shan in the territory given to the tribe of Manasseh. All the men of this city were destroyed because they did not obey the command of God to assemble at Mizpah (Jgs 21:8–14). Later Saul freed the city from the Ammonites (1Sm 11:1–11). The people of this city remembered Saul and gave him a decent burial (1Sm 31:11–13).

JABIN (JAY-bin; he discerns). 1. A king of Hazor whom Joshua defeated (Jsh 11:1–14).

2. Another king of Hazor whose general, Sisera, was defeated by Deborah and Barak (Jgs 4).

JACHIN (JAY-kin). 1. The name of several minor Old Testament characters, including a son of Simeon (Gn 46:10).

2. Jachin and Boaz were the names of the two large pillars that stood in front of Solomon's temple (1Ki 7:15–22).

JACOB (JAY-kuhb; supplanter). The son of Isaac and Rebekah and the younger twin of Esau (Gn 25:21–26). Jacob bought the birthright from Esau for a pot of lentil stew and, with his mother's help, tricked Isaac into giving him the blessing of the firstborn son (Gn 25:29–34; 27:1–41). Then Jacob fled to Haran. On the way he had a vision of a ladder reaching to heaven (Gn 27:42–28:22). At Haran Jacob worked for his Uncle Laban at least 20 years—14 years to earn the right to marry Laban's daughters, Rachel and Leah, and six more to acquire flocks of his own (Gn 29:1–30). Jacob had at least 12 sons and one daughter by his wives and his wives' maids. Leah was the mother of Reuben, Simeon, Levi, Judah, Issachar, Zebulun, and Dinah. Rachel was the mother of Joseph and Benjamin. Leah's maid, Zilpah, was the mother of Gad and Asher, and Rachel's maid, Bilhah, was the mother of Dan and Naphtali (Gn 29:31–30:24; 35:16–26).

Jacob fled from Laban back to Canaan, wrestling with God one night on the way (Gn 30:25–32:32). Jacob reconciled with his brother, Esau, and settled in Canaan (Gn 33). Jacob worshiped the true God and was blessed by Him (Gn 35:9). God changed Jacob's name to Israel (Gn 35:10).

The story of Jacob's life overlaps in Genesis with the story of his son Joseph's life in Egypt (Gn 42–46). Before he died, Jacob gave a prophetic blessing to each of his sons (Gn 49). See pp. 16, 24, 148.

2. The name Jacob is also used as a symbol for the Israelites (Nu 23:10; Ps 59:13).

3. The father of Joseph of Nazareth, and the paternal, earthly grandfather of Jesus (Mt 1:15–16).

JADDUA (ja-DYOO-ah; known). The name of the last high priest mentioned in the Old Testament (Ne 12:11, 22).

JAEL (JAY-uhl; wild goat). The wife of Heber. Jael killed Sisera, the general of Jabin's troops, with a tent peg (Jgs 4:17–27).

JAIR (JAY-ur; enlighten). One of the judges of Israel (Jgs 10:3–5). See p. 88.

JAIRUS (JAY-uh-ruhs; the Greek form of the name Jair). The ruler of the synagogue, probably at Capernaum, whose daughter was raised by Jesus (Mk 5:22; Lk 8:41). See pp. 294–95, 321.

JAMBRES (JAM-breez). The name of one of the Egyptian magicians who opposed Moses (2Tm 3:8–9; cf. Ex 7:9–13).

JAMES (JAMZ; the Hebrew form of this name is Jacob). 1. The son of Zebedee who was called away from the family fishing business along with his brother to be a disciple (Mt 4:21). James, his brother John, and Peter formed the inner circle of disciples who were closest to Jesus. James witnessed the transfiguration of Jesus (Mk 9:2–9), the raising of Jairus's daughter (Mk 5:37–39), and Jesus' agony in Gethsemane (Mt 26:37). He was killed by Herod Agrippa I about AD 43. Jesus nicknamed James and his brother the "Sons of Thunder" (Mk 3:17). See p. 286.

2. James, the son of Alphaeus and Mary, another of the 12 disciples of Jesus (Mk 3:18; Ac 1:13). Often referred to as James the Less, he is distinguished from the other disciple named James as being either younger or smaller or both (Mk 15:40). See p. 287.

3. One of the brothers of the Lord (Mt 13:55). He apparently did not believe in Jesus as the Son of God until after His resurrection, possibly being converted by one of Jesus' postresurrection appearances (Jn 7:5; Ac 1:13–14; 1Co 15:5, 7). James became a leader of the Early Church, especially the church at Jerusalem (Gal 1:18–19; 2:12). He served as chairman of the Jerusalem Council (Ac 15:13, 19–23). It is generally thought that James wrote the Letter of James (Jas 1:1). See

pp. 308, 368, 426.

JAMES, LETTER OF. James wrote this letter to comfort the Jews outside Israel who were undergoing trials. In the letter he warns them against spiritual laziness and having faith in name only—faith that takes no action. See pp. 426–28.

JANNES (JAN-eez). The name of an Egyptian magician who opposed Moses (2Tm 3:8–9; cf. Ex 7:9–13).

JAPHETH (JAY-feth; beauty or enlarged). One of Noah's three sons and the father of Gomer, Magog, Madai, Javan, Tubal, Meshech, and Tiras (Gn 6:10; 10:2). His descendants occupied the islands and coastlands of the Gentiles; they were the Indo-European peoples (Gn 10:5). Japheth's obedient behavior brought him the blessing of his father (Gn 9:20–27). See p. 12.

JAPHIA (jah-FIGH-ah; shining). 1. A king of Lachish whom Joshua put to death (Jsh 10:3–26).

2. A son of King David (2Sm 5:15).

3. An ancient town located near Nazareth (Jsh 19:12).

JASHAR (JAY-shur; upright). The author of a lost poetical book that was used in writing the historical books of the Old Testament (Jsh 10:13; 2Sm 1:18).

JASON (JAY-suhn; healing). A Christian who showed Paul hospitality at Thessalonica and received harsh treatment from the Jews (Ac 17:5–9). He is probably the same Jason mentioned in Rm 16:21.

JASPER. A type of quartz usually stained deep shades of red, brown, green, and yellow. In ancient times jasper included other types of rock as well. Jasper was used for decorative purposes (Ex 28:20; Ezk 28:13; Rv 4:3).

JAVELIN (JAV-lin). A short, light spear (Jb 41:26). See p. 108. *See also* ARMOR, ARMS.

JEBUS (JEE-buhs). The name of Jerusalem when occupied by the Jebusites (Jsh 15:63; 18:28; Jgs 19:10). The city was small in comparison to the size of Jerusalem at Solomon's time. *See also* ZION 1. See p. 79.

JEBUSITES (JEB-yoo-zights). A mountain tribe of Canaan that lived at Jebus (Gn 10:16; 15:21; Nu 13:29; Jsh 11:3). Joshua killed their king and assigned their territory to Benjamin (Jsh 10:23–27; 18:16, 28). See p. 79.

JECONIAH (jek-o-NIGH-ah; Lord establishes). A variant spelling of the name Jehoiachin. Jeconiah, or Jehoiachin, was a king of Judah (1Ch 3:16–17; Jer 24:1; 27:20; 28:4; 29:2). *See also* JEHOIACHIN.

JEDIDAH (ji-DIGH-dah; beloved). The mother of Josiah (2Ki 22:1).

JEDIDIAH (jed-i-DIGH-ah; beloved by the Lord). The name Nathan gave to Solomon (2Sm 12:25).

JEGAR-SAHADUTHA (JEE-gahr-say-hah-DYOO-thah; heap of witness). The Aramaic name Laban gave to the heap of stones he piled up as a memorial covenant between him and Jacob. Jacob called it Galeed (Gn 31:47–48).

JEHEZKEL (ji-HEZ-kel; God strengthens). The head of the twentieth division of priests (1Ch 24:16).

JEHOAHAZ (ji-HO-ah-haz; Lord has laid hold of). 1. The son and successor of Jehu and the eleventh king of Israel (2Ki 10:35; 13:1). Jehoahaz did what was evil in the sight of the Lord and continued the idolatry of Jeroboam. Because of this, God became angry with Israel and allowed Hazael, king of Syria, and Ben-hadad, his son, to campaign successfully against them (2Ki 13:1–9). See p. 125.

2. The son and successor of Josiah and the seventeenth king of Judah. His reign of three months was evil. After this time he was deposed by Pharaoh Neco and taken captive to Egypt (2Ki 23:30–34; 2Ch 36:1–4). In 1Ch 3:15 and Jer 22:10–12 he is referred to as Shallum. He is also called a young lion (Ezk 19:1–4). See pp. 125, 202.

JEHOIACHIN (ji-HOI-ah-kin; Lord establishes). The son and successor of Jehoiakim and the nineteenth king of Judah. During his short reign of three months and a few days, he did that which was evil in the sight of the Lord. Then Nebuchadnezzar carried him away into captivity and put him into prison. When Evil-merodach ascended the throne of Babylon a number of years later, he released Jehoiachin (2Ki 24:8–16; 25:27–30; 2Ch 36:9–10; Jer 39:2; 52:28–34; Ezk 17:12). See pp. 120, 125, 202. *See also* JECONIAH.

JEHOIADA (ji-HOI-ah-dah; Lord has known). The high priest at the time Athaliah usurped the throne. Jehoiada's wife hid the young prince Joash while Jehoiada planned and carried out the revolt that led to Athaliah's overthrow. Then Joash became the rightful king. Jehoiada was Joash's uncle, and while Jehoiada lived, Joash was faithful to the Lord (2Ki 11:1–12:16; 2Ch 22:10–24:22).

JEHOIAKIM (ji-HOI-ah-kim; Lord establishes) The son of Josiah and the eighteenth king of Judah. His name was originally Eliakim. When his father died, the people put Jehoahaz, Jehoiakim's younger brother, on the throne. But when Pharaoh Neco took Jehoahaz captive to Egypt after three months, he made Eliakim, whose name he changed to Jehoiakim, the new king. Jehoiakim did what was evil in the eyes of the Lord and went back to idol worship. He also heavily taxed his people so that he could pay tribute to Pharaoh Neco.

In 605 BC, Nebuchadnezzar defeated Neco in battle at Carchemish and advanced on Jerusalem. Jehoiakim then became Nebuchadnezzar's servant and paid tribute to him. Three years later Jehoiakim rebelled against Babylonian rule. When he died, his body received the burial of a donkey (2Ki 23:34–37; 24:1–6; 2Ch 36:4–8; Jer 1:3; 22; 24–28; 35–37; 45–46; 52; Dn 1:1–2). See pp. 202–03, 125, 249.

JEHOIARIB (ji-HOI-ah-rib; Lord pleads). The head of the first division of temple priests (1Ch 9:10; 24:7).

JEHORAM (ji-HO-ram). *See* JORAM.

JEHOSHAPHAT (ji-HAHSH-ah-fat; the Lord has judged). The son of Asa and fourth king of Judah. Jehoshaphat reigned 25 years and is described as a good king. In the third year of his reign, he sent princes and Levites to teach the people the Law. He made peace with Israel and removed the high places and idols out of Judah. After visiting Ahab, king of Israel, Jehoshaphat was persuaded to join armies with Ahab against the Syrians. On Jehoshaphat's return home the prophet Jehu rebuked him for joining forces with Ahab and Ahaziah. Jehoshaphat died around 848 BC and was succeeded by his son Jehoram (1Ki 15:24; 2Ki 8:16, 26; 2Ch 17–21:1; Mt 1:8). See pp. 53, 125, 142.

JEHOSHAPHAT, VALLEY OF. A symbolic name for a valley where the Lord will gather all nations for judgment (Jl 3:2, 12).

JEHOSHEBA (ji-HAHSH-i-bah; the Lord is an oath). The wife of the high priest Jehoida and the daughter of Jehoram and sister of Ahaziah, both kings of Judah. When Ahaziah was murdered, Jehosheba hid Joash, Ahaziah's son, from Athaliah until Joash could safely be proclaimed king (2Ki 11:2).

JEHOVAH (ji-HO-vah). A common English word for one of God's names. It is a combination of the Hebrew consonants YHWH (which were probably pronounced YAH-weh and translated "Lord") and the vowel points of *Adonai*, the word the Hebrew people said whenever they saw YHWH in the text. The Hebrews took seriously the commandment to keep God's name holy. That is why they spoke the word *Adonai* whenever they encountered God's name *YHWH* in their writings.

YHWH is derived from the verb *to be* and indicates God is eternal (Ex 3:13–15). It is God's personal name for Himself, the one He uses when dealing with His people. To know the name *YHWH* is to know God manifesting Himself to His people in grace and love (Ps 9:10; Jer 16:21). See p. 5.

JEHOVAH-JIREH (ji-HO-vah-JIGH-re; the Lord will provide). The name Abraham gave to the place where he put Isaac on the altar (Gn 22:14).

JEHU (Je-hu; Lord is he). 1. A prophet who rebuked Baasha and Jehoshaphat (1Ki 16:1, 7, 12; 2 Ch 19:1–3).

2. The tenth king of Israel. He was a son of Jehoshaphat, a grandson of Nimshi, and a commander in Ahab's army. Because of Ahab's wickedness, God told Elijah to anoint Jehu king over Israel and commission him to destroy the house of Ahab (1Ki 19:16–17).

After being anointed king, Jehu killed Jehoram of Israel (Ahab's son), Ahaziah of Judah, Jezebel (Ahab's wife), Ahab's heirs, and the prophets of Baal. Jehu, however, made no attempt to walk in the Lord's ways. He assembled all the people and said to them: "Ahab served Baal a little, but Jehu will serve him much" (2Ki 10:18). Jehu also paid tribute to Shalmaneser III, king of Assyria (2Ki 9–10; 2Ch 22:7–9). See p. 125.

JEHUDI (ji-HYOO-digh; Jew). A messenger sent by the court of King Jehoiakim to ask Baruch for the scroll Jeremiah had written (Jer 36:14–23).

JEPHTHAH (JEF-thah; he opens). One of the judges of Israel. Jephthah was an illegitimate son who was driven from home by his brothers, the legitimate heirs. Jephthah went to the land of Tob, where he lived until the elders of the tribes of Israel called him back to fight the Amorites. Jephthah rashly promised God that, if he were permitted to win the war with the Amorites, he would offer as a burnt offering whatever first came to him from out of his house when he returned home. Jephthah did defeat the Amorites, and upon his return home was first greeted by his daughter, his only child. Because of his promise, Jephthah offered her to the Lord, though how is debated. Jephthah judged Israel six years. Then he died and was buried in Gilead (Jgs 11:1; 12:7; Heb 11:32). See p. 88.

JERAHMEEL (ji-RAH-mi-el; God has mercy). One of the officers Jehoiakim sent to arrest Jeremiah and Baruch (Jer 36:26).

JEREMIAH (jer-i-MIGH-ah; Lord exalts or appoints). One of the major Hebrew prophets. Jeremiah lived from about 640 to 580 BC. He was the son of Hilkiah, a priest of Anathoth in the territory of Benjamin (Jer 1:1). In the thirteenth year of King Josiah's reign, Jeremiah was called to prophesy by a vision in which God told him he was "to destroy and to overthrow, to build and to plant" (Jer 1:4–10).

Jeremiah continued in his prophetic office during the days of the last kings of Judah (Josiah, Jehoahaz II, Jehoiakim, Jehoiachin, and Zedekiah), approximately 50 years. He supported and probably assisted in Josiah's reforms (2Ki 23). He warned Jehoiakim not to be friends with Egypt and depend on it because the Chaldeans would be successful in their attack against Jerusalem. Jeremiah dictated a scroll of his prophecies to Baruch. When the scroll was eventually read to the king, he cut off a section at a time and threw it into the fire until the entire scroll was destroyed (Jer 36).

In the days of Zedekiah, the princes persecuted Jeremiah (Jer 37–38). After Jerusalem was captured in 605 BC by the Chaldeans, Nebuchadnezzar showed Jeremiah great kindness (39:11–12). Jeremiah finally was taken to Egypt, where he probably died (43:6–7). See pp. 139, 202–03, 209.

JEREMIAH, BOOK OF. A book of prophetic sermons and autobiographical and historical material written by the prophet Jeremiah. See pp. 202–04.

JERICHO (JER-uh-ko; place of fragrance or moon-city). A city near the Dead Sea about 825 feet below sea level and 6 miles west of the Jordan River. Jericho has been examined by archaeologists and is regarded as the oldest known city in the world.

Joshua conquered Jericho and later gave it to the tribe of Benjamin (Jsh 2–6; 18:21). Later, during Ahab's reign, Hiel rebuilt the city (1Ki 16:34). Jericho is frequently mentioned in the Scriptures (2Ki 2:1–22; 25:5; Ezk 2:34; Mt 20:29; Mk 10:46; Lk 10:30). See pp. 80–82, 84–85.

JEROBOAM (jer-o-BO-ahm; he pleads people's cause). 1. Jeroboam I, the first king of Israel after the division of the kingdom. As a young man, Jeroboam was industrious and able. Consequently, Solomon, who was busy in building operations in Jerusalem, made Jeroboam superintendent over all the forced labor assigned to the house of Joseph (1Ki 11:27–28). One day on the road outside Jerusalem, Jeroboam met the prophet Ahijah, who told him the kingdom would be divided, and Jeroboam would become king of 10 of the tribes (1Ki 11:29–40).

When Solomon heard this news, he wanted to kill Jeroboam, and so Jeroboam fled to Egypt (1Ki 11:40). After Solomon's death, Jeroboam did become king of the 10 northern tribes. He made Shechem his capital and Tirzah the place where he lived (1Ki 12:1–25). Jeroboam was afraid the people would be won back to the house of David and kill him if they went to Jerusalem to worship, so he built worship centers containing golden calves in Bethel and Dan (1Ki 12:25–33). The prophet Ahijah foretold Jeroboam's downfall (1Ki 13). See pp. 123, 125.

2. Jeroboam II, the son and successor of Jehoash and the thirteenth king of Israel. Jeroboam was successful in war with Syria and other nations and extended Israel's territory. Amos prophesied during Jeroboam's reign against the moral corruption and idolatry that continued under Jeroboam. Hosea also began his prophetic work during Jeroboam's lifetime. Excavations at Samaria show the splendor of that time (2Ki 14:23–29). See pp. 125, 233, 238.

JERUSALEM (ji-ROO-sah-lem). The capital of the united kingdom of Israel and Judah and of Judea. According to the Tel el Amarna letters it was originally called

U-ru-sa-lim, which means city of peace. It sits on a 2,550-foot-high rocky plateau 33 miles east of the Mediterranean Sea and 14 miles west of the Dead Sea.

Jerusalem's water is supplied by the Gihon Spring in the Kidron Valley and by En-rogel, a spring near the join of the Kidron and Hinnom valleys. There are reservoirs within the city. During Hezekiah's reign a tunnel was cut in the rock to conduct water from the Gihon to the upper pool of Siloam (2Ch 32:30).

The Jerusalem David took from the Jebusites consisted of only the southeast corner of present-day Jerusalem. Located on a hill south of Ophel, it was 1,250 feet long and 400 feet wide (1Ch 11:4–8). Solomon extended its walls to protect his palaces and temple (1Ki 3:1; 9:15). Manasseh also extended the wall of Jerusalem (2Ch 33:14). After it had been broken down by Nebuchadnezzar, Nehemiah rebuilt the wall out of old material, extending it on the north. Herod built or extended the walls as they were in the time of Christ. The modern walls of the city were built by Suleiman the Magnificent in AD 1542. The temple stood on Mount Zion.

In its history Jerusalem has been known by many different names. It is considered the Salem of Melchizedek (Gn 14:18). It is also called Salem (Ps 76:2), Jebus (Jgs 19:10–11), the city of David (1Ki 8:1; 2Ki 14:20; 2Ch 25:28), Zion (Ps 48:2), the city of God (Ps 46:4), the city of the great King (Mt 5:35), and the holy city (Ne 11:1). See pp. 113, 139, 271–72, 303, 325, 353, 368.

JERUSALEM, THE NEW. The city of God. It is described as coming down from heaven and as the mother of believers (Gal 4:26; Rv 21:2, 10). Cf. Heb 11:8–10; 12:22–24. See pp. 444–45.

JESHUA (JESH-yoo-ah; Lord is salvation) 1. *See* JOSHUA.

2. The head of the ninth division of priests (1Ch 24:11; Ezr 2:36; Ne 7:39).

JESHURUN (JESH-yoo-run; upright). A poetical name for Israel that represents Israel as a righteous people (Dt 32:15; 33:5, 26; Is 44:2).

JESSE (JES-ee). The son of Obed and grandson of Ruth (Ru 4:17, 22; Mt 1:5). David was the youngest of eight sons (1Sm 16:11–13; 17:12). See pp. 97, 122.

JESUS CHRIST (JEE-zuhs KRIGHST). The biblical names and titles for Jesus tell us who He is and what He does for humanity. Some of the most important of His names and titles are:

1. *Jesus*. The word *Jesus* is Greek for the Hebrew name Joshua, which means "savior." An angel gave the name to Joseph to use for Mary's firstborn Son (Mt 1:21, 25; Lk 1:31), called "Jesus of Nazareth" because Jesus was a common name at the time (e.g., Ac 13:6). See pp. xvi, 5.

2. *Christ*. Christ is Greek for the Hebrew name *Mashiah*, which means "anointed one." Jesus is fully anointed with the Spirit of God (Jn 3:34). Thus, He is the promised Mashiah or Messiah (Mt 16:13–23; Lk 2:25–26; Jn 1:35–41). This name/title functions as a confession. See p. 432. *See also* MESSIAH.

3. *Logos*. Jesus is referred to as Logos, which in Greek means "word" (Jn 1:1–14; 1Jn 1:1; Rv 19:13). This name is used in the New Testament to identify Jesus as the eternal Second Person of the Trinity. As the Logos, Jesus is the living Word of God who creates and preserves life (Ps 147:15–18; Mt 8:24–27; 9:1–8; Jn 1:3; Col 1:15–20). The Spirit of the eternal Word also inspired the prophets of old (1Pt 1:10–11).

4. *Son of God*. This title is applied to Jesus in a unique sense (Mt 11:27;

16:16; 21:33–41; Jn 1:14, 18; 3:16–18). It says that Jesus as the Son is equal to God the Father (Jn 10:30; 12:45; 14:8–11; 17). He is the Second Person of the Trinity eternally born of God the Father (Jn 1:18; Rm 8:3). He has the same characteristics, works, and honor as God the Father (Mt 9:18; Jn 5:17, 21, 23, 25; 21:17; Col 1:15–20). See pp. 281, 320, 339, 436.

5. *Son of Man*. Jesus used this title to emphasize His humanity, especially in connection with His ministry (Lk 9:58; 19:10), power (Mt 9:6; 12:8), death (Mk 14:21; Lk 22:48; Jn 3:14), resurrection (Mt 17:9; Mk 9:9), ascension (Jn 6:62), and second coming and judgment (Mt 25:31). As the new Adam, Jesus brought into existence the new humanity (Rm 5:12–21; 1Co 15:22; Php 2:5–11). As man, He shared in the flesh and blood of man (Heb 2:14). Jesus is God and man in one person (Jn 1:14; Col 2:9; 1Tm 2:5). See pp. 219, 239, 324, 443.

6. *Servant of God*. Jesus is the Servant of God because He did what God willed, especially saving humanity (Mt 12:18; Mk 14:32–42; Jn 1:29; 4:34; 5:30). For this reason He is the ultimate fulfillment of Isaiah 53 (Mk 8:31; 10:33; Rm 4:25). See pp. 191, 261, 312.

7. *Savior*. Jesus is the promised Savior (Lk 2:11). Through His life, death, resurrection, and preaching He saves those who believe in Him from sin, wrath, and death (Mt 1:21; Lk 19:10; Jn 4:42; Ac 4:12; 11:14; 16:31; Rm 5:9–10; 10:9–10; 2Tm 1:10). See pp. 4, 258, 315, 445, 449.

8. *Mediator*. Jesus is the Mediator between God and people (Gal 3:19; 1Tm 2:5; Heb 8:6; 9:15; 12:24). As Prophet, Priest, and King, Jesus brings people to God. (See also offices of Prophet, Priest, and King below.)

9. *Lamb of God*. Jesus is the Lamb of God sacrificed for the sins of the world (Jn 1:29, 36; Ac 8:32; 1Co 5:7; 1Pt 1:19; Heb 7:27). Cf. Ex 12; Is 53:7. See pp. 28, 63, 174, 449.

The work of Jesus Christ may be described in terms of the three offices He fills. As *Prophet*, Jesus announces the kingdom of God through His words and actions. He reveals to people God's anger over sin and God's love in Him. Christ carries on His prophetic work today through the preachers of the Church. As *Priest*, Christ fulfilled all righteousness and paid for the sins of all people by offering up to God the sacrifice of His own life, death, and resurrection in their place (Rm 4:25; 2Co 5:19; Heb 7). Now He continues to intercede for humanity before God the Father (Rm 8:34; 1Jn 2:1). As *King*, Christ rules the whole world through His power (Mt 28:18; Eph 1:22; Heb 1:3), the Church on earth through His grace (Mt 16:18–19; 28:19–20; Mk 16:15; Rm 1:16–17; 14:17–18), and the Church in heaven through His glory (Mt 25:34; Jn 17:24; 2Tm 4:18; Rv 5:12–13; 21:4).

Further, the work of Jesus Christ may be described in terms of two states of being. During His state of *humiliation*, which began at the moment of the incarnation and continued through His death, Jesus in His human nature did not fully and always use all of the divine characteristics given to Him through His divine nature (Php 2:6–8). Beginning with His being made alive in the tomb and His descent into hell, Jesus began to fully and constantly use all His divine characteristics (Php 2:9–11; Eph 4:8). This is called Christ's state of *exaltation*.

JETHRO (JETH-ro; excellence). A priest and prince of Midian and the father-in-law of Moses. After Moses fled from Egypt, he came to Midian, where he met Jethro. Jethro gave Moses his daughter Zipporah in marriage. Later, after Moses had led the Israelites out of Egypt and they were camping in the wilderness, Jethro came to Moses and gave him advice on how to govern the people (Ex 18).

Jethro was probably a surname or title; Reuel or Raguel was his personal name (Ex 2:18; Nu 10:29). See pp. 89–90, 149.

JEW (JYOO). Originally someone who belonged to the tribe or kingdom of Judah as opposed to those of the Northern Kingdom (2Ki 15:36; 16:6). After the Babylonian captivity, since the majority of the Israelites returning were from Judah, the meaning of the name Jew was extended. It was applied to anyone of the Hebrew race who returned from captivity.

Hebrew denotes those who descended from Abraham; *Israel* denotes those who descended from Jacob; and *Jew* denotes those who descended from the tribe or kingdom of Judah. The word *Jew* is not applied to Gentile converts as *Israel* is. See p. 148. *See also* HEBREWS; ISRAEL.

JEZEBEL (JEZ-uh-buhl; unmarried or unexalted). Ahab's wicked wife (1Ki 16:31). Jezebel's father was Ethbaal, the king of Tyre and Sidon and a priest of Astarte.

Jezebel worshiped the gods of her father. Ahab built altars to Baal in Samaria to please Jezebel, and 450 prophets of Baal and Astarte were invited to eat at her table (1Ki 16:31–32; 18:19). Jezebel killed the prophets of the Lord and opposed Elijah (1Ki 18:13; 19:1–2). When Ahab coveted Naboth's vineyard, Jezebel planned and carried out a way to have Naboth put to death so that Ahab could take over (1Ki 21).

Because of these murders and other wicked acts, Elijah prophesied that Jezebel would die and the dogs would eat her by the wall of Jezreel (1Ki 21:23). Eleven years after Ahab's death, Jehu killed Jezebel, and Elijah's prophecy was fulfilled (2Ki 9:7, 30–37).

JEZREEL (JEZ-ri-el; God sows). A city of Issachar about five miles north of Jerusalem (Jsh 19:18; 1Sm 29:1). The kings of Israel had a palace there (2Sm 2:9; 1Ki 18:45–46; 21:1). Naboth's vineyard was nearby.

JEZREEL, VALLEY OF. A plain 20 miles long and 14 miles wide between the ridges of Gilboa and Moreh (Jsh 17:16; Jgs 6:33; Hos 1:5).

JOAB (JO-ab; Lord is father). The son of David's half-sister Zeruiah and the brother of Asahel and Abishai (2Sm 2:18). Joab killed Abner out of vengeance for the death of his brother Asahel, whom Abner had killed at the battle of Gibeon (2Sm 3:22–39). David made Joab commander-in-chief of the armies of all Israel as a reward for his part in the attack on Jebus (1Ch 11:4–9). Under Joab's leadership, Israel defeated Syria, Edom, and Ammon (2Sm 10; 12:26–31).

Joab arranged Uriah the Hittite's death according to David's orders (2Sm 11). He killed Absalom and Amasa (2Sm 18:9–15; 20:4–13). When Adonijah tried to take the throne, Joab sided with him against David (1Ki 1). On his deathbed, David said he wanted Joab brought to justice for the unjust murders of Abner and Amasa. Solomon, carrying out this wish, had Joab put to death (1Ki 2:28–34).

JOASH (JO-ash; Lord has given). 1. The son of Ahaziah and the eighth king of Judah (2Ki 11:2). When Joash was a baby, his father was murdered. Joash was saved from the same fate by his Aunt Jehosheba, the wife of the high priest Jehoiada: Jehosheba hid Joash in the temple for six years. Then through Jehoiada's efforts, Athaliah was put to death, and Joash was rightfully crowned king.

Under the guidance of Jehoiada, Joash restored worship of the Lord. After

Jehoiada's death, however, Joash turned his back on the Lord and led his people into idolatry. When Zechariah, Jehoiada's son, denounced Joash for his idolatry, Joash had him put to death. Joash reigned about 37 years. He was killed by his servants (2Ki 11–12; 2Ch 24). See pp. 125, 142.

2. The son of Jehoahaz and the thirteenth king of Israel. Joash followed in the sins of Jeroboam by continuing the worship of the calves at Bethel and Dan. He respected Elisha, however, and went to see him when the prophet was dying. Elisha told Joash to strike the ground with some arrows. The number of times Joash struck the ground symbolized the victories he would win over the Syrians, the Moabites, and Amaziah of Judah.

Joash reigned about 16 years. He died in peace, and his son, Jeroboam II, took the throne (2Ki 13–14; 2Ch 25:17–28). See pp. 125, 136.

JOB, BOOK OF. A book belonging to the Wisdom Literature of the Old Testament. It is a great literary masterpiece, containing dramatic, lyric, and epic poetry.

The book, named after its chief character, Job, gives an account of Job's suffering and the reasons for it. It asks the questions: How is the suffering of the righteous compatible with a just God? Is human conduct justly rewarded or punished on earth? Job concludes that as he knows God, so God knows him; that his redeemer lives and he shall see God; and that though God's rule is mysterious, He rules for best. See pp. 160–63.

JOBAB (JO-bab). A king who joined with Jabin and Hazor to fight Joshua (Jsh 11:1).

JOCHEBED (JOK-i-bed; the Lord is glory). The mother of Moses and Aaron (Ex 6:20; Nu 26:59).

JOEL (JO-el; the Lord is God). The son of Pethuel and author of the second book of the Minor Prophets (Jl 1:1). Little is known about Joel outside of his prophecy. See pp. 88, 230.

JOEL, BOOK OF. The second book of the Minor Prophets as they appear in the Old Testament. It was written by the prophet Joel.

The book opens with a description of a plague of locusts, which Joel views as a punishment for sin. Joel urges the people to repent of their sins and has a vision of Judgment Day. He also prophesies of the day when God would pour out His Spirit on all flesh (Jl 2:28–32). Peter quotes this prophecy in his Pentecost sermon (Ac 2:16–21). See pp. 230–31.

JOHANAN (jo-HAY-nuhn; the Lord is merciful). A Jewish chief who warned Gedaliah, the governor of Judah, of a plot to murder him (2Ki 25:23; Jer 40:8–41:16). Later Johanan took Jeremiah and some other countrymen to Egypt (Jer 40–43).

JOHN (JON; the Lord has been gracious). 1. The father of the apostle Peter (Jn 1:42; 21:15–17).

2. John the Baptist, the forerunner of Jesus. John was the son of Elizabeth and Zechariah, the priest, both of whom were descendants of Aaron (Lk 1:5–25, 56–80). Following the pattern of Elijah, John lived as a Nazirite in the desert (Mt 11:12–14; 17:11–12; Lk 1:17). He began his ministry in the fifteenth year of Tiberius Caesar in the region around the Jordan (Lk 3:1–3). John preached the baptism of repentance and the coming of the kingdom of heaven (Mt 3:1–12; Lk 3:4–14). He baptized Jesus in the Jordan River and witnessed to Him as the promised Messiah (Mt 3:13–17; Mk 1:9–10; Lk 3:21; Jn 1:24–42). See pp. 62, 130.

John rebuked Herod for living in sin with Herodias, Herod's sister-in-law. This made Herod angry, so he put John in jail (Mk 6:17–20). Because of what John had said to Herod, Herodias also had a grudge against John and wanted to kill him. She told her daughter, who had pleased Herod with her dancing, to ask for the head of John the Baptist on a platter. Her daughter did this, and Herod gave the order to behead John (Mt 14:6–12; Mk 6:21–28).

Jesus highly praised John (Mt 11:7–14; Lk 7:24–28).

3. John the apostle, a son of Zebedee and Salome and the brother of James (Mt 4:21; 27:56; Mk 15:40; Ac 12:1–2). John was from Galilee, probably Bethsaida, and was a fisherman by trade (Mk 1:19–20; Lk 5:10; Jn 1:44). John the Baptist introduced John the apostle to Jesus with the words: "Behold, the Lamb of God!" (Jn 1:35–36). John followed Jesus and was called by Him to be an apostle (Jn 1:43; 2:2, 12, 23; 4:5). Jesus named John and his brother James *Boanerges*, which means "Sons of Thunder" (Mk 3:17).

John was among the three whom Jesus chose to be with Him at the raising of Jairus's daughter, at His transfiguration, and at Gethsemane (Mt 17:1; 26:37; Mk 5:37; 9:2; Lk 8:51; 9:28).

One time when Jesus was rejected in a Samaritan village, John and James asked if Jesus wanted them to call down fire from heaven to burn the village. Jesus rebuked them (Lk 9:54). Another time John, James, and their mother asked Jesus for places of honor in His future kingdom (Mt 20:20–21; Mk 10:35–45). John helped prepare the Passover for Jesus and His disciples on the night before Jesus' crucifixion (Lk 22:8).

John has been identified as the beloved disciple. At the Last Supper he sat next to Jesus (Jn 13:23). Later, when Jesus was taken prisoner, John followed the soldiers and was able to go along with Jesus into the court of the high priest (Jn 18:15–16). At the cross John stood near Mary, Jesus' mother. When Jesus asked John to look after Mary, John accepted the trust (Jn 19:26–27).

John was the first disciple to believe that Jesus had risen from the dead (Jn 20:1–10). With the other disciples, he saw the risen Christ on the night of His resurrection and again a week later (Lk 24:33–43; Jn 20:19–30). After a night of fishing with the disciples on the Sea of Galilee, John was the first to recognize Jesus as He stood on the beach (Jn 21:1–7). After Jesus' ascension John waited for some time in the Upper Room in Jerusalem with the other apostles, and after Pentecost he became a missionary with Peter (Ac 1:13; 3:1–4:22; 8:14–17; Gal 2:9).

John lived to an old age. He wrote the fourth Gospel, the three letters bearing his name, and the Book of Revelation. See pp. 287, 338, 437–38, 441.

JOHN, GOSPEL OF. It is generally believed that the apostle John, "the disciple whom Jesus loved," wrote this Gospel. The author of the book was an eyewitness of the events he describes. His stated purpose for writing it is to show that Jesus is the Christ, the Son of God, so that those believing this might have life in His name (Jn 20:30–31). With this in mind, John presents the acts and words of Jesus, revealing the unique person of Christ and His significance to the world.

John describes Jesus as the eternal Word (1:1–18), the Messiah (1:41–51; 4:25–26; 10:22–25; 17:3), the Son of Man (3:12–15; 5:22–27; 6:62; 12:27–36), and the Son of God (3:16; 5:17–31; 8:58; 10:29–39; 14:1). See pp. 338–40.

JOHN, FIRST LETTER OF. According to the Early Church Fathers, the apostle John wrote this letter near the end of the first century. He wrote it to warn against false teachers (Gnostics) and to strengthen his readers in their Christian loyalty. The keynote of the letter is faith and love. See pp. 437–38.

JOHN, SECOND LETTER OF. John wrote this letter to encourage his readers to walk in light and to warn them against error. The "elect lady" may refer to a woman or a church. See pp. 437–38.

JOHN, THIRD LETTER OF. This letter is addressed to Gaius and commends him for his Christian life and for his service to the evangelists John sent. In the letter John also censures Diotrephes for his bad conduct and praises Demetrius. See pp. 437–38.

JOKTAN (JOK-tuhn; small). A person who descended from Shem through Eber (Gn 10:25–30). He is the ancestor of 13 Arabian tribes.

JONAH (JO-nah; dove). A son of Amittai of Gath-hepher and a prophet of Israel. Jonah predicted the recovery of the land of Israel to its ancient borders through the efforts of Jeroboam II. He also preached to Nineveh (2Ki 14:23–25; Jnh 1:1). His prophecy is recorded in the Book of Jonah. See pp. 139, 144, 238–41.

JONAH, BOOK OF. The fifth book of the Minor Prophets. It is typological in character. Its purpose is to teach that God's grace and mercy is not limited to Israel but extends to all.

The Book of Jonah differs from the other prophetic books. They are mainly prophetic with a minimum of narrative; Jonah is the opposite. See pp. 238–41.

JONATHAN (JON-ah-thuhn; the Lord has given). The oldest son of King Saul (1Sm 13:16; 14:49; 1Ch 8:33). Jonathan was a great military commander. He successfully fought the Philistines (1Sm 13–14).

Jonathan is best known for his devotion to David. Although Jonathan was the rightful heir to the throne, he stripped himself of his royal robe, girdle, and sword and pledged his loyalty to David (1Sm 18:4; 20:42). Later, when Saul wished to kill David, Jonathan defended him from Saul's anger (1Sm 19:1–7; 20). Jonathan was killed with Saul in a battle with the Philistines at Mount Gilboa (1Sm 31:2–10; 2Sm 1:17–27). See pp. 102, 113.

JOPPA (JOP-ah; beauty). An ancient walled seaport about 34 miles northwest of Jerusalem. It was assigned to the tribe of Dan. Simon Peter did missionary work there (Ac 9:36–11:18). Joppa, which is mentioned in both the lists of Thutmose III and the Amarna Letters, is modern-day Joffa (Jsh 19:46; 2Ch 2:16; Ezr 3:7; Jnh 1:3). See p. 294.

JORAM (JO-ruhm; the Lord is high). 1. The son of Ahab and the ninth king of Israel. With the help of the kings of Judah and Edom, Joram defeated the Moabites (cf. "Jehoram" in 2Ki 3:1–27). He was also undoubtedly the king to whom Naaman came to be cured of his leprosy and who sent the Syrians home unharmed (2Ki 5; 6:8–23). Jehu killed Joram and threw his body into Naboth's vineyard (2Ki 9:14–26). See p. 125.

2. The son of Jehoshaphat and fifth king of Judah. Shortly after Joram became king, he killed all his brothers and some other princes of Israel. Joram married a daughter of Ahab who led him into idolatry. During his reign, Joram was harassed by the Edomites, the Philistines, and the Arabs (cf. "Jehoram" in 2Ki 8:16–24;

2Ch 21). See p. 125.

JOSEPH (JO-zuhf; he adds). 1. The son of Jacob and Rachel (Gn 30:22–24). Joseph was Jacob's favorite child (Gn 37:3–4). When Joseph was 17, his father sent him to the place where his brothers were looking after their flocks. Because his brothers were jealous of Joseph, they sold him into slavery to a caravan of merchants going to Egypt (Gn 37).

In Egypt, Joseph became the slave of Potiphar, the captain of Pharaoh's guard. Falsely accused by Potiphar's wife, Joseph was put into prison for years. In prison Joseph became friends with the jailer. God gave Joseph the ability to interpret the dreams of the chief baker and chief butler who were in prison with Joseph. Two years later, when Pharaoh had two prophetic dreams, the jailer remembered Joseph and told Pharaoh about him. After Joseph correctly interpreted the dream, Pharaoh made him a high officer in the kingdom (Gn 39–41).

When famine struck the land and Joseph's brothers came to Egypt for food, Joseph saved them from starving (Gn 42–45). Joseph arranged for his family to come to Egypt and settled them in Goshen (Gn 47). Joseph died at age 110. When the people of Israel left Egypt, they took Joseph's bones with them and buried them at Shechem (Jsh 24:32). See pp. 16, 21, 132.

2. The husband of Mary, Jesus' mother (Mt 1:16; Lk 3:23). Joseph was a carpenter who lived in Nazareth (Mt 13:55). When he found out that Mary was expecting a child, Joseph was going to put her away without public exposure. But when an angel assured Joseph that the child Mary was carrying was of the Holy Spirit, Joseph took her for his wife (Mt 1:18–25). Joseph took Mary with him when he went to Bethlehem to be taxed. There Jesus was born (Lk 2:4–6).

Forty days after Jesus' birth, Joseph and Mary presented Jesus in the temple (Lk 2:22–40). When an angel warned Joseph in a dream that Herod was going to kill baby Jesus, Joseph fled with Mary and Jesus to Egypt (Mt 2:13–18). After Herod had died and the danger was past, they returned to Nazareth (Mt 2:19–23). When Jesus was 12 years old, Joseph and Mary took Him to Jerusalem (Lk 2:41–52). See pp. 306–07.

3. Joseph of Arimathea, a member of the Sanhedrin and a secret disciple of Jesus. Jesus was buried in Joseph's new tomb (Mt 27:57–60; Mk 15:42–46; Lk 23:50–53).

4. A "brother of the Lord" (Mt 13:55; 27:56). He is also called Joses (Mk 6:3; 15:40, 47).

5. The personal name of Barnabas (Ac 4:36).

JOSES (JO-seez; Gk for Joseph). 1. *See* JOSEPH 4.

2. *See* JOSEPH 5.

JOSHAPHAT (JOSH-ah-fat; the Lord has judged). A priest who blew the trumpet before the ark when it was brought to Jerusalem (1Ch 15:24). See p. 125.

JOSHUA (JOSH-yoo-ah; the Lord is salvation. Later Jeshua, Jesus). 1. The helper and successor of Moses. Joshua, an Ephraimite, was the son of Nun (Ex 33:11; Nu 13:8, 16; 1Ch 7:27). Joshua commanded the Israelites in their attack against the Amalekites (Ex 17:8–16). As Moses' attendant, he went part of the way up Mount Sinai with Moses (Ex 24:13; 32:17). Joshua was also in charge of the tabernacle (Ex 33:7–11).

As a leader of Ephraim, Joshua was among the spies sent to report on the land of Canaan. Of the 12 spies sent, only he and Caleb urged the people to go and take the land (Nu 13; 14:7–10). Moses appointed Joshua as his successor (Dt 31; Jsh 1). On the death of Moses, Joshua made plans for crossing the Jordan.

After entering Canaan, Joshua conquered the land by leading the Israelites into a number of battles. Then he supervised the allotment of the conquered territory as it was divided among the tribes (Joshua). Joshua asked for and obtained for himself the town of Timnath-serah (Jsh 19:50). He died at 110 years of age and was buried in Timnath-serah (Jsh 24:29). See pp. 59, 74–75.

JOSHUA, BOOK OF. The first book in the Hebrew division of the Old Testament known as the Former Prophets. In the English canon it is the first of the historical books.

The purpose of the book is to teach God's will for Israel and to show how He gave His people the land He had promised them. See pp. 74–76.

JOSIAH (jo-SIGH-ah; the Lord supports). The son of Amon and Jedidah and the sixteenth king of Judah. Josiah came to the throne of Judah when he was eight years old and reigned for 31 years (2Ki 22:1). In the eighth year of his reign he began to seek the God of David, and four years later he set about to suppress idolatry in Judah and Israel (2Ch 34:3).

In his eighteenth year of reign he decided to repair the temple. While engaged in this activity, workmen found the Book of the Law and handed it over to Shaphan, the scribe, who read it to the king. Josiah gathered together "all the elders of Judah and Jerusalem. . . . the inhabitants of Jerusalem and the priests and the Levites, all the people both great and small. And he read in their hearing all the words of the Book of the Covenant that had been found in the house of the Lord" (2Ch 34:29–30). This reading of the Law stimulated worship reforms anew.

In 609 BC Josiah's leadership was ended when Pharaoh Neco defeated and killed him in battle at Megiddo (2Ki 22–23; 2Ch 34–35). See pp. 124–25, 142, 202, 249.

JOTBATHAH (JOT-bah-thah; pleasantness). One of the places Israel set up camp. It may have been near Ezion-geber (Nu 33:33–34; Dt 10:7).

JOTHAM (JO-thuhm; Lord is upright). 1. The son of Gideon. When Shechem made Abimelech king, Jotham told the parable of the trees and bramble (Jgs 9). See p. 189.

2. The eleventh king of Judah. He began reigning as a regent of his father, King Uzziah, while Uzziah was a leper. Later he was the sole king. Jotham is described as good because he followed the Lord. He fortified Jerusalem, built fortresses in Judah, and fought successfully against the Ammonites (2Ki 15:32–38; 2Ch 27).

Jotham lived during the time of Isaiah, Hosea, and Micah (Is 1:1; Hos 1:1; Mi 1:1). He was an ancestor of Jesus (Mt 1:9). See p. 242.

JOURNEY. *See* MEASURES 1h.

JUBAL (JYOO-buhl). A son of Lamech and perhaps the inventor of musical instruments (Gn 4:19–21).

JUBILEE (JYOO-buh-lee; blast of trumpets). Every fiftieth year in Israel was to be celebrated as a year of jubilee. This year was announced by a blast on the trumpet.

Three things characterized this year: (1) The land rested for the year. (2) Property that people had to sell because of poverty was to be returned to them. (3) All Israelite slaves were to be set free (Lv 25:8–55; 27:16–25; cf. Ezk 46:17). See p. 99.

JUDAH (JYOO-dah; praise). 1. The fourth son of Jacob and Leah (Gn 29:35). When Joseph's brothers were planning to kill Joseph, Judah suggested they sell him to the Ishmaelites instead (Gn 37:26–27). Judah married a Canaanite woman and had three sons with her. After his two older sons and his wife had died, Judah had twin sons by his daughter-in-law Tamar (Gn 38).

Judah became a leader of his family (Gn 43:3–10; 44:16–34). Jacob bestowed the blessing of the birthright on Judah. This blessing is usually understood as a messianic prophecy (Gn 49:9–10). See p. 17.

2. The tribe that descended from Judah. It occupied the greater part of southern Israel (Jsh 15:20–63). David and Solomon were two kings of Israel that came from the tribe of Judah. Jesus also came from the tribe of Judah through Boaz, Jesse, and David (Lk 3:23–32).

3. The kingdom of Judah, which began when the 10 northern tribes withdrew from Rehoboam around 912 BC and lasted until 587 BC when Jerusalem fell. In 538 BC, Cyrus permitted the Jews to return to their homeland (1Ki 12–22; 2Ki; 2Ch 11–36; Ezr; Ne).

JUDAS (JYOO-dahs). 1. *See* JUDAH 1.

2. Judas Iscariot, the disciple who betrayed Jesus (Mt 10:4; Lk 6:16). Iscariot is thought to mean man of Kerioth. Judas was the treasurer for Jesus and the apostles (Jn 12:4–6; 13:29). He became greedy, however, and took money from the group moneybag for himself (Jn 12:3–8). Judas betrayed Jesus for 30 pieces of silver but then regretted his deed and hanged himself (Mt 26:47–49; 27:3–5; Ac 1:17–18). See p. 287.

3. The brother of Jesus (Mt 13:55; Mk 6:3). See pp. 439–40. *See also* JUDE, LETTER OF.

4. One of the 12 apostles. He was also apparently referred to as Thaddaeus since this name appears in lists in the place that corresponds to Judas (Mt 10:3; Mk 3:18). Judas was the son or perhaps brother of James (Lk 6:16).

5. A man in Damascus to whom Paul went after his conversion (Ac 9:11).

JUDE (JYOOD). *See* JUDAS 3; 4.

JUDE, LETTER OF. The author of this letter gives his name as Jude, the brother of James, and calls himself a servant of Jesus Christ. He is commonly identified with Judas, the brother of Jesus. See pp. 439–40.

JUDEA (jyoo-DEE-ah). The term used in Ezr 9:9 for the province to which the tribes of Judah and Benjamin returned. It is usually called Judah (Ezr 5:8; Ne 2:7).

At the time of Christ, Judea was the southern division of the three regions into which the Roman province of Israel was divided, the other two being Galilee and Samaria. Judea was about 55 miles long and wide. It was located east of the Jordan River and Dead Sea, from Beersheba in the south to 10 miles north of the Dead Sea in the north. See pp. 271–72, 275–76, 306, 353.

JUDGES. The governors, leaders, and deliverers of the Israelites between the time of Joshua and Saul. They included Othniel, Ehud, Shamgar, Deborah, Barak, Gideon, Abimelech, Tola, Jair, Jephthah, Ibzan, Elon, Abdon, and Samson. The high priest

Eli and the prophet Samuel also functioned as judges. The activity of the judges is described in the Book of Judges. See pp. 86, 91.

JUDGES, BOOK OF. A historical book in the Old Testament that is placed among the Former Prophets, following the Book of Joshua. Taking its name from the title of the people who ruled Israel from the death of Joshua to the time of Samuel, the Book of Judges tells the story of the history of Israel during that period.

The book covers a period of about 300 years. Since more than one judge may have ruled in different areas at the same time, it is difficult to arrive at an exact chronology for the book. See pp. 86–88.

JUDGMENT. In the Old Testament, the word *judgment* occasionally refers to the administration of justice (2Sm 15:4; 1Ki 3). It usually refers, however, to keeping people in a right relation to the covenant (Is 41:1; 58:2). The prophets describe God as bringing judgment upon a disobedient people. The purpose of God's judgment is to purify, not destroy, His people. God's judgment preserves a faithful remnant (cf. Is 6:13).

God's judgments point to the final judgment, the Day of the Lord, the day when His judgment will come upon all who are unjust and disobedient. On that day God will vindicate His divine rule (Is 25; Zec 14).

In the New Testament, the word *judgment* sometimes refers to the administration of law (Jn 18:31; Ac 23:3). Usually it refers to the judgment of God and includes the salvation of believers (Lk 18:1–8; Rm 1:18–32; 1Co 11:29–32; 2Th 1:5–10). God's judgment culminates in the final judgment (Mt 11:20–24; 25:31–46; Jn 16:11; 1Th 4:13–18). It belongs to God and is administered by Christ (Mt 18:35; Rm 14:10). God's judgment is salvation to believers, condemnation to unbelievers (Mt 25:31–46). God's judgment is based on whether an individual keeps the Law perfectly (Mt 25). But since the Law has been fulfilled only by Christ, a person's relationship to Him is the decisive factor (Mt 10:32–33; Rm 8:1–17; Gal 5:13–25).

JUDGMENT HALL. *See* PRAETORIUM.

JUDITH (JYOO-dith; praised Jewess). Esau's wife (Gn 26:34).

JULIUS (JYOOL-yuhs; soft-haired). A Roman centurion of the Augustan band who conducted Paul and other prisoners to Rome (Ac 27).

JUSTIFICATION. The gracious act of God by which He pronounces all people to be not guilty of their sin (2Co 5:19). The basis for His acquittal is that Jesus Christ fulfilled the Law in humanity's place and paid the penalty for all people's sin (Rm 5:12–20). An individual gains the benefits of Christ's substitutionary life and death through the instrument of faith, which God gives him or her by the Holy Spirit working through the Gospel (Rm 1:16; 3:21–25; 5:1; Eph 2:8–9). See p. 414. *See also* RECONCILIATION.

JUTTAH (JUT-ah; extend). A town in Judah about 5 1/2 miles southwest of Hebron. It was assigned to the priests (Jsh 15:55; 21:16). It may be the same as the "town in Judah," where John the Baptist was born (Lk 1:39). Today it is known as Yuttah.

K

KAB. *See* MEASURES 2b.

KADESH (kay-DESH; consecrated). Known as En-mishpat in early times, Kadesh was in the desert about 70 miles south of Hebron (Gn 14:7). Hagar fled to the region around Kadesh (Gn 16:7, 14). Israel wandered in this area for 37 years, twice stopping to set up camp at Kadesh (Nu 13:25–26; Dt 1:46). Miriam died at Kadesh (Nu 20:1). There, rather than speaking to the rock as the Lord had told him to do, Moses struck it to bring forth water (Nu 20:2–13). This displeased the Lord. The waters were called Meribah, which means strife. Kadesh is often called Kadesh-barnea (Nu 32:8; Dt 2:14).

KADESH-BARNEA (KAY-desh-BAHR-ni-ah). *See* KADESH.

KARKOR (KAHR-kawr; soft level ground). The place east of the Jordan River where Gideon attacked Zebah and Zalmunna (Jgs 8:10).

KEDAR (KEE-dur; dark). 1. One of Ishmael's sons (Gn 25:13; 1Ch 1:29).

2. An Arabian tribe that descended from Kedar. The people of this tribe lived in black tents and had flocks and camels (Sg 1:5; Is 21:13–17; 42:11; 60:7; Jer 49:28–29).

KEDEMAH (KED-i-maa; eastward). Ishmael's son and the tribe that descended from him (Gn 25:15; 1Ch 1:31).

KEDESH (KEE-desh; sacred place). 1. A Canaanite city northwest of Lake Huleh that Joshua conquered during his northern campaign. Having captured the city, Joshua put its king to death (Jsh 12:22). Kedesh was given to the tribe of Naphtali and made a city of refuge (Jsh 19:37). Years later Tiglath-pileser captured it (2Ki 15:29). Also called Kedesh-naphtali, it was the home of Barak (Jgs 4:6).

2. A town in southern Judah, probably the same as Kadesh.

KEILAH (ki-IGH-lah). A city in the lowlands of Judah (Jsh 15:44). David delivered it from the Philistines (1Sm 23:7–13).

KENAZ (KEE-naz). A descendant of Esau and an ancestor of the Kenizzites (Gn 15:19; 36:15).

KENITES. A tribe of Midianites related to the Kenizzites (Gn 15:19). The Kenites had extraordinary skill in metal work. Moses' father-in-law was a Kenite (Jgs 1:16). Hobab the Kenite guided the Israelites on their march through the desert (Nu 10:29–32; Jgs 1:16; 4:11). The Kenites were on friendly terms with the Israelites. They settled in Wadi Arabah, near Hebron, in Naphtali, and in southern Judah (Nu 24:20–22; Jgs 1:16; 4:11; 1Sm 15:6; 27:10; 30:29).

KENIZZITES (KEE-niz-ights). Descendants of Kenaz (Gn 36:11). The Kenizzites were a tribe that lived in southern Canaan before Israel. It seems that they were conquered by and merged with the Edomites (Gn 15:19; Dt 2:12). Part of the tribe, however, may have merged with Judah. Caleb and Othniel were Kenizzites (Nu 32:12; Jsh 14:6; 15:17).

KERIOTH-HEZRON (KEE-ri-oth-HEZ-ron). A city in southern Judah (Jsh 15:25). Most likely Judas Iscariot came from there.

KETURAH (kuh-TYOO-rah; incense). Abraham's second wife. She was the mother of six sons, the ancestors of the eastern nations (Gn 25:1–6; 1Ch 1:32–33). See p. 89.

KEY. An Oriental key was made of a piece of wood. It had pegs to fit the corresponding holes in a wooden bolt (Jgs 3:25; Is 22:22). The key is a symbol of power and authority (Is 22:22; Lk 11:52; Rv 3:7).

The keys of the kingdom are power Christ gives to the Church through the apostles to open heaven by forgiving the sins of penitent Christians or to close heaven by retaining the sins of the impenitent (Mt 16:19; 18:18). See p. 433.

KID. A young goat used for sacrifice (Jgs 13:15–19). It was also a favorite food item (Gn 38:17; Lk 15:29).

KIDNEY. An internal organ that, along with the fat around it, was used for a burnt offering (Ex 29:13, 22; Lv 3:4–15). People regarded the kidney as the seat of emotion and desire (Jb 16:13).

KIDRON, BROOK. A valley and winter brook that begins northwest of Jerusalem. It then joins with the Valley of Hinnom and runs 20 miles to the Dead Sea. The Kidron was a burial ground and dumping place for destroyed idols and their altars (1Ki 15:13; 2Ki 23:6; 2Ch 29:16; 30:14). When David was being chased by Absalom, he fled across the Kidron (2Sm 15:23). Jesus crossed over it on His way to Gethsemane (Jn 18:1).

KING. The Lord was the King of Israel (Dt 33:1–5; 1Sm 8:7; 10:19; 12:12). Later, the Israelites wanted to be like other nations and have a human king. So God allowed them to have kings to rule over them; nevertheless, these kings were accountable to the Lord. They were subject to tribal politics, the moral law, and prophetic warnings (2Sm 12; 1Ki 12:16; 21:20–24).

Israel had kings to rule them from about 1020 to 587 BC, beginning with Saul and ending with Zedekiah. Their kings had scepters, crowns, thrones, and palaces (1Ki 2:19; 7:1–12; 2Ki 11:12; Ps 45:6). The kings' officers included such people as army officers, a captain of the bodyguard, a secretary, overseers, and counselors (1Sm 14:50; 2Sm 8:17; 15:12; 20:23–24; 1Ki 4:6). See pp. 114, 125.

KINGDOM OF GOD. This theological term refers to the fact that God is the Creator of the world and everything in it and rules over all things with unlimited power. He especially rules over His people as their Creator, Redeemer, and Sanctifier.

The development of this concept can be traced through the Old Testament. God is described as King over the whole earth (Nu 23:21; Dt 33:5; Ps 47:7). Specifically, His Lordship over Israel, His chosen nation, is seen (1Sm 12:12; Is 44:6). In turn, the Israelites hoped for the coming of the kingdom of God—they looked for a redeemer or Messiah who would establish the kingdom of God.

During the time of the kings, these rulers were God's representatives, responsible to Him and ruling in His stead. David, for instance, was a type of ideal king or Messiah, ruling the kingdom subject to God's will and law. None of the kings, however, not even David, were perfect representatives of God. Nor were the people of Israel perfect. Thus it became clear that the kingdom of Israel did not equal the kingdom of God.

The prophets pointed out that God's kingdom is really a spiritual kingdom that includes all nations (Is 2:4; 9; 11; 61; Jer 23:5–6; Zec 9:10). The New Testament pictures God's kingdom as the Holy Spirit in the hearts of His people. Numerous Bible passages speak of the rule of God (Mt 12:28; Mk 4:11; Lk 9:27, 11:20).

When John the Baptist said the kingdom of God was near, he was telling people that God was laying the foundation for His rule in human hearts through the Messiah. Jesus is that Messiah. He is the fulfiller of the Kingdom and the one who brings God's kingdom to people (Mt 12:28; Lk 9:27; 17:20–21). Jesus said, "The time is fulfilled, and the kingdom of God is at hand; repent and believe in the Gospel" (Mk 1:15). People enter the kingdom of God by repenting of their sins and believing in Jesus as their Savior (Jn 3:3–5; cf. "kingdom of heaven" in Mt 18:3–4). As members of the kingdom of God, the Holy Spirit works in them, and they become more and more Christlike (Mt 5–7; Lk 9:60–62).

The kingdom of God is, at times, spoken of as a future blessing and, at times, as a present reality (Mt 7:21; 8:11; Lk 16:16; 17:20). The Church proclaims the kingdom of God by witnessing to Christ. See pp. 447–48.

KINGS, FIRST AND SECOND BOOK OF. At first, these were one book, the last in the division known as the Former Prophets. They were divided into two, however, in the Septuagint. They describe the religious history of Israel during the period of the kings and show that the Lord carries out His threats and keeps the promises of "His holy covenant." See pp. 120–24.

KINGS OF JUDAH AND ISRAEL. These kings can be divided into three groups: the kings of the united kingdom of Israel; the kings of Judah, the Southern Kingdom; and the kings of Israel, the Northern Kingdom.

1. The kings of the united kingdom and the approximate dates they ruled:

Saul	1048–1009 BC
David	1009–970
Solomon	970–931

2. The kings of Judah and the approximate dates they ruled:

Rehoboam	931–914 BC
Abijam	914–911
Asa	911–870
Jehoshaphat	873–848
Jehoram	853–841
Ahaziah	841
Athaliah	841–835
Joash	835–796
Amaziah	796–767
Azariah (Uzziah)	792–740
Jotham	750–735
Ahaz	735–715
Hezekiah	715–686
Manasseh	696–642
Amon	642–640
Josiah	640–609
Jehoahaz	609
Jehoiakim	609–598

Jehoiachin	598–597
Zedekiah	597–587

3. The kings of Israel and the approximate dates they ruled:

Jeroboam I	931–910 BC
Nadab	910–909
Baasha	909–887
Elah	886–885
Zimri	885
Tibni	885–880
Omri	885–874
Ahab	874–853
Ahaziah	853–852
J(eh)oram	852–841
Jehu	841–814
Jehoahaz	814–796
Joash	798–782
Jeroboam II	793–753
Zechariah	753
Shallum	752
Menahem	752–742
Pekah	742–732
Pekahiah	742–740
Hoshea	732–722

See p. 125.

KIRIATH-ARBA (KIR-i-ath-AHR-bah; city of Arba). An ancient name for Hebron (Gn 23:2; Jsh 14:15; Jgs 1:10; Ne 11:25).

KIRIATH-JEARIM (KIR-i-ath-JEE-ah-rim; city of thickets). A Gibeonite town near Mount Jearim (Jsh 9:17). It was known by different names, e.g., Baalah (Jsh 15:9), Kiriath-baal (Jsh 18:14), and Baale-judah (2Sm 6:2). Kiriath-jearim was assigned to Judah first and then later to Benjamin (Jsh 15:60; 18:20). The ark of the covenant remained there for 20 years (1Sm 6:19–7:2).

KISH (KISH). A Benjaminite; the father of Saul (1Sm 9:3; 10:11; Ac 13:21). Kish was the son of Abiel; however, the Bible sometimes refers to him as the son of Ner (1Sm 9:1; 1Ch 8:33; 9:39). See p. 114.

KITTIM (KIGHT-tim). 1. The descendants of Javan. These people lived on Cyprus and other islands and on the coasts along the eastern part of the Mediterranean Sea (Gn 10:4; Nu 24:24; 1Ch 1:7; Dn 11:30). The name Kittim was applied to these places too (cf. Is 23:12; Jer 2:10).

2. Macedonia or the Macedonian people. *See also* MACEDONIA.

KNEADING BOWL. A shallow dish made of clay or wood that was used to knead dough (Ex 8:3).

KNEE, KNEEL. "To bend the knee" or kneel indicated an attitude of worship, prayer, awe, or subjection (Gn 41:43; 2Ch 6:13; Ps 95:6; Is 45:23; Mt 17:14; Php 2:10).

KNIFE. In ancient times knives were made of flint (Jsh 5:2–3). The Philistines used metal knives. These did not become common in Israel until the time of the later kings. Knives were used for killing, cutting, pruning, and shaving (1Ki 18:28; Is 18:5; Ezk 5:1).

KOHATH (KO-hath). One of Levi's sons (Gn 46:11; Ex 6:16–18; Nu 3:17). His descendants, the Kohathites, were one of the three divisions of Levites. Moses and Aaron were Kohathites (Ex 6:18–20).

KORAH (KO-rah; ice or baldness). A Levite who secretly plotted with Dathan and Abiram against Moses. As punishment for this, as well as to show that Moses was His appointed leader, God allowed the earth to open up and swallow Abiram and Dathan and their households and Korah and his servants. Korah's sons, however, were not destroyed (Nu 16). See p. 57.

KORAHITE (KO-ra-ight). Someone who descended from the Levite Korah. Heman and Samuel were both Korahites (1Ch 6:33–38). The Korahites became famous temple singers (1Ch 15:17; 16:41–42; titles of Ps 42; 44–49; 84–85; 87–88).

L

LABAN (LAY-buhn; white). Abraham's great-nephew and Rebekah's brother (Gn 24:29; 25:20). Laban lived at Haran (11:31–32; 24:4, 10). He allowed Rebekah to go with Abraham's servant to Canaan to become Isaac's wife (ch. 24). Later, Isaac and Rebekah's son Jacob worked for Laban for 20 years. As payment for this service, Jacob received cattle and also his wives, Leah and Rachel (chs. 29–31). See pp. 12, 19.

LABOR. The Bible describes labor as honorable (Ps 128:2; Pr 21:25; cf. 1Th 4:11). God's work of creation is called work (Gn 2:2). Jesus points to God's continued work in the world, that is, His providential care, to defend working on the Sabbath (Jn 5:17). Workers were protected by laws (Dt 24:14) and were a subject of Jesus' parables (Mt 20:1).

LACHISH (LAY-kish). A royal city of the Canaanites located at Tell ed-Duweir, 30 miles southwest of Jerusalem and 15 miles west of Hebron. It was one of the largest cities of ancient Judah. Under Joshua, the Israelites captured Lachish and killed its king (Jsh 10:3–35). Years later, shortly after the division of the kingdom, Rehoboam strengthened the defenses of Lachish (2Ch 11:9). Amaziah, king of Judah, fled there and was slain (2Ki 14:19). Around 701 BC, Sennacherib, the king of Assyria, captured Lachish (2Ki 18:14, 17). Nebuchadnezzar destroyed Lachish along with Jerusalem two times: once in 597 BC and then again in 587 BC (2Ki 24–25; Jer 34:7). When the exiles returned from captivity, they once again lived in Lachish (Ne 11:30). The city, however, never regained its former importance.

Archaeologists have found many important items at Lachish. One find, the Lachish Letters, are written in Hebrew and belong to Jeremiah's time.

LAISH (LAY-ish; lion). A city in the extreme north of Israel. The people of the tribe of Dan captured it and renamed it Dan (Jgs 18:7–29).

LAMB. A young sheep. Lamb's meat was used for food and sacrifices, particularly at Passover (Gn 22:7; Ex 12:3–5; 29:38–41; Lv 3:7; 2Sm 12:4). Lambs used for sacrifices had to be perfect, without blemish. They pointed to Christ, the Lamb of God, who takes away the sin of the world (Jn 1:29; Rv 5:6, 8). Christians, particularly children, are compared to lambs (Jn 21:15). See pp. 28, 37–38, 61, 63.

LAMENTATIONS. The English Bible places this book after the Book of Jeremiah, as it was written by Jeremiah also. In the Hebrew Scriptures it appears between Ruth and Ecclesiastes. The book laments the destruction of Jerusalem and the suffering of the people there. It acknowledges that God is just in allowing suffering to result from sinfulness (Lm 1:18, 22; 2:17; 3:33; 4:13, 22). The five chapters are really five poems, of which the first four are based on letters from the Hebrew alphabet. See pp. 209–10.

LAMP. A container holding liquid and a wick. Lamps were burned to give light (Ex 27:20; 2Ki 4:10). Lamps in the tabernacle and temple were made of gold (Ex 25:31–40; 37:17–24). They burned olive oil (Ex 27:20). In the Bible a lamp is also a symbol for God's Word (Ps 119:105), His guidance (Ps 18:28), and wise leaders (Jn 5:33–35). See pp. 23, 40, 170, 259, 430.

LANCE. A javelin or light spear (1Ki 18:28).

LANDMARK. An object, such as a stone or stake, that marked the boundary of an area of land. Landmarks were not to be removed (Dt 19:14; 27:17; Hos 5:10).

LANGUAGE. Words, spoken or written to convey ideas. Language is a gift of God, but the differences among languages were originally a result of sin (Gn 11:1–9). Many languages were spoken during Old Testament times. Sumerian, Akkadian, Egyptian, Phrygian, Phoenician, Canaanite, and Hittite are only a few. The chief languages spoken in Israel during New Testament times were Aramaic, Hebrew, Greek, and Latin (Jn 19:20).

LAODICEA (lay-ahd-i-SEE-ah). A wealthy city located in the Lycus Valley of Asia Minor. It was probably founded by Antiochus II and named by him for his wife (Col 2:1; 4:15; Rv 1:11; 3:14–22).

LAPPIDOTH (LAP-i-doth; torches). Deborah's husband (Jgs 4:4).

LAST DAY. *See* JUDGMENT; ESCHATOLOGY.

LAST TIMES. *See* ESCHATOLOGY.

LATIN (LAT-in). The language spoken by the Romans (Jn 19:20).

LAW. 1. God's will for His creation, revealed to people in His judgments, words, rules, and acts (Ex 20:1–17; 21:1; Dt 7:6–16; Ps 19; 119; Is 1:10). See p. 28.

2. The Torah, the first five books of the Old Testament (Mt 5:17; Lk 16:16).

3. The Old Testament (Jn 10:34; 12:34).

4. The Ten Commandments given to Moses (Ex 20:2–17; Dt 5:6–21; Jn 7:19). The commandments summarize God's requirements of people—what their relationship to God, to one another, and to the rest of creation should be (Lv; Dt).

Jesus showed respect and love for the Law. He pointed out its deeper meaning for people (Mt 5:17–48). Paul emphasized that the Law shows the sinfulness of people because they can never keep it perfectly. Moreover, the Law is unable to provide victory over sin (Rm 3–7; Gal). It does prepare one for the Gospel (Gal

3:24). *See also* APPEAL; JUDGMENT; RIGHTEOUSNESS.

The Law has three purposes or uses. It curbs sinful human behavior and preserves civil society (Gn 9:6; Rm 2:14–15; 1Tm 1:9). The Law also shows us our sin or acts as a mirror (Rm 3:20; 7:7). Finally, the Law guides and directs Christian behavior according to God's will (Ps 119:9, 105). See p. 336.

LAWYER. A professional interpreter of the Old Testament, often a scribe (Mt 22:35; Lk 10:25).

LAYING ON OF HANDS. An act symbolizing dedication or blessing. It was used to dedicate priests to their office and animals to the Lord (Lv 1:4; Nu 8:5–20). Through the laying on of hands, blessings of various kinds were given and people were set apart for special service (Gn 48:5–20; Mk 10:16; Lk 4:40; Ac 6:6; 13:3; 1Tm 4:14; 2Tm 1:6; Heb 6:2). See p. 412.

LAZARUS (LAZ-ah-ruhs; God has helped). 1. The brother of Mary and Martha. After Lazarus died, Jesus came to his town and brought him back to life (Jn 11–12:11). See pp. 293–5, 321, 340.

2. The name of the beggar in the parable Jesus told about a rich man and a beggar (Lk 16:19–31).

LEAH (LEE-ah; languid). Laban's older daughter. Through a trick of her father, Leah was passed off on Jacob as his bride (Gn 29–30; 49:31). See pp. 17, 19, 21.

LEAVEN (LEV-uhn). A substance used to make dough rise (Ex 12:15, 20; Mt 13:33). The Israelites removed leaven from their houses during Passover and did not use it in meal offerings (Lv 2:11). It was a symbol of corruption and moral influence, whether good or bad (Mt 13:33; 16:6, 12; 1Co 5:6–8). See pp. 38, 335, 447.

LEBANON (LEB-ah-nuhn; white). The snow-clad mountain ranges of Lebanon and Anti-Lebanon run 110 miles along the coast of Syria between the Taurus Mountains and the lower mountain ranges of Israel. Some peaks reach 10,000 feet. Mount Hermon is the southern spur of the Anti-Lebanon range. The Lebanons formed the northern boundary of Israel (Dt 1:7). They are known especially for their cedars (Jgs 9:15; 1Ki 5). See pp. 116, 147, 224.

LEGION. 1. The largest single unit in the Roman army (about 6,000 men).

2. A great number (Mt 26:53; Mk 5:9).

LEHI (LEE-high; jawbone). The place where Samson killed the Philistines with a donkey's jawbone (Jgs 15:9–19).

LEMUEL (LEM-yoo-uhl; belonging to God). The unidentified king who wrote Proverbs (Pr 31:1–9). He may have been Solomon. See p. 175.

LEPROSY (LEP-ro-see). A dreadful skin disease. Leprosy usually began with scabs that scarred the skin and made the hair around the affected area turn white. Often raw flesh appeared (Ex 4:6; Lv 13:10, 14–16, 24).

The leprosy referred to in the Bible probably included skin diseases other than what is commonly known as leprosy today (Lv 13:14). The leprosy of garments may have been mold or mildew (Lv 13:47–59; 14:33–37). Jesus healed lepers (Mt 8:2–4; Lk 17:11–19). See p. 51.

LETTER. *See* EPISTLE.

LEVI (LEE-vigh; joined). Jacob's third son by Leah (Gn 29:34). Born in Haran, Levi went with his family on the return to Canaan. He joined his brothers in the plot against Joseph (Gn 37). Levi had three sons: Gershon, Kohath, and Merari (Gn 46:11; 1Ch 6:16–48). He died in Egypt (Ex 6:16). See pp. 17, 149.

LEVIATHAN (li-VIGH-ah-thuhn). A sea monster (Ps 104:26). Poetical passages in the Bible describe it as somewhat similar to a crocodile or serpent (Jb 41; Is 27:1). Symbolically, Leviathan represents unrestrained power or evil (Jb 3:8; Ps 74:14; 104:26; Is 27:1). *See also* BEAST 4.

LEVIRATE MARRIAGE (LEV-uh-rayt MAR-ij). When an Israelite man died without any male children, the nearest male relative was supposed to marry the deceased's wife. The first son born of this union was then the heir of the woman's first husband (Dt 25:5–10). See p. 99.

LEVITES (LEE-vights). The descendants of Jacob's son Levi. Levi's three sons, Gershon, Kohath, and Merari, each became heads of a tribal family (Ex 6:16–25; Lv 25:32; Nu 35:2–8; Jsh 21:3). They became substitutes for the firstborn of their fellow Israelites in all duties pertaining to God (Nu 3:11–13; 8:16). Their duty was to preserve the law of the Lord and His worship (Lv 10:11; Dt 17:18; 31:9–13). Each family descending from the three sons had different duties assigned to them (Nu 3:5–39).

Aaron and Moses were Levites of the family of Kohath. The priests descended from this family through Aaron and his sons (Ex 28:1; Nu 18:7). They received no tribal territory but were assigned 48 cities and tithes (Lv 27: 30–33; Nu 18:20–24; 35; Dt 10:9). See pp. 43, 149.

LEVITICUS (li-VIT-i-kuhs). The third book of the Pentateuch. Leviticus was the manual for the priesthood. The Book of Leviticus stresses the holiness of God and the demand for holiness that God expects from His covenant people: "You shall be holy, for I the Lord your God am holy" (Lv 19:2). The book also spells out the means for attaining this holiness. The barrier between a holy God and an unholy people is removed by making amends for sin. This is symbolized by the vicarious sacrifice of animals by the priests. See pp. 43–45.

LEVY. A contribution to the Lord taken from the spoils of war on at least one particular occasion (Nu 31:25–31).

LIBERTY. Freedom, the opposite of slavery or bondage. Although the Israelites often were in bondage, they prized liberty. Those who had become slaves were to be freed in the year of jubilee (Lv 25:8–17).

Old Testament prophecies about liberty have a spiritual meaning, which is fulfilled in Christ (Is 61:1, Lk 4:18; Jn 8:31–36). Jesus frees people from Satan, sin, death, judgment, fear, and the Law (Jn 1:29; Ac 26:18; Rm 6–8; Gal 3). In matters that are neither commanded nor forbidden in God's Word, a Christian has freedom (Rm 14; 1Co 8). *See also* ADIAPHORA.

LIBYA (LIB-ee-ah). A country in North Africa west of Egypt (Ezk 30:5; Ac 2:10).

LIBYANS (LIB-i-uhns). People who live in Libya (Na 3:9).

LIEUTENANT (lu-TEN-uhnt). *See* SATRAP.

LIFE. 1. The Bible refers to the physical life of plants, animals, and humans as that quality which makes it possible for them to breathe, eat, grow, and reproduce (Gn 6:17; Ex 1:14; Jb 3:20–21; Ec 2:17).

2. The Bible also talks about the spiritual or eternal life of man. It is the gift of God that one has by grace through faith in Jesus Christ (Eph 2:8–10; Jn 17:3; 1Jn 5:12). The person who believes in Jesus as Savior never dies (Jn 11:25–26). See pp. 294, 320, 390, 414.

3. Christ is the source of all life (Jn 1:4; 11:25; Col 3:4). See pp. 294, 337, 339, 351, 422.

LIGHT, DARKNESS. God made natural light. It is a blessing that makes life as we know it possible. Light is often used to describe God, the highest good, from whom every good gift comes (Jas 1:17). Jesus is the Light of the world (Jn 1:4–9). God's Word and believers are spoken of as lights (Ps 119:105; Mt 5:14–16). Living a godly life is described in terms of putting on the armor of light or walking in the light (Rm 13:11–14; 1Jn 1:7).

Darkness, on the other hand, is symbolic of evil and all the results of the power of evil: spiritual blindness, evil deeds, death, hell, and suffering (Jb 10:21–22; Jl 2:2; Mt 22:13; Lk 22:53; Jn 3:19–20; 1Jn 1:6).

See pp. 93, 350, 430, 445.

LIME. The mountains of Palestine contain a large amount of limestone. The Israelites burned this limestone to make lime plaster and the like (Is 33:12; Am 2:1). See p. 22.

LINEAGE. *See* GENEALOGY.

LINEN. A thread or cloth made from flax. Linen was used to make clothing, priestly garments, the temple veil, choir robes, and burial cloths (Gn 41:42; Ex 28:5–42; 2Ch 3:14; 5:12; Mk 15:46). It was a symbol of wealth and purity (Lk 16:19; Rv 19:8, 14). See pp. 40, 150.

LITTER. A couch or chair used to carry people (Sg 3:7; Is 66:20).

LIVER. An internal organ of the body. The liver was used in sacrifice and for divination (Lv 3:4–15; Ezk 21:21). It was thought to be the center of life and feeling (Pr 7:23).

LO-AMMI (lo-AM-ee; not my people). The symbolic name of Hosea's third child (Hos 1:9).

LOANS. Something, especially money, that is lent. During Old Testament times the Hebrews were encouraged to make loans to their needy neighbors. If the Israelites became poverty-stricken, they could sell themselves as servants. After seven years, however, Israelite servants were to be released, and in the year of jubilee their debts were to be canceled (Lv 25:39–41; Dt 15:1–11; 23:19).

The Israelites were not allowed to charge interest to other Israelites but could charge it to strangers. Charging interest on a loan was looked down upon (Ne 5:7; 10; Ps 15:5; Ezk 22:12). See pp. 45, 99.

LOGOS (LAHG-ahs). *See* JESUS CHRIST.

LOIN. Part of the back of the body between the hips and false ribs. Before walking or working, a man usually tied loose clothing at his loins.

LOIS (LO-is; pleasing). Timothy's grandmother (2Tm 1:5).

LORD. Various Hebrew and Greek names in the Bible are expressed by the English word *Lord*. 1. LORD (printed often in capital letters in the Bible) is God's personal name. It comes from the Hebrew word *Yahweh*. Some Bible versions use *Yahweh* instead of LORD.

2. Lord translates the Hebrew word *'adon*. It means master or my master, my Lord, and denotes ownership by human beings or God (Ps 110:1; 114:7).

3. *'Adonai* is the word the Israelites said whenever they saw the consonants of *Yahweh* (YHWH).

4. The Greek word *Kurios* is also translated as Lord. It is the word used for a human master or for God as the ruler (Mt 8:25; 21:9). It is also the word used for Christ, who by His death and resurrection is the Lord (Rm 14:9). See pp. 4–5, 24. *See also* JEHOVAH; JESUS CHRIST.

LORD OF HOSTS. *See* HOST 2.

LORD'S DAY. That day associated with the resurrection of Jesus and the outpouring of the Holy Spirit on the disciples (Ac 2:1–41). The Lord's day is the first day of the week. It was set aside for worship, though some people still observed the Sabbath (Ac 20:7; Rv 1:10; cf. Rm 14:5; 1Co 16:2; Gal 4:10). *See also* SUNDAY.

LORD'S PRAYER. The prayer Jesus taught His disciples as a pattern for their prayers (Mt 6:9–13; Lk 11:2–4). See p. 143.

LORD'S SUPPER. Christ instituted this supper on the night of His betrayal as a ful fillment of the paschal feast. It is a proclamation of His death for the sins of the world (1Co 11:26). In this meal Christ gives His body and blood together with the bread and wine (Lk 22:19–20; 1Co 10:16–17; 11:20–26). Before going to the Lord's Supper, believers in Christ are to examine themselves to see whether they are truly sorry for their sins, truly believe in Jesus Christ as Savior, and share the same confession of those at the altar (1Co 11:27–32). Christians who trust in the blessings Christ promises to give in this meal and partake of it in faith receive the forgiveness of sins, life, and salvation, and a strengthening of their faith.

The Lord's Supper is also called the breaking of bread (Ac 2:42; 20:7; 1Co 10:16), Communion (cf. "participation" in 1Co 10:16), Eucharist (cf. "blessing" in 1Co 10:16), and the table of the Lord (1Co 10:21). See pp. 38, 83, 173, 335, 387.

LO-RUHAMAH (lo-ryoo-HAY-mah; no mercy). The symbolic name given to Hosea's daughter (Hos 1:6, 8).

LOT (LOT; may mean "covering"). 1. Haran's son; Abraham's nephew (Gn 11:27–31). Lot went with Abraham to Egypt and Canaan (Gn 13:1–7). In Canaan, Lot and his family settled in the Jordan Valley (Gn 13:8–13). Before the Lord destroyed Sodom and Gomorrah, He sent two angels to help Lot and his family escape. Only Lot and his two daughters made it to safety (Gn 19). Lot was an ancestor of Moab and Ammon (Gn 19:36–38). See pp. 12, 18.

2. A way people in Bible times decided an issue or figured out the divine will in a matter (Jsh 18:6–28; Jnh 1:7; Mt 27:35; Ac 1:26). See pp. 50, 157, 327.

LOVE. Various types of love are referred to in the Bible. The Old Testament talks about God's steadfast love for His covenant people (Dt 7:7–9, 12). The Greek word *agape* represents God's undeserved love for sinful people (Jn 3:16; 1Jn 4:8). This is the kind of love Christians are to have—a self-giving, sacrificial concern for another person (Mt 5:44–45; 1Co 13; 1Jn 4). One may also have a noble, unselfish love or brotherly love (Jn 5:20; Ti 3:15). Those loved by God show love toward others. See pp. xxiii, 4, 72, 427–28, 438.

LOVE FEAST. A common meal early Christians shared with one another that was connected with the Lord's Supper (Jude 12; cf. 2Pt 2:13). These meals were held to express and deepen their brotherly love for one another. See p. 354.

LUKE. A doctor who was Paul's companion. Luke wrote the Gospel according to Luke and the Acts of the Apostles. From his writings it seems that he was a well-educated man. He was a Gentile Christian, probably a Greek, whom the New Testament mentions three times by name (Col 4:14; Phm 24; 2Tm 4:11). It seems Luke accompanied Paul on his missionary journeys at times. In Ac 16:6–10 we learn that he joined Paul at Troas. Later, when Paul was on his third missionary trip, Luke joined him again at Philippi (Ac 20:5–6). See pp. 323–24, 352.

LUKE, GOSPEL ACCORDING TO. The third book of the New Testament. The vocabulary, style, and dedication to Theophilus indicate that Luke and Acts were written by the same person. Traditionally this person is thought to be Luke. At the beginning of the Gospel, Luke says that he collected the information in it from eyewitnesses (Lk 1:2). See pp. 323–25.

LYCAONIA (lik-ay-O-ni-ah; wolf land). A high, rugged tableland of Asia Minor that was annexed to Galatia in 35 BC. Paul visited this district and preached in three of its cities: Iconium, Derbe, and Lystra (Ac 13:51–14:23).

LYCIA (LISH-i-ah). A province of southwest Asia Minor (Ac 27:5).

LYDIA (LID-i-ah). A woman in Philippi who made her living by selling purple dyes. She was Paul's first convert in Europe to Christianity. Paul stayed in her house when he was in Philippi (Ac 16:14–15, 40). See pp. 376, 409.

LYRE (LI-er). A stringed musical instrument (1Sm 10:5; Ps 57:8; 71:22; Dn 3:5). *See also* MUSIC. See p. 168.

LYSIAS, CLAUDIUS (LIS-i-as KLAW-di-uhs). The chief captain of the Roman soldiers in Jerusalem. He rescued Paul from a mob and sent him to Caesarea (Ac 21–24).

LYSTRA (LIS-trah). A Roman colony in Lycaonia (Ac 14:6–21; 16:1–2; 2Tm 3:11). See pp. 360–61, 366–67, 375, 393, 407.

M

MAACAH (MAY-ah-kah; oppression). 1. David's wife and Absalom's mother (2Sm 3:3; 1Ch 3:2).

2. Rehoboam's wife, Abijah's mother, and Absalom's granddaughter (1Ki 15:2, 10, 13; 2Ch 11:20–22). She is also referred to as Micaiah (2Ch 13:2).

MAASEIAH (MAY-ah-SEE-yah; work of the LORD). 1. A captain who helped Jehoiada overthrow Athaliah (2Ch 23:1).

2. The governor of Jerusalem during Josiah's reign (2Ch 34:8).

3. A priest who was a co-worker of Ezra (Ne 8:4; 12:41).

4. The father of the false prophet Zedekiah (Jer 29:21).

MAAZIAH (may-ah-ZIGH-ah; may mean decision of the LORD). The head of the twenty-fourth division of priests (1Ch 24:18).

MACCABEES (MAK-ah-beez; may mean hammer). A Hasmonean Jewish family that led a revolt against Antiochus IV, king of Syria. They won freedom for the Jews and ruled Judea from 164 to 134 BC.

The term *Maccabeus* was first given to Judas, the third son of the family. Later it was used of his entire family, as well as others who had a part in the rebellion. The history of the Maccabees is found in the Books of the Maccabees in the Apocrypha. See p. 271.

MACEDONIA (mas-i-DO-ni-ah). A country in the Balkan Peninsula north of Greece. Philip ruled Macedonia from 359 to 336 BC, and his son Alexander the Great ruled it from 336 to 323 BC. In 168 BC Macedonia became a Roman province. Paul often visited there (Ac 16:9–12; 20:1–6; Rm 15:26; 1Co 16:5; 2Co 1:16; Php 4:15; 1Tm 1:3). See pp. 360–61, 375–76, 404.

MACHIR (MAY-kir; sold). The son of Manasseh (Gn 50:23). The Machirites descended from him (Nu 26:29).

MACHPELAH (mak-PEE-lah; double). A cave Abraham bought that was located in the western part of Hebron. Abraham, Sarah, Isaac, Rebekah, Jacob, and Leah were buried in this cave (Gn 23; 25:9–10; 49:30–31; 50:13). An Islamic mosque now stands over the site.

MAGDALENE. *See* MARY 3.

MAGIC. The use of spells, charms, and the like that supposedly gives one powers to make things happen in an unusual way (cf. "magicians" in Gn 41:8; Ex 7:11, 22; 8:7, 18; Ac 13:6–12). Magic includes necromancy (trying to tell the future by getting messages from the dead; 1Sm 28:8), exorcism (driving out evil spirits; Ac 19:13), dreams (Dt 13:1–4), shaking arrows (Ezk 21:21), divination (trying to tell the future; Dt 18:10, 14), witchcraft (Lv 19:26; Is 47:9), astrology (believing that the sun, moon, and stars affect peoples' lives; Dn 2:27; 4:7), and divining by rods (Hos 4:12). See pp. 34–35.

MAGICIAN. A title the Babylonians, Medes, and Persians gave to their priests and learned men (Dn 2:2, 10; 5:11). The magicians studied astrology and astronomy and interpreted dreams and omens. They were important men who advised rulers.

When Jesus was born, the Wise Men, sometimes called Magi, came from the East to worship Him (Mt 2:1–11). In New Testament times the words *magi* or *magos* were also applied broadly to anyone who used the methods of these priests and learned men from the East (Ac 8:9; 13:8). See pp. 34–35. *See also* WISE MEN.

MAGISTRATE. The chief official in a Roman colony (Ac 16:25–40). See pp. 399–400.

MAGOG (MAY-gog; Gog's land). 1. People who descended from Japheth (Gn 10:2; 1Ch 1:5).

2. Gog's land is often identified with Scythia, the place where the Magog

lived, or with Lydia (Ezk 38; 39:1, 11). The word *Magog* is also used symbolically for the final struggle of the forces of evil against the people of God (Rv 20:7–9).

MAHALATH (MAY-hah-lath). 1. The daughter of Ishmael and wife of Esau (Gn 28:9). She is also referred to as Basemath (Gn 36:3).

2. The wife of Rehoboam (2Ch 11:18).

3. The title of Pss 53 and 88. The term probably refers to a familiar melody.

MAHANAIM (may-hah-NAY-im; two camps). A place east of the Jordan River on the boundary between Gad and Manasseh (Jsh 13:26, 30). After Jacob left Laban, the angels of God met him at Mahanaim (Gn 32:2). Later Mahanaim was assigned to the priests as a Levitical city (Jsh 21:38). Ishbosheth ruled there, and when David was fleeing from Absalom, he went to Mahanaim (2Sm 2:8; 17:24; 1Ki 2:8).

MAHER-SHALAL-HASH-BAZ (MAY-hur-SHAL-al-hash-baz; the spoil speeds, the prey hastens). The symbolic name Isaiah gave to his second son (Is 8:1–4).

MAHLON (MAH-lon; sickly). The son of Elimelech and Naomi and the first husband of Ruth (Ru 1:2; 4:10). See p. 99.

MAID, MAIDEN. 1. A female servant or slave (Jb 19:15; Is 24:2). See pp. 17, 19, 89.

2. A virgin (Gn 24:16) or young woman (cf. 2Ch 36:17; Jer 2:32).

3. Possibly, a prostitute (cf. Am 2:7).

MALACHI (MAL-ah-kigh; my messenger). A prophet who wrote the last book in the Old Testament. Nothing is known about Malachi except what is written in his book. He is thought to have lived around the time of Nehemiah. See pp. 139, 264.

MALACHI, BOOK OF. The twelfth book of the Minor Prophets, probably written around Nehemiah's time. It speaks to specific moral and religious abuses and to their underlying cause: religious apathy. See pp. 264–66.

MALCHIJAH (mal-KIGH-jah; Lord is king). 1. The head of the fifth division of priests (1Ch 24:1, 9).

2. A prince into whose dungeon Jeremiah was thrown (Jer 21:1; 38:1, 6).

MALCHUS (MAL-kuhs; king). A servant of the high priest. On the night Jesus was betrayed, Peter cut off Malchus's ear in the Garden of Gethsemane (Jn 18:10).

MALTA (MAL-tah). The island where Paul was shipwrecked (Ac 28:1). See pp. 360–61.

MAMMON (MAM-uhn; wealth). Riches, particularly those that make people greedy and selfish (cf. Mt 6:24; Lk 16:9, 11, 13).

MAMRE (MAM-ri; perhaps strength). 1. An Amorite living at Mamre. He helped Abraham (Gn 14:13, 24).

2. A place where Abraham lived that was near or in Hebron (Gn 13:18; 14:13; 18:1; 35:27; 50:13).

MAN. A being that God created in His own image and likeness (Gn 1:26–27; 9:6; 1Co 11:7; Col 3:10). Man is dependent upon God (Mt 6:26–30; Ac 17:24–28). Man has a body (Mt 6:25), flesh (Rm 1:3), soul, spirit (Gn 2:7; Mt 10:28), and intelligence (Jn 12:40; Rm 2:15).

Man fell into sin and lost the image of God (Gn 3; Rm 5:15–21). As a result, man refuses to honor and thank God but worships created things instead (Rm 1:19–25). Because of sin man also dies (Rm 5:17). In His Law God shows man that he is a sinner, cut off and turned in the opposite direction from his Creator (Rm 7:14–24). But out of grace, God saves those who have faith in Jesus as their Savior and conforms them to His Son's image (Rm 5:15–21; 8:29; 1Co 15:48–49; Col 1:15; 3:10).

MAN OF LAWLESSNESS. An enemy of Christ who makes himself out to be greater than God. He is found within God's temple and shows himself as God. He works with power and signs, bringing rebellion against God, deception, and delusion. The man of lawlessness will be uncovered at the end of time when Christ comes in glory (2Th 2:3–12; cf. Dn 7; 1Jn 2:18). See p. 405. *See also* ANTICHRIST.

MAN, SON OF. *See* JESUS CHRIST.

MANASSEH (mah-NAS-eh; cause to forget). 1. The first son of Joseph and Asenath (Gn 41:50–51). Manasseh and his brother, Ephraim, were blessed by Jacob (Gn 48:8–22). See pp. 19, 21.

2. The tribe that descended from Manasseh (Gn 50:23; Nu 26:28–34; Jsh 17:1).

3. The son of Hezekiah and fourteenth king of Judah. Manasseh was a wicked ruler. He brought back many forms of heathen worship. As punishment for his evil ways and idol worship, God let Manasseh's enemies, the Assyrians, carry him into captivity (2Ki 21; 2Ch 33; Mt 1:10).

MANASSITES (mah-NAS-ights). Descendants of Manasseh (Dt 4:43; 2Ki 10:33).

MANGER (MAYN-jur). A feeding place for cattle (Lk 2:7–16; 13:15). See pp. 328–29.

MANNA (MAN-ah;). A special food God miraculously provided for the Israelites while they were in the wilderness. It was white and finely flaked, like frost (Ex 16:14–36; Nu 11:7–9; Dt 8:3; Jsh 5:12). Jesus is described as the true manna from heaven (Jn 6:31–40). See pp. 63–65, 83.

MANOAH (mah-NO-ah; rest). Samson's father (Jgs 13).

MARA (MAY-rah; bitter). The name Naomi gave to herself (Ru 1:20).

MARAH (MA-rah; bitter). A spring in the wilderness of Shur where the Hebrews found water (Ex 15:22–25; Nu 33:8–9).

MARANATHA (mar-ah-NATH-ah). An expression meaning "Our Lord, come!" *See also* ANATHEMA MARANATHA.

MARK. The writer of the second Gospel. John was his Jewish name; Mark was his Roman name. Sometimes he is referred to by both names: John Mark (Ac 12:12, 25; 13:5; 1Pt 5:13). The young man mentioned in Mk 14:51–52 may be Mark.

John Mark's mother, Mary, had a home in Jerusalem (Ac 12:12–17). John Mark went with Barnabas, his cousin, and Paul, his spiritual father, on part of the first missionary journey (Ac 12:25; 13:1; Col 4:10; 1Pt 5:13). He left them, however, before the trip was over and returned to Jerusalem (Ac 13:13). This resulted in an argument between Barnabas and Paul (Ac 15:36–41). As a result, Barnabas let Paul go on the second missionary journey without him, and Barnabas took John Mark and went to Cyprus (Ac 15:39). Later Mark became Paul's helper (2Tm 4:11; Col 4:10; Phm 24).

According to tradition, Mark presented Peter's story of Christ in his Gospel (cf. 1Pt 5:13). Mark is also said to have been the founder of the church of Alexandria. See pp. 281, 311–12, 360.

MARK, GOSPEL ACCORDING TO. The second and shortest of the four Gospels. According to tradition, John Mark wrote this Gospel to present Peter's story of Christ. The author of the book knows Jewish thought and life well. The book, however, is primarily addressed to Gentile Christians. See pp. 311–13.

MARKET, MARKETPLACE. A place in cities where goods were traded or sold and where people came together to visit (Ps 55:11; Mt 11:16; Lk 11:43; Ac 16:19). Paul also reasoned and debated with those in the marketplace (Gk *agora*; Ac 17:17). Archaeologists have excavated numerous sites that were marketplaces, since every city or town had one. See pp. 382, 388.

MARRIAGE. A lifelong union between a man and a woman, instituted by God (Gn 1:26–31; 2:18–25; Mt 19:5). God provides blessings through marriage: children, help, and companionship (Gn 1:28; 2:18–24; 29:32; 30:1). Sexual relations between a husband and his wife are God-pleasing (Pr 5:15–19; 1Th 4:1–5; Heb 13:4).

The union of one man and one woman until one of them dies is God's ideal intention for marriage (Gn 2:24; Pr 31:10–31; Mt 19:5–6; 1Tm 3:2). Nevertheless, men in Bible times sometimes had more than one wife (Gn 4:19; 30; 1Ki 11:3).

The Israelites were not allowed to marry Canaanites or close relatives (Lv 18; 20; Dt 7:3–4). There were also certain legal restrictions on marrying people of other nations (Dt 23:3–8). After the exile, Israelite men were told to divorce their foreign wives (Ezr 9–10).

Although divorce is not part of God's plan, it is allowed for certain reasons (Dt 24:1–4; Ezr 10:11–44; Mt 19:3–9). Unless one's husband or wife has been sexually unfaithful, to divorce him or her is adultery (Mt 5:31–32; 19:3–10; Mk 10:2–12; Lk 16:18).

In Bible times marriage customs differed from today. Fathers often picked wives for their sons. An engagement between a man and woman involved a legal agreement that was confirmed by an oath and dowry. After this the two were considered man and wife. They did not live together as man and wife, however, until they were actually married. When the bridegroom took his bride from her father's house to his own, the people joined in a marriage celebration (Is 61:10; Sg 3:11; Mt 25:1–13).

The Scriptures picture the covenant union between God and Israel as a marriage (Is 62:1–5; Jer 2:2). In the New Testament the Church is called the Bride of Christ (Lk 5:34; 2Co 11:2; Rv 21:2). See pp. 184, 228–29, 341, 409–10.

MARRIAGE, LEVIRATE. *See* LEVIRATE MARRIAGE.

MARTHA (MAHR-thah; lady). The sister of Mary and Lazarus (Lk 10:38–41; Jn 11; 12:2). See pp. 325, 409.

MARTYR (MAHR-tur; witness). A person who witnesses to his or her faith in Christ by dying for it (Rv 17:6). Cf. Ac 22:20. See pp. 272, 286–87, 355, 372, 433.

MARY (MAIR-ee; rebellion). Miriam in the Old Testament. In the New Testament a number of women are named Mary. 1. Mary, mother of Jesus. She was the wife of

Joseph, a descendant of King David (Mt 1:18–25; Rm 1:3) and a relative of Elizabeth, John the Baptist's mother (Lk 1:27, 36).

Mary gave birth to Jesus at Bethlehem (Mt 1:18, 20; Lk 2:1–20). At the proper time Mary and Joseph brought Jesus to the temple in Jerusalem for His presentation to the Lord (Lk 2:22–38). Shortly after the visit of the Wise Men, an angel warned Joseph in a dream to flee to Egypt because Herod was going to kill Jesus. So Mary and Joseph took Jesus and went to Egypt (Mt 2:13–15). After Herod died, they returned to the land of Israel and lived at Nazareth (Mt 2:19–23; Lk 2:39–40). When Jesus was 12 years old, Mary and Joseph took Him to Jerusalem for the Feast of the Passover (Lk 2:41–50).

Mary was at the wedding in Cana where Jesus performed His first miracle (Jn 2:1–12). When Jesus was dying on the cross, He asked John to look after Mary (Jn 19:25–27). After Jesus' ascension Mary met with other believers in the Upper Room for prayer (Ac 1:14).

Mary is called blessed among women (Lk 1:28, 42, 48). She carefully considered and thought about Jesus' mission and work and believed in His powers (Lk 2:51; Jn 2:3–5). Jesus stressed His spiritual relationship to Mary rather than His earthly one (Mt 12:46–50; Lk 8:20–21; 11:27–28). See pp. 308, 328–31, 409, 434.

2. Mary, the wife of Clopas and mother of James and Joses (Mt 27:56; Mk 15:40). She was one of the women at Jesus' crucifixion and burial (Mt 27:61; Mk 15:47). Early on the morning of Jesus' resurrection she went to His grave only to discover that He was not there; He had risen (Mt 28:1; Mk 16:1; Lk 24:1).

3. Mary Magdalene, a woman who came from Magdala on the southwest coast of the Sea of Galilee. Mary became a devoted follower of Jesus after He cast seven demons out of her (Mk 16:9; Lk 8:1–2). She is often regarded as the sinful woman who anointed Jesus' feet and wiped them with her hair (Lk 7:37–50). No one knows this for sure, however, since the biblical account does not name this woman. Mary was among the women who witnessed the crucifixion and burial of Jesus (Mt 27:56, 61; Mk 15:40, 47; Jn 19:25). On the morning of His resurrection she went to His tomb (Mt 28:1; Mk 16:1; Lk 24:1; Jn 20:1). She was the first person to whom the risen Lord appeared (Mk 16:9; Jn 20:11–29). See p. 316.

4. Mary of Bethany, the sister of Lazarus and Martha (Jn 11:1). While Martha prepared the dinner, Mary sat at Jesus' feet and listened to His teaching (Lk 10:38–41). On another occasion Mary anointed Jesus' feet with ointment (Jn 12:1–8). See p. 409.

5. Mary, mother of John Mark and sister of Barnabas (cf. Col 4:10). Mary lived in Jerusalem. When Peter was in prison, Christians met in her home to pray for his release. While they were gathered there, Peter surprised them by knocking at the door. After they had gotten over their amazement, they let Peter in and listened to him describe how the Lord had brought him out of prison (Ac 12:12–17).

MASTER. Various words in the Bible are translated as master. Consequently, when the word *master* is used in English Bibles, it may mean any of the following: master of a house or husband (Jgs 19:22; Mt 13:27); ruler, owner, or lord (Gn 24:14, 27; 39:20; 2Ki 19:4; Mt 24:45); superior or supervisor (Lk 5:5; 8:24). See pp. 299, 417, 447.

MATTANIAH (mat-ah-NIGH-ah; Lord's gift). The original name of King Zedekiah (2Ki 24:17).

MATTHEW (MATH-yoo; gift of the Lord). The son of Alpheus. Matthew, who was also referred to as Levi, was a tax collector at Capernaum. One day Jesus called him to be His disciple (Mt 9:9–13; Mk 2:14–17; Lk 5:27–32). Jesus made Matthew an apostle along with the other 12 disciples (Mt 10:3; Lk 6:15; Ac 1:13). See pp. 286, 302–03, 306–07, 389.

MATTHEW, GOSPEL ACCORDING TO. The first of the four Gospels. Matthew wrote this account for Jewish converts to Christianity to show that Jesus was the Messiah promised in the Old Testament. Matthew focuses on Jesus' teaching, whereas the Gospel of Mark focuses on what Jesus did. See pp. 302–04, 434, 447.

MATTHIAS (ma-THIGH-uhs; gift of Lord). The apostle whom the disciples chose to fill the place of Judas Iscariot after Judas killed himself (Ac 1:15–26). See p. 362.

MEASURES. Biblical measurements can be divided into three categories: length, dry ingredients, and liquids.

1. LENGTH
   a. A fingerbreadth equaled about three-fourths of an inch.
   b. A handbreadth equaled four fingerbreadths (about three inches).
   c. A span was the distance from the tip of the thumb to the tip of the little finger when the fingers were stretched apart (about 9 inches).
   d. A cubit equaled 6 handbreadths (about 18 inches). See p. 13.
   e. A reed equaled 6 cubits (about 9 feet).
   f. A pace was the distance of 1 step (about 30 inches).
   g. A little way (cf. Gn 48:7) was the distance one could walk in 2 hours.
   h. A day's journey was the distance traveled in one day (about 20 miles).
   i. A furlong or stadion was about 600 feet.
   j. A fathom was the distance between two hands when held wide apart (about 5 to 6 feet).
   k. A mile was 1,000 paces (about 4,854 feet).
   l. A Sabbath day's journey was 3,000 feet (Jsh 3:4).
2. DRY MEASURES
   a. A handful was the amount that could be held in one hand.
   b. A kab was equal to about 1 quart.
   c. A seah was equal to 7 kabs (about 7 quarts).
   d. An ephah was equal to about three-fifths of a bushel.
   e. An omer was one-tenth of an ephah (about 2 quarts).
   f. A homer was 10 ephahs, or the load of a donkey (about 6 bushels).
   g. A choenix equaled about 1 quart.
   h. A modius probably equaled about 1 peck.
   i. A saton or measure equaled about a peck.
   j. A cor equaled a homer (about 6 bushels).
3. LIQUID MEASURES
   a. A log was the amount displaced by 6 hen's eggs (about one-third of a quart).
   b. A hin equaled one-sixth of a bath (about 4 quarts).
   c. A bath equaled 1 ephah (about 6 gallons).
   d. A firkin was about 9 or 10 gallons.

e. A sextarius was about 1 pint.

MEDAD (MEE-dad). One of the elders Moses chose to help him govern the people. Medad was a prophet (Nu 11:26–27).

MEDAN (MEE-dan). The son of Abraham and Keturah (Gn 25:2; 1Ch 1:32).

MEDE (MEED). A person who came from Media (2Ki 17:6; Est 1:19; Is 13:17; Dn 5:31). See p. 248.

MEDIA (MEE-di-ah). A country in Asia northwest of Persia and south of the Caspian Sea. The people who lived there were famous for the horses they bred. In 612 BC the Medes captured Nineveh. Under Nebuchadnezzar's rule, the Median Kingdom stretched from the Persian Gulf to the Caspian Sea (Est 1:3, 14, 18; 10:2; Is 21:2; Dn 8:20).

MEDIATOR (MEE-di-ay-tur). A person who acts as a go-between (1Sm 2:25; Jb 33:23; Is 43:27). Christ is the mediator of the new covenant. Through Him God and people are brought back into a right relationship with each other (1Tm 2:5; Heb 8:6; 9:15; 12:24). See p. 68. *See also* JESUS CHRIST.

MEDICINE. In the Scriptures, the word *medicine* is used primarily in a figurative sense (Pr 17:22; 30:13; Jer 46:11). See p. 314. *See* DISEASE; PERFUMER.

MEDITERRANEAN SEA (med-uh-tuh-RAY-ni-uhn). The sea that lies between Europe and Africa. It is also referred to as the sea, the Great Sea, the western sea, and the Sea of Philistines (Ex 23:31; Nu 34:6; Dt 11:24; Ac 10:6). See pp. 146–47, 247, 284, 307, 361.

MEDIUM. A person who claims to be able to call forth the spirits of the dead for consultation (Lv 19:31; 20:6, 27; Dt 18:11; 1Sm 28:3; 2Ki 21:6). *See also* NECROMANCY.

MEGIDDO (mi-GID-o; place of troops). A city that overlooked the Plain of Esdraelon. It was situated on two important trade routes (Jsh 12:21; 17:11; Jgs 1:27). Solomon strengthened its fortifications (1Ki 9:15). When Ahaziah, king of Judah, was wounded by Jehu's men, he fled to Megiddo, where he died (2Ki 9:27).

Megiddo was also the scene of a battle between Pharaoh Neco and King Josiah (2Ki 23:29; 2Ch 35:22). *See also* ARMAGEDDON.

MEHUJAEL (mi-HYOO-yay-el). Cain's grandson (Gn 4:18).

MELCHIZEDEK (mel-KIZ-uh-dek; king of righteousness). The king of Salem (Jerusalem) and priest of God. Melchizedek blessed Abram and received tithes from him (Gn 14:17–20). He is a type of Christ, the priest-king (Ps 110:4; Heb 5:6–10; 6:20; 7). See pp. 15, 149, 423.

MEMPHIS (MEM-fis; place of good). An ancient city of Egypt located on the Nile River about 10 miles north of Cairo. The prophets spoke of it negatively (Is 19:13; Jer 2:16; 44:1; 46:14; 19; Ezk 30:13, 16).

MENAHEM (MEN-ah-hem; comforter). The sixteenth king of Israel, who gained the throne by killing King Shallum. Menahem paid tribute to Pul (Tiglath-pileser) to keep him from invading the land. He also practiced calf worship. The Scriptures evaluate Menahem's reign by saying that "he did what was evil in the sight of the Lord" (2Ki 15:14–22). See p. 125.

MENE, MENE, TEKEL, AND PARSIN (MEE-ni, MEE-ni, TEK-il, and PAHR-sin). Four Aramaic words that suddenly appeared on a wall at Belshazzar's feast (Dn 5:25–28). They probably mean "numbered, numbered, weighed, and divisions."

MEPHIBOSHETH (mi-FIB-o-sheth; destroying shame). 1. The son of Saul and Rizpah (2Sm 21:8).

2. Jonathan's son. He was accidentally crippled after Saul's death. David honored Mephibosheth and provided for him by giving him Saul's estates (2Sm 4:4; 9:6–13; 16:1–4; 19:24–30; 21:7). He is also referred to as Merib-baal (1Ch 8:34; 9:40).

MERAB (MEE-rab; increase). Saul's daughter (1Sm 14:49). *See also* MICHAL.

MERATHAIM (mer-ah-THAY-im; double rebellion). A name for Babylon (Jer 50:21).

MERCY. 1. The Hebrew word *hesed* means God's undeserved favor and love within the covenant relationship. *See also* STEADFAST LOVE.

2. Various other Hebrew and Greek words are translated into English as "mercy." They convey the idea of compassion or sympathy, pity, pardon or forgiveness, and showing favor (Gn 19:16; Dt 13:17; Jb 8:5; Ps 23:6; Mt 5:7; Col 3:12).

MERCY SEAT. The covering of the ark (Ex 25:17–22; 26:34; 37:6–9). It reminded the people of God's gracious act of "covering" sin. On the Day of Atonement, the high priest burned incense before the Mercy Seat and sprinkled blood on it. By doing this, he made atonement for his sins and the sins of the nation in the presence of the Lord, who appeared in a cloud upon the Mercy Seat (Lv 16). The blood of Christ, shed for the sins of the world, is the real atonement (Heb 9). See pp. 30, 65.

MERIBAH (MER-i-bah; strife). 1. A place where God gave Israel water from a rock. It was near Rephidim (Ex 17:1–7).

2. Meribah of Kadesh. *See* MERIBATH-KADESH.

MERIBATH-KADESH (MER-i-bath-KAY-desh, Meribah of Kadesh). A place near Kadesh-barnea in the Desert of Zin. The people of Israel were thirsty there, so God told Moses to speak to the rock. But Moses struck the rock instead. Water flowed from it for the people to drink. Because of his disobedience, however, Moses was forbidden to enter the Promised Land (Nu 20:1–13; Dt 32:51).

MERODACH (mi-RO-dak). Marduk, the chief god of the Babylonians (Jer 50:2).

MEROM (MEE-rom; height). A place north of the Sea of Galilee where Joshua defeated the kings of northern Canaan (Jsh 11:5–7).

MESHACH (MEE-shak). The Babylonian name given to Mishael, one of Daniel's friends (Dn 1:7). Because Meshach refused to worship the golden image King Nebuchadnezzar set up on the plain of Dura, he was thrown into a fiery furnace (Dn 3). See pp. 121, 137, 217, 224.

MESHULLAM (mi-SHUL-am; friend). A common name in the Old Testament. A number of men with this name lived during Ezra's time. Ezra sent one of them to get Levites for the temple in Jerusalem (Ezr 8:16).

MESHULLEMETH (mi-SHUL-i-meth; friend). The wife of King Manasseh of Judah and mother of Amon (2Ki 21:19).

MESOPOTAMIA (mes-o-po-TAY-mi-ah; between rivers). The name applied to the upper part of the land between the Tigris and Euphrates rivers (Gn 24:10; Dt 23:4; Jgs 3:8–11; Ac 2:9; 7:2). The Hebrews called it Aram-naharaim. Today it is Iraq.

MESSIAH (muh-SIGH-ah; anointed one). In the Old Testament this term describes any high official, such as a prophet, priest, or king, who was consecrated to his office by being anointed with oil. The term came to be used in a special sense, however, of a great prophet from David's family, anointed by God, and filled with His Spirit (Dt 18:15–18; 2Sm 7:12–14; Is 11:2). This Messiah would deliver God's judgment on the wicked, restore God's kingdom to the people of Israel, and enable them to live perfectly as God's chosen people. Moreover, He would usher in a time of universal peace, goodwill, and well-being (Is 11). Many nations would come to Him (Is 11:10; 60:1).

The Old Testament also pictures the Messiah as the Savior and Suffering Servant, the one who would suffer and die for the sins of the people (Is 25:9; 53; 63:1–5). He would be the Creator of a spiritual kingdom for all people (Is 60; Jer 33:15–26).

Jesus fulfills the biblical prophecies concerning the Messiah. He is the Promised One of God (Lk 4:18; Ac 4:27). Through His threefold office of Prophet, Priest, and King, He ushers in God's spiritual kingdom. Through His suffering and death, He redeems people from their sins and brings peace and well-being between God and humanity (Lk 1:53; 7:18–25; Jn 3:16–21). See pp. 69, 200, 219, 242, 303. *See also* ANOINT 5; JESUS CHRIST.

METHEG-AMMAH (MEE-theg-AM-ah). A town that David took from the Philistines (2Sm 8:1). It was probably Gath (1Ch 18:1).

METHUSELAH (mi-THYOO-zuh-lah; man of dart). The son of Enoch, father of Lamech, and grandfather of Noah. He lived 969 years, which is the longest recorded age of any person (Gn 5:21–27; 1Ch 1:3; Lk 3:37). See p. 12.

MIBSAM (MIB-sam; sweet odor). The fourth son of Ishmael and grandson of Abraham (Gn 25:13; 1Ch 1:29).

MICAH (MIGH-kah; who is like Lord). A prophet from Moresheth who wrote one of the shorter prophetic books in the Old Testament (Mi 1:1; Jer 26:18). Micah began his work a little later than Hosea and Isaiah, prophesying during the reigns of Jotham, Ahaz, and Hezekiah. See p. 242.

MICAH, BOOK OF. The sixth book of the Minor Prophets. In his book Micah emphasizes God's judgment on the wicked and His salvation for all. He also foretells that the Messiah will be born in Bethlehem (Mi 5:2). He prophecies doom for Samaria and Jerusalem while promising the deliverance that will come through David's line. See pp. 242–43.

MICAIAH (MIGH-KAY-yah; who is like the Lord). 1. A prophet who predicted the death of King Ahab (1Ki 22:7–28; 2Ch 18:6–27).

2. The man who reported Jeremiah's prophecies to the Jewish princes (Jer 36:11–13).

MICHAEL (MIGH-kuhl; who is like God). An archangel who fought for Israel (Dn 10:13, 21; 12:1). Michael also disputed with the devil for Moses' body and defeated him, and successfully fought the dragon and the enemies of God's people (Jude 9; Rv 12:7). See p. 196.

MICHAL (MIGH-kuhl; Michael). The daughter of Saul and wife of David (1Sm 14:49; 18:20–27). *See also* MERAB.

MICHMAS, MICHMASH (MIK-mas, MIK-mash; treasury). A town near the Mount of Bethel, about 7 miles north of Jerusalem. A notable battle between the Philistines and the Israelites occurred there. Through Jonathan's strategy the Philistines were defeated (1Sm 13–14). After the captivity Jewish exiles returned to Michmas and lived there (Ne 11:31).

MIDIAN (MID-i-uhn; strife). One of the sons of Abraham and Keturah (Gn 25:2). See p. 89.

MIDIANITES (MID-i-uhn-ights). A race of people that descended from Midian (Ex 3:1; Nu 22:4; Jgs 7:13). They were merchants who lived south of Moab and east of the Gulf of Aqabah, though the boundary of their land did shift (Gn 37:25–36). Moses fled from Egypt to Midian, where he married Zipporah (Ex 2–4). The Midianites were defeated first by the Israelites and then by Gideon (Nu 22–25; 31; Jgs 6–8). See pp. 89, 117.

MIKLOTH (MIK-loth; rods). David's chief officer (1Ch 27:4).

MILCAH (MIL-kah; counsel). A daughter of Haran, Abraham's brother, and the sister of Lot. Milcah married her uncle Nahor, and together they had eight children. Rebekah and Laban were her grandchildren (Gn 11:29; 22:20–23; 24:15, 24, 47). **MILCOM** (MIL-kom; their king). A heathen god who was worshiped by the Ammonites (1Ki 11:5, 33; 2Ki 23:13; Jer 49:1, 3). Solomon introduced his worship into Israel. Milcom is sometimes identified with Molech. *See also* MOLECH.

MILE. *See* MEASURES 1k.

MILETUM, MILETUS (migh-LEE-tuhm, migh-LEE-tuhs). A city on the seacoast of Ionia about 36 miles south of Ephesus. Paul stopped there (Ac 20:15, 17; 2Tm 4:20).

MILLENNIUM (1,000 years). The term applied to that period, before or after the final resurrection and judgment, when Christ will supposedly appear on earth with the saints and rule for 1,000 years. It is based on a misinterpretation of Rv 20:1–7.

MINA (MIGH-nah). A Babylonian weight used in Palestine that was equal to about 60 shekels (1Ki 10:17; Ezr 2:69; Ne 7:71). A light mina was about 500 grams, and a heavy mina was about 1,000 grams (Ezk 45:12). In the New Testament, it equaled about 100 drachmas (Lk 19:13–15).

MINISTER. 1. A person who serves or waits on another. Joshua was Moses' minister (Ex 24:13; Jsh 1:1).

2. A person who is active in service to God or the state. Priests performed a ministry (Ex 28:43; Dt 10:8). Prophets and kings were also consecrated for sacred service. *See also* KING; PRIEST; PROPHET.

3. In the New Testament the usual word for ministry is *diakonia* or service. The New Testament distinguishes between the ministry or service rendered in the public sphere for the good of all, such as the government might perform (Rm 13:6), and the service or ministry rendered by God's special ministries in Word

and Sacrament: apostles, evangelists, pastors, teachers, elders, bishops, and deacons (Lk 6:13; Ac 14:23; 21:8; Rm 12:7; 1Co 12:28–31; 2Co 6:13–10; Php 1:1; 1Tm 3:1–8; 5:17; 2Tm 4:5; Jas 3:1). While all Christians are called to speak the glory of Him who called them out of darkness, God especially call the apostles and pastors to preach publicly (cf. 1Co 1:17; 9:16; 1Tm 2:7; 2Tm 1:11; 4:2). See pp. 412, 416.

MIRACLE. An event that causes wonder; something that takes place outside of the laws of nature (cf. "sign" in Jn 4:48; Ac 2:19; 2Co 12:12).

The Old Testament describes a miracle as an extraordinary manifestation of God's presence (Ex 4:21; 7:9; Ps 105:27; cf. Nu 16:30; Jsh 10:10–14; 2Ki 20:8–11). God's people recognized miracles as God's work because of their faith in Him (cf. Ex 7–12; Jgs 6:17–21, 36–40; 1Ki 18:38–39).

The New Testament depicts miracles as acts of power, signs, and wonders (Act 19:11; cf. "signs" in Lk 21:25; Jn 2:11). Their significance could be understood only by those who had faith in Jesus Christ (Jn 6:26; 11:25–27, 38–40; 20:30–31). See pp. 28, 293–95, 320–21, 340.

MIRIAM (MIR-i-uhm; rebellion). The sister of Moses and Aaron. After the Israelites had passed unharmed through the Red Sea, Miriam led the women, with tambourines and dancing, in a song of victory (Ex 15:20–21). Miriam was a prophetess. When she criticized Moses for marrying a Cushite woman, she was punished with leprosy. But Moses asked God to make her better, and Miriam was healed after seven days (Nu 12:1–15). When Miriam died, she was buried at Kadesh (Nu 20:1). See pp. 59, 168.

MISHAEL (MISH-ay-el; who is like God?). 1. Moses' uncle (Ex 6:22; Lv 10:4–5).

2. The Hebrew name of Meshach, one of the three men thrown into the fiery furnace for refusing to worship the golden idol King Nebuchadnezzar set up on the Plain of Dura (Dn 1:7; 3).

MISHMA (MISH-mah; hearing). A son of Ishmael and the founder of an Arabian tribe (Gn 25:14; 1Ch 1:30).

MITRE. *See* TURBAN.

MIZPAH, MIZPEH (MIZ-pah, MIZ-pe; tower). The heap of stones Jacob piled together in Gilead as a witness of the covenant between him and Laban. Laban called it Jegar-sahadutha; Jacob called it Galeed, which means "cairn of testimony."

The Mizpah blessing/curse, "The Lord watch between you and me, when we are out of one another's sight," was spoken there (Gn 31:44–49). The location may be that of Ramoth-gilead.

MOAB (MO-ab). Lot's son by his daughter (Gn 19:30–38). Moab was the ancestor of the Moabites, people who lived on a well-watered tableland east of the Jordan (Nu 21:13–15). The Moabites were the ones who refused the Israelites passage through their land when the Israelites were on their way to Canaan (Jgs 11:17–18). Later they sent Balaam to curse Israel (Nu 22–24). During the period of the judges, Moab controlled Israel for 18 years (Jgs 3:12–14). See pp. 58, 94, 117.

David defeated the Moabites and made them pay tribute (2Sm 8:2, 12; 1Ch 18:2, 11). The Moabites were enemies of Israel (2Ki 1:1; 24:2; 2Ch 20:1–30). The prophets spoke against them in a strong way (Is 15–16; Jer 9:26; 48; Ezk

25:8–11; Am 2:1; Zep 2:8–11). Ruth, the mother of Obed and an ancestress of Jesus, was from Moab (Ru 1:4).

MOABITE STONE (MO-ub-ight). A two-by-four foot black asphalt slab erected around 850 BC by Mesha, king of Moab. The stone, which is inscribed with the Moabite language (a language that is almost the same as Hebrew), describes the events of 2Ki 3:4–27.

MOLECH (MO-lek; king). A heathen god worshiped especially by the Ammonites. Sacrificing children to this god was a common worship practice. This practice was forbidden by Hebrew law (Lv 18:21; 20:1–5). Nevertheless, an altar was built to Molech in the Valley of Hinnom, and Manasseh worshiped him there, burning his sons as an offering to the god (2Ch 33:6).

When Josiah was king, he stamped out idol worship and tore down the altar built to Molech (2Ki 23:10). The prophets spoke strongly against the worship of Molech (Jer 7:29–34; 19:1–13; Ezk 20:26–39). This god is also referred to as Moloch (Ac 7:43). See p. 77.

MONEY. In early times bartering, or trading one thing for another, was the system of exchange. Cattle, produce, and weighed metal were used for this (Gn 13:2; 26:16; 1Ki 5:11; 1Ch 21:25). Coined money came into use after the exile (Ezr 1:4). To begin with, the Israelites used the coins of the country that had conquered them. During New Testament times coins from various countries were in use. See pp. 282–83, 319. *See also* MONEY-CHANGER.

MONEY-CHANGER. A person who for a fee changed foreign money into coins that could be used in the temple (Mt 21:12; Mk 11:15; cf. Ex 30:13–15). See p. 389.

MONOTHEISM (MON-o-thee-iz'm; one God). The belief that there is only one God. *See also* GOD; GODS, FALSE.

MONTH. *See* TIME.

MOON. The principal light of the night, given to mark seasons, days, months, years, and signs (Gn 1:14; Ps 104:19; Jl 2:10; Mt 24:29; Lk 21:25).

Many heathen nations worshiped the moon, but this practice was forbidden to the Israelites (Dt 4:19; 17:3). Nevertheless, during the period of the kings, moon worship was also practiced by some of the Israelites (2Ki 23:5; Jer 8:2).

MORASHTITE (mo-RASH-tight). *See* MICAH.

MORDECAI (MAWR-di-kigh). A Benjaminite who was the uncle and foster father of Esther (Est 2:5–7). Mordecai saved King Ahasuerus's life by letting him know through Esther about two men who were plotting to kill him (Est 2:21–23). Mordecai also helped save the Jews from Haman's plot to destroy them (Est 3–10). The Feast of Purim reminds the Jewish people of this deliverance. See pp. 153, 157.

MOREH (MO-re). An oak tree or plain near Shechem (Dt 11:30). Abraham camped there when he arrived in Canaan (Gn 12:6).

MORESHETH (MO-resh-eth; possession of). *See* MICAH.

MORIAH (mo-RIGH-ah). The place where Abraham went to offer Isaac as a sacrifice to the Lord (Gn 22:2). It probably is the hill in Jerusalem on which Solomon built the temple (2Ch 3:1).

MORNING. *See* TIME.

MOSES (MO-ziz; drawn out or child). The great Israelite leader, lawgiver, and prophet through whom God delivered the Israelites from Egyptian slavery and prepared them for entrance into the Promised Land. Moses was born in Egypt to Israelite parents of the tribe of Levi. Since Pharaoh had ordered the death of all Hebrew baby boys, Moses' mother put him afloat in a basket on the Nile River. Pharaoh's daughter discovered baby Moses and adopted him as her own (Ex 2:1–10). Moses received a fine education in the Egyptian court (Ac 7:22). This helped to prepare him for his later leadership of the Israelites.

When Moses was older, he killed an Egyptian who had struck one of Moses' Hebrew countrymen. The next day, fearing for his life, Moses fled to Midian.

Moses spent the next 40 years of his life in Midian. There he married Zipporah, the priest Jethro's daughter. Moses and Zipporah had two sons (Ex 2:11–25). The time spent in Midian was a period of preparation for Moses. He grew familiar with wilderness life, its climate, and resources. At the end of this period, God spoke to Moses from a burning bush and called him as leader of Israel (Ex 3–4).

In a series of 10 plagues the Lord countered Pharaoh's attempt to keep the Hebrew people as slaves in Egypt. Finally, when the Lord passed over the Israelites but put to death all the firstborn of the Egyptians, Pharaoh said the Hebrew people could go. The Passover was instituted to remind the Israelites of this event (Ex 5–15).

Moses led the Israelites through the Wilderness of Shur (Ex 15:22–26). At Sin, God provided manna for the people to eat (Ex 16). Next the Israelites traveled to Rephidim and from there to the wilderness at Sinai, where they set up camp (Ex 17–19:2).

At Sinai, Moses received God's law for the people. It spelled out how they were to live in a covenant relationship with God (Ex 20–25). There Moses also received instructions for building the tabernacle and regulations for the priesthood and the altar (Ex 26–30). When Moses left the mountain and went back to the people, he found them worshiping a golden calf (Ex 32).

God renewed the covenant with His people (Ex 34). Then they began to build the tabernacle and make holy clothing for the priests (Ex 35–38:40; 39).

Moses took a census of the people (Nu 1–2). Later, at God's command, they left the wilderness at Sinai (Nu 10). At various times Moses' actions or leadership were opposed. Miriam and Aaron spoke against him for marrying a Cushite woman. God punished Miriam with leprosy for this act. But when Moses asked God to heal her, God did so after seven days (Nu 12). Later, Korah, Dathan, and Abiram also spoke out against Moses. Because of this, the Lord opened the earth and swallowed them up. In this way God showed the Israelites that Moses was indeed His chosen servant (Nu 16–17).

When they left Mount Hor to go around the land of Edom, the people once again spoke against God and Moses, saying, "Why have you brought us up out of Egypt to die in the wilderness?" (Nu 21:4–5). God punished them for their complaints and lack of trust by sending fiery serpents to bite them. Many of the people died. Moses prayed for the people and was told to set up a bronze serpent on a pole. Those bitten by real snakes would live if they looked at this bronze serpent (Nu 21:6–9).

Because Moses sinned at Meribah, he was not allowed to enter the Promised Land. Joshua, the man Moses named as the new leader of the Israelites, would be the one to lead the people into Canaan. God did allow Moses to see the Promised Land, however, before his death (Nu 20:27). Moses died on Mount Nebo (Dt 34).

Both the Old and New Testaments indicate that Moses wrote the first five books of the Old Testament called the Pentateuch (Gn–Dt; Lk 24:27, 44; Jn 5:45–47). After his death, Moses' greatness was recognized by all (Jer 15:1; Heb 3:2). Along with Elijah, Moses appeared on the Mount of Transfiguration with Jesus (Mt 17:3–4). Moses is the great lawgiver with whom Christ is compared and contrasted (Ac 3:22; 2Co 3:12–18; Gal 3–4; Heb 3). See pp. 26–29.

MOTHER. The Israelites, unlike many other nations, held mothers in respect (Ex 20:12). The word *mother* is sometimes used in a wider sense to mean grandmother or some other female ancestor (Gn 3:20; 1Ki 15:10) or a woman who acted kindly toward a person in need (Jgs 5:7).

It is also used figuratively for nation, city, and the new Jerusalem (Is 50:1; Gal 4:26–31; Rv 17:5). See pp. 409–10.

MOTHER-OF-PEARL. *See* ALABASTER.

MOUNTAIN. Much of Israel is hilly or mountainous. The best-known mountain range of Syria, the Lebanon range, formed the northwest boundary of the Promised Land (Dt 1:7; Jsh 1:4). The mountains consist of two ranges that begin at the northeast corner of the Mediterranean and extend northeast to southwest through Israel. During the Greek period the name Lebanon was restricted to the western range while the eastern range was called the Anti-Lebanon. Often the peaks of mountains had names, for example, Mount Zion, Mount of Olives, Mount Hermon, Mount Tabor, and Mount Sinai. Many of these are no more than hills.

Mountains were places of refuge (Gn 14:10). They were used as lookouts and as sites for assemblies, camps, and cemeteries (Jgs 9:7; 1Sm 17:3; 2Ki 23:16; Is 18:3). Mount Ebal was the mountain from which the people recited the curses of the Law; Mount Gerizim, the blessings (Dt 27:4–26). Sinai and Zion were God's mountains (Ex 24:13; Ps 68:16; Is 27:13).

Mountains symbolize strength, persons in authority, proud persons, the righteousness of God, and the messianic reign (Ps 36:6; 72:3; Is 2:2, 14; Jer 3:23).

MOURNING. During Bible times people showed grief for a dead person in the following ways: tearing their own clothing, putting on sackcloth and ashes, cutting their bodies, shaving their heads, crying loudly, and building fires (Gn 37:34; Ex 12:30; Dt 14:1; 2Ch 16:14; Mi 1:10). Often professional mourners were hired (2Ch 35:25; Mt 9:23). Mourning lasted 7, 30, or 70 days (Gn 50:3; Dt 34:8; 1Sm 31:13).

MULE. A cross between a horse and a donkey. It is not mentioned in the Bible before the time of David but was in common use then (2Sm 13:29; 18:9; 1Ki 1:33, 38, 44; Ezr 2:66).

MURDER. The act of killing another person. Murder is forbidden (Ex 20:13; Dt 5:17). During Old Testament times those who did take another person's life received the death penalty (Gn 9:6; Ex 21:14). A person who killed someone else without meaning to do so could find freedom from the death penalty in cities of refuge (Nu 35:9–34; Dt 19:1–10). See pp. 162, 333, 400.

MUSIC. Music has existed from earliest times (Gn 4:21). Folk music celebrated victories (Jgs 5; 1Sm 18:6–7). Music was used at special occasions, such as feasts, weddings, and funerals (Gn 31:27; 2Sm 19:35; Jer 7:34; Mt 9:23).

David organized a sacred choir and appointed instrumental musicians (1Ch 6:31–48; 16). The use of these was continued by Solomon, Jehoshaphat, Hezekiah, Josiah, Ezra, and Nehemiah.

Various instruments were used in biblical times, for example, lyres, harps, trumpets, pipes, flutes, oboes, tambourines, and cymbals. During the New Testament period people played flutes at funerals and to accompany dancing (Mt 9:23; Lk 7:32). Harps were symbols of praise (Rv 5:8; 14:2). Music and hymns played an important role in the worship life of Israel (Mt 26:30; Eph 5:19). See pp. 168–70.

MYRA (MIGH-rah). A seaport of Lycia where Paul changed ships when he was being taken prisoner to Rome (Ac 27:5). See p. 361.

MYRRH (MUR). A yellow-brown resin used for perfume, embalming, and anointing (Ex 30:23; Sg 3:6; Mt 2:11; Jn 19:39; Rv 18:13). See pp. 329, 348.

N

NAAMAH (NAY-ah-mah; pleasantness). The wife of Solomon and mother of Rehoboam (1Ki 14:21, 31; 2Ch 12:13).

NAAMAN (NAY-ah-muhn; pleasantness). One of the commanders of Ben-hadad II. He was cured of leprosy by Elisha (2Ki 5:1–19; Lk 4:27). See p. 132.

NABOTH (NAY-both). A man living in Jezreel who owned a vineyard near King Ahab's palace. When Naboth refused to sell Ahab his vineyard or exchange it for other land, Queen Jezebel plotted a way to get the land. She had Naboth stoned for blasphemy so that Ahab could take over the vineyard (1Ki 21:1–24; 2Ki 9:21–26).

NADAB (NAY-dab; liberal). 1. A son of Aaron. He was a priest who went up Mount Sinai with Moses. When Nadab and his brother offered unauthorized fire on the altar, they were killed (Ex 6:23; 24:1, 9–11; 28:1; Lv 10:1–7; Nu 26:60–61).

2. The second king of Israel. He was the son of Jeroboam and the one who succeeded him to the throne. Nadab "did what was evil in the sight of the Lord." He reigned over Israel two years. Then Baasha killed him and took over his throne (1Ki 14:20; 15:25–31). See p. 125.

NAHOR (NAY-hawr; snoring). 1. Abraham's grandfather (Gn 11:22–25; Lk 3:34).

2. Abraham's brother (Gn 11:26–29; 22:20; Jsh 24:2). See pp. 12, 18.

NAHSHON (NAH-shon). A leader of the tribe of Judah in the wilderness (Nu 1:7; 2:3; 7:12; 10:14). His sister married Aaron (Ex 6:23).

NAHUM (NAY-hum; full of consolation). A prophet from Elkosh who prophesied to Judah between 663 and 612 BC (Na 1:1; 3:8–11). He wrote the Book of Nahum. See p. 245.

NAHUM, BOOK OF. The seventh book of the Minor Prophets. Written by the prophet Nahum, the book contains his prediction of the downfall of Nineveh, the capital of Assyria. Nahum insists that the Lord is a jealous God whose judgment will fall on those who oppose Him, but who is a stronghold to those who trust in Him (1:2–8). See pp. 245–46.

NAIN (NAY-in; beauty). A city in Galilee. Jesus raised a widow's son from death near Nain (Lk 7:11–17). See pp. 291, 294–95, 321.

NAIOTH (NAY-oth; shepherd dwellings). A place in Ramah where Samuel and his prophets lived (1Sm 19:18–20:1).

NAKED, NAKEDNESS. Without any clothing, without an outer garment, or poorly clothed (Gn 2:25; Mt 25:36; Jn 21:7).

Figuratively the word *naked* depicts a lack of power or spiritual poverty (Gn 42:9; Rv 3:17).

NAME. In biblical times a name often expressed something about the person named (Gn 2:20; Is 40:26). When an individual's name was changed, it reflected a change in the person's being. For instance, God gave Abram (exalted father) the name Abraham (father of a multitude) to show that He had established His covenant of grace with Abraham (Gn 17:5; 35:10).

God's names reveal His nature (Ex 3:13–15), will (Ps 22:22; Jn 17:6, 26), and attributes (Ex 33:19; Ps 8:1, 9; 1Tm 6:1). God is present where His name is present (Is 18:7; 30:27). See pp. 4–5, 17–21, 24, 286–87, 431.

NAOMI (nay-O-mi; my pleasantness). Ruth's mother-in-law (Ru 1–2; 3:1; 4:3–17). See p. 93.

NAPHTALI (NAF-tah-ligh; my unresting). 1. A son of Jacob and Bilhah (Gn 30:8; 46:24). See p. 19.

2. The tribe of Naphtali was given land in northern Israel. Zebulun and Asher were to its west; the upper Jordan and Sea of Galilee to its east (Jsh 19:32–39). Barak came from this tribe (Jgs 4:6). Naphtali was the first tribe captured by the Assyrians under Tiglath-pileser (2Ki 15:29).

NATHAN (NAY-thuhn; he gave). 1. A prophet during the reigns of David and Solomon. When David consulted him about building the temple, Nathan told David to leave this job for his son (2Sm 7:1–7). Nathan also rebuked David for his adultery with Bathsheba (2Sm 12:1–14). When David grew old and Adonijah tried to get his throne, Nathan stepped in and through Bathsheba secured the succession for Solomon (1Ki 1:8–45). Nathan also recorded the life of David and the history of the reign of Solomon (1Ch 29:29; 2Ch 9:29). See pp. 113, 118.

2. One of David's sons (1Ch 3:5; Lk 3:31).

NATHANAEL (nah-THAN-ay-el; gift of God). One of Jesus' 12 disciples (Jn 1:45–51; 21:2). It is thought that Nathanael and Bartholomew were the same person. See p. 286.

NATIONS. In the Old Testament this word is often used for Gentiles, people who are not of the Jewish race (Ex 34:24; Is 43:9; Jer 10:1–25). See pp. 78–79.

NAVE (NAYV). The Holy Place of the temple (1Ki 6:3, 5, 17, 33; 2Ch 3:4–5, 13).

NAZARENE (naz-ah-REEN). Someone who came from Nazareth. Jesus was a Nazarene (Mt 2:23; Mk 14:67). See p. 110.

NAZARETH (NAZ-ah-reth). The town in Galilee where Mary and Joseph lived and where Jesus grew up (Mk 1:9; Mt 4:13; Lk 1:26; 2:4, 51). Jesus is often referred to as Jesus of Nazareth (Lk 18:37; Jn 1:45–46; Ac 2:22). See pp. 281, 284–85, 290–91, 410.

NAZIRITE (NAZ-i-right; separated). An Israelite who bound himself or herself by a vow to be set apart from others for the service of God, either for life or for a set amount of time. Nazirites could not drink alcoholic beverages or cut their hair. They also had to avoid contact with the dead and abstain from eating unclean food (Nu 6:1–21; Am 2:11–12). Samson and John the Baptist were both Nazirites from birth (Jgs 13; Lk 1:15). See pp. 110–12

NEAPOLIS (ni-ap-O-lis; new city). The seaport of Philippi to which Paul sailed after being given a vision to preach the Gospel in Macedonia (Ac 16:11).

NEBAT (NEE-bat; viewed). The father of Jeroboam I (1Ki 11:26).

NEBO (KNEE-bo). 1. The Babylonian god of learning (Is 46:1).

2. The name of the mountain located in Moab that Moses climbed to view the Promised Land before he died (Dt 32:49–50; 34:1–5). *See also* PISGAH, MOUNT.

NEBUCHADNEZZAR (neb-yoo-kuhd-NEZ-ur; defend the boundary). Nabopolasser's son and the ruler of the Neo-Babylonian Empire from 604 to 562 BC. In 605 BC Nebuchadnezzar defeated Pharaoh Neco at Carchemish. Then in 603 BC he made Jehoiakim his servant (Dn 1:1; 2Ki 24). After a few years of paying taxes to Nebuchadnezzar, Jehoiakim revolted. Nebuchadnezzar returned to Judah and in 587 BC destroyed Jerusalem and carried the people into captivity (2Ki 24:11–16; 25:1–21). Nebuchadnezzar is frequently mentioned in the Old Testament (1Ch 6:15; 2Ch 36; Ezr 1:7; Ne 7:6; Est 2:6; Jer 21–52; Dn 1–5). See pp. 121, 124, 211, 216–17, 236.

NEBUSHAZBAN (neb-yoo-SHAZ-ban; Nebo save). A rabsaris, an important officer in Nebuchadnezzar' s court (Jer 39:13).

NECO (NEE-ko). *See* PHARAOH 8.

NECROMANCY (NEK-ro-man-see). A form of witchcraft. A necromancer was a person who consulted the dead for information (Dt 18:11; 1Sm 28:1–25). *See also* MEDIUM.

NEGEB (NEG-eb; dry). A grazing region lying south of Hebron (Gn 12:9; 13:1; 20:1). See pp. 78, 146.

NEHEMIAH (nee-hi-MIGH-ah; the Lord comforts). The son of Hachaliah and the cupbearer of Artaxerxes Longimanus (Ne 1:1; 2:1). When Artaxerxes found out that Nehemiah was distressed at Jerusalem's state of ruin, he allowed Nehemiah to return there. Nehemiah arrived in Jerusalem in the twentieth year of Artaxerxes' reign; in 445 BC, Nehemiah became the governor of Judah (Ne 2:1–10). He organized the Jewish community to carry out the task of rebuilding Jerusalem's walls (Ne 1–4; 6). He also instituted reforms and restored worship and the Law (Ne 5; 8–13). See pp. 151–52.

NEHEMIAH, BOOK OF. Nehemiah is part of the third division of the Hebrew Scriptures known as the Writings. It describes how God restored the Law, worship, government, and the walls of Jerusalem through the efforts of Nehemiah and other leaders after the Israelites' return from captivity. See pp. 151–52.

NEHUSHTAN (ni-HUSH-tuhn; piece of bronze). This was the name Hezekiah gave to the brass serpent made in Moses' time. Hezekiah destroyed it because the people were worshiping it rather than the Lord (2Ki 18:4).

NEIGHBOR. The Old Testament describes one's neighbor as someone who lives nearby or as a fellow Israelite (Ex 11:2; Dt 15:1–11). The duty to love one's neighbor as oneself included both Israelites and foreigners (Lv 19:18–34).

The New Testament describes one's neighbor as every person for whom Christ died, that is, everyone (Lk 10:25–37). Because Christ died for all, love is to be extended to everyone (Mt 5:43–48). Anything done for the neighbor is done for Christ (Mt 25:31–46). See pp. 72, 336, 428.

NEPHILIM (NEF-uh-lim). *See* GIANTS.

NER (NUR; lamp). 1. The son of Abiel, father of Abner, and uncle of Saul (1Sm 14:50–51; 26:5, 14; 2Sm 2:8, 12).

2. Saul's grandfather (1Ch 8:33; 9:35–36, 39).

NERO (NEE-ro). The Roman emperor from AD 54 to 68. His full name was Nero Claudius Caesar Augustus Germanicus, but he was usually referred to as Caesar (Ac 25:11; Php 4:22). See pp. 421, 429.

NEW BIRTH. *See* CONVERSION.

NEW MAN. This term refers to the Christian believer who is created anew by God's grace. Christ's death and resurrection makes the existence of this new man possible (Rm 5:10; 8:34–39). By faith in Christ, the believer dies to the old life and rises to the new life, becoming a new creature (2Co 5:17; Gal 6:15). Baptism works this conversion (Rm 6:1–4). The new man is a member of the Church, Christ's body (Eph 2:15). His new life in Christ is shown in how he lives. It is constantly renewed in Christ (Rm 6:5–11; Col 3:10–11).

NEW TESTAMENT. 1. The books of the Bible from Matthew to Revelation. See pp. xviii–xx, xxiv–xxv, 2–3, 281.

2. The new testament, or new covenant, is a term describing the work of Christ, by whose life, death, and resurrection God's grace is brought to all people (Jer 31:31–34; 2Co 3; Gal 4; Heb 7:20–22). The Holy Spirit brings people into this covenant by creating faith in their hearts by means of the Word (Jn 3:5; Rm 1:16–17; 15:16; 1Co 2:10; 2Th 2:13). The Lord's Supper is the new testament made visible (Mt 26:26–28; 1Co 11:25). See pp. 281, 387. *See also* COVENANT.

NEW YEAR. *See* TIME.

NICANOR (ni-KAY-nawr; conqueror). One of the seven men chosen by the church in Jerusalem to look after the widows and the poor (Ac 6:5). See p. 412.

NICODEMUS (nik-o-DEE-muhs; victor over people). A leading Pharisee and member of the Sanhedrin. He visited Jesus one evening and talked with Him. Jesus told Nicodemus about the new birth necessary to enter the kingdom of God (Jn 3:1–21). When Jesus was on trial before the Sanhedrin, Nicodemus spoke up for Him, though in a roundabout way (Jn 7:50–52). After Jesus' death, however, Nicodemus helped Joseph of Arimathea with the burial (Jn 19:39–42). See p. 269.

NICOLAITANS (nik-o-LAY-uh-tuhns). A Gnostic sect in the churches at Ephesus and Pergamum. Their teachings were harshly spoken against by John (Rv 2:6, 14–15).

NICOLAUS (NIK-o-luhs, nik-o-LAY-uhs; victor over people). A proselyte at Antioch. He was one of the seven men chosen by the church at Jerusalem to take care of the widows and the poor (Ac 6:5). See p. 412.

NICOPOLIS (ni-KOP-o-lis; city of victory). A Roman town in Epirus that was founded by Caesar Augustus in 31 BC (Ti 3:12).

NILE (NIGHL). The main river of Egypt and Africa. It is 4,050 miles long. The Nile's yearly overflow leaves deposits of rich soil that make the land of northern Egypt fertile.

The people in ancient times worshiped the Nile as a god. Moses was placed on the Nile in a basket made of papyrus (Ex 2:3). During one of the plagues the waters of the Nile were turned to blood (Ex 7:20–21). The Nile was also famous for the papyrus that grew along its banks. From it, the people made papyrus writing material (Is 19:7). See pp. 33–34, 132, 193, 206.

NIMROD (NIM-rod). A son of Cush. Nimrod was a hunter, builder, and founder of the kingdoms in Shinar (Gn 10:8–12; 1Ch 1:10; Mi 5:6). Many places in Mesopotamia were named Nimrod. See p. 247.

NINEVEH (NIN-uh-vuh). The capital of Assyria. It was located on the Tigris River and was founded by Nimrod (Gn 10:9–11). Sargon II, the ruler of Assyria from 721 to 705 BC, made Nineveh the capital of Assyria. From 705 to 626 BC Nineveh was strengthened and made beautiful by Sennacherib, Esarhaddon, and Ashurbanipal. In 612 BC the city was destroyed by the Babylonians, Scythians, and Medes. Nineveh is mentioned numerous times in the Bible (2Ki 19:36; Is 37:37; Jnh; Na; Zep 2:13; Mt 12:41; Lk 11:30, 32). See pp. 238, 240–41, 245–48.

NOAH (NO-ah; rest). The son of Lamech (Gn 5:28–32). When Noah was 480 years old, God warned him that the world was going to be destroyed by water. Then He gave Noah instructions on how to build the ark. While building the ark, Noah warned people to repent of their wickedness (Gn 6:1–9, 12–22; 1Pt 3:20; 2Pt 2:5). After 120 years God led Noah, Noah's wife, their sons, and their sons' wives into the ark. Then God directed the animals into the ark. When all were safely aboard, God shut the door. In this way He saved Noah and his family from the flood, which destroyed everything outside the ark (Gn 7–8).

After the rain stopped and the waters went down, Noah, his family, and the animals were allowed to leave the ark. Noah and his family repopulated the earth (Gn 9:10). Noah lived to be 950 years old. See pp. 12–15.

NO-AMON (no-AY-mon). *See* THEBES.

NOD (NOD; exile). The region east of Eden where Cain went to live after he had killed Abel (Gn 4:16).

NORTHEASTER. A tempestuous wind that eventually caused St. Paul to be shipwrecked on his journey to Rome (Ac 27).

NUMBERING. *See* CENSUS.

NUMBERS. The Hebrew people used letters of the alphabet for numbers. Their numbers often had religious or symbolical meaning. For example, 10 was regarded as a sacred number, and 40 was a number of completeness (Ex 24:18; 1Ki 19:8; Mt 25:1–3). See pp. 112, 289.

NUMBERS, BOOK OF. The fourth book of the Pentateuch. It is called Numbers because it records two numberings of the Israelites. The Hebrew name for this book is "In the Wilderness."

This book contains various laws, the numbering of the tribes, and the Israelites' journey from Sinai to Palestine. See pp. 57–59.

NUN (NUN; fish). Joshua's father (Ex 33:11; 1Ch 7:27).

OATH. A solemn appeal to God, a person, or an object to witness the truth of a statement or the binding character of a promise (Gn 21:23; Ex 22:11; 2Sm 11:11; Mt 5:34). Oaths of the covenant were worked out in a careful and detailed way (Gn 21:28–31). Swearing by God's name showed loyalty to Him (Dt 6:13). See p. 111.

OBADIAH (o-bah-DIGH-ah; worshiper of the Lord). 1. One of Ahab's officers who was a friend to Elijah and the prophets of the Lord (1Ki 18:3–16).

2. A prophet of Judah who wrote the Book of Obadiah (Ob 1:1). See pp. 139, 236.

OBADIAH, BOOK OF. The fourth book of the Minor Prophets as they appear in the Old Testament. It tells of Edom's destruction because of its constant hostility toward Israel. See pp. 236–37.

OBED (O-bed; worshiper, servant). The son of Boaz and Ruth and the grandfather of King David (Ru 4:17, 21–22; 1Ch 2:12; Mt 1:5). See pp. 97, 122.

OBED-EDOM (O-bed-EE-dum). A man from Gath into whose home David had the ark of the covenant carried after Uzzah had been struck dead for touching it. The ark remained in Obed-edom's house for three months, and God greatly blessed Obed-edom and all his household (2Sm 6:10–12).

OBEDIENCE. The act of obeying. The complete, willing response to God is the duty of all people (Dt 4:30; Jer 7:23; 1Jn 5:2). Man disobeyed God, however, and fell into sin (Gn 3). From that point forward the natural state of humanity has been disobedience toward God (Rm 1:24; 5:19). Christ obeyed the Father and obtained the forgiveness of sins for all people (Rm 5:19; Php 2:8; Heb 5:8). Throughout the Bible obedience is linked to faith (Rm 1:5; 1Pt 1:14). Christians show obedience in the home, to the state, in the church, and to others (Rm 13:1–7; Eph 5:21; 6:1; Heb 13:17; 1Pt 3:6). See pp. 27–28, 243, 257.

OBEISANCE (o-BEE-suhns). *See* BOW 2.

ODOR. Any smell, either pleasant or unpleasant (Jn 11:39; cf. "aroma" in Gn 8:21; Nu 15:3–24).

OFFERING. *See* SACRIFICE.

OFFICES OF CHRIST. *See* JESUS CHRIST.

OINTMENT. Usually perfumed olive oil was used to dress the hair and make the skin smell sweet, to prepare bodies for burial, and to anoint people (Est 2:3–12; Mt 26:6–13; Lk 23:56). The balm of Gilead and eye salve were two medicines (Jer 8:22; cf. "salve" in Rv 3:18). See pp. 314, 318. *See also* MEDICINE; PERFUMER.

OLD TESTAMENT. 1. The 39 books from Genesis to Malachi that make up the first part of the Bible. Most of the Old Testament was written in Hebrew except for a few sections in Ezra and Daniel, which were written in Aramaic. See pp. xvi–xxv, 2–7, 268, 281, 303.

2. The covenant of Moses. *See also* COVENANT.

OLIVE. *See* ORCHARD.

OLIVES, MOUNT OF; OLIVET (AHL-i-vet). A ridge about one mile long on the eastern side of Jerusalem, separated from it by the Valley of Kidron. Gethsemane, Bethphage, and Bethany are on its slopes (2Sm 15:30; Zec 14:4; Mt 21:1; 24:3; Mk 11:1; Lk 22:39; Jn 8:1; Ac 1:12). See p. 315.

OMEGA (o-MEG-uh). *See* ALPHA.

OMER (O-mur). *See* MEASURES 2e.

OMNIPOTENCE (ahm-NIP-o-tuhns). All-powerful. Only God has limitless power and authority (cf. Gn 17:1; Mt 19:26; Eph 1:21–22). See p. 195.

OMNIPRESENCE (ahm-ni-PREZ-uhns). The attribute of being in all places at once. God is omnipresent; that is, He is everywhere (cf. Ps 139:7–10; Pr 15:3; Ac 17:27–28). See p. 165.

OMNISCIENCE (ahm-NISH-uhns). The term used to describe God's complete knowledge of all things (cf. 1Sm 2:3; Mt 10:30; Ac 15:18; Eph 1:4).

OMRI (OM-righ). The sixth king of Israel, who reigned from about 885 to 874 BC. Before gaining the throne, Omri was a general in the Israelite army of King Elah. During one battle, news arrived that Zimri had killed Elah. At once the prophets and army proclaimed Omri the new king of Israel.

During his reign Omri moved the capital from Tirzah to Samaria. He is described as doing "evil in the sight of the LORD, . . . more evil than all who were before him" (1Ki 16:16–28). See p. 125.

ON (ON). A city in the Delta of Egypt about 19 miles north of Memphis. It was also called Heliopolis (Jer 43:13). On was the main religious center for sun worship. Joseph's wife, Asenath, was the daughter of a priest of On (Gn 41:45, 50).

ONESIMUS (o-NES-i-muhs; useful). Philemon's slave. It seems that Onesimus robbed his master and then ran away to Rome. In Rome he came in contact with Paul and became a Christian. Paul persuaded Onesimus to return to Philemon and wrote the Letter to Philemon on Onesimus's behalf (Col 4:9; Phm). See p. 417.

ONESIPHORUS (on-i-SIF-o-rus; profit bringing). A Christian from Ephesus who ministered to Paul when Paul was in prison in Rome (2Tm 1:16–18; 4:19).

ONYX (ON-iks). A precious stone, perhaps some type of quartz, which was put on the high priest's shoulder pieces and breastpiece (Gn 2:12; Ex 28:9; 35:9; 1Ch 29:2).

OPHRAH (AHF-rah). Gideon's hometown. It was located in Manasseh (Jgs 6:11, 24; 8:27, 32).

ORACLE (AHR-ah-k'l). A place, such as the Most Holy Place, a message or word of God, a prophecy or some other way in which God communicated His will to His people (2Sm 16:23; 1Ki 6; Is 14:28; 15:1; Ezk 12:10; Ac 7:38; Rm 3:2; 1Pt 4:11).

Heathen oracles are also mentioned in the Bible (cf. Jgs 17:1, 5; 8:27; 2Ki 1:2). Israel is rebuked for consulting these false oracles (cf. Hos 4:12; Hab 2:19). See p. 249.

ORCHARD. The place where fruit- or nut-bearing trees are grown. Olives, figs, dates, pomegranates, citrus fruit, almonds, and walnuts were among the fruits and nuts grown in Palestine.

The olive harvest began in August when the whitish fruit was knocked from the trees. The oil was taken out of the olives by placing the fruit in a stone basin or on a concave stone and then crushing it with another stone. Olive oil was used in ceremonial anointings, as fuel for lamps and torches, for anointing the body and head, and in salves for wounds (Ex 27:20; 29:7; 1Sm 16:13; Lk 7:46; 10:34). The olive was a symbol for peace, wealth, and success (Gn 8:11; Ps 52:8).

Various types of figs were grown in Palestine (1Ki 4:25; Ps 105:33). The first crop was ready to harvest in May (Is 28:4; Na 3:12). The regular crop was ready in late July or mid-August, and sometimes a third crop was ready in late fall. The sycamore fig had smaller fruit (Am 7:14). Figs were dried for year-round use.

Date palms grew wild along the Mediterranean Sea, the Jordan Valley, and in desert oases. Dates were dried and caked for use in the winter. Palm tree branches were brought to Passover celebrations (Mt 21:8; Mk 11:8; Jn 12:13).

Pomegranates are often mentioned in the Old Testament (Hg 2:19). The people made wine from the juice of this fruit (Sg 8:2). In a number of passages the pomegranate is referred to as an apple (Pr 25:11; Sg 2:3, 5; Jl 1:12).

Almonds and walnuts were both common in Palestine. Almonds were particularly plentiful (Gn 43:11; Ex 25:33; Jer 1:11).

See pp. 230–315.

ORDINATION (awr-duh-NAY-shuhn). The act of conferring a sacred office upon a person. Old Testament priests were ordained to office (Ex 28:41; Nu 3:3). Rams were sacrificed at these ordinations (Ex 29:22–34; Lv 8:22–33).

In the New Testament, deacons, missionaries, and elders were ordained to office, referred to as "laying on hands" (cf. Ac 6:6; 13:3; 14:23). See pp. 412, 416.

ORPAH (AWR-pah; fawn). The daughter-in-law of Naomi and sister-in-law of Ruth (Ru 1:4–14).

OSNAPPAR (os-NAP-ur). The king of Assyria mentioned in Ezr 4:10. Osnappar is usually identified with Ashurbanipal, Sennacherib's grandson. Ashurbanipal ruled Assyria from 668 to 627 BC.

OTHNIEL (OTH-ni-el; God's powerful one). The son of Kenaz and first judge of Israel (Jsh 15:17; 1Ch 4:13). Othniel captured the town of Kiriath-sepher (Jsh 15:15–17; Jgs 1:11–13). Later he delivered Israel from the Mesopotamians (Jgs 3:8–11). See p. 88.

P

PACE. *See* MEASURES 1f.

PADDAN-ARAM (PAD-uhn-AY-RAM; plain of Aram). The plain surrounding Haran in Mesopotamia. It was the home of Rebekah and Laban (Gn 25:20; 28:2–7; 31:18; 33:18; 35:9; 46:15). See p. 146.

PAGAN. *See* GENTILES.

PAGIEL (PAY-gi-el; meeting with God). The chief of the tribe of Asher when it was in the wilderness (Nu 1:13; 2:27; 7:72, 77).

PALACE. *See* ARCHITECTURE; HOMES.

PALESTINE (PAL-uhs-tighn). The name comes from Philistia, the area along the coast where the Philistines lived (Ps 60:8). The older name for this region was Canaan (Gn 12:5). After the conquest it became known as the land of Israel (1Sm 13:19). The Book of Zechariah refers to it as the holy land (Zec 2:12), and during the Greco-Roman times it was called Judea.

Biblical Palestine was about 70 miles wide and 150 miles long. It lay south of the Lebanon Mountains, northeast of Egypt, north of the Sinai Peninsula, and east of the Arabian Desert. It was divided into five regions: the coastal plain on the west, the Shephelah, the central range, the Jordan Valley, and the eastern plateau.

Because of the variation in elevation from Mount Hermon's 9,101 feet above sea level to the Dead Sea's 1,290 feet below sea level, the climate of Palestine varies greatly. The mean temperature of Jerusalem is 65 degrees F, whereas the Jordan Valley is tropical in climate. There are two seasons: winter (November–April) and summer (May–October). Winter is mild and rainy; summer is hot and dry.

In the days of Abraham, Palestine was inhabited by the Canaanites, Amorites, Hittites, Horites, and Amalekites. The Israelites conquered Palestine under Joshua and under the judges and kings. From 587 to 166 BC Palestine fell under foreign rule. Then the Maccabees reigned from 166 to 63 BC, at which time the Romans took over until AD 325. During New Testament times Palestine was divided into three parts: Judea, Samaria, and Galilee. See pp. 104, 116, 193, 304–05.

PALSY. *See* DISEASE.

PALTI (PAL-tigh; delivered). The man to whom Saul gave David's wife Michal (1Sm 25:44).

PAMPHYLIA (pam-FIL-i-ah; every race). A coastal plain along the Mediterranean in southern Asia Minor. Some of the people at Pentecost were from Pamphylia (Ac 2:10). On his first missionary trip Paul preached at Perga, the chief city of Pamphylia (Ac 13:13; 14:24; 15:38). See pp. 360–61, 446.

PAPER. *See* PAPYRUS.

PAPHOS (PAY-foss). The capital city of Cyprus (Ac 13:6, 13). See pp. 360–61.

PAPYRUS (pah-PIGH-ruhs). An 8- to 10-foot-high sedge or reedlike plant that grew along the Nile River in ancient times. The people of that time made paper from this plant (Jb 8:11; Is 18:2). Moses' basket was probably made of papyrus (Ex 2:3). See pp. 206–07.

PARABLE. A method of speech that compares two objects for the purpose of teaching a moral or religious truth (Mt 15:14–15; Mk 13:28). It is an earthly story with a heavenly or spiritual meaning. Although the events and characters in a parable are true to nature, not every detail of the story has a spiritual meaning. Rather there is only one main point of comparison (Mt 13; Lk 15). Jesus often spoke in parables to teach the people about Himself and the kingdom of heaven. Parables were also used in the Old Testament (Ezk 17).

A parable differs from a fable, myth, allegory, and proverb. See pp. 392, 447. *See also* ALLEGORY; FABLE; PROVERB.

PARACLETE (PAR-ah-kleet; comforter). *See* HELPER.

PARADISE (PAR-ah-dighs; park). A park, orchard, or pleasure ground. The Garden of Eden was a paradise (Gn 2:8–17; Rv 2:7). In the New Testament the word *paradise* is used to describe heaven, the home of those who die in Christ (Lk 23:43; 2Co 12:3–4; Rv 2:7). See 82, 220–21, 391–92.

PARBAR (PAHR-bahr; open place). Some building or place on the west side of the outer court of the temple (cf. "colonnade" in 1Ch 26:18).

PARDON. *See* FORGIVENESS; JUSTIFICATION.

PARMENAS (PAHR-mi-nas; faithful). One of the seven men chosen by the Early Church to look after widows and poor people (Ac 6:5). See p. 412.

PAROUSIA (pah-ROO-zhi-ah; presence or coming). A Greek word used in the New Testament to describe the second coming of Christ in glory and power to judge the world at the end of time (cf. "coming" in Mt 24:27–39; 1Co 15:23; 1Th 4:15–17; Jas 5:8; 2Pt 3:4; 1Jn 2:28). *See also* ADVENT OF CHRIST 3; DAY OF THE LORD 2; JESUS CHRIST; JUDGMENT.

PARTHIANS (PAHR-thi-uhns). People who lived in southwest Asia, southeast of the Caspian Sea. Today that country is Iran. Parthians were present on the Day of Pentecost (Ac 2:9).

PASHHUR (PASH-ur). 1. A son of Immer. Pashhur was a priest. Because Jeremiah's prophecies angered Pashhur, he had the prophet beat and put in stocks (Jer 20:1–6).

2. The son of Malchiah. He was among the court princes in Zedekiah's reign who sought to put Jeremiah to death (Jer 21:1; 38:1, 4).

PASSION (suffering). The sufferings of Christ, beginning with His agony in the Garden of Gethsemane and ending with His death on the cross (Ac 1:3). *See also* JESUS CHRIST. See pp. 332–34.

PASSOVER. The first of three yearly festivals at which all the Jewish men were to come to the sanctuary (Ex 23:14–17; Dt 16:16). It was instituted to keep alive the memory of the "passing over" of Israel when all the firstborn of Egypt were put to death (Ex 12; 13:3–9). The ritual involved with this feast is described in Ex 12:3–20. Passover began at sunset on the 14th day of Nisan (Lv 23:5). Passover is also called the Feast of Unleavened Bread (Ex 23:15; Dt 16:16).

Christ and the Lord's Supper are the Christian's Passover (Lk 22:1–20; 1Co 5:7). See pp. 37–38, 56, 84, 173, 333, 335.

PASTORAL EPISTLES. The name given to three of Paul's letters: 1 Timothy, 2 Timothy, and Titus. These letters show Paul's concern for the pastoral work of the church. See pp. 407–09, 413–14.

PATARA (PAT-ah-rah). A seaport on the southwest coast of Lycia (Ac 21:1).

PATMOS (PAT-mahs). A small island in the Aegean Sea off the southwest coast of Asia Minor. According to tradition, the Emperor Domitian banished John there in AD 95 (Rv 1:9). See p. 441.

PATRIARCH (PAY-tri-ahrk; father-ruler). The father or chief of a race. The name is given to the fathers of the human race both before and after the flood (Gn 4–5; 11). Scripture also gives this name to the founders of the Hebrew race and nation: Abraham, Isaac, Jacob, the 12 sons of Jacob, and King David (1Ch 1:28, 34; Ac 2:29; 7:8–9; Heb 7:4). See pp. 18–19.

PAUL (PAWL; little). The apostle to the Gentiles (Rm 11:13; Gal 1:16; 2:2, 8–9).

Paul's given name was Saul. He was born in Tarsus to Jewish parents (Ac 21:39; 22:3). Paul's father was a Pharisee from the tribe of Benjamin (Php 3:5). He also held Roman citizenship, a privilege that he passed on to Paul (Ac 22:28; 23:6). Not too much is mentioned about Paul's relatives. From Ac 23:16, we learn that he had a sister and a nephew. Paul also mentions three relatives, two of which were Christians before Paul and well-known among the apostles (Rm 16:7, 11).

As a child, Paul was schooled in reading, writing, arithmetic, and particularly in religion. Later he went to Jerusalem and became a student of Gamaliel, a famous teacher known for his tolerant ways (Ac 5:34–40; 22:3). As a student of Gamaliel, Paul studied the Holy Scripture and its various interpretations by famous rabbis. After this Paul likely returned to Tarsus, where he learned the trade of tentmaking (Ac 18:3).

Paul was present at the stoning of Stephen, the first Christian martyr (Ac 7:58; 9:13; 26:10–11; Gal 1:13). Owing to his intense hatred of the Christians, a sect whom he thought to be a serious threat to the Jewish religion, Paul began to treat Christians in a cruel and harsh way. He sought them out in Jerusalem and other cities and then had them put in prison or even put to death (Ac 8:1–3; 9:1–2, 13–14; 22:1–5; 26:9–12).

One day while Paul was on his way to Damascus to arrest the Christians there, the glorified Jesus appeared to him and asked Paul why he was persecuting Him. Paul became a Christian and, a few days later, was baptized by Ananias (Ac 9; 22:1–16; 26:1–20; 1Co 15:8–10; Gal 1:12–16; Eph 3:1–8).

Then Paul went to Damascus, where he met with the Christian disciples and preached in the synagogues about Jesus, the Son of God (Ac 9:15; 26:16–20). After this Paul went to Arabia (Gal 1:17). Upon his return to Damascus, Paul continued to preach the Gospel but was forced to flee because of angry enemies who were trying to kill him (Ac 9:23–25). Paul then went to Jerusalem, and from there he set sail for Tarsus (Ac 9:26–30. Cf. Ac 15:41). It seems that Paul spent a number of years there.

Barnabas brought Paul to Antioch to help him in serving the Christian church there (Ac 11:25). When the church at Antioch heard that the believers in the church at Jerusalem were suffering from a famine, they took up a collection for them and appointed Paul and Barnabas to take it to them (Ac 11:29–30). Soon after their return from Jerusalem, Paul and Barnabas were sent on the first missionary trip to Asia Minor. John Mark went along with them on part of this journey (Ac 13:13–14). When they returned to the church at Antioch, they reported to it how God "had opened a door of faith to the Gentiles" (Ac 14:27).

Not long after this, Jewish Christians from the church in Jerusalem came to Antioch. They said that Gentile converts must keep the Law. Paul went up to Jerusalem and attended the council, which reached a decision regarding Jewish laws for Gentile Christians (Ac 15).

Paul made two other missionary journeys, traveling to Asia Minor, Macedonia, and Greece (Ac 16–20). After his last trip, he went to Jerusalem for a visit. There he was almost killed by a mob. Roman soldiers came to break up the crowd and arrested Paul. Before taking him away, however, they allowed Paul to speak to his angry countrymen. Paul recounted to them his family background and how God had chosen him to tell others about Christ, the promised Messiah (Ac 21:37–22:21).

Paul was then sent before the Sanhedrin (Ac 22:30–23:10). Upon learning of a plot to kill Paul, the Roman officer in charge sent Paul to Caesarea. There Paul was brought before Felix, the Roman governor of Judea. Paul was kept under house arrest for a few years. When the new governor of Judea arrived to replace Felix, Paul was brought before him. His name was Festus. Paul appealed to his Roman citizenship and asked to be sent to Rome to be heard by the emperor (Ac 25:6–12). Before he was sent to Rome, however, Agrippa and his sister, who were visiting Festus, asked to hear Paul speak. After listening to Paul, Agrippa declared that he thought Paul was innocent. But since the appeal to Rome had already been made, Paul had to be sent there (Ac 26).

And so Paul was sent to Rome (Ac 27–28). It seems likely that Paul was set free after his first trial and made additional missionary journeys (Php 2:24; 1Tm 1:3; 3:14; 2Tm 4:20; Ti 3:12; Phm 22).

According to tradition, Paul died in Rome around AD 68 (2Tm 1:8, 15; 4). He is the author of most of the letters in the New Testament. See pp. 353, 360–61, 366–67, 372–78, 399–400.

PAULUS (PAWL-uhs). *See* SERGIUS PAULUS.

PEACE. A word often used in the Bible in a variety of ways. It can mean a period of calm and quiet as opposed to war (Mt 5:9; 2Co 13:11; 1Tm 2:2). It is also used to describe that state of spiritual tranquility and harmony that God gives when He brings one into a right relationship with Himself (Nu 6:26). Christ is the Christian's peace with God (Eph 2:14–17). Through His death on the cross He has earned the forgiveness of sins for all people, making peace between God and people (Col 1:20). This peace is worked in believers by the Holy Spirit through faith and shows itself in their lives (Jn 20:19, 22; Rm 12:18; 14:19; 1Co 7:15; Gal 5:22; Eph 4:3; 1Th 5:13). See pp. 136, 234, 241, 269, 449.

PEACE OFFERING. An animal that was sacrificed to God as a thank offering for some blessing, as a result of some promise or vow made to God or as an expression of love for God (Lv 3; Jgs 20:26; 2Sm 24:25). *See also* SACRIFICE.

PEDAIAH (pi-DAY-yah; the Lord saved). 1. The grandfather of King Jehoiakim (2Ki 23:36).

2. Zerubbabel's father (1Ch 3:19).

PEKAH (PEE-kah; opening). The 18th king of Israel. Pekah gained the throne by murdering Pekahiah. He aligned himself with the king of Damascus against the king of Judah. Pekah reigned about 20 years and then was killed by Hoshea, who became the next king (2Ki 15:25–31; 16; 2Ch 28:5–15).

PEKAHIAH (pek-ah-HIGH-ah; the Lord opens). The 17th king of Israel. He took over the throne from his father, Menahem. He ruled about two years and then was murdered by Pekah, who wanted his throne (2Ki 15:22–26).

PELEG (PEE-leg; division). A son of Eber (Gn 11:16–19; 1Ch 1:19, 25). "In his days the earth was divided" (Gn 10:25). This statement may refer to the time God confused the language and scattered the descendants of Noah.

PEN. Either a stylus or graving tool used for cutting letters on stone or a reed pen used for writing on papyrus (Jb 19:24; Ps 45:1; Jer 8:8; 3 Jn 13). See p. 207.

PENCIL. A tool that a carpenter used for marking lines (Is 44:13).

PENNINAH (pi-NIN-ah; coral). One of Elkanah's two wives (1Sm 1:2–6). His other wife was Hannah.

PENNY. Bronze or copper Roman coin worth a penny or less (Mt 5:26; 10:29; Lk 12:6; cf. "copper coin" in Lk 21:1–4). *See* DENARIUS.

PENTATEUCH (PEN-tah-tyuk). The first five books of the Old Testament: Genesis, Exodus, Leviticus, Numbers, and Deuteronomy. The Hebrew people called this collection of books the Torah, or the Law. Both the Old Testament and the New Testament speak of these books as being written primarily by Moses (Jsh 8:31; Ezr 6:18; Lk 24:27; Jn 5:45–47). See p. 10.

PENTECOST (PEN-ti-kawst; 50th day). 1. The Jewish Feast of Weeks, which was celebrated 50 days after the Feast of Passover (Ex 34:18–26; Dt 16:10). It is also known as the Feast of Harvest and the day of Firstfruits (Ex 23:16; Nu 28:26). See pp. 174, 362–63.

2. The 50th day after Easter Sunday. On this day the Holy Spirit was outpoured on the disciples, and many people came to faith in Christ (Ac 2; 1Co 16:8). This first Pentecost fell on the same day as the Feast of Harvest. See pp. 362–63.

PENUEL (pi-NYOO-uhl; face of God). The place, east of the Jordan, where Jacob wrestled with God (Gn 32:31; Jgs 8:17; 1Ki 12:25).

PERDITION (pur-DISH-uhn). *See* HELL; JUDGMENT.

PERDITION, SON OF. *See* DESTRUCTION, SON OF.

PEREZ-UZZA (PEE-rez-UZ-ah; breach of Uzzah). The name David gave to the place where Uzzah was struck dead for touching the ark of the covenant (2Sm 6:8; 1Ch 13:11).

PERFUMER. A person who mixed ointments and oils for the holy place (Ex 30:25, 35; 31:11; 37:29; Ne 3:8). They also made perfumes for burial spices and, according to excavation finds, medicinal herbs (2Ch 16:14).

PERGA (PUR-gah). A city of Pamphylia. Paul and Barnabas passed through Perga on their first missionary journey. This is also the place where John Mark left them to return home (Ac 13:13; 14:25). See pp. 360–61.

PERGAMUM (PUR-gah-muhm). A city in Mysia in Asia Minor. It is the third of the seven churches of Asia mentioned in the Book of Revelation (1:11; 2:12–17). Today it is called Bergama. See p. 446.

PERSIA (PUR-zhah; land of Aryans). To begin with, Persia was only the land around the Persian Gulf. Cyrus II, also known as Cyrus the Great, built the Persian Empire by conquering Media and Babylonia. This empire dominated Asia from 538 to 331 BC.

Cyrus allowed the Hebrew exiles in Babylonia to return to their land (2Ch 36:22–23; Ezr 1; Is 41:2; 44:28; 45). Darius I gave them permission to rebuild the temple at Jerusalem (Ezr 6). Darius's son, Xerxes I, was the next Persian ruler. He was probably the same person as the Ahasuerus mentioned in Est 1:1. Under Artaxerxes I, Ezra was allowed to lead more exiles back to Jerusalem. Nehemiah was also permitted to return to Jerusalem, where he organized the rebuilding of the city walls (Ezr 7–8; Ne 2:1–8). See p. 268.

PETER (PEE-tur; rock). One of the 12 disciples and a leader in the Early Church. He received the name Peter from Jesus at their first meeting. Peter's given name, however, was Simon or Simeon (Mt 4:18; Mk 1:16; Jn 1:41). He was also referred to as Cephas, which means "rock" (Jn 1:42; 1Co 1:12). Peter was the son of Jonas or John (Mt 16:17; Jn 1:42; 21:15–17). He lived in Bethsaida, where, together with his brother Andrew, he made his living as a fisherman on the Sea of Galilee (Mt 4:18; Mk 1:16; Lk 5:1–11; Jn 1:44).

Peter was first introduced to Jesus by Andrew and called to discipleship by Jesus at the Sea of Galilee (Mt 4:18–22; Mk 1:16–20; Jn 1:40–42). Later, along with the other 11 disciples, Jesus called him to be an apostle (Mt 10:2–4; Mk 3:13–19; Lk 6:13).

Because of Peter's personality, he seemed to be a natural leader among the disciples. On one occasion he walked on the sea toward Jesus. As his doubts began to grow, however, he began to sink, and Jesus had to put out His hand to save Peter (Mt 14:25–33). At Caesarea Philippi, when Jesus asked the 12 disciples what they thought of Him, Peter answered, saying, "You are the Christ, the Son of the living God" (Mt 16:16). Jesus praised Peter for his God-given confession of faith and said that He would build His Church on it (Mt 16:13–19; Mk 8:27–29; Lk 9:18–20). When Jesus began to tell the disciples about how He must suffer and die, Peter rebuked Him and said, "Far be it from You, Lord! This shall never happen to You." Jesus sharply scolded Peter for this (Mt 16:21–23).

Along with James and John, Peter was a member of the inner circle of disciples (Mt 16:15–16; 17:1). He was present at Jesus' transfiguration, in the Garden of Gethsemane, and at the high priest's palace, where Jesus was taken after His arrest (Mt 17:1; 26:37, 69; Mk 9:2; 14:33, 66; Lk 9:28; 22:54; Jn 18:16). While in the courtyard of the high priest's palace, Peter denied Jesus three times (Mt 26:69–75; Mk 14:70–72; Lk 22:59–62; Jn 18:26–27).

Peter was the first of the 12 disciples to whom Jesus appeared after His resurrection (Lk 24:34; 1Co 15:5). On Pentecost, Peter preached the Spirit-inspired message to the crowds of listening people (Ac 2). He was also one of the chief leaders in the Early Church (Ac 1–12; 15). According to tradition, Nero had Peter put to death in Rome around AD 65. See pp. 286, 429–33.

PETER, FIRST LETTER OF. Peter wrote this letter to the Christians suffering persecution in five provinces of Asia Minor: Pontus, Galatia, Cappadocia, Asia, and

Bithynia (1Pt 1:1). In his letter Peter tries to encourage them by stressing the comfort and hope they have in Jesus Christ, their Savior. See pp. 429–30.

PETER, SECOND LETTER OF. A general letter written by Peter to warn its readers against false teachers and to remind them of the truths they had been taught about Jesus so that they might grow in His grace and trust His promises. See pp. 429–30.

PHANUEL (fah-NYOO-el; face of God). The father of the prophetess Anna (Lk 2:36).

PHARAOH (FAIR-o, great house). The title of Egyptian rulers (Gn 12:15; 41:39, 42; Ac 7:10). At birth individual names were given to the pharaohs, for instance, Pharaoh Neco and Pharaoh Hophra. A number of these Egyptian rulers are referred to in the Bible.

1. Pharaohs are mentioned in connection with Abraham and Joseph (Gn 12:14–20; 40–41). The names of these pharaohs are unknown.

2. Also unknown is the name of the pharaoh of the oppression. He may have been Seti I or Thutmose III.

3. Another pharaoh is mentioned when the children of Israel left Egypt under Moses. This ruler may have been either Rameses II or Amenhotep II.

4. Another pharaoh defeated the Canaanites of Gezer and gave the city as a dowry to his daughter, Solomon's wife (1Ki 3:1; 7:8; 9:16).

5. Pharaoh Shishak, who began ruling Egypt during the latter part of Solomon's reign, used the division of the kingdom after Solomon's death for his own benefit. While the country was politically weakened, he invaded Jerusalem (1Ki 14:25–26; 2Ch 12:2–9).

6. Zerah invaded Judah in the days of King Asa but was defeated by him (2Ch 14:9–15; 16:8).

7. Before Tirhakah became pharaoh, he did battle with Sennacherib, king of Assyria (2Ki 19:9).

8. Pharaoh Neco killed King Josiah and, when Josiah's son, Jehoahaz, became king, Neco dethroned him and carried him off to Egypt. Next Jehoiakim was made king. In 605 BC Nebuchadnezzar, king of Babylonia, defeated Neco at Carchemish (2Ki 23:29–35; 24:7; 2Ch 35:20–36:4; Jer 46:2).

9. Pharaoh Hophra was the ruler of Egypt while Jeremiah was a prophet in Judah. Jeremiah spoke against him (Jer 44:30).

See pp. 16, 27, 32, 34–36, 89.

PHARAOH'S DAUGHTER. 1. The woman who found baby Moses on the Nile River and raised him as her own child (Ex 2:5–10). See p. 132.

2. One of Solomon's wives (1Ki 3:1).

PHARISEES (FAR-uh-see; separated). One of the three leading Jewish parties during Jesus' time. It is believed that this strict and influential sect had its beginning during the time of the Maccabees.

The Pharisees believed that people had the ability to do good or evil, and that, by keeping the Law in an outward manner, they could of themselves earn God's favor. For this reason they stressed keeping God's Law and the oral law and put great emphasis on observing such rituals as washing, tithing, and fasting. They also avoided contact with non-Pharisees. They believed in the existence of angels and taught the immortality of the soul, two doctrines disputed by their rival party, the Sadducees (Mt 9:11–14; 12:1–8; 16:1–12; 23; Lk 11:37–54; Ac 15:5; 23:6–8). See pp. 269, 308–10.

PHILADELPHIA (fil-ah-DEL-fi-ah; brotherly love). A city of Lydia in Asia Minor. It was the location of one of the seven churches addressed in the Book of Revelation (Rv 1:11; 3:7–13). See p. 446.

PHILEMON (fi-LEE-mun; friendship). One of Paul's converts who lived in Colossae and had a church in his house. Paul addressed a letter to Philemon when he sent Philemon's runaway slave, Onesimus, back to him (Phm). See p. 417.

PHILEMON, LETTER OF PAUL TO. A letter Paul wrote to Philemon on behalf of Philemon's runaway slave, Onesimus. In the letter Paul asks Philemon to forgive Onesimus and receive him back as a brother in the faith. See pp. 417–18.

PHILIP (FIL-uhp; lover of horses). 1. One of the 12 apostles. He came from Bethsaida on the Sea of Galilee and was likely a close friend of Andrew and Peter (Jn 1:44; 12:21). Philip was called to be a disciple near Bethany beyond the Jordan (Jn 1:41–43). Some time later Jesus called him to be an apostle (Mt 10:3; Mk 3:18; Lk 6:14).

When Jesus was about to perform the miracle of feeding the 5,000, He tested Philip's faith by asking, "Where are we to buy bread, so that these people may eat?" (Jn 6:5–7). On the day of Jesus' triumphal entry into Jerusalem, Philip brought some Greeks who wished to meet Jesus to Him (Jn 12:20–23). While Jesus was talking to His disciples on the night before He was crucified, He told them that by knowing Him they knew the Father. Philip, however, did not understand this and asked Jesus to show them the Father (Jn 14:8–12). The last information the New Testament gives about Philip is that he was among the apostles in the Upper Room after Jesus' ascension (Ac 1:13). See p. 286.

2. The evangelist who came from Caesarea. Philip was one of the seven men chosen to look after the needs of widows and the poor in the Early Church. See p. 412.

Philip preached the Gospel in Samaria. He cast out demons and healed sick people just as the apostles did. God used him to bring the Ethiopian eunuch to faith in Christ (Ac 6:5; 8:4–40; 21:8–9). See pp. 357–59.

PHILIPPI (fuh-LIP-igh). A Macedonian city that was made a Roman colony by Octavius and granted citizenship privileges. Paul visited this city and made various converts there, among whom were Lydia and the Philippian jailor (Ac 16:12, 20:6; Php 1:1; 1Th 2:2). See pp. 360–61, 375–76, 397–99.

PHILIPPIANS, LETTER OF PAUL TO. A letter Paul wrote while he was in prison to thank the Philippians for sending a gift to him through Epaphroditus. In the letter Paul expresses his joy in Christ and offers the Philippians spiritual advice for the Christian life. See pp. 397–98.

PHILISTIA (fuh-LIS-ti-ah). The land of the Philistines, an area along the coast of Canaan about 50 miles long and 15 miles wide. It extended from Joppa to south of Gaza and had five great cities: Gaza, Ekron, Ashdod, Ashkelon, and Gath (Jsh 13:2–3; 1Sm 6:17).

The Philistines were a non-Semitic people who came from Caphtor (or Crete) around 1175 BC. They were a warlike people, knowledgeable in making iron tools and weapons. Since Israel did not have these types of weapons until the time of David, the Philistines dominated them during the period of the judges (Jgs 13:1). Israel was set free from Philistine control by various deliverers, such as Shamgar, Samson, and Samuel (Jgs 3:31; 13–16; 1Sm 7:1–14). Later, the Philistines were defeated by Jonathan and conquered by David, who made them pay tribute (1Sm 13–14; 17–18). The Philistines regained their power during the period of the divided monarchy (1Ki 15:27; 2Ch 21:16; 28:18). See p. 104.

PHILISTINES (fuh-LIS-tinz). The people of Philistia. *See also* PHILISTIA. See p. 104.

PHILOSOPHY (fuh-LOS-o-fee). The study of humanity's thinking about the meaning of life. In the Bible the word *philosophy* is used only in Col 2:8. Other passages in the New Testament, however, refer to various philosophical movements. The Epicureans and Stoics are mentioned in Ac 17:18. A chief threat to Christianity came from Gnostic (Col 2:8) and syncretistic thought (1Co 1:18–25; 1Tm 6:20). See pp. 161, 244, 269–70.

PHINEHAS (FIN-i-uhs). 1. The son of Eleazar and grandson of Aaron. Phinehas ran a spear through an Israelite man and the Midianite woman he had brought into the camp. This ended a plague that had been sent as a judgment against the idolatry into which the Midianite women were leading the Israelites. For this reason God promised Phinehas and his descendants an everlasting priesthood (Nu 25:1–8; 31:6; Jsh 22:13; Jgs 20:28). Except during the time of Eli, the descendants of Phinehas held the high priesthood until AD 70. See p. 150.

2. A wicked son of Eli. Both he and his brother were unfaithful priests who were killed by the Philistines (1Sm 1:3; 2:34; 4:11–22).

PHOEBE (FEE-bi; pure, radiant). A deaconess at Cenchrea. She was perhaps the first deaconess of the Christian Church and was highly spoken of by Paul (cf. "servant" in Rm 16:1–2).

PHOENICIA (fi-NISH-i-ah; bloodred, purple, or palm). A country along the Mediterranean coast, about 120 miles long, that went from Arvad to the Ladder of Tyre. In the New Testament it extended to Dor.

The people who lived in Phoenicia were Semitic in background. They were well-known seagoers who founded Carthage and places in Spain and may even have reached England. Sidon was a city of Phoenicia. The Phoenicians were also famous shipbuilders and carpenters (1Ki 5:6; Ezk 27:9). Phoenicia was a trading center of the nations (Is 23:3; Ezk 27:25). Because the Phoenicians went to other lands and people from other lands came to Phoenicia, the Phoenician culture, its alphabet, dyes, numbers, weights, measures, and architecture spread.

The Phoenicians worshiped the idols El, Baal, Anath, Astarte, and Asherah. Jezebel, Ahab's wife, brought this worship to Israel (1Ki 16:31; 18:19). Hiram, one of the Phoenician kings, was friendly with David and Solomon (2Sm 5:11; 1Ki 5:1–12; 2Ch 2:3–16). Another Hiram, a craftsman and architect, helped Solomon build the temple (1Ki 7:13–47; cf. "Huram-abi" in 2Ch 2:13–14). After Elijah had told King Ahab about a coming drought, Elijah fled to Phoenicia, where a widow looked after him (1Ki 17:9).

Jesus visited the regions of Phoenicia and healed a Syrophoenician woman there (Mk 7:24–30). Paul visited the Christians in Phoenicia (Ac 15:3; 21:2–7). See pp. 285, 360–61.

PHRYGIA (FRIJ-i-ah). A province in Asia Minor that once included the greater part of Asia Minor. It was obtained by Rome in 133 BC. Paul visited Phrygia on several of his missionary journeys (Ac 2:10; 16:6; 18:23). See pp. 360, 375.

PHYLACTERY (fi-LAK-tur-ee). *See* FRONTLET.

PIECE OF GOLD OR SILVER. A certain amount of precious metal, either in coin or uncoined form. The phrases "a piece of gold" or "a piece of silver" are used in the Bible because the exact amount of money is unknown. In the Old Testament the original text often said "1,000 of silver," or "1,000 of gold" (Gn 20:16). In the New Testament a piece of silver commonly meant a drachma (Lk 15:8–9), shekel, or denarion (Mt 26:15; 27:3–9). See pp. 262, 287.

PILATE (PIGH-laht; armed with javelin). Pontius Pilate, the fifth procurator or representative of the Roman government in Judea (AD 26–36). Although Pilate found Jesus innocent of the accusations brought against Him, he nevertheless gave in to the peoples' wishes and condemned Jesus to death on the cross (Mt 27; Mk 15; Lk 3:1; 13:1; 23; Jn 18–19; Ac 3:13; 4:27; 13:28; 1Tm 6:13). See pp. 272–73, 332.

PILGRIMAGE. 1. The Jewish people were expected to make the pilgrimage or trip to the temple in Jerusalem for the great feasts (Dt 16:16; Ps 120–134; Ac 2:5–11). See pp. 173–74, 325.

2. In the New Testament Christians are referred to as pilgrims or sojourners on the road to heaven (Heb 11:13; 1Pt 2:11).

PILLAR. 1. A monument that marked a sacred spot or a grave or was put up as a memorial (Gn 28:18; 31:45; 35:20; 2Sm 18:18).

2. Pillars or columns that supported buildings (Jgs 16:25–30; 1Ki 7; 2Ki 11:14). See pp. 40, 259, 365.

3. A pillar of cloud by day or fire by night that guided the Israelites during the exodus and showed God's presence (Ex 13:21; 14:19–24).

PINNACLE. Something shaped like a wing on a building, roof, battlement, or temple. The devil took Jesus to the pinnacle of the temple and said to Him, "If You are the Son of God, throw Yourself down" (Mt 4:5; Lk 4:9).

PIPE. A musical instrument of the woodwind category (Gn 4:21; Jb 21:12; 30:31). See pp. 168, 172. *See also* MUSIC.

PISGAH, MOUNT (PIZ-gah). Part of the Abarim mountain range that looks out over Jericho (Nu 21:20; 23:14; Dt 3:17; 4:49; 34:1; Jsh 12:3; 13:20). It is near Mount Nebo, the mountain from which Moses viewed the Promised Land (Dt 3:27). See p. 69.

PISHON (PIGH-shon). One of the four rivers of Eden (Gn 2:11).

PISIDIA (puh-SID-i-ah). An area in southern Asia Minor north of Pamphylia. Paul visited there on his first two missionary journeys (Ac 13:14; 14:24). See p. 360.

PIT. 1. A hole that was dug for a well or cistern. Often these holes were used for prisons, burials, or traps (Gn 37:24; 2Sm 23:20; Ps 28:1; Is 24:22; Ezk 19:8). See p. 89.

2. The word *pit* is also used in the Old Testament to mean death, grave, or existence beyond death (Jb 33:18–30; Ps 28:1; 30:3; Is 14:15, 19). *See also* ABYSS; SHEOL.

PITCH. Asphalt or bitumen (Is 34:9). Pitch was used to make vessels watertight (Gn 6:14; Ex 2:3; Is 34:9).

PITHOM (PIGH-thom; dwelling of Atum, sun-god). An Egyptian store-city in Goshen. It held supplies of grain for armies and perhaps for caravans (Ex 1:11).

PLAGUE. Something that causes trouble or suffering (Ex 11:1). Often a plague was a quickly spreading disease that made many people severely ill or caused them to die (1Sm 5; 2Sm 24:13–25). The ten plagues on Egypt were the means God used to convince the pharaoh to let the Israelites go (Ex 7–12). See pp. 27, 34–36, 230–31.

PLANE. A tree that grows along the water in Syria and Mesopotamia. The word *plane* is sometimes translated as chestnut or pine (Gn 30:37; Is 41:19; 60:13; Ezk 31:8).

PLEDGE. 1. Something given to be held as security for a loan (Dt 24:10–13, 17). *See also* LOANS.

2. A wager (2Ki 18:23; Is 36:8).

PLEIADES (PLEE-yah-deez; cluster). The stars in the constellation Taurus (Jb 9:9; 38:31; Am 5:8).

PLOW. *See* AGRICULTURE.

PLOWSHARE. A stone or the point of a plow (1Sm 13:20; Is 2:4; Mi 4:3). *See also* AGRICULTURE.

POETRY. Features of Hebrew poetry include its rhythm, parallelism, alliteration, and rhyme or other wordplays. Job, Psalms, Proverbs, Ecclesiastes, Song of Solomon, and sections in the prophets are examples of Hebrew poetry. See pp. 165–66, 176, 179–82, 189, 233, 249.

POMEGRANATE (POM-gran-it). *See* ORCHARD.

PONTIUS (PON-shuhs). *See* PILATE.

PONTUS (PON-tuhs; sea). A region of northeast Asia Minor. During New Testament times it was a Roman province (Ac 2:9; 1Pt 1:1). Aquila, one of Paul's helpers, came from Pontus (Ac 18:2). See p. 429.

POOR. Old Testament law would prevent poverty and begging (Dt 15:4; cf. Ps 37:25; Pr 20:4). Laziness, some great trouble or disaster, and cruel or unjust treatment are cited as causes of being poor (Jgs 10:6–17; Pr 10:4; 14:23; Is 5:8; Mt 23:14).

Although it is true that God promises to bless His people (Dt 28:1–14) and that hard work and wisely managing one's resources often benefit the person who does so, poor people were still present in Israel throughout its history. Laws protected the poor. For instance, when crops were harvested, some of the yield was to be left for the fatherless and widows (Lv 19:9–10; Dt 24:19–22). Every seventh year fields and orchards were to lie fallow so the poor could eat (Ex 23:11; Lv 25:6). During the year of jubilee, land that people sold because they needed the money was to be returned to them (Lv 25:8–30). The poor were to receive their wages on time, and they were not to be charged interest (Ex 22:25–27; Dt 24:14–15).

Scripture praises the person who has mercy on the poor (Ps 41:1; Pr 14:21; 29:7). See pp. 234, 323–31, 354, 410, 426.

PORCH. A passageway from a street to the inner hall or an area protected by a roof, such as a veranda, a colonnade or portico, or a vestibule or hall (Jgs 3:23; 1Ki 7:6; 1Ch 28:11; Jn 5:2). See pp. 259, 325, 365, 382.

POST. A position from which soldiers would keep watch to protect the town or city (2Ch 23:18; Ne 7:3). Also figurative (Ezk 46:2).

POT. A clay or metal vessel used for holding liquid or dry ingredients (Jgs 6:19; 2Ki 4:38; Jb 41:20, 31; Lm 4:2).

POTIPHAR (POT-uh-fur; who is of the sun). The captain of the pharaoh's guard during Joseph's time (Gn 37:36; 39:1).

POTIPHERA (po-TIF-ur-ah; who is of the sun). The Egyptian priest of On, whose daughter, Asenath, became Joseph's wife (Gn 41:45, 50; 46:20).

POTTER, POTTER'S FIELD, POTTER'S WHEEL, POTTERY. *See* TRADE.

POVERTY. *See* POOR.

PRAETORIAN GUARD (pri-TO-ri-uhn). *See* IMPERIAL GUARD.

PRAETORIUM (pri-TO-ri-uhm). The headquarters of a general. 1. The palace in Jerusalem occupied by Pontius Pilate (cf. "headquarters" in Mt 27:27; Mk 15:16; Jn 18:28).

2. Herod's palace at Caesarea (Ac 23:35).

PRAYER (PRAIR). Speaking with God. Moses' prayers were largely intercessory, that is, speaking to God on behalf of the people (Ex 32:11–13, 31–32; Nu 11:11–15; Dt 9:18–21). The psalms are examples of the covenant people's prayers to their covenant God. These prayers are usually a result of some experience seen in its spiritual depth and are often closely related to sacrifice (Gn 12:8; 26:25) and the temple (1Ki 8:30, 33; Ps 5:7).

The New Testament teaches that prayer is to be spoken in the name of Jesus since sinful people cannot approach God on their own merits (Jn 14:13; 15:16). They approach only through Christ, who has bought humankind back from their sins and put them in a right relationship with God (Gal 4:1–7). Christ taught the disciples the Lord's Prayer (Mt 6:9–13; Lk 11:1–4). It is an example of proper approach and manner for speaking to God. Christ intercedes for believers before the Father (Rm 8:34; Heb 4:14–16; 7:25). The Holy Spirit who dwells within all Christians also intercedes for them according to the will of God (Rm 8:15–16, 26–27).

Prayers can be formal (Ps; Mt 6:9–13; 26:30) or spoken freely from one's own thoughts and concerns (Jn 17; Lk 18:13; 1Th 5:17). They can be said together by a large group of believers or alone by an individual (Mt 6:6; 14:23; Ac 1:14; Phm 4); they can be said at set times and places (Ac 2:42; 6:4; 16:13) or at all times and places (Eph 6:18; 1Th 5:17; 1Tm 2:8).

The Bible mentions various ways in which prayers can be said: with uplifted hands, while kneeling, while lying flat on the ground, or while standing (1Ki 8:54; Ps 28:2; Mt 6:5; 26:39; Ac 9:40; 1Tm 2:8). See pp. 143–44, 251–52.

PREACHER, PREACHING. One who speaks God's message or the act of speaking for God.

In the Old Testament prophets proclaimed God's message—the Law and the Gospel. They spoke about God's will for people, proclaimed His judgment on those who had sinned, and spoke His promises (Ezk 20:46; Jer 11:6).

In the New Testament preaching centered in the person and work of Jesus Christ (Ac 2:14–40; 3:11–26). Again, the message included both the Law and the Gospel (Mt 4:17; Lk 3:3–14; 4:18; Ac 2:14–40; 17:22–31). See pp. 118, 156, 186, 363, 415.

PREDESTINATION (pri-des-tuh-NAY-shuhn). God's act before the beginning of the world in choosing from sinners those whom He would save (Eph 1:4–5). God does this by (1) providing for the salvation of the world through Christ, (2) offering the merits and benefits of Christ's work to individuals through the Word and Sacraments, (3) working faith in the hearts of individuals through the Holy Spirit, (4) graciously receiving those who are sorry for their sins and who trust and believe in Christ as their Savior, (5) making individuals more and more holy by the Holy Spirit's work in them, (6) protecting them from the work of the devil and the sinful world, (7) keeping them in the faith until the end through the work of the Holy Spirit in Word and Sacrament, and (8) saving these individuals eternally (Mt 20:16; 22:14; Mk 13:20–22; Ac 13:48; Rm 8:28–30; 9:11; 11:15; Eph 1:4–5, 11; 2Th 2:13; 2Tm 1:9; 2:10, 19; 1Pt 1:2). *See also* ELECT, ELECTION.

PRESBYTER (PREZ-buh-tur). *See* ELDER.

PRIEST. One who represents the people before God. Originally individuals or heads of families carried out the work of a priest (Gn 4:3–4; 12:7; 13:18; 26:25; 33:20). Then through Moses God appointed Aaron and his sons and their descendants as priests (Ex 28:1). Aaronic priests had to meet high standards (Lv 21:16–24). Consecrated for this task, they wore special clothing in the sanctuary, taught the people, and inquired of God's will (Ex 28–29).

The priesthood was grouped into 24 divisions, each serving a week at a time (1Ch 24:1–19). Kings, judges, and prophets also made sacrifices to God (Jgs 6:17–21; 13:15–20; 2Sm 6:17; 1Ki 18:30–38).

The chief priest, or high priest, was in charge of all the other priests. He offered the sin offering, made sacrifice on the Day of Atonement, and discovered the will of God through Urim and Thummin (Lv 4; 16; Nu 27:21; Ne 7:65). The high priest wore the regular priestly clothing plus breastplate, ephod, sash, and turban(Ex 28). *See also* AARON.

In the New Testament Jesus Christ is the only high priest. Since He sacrificed Himself for the sins of the people and this sacrifice need never be repeated, there is no longer a need for the Levitical priesthood; it has been done away with in Christ (Jn 14:6; 1Tm 2:5–6; Heb 5:7–10). *See also* JESUS CHRIST (office of priest).

The New Testament also teaches the priesthood of all believers. Christians share in Christ's priestly activity by bringing the Gospel to people (Eph 2:18; Heb 10:19–25; 13:15; 1Pt 2:5, 9; Rv 1:5–6). See pp. 28, 50, 149–50

PRIEST, HIGH. *See* PRIEST.

PRINCE. A ruler or chief person, such as the head of a family or tribe, a king, a ruler, a governor, a magistrate, a satrap, or a royal descendant (Gn 25:16; Nu 22:8; 1Sm 9:16; 2Ki 10:13; 2Ch 12:5–6; Est 1). The Messiah is called "the Prince of Peace" (Is 9:6). The devil is called "the prince [or ruler] of demons" (Mt 9:34). See pp. 89, 200, 303.

PRISCA, PRISCILLA (PRIS-kah, pri-SIL-ah; little old woman). Wife of Aquila. Priscilla and her husband were tentmakers and Christian friends of Paul, whom they helped on a number of occasions (Ac 18:2, 18; Rm 16:3; 2Tm 4:19). They had a church in their house and together taught Apollos more about the Christian faith (Ac 18:26; 1Co 16:19). See pp. 360, 376, 421.

PRISON. A place where persons who are suspected of committing a crime or who have been accused of one are kept. 1. The oldest prisons mentioned in the Bible were wells or dungeons (Gn 37:24; Jer 38:6–13). During the period of the kings prisons were located in the palace or in private houses (1Ki 22:27; Jer 32:2; 37:15). The Herods and Romans had royal prisons (Lk 3:20; Ac 12:4; cf. "praetorium" in Ac 23:35). See pp. 355–57, 383.

2. Another word for abyss, the place where Satan lives (1Pt 3:19; Rv 20:7).

PROCHORUS (PROK-o-ruhs; leader of chorus). One of the seven men chosen by the Early Church to look after widows and probably the poor in general (Ac 6:5). See p. 412.

PROCONSUL (pro-KAHN-suhl). The governor of a Roman province administered by the Senate (Ac 13:7–8, 12).

PROMISE. The most important promise in the Bible is God's assurance that He would send a deliverer, or Messiah, to save His people (Gn 3:15; 12:3; Rm 4:13; 9:8; Gal 3:14–19). The promises in the Old Testament concerning the Messiah are fulfilled in Christ Jesus (Ac 13:23, 32–33; Rm 1:2–3; 15:8; Gal 3:14; 2Co 1:20). Those who believe in Jesus as their Savior are called heirs, or children, of the promise (Rm 4:16; Gal 3:16, 26–29; 4:28). By God's grace, through faith, they receive many blessings, including the forgiveness of sins, the indwelling of the Holy Spirit, and life everlasting (1Co 3:16; Gal 3:1–14; 1Jn 1:7). See pp. 162, 172, 315, 442–43, 446.

PROPHET (PRAHF-it; seer, announcer, spokesman). A person called by God to speak for Him to the people. Prophets spoke God's Word of judgment, calling people to account for their sins (2Sm 12; Is 58:1; Ezk 3:17), and His Word of mercy (Is 40; 53). Their work involved forth-telling and, to a lesser degree, foretelling. They constantly emphasized God's work in the course of history, particularly His plan of salvation through the Messiah, Jesus Christ.

The Old Testament prophets came from all walks of life (Am 1:1). Many of them wrote books of the Bible which have been named for them. The Old Testament also mentions schools of prophets (1Sm 19:19–20; 2Ki 2:3–5; 4:38; 6:1). See pp. 118, 130–31, 139, 186–88, 192.

PROPITIATION (pro-pish-i-AY-shuhn; cover, incline toward). The act of keeping God from being angry by satisfying His justice and holiness so that He can forgive sins. Sin causes a separation between God and people; it is necessary that human guilt be removed in order to restore a right relationship between them. In the Old Testament, the sacrificial system served this function, though God also forgave people without sacrifices being offered (cf. "atonement" in Lv 14:18; 17:11; 19:22; Is 6:7; 27:9; Ezk 16:63). These sacrifices pointed forward to the supreme sacrifice of God's Son, Jesus Christ, who died for the sins of the world. Christ's death and resurrection once and for all removed the barrier between God and all people (Rm 3:25; 1Jn 2:2; 4:10).

PROSELYTE (PRAHS-uh-light). In the Old Testament, referred to as sojourners. *See* SOJOURNER.

In the New Testament, proselytes included people who observed some or all features of the Jewish religion (Mt 23:15; Ac 2:11) and those who simply feared God (cf. Ac 10:2). Some proselytes believed that the God of Israel was the true God but they had not received circumcision. See p. 412

PROSTITUTE (PRAHS-tuh-tyoot). A person who offers sexual favors for money, especially a woman who offers herself to a man for money. There were both common and religious prostitutes in the ancient world (Dt 23:17–18; Hos 4:14). The Scripture often speaks of prostitutes and prostitution as a symbol for disobedience and unfaithfulness (Ex 34:15; Ezk 16; 23; Hos 4:15). The sin of prostitution is forbidden in Scripture many times (Lv 21:7, 9, 14; 1Co 6:18–20). See p. 226.

PROVERB (PRAHV-urb). Generally a short saying expressing a familiar or useful truth (Gn 10:9; 1Sm 10:12; Dt 28:37; Pr). See p. 175.

PROVERBS, BOOK OF. A book in the Bible containing proverbs and practical advice "to know wisdom and instruction" (1:2). It notes that a wise person recognizes God in all things. Most of the proverbs in the book were written by King Solomon. See pp. 175–77.

PROVIDENCE (PRAHV-uh-duhns). The activity of God whereby He preserves, governs, and directs His entire creation (Jb 9:5; Ps 104:10–25; 145:15; Mt 4:4; 6:26–28; Lk 12:6–7; Ac 17:25–28; Heb 1:3). See pp. 16, 61, 131, 155, 174.

PROVINCE. A unit of a country, for instance, the provinces of the Roman Empire. Persian provinces were also called satrapies (Ezr 2:1; 5:8; Ac 23:34; 25:1). See pp. 219, 224.

PSALMS, BOOK OF (song of praise, poem sung to music of stringed instruments). The longest book of the Writings division of the Hebrew Scriptures. The authors of the various psalms are given in their titles. Bible scholars think the titles of the psalms may refer to musical directions or instruments, melodies, or liturgical instructions or occasions. Some think these titles may be simply descriptive. In the Hebrew Psalter the psalms are divided into five books. See pp. 164–67.

PTOLEMY (TAWL-i-mee). The common name of the Macedonian kings who ruled Egypt after the death of Alexander the Great in 323 BC until 30 BC, the year of Cleopatra's death.

PUBLICAN (PUHB-li-kuhn). See p. 389. *See* TAX COLLECTOR.

PURIM (PYOO-rim). A Jewish festival commemorating the deliverance of the Jews by Esther (Est 3:7; 9:24–32). The name comes from Pur, meaning lot (Est 9:24–26). See pp. 153, 157–58.

QUART. *See* MEASURES 2; 3.

QUEEN OF HEAVEN. A Semitic goddess of fertility. She was likely Astarte of Canaan or Ishtar of Babylonia (Jer 7:18; 44:17–25). See p. 77.

QUEEN OF THE SOUTH. The queen of Sheba (Mt 12:42; Lk 11:31. See also 1Ki 10:1–13; 2Ch 9:1–12). See p. 123.

QUIRINIUS, PUBLIUS SULPICIUS (kwigh-RIN-i-uhs PUB-li-uhs sul-PISH-UHS). The governor of Syria at the time Caesar Augustus issued the decree for the census in which Joseph enrolled (Lk 2:2).

QUIVER (KWIV-ur). *See* ARCHERY.

R

RAAMSES (ray-AM-seez). A store-city the Hebrews built in northeast Egypt while they were slaves there (Ex 1:11). It was the capital of the Nineteenth Dynasty. It is also referred to as Rameses (Gn 47:11; Ex 12:37; Nu 33:3, 5).

RABBI (RAB-igh; my master). A title of respect the Jewish people gave to their spiritual leaders and instructors (Mt 23:7–8; Mk 10:51; Jn 1:38, 49; 3:2, 26; 6:25). John explains *rabbi* and *rabboni* as meaning "master" (Jn 4:31; 9:2; 11:8; 20:16). See pp. 298–300.

RABBONI (ra-BO-nee). *See* RABBI.

RAB-SARIS (RAB-sah-ris; chief eunuch). The title of Assyrian officials who held high positions in the court (2Ki 18:17; Jer 39:3, 13).

RABSHAKEH (RAB-shah-ke; chief officer). The title of Assyrian military officials who held high positions (2Ki 18:17–37; 19:4–8; Is 36; 37:4, 8).

RACHEL (RAY-chuhl; ewe). The favorite wife of Jacob; mother of Joseph and Benjamin. Rachel was the younger daughter of Laban, Jacob's uncle. This made her Jacob's cousin (Gn 29–35; Jer 31:15). See pp. 17–21, 105, 212.

RADDAI (RAD-ay-igh; trampling). One of David's brothers (1Ch 2:14).

RAHAB (RAY-hab; broad). 1. A woman who had a house on the wall of Jericho during the time of the conquest. For her help in hiding Israelite spies in her home, Rahab's life and the lives of her family were spared (Jsh 2:1–21; 6:17–25). She is likely the Rahab who married Salmon and became the mother of Boaz, an ancestor of Jesus (Ru 4:21; Mt 1:5). See pp. 75, 82.

2. Meaning "violent one." A mythical monster representing sea power and violence (Jb 26:12; Ps 89:10). The name is also applied to Egypt (Ps 87:4; Is 30:7).

RAIN. The rainy season in Palestine extends from October through April. The early rain occurs in October and November (Ps 84:6; Is 30:23; Jer 5:24); the spring rain comes in March and April (Jb 29:23; Pr 16:15; Jer 3:3; Zec 10:1).

In the Bible *rain* is often a picture word for teaching and counsel, for the Word, for righteousness and peace, for blessings on believers, for judgments that destroy, and for nagging (Dt 32:2; Jb 20:23; 29:21–25; Ps 72:6; 84:5–6; Pr 19:13; Is 55:10; Ezk 38:22).

RAINBOW. The sign of God's covenant with Noah. The rainbow is a reminder that God will never again flood the whole earth (see "bow" in Gn 9:12–17). See p. 16.

RAM. A male sheep. The ram was a source of food and sacrifice (Gn 15:9; 22:13; 31:38). The skins of rams were used as coverings for the tabernacle; their horns, for trumpets (Ex 26:14; Josh 6:4–20).

RAMAH (RAY-mah; height). 1. A town of Benjamin 5 miles north of Jerusalem. It was near Deborah's palm tree and Rachel's tomb (Jsh 18:25; Jgs 4:5; 19:10–15; 1Ki 15:17–22; Jer 31:15; 40:1; Mt 2:18). Benjaminites lived in Ramah after the captivity (Ezr 2:26; Ne 7:30). Today it is called el-Ram.

2. A town in the mountains of Ephraim. It was where Samuel was born, lived, and buried. In 1Sm 1:1 it is called Ramathaim-zophim to distinguish it from other towns of similar name. It may be the same as Arimathea, a place mentioned in the New Testament.

RAMESES (RAM-i-seez). *See* PHARAOH 3.

RAMOTH-GILEAD, RAMOTH IN GILEAD (RAY-moth-GIL-i-uhd; heights of Gilead). An Amorite city east of the Jordan and a Levitical city of refuge in Gad (Dt 4:43; Jsh 20:8; 21:38). It was the home of Jephthah and the place where Solomon's tax gatherer lived (Jgs 11:34; 1Ki 4:13). King Ahab was killed there (1Ki 22:1–38). It was also known as Ramah, Ramath-mizpeh, and Mizpah or Mizpeh (Jsh 13:26; Jgs 10:17; 2Ki 8:29).

RANSOM. The price paid for getting someone or something back (Ex 21:30. Cf. 1Co 6:19–20). See p. 191.

RAPHAEL (RAF-ay-el). An archangel who appears in the apocryphal Book of Tobit.

REAP. *See* AGRICULTURE.

REBA (REE-bah; fourth). A Midianite king who, at Moses' command, was killed by Israel in Moab (Nu 31:8; Jsh 13:21).

REBEKAH (ri-BEK-ah; noose). The daughter of Bethuel, wife of Isaac, and mother of Esau and Jacob (Gn 22:23; 24; 25:21–26). See pp. 12–13, 19.

RECONCILIATION (rek-UN-sil-i-AY-shuhn). The removal of the barrier, caused by sin, between God and humanity. Christ's death on the cross for the sin of the world is the way this barrier was removed. An individual appropriates the forgiveness earned by Christ for himself or herself by grace through faith (Rm 5:11; 2Co 5:18–19; Eph 2:16). See pp. 65, 78, 449.

RECORDER. An official of high rank who wrote down important events and kept the public documents (2Sm 8:16; 20:24; 1Ki 4:3; 2Ki 18:18, 37; 1Ch 18:15; Is 36:3, 22). See p. 383.

RED SEA. Body of water, 1,350 miles long, extending from the Gulf of Suez to the Indian Ocean. It has two arms: the Gulf of Suez and the Gulf of Aqabah. The name *Red Sea* may refer to either the Gulf of Suez (Nu 33:10–11), the Gulf of Aqabah (1Ki 9:26), the entire Red Sea (Ex 23:31), or nearby lakes. See pp. 28, 31.

REED. Tall grasses, flags, or rushes. *Reed* is used as a picture word for uncertain support, fickleness, and weakness or helplessness (2Ki 18:21; Is 36:6; 42:3; Mt 11:7; 12:20; Lk 7:24). See pp. 168, 206–07.

REDEEMER, REDEMPTION (ri-DEEM-ur, ri-DEMP-shuhn). The buying back of humanity from sin and death by Christ, who paid the price with His perfect obedience and His sacrificial death on the cross (Rm 3:24; Gal 3:13; cf. "ransom" in Eph 1:7; 1Pt 1:18–19). See pp. 27, 38, 41, 320, 336.

REFINER. Someone who worked with precious metals (Mal 3:2–3). *See also* TRADE.

REFUGE, CITIES OF. Six Levitical cities designed to provide temporary shelter for those who had accidentally killed someone (Nu 35:6, 11–32; Dt 4:43; 19:1–13; Jsh 20). They were Kadesh (Naphtali), Shechem (Ephraim), Hebron (Judah), Golan (Manasseh), Ramoth-gilead (Gad), and Bezer (Reuben). See p. 58. *See also* MURDER.

REGENERATION (ri-jen-ur-AY-shuhn). To be born again, restored, renewed, completely made over. Regeneration is an act of God the Holy Spirit, who works through Word and Sacraments to bring a sinful, self-centered person into union with Christ Jesus through faith (Jn 1:13; 3:1–12; 1Pt 1:23).

REHOBOAM (ree-ho-BO-am; enlarger of people). Son of Solomon and Naamah (1Ki 14:21, 31; Mt 1:7). Rehoboam was the last king of the united kingdom of Israel. When he took over after his father's death, Rehoboam refused to listen to the people and lower their taxes. So the ten northern tribes rebelled and made Jeroboam their king. Rehoboam became the first king of the Southern Kingdom of Judah, the two remaining tribes (1Ki 12; 14; 2Ch 10–12). Rehoboam made his kingdom and cities stronger. In the fifth year of Rehoboam's reign, however, King Shishak of Egypt captured the fortified cities of Judah and Jerusalem (1Ki 14:25–27). See pp. 122, 125.

RELIGION. Humanity's recognition of its relationship to a supreme being and the expression of that relationship in faith, worship, and life. Religion may be true or false (Ac 17:22; 26:5; Rm 1:18–25; Jas 1:26–27). See pp. 79, 149, 384,399, 424.

REMNANT (REM-nuhnt). Something left over. 1. People who survived a period of deep trouble (Jsh 12:4; 13:12).

2. The small number of people who survive God's judgment and remain faithful to Him. Because of God's love for His people, believers will be added from all peoples to form the Church (Is 10:20–23; 11:11–12; Zec 8:12; Rm 9:27; cf. Jer 32:38–39; Zep 3:13).

See pp. 93–94, 203, 205, 243.

REPENTANCE (ri-PEN-tuhns). A total change of heart and life that God works in an individual who does not believe or trust in Him by turning him or her around to believe and trust in Him. Repentance includes both sorrow for one's sins and faith in Christ through whom forgiveness is granted (Mk 1:4; Lk 3:3, 8; Ac 5:31). See pp. 57, 69, 87, 281, 337.

REPHIDIM (REF-i-dim). A place between Sin and Sinai where Israel camped (Ex 17:1; 19:2; Nu 33:14–15). See p. 30.

RESIN (REE-sen). An Assyrian city built by Nimrod. It was probably a suburb of Nineveh (Gn 10:11–12).

RESURRECTION (rez-uh-REK-shuhn). A return to life after one has died. Because Christ rose from the dead, believers can be sure they, too, will rise from the dead and enjoy eternal life with Christ. The Bible describes the resurrected body as a spiritual body (Rm 6:3–11; 1Co 15). All people, both believers and nonbelievers, will rise from the dead and be judged (2Co 5:10). See pp. 391–92.

REUBEN (ROO-ben; see a son). Jacob's firstborn son by his wife Leah (Gn 29:32). Reuben brought mandrakes to his mother, which she used to get Jacob to make her pregnant so she could have another child (Gn 30:14–16). Reuben sinned by having sexual relations with his father's concubine (Gn 35:22; 49:3–4). When his brothers wanted to kill Joseph, Reuben spoke up and suggested that they throw him into a pit instead. Reuben's intention was to release Joseph and let him return home (Gn 37:22, 29–30).

Many years later when Joseph, whom they did not recognize, asked his brothers to bring Benjamin to Egypt, Reuben assured his father of Benjamin's safety (Gn 42:36–38).

The tribe of Reuben settled east of the Jordan River, an area suited for raising flocks and herds (Nu 1:20–21; Jsh 13:15–23). In her song Deborah refers to the Reubenites' lack of help in the battle with Sisera (Jgs 5:15–16). A number of years later the Assyrians took the Reubenites away into captivity (1Ch 5:26). See pp. 17, 19.

REUBENITES (ROO-ben-ights). Descendants of Reuben (Nu 26:7; Jsh 1:12).

REUEL (ROO-el; God's friend). 1. One of Esau's sons and the ancestor of the Edomite clan (Gn 36:4, 10, 13, 17).

2. The father-in-law of Moses (Ex 2:18). *See also* JETHRO.

REVELATION (rev-uh-LAY-shuhn). The way in which God makes Himself and His ways known to people. God reveals something of Himself to all people through nature, their consciences, and history. God reveals Himself and His will in a special way to particular people at particular times through visions, phenomena, dreams, angels, words, prophecies, and by appearing in human form (Gn 16:9; 18:9; 28:12–16; Ex 3:4; 19:18; Is 6). In particular, God reveals Himself through the Bible and Jesus Christ, the Word made flesh. See pp. xvii–xviii, 2, 4–6, 10–11, 39.

REVELATION, BOOK OF. The last book of the New Testament. John wrote Revelation to seven churches in Asia Minor while he was an exile on the island of Patmos (Rv 1–3). The book is apocalyptic in nature (*see* APOCALYPIC LITERATURE). Its divine message is conveyed through the use of symbols and visions. Dealing with the past, present, and future, the purpose of the book is to prepare people for the great trouble and misery that they will face as God's people. See pp. 441–43.

REWARD. Something given in return for something done. Being paid is a reward for work (Lk 10:7; 1Tm 5:18). God's punishment is the reward for people's sinfulness (Lk 23:41; cf. "recompense" in Rv 22:12). The Bible also speaks about the reward of grace. Although people do not deserve it, God graciously provides for their salvation through Christ Jesus. Those who believe in Jesus receive life and salvation (1Co 9:18; Col 3:24). This new life shows itself in fruits of faith, the way in which God crowns His work in the believer (Mt 6:4; Mk 9:41; Lk 6:23; 1Co 3:14).

REZIN (REE-zin). Last king of Damascus. Rezin ruled Syria from 735 to 732 BC. He aligned his country with Israel against Judah. Tiglath-Pileser, king of Assyria, besieged Damascus and when he finally captured it, killed Rezin and took his people into captivity (2Ki 15:37; 16:5, 9; Is 7:1–9; 8:6–8).

RHODA (RO-dah; rose). A young woman who worked in the home of Mary, John Mark's mother. When Peter was miraculously released from prison and went to Mary's home, Rhoda opened the door when he knocked on it (Ac 12:12–15).

RHODES (RODZ; roses). An island at the southwestern tip of Asia Minor that is famous for its huge statue of Helios (Ezk 27:15). Rhodes was a center for commerce, literature, and art. Paul stopped there once (Ac 21:1).

RIDDLE (dark or hidden saying). In the Bible a riddle is any saying in which the meaning is not at first clear (Jgs 14:12–19; Dn 8:23). Proverbs, musical meditations, oracles, parables, and hard questions are all riddles (Nu 12:8; 1Ki 10:1; 2Ch 9:1; Ps 49:4; Pr 1:6). See pp. 180, 219.

RIGHT HAND. A phrase for describing God's activity in carrying out His purposes (Ex 15:6; Ps 98:1). Jesus' session to the right hand of God shows Jesus' power (Ac 2:25; 7:55–56; Heb 1:3). See pp. 6, 21.

RIGHTEOUS. That which is right (Mt 27:19; Php 1:7) or in accordance with the Law and ceremonies (Mk 2:17; Lk 5:32; Rm 5:7). The term is particularly used to describe people who are in a right relationship with God through faith (Gn 15:6; Rm 1:17). See pp. 27, 308, 333, 445.

RIGHTEOUSNESS (RIGH-chuhs-ness; the quality of rightness). God is holy and right in His nature because He is God. He makes His righteousness known to people through His work on their behalf (Jer 23:6; Hs 2:19). He saves them from their earthly and spiritual enemies (Is 40–55).

Jesus is our righteousness, the One who puts us in a right relationship to God (Rm 1:16–17; 3:2 1–26; 1Co 1:30; 1Pt 2:24). See pp. 4, 110, 157, 347, 445.

RIMMON (RIM-un; thunderer). An Assyrian storm god (2Ki 5:18).

RING. A piece of jewelry (Jas 2:2; Lk 15:22). When rings were engraved with the symbol of the owner, they became symbols of power and authority. They were used as seals and signets (Gn 41:42; Est 3:10, 12; 8:2, 8, 10; cf. "signet" in Dn 6:17).

RIVER. A flowing body of water, such as a stream, a channel, or a brook (Gn 2:10–14; Ps 119:136; Ezk 47:1–12; Am 6:14). The word *river* is also a picture word for a great deal of good or evil (Jb 20:17; Ps 36:8; 69:2; Is 43:2). See pp. 33–34, 62, 146, 305, 444. *See also* EUPHRATES; NILE.

ROAD. A path, a well-traveled road, or a highway made by a ruler or by people (Nu 20:17; 21:22; Dt 19:3).

The Romans built an elaborate network of roads across their empire. The ones in Palestine were used by traders, armies, and travelers. Some well-known roads were those extending from Jerusalem to Jericho and beyond, from Jerusalem to Joppa, from Damascus to Ptolemais, from Ptolemais to Egypt, and from Galilee to Judea. See pp. 272, 306, 336, 357, 381.

ROD. A branch, stick, staff, or shoot. A shepherd's rod was a sturdy club that he used for guiding, defending, and counting his flock (Ps 23:4; Ezk 20:37; cf. Lv 27:32).

A *rod* or *shoot* is a picture word for the messianic ruler (Is 11:1). *Rod* is also a picture word for power and great trouble (Jb 9:34; Ps 2:9). See pp. 109, 171.

ROE. *See* GAZELLE; ROEBUCK.

ROEBUCK. A small deer (Dt 14:5; 1Ki 4:23). *See also* GAZELLE.

ROMAN (RO-mahn). 1. A person who was born in Rome or had Roman citizenship. *See* CITIZEN 2.

2. A Roman official (Jn 11:48; Ac 28:17).

ROMAN EMPIRE. *See* ROME.

ROMANS, LETTER OF PAUL TO. A letter Paul wrote from Greece to the Romans, whom he planned to visit (Ac 20:2, 3; Rm 1:1, 10, 11; 15:14–33). In this letter, Paul explains the Gospel in detail, describing the righteousness of God that justifies sinful humanity by grace through faith. See pp. 379–81.

ROME (ROM). The capital of the Roman Empire, situated on the Tiber River in Italy about 17 miles from the Mediterranean Sea. Rome was founded in 753 BC. From 753 to 509 BC, it was a monarchy; from 509 to 531 BC, a republic; and from 31 BC until its fall, an empire.

The Roman Empire extended over the whole Mediterranean world, providing a large network of roads, peace, trade, and a common government. This aided in the spread of the Gospel.

Under Augustus, the provinces of the empire were divided into senatorial provinces ruled by a proconsul (Ac 13:7; 18:12; 19:38) and imperial provinces ruled by a governor (Mt 27:2; Lk 2:2; Ac 23:24).

Under Roman rule, cities, reservoirs, aqueducts, roads, and public buildings were constructed in Israel. The Bible refers to four emperors: Augustus (Lk 2:1), Tiberius (Lk 3:1), Claudius (Ac 11:28), and Nero (Ac 25:11–12). See pp. 269, 271–74, 354–55, 381–83, 399.

ROSE. Many authorities believe roses grew in Palestine during Bible times. The identity of the flower mentioned in Sg 2:1 and Is 35:1, however, is unknown.

RUE (RU). A plant grown for its use in medicine and seasonings (Lk 11:42).

RUFUS (RU-fuhs; red). Son of Simon of Cyrene (Mk 15:21). The Rufus mentioned in Rm 16:13 may be the same person.

RUHAMAH (roo-HAH-mah). Hosea's daughter. Her name means "she has received mercy" (Hos 2:1; cf. Rm 9:25; 1Pt 2:10). *See also* LO-RUHAMAH.

RUSH. *See* PAPYRUS; REED.

RUTH (ROOTH; may mean friendship). A woman from Moab who married Mahlon, a son of Elimelech and Naomi. When both Ruth and Naomi's husbands died, Ruth decided to return to Judah with Naomi. She told Naomi: "Where you go I will go, and where you lodge I will lodge. Your people shall be my people, and your God my God" (Ru 1:16). Ruth married Boaz and became the mother of Obed, an ancestor of both David and Jesus (Ru; Mt 1:5). See pp. 93–94.

RUTH, BOOK OF. One of the books in the division of the Old Testament known as the Writings. This book tells the story of Ruth, the woman from Moab who became the ancestor of David and Christ (Ru; Mt 1:5). See pp. 93–94.

S

SABAOTH (SAB-ay-ahth; hosts). A Hebrew name for God that means Lord of hosts. *See* HOST 2.

SABBATH (SAB-ahth; rest, cessation). The weekly day of rest corresponding to the seventh day upon which God rested after creation (Gn 2:3; Ex 20:11; 31:17). The first time the Sabbath is mentioned by name occurs at the time when a double amount of manna was given on the sixth day to the people of Israel in the Wilderness of Sin. When they told Moses what had happened, he said: "This is what the LORD has commanded: 'Tomorrow is a day of solemn rest, a holy Sabbath to the LORD' " (Ex 16:23). The command to keep the Sabbath holy was repeated on a number of occasions (Ex 20:8–11; Lv 19:3, 30; 23:3; Dt 5:12–15).

The people observed the Sabbath by stopping their work, by gathering together for worship, and by increasing their offerings (Ex 16:29; 20:10; 35:3; Nu 15:32–36; 28:9–10; Am 8:5). The penalty for not observing the Sabbath was death (Ex 31:15).

The Day of Atonement on the tenth day of the seventh month was also a Sabbath (Lv 23:32).

The Sabbath day is a picture for the believer's entrance into God's rest fulfilled in Christ (Col 2:16; Heb 4). See pp. 30, 48, 424–25.

See pp. 30, 46, 48, 348, 424–25.

SABBATH DAY'S JOURNEY. *See* MEASURES 1l.

SABBATICAL YEAR (sa-BAT-i-kuhl yeer). Every seven years the Jewish people observed the Sabbatical year. During this year the land rested, the poor received what grew, and people in debt were released from what they owed (Ex 23:10–11; Lv 25:2–7; Dt 15:1–18).

SABEANS (sah-BEE-uhnz). Semitic people who lived in southwest Arabia. The Sabeans or people of Sheba ran caravans in the Middle East. The Bible describes them as murderous bandits and slave dealers (Jb 1:15; Jl 3:8). The queen of Sheba who visited Solomon was queen of the Sabeans (1Ki 10; 2Ch 9; Mt 12:42; Lk 11:31).

SACKCLOTH. Coarse cloth made out of goat's hair and woven into sacks (Gn 42:25). People wore sackcloth to mourn a death (Gn 37:34; 2Sm 3:31; 2Ki 6:30; Ne 9:1; Jb 16:15; Mt 11:21; Rv 11:3). See p. 241.

SACRAMENT (SAK-rah-ment). A word the church uses to describe a sacred act instituted by God where visible means are connected to His Word. In a sacrament God offers, gives, and seals to the individual the forgiveness of sins earned by Christ. *See* BAPTISM; LORD'S SUPPER. See pp. 83, 387.

SACRIFICE (SAK-ruh-fighs). An act of worship where a person presents an offering to God. Sacrifices were practiced from ancient times and expressed thankfulness to God (cf. "offering" in Gn 4:3–4; 8:20–22). They were offered on many occasions, for example, on a pilgrimage, at a time of rejoicing, when making a treaty, before battle, and after God had appeared to an individual (Gn 31:54; 1Sm 1:3; 20:6; cf. Gn 12:7; 1Sm 7:9).

Sacrifices were offered for various purposes. Among the main ones mentioned in the Old Testament are the sin offering (Lv 4), the guilt offering (Lv 5:15–6:7; 14:12; Nu 6:12), the burnt offering (Lv 1; 6:8–13), the peace offering (Lv 7:11–34), the meal and drink offerings (Lv 6), and the red heifer offering (Nu 19). Offerings were sacrificed upon the altar morning and evening, at each Sabbath and new moon, and at the three leading festivals (Ex 29:38–42; Nu 28–29).

All sacrifices point to and are fulfilled in Christ, the Lamb of God sacrificed for the sins of the world (Heb 9:10–28). See pp. 37, 39, 42, 49, 297.

SADDUCEES (SAD-yoo-seez). One of the three leading Jewish religious parties at the time of Christ. Although a small group, they were influential. Unlike the Pharisees, the Sadducees believed only what was in the written law; they were opposed to tradition and denied belief in the resurrection, angels, and spirits (Mk 12:18; Lk 20:27; Ac 23:8). They stressed moral freedom. Both John the Baptist and Jesus spoke against them (Mt 3:7–8; 16:6, 11–12). See p. 269.

SAINT. 1. Those faithful to God in the Old Testament are called saints (2Ch 6:41). See p. 13.

2. People, such as priests, who were set apart for God's service (cf. "holy" in Ps 106:16; 1Pt 2:5).

3. Members of the Jerusalem congregation (Ac 9:13; 1Co 16:1). See p. 398.

4. Those who believe in Christ (Rm 1:7; 1Co 1:2; 2Co 1:1). See p. 392.

SAKKUTH (SAK-uth). A false god worshiped by Israel (Am 5:26).

SALAMIS (SAL-ah-mis). A city on Cyprus that Paul visited on his first missionary journey (Ac 13:5). See pp. 360–61.

SALEM (SAY-lem; peace). The city of which Melchizedek was king. It was probably Jerusalem (Gn 14:18; Ps 76:2; Heb 7:1–2). See p. 423.

SALMON (SAL-muhn). The father of Boaz (Ru 4:21; Mt 1:4; Lk 3:32). See pp. 97, 122.

SALOME (sah-LO-mi; of Solomon). 1. The wife of Zebedee and mother of James and John (Mk 15:40). Salome was among the women who witnessed the crucifixion of Jesus (Mt 27:56). Later she purchased spices to anoint His body (Mk 16:1).

2. The daughter of Herodias. Salome's dancing pleased Herod so much that he granted her request for the head of John the Baptist (Mt 14:6; Mk 6:22).

SALT. Salt was used as a seasoning and preservative and for sacrifices (Lv 2:13; Nu 18:19; Jb 6:6; Mt 5:13).

Lot's wife was turned to salt (Gn 19:26). The site of Shechem was sown with salt to keep it from producing vegetation (Jgs 9:45; Ezk 47:11). The disciples of Christ are called the salt of the earth (Mt 5:13; Mk 9:50; Lk 14:34). See pp. 32, 85, 106, 386.

SALT SEA. The name given to the Dead Sea because of its high salt content. Fed by the Jordan River, the Salt Sea is 46 by 9 1/2 miles long, 1,292 feet below sea level, and 1,300 feet deep. Since there is no outlet, the water is bitter and buoyant (Gn 14:3; Nu 34:3; Jsh 15:2). It is called by various names: Sea of Arabah (Jsh

3:16; 12:3), Sea (Ezk 47:8), and eastern sea (Ezk 47:18; Jl 2:20; Zec 14:8). See pp. 124, 285, 294.

SALVATION (sal-VAY-shuhn). Deliverance from any type of evil, both physical and spiritual (Ex 14:13, 30; Jb 22:29; cf. Is 49:25). Spiritual deliverance or salvation includes rescue from sin (Mt 1:21; Ac 4:12; Heb 2:10), death (Rm 6:9; 8:2; 1Co 15:54–57), evil (Gal 1:4; 2Tm 4:18), and the power of darkness (Col 1:13). It is a gift of God's grace through faith in Christ (Ac 16:31; Rm 5:1) and marks the entrance into spiritual, eternal life (cf. Jn 5:24; Col 3:9–10). See xvi, 4, 6, 60, 289, 363.

SALVE. *See* OINTMENT.

SAMARIA (sah-MAIR-i-ah; watch-mountain). 1. The capital city of Israel's Northern Kingdom. It was built by Omri on a tableland five and a half miles northwest of Shechem. Samaria is repeatedly rebuked for its luxury and evil ways (1Ki 17–19; 21; 2Ki 3:3–9; Is 7:9; Jer 31:5; Ezk 23:33; Hos 8:5–6; Am 3:1–12). Today it is called Sebastia. See p. 242.

2. The entire area occupied by the Northern Kingdom of Israel, or the ten tribes (1Ki 13:32).

3. The region where the Samaritans lived after they returned from captivity. *See also* SAMARITANS. See p. 344.

SAMARIA, MOUNTAINS OF. *See* EPHRAIM, MOUNT.

SAMARITANS (sah-MAR-uh-tuhns). In 2Ki 17:29 a Samaritan refers to a person belonging to the ten tribes, or the old Northern Kingdom of Israel. Later Samaritans included a small leftover group of Jewish people who returned to Samaria after the captivity along with peoples from Babylonia, Syria, Elam, and other Assyrian lands (2Ki 17:24–34). Since all these people intermingled, they were despised by their Jewish neighbors to the south (Ne 4:1–3; Mt 10:5; Jn 4:9–26; 8:48). See pp. 344–45.

SAMOS (SAY-mahs; height). A mountainous island off the coast of Lydia. Paul stopped at Samos on his third missionary journey (Ac 20:15). See pp. 360–61.

SAMOTHRACE (SAM-o-thrays). An island between Troas and Neapolis where Paul and his party spent the night on their voyage to Macedonia (Ac 16:11). See pp. 360–61, 375.

SAMSON (SAM-s'n; sunlike). A judge of Israel for 20 years. He was the son of Manoah from the tribe of Dan and a Nazirite from birth. Samson married a Philistine woman from Timnah. But later, when her father gave her to another, Samson burned the Philistine fields in revenge. Then the Philistines tried to capture him, but Samson broke the ropes binding him and, taking a donkey's jawbone, killed 1,000 Philistine men. Samson also performed great feats of strength. On one occasion he carried the heavy gates and two posts of the city of Gaza to the top of the hill that is before Hebron.

Samson fell in love with a Philistine woman named Delilah. She tricked him into telling her the source of his strength and then betrayed him into the hands of her countrymen. They cut off Samson's hair, blinded him, and put him to work grinding in the mill at the prison of Gaza.

On one occasion when the Philistines were making public sacrifice to their god Dagon, they called for Samson to make sport of him. Since his hair was beginning to grow, Samson was again fulfilling his Nazirite vow. He prayed to God, asking Him for strength one more time. Then Samson pushed against the pillars that supported the roof and brought the whole temple to Dagon down, killing himself and about 3,000 Philistines who were present (Jgs 13 16; Heb 11:32). See pp. 88, 111–12.

SAMUEL (SAM-yoo-uhl; God has heard). Samuel is often referred to as the last of the judges and the first of the prophets after Moses (1Sm 3:20; 7:6; Ac 3:24). He was a Levite, the son of Elkanah and Hannah (1Sm 1:19–20). When he was still young, Samuel's mother brought him to Eli the priest, who educated Samuel and took care of him (1Sm 3).

Samuel anointed both Saul and David as kings of Israel (1Sm 10; 16:13). When Samuel died, all Israel mourned for him; the people buried him in Ramah, his home city (1Sm 25:1). See pp. 100–2, 187.

SAMUEL, FIRST AND SECOND BOOK OF. Two historical books of the Old Testament that tell the history of Israel from the time of Eli to David's old age. Although these books are named for Samuel, he was not their author (1Sm 25:1; 28:3). See pp. 100–3.

SANBALLAT (san-BAL-uht; Sin [the moon god] has given life). A Persian officer who tried to defeat Nehemiah's plans for rebuilding the walls of Jerusalem (Ne 2:10; 4:1–9; 6:1–14; 13:28).

SANCTIFICATION (sangk-tuh-fi-KAY-shuhn). The Hebrew word for sanctification means separation from the world and that which is sinful, and consecration to a sacred purpose by the Lord (Ex 31:13; cf. "consecrate" in 1Ch 15:14; 2Ch 5:11; 29:15).

In the wide sense the Greek word for sanctification includes the entire process of God's grace whereby spiritually dead people, through the work of the Holy Spirit in the Word and Sacrament, are reborn to spiritual life and made perfect in life eternal (Ac 26:18; Eph 5:26; 2Th 2:13; Heb 10:14).

In the narrower sense, sanctification is the spiritual growth, worked by God the Holy Spirit, that follows after a person has come to faith in Christ; it does not include justification itself (Rm 6:15–23; Gal 5:22–23; Php 2:13; 2Pt 3:18). See pp. 38, 41, 363.

SANCTUARY (SANGK-tyoo-er-ee). A holy place set aside for the worship of God. The sanctuary was the earthly place where God chose to dwell among His people. The Promised Land, the tabernacle, the whole temple, and particularly the Most Holy Place in the tabernacle and temple are called sanctuaries (Ex 15:17; Lv 4:6; 1Ki 6:16; 2Ch 20:8). Judah is also God's sanctuary (Ps 114:2).

The author of the Letter to the Hebrews explains that the earthly sanctuary was only a type of the true sanctuary—access to God through Christ, the believer's High Priest (Heb 8:1–5; 9:1–8). See pp. 142–43, 298.

SANDAL. Leather sandals usually fastened to the foot with straps known as thongs (Ex 3:5; Jsh 5:15; Is 20:2). Occasionally the Bible uses the word *shoe* rather than sandal (Ps 60:8; 108:9; Ezk 24:17, 23; Lk 15:22; Eph 6:15). See pp. 206, 318.

SANHEDRIN (SAN-hi-drin; council). *See* COUNCIL 2.

SAPPHIRA (sa-FIGH-rah; beautiful). The wife of Ananias. Within a period of a few hours, both she and her husband fell dead at Peter's feet because they had lied (Ac 5:7–10).

SARAH (SAIR-ah; princess). The wife of Abraham and mother of Isaac (Gn 11:29; 21:2–3). Her given name was Sarai, but God changed it to Sarah (Gn 17:15–16). When Sarah's maid, Hagar, became pregnant with Abraham's child, she began to think she was better than Sarah. Sarah, in turn, treated Hagar cruelly and sent her away (Gn 16:5–16; 21:9–21).

When Sarah was 90, God kept His promise to her and Abraham and blessed them with a son, Isaac. Sarah lived 127 years. After she died, Abraham buried her at Machpelah (Gn 23). The writer of Hebrews praises Sarah for her great faith (Heb 11:11). See p. 24. *See also* ABRAHAM.

SARAI. *See* SARAH.

SARDIS (SAHR-dis). One of the seven churches to which the Book of Revelation is addressed (Rv 1:11; 3:1–6). Sardis was a city of western Asia Minor located about 50 miles east of Smyrna. It was known for its manufacture of textiles, gold jewelry, and minted coins. Sardis was also a patron of the mystery cults. See pp. 298, 446.

SARGON II (SAHR-gahn). One of the kings of Assyria. He was born in 771 BC and died in 705 BC. In 721 BC he took over the throne from his brother Shalmaneser V and completed the conquest of Samaria begun by Shalmaneser (2Ki 17:5; Is 20:1).

Sennacherib, Sargon's son, succeeded Sargon to the throne. See p. 248.

SATAN (SAY-tahn; adversary). The chief of the fallen angels, beings of great power (Lk 11:18; cf. Mt 8:28–29; 9:34). Satan is the enemy of God, humanity, and all that is good (Jb 1:6, 12; 2:1; Zec 3:1).

Satan is named and described in other ways. He is called the devil (Mt 13:39; 25:41; 1Pt 5:8), a murderer and liar (Jn 8:44), Abaddon, or Apollyon, the angel of the bottomless pit (Rv 9:11), Beelzebul (Mt 12:27), Belial (2Co 6:15), the dragon (Rv 12), the evil, or wicked, one (Eph 6:16; 1Jn 2:13), the ruler of this world (Jn 12:31), the prince of power of the air (Eph 2:2), and a serpent (Rv 12:9). See pp. 162, 312.

SATRAP (SAY-trap). An official person in the Persian Empire who was sent by the Persian king to rule several small provinces that had a combined government. These provinces were called satrapies, and the satrap had complete civil and military control over them (Ezr 8:36; Est 3:12; 8:9; Dn 3:3).

SAUL (SAWL; asked). The first king of Israel. Saul was the son of Kish and came from the tribe of Benjamin (1Sm 8–9). Samuel anointed him to be king of Israel, and then later, after Samuel had brought all the tribes of Israel together, the people chose Saul by lot to be their king (1Sm 9:27; 10:1–13, 17–27). Under Saul's leadership, the Israelites defeated the Ammonites, Philistines, Moabites, Zobah, and Amalekites (1Sm 11–14).

When Saul disobeyed by offering the burnt offering himself rather than waiting for Samuel to do it, Samuel rejected him as the one from whom the kingdom of Israel would be established (1Sm 13:1–14). As Saul's power declined and David's popularity grew, Saul became jealous of David (1Sm 16–31). In a battle between the Israelites and Philistines, Saul was seriously wounded and killed himself by falling on his own sword (1Sm 31). See pp. 101–2, 114–15.

SAVIOR (SAYV-yur). 1. One who saves from danger or evil (2Ki 13:5).

2. In Ps 106:21 God is referred to as Israel's Savior. Jesus is called our Savior (Lk 2:11; Jn 4:42; 1Tm 1:1; 2Pt 1:1). See pp. 164, 429, 440, 445, 449. *See also* JESUS CHRIST; SALVATION.

SAW. *See* TRADE.

SCAB. *See* DISEASE.

SCALES. *See* DISEASE; WEIGHT.

SCAPEGOAT. *See* AZAZEL.

SCHISM (SIZ'm). *See* HERESY.

SCOURGING (SKURJ-ing). Severe punishment with a whip of cords or thongs (Mt 27:26; Mk 15:15; cf. Mt 23:34; Jn 19:1; Heb 11:36). Under Old Testament Law, a person could be whipped no more than 40 times (Dt 25:3; 2Co 11:24). It was unlawful to scourge a Roman citizen (Ac 22:24–25). See pp. 333–34.

SCRIBE. A person who copied records, books, and the like before printing presses were invented. In Jewish times scribes served as recorders, secretaries, and clerks (1Ch 24:6; 27:32).

After the exile, scribes faithfully copied the Scriptures to preserve them for future generations. They became interpreters of the Law and powerful leaders in Israel (Ezr 7:6, 11; Ne 8:1–13; 13:13; Mt 16:21; 26:3; Ac 4:5). See pp. xxvii, 120, 269, 283, 389.

SCRIPTURE. Something that is written down. The Old Testament and New Testament of the Bible are called Scripture. See pp. xv–xxv, 23, 281, 336.

SCROLL. A book made of sheets of skins, papyrus, or parchment sewn together to make a strip about 11 inches wide and several feet long. These sheets were rolled on sticks to make a book, a roll, or a scroll (Is 34:4; Jer 36; Ezk 3:1–3; Rv 5; 10:1–10). See pp. xxvi–xxvii, 225, 299, 326, 389.

SCROLLS, DEAD SEA. Very old manuscripts first found in AD 1947 in caves around the Dead Sea. These manuscripts contained parts of the Old Testament, commentaries, and other writings. See pp. 201, 270.

SCURVY. *See* DISEASE.

SEA. A large, deep body of water (Gn 1:26; Ex 10:19; Dt 30:13; Jb 12:8). *See also* GALILEE, SEA OF; MEDITERRANEAN SEA; MEROM; RED SEA; SALT SEA.

SEAL. A stamp or a ring with a raised design on it that was used to make an impression on something. People in authority used seals to secure or authenticate various items (Jb 38:14). At the request of some Pharisees, Pilate sealed Jesus' tomb so that His disciples could not break into it and take His body without someone knowing about it (Mt 27:66).

SECOND COMING OF CHRIST. *See* ADVENT OF CHRIST 3; ESCHATOLOGY; PAROUSIA.

SECOND QUARTER. A suburb of Jerusalem (2Ki 22:14; 2Ch 34:22).

SECT (SEKT). A religious party that has its own set of beliefs. The Pharisees (cf. Ac 15:5) and the Sadducees (cf. Ac 5:17) were two sects of Judaism in Jesus' day. Some of the people in early New Testament times referred to Christians as a sect of the Nazarenes (Ac 24:5, 14). See pp. 269–70, 399.

SEER (SEE-ur). *See* PROPHET.

SELAH (SEE-lah; may mean lift up). This word is often found in the Psalms (Ps 9:16) as well as in Hab 3:3, 9, 13. The meaning of the word is uncertain, though it may be an instruction for singers or musicians. See p. 169.

SELEUCIA (si-LYOO-shi-ah). A seaport of Syrian Antioch about 16 miles west of Antioch. It was founded by Seleucus Nicator. Paul and Barnabas sailed from Seleucia on their first missionary journey (Ac 13:4). See pp. 360–61.

SENATE. *See* COUNCIL 2.

SENNACHERIB (suh-NAK-ur-ib; Sin, the moon god, has increased brothers). The son of Sargon II and the king who ruled Assyria from 704 to 681 BC. After taking over the throne, Sennacherib dealt with revolts throughout his empire and extended the conquered territories of Assyria as far as the Mediterranean. During Hezekiah's reign, he invaded Judah. The Lord, however, saved Jerusalem by sending His angel to strike down the Assyrian army, forcing Sennacherib to return home (2Ki 18–19; Is 36–37). In his annals Sennacherib describes his victories in Judah. See p. 200.

SEORIM (si-O-rim). The head of the fourth division of priests (1Ch 24:8).

SEPHARVAIM (sef-ahr-VAY-im). A place near Riblah. The Assyrians brought people from Sepharvaim to colonize Samaria (2Ki 17:24–34; 18:34; 19:13; Is 37:13).

SEPTUAGINT (SEP-tyoo-ah-jint). The Greek translation of the Old Testament, prepared at Alexandria, Egypt, in the third century BC. The abbreviation for this translation is LXX, which means "70." See pp. xx, 151, 270.

SERAIAH (si-RAY-yah; soldier of Lord). 1. One of the men sent to arrest Jeremiah and Baruch (Jer 36:26).

2. A prince who was taken captive to Babylon when Jerusalem fell (Jer 51:59–64).

SERAPHIM (SER-ah-fim). An order of angels. Isaiah saw seraphim standing around God's throne (Is 6:2–7). See p. 196.

SERGIUS PAULUS (SUR-ji-uhs PAWL-uhls). The Roman proconsul of Cyprus, a senatorial province in Paul's time (Ac 13:7–12).

SERPENT. A snake, a creature that creeps on its belly (Gn 3:14). A number of serpents are mentioned in the Bible, for instance, the asp or perhaps cobra (Dt 32:33), the adder (Ps 58:4; 91:13), and the viper (Gn 49:17; Jb 20:16).

Serpents are a symbol of evil, great harmfulness, and poison (Gn 49:17; Ps 58:4; Pr 23:32; Mt 23:33). They are described as subtle and wise (Gn 3:1; Mt 10:16). A serpent deceived Eve (Gn 3). The bronze serpent Moses attached to the top of a pole when the children of Israel were in the wilderness was a type of Christ (Nu 21:4–9; Jn 3:14). When an Israelite who had been bitten by a real snake looked at the bronze serpent, he or she was healed. See p. 198.

SERUG (SEE-rug; branch). Father of Nahor and ancestor of Abraham (Gn 11:20, 23; 1Ch 1:26; Lk 3:35). See p. 12.

SERVANT. A general term used of both slaves and persons who worked for wages. The Israelites acquired slaves through purchase and war (Lv 25:44–45; Nu 31:25–47). When slaves had children, their children also were slaves (Gn 14:14; Ec 2:7). Israelites became slaves through poverty, theft, and birth (Ex 21:1–11; 22:3; Lv 25:39, 47; 2Ki 4:1). Laws in the Old Testament protected servants (Ex 20:10; Lv 25:55). Often they were treated as members of the household (Gn 24; 30; 32:16; 1Sm 9:5, 8).

In New Testament times it was common practice for people to have slaves and servants (Mk 1:20; 14:66; Jn 18:10–18; Ac 12:13–15). Jesus was kind to servants (Mt 8:5–13), often referring to them in His parables (Mt 18:23–35; 24:45–51; Mk 13:34–37; Lk 20:9–16).

The New Testament stresses that faith in Christ removes the barrier between master and servant (Gal 3:28; Phm).

See pp. 17, 132, 160, 219.

SERVANT OF THE LORD, OF CHRIST, OF THE CHURCH. 1. Any agent of the Lord, such as Abraham, Moses, and the prophets (Ex 4:10; Ps 105:42; Zec 1:6). Chiefly, however, the term is used as a title for those who serve Christ (Rm 1:1; 2Co 11:23; Col 4:12; Ti 1:1; 2Pt 1:1; Rv 1:1).

2. Ministers in the church (Col 4:7; cf. 1Th 3:2).

See pp. 29, 75, 414–16.

SERVANT, SUFFERING. Jesus is the fulfillment (Mt 12:18; cf. Lk 22:37) of the Suffering Servant spoken about in the Old Testament (Is 42:1–4; 52:13–53:12). See p. 312.

SETH (SETH). The third son of Adam and Eve (Gn 4:25–26; 5:3–8; 1Ch 1:1; Lk 3:38). See p. 12.

SEVEN. A number the Scriptures use symbolically for plenty or completeness (Gn 4:15, 24; Mt 18:21–22).

Seven can mean seven exactly or another number rounded off to seven (1Sm 2:5; Mt 12:45). Often seven and multiples of seven are used for religious cycles (Gn 2:2). See pp. 14, 45–46, 112, 128, 137. *See also* JUBILEE; NUMBERS; SABBATH.

SEVENTY-TWO, THE. Disciples sent on a special mission by Jesus (Lk 10). See p. 289.

SHABBETHAI (SHAB-i-thigh; of the Sabbath). A Levite during Ezra's time who favored the position that the Israelites should divorce their foreign wives. Shabbethai also played a chief role in rebuilding the temple and reading the law (Ne 8:7).

SHADES (silent ones). The dead in Sheol (Is 14:9; 26:14).

SHADRACH (SHAY-drak). The Babylonian name given to Hananiah, one of Daniel's three friends (Dn 1:7). Shadrach was thrown into the fiery furnace for refusing to worship the statue that King Nebuchadnezzar had set up (Dn 3). See pp. 121, 137, 217, 224.

SHALLECHETH (SHAL-i-keth; casting out). The west gate of the temple (1Ch 26:16).

SHALLUM (SHAL-uhm; pacified). 1. The 15th king of Israel. After killing Zechariah, Shallum ruled for one month and then was killed himself by Menahem (2Ki 15:10–15). See p. 125.

2. The son of Zadok, a high priest, and an ancestor of Ezra (1Ch 6:12–13; Ezr 7:2). In 1Ch 9:11 and Ne 11:11 he is referred to as Meshullam.

3. Husband of the prophetess Hulda (2Ki 22:14; 2Ch 34:22). He was probably Jeremiah's uncle (Jer 32:7).

4. Another name for Jehoahaz II, the son of Josiah. He was king of Judah (1Ch 3:15; Jer 22:11).

5. A ruler of half of Jerusalem who, with his daughters, helped repair the walls of Jerusalem (Ne 3:12).

SHALMAN (SHAL-muhn). *See* SHALMANESER 2.

SHALMANESER (shal-muhn-EE-zur). The title of a number of Assyrian kings. 1. Shalmaneser III, the first Assyrian king to come into conflict with the Israelites, ruled Assyria from 858 to 824 BC. He conquered the Hittites as far as the Mediterranean. The Syrian league was formed to stop him in the west. Among others, Ben-hadad of Damascus and Ahab of Israel opposed him. Nevertheless, Shalmaneser defeated Hazael, Ben-hadad's successor, and made Israel pay tribute.

2. Shalmaneser V was the king of Assyria from 726 to 722 BC. He besieged Samaria. The city likely fell to him shortly before his death, or it may have fallen to his successor, Sargon. After the fall of Samaria, the ten northern tribes were carried into captivity (2Ki 17:3; 18:9). In Hos 10:14, Shalmaneser is referred to as Shalman.

SHAMGAR (SHAM-gahr). The son of Anath. He killed 600 Philistines with an oxgoad (likely over a period of time), preparing the way for the deliverance of Israel by Deborah and Barak (Jgs 3:31). See p. 88.

SHAMMUA (sha-MYOO-ah; fame). 1. A Reubenite spy (Nu 13:4).

2. A son of David and Bathsheba (2Sm 5:14; 1Ch 14:4). In 1Ch 3:5 he is referred to as Shimea.

SHAPHAN (SHAY-fan; rock badger). A scribe and secretary during Josiah's reign. When the book of the Law was found, Shaphan first read it privately and then took it to King Josiah (2Ki 22:8–10). After hearing its contents, Josiah sent Shaphan, along with some others, to ask Huldah the prophetess what it meant (2Ki 22:14–20).

SHAPHAT (SHAY-fat; he has judged). The father of the prophet Elisha (1Ki 19:16; 2Ki 3:11).

SHAREZER (shah-REE-zur; protect king). The son and murderer of Sennacherib, the Assyrian king (2Ki 19:37; Is 37:38).

SHARON (SHAIR-uhn; plain). A coastal plain between Joppa and Carmel. It was about 50 miles long and 6–12 miles wide (1Ch 27:29; Is 33:9; 35:2; Ac 9:35).

SHAVEH, VALLEY OF (SHAY-ve; plain). A place, probably near Jerusalem, where Melchizedek met Abraham (Gn 14:17).

SHAVSHA (SHAV-shah). One of David and Solomon's scribes (1Ch 18:16). He is probably the same person as the secretary Seraiah, the secretary Sheva, and the secretary Shisha (2Sm 8:17; 20:25; 1Ki 4:3).

SHEALTIEL (shi-AL-ti-el; I have asked God). A son of Jeconiah, or Jehoiachin, or possibly of Neri (1Ch 3:17; Mt 1:12; Lk 3:27). Shealtiel was probably the legitimate successor of Jehoiachin, and when Shealtiel died, the right to the throne passed to Zerubbabel (Ezr 3:2; 1Ch 3:17–19).

SHEAR-JASHUB (SHEE-ahr-JAH-shub; remnant shall return). A symbolical name Isaiah gave to his son (Is 7:3).

SHEBNA, SHEBNAH (SHEB-nah; tenderness). King Hezekiah's secretary and the steward of his house. Isaiah rebuked him (2Ki 18:18–26, 37; 19:2; Is 22:15–25; 36:3, 11, 22; 37:2).

SHECHEM (SHEE-chem; shoulder). A town in the hill country of Ephraim in the pass between Mount Ebal and Mount Gerizim. Shechem was a Levitical city of refuge (Gn 12:6; 35:4; Jsh 20:7; Jgs 9:7; Ac 7:16).

Shechem was the first place Abraham camped after leaving Haran. Although the Canaanites were in the land at that time, the Lord appeared to Abraham and told him He would give the land to Abraham's descendants (Gn 12:6–7). Later, Jacob bought ground at Shechem, and Joseph was eventually buried there (Gn 33:18–20; Jsh 24:32).

Today it is the site of Tell Balatah, located near Neapolis and Nablus. See pp. 17, 30, 139.

SHEEP. Sheep were domesticated early (Gn 4:2). The patriarchs and their descendants herded flocks of these animals (Gn 12:16; Ex 10:9; 1Ch 27:30–31). Sheep were valuable property, since they were a source of food, clothing, and tribute (Lv 13:47; 1Sm 14:32; 2Ki 3:4). They were also used as sacrifices in worship (Ex 20:24; Lv 9:3). The sheep's horns were used for trumpets and as containers for liquids (Jsh 6:4; 1Sm 16:1). Sheepshearing time was an occasion for great festivity (1Sm 25:4, 11, 36).

Sheep and shepherds are often used in a figurative way in the Bible (2Ch 18:16; Ps 23; 119:176; Mt 9:36; Jn 10). See pp. 54, 171–72, 347, 350–51.

SHEEPFOLD. An enclosure where sheep were kept, especially at night, for protection and when they were to be sheared (Nu 32:16; Jgs 5:16; 1Sm 24:3; Ps 78:70; Jn 10:1). See p. 172.

SHEEP GATE. One of the gates of Jerusalem (Ne 3:1, 32; 12:39).

SHEKEL (SHEK-uhl; weight). 1. A weight used for metals. It weighed about half an ounce (Ex 30:13; 2Sm 14:26).

2. A coin (Mt 17:27). See p. 283.

SHEM (SHEM). One of Noah's sons (Gn 5:32; 10:1; Lk 3:36). Shem received a blessing from God: from his line of descent would come the chosen people (Gn 9:21–27). Shem is the ancestor of the Hebrews, the Aramaeans, and the Arabs. See p. 12.

SHEMAIAH (shi-MAY-yah; Lord has heard). 1. One of God's prophets. Shemaiah told Rehoboam, king of Judah, not to attempt regaining control of the ten northern tribes of Israel, which had revolted (1Ki 12:22; 2Ch 11:2; 12:5, 7, 15).

2. The father of the prophet Uriah (Jer 26:20).

3. A false prophet among the exiles in Babylon who opposed Jeremiah (Jer 29:24–32).

4. One of the men Ezra sent to Iddo to ask for Levites and temple ministers (Ezr 8:16).

SHEMER (SHEE-mur; guardian). A person who owned a hill in Samaria that Omri, king of Israel, bought (1Ki 16:24).

SHEMINITH (SHEM-i-ninth; eighth). A musical term. It may refer to an octave, a scale, or the strings of an instrument (1Ch 15:21; titles of Ps 6; 12).

SHEMUEL (shi-MYOO-uhl; heard of God). The Hebrew pronunciation of the name Samuel. Both spellings may occur for various people in English translations of the Old Testament (1Ch 6:33; 7:2).

SHENAZZAR (shi-NAZ-ur; Sin [the moon god] protect). A son of Jehoiachin (Jeconiah), who was likely born in captivity (1Ch 3:18).

SHEOL (SHEE-ol; perhaps meaning dig or ask). 1. The Old Testament name for the place where people go when they have died. It is translated in a number of ways, for instance, as grave and as the realm of the dead, a place full of darkness where the dead are (Dt 32:22; Jb 7:9; 17:16; 11:8; Ps 89:48; Is 38:10).

2. The people who are in Sheol (Is 14:9). *See also* ESCHATOLOGY; ETERNAL LIFE; HADES; HELL.

SHEPHATIAH (shef-ah-TIGH-ah; Lord has judged). 1. One of David's sons (2Sm 3:4; 1Ch 3:3).

2. A prince who was among those who advised Zedekiah to put the prophet Jeremiah to death (Jer 38).

SHEPHELAH, THE (shi-FEE-lah; low). The land between the central highlands of Israel and the Mediterranean plain (1Ki 10:27; 1Ch 27:28; 2Ch 1:15; 9:27; 26:10; Jer 17:26; 32:44; Ob 19).

SHEPHERD. A person who makes his living by looking after sheep. The shepherd was an important person in Bible times (Gn 29:6–7; 30:29–30; Ex 2:16–22). He led his sheep to pasture and water; he looked after them and protected them from danger (Gn 29:7; Ex 2:16; 1Sm 17:34; Ps 23; Jn 10:1–15). When a sheep was lost, the shepherd went out to search for it (Ps 119:176; Lk 15:1–7). At night, he brought the sheep home, checking to see they were all there by counting them as they passed under his shepherd's rod or staff (Lv 27:32; Ezk 20:37).

Shepherding was often dangerous work (Gn 31:40; 1Sm 17:34; Jn 10:11–13). For this reason a shepherd equipped himself with a sheepskin mantle, a crook, and a pouch in which he carried his slingshot, his food, and the oil for medicating scratches, cuts, and bruises on his sheep. Frequently, he was assisted in his work by a dog (Jb 30:1). The chief shepherd, overshepherd, or overseer was the person in charge of a number of shepherds and the flocks for which they cared (1Ch 27:30–31).

The word *shepherd* is also used figuratively in the Bible. God, a king, ministers, and Christ are all referred to as shepherds (Is 44:28; 56:11; Jer 23:4; 31:10; Jn 10:14; Heb 13:20; cf. Ac 20:28–30). See pp. 110, 171–72, 347.

SHEREBIAH (sher-i-BIGH-ah; Lord has sent heat). A Levite who joined Ezra at Ahava on his return to Jerusalem. Ezra entrusted him with the gifts for the temple (Ezr 8:18, 24). Later, Sherebiah sealed the covenant with Nehemiah (Ne 8:7; 9:4–5; 10:12; 12:8, 24).

SHESHBAZZAR (shesh-BAZ-ur; may mean sun god or guard lord). A prince of Judah at the time Cyrus made the decree allowing the Jews to return to Jerusalem. Cyrus made Sheshbazzar a governor and gave him the sacred vessels for the temple. Sheshbazzar also helped lay the foundation of the temple in Jerusalem. He is often identified with Zerubbabel (Ezr 1:8; 5:14, 16). See pp. 146–47.

SHIBAH (SHIGH-bah; seven, oath). A well that Isaac's servants dug at Beersheba (Gn 26:31–33).

SHIELD. *See* ARMOR, ARMS.

SHIGGAION, SHIGIONOTH (shi-GAY-yahn, shig-i-O-nahth; wandering). A musical term perhaps referring to the music or meter of a piece (title of Ps 7; Hab 3:1).

SHIHOR (SHIGH-hawr; black). *See* NILE.

SHILOH (SHIGH-lo; peace). 1. A place about nine miles north of Bethel. It was the site of Israel's early sanctuary and the place where the ark of the covenant was kept for about 300 years (Jsh 18:1, 8–10; Jgs 21:19–23). Eli and Samuel lived at Shiloh and ministered in the temple there (1Sm 3). Shiloh was also the home of the prophet Ahijah. He was the one who told Jeroboam that God was going to make him king over the ten northern tribes (1Ki 11:29–34; 14:1–18). By Jeremiah's time it seems that Shiloh lay in ruins (Jer 7:12–14; 26:6–9). See p. 76.

2. A word of uncertain meaning. Many people think it refers to the Messiah (cf. Gn 49:10).

SHIMSHAI (SHIM-shigh). A scribe and leader in Samaria who wrote a letter to Artaxerxes complaining about the rebuilding of the temple (Ezr 4:8–9, 17, 23).

SHINAR (SHIGH-nur). An alluvial plain of southern Babylonia where the cities Babel, Erech, Accad, and Calneh were located (Gn 10:10; Dn 1:2). The tower of Babel was built on this plain. During Abraham's time, Amraphel was king of Shinar (Gn 14:1, 9). Many years later, some of the Jews were taken captive to Shinar (Zec 5:11).

SHIP. *See* BOATS.

SHITTAH, SHITTIM (SHIT-ah, SHIT-im; acacia). A tree that grew in the Jordan Valley, in the wilderness of Sinai, and in the area around the Dead Sea. The acacia was one species of shittah tree. Its wood was hard, fine grained, and insect repelling. The Hebrews used acacia wood to build the tabernacle, the ark, the altars, the tables, and the bars and pillars (Ex 25:5–28; 26:15–37; Is 41:19).

SHITTIM (SHIT-im; acacias). The last place Israel camped before entering Palestine. From Shittim Joshua sent spies to look over the defenses of Jericho, and then Israel broke camp to cross over the Jordan (Nu 25:1; Jsh 2:1; Mi 6:5). In Nu 33:49, it is referred to as Abel-shittim.

SHOBAL (SHO-bal). The son of Hur and founder of Kiriath-jearim (1Ch 2:50; 4:1–2).

SHOBI (SHO-bigh; one who leads captive). An Ammonite who brought food and other provisions to David and the people with him when they stopped at Mahanaim (2Sm 17:27).

SHOE. *See* SANDAL.

SHOWBREAD. A translation for the Hebrew words that literally mean "bread of the presence" (Nu 4:7; 1Ch 9:32; 23:29; cf. Ex 25:30; 35:13; 39:36). The showbread consisted of 12 loaves of fresh, unleavened bread that were placed in two stacks on the table of acacia wood in the Holy Place every Sabbath. The old loaves were eaten by the priests (Ex 25:30; 1Sm 21:1–6; Mt 12:3–4). See p. 126.

SHUA (SHU-ah; wealth). A Canaanite who was Judah's father-in-law (Gn 38:2).

SHUAH (SHU-ah; depression). A son of Abraham and Keturah (Gn 25:2). An Arab tribe, probably the Shuhites, descended from him.

SHUR (SHOOR; wall). A region in the wilderness south of Israel and east of Egypt. The Israelites marched through this area for three days after crossing the Red Sea (Gn 16:7; 25:18; Ex 15:22). See pp. 30, 89, 146, 193.

SHUSHAN (SHU-shan; lily). *See* SUSA.

SHUSHAN EDUTH (SHU-shan-EE-duth; lilies of the Testimony). The title of Psalm 60. Although its meaning is uncertain, it may be a musical term, perhaps referring to the melody.

SIDON (SIGH-d'n; fishery). An ancient Canaanite city situated on the Mediterranean coast about 22 miles north of Tyre. It was assigned to the tribe of Asher, but they never succeeded in conquering the Canaanite people living there (Jgs 1:31; 10:12; 18:7, 28). When Solomon was building the temple, he hired people from Sidon to cut timber for it (1Ki 5:6; 1Ch 22:4).

The Sidonians worshiped the false goddess Ashtoreth. Their religion corrupted the Israelites, who began to worship Ashtoreth also (1Ki 11:5). Jezebel, Ahab's wife, came from Sidon. Under her influence, Ahab built an altar to Baal in Samaria and worshiped him (1Ki 16:31). Sidon was spoken against by the prophets (Jer 27:3; Jl 3:4–6).

Sidon is also mentioned in the New Testament. Christ visited there, and Paul stopped at the port at Sidon (Mt 15:21; Ac 27:3). Today it is called Saida. See p. 361.

SIEGE. Surrounding a city with an army in order to capture it. In Israel's early days, sieges lasted only a short time (2Ki 6:24; 2Sm 20:15). Later siege engines, protected ladders, and battering rams were built to help the army take over the city (2Ch 26:14). See pp. 121, 421. *See also* ARMOR, ARMS; ARMY; WAR.

SIEVE (netted or shake). A utensil made of rushes, horsehair, or string that was used for sifting materials, such as grain (Is 30:28; Am 9:9). See p. 96.

SIGNET. *See* RING.

SILAS (SIGH-lahs; sylvan). An important member of the Christian church in Jerusalem. Silas went with Paul to Antioch to tell the Christians there the decision of the Jerusalem council (Ac 15:22, 27, 32). He also accompanied Paul on the second missionary journey (Ac 16–18). Silas is also referred to as Silvanus (2Co 1:19; 1Th 1:1; 2Th 1:1; 1Pt 5:12). See pp. 375, 399–400, 421.

SILOAM (si-LO-am; shooting forth, sent). A pool at Jerusalem on the southern side of the temple. It received its water from En-rogel through a 1,780-foot tunnel built during Hezekiah's reign (Jn 9:7). In Is 8:6 it is referred to as Shiloah and in Ne 3:15 as Shelah. Today it is called Birket Silwan.

SILVANUS (sil-VAY-nuhs). *See* SILAS.

SILVER. A precious metal used from early times for money, ornaments, crowns, trumpets, vessels, and items in the tabernacle (Gn 23:16; 24:53; 44:2; Ex 26:19; 27:10; 38:19; Nu 10:2; Jb 28:15; Zec 6:11). Some idols were also made of silver (Ps 115:4). See pp. 40–41, 76, 190, 319, 377.

SIMEON (SIM-ee-uhn; hearing). 1. One of Jacob and Leah's sons (Gn 29:33). Simeon and his brother Levi killed the people of Shechem because of what one of them had done to Dinah, their sister (Gn 34:24–31). During Israel's famine Joseph kept Simeon hostage in Egypt in order to make sure the rest of his brothers would return (Gn 42:24). When Jacob was dying, he foretold that the tribe of Simeon would be scattered in Israel (Gn 49:5–7). See p. 17.

2. The tribe of Simeon. Members of this tribe descended from Simeon (Nu 1:22–23). The tribe of Simeon received cities and villages in Judah and in the neighborhood of Beersheba (Jsh 19:1–9; 1Ch 4:28–33).

3. A righteous and devout man to whom God revealed that he would not die until he had seen the Christ child. When Mary and Joseph brought the baby Jesus to the temple, Simeon came in and recognized Him as the promised Messiah. He uttered the blessing known as the *Nunc dimittis* (Lk 2:25–35). See p. 331.

4. Simeon Niger, a Christian at Antioch (Ac 13:1).

5. *See* PETER.

SIMON (SIGH-muhn; hearing). 1. *See* PETER.

2. Simon the Canaanite, or Simon the Zealot, one of the apostles (Mt 10:4). See p. 287.

3. A brother of Jesus (Mt 13:55; Mk 6:3).

4. A Pharisee who invited Jesus to his home for a meal. While Jesus was there, a woman came in and anointed His feet (Lk 7:36–50).

5. Simon of Cyrene, the man who carried Jesus' cross for Him (Mt 27:32; Mk 15:21; Lk 23:26).

6. Simon Magus, a sorcerer of Samaria. When Simon saw that the Holy Spirit was given through the laying on of hands, he tried to buy the power from the apostles. Peter sharply rebuked him for this and told him to repent (Ac 8:9–24).

7. A tanner at Joppa. Peter stayed at his house for many days (Ac 9:43).

SIN, I (SIN). A desert plain lying inland from the Red Sea. The Israelites passed through the Wilderness of Sin on their way from the Red Sea to Mount Sinai (Ex 16:1; 17:1; Nu 33:11–12). See p. 30.

SIN, II. Sin is both doing what God forbids and failing to do what He commands (Rm 1:18–32; 1Jn 3:4). Since God's law tells us what He wants us to do and not to do, sin is breaking God's law. It is a condition as well as an act.

When Adam and Eve yielded to the devil's temptation and fell into sin, they lost the image of God; they were no longer holy and innocent. Because of their sin, they came under God's just anger and curse. Also by their act of disobedience, sin entered the world, and through it, misery, suffering, and death came upon the entire human race (Gn 3; Ps 51:5; Rm 3:9–23; 5:21; 6:6–17; 7:21–23).

From Adam all people receive both hereditary guilt (Rm 5:12) and a total corruption of the human nature, called original sin. Original sin is the evil condition of our nature that we have by being born of human parents also corrupted by sin. It consists of an alienation from God (Rm 1:18–24; 8:7) as well as a natural liking for doing evil (Rm 1; 7:14). It expresses itself in actual sinful deeds contrary to God's will as found in His law (Rm 3:20; 4:15; 7:7; 1Jn 3:4).

Sin is against God (Gn 39:9; 2Sm 12:13; Ps 51:4). Because of original sin, people by nature cannot fear, love, or trust in God or love their neighbor (1Jn). Because of sin everyone deserves temporal and eternal death. "The wages of sin is death" (Rm 6:23). Only through faith in Christ, who both kept God's law perfectly and suffered the punishment for the sins of the world, does one escape the results of sin. "But the free gift of God is eternal life in Christ Jesus our Lord" (Rm 6:23). See pp. 4, 13, 15–16, 347–48, 380.

SIN OFFERING. *See* ATONEMENT, DAY OF; SACRIFICE.

SIN, UNPARDONABLE. A sin that excludes the possibility of repentance. The Bible often refers to this sin as the sin against the Holy Spirit. This sin is committed when the Holy Spirit has clearly revealed the divine truth to the sinner, and yet the sinner still consciously persists in his or her evil ways, opposing God and His will. It is the rejection of the Gospel by a hardened sinner who has been convinced of its truth (Mt 12:31; Mk 3:29; Lk 12:10; 1Jn 5:16).

SINAI (SIGH-nigh; may possibly mean thorny or Sin, the moon god). The mountain on which the Law was given. Mount Sinai was probably a peak in the mountain range Horeb (Ex 3:1; 17:6; Dt 1:6; 4:10). The Ten Commandments were given from its peak, and the covenant between the Lord and Israel was ratified at its base (Ex 20:1–24:8). The location of Mount Sinai is uncertain. The Sinai Peninsula lies between the Red Sea, the Gulf of Aqaba, and the Gulf of Suez. See pp. 5, 26–27, 30.

SIRAH (SIGH-rah; recession). A well about one mile north of Hebron. Here, Joab killed Abner (2Sm 3:26).

SISERA (SIS-u-rah). A Canaanite who was the captain of the army of King Jabin of Hazor. Under Deborah's direction Barak united his forces and met with Sisera in battle. When Sisera's forces were killed or scattered, he ran away on foot. Jael, the wife of Heber, killed Sisera while he slept (Jgs 4–5; 1Sm 12:9; Ps 83:9). See p. 136.

SISTER. 1. Full sister or half sister (Gn 20:12; Dt 27:22).

2. Wife (Sg 4:9).

3. A woman of the same tribe (Nu 25:18).

4. A female fellow Christian (Rm 16:1).

See pp. 17, 168, 308, 418, 442.

SLEEP. 1. Physical rest (Ps 4:8; Pr 24:33; Jn 11:13). See pp. 112, 324.

2. Death (1Ki 1:21; Ps 13:3; Jer 51:39; Jn 11:11). See pp. 391–92, 405–06.

3. Spiritual laziness or stupidity (Rm 13:11; 1Th 5:6). See p. 203.

SMYRNA (SMUR-nah; myrrh). An ancient Ionian city about 40 miles north of Ephesus. After lying in ruins for a number of years, it was rebuilt by Alexander the Great in 320 BC. John addresses the church at Smyrna in the Book of Revelation (1:11; 2:8–11). See p. 446.

SNOW. Snow is common in the hilly country of Israel (2Sm 23:20; Is 55:10). It is often mentioned in poetical sections of Scripture and in metaphors (Jb 37:6; 38:22; Ps 51:7; 147:16; Is 1:18; Mt 28:3). See pp. 175, 195.

SODOM (SAHD-uhm). A city, along with Gomorrah, Admah, Zeboiim, and Zoar, that was located in the plain of Siddim (Gn 13:12). Although the exact site of Sodom is unknown, many think it was located on the southeast end of the Dead Sea. In Gn 14:2, it is described as a royal city. Abraham's nephew Lot lived there (Gn 13:11–13). When God destroyed Sodom because of its wickedness, only Lot and his two daughters escaped (Gn 19). The Bible repeatedly uses Sodom as an example of wickedness (Dt 29:23; Is 1:9; 3:9; Jer 50:40; Ezk 16:46; Mt 10:15; Rm 9:29; 2Pt 2:6). See pp. 15, 143, 146.

SOJOURNER (so-JYOOR-nur). A stranger or foreigner in the land of Israel who obeyed certain rules (Ex 20:10; Lv 17:10, 15; 18:26; 20:2; 22:18; 24:16). Although there were exceptions (Dt 23:3, 8), they could become part of Israel if they underwent the rite of circumcision (Ex 12:48–49). *See also* FOREIGNER; PROSELYTE.

SOLDIER (SOL-jur). *See* ARMY.

SOLOMON (SAHL-o-muhn; peaceable). Third and last king of the united kingdom of Israel. Solomon was the son of David and Bathsheba. When Solomon was born, Nathan named him Jedidiah, which means "beloved of the Lord" (2Sm 12:24–25; 1Ki 4:1; 1Ch 3:5). After Solomon was made king, he put to death those who had plotted to take the throne from him: his brother Adonijah and Adonijah's followers Joab and Shimei. He also removed Abiathar, the priest, from office (1Ki 1:5–40; 2).

Solomon married numerous women, one of whom was the daughter of the Egyptian pharaoh (1Ki 3:1). Early in his reign Solomon was faithful to the Lord. He worshiped the Lord, offering up burnt offerings and praying to Him. When God told Solomon in a dream to ask whatever he wished of Him, Solomon chose wisdom so that he could rule his kingdom better (1Ki 3:3–12). God answered his request, blessing Solomon with "wisdom and understanding beyond measure. . . . He was wiser than all other men" (1Ki 4:29–31).

With the help of King Hiram of Tyre, Solomon built the temple in seven years. He also built a palace for himself (1Ki 5–8; 2Ch 2–7). Solomon showed wisdom in government and commerce (1Ki 4:2–19; 10:11–29; 2Ch 9:10–22). He also had interests and abilities in botany and zoology (1Ki 4:33). In addition to this, Solomon was a great writer. Among other writings, the Book of Proverbs and Psalms 27 and 127 were likely written by him.

In his old age, however, Solomon began to fall away from the Lord. Under the influence of his foreign wives, he was tempted to worship other gods; he built altars to Chemosh and Molech and worshiped Ashtoreth. The Lord grew angry with Solomon. As judgment on Solomon's idolatry, God said He would take the kingdom of Israel from Solomon's descendants. Only one tribe would remain for them to rule (1Ki 11:1–13). See pp. 103, 127, 141, 165, 178.

SOLOMON, SONG OF. The full title of this book of the Old Testament is "The Song of Songs, which is Solomon's" (1:1). It is also called "Canticles," which comes from the Latin for "Song of Songs." Historically Bible scholars have interpreted this book in a number of ways, for example, allegorically.

The allegorical interpretation was developed in the eighteenth century. According to it the bride represents the Church and the bridegroom represents Christ (Is 54:5; 62:5; Jer 2:2; Hos 2:19, 20; Mt 9:15; Jn 3:29; 2Co 11:2; Eph 5:25–32; Rv 19:7; 21:2). See pp. 181–82.

SOLOMON'S PORTICO. A colonnade on the east side of Herod's temple (Ac 3:11; 5:12; cf. Jn 10:23). See pp. 364–65.

SON. 1. A male child; one's immediate descendant (Gn 27:1). See pp. 16–17, 275–76, 286, 409.

2. A descendant further removed than one's own child (2Ki 9:20; cf. Mal 3:6). See pp. 17, 149.

3. A spiritual son (2Ki 2:3; 1Tm 1:18; 2Tm 2:1). See pp. 407, 413.

4. An address to a younger person (1Sm 3:6).

5. A member of a profession (Ne 12:28).

6. A follower (Nu 21:29).

7. An adopted son (Ex 2:10). See p. 132.

8. A native (Lm 4:2).

9. *See* JESUS CHRIST.

SON OF GOD. 1. Adam (Lk 3:38).

2. Angels (Jb 38:7).

3. Believers (Rm 8:14; 2Co 6:18; Gal 4:1–7). *See also* ADOPTION.

4. *See* JESUS CHRIST.

SON OF MAN. 1. A human being (Nu 23:19; Jb 25:6; Ps 8:4; Dn 8:17).

2. Used in a messianic sense in Dn 7:13–14. Jesus applies the term to Himself numerous times. See pp. 219, 239, 324, 443. *See also* JESUS CHRIST.

SONG. *See* MUSIC; PSALMS, BOOK OF.

SONG OF ASCENTS (DEGREES). *See* ASCENTS, SONG OF.

SONG OF SONGS. *See* SOLOMON, SONG OF.

SONSHIP. *See* ADOPTION; SON OF GOD.

SOOTHSAYER (SOOTH-say-ur). *See* DIVINATION.

SOPHERETH (so-FEE-reth; secretariat). A name or title given to some of Solomon's servants (Ne 7:57).

SORCERER (SAWR-sur-ur). *See* DIVINATION; MAGIC.

SOSTHENES (SOS-thi-neez; savior). A ruler of the synagogue at Corinth (Ac 18:17). He may have been the man mentioned in 1Co 1:1, who was Paul's coworker.

SOUL, SPIRIT (sometimes translated life or ghost). The word *soul* comes from the Hebrew word *nephesh* and the Greek word *psuche*. The soul is not separate from the body; rather it is that which gives it life: it animates the flesh. It is the inner person as distinguished from the flesh (Jb 14:22). Through the breath of God, people and animals become living beings or souls (Gn 2:7). The soul is described as living and dying and as life itself (Gn 12:13; 44:30; Is 53:12; Ezk 18:4; Ac 20:10). The soul departs at death (Gn 35:18; Lk 12:20). The soul is the seat of the appetites, emotions, and passions (Ps 107:9; Mt 22:37; Lk 12:19; Jn 12:27). It can be lost and saved (Mk 8:35–36).

Spirit is a translation of the Hebrew word *ruah* and the Greek word *pneuma*. It is often translated as breath or wind (Jb 15:30; 2Th 2:8). The spirit of life is created and preserved by God (Jb 10:12; 27:3; Zec 12:1). It is those inner aspects of one's personality and the seat of one's moral character (Ezk 11:19; 18:31; Mk 2:8; 1Co 5:3–5). The spirit returns to God at death (Ec 12:7; Mt 27:50; Jn 19:30). The Spirit of God gives special gifts to people (Ex 31:3; Jb 32:8).

At times soul and spirit are used as synonyms (Lk 1:46–47); at other times they are contrasted (1Co 15:44–45). Both demonstrate one life principle from two points of view. See pp. 162, 175, 220, 252, 391. *See also* DEATH; ESCHATOLOGY; ETERNAL LIFE; HOLY SPIRIT.

SPAN. *See* MEASURES 1c.

SPICES. Pleasant-smelling gums, barks, and the like that were used during biblical times in ceremonies, in medicines, for embalming, for anointing, and for grooming oneself (Gn 37:25; 43:11; Sg 4:14; Mk 16:1; Jn 19:39–40). See pp. 170, 318.

SPIDER. A spider's web is a picture word for the foolishness of wickedness (Jb 8:14; Is 59:5).

SPINNING. *See* TRADE.

SPIRIT. *See* HOLY SPIRIT; SOUL, SPIRIT.

SPIRIT, HOLY. *See* HOLY SPIRIT.

SPIRITUAL GIFTS. Gifts and abilities that the Holy Spirit gives to Christians to equip them for service in the Church (1Co 12). See p. 385.

SPOIL. *See* BOOTY.

SPOT. 1. A mark or blot that spoils an animal or person (Gn 30:32–39; Lv 13:2–39).
2. A physical or moral flaw (Lv 13). *See also* BLEMISH.

STADIUM (STAY-di-uhm). *See* MEASURE 1i.

STAFF. *See* ROD.

STAIRS, STAIRWAY. *See* HOMES.

STANDARD. Banners that marked to which tribe each camp belonged (Nu 1:52; 2).

STAR. The Bible speaks of a star as any heavenly body except the sun and the moon. The Israelites recognized stars as the work of God and observed them from patriarchal times (Gn 1:16). For instance, God told Abraham his descendants would be as numerous as the stars, and Joseph dreamed the sun, the moon, and 11 stars had bowed down to him (Gn 15:5; 37:9).

Stars are also used as picture words for brightness, multitudes, and important persons (Gn 22:17; 37:9; Nu 24:17; Ps 147:4; 148:3; Dn 8:10; 12:3; Rv 6:13). The star of the east led the Wise Men to Bethlehem after Jesus was born (Mt 2:2–10). See pp. 58, 220, 328–29, 430. *See also* ASTROLOGERS; MAGICIAN.

STEADFAST LOVE. The Hebrew word for this is *hesed*. Although difficult to translate into English, *hesed* has the basic sense of that loving kindness, mercy, and faithfulness of God expressed in the act by which He chose Israel, established a covenant relationship with the people of Israel, promised them salvation, and bound Himself to loving them and showing them mercy. Those who have been called by grace into this covenant relationship with God respond in love to God and their fellow human beings (Gn 24:12–27; Ex 20:6; Ps 5:7; 26:3; Jer 16:5). Often this word is translated by "loving kindness" or "mercy" as well as "steadfast love." See p. 165. *See also* GRACE; LOVE; MERCY.

STEPHEN (STEE-vuhn; crown). One of the seven deacons chosen by the Early Church to minister to the needs of the Greek-speaking widows and probably the poor in general. Stephen himself was likely a Greek-speaking Christian. The New Testament describes him as a man of great faith, wisdom, and power (Ac 6:3–8). Some people who belonged to the synagogue of the Freedmen, as well as Jews from Cyrene, Alexandria, Cilicia, and Asia, debated with Stephen. Accusing him of blasphemy against Moses and God, they stirred up the people to bring Stephen before the council (Ac 6:9–15).

Stephen gave a remarkable defense, explaining that Christianity was the fulfillment of Jewish history. His words angered his accusers, who took him outside the city and stoned him to death. The young man Saul (Paul) watched the proceedings and approved of Stephen's death (Ac 7–8:1). See pp. 372, 412.

STEW. A meal made of fruit and vegetables (Gn 25:29–30, 34; 1Ki 4:38–40; Hg 2:12).

STOICS (STO-iks; porch scholars). A school of Greek philosophy founded by Zeno. Stoics taught that virtue was the highest good. Through it they believed that one's actions were brought into harmony with nature and universal reason. Their religion was pantheistic, that is, they believed God is in everything.

Stoics were known for their austere ethics, for their rigid control of feelings, and for hiding their emotions. They were unmoved by pleasure or pain. When Paul was in Athens, he talked with some Stoics (Ac 17:18–32).

STRAIGHT STREET. A street of Damascus (Ac 9:11).

STRONG DRINK. Any alcoholic beverage (Nu 28:7). It was usually made from grapes, barley, honey, or dates. Strong drink was forbidden to priests before they entered the sanctuary and to Nazirites (Lv 10:9; Nu 6:3; Jgs 13:4, 7; Lk 1:15). See p. 111.

STUMBLING BLOCK. 1. In Old Testament usage a stumbling block is any object that causes a person to fall (Lv 19:14).

2. In the New Testament Jesus and the cross are described as stumbling blocks (1Co 1:23). God's way of salvation through Jesus and the cross does not meet people's expectations or wishes. Individuals cannot be saved through their own reason or works, only by grace through faith in Christ's redeeming work for them. This is a "stumbling block" for them.

3. An occasion for inner conflict or sin (Rm 14:13; 1Co 8:9).

SUCCOTH (SUK-ahth; booths). 1. The place east of the Jordan near Damiyeh where Jacob built a house for himself and booths for his cattle on his return from Mesopotamia to Canaan (Gn 33:17). Later, it was assigned to the Gadites (Jsh 13:27). During the time of Gideon, Succoth was an important town. When the people of Succoth refused to help Gideon, he punished the town severely (Jgs 8:5–16).

2. The first place Israel camped after leaving Rameses (Ex 12:37; 13:20; Nu 33:5–6). See p. 30.

SUFFERING. A result of the alienation between God and people caused by sin (Jb 10:2; Ps 51:4). Although the root cause for suffering is spiritual, people suffer both physically and morally (Gn 3:1–6; Jb; Mt 27:27–30, 39–44). Christ paid the penalty for the sins of the world by suffering and dying on the cross (Ps 22; Mt 27:45–46). Since it will not be until the next life that the effects of sin are totally removed, Christians still suffer in this world. Christian suffering, however, is understood by faith (Rm 8:24; 2Co 1:5–14). Suffering teaches Christians to rely on and trust in God. Paul writes: "We felt that we had received the sentence of death. But that was to make us rely not on ourselves but on God who raises the dead. He delivered us from so deadly a peril . . . [that] on Him we have set our hope that He will deliver us again" (2Co 1:9–10). People who do not believe in Christ will suffer eternally. See pp. 130, 160–61, 236–37, 252, 312–13.

SULFUR. A chemical element commonly used figuratively for destruction and punishment (Jb 18:15; Ps 11:6; Is 34:9; Rv 21:8). See p. 85.

SUN. The greater light of the day created and preserved by God (Gn 1:16; Ps 74:16; 104:19; Jer 31:35; Mt 5:45). The sun helps crops and vegetation to grow but also burns them (Dt 33:14; Jnh 4:8). In Old Testament days both the Hebrews and other nations worshiped the sun (2Ki 21:3, 5; 23:5; Jb 31:26–27).

The sun is also a picture word for the glory of Christ, heavenly beings, and the saints (Mt 13:43; 17:2; Rv 1:16; 10:1; 12:1).

When a person died before he or she reached old age, it was compared to the setting of the sun during daytime (Jer 15:9; Am 8:9; Mi 3:6). A darkened sun was symbolic of some great disaster or trouble (Ezk 32:7; Jl 2:10, 31). See pp. 76, 232, 266, 281, 445.

SUNDAY. The first day of the week. At first, the early Christians worshiped on both the seventh day of the week, the Sabbath, and the first day of the week, the day upon which Christ rose from the dead. Eventually they stopped meeting on the seventh day. The word *Sunday* is of pagan origin. See pp. 354, 424–25. *See also* LORD'S DAY.

SUPPLICATION (SUP-li-KAY-shuhn). A prayer for mercy or favor in some special need (Eph 6:18; 1Tm2:1; 5:5; cf. 1Ki 8:28–54; Jb 8:5; Ps 6:9). *See also* PRAYER. See pp. 165, 251, 253, 398.

SUSA (SYOO-sah). The capital of Elam and later, under Cyrus, one of the capitals of the Persian Empire (Ne 1:1; Est 1:2; Dn 8:2). Today it is called Shush. See pp. 146–47.

SWEARING. *See* OATH.

SWORD. *See* ARMOR, ARMS.

SYCAMORE (SIK-ah-mor). A fig tree. It was valued for its small, edible fruit and light, durable wood (1Ki 10:27; 1Ch 27:28; Ps 78:47; Lk 19:4). See p. 233. *See also* ORCHARD.

SYNAGOGUE (SIN-ah-gog; led together). A Jewish place for worship and for social gathering. The synagogue served as the place for worship and instruction in both God's law and the civil and moral law. The synagogue as a meeting place and building likely began during the captivity when people could not get to the temple in Jerusalem for worship (cf. Ezr 8:15; Ne 8:2; 9:1).

The furnishings of the synagogue included a chest for the sacred books, a reading platform with a lectern, seats for the congregation, and lamps and trumpets. The ruler of the synagogue, the attendant, and the almoner were the officers in charge of the synagogue. When the people came for worship, they observed the following order of service: a recitation of the Shema, prayer, a reading from the Law, a reading from the prophets, and the benediction. See pp. 298–300, 325–27. *See also* EDUCATION.

SYRACUSE (SIR-ah-kyoos). A leading city on the east coast of Sicily where Paul stayed for three days on his voyage to Rome (Ac 28:12). See pp. 360–61.

SYRIA (SIR-i-ah). In the Old Testament Syria was called Aram. It was that territory bounded by the Taurus Mountains, the Euphrates River, the Arabian Desert, and the Mediterranean Sea. David conquered it, but under Solomon it became independent (2Sm 8; 10; 1Ki 11:23–25). Syria was a continual enemy of the Israelites (1Ki 15:18–20; 20; 22; 2Ki 6:8–33; 7; 9:14, 15; 10:32, 33; 13). See pp. 147, 271, 360–61, 372, 375.

SYRIAC (SIR-i-ak). The language spoken in Syria; Aramaic (Dn 2:4).

SYROPHOENICIAN (sigh-ro-fi-NISH-uhn). A person who lived in northern Phoenicia. The Syrophoenicians were absorbed into the Syrian kingdom (Mk 7:26).

T

TAANACH (TAY-ah-nak). A Canaanite city about 5 miles southeast of Megiddo. Joshua conquered Taanach and gave it to Manasseh and the Kohathite Levites (Jsh 12:21; 17:11; 21:25). The battle between Barak and Sisera was fought near Taanach (Jgs 5:19).

TABEEL (TAY-bi-el; God is good). The father of the one whom Rezin of Syria and Pekah of Israel proposed to put on the throne of Judah as their puppet king (Is 7:6).

TABERAH (TAB-i-rah; burning). A place in the wilderness where Israel camped. Here the fire of the Lord burned some people who complained. Taberah is also called Kibroth-hattaavah (Nu 11:3, 34; Dt 9:22).

TABERNACLE (TAB -ur-nak' l). 1. *See* TENT OF MEETING.

2. The movable sanctuary in the form of a tent. God directed Moses to make the tabernacle so that He would have a place to live as King among His people (Ex 25:8–9). Because it contained the ark and two tables of the Law, the tabernacle was sometimes referred to as the tent, or tabernacle, of testimony (Ex 38:21; Nu 9:15; 17:7; 18:2). Other names for it include the tent of meeting or the tabernacle of congregation, the house of the Lord, the sanctuary, and the temple (Ex 23:19; 25:8; 29:42, 44; 1Sm 1:9; 3:3).

A description of the tabernacle is found in Ex 26:1–27:19. The tabernacle stood in a court that was 100 cubits long by 50 cubits wide. The court was enclosed by acacia pillars 5 cubits high that had silver bands and hooks connected at the top by silver-covered rods. From these rods hung sheets of fine linen, embroidered on the east entrance. The frame of the tabernacle was 30 cubits long by 10 cubits wide by 10 cubits high. It was made of gold-covered acacia wood, covered on the outside with double blankets of skin and on the inside with embroidered linen tapestry. The tabernacle was divided into the Holy and Most Holy Places by a linen veil embroidered with cherubim.

The altar of burnt offering stood in the court between the court entrance and the tabernacle. A basin (the place where priests washed) stood halfway between the altar and the tabernacle. The table of showbread, the golden candlestick, and the altar of incense were kept in the Holy Place, while the ark of the covenant was kept in the Most Holy Place.

The tabernacle was set up at Sinai the second year after the Israelites left Egypt (Ex 40:2, 17). During the time of the conquest the tabernacle was stationed at Gilgal and Ebal (Jsh 4:9; 8:30–35). Later, it was stationed at Shiloh, Nob, and Gibeon (Jsh 18:1; 1Sm 4:17, 22; 21:1; 1Ch 16:39; 21:29). Under David the ark of the covenant was moved to the new tabernacle in Jerusalem. When the temple was built, the ark was placed in it (2Sm 6:17; 1Ch 15:1). See pp. 39–42, 128, 149–50.

TABERNACLES, FEAST OF. *See* BOOTHS, FEAST OF.

TABITHA (TAB-i-thah; gazelle). *See* DORCAS.

TABLE. 1. *See* SHOWBREAD; TABERNACLE.

2. A table spread with food (Jgs 1:7; 1Ki 2:7; Mt 15:27; Mk 7:28; Lk 16:21). See pp. 110, 123.

3. *See* LORD'S SUPPER.

4. A table the moneychangers used for their business (Mt 21:12).

TABOR (TAY-bur). A limestone mountain in Galilee about 6 miles east of Nazareth (Jsh 19:22). It is 1,843 feet above sea level. Barak gathered 10,000 men together on Mount Tabor (Jgs 4:6–14). Gideon's brothers were murdered there (Jgs 8:21). See pp. 284–85, 291, 435.

TAHATH (TAY-hath; that which is beneath). One of the places in the wilderness where Israel camped (Nu 33:26–27).

TALENT. The largest metal weight in Bible times (Mt 25:14–30). A talent of gold was worth about 15 times as much as a talent of silver. A talent of silver represented wealth; a talent of gold meant fabulous riches. See p. 127.

TALITHA CUMI (tah-LIGH-thah KOO-mi). An Aramaic expression that means "Little girl . . . arise" (Mk 5:41).

TAMAR (TAY-mur; palm tree). 1. The wife of Er, son of Judah. When she was left a widow, Tamar tricked her father-in-law, Judah, into making her pregnant. She became the mother of Perez and Zerah (Gn 38:6–26; Nu 26:20–21; Mt 1:3). See pp. 97, 212.

2. Absalom's sister (2Sm 13; 1Ch 3:9).

3. The daughter of Absalom and mother of Maacah (2Sm 14:27; 2Ch 13:2).

TAMBOURINE (tam-boo-REEN). A percussion instrument used to mark time (Gn 31:27; Ps 81:2). See p. 168.

TANNER. *See* TRADE.

TAPHATH (TAY-fath; drop). Solomon's daughter (1Ki 4:11).

TARES. *See* WEEDS.

TARSHISH (TAHR-shish; foundry, refinery). 1. A place on the Mediterranean, perhaps in Spain or Tunisia (2Ch 9:21; 20:36–37; Ps 72:10). Jonah fled to Tarshish (Jnh 1:3). See p. 240.

2. The "ships of Tarshish" were large, seagoing ships which carried refined ore or other cargo (1Ki 9:26; 10:22; 22:48; 2Ch 9:21).

TARSUS (TAHR-suhs). The chief city of Cilicia, located on the Cydnus River. It was a free city and a great commercial center. Known for its educational system, its schools were almost as good as those of Athens and Alexandria. Tarsus was the home of Paul, who no doubt benefited from all his city had to offer (Ac 9:11, 30; 11:25; 21:39; 22:3). See pp. 358, 361, 372, 399.

TAX COLLECTOR. A person who collected taxes for the Roman government. The Romans used a tax-farming system, employing the natives of a particular country or area to collect taxes for them. For instance, in Palestine the tax collectors were usually Jews. Tax collectors had two marks against them: not only were they collecting taxes, but they were doing this for Rome, a government hated by their fellow countrymen because of its control over their land. As a result they were also looked down upon, even hated, by their own countrymen (Mt 9:10; 18:17; Lk 3:12–13; 19:2). See pp. 308–10, 389.

TAXES. Under the judges the Israelites paid taxes to support the priests and tabernacle.

Under the kings taxes were collected from various sources to support the kingdom. These included the following:

1. Taxes in kind levied on the produce of fields and flocks (1Ki 4:7–28)
2. Military service (1Sm 8:12; 1Ch 27:1)
3. Special gifts (1Sm 10:27; 16:20)
4. Duties paid by merchants (1Ki 10:15)
5. Tribute and services exacted by subject people (2Sm 8:6, 14)
6. Monopoly of certain trade (1Ki 9:28; 22:48)

Under the Persian Empire, the satraps paid a fixed sum into the royal treasury. This sum was collected from the people by tribute, customs, and toll (Ezr 4:13, 20). The priests, Levites, and Nethinim, however, were exempt (Ezr 7:24).

The Egyptians and Syrians sold the right to tax to the highest bidder at auction. That person who promised to collect the most revenue from a province was authorized to do so and given military power to enforce his demands.

The Romans practiced tax farming (Mt 17:24; 22:17). See pp. 50, 308–10, 389. *See also* CENSUS; TAX COLLECTOR.

TEKOA, TEKOAH (ti-KO-ah). A town in Judah about 6 miles south of Bethlehem (2Sm 14:2, 4, 9). It was fortified by King Rehoboam and was the home of the prophet Amos (2Ch 11:6; Am 1:1). Today it is Tekia. See p. 233.

TEL-ABIB (tel-AY-bib; grain heap). A place on the Chebar Canal where Ezekiel lived (Ezk 3:15).

TEMAN (TEE-muhn; south). 1. Esau's grandson and a prince of Edom (Gn 36:11, 15, 42; 1Ch 1:36).

2. A district in northern Edom where Teman's descendants lived (Ezk 25:13; Am 1:12). The people of Teman were noted for their wisdom (Jb 2:11; Jer 49:7).

TEMPLE. David wanted to build the temple so the Lord would have a permanent house instead of a tent. With this in mind, he gathered together the materials for it (2Sm 7; 1Ch 17; 22; 28:12–19; 29:1–9). But it was Solomon, his son, who actually built the temple on Mount Moriah with the help of Hiram of Tyre. The temple proper was 60 cubits long, 20 cubits broad, and 30 cubits high. It was built of stone from a quarry. The roof was made of cedar; the floor was carved with cypress overlaid with gold; and the inside walls were lined with carved cedar overlaid with gold.

The Most Holy Place, or inner sanctuary, was a cube, each side measuring 20 cubits. It contained two cherubim made of olive wood and overlaid with gold and the ark with the mercy seat.

The Holy Place, separated from the Most Holy Place by a cedar door and a veil, was 40 cubits long, 20 cubits wide, and 30 cubits high. It contained an altar of incense made of cedar and overlaid with gold, 10 golden seven-lamp candlesticks, and 10 tables for showbread.

On the east, west, and south sides of the temple was a three-story building containing rooms for officials and storage. On the north side before the front entrance was a portico with two pillars, Jachin and Boaz.

The temple had two courts: the inner, or upper court for the priests, containing the altar of burnt offering and a molten sea, and around this inner court was the outer court for Israel (1Ki 6–8; 2Ch 3–7).

This temple, known as Solomon's temple, was burned by the Babylonians. Zerubbabel's temple was larger than Solomon's but less magnificent (Ezr 3–6).

Herod rebuilt, enlarged, and made Zerubbabel's temple more beautiful. Herod's temple had an outer court where Gentiles often gathered, a court of women, and an inner court. The gate called Beautiful was on the east side of this temple (Ac 3:2). See pp. 123–29, 146, 259, 325–27, 364–65. *See also* NAVE.

TEMPLE SERVANTS. A group of servants or slaves who performed menial tasks in the temple (1Ch 9:2; Ezr 2:43–58; 8:17–20; Ne 7:46–56)

TEN COMMANDMENTS. The Ten Commandments were given by God to Moses on Mount Sinai and written on tablets of stone (Ex 20; 31:18; 32:15–19; Dt 10:1–5). The Ten Commandments form the basis of God's Law. In the Old Testament they are also referred to as the words (Ex 20:1; 34:28). In the New Testament, they are called commandments (Mt 19:17; Eph 6:2). Jesus' interpretation of the commandments is found in Mt 5:17–48; 19:16–22; Mk 2:24–27; Lk 6:1–10; 13:10–16. Perfect love is the fulfillment of the commandments (Mt 22:35–40). See pp. 70–72, 336.

TENT OF MEETING. A provisional tent where the Lord met with His people (Ex 33:7–11; 34:34–35). See pp. 76, 128.

TERAH (TEE-rah; ibex). 1. The father of Abraham, Nahor, and Haran (Gn 11:26; 1Ch 1:26; Lk 3:34). Terah, who lived in Ur of the Chaldees, served idols (Jsh 24:2). See p. 12. He moved with Abraham and Lot from Ur to Haran, where he died at the age of 205.

2. A place in the wilderness where Israel camped (Nu 33:27–28).

TERAPHIM (TER-ah-fim). Household idols. They were figurines in human form which varied in size (Ezk 21:21; cf. Gn 31:19, 32–35; 1Sm 19:13).

TERTIUS (TUR-shi-uhs; third). Paul's scribe. At Paul's dictation Tertius wrote down Paul's Letter to the Romans (Rm 16:22).

TERTULLUS (TUR-TUL-uhs; little third). The Roman lawyer hired by Jewish authorities to prosecute Paul before Felix (Ac 24:1–8).

TESTAMENT. 1. Will (Heb 9:16–17).

2. Covenant (Heb 8:6–10).

3. The books of the Bible pertaining to the Old Covenant (Genesis through Malachi) and the New Covenant (Matthew through Revelation). The Old and New Covenants are more accurate descriptions for the Old and New Testaments. *See also* COVENANT.

See pp. xviii–xix, xxiv, 2–4.

TESTIMONY. 1. Divine commands (Dt 4:45; 6:17).

2. The Decalogue or divine law as found in the ark. The two tables of the law are called the testimony (Ex 25:16). See p. 65.

3. Legal evidence; witness (Mt 26:59).

TETRARCH (TET-rahrk; ruler of one quarter). One who ruled over a small territory (Mt 14:1; Lk 3:1; Ac 13:1). See p. 275.

THADDAEUS (tha-DEE-uhs; wise). *See* JUDAS 4.

THEBES (THEEBZ). An ancient city of Upper Egypt referred to as No in the Bible. Thebes was built on both sides of the Nile and is well known for its temples and other ruins (Jer 46:25; Ezk 30:14–16; Na 3:8).

THEOCRACY (thee-OK-rah-si; ruled by God). The form of government in the Old Testament where God Himself ruled His people and where all power and authority rested in Him (1Sm 8:4–9; 12).

THEOPHILUS (thee-OF-uh-luhs; friend of God). An unknown person, perhaps an official, to whom Luke and Acts are addressed (Lk 1:3; Ac 1:1). See p. 324.

THESSALONIANS, FIRST LETTER OF PAUL TO. Paul wrote this Letter to the Thessalonians while he was in Corinth. His purpose for writing the letter was to encourage the Thessalonians to good conduct and to comfort them concerning those who had died. See pp. 404–06.

THESSALONIANS, SECOND LETTER OF PAUL TO. Paul wrote his second Letter to the Thessalonians to correct their wrong ideas about the return of Christ. See pp. 404–06.

THESSALONICA (thes-ah-lo-NIGH-kah; victory of Thessaly). A city on the Thermaic Gulf in Macedonia. Thessalonica was a commercial city, a chief port of Macedonia, and a free city in the Roman Empire. It was ruled by politarchs (Ac 17:1–8). Today it is known as Salonika. See pp. 360–61, 404–05.

THOMAS (TOM-ahs; twin). One of the twelve disciples. He was also known as Didymus, the Greek name for twin. Thomas showed great love for Jesus. When the other apostles were unable to talk Jesus out of going to Bethany to heal Lazarus because of the danger, Thomas said, "Let us also go, that we may die with Him" (Jn 11:16). Thomas doubted Jesus' resurrection since he was not present with the other apostles when Jesus showed Himself to them (Jn 20:24–25). Later, Thomas was with the apostles when Jesus appeared again; Thomas exclaimed, "My Lord and My God" (Jn 20:28). Thomas was with the apostles after the ascension (Ac 1:13). According to tradition Thomas preached in Parthia. See p. 287.

THORNS AND THISTLES. There are 22 Hebrew words for thorns, thistles, briers, etc., which grow in great quantities in Israel (Gn 3:17–18). Figuratively, thorns and thistles are descriptive of a waste place, wickedness, divine visitation, a messenger of Satan, and troubles (Nu 33:55; 2Sm 23:6; Pr 22:5; 24:31; 2Co 12:7). See pp. 60, 332, 334, 374.

THRESHING, THRESHING FLOOR. *See* AGRICULTURE.

THUNDER. In Palestine thunder is rare in the summer. In Bible times, when thunder did occur, it served as a sign from God (1Sm 12:17–18). Thunder accompanied the giving of the Law (Ex 19:16; 20:18). Thunder is described poetically as the voice of God and is a picture word for glory and power (Ex 19:16; Jb 37:2; Ps 18:13; Rv 8:5). See p. 165.

THYATIRA (thigh-ah-TIGH-rah; burning incense). A city of Asia Minor on the Lycus River in northern Lydia. It was known for its purple dyeing and weaving. Lydia, a seller of purple dye at Philippi, was from Thyatira (Ac 16:14). One of the seven churches mentioned in the Book of Revelation was in Thyatira (Rv 2:18–29). See pp. 361, 376, 446.

TIBERIAS (tigh-BEER-i-uhs). A city built by Herod Antipas on the western shore of the Sea of Galilee. Herod named the city after the ruling emperor at that time: Tiberius Caesar. After AD 70, Tiberias became a center for Jewish learning, and later the Sanhedrin was transferred there (Jn 6:1, 23; 21:1). Today it is called Tabariyeh.

TIBERIAS, SEA OF. *See* GALILEE, SEA OF.

TIBERIUS (tigh-BEER-i-uhs). Tiberius Caesar was the second emperor of the Roman Empire. He was born in 42 BC and was the reigning emperor at the time of Christ's death (Lk 3:1; Jn 19:12, 15). See pp. 282, 319.

TIBNI (TIB-nigh). Omri's unsuccessful competitor for the throne of Israel (1Ki 16:21–22).

TIGLATH-PILESER III (TIG-lath-pigh-LEE-zur; trust is [Ninip] the son of E-Sarra). The Assyrian king who ruled Assyria from 744 to 727 BC. He extended the Assyrian Empire and was recognized as king even in Babylon, where he was referred to as Pul (2Ki 15:19; 1Ch 5:26). Tiglath-pileser broke the coalition of Uzziah, king of Judah, and made him pay tribute. Later, when Ahaz was king of Judah, Pekah of Israel and Rezin of Syria joined forces to conquer Judah. Ahaz paid Tiglath-pileser a large sum of money to defend him and his country from the armies of Pekah and Rezin (2Ki 16:7–10).

TIGRIS (TIGH-gris). One of two rivers of Babylonia, the other one being the Euphrates. See pp. 193, 222, 246–47.

TIME. Time and seasons are mentioned early in the Bible (Gn 1:5, 14–16; 8:22; Ex 34:21; Ps 74:17). Ancient people calculated time by dating such things as important events, the reign of kings and rulers, and natural phenomena like earthquakes (Ex 12:40; 1Ki 6:1; 2Ki 3:1–2; Am 1:1; Lk 3:1–2). They followed a lunar year, consisting of 354 days, 8 hours, and 38 seconds. The lunar year was divided into 12 lunar months with seven intercalary months added over 19 years.

The Hebrew month began with the new moon. Before the exile the Hebrews used numbers to name the months; after the exile, they used names. The sacred year began with Nisan (March–April); the secular year, with Tishri (September–October). Months were divided into weeks of seven days. The week ended with the Sabbath (Ex 20:11; Dt 5:14–15).

The day was reckoned from either sunset to sunset or dawn to darkness (Gn 1:5; 8:22; Ex 12:18; Jn 11:9). It was divided into morning, noon, and evening (Ps 55:17). Night was the time of darkness. It was divided into periods called watches (Ex 14:24; Jgs 7:19; Mk 13:35; Lk 12:38).

Sundials were used to divide the day (2Ki 20:11; Is 38:8). See pp. 3, 46–47, 56.

TIMNATH-SERAH (TIM-nath-SEE-rah; double portion). A city in Ephraim given to Joshua as his inheritance. It was his home and burial place (Jsh 19:50; 24:30). In Jgs 2:9, it is called Timnath-heres.

TIMOTHY (TIM-o-thee; venerating God). Paul's companion, assistant, and friend whom he affectionately spoke of as his "beloved and faithful child in the Lord" (1Co 4:17). Timothy's mother was a devout Jewish woman; his father was a Greek (Ac 16:1–3). When he was a child, his mother, Eunice, and grandmother Lois instructed Timothy in the Jewish religion (2Tm 1:5; 3:15). Through Paul's witness to the Gospel, Timothy became a Christian (1Co 4:17; 1Tm 1:2). After his conversion, Timothy became active in Christian work at Lystra and Iconium. When Paul visited Lystra on his second missionary trip, he found Timothy well spoken of by the Christians in these places (Ac 16:1–2). Paul decided to take the young man with him, and Timothy was set apart for church work by the laying on of hands (1Tm 4:14; 2Tm 1:6). Paul also circumcised Timothy in order not to offend the Jews (Ac 16:3).

Paul frequently mentions Timothy in his writings (Php 1:1; Col 1:1; 1Th 3:2; 2Th 1:1; Phm 1). He also addresses two letters, 1 and 2 Timothy, to his friend. According to tradition, Timothy was a bishop at Ephesus. See p. 407.

TIMOTHY, FIRST LETTER OF PAUL TO. Paul wrote this letter to Timothy while Timothy was in charge of the church at Ephesus. In the letter Paul gives Timothy instructions for his office and warns him against false teachers. See pp. 407–09.

TIMOTHY, SECOND LETTER OF PAUL TO. Paul wrote this letter to encourage Timothy to be faithful in his work and to urge him to come to Rome with Mark. See pp. 407–09.

TIRZAH (TUR-zah; delightfulness). A city that originally belonged to the Canaanites. Joshua captured Tirzah and killed its king (Jsh 12:24). Jeroboam I made Tirzah his capital, and it remained the capital of the kings of Israel until Omri built Samaria. Tirzah was located five miles east of Samaria and is probably modern-day Tell el-Far'ah. See p. 139.

TISHBITE (TISH-bight). Elijah is referred to as a Tishbite, someone from the town of Tishbe or a town similar to that name (1Ki 17:1; 21:17; 28). See p. 130.

TITHE (TIGHTH). A tenth part of one's income. Abram gave tithes to Melchizedek; Jacob promised tithes to God (Gn 14:20; 28:22; Heb 7:2, 6). See pp. 98–99.

According to Mosaic Law a tenth of all produce of the land and herds was sacred to the Lord (Lv 27:30–33). This tithe was used to support the Levites (Nu

18:21–24). A tenth of it went for the priests (Nu 18:25–32). Additional tithes were used for festivals and for the poor (Dt 12:5–18; 14:22–29). The Pharisees also tithed mint, anise, cumin, and rue (Mt 23:23).

TITTLE. *See* DOT.

TITUS (TIGH-tuhs). A Gentile convert to Christianity who became Paul's friend and helper. Titus went with Paul and Barnabas to Jerusalem at the time of the council. Since Titus was born of Greek parents, he was uncircumcised (Gal 2:3–5). This offended the Judaizers at the council; however, the Church refused to make Titus submit to circumcision, siding with Paul, who maintained the freedom of Gentiles from the Mosaic Law (Gal 2:1, 3–5). Titus was sent to Corinth to solve the problems there and then rejoined Paul in Macedonia (2Co 2:13; 7:6, 13–14; 8:6, 16; 12:18). Later Titus was left behind in Crete to organize the churches there. Paul wrote his letter to Titus while Titus was in Crete (Ti 1:4–5). The last mention of Titus indicates that he went to Dalmatia (2Tm 4:10). According to tradition Titus was the bishop of Crete. See pp. 407, 413.

TITUS, LETTER OF PAUL TO. Paul wrote this letter to Titus while Titus was in charge of the churches on Crete. The letter is a manual for ministers and congregations. See pp. 413–14.

TOMB. *See* BURIAL.

TOOTH. In the Bible a tooth illustrates the law of retaliation (Ex 21:24; Mt 5:38). When referred to in a figurative way, teeth also means "plenty" or "oppression" (Gn 49:12; Pr 30:14). The teeth of beasts are figurative for cruelty (Dt 32:24; Jb 4:10). Cleanness of teeth is a picture of famine; gnashing of teeth, a picture of rage or despair (Jb 16:9; Am 4:6; Mt 8:12).

TORCH. A light that could be carried from place to place (Jgs 7:16; Ezk 1:13; Dn 10:6; Jn 18:3).

TOWER OF BABEL. *See* BABEL 2.

TOWN CLERK. An official in Ephesus who was second in rank to the president of the council (Ac 19:35–41).

TRADE. In Israel trades were often carried out in the home. Mats and baskets were handwoven from straw or rushes. Wool, flax, and cotton were washed, combed, and spun into yarn. Then the yarn was woven on a loom into material.

Carpentry was also carried out in the home. The carpenter made agricultural machinery, woodwork for the house, furniture, and wooden utensils. Because of the lack of good timber in Israel, its carpenters could not produce as fine a product as carpenters from countries where good wood was plentiful. When David built his palace and when Solomon built the temple, they hired carpenters from heavily wooded Phoenicia, where the carpenter's trade had reached its height (2Sm 5:11; 1Ki 5:2–8).

Other trades in Bible times were those of the potter and brickmaker. Since Israel has a good supply of clay, many items were made from it (Gn 24:14–20; Lv 6:28; 1Ki 17:12). Clay was dug from a field that became known as a potter's field because of it. Pottery was roughly shaped by hand or worked on a potter's wheel, then dried and baked in a kiln (Jer 18:3–6). Brick was molded in wooden molds and then baked in loosely built stacks or in kilns (Ex 9:8–10).

Metal casting and forging, tanning, stonecutting, gem cutting, leather working, and tentmaking were other common trades in Bible times. The leather worker made sandals, parts of armor, aprons, belts, shoes, and purses (Gn 3:21; 2Ki 1:8, Mt 3:4). Tentmakers used such items as knives, shears, and needles and thread to make their tents. The best tents were woven of goats' hair and were usually dark in color (Ex 25:4; Ac 18:3).

TRADITION (trah-DISH-uhn). 1. Interpretations of the Old Testament law (Mt 15:1–9; Gal 1:14). See pp. 52, 63, 178.

2. Apostolic teaching or truths handed down in the Church by those who were witnesses to Christ (1Co 11:2; cf. Lk 1:2; Rm 6:17; 1Co 15:3–9; 2Pt 2:21). See pp. 286–87, 315, 338, 374.

TRANSFIGURATION (trans-fig-yoo-RAY-shuhn). The name given to the time when Jesus was visibly glorified in the presence of His three disciples. Jesus' transfiguration likely occurred on Mount Hermon (Mt 17:1–13; Mk 9:2–13; Lk 9:28–36). See pp. 336, 434–36.

TREASURE. Anything that is collected in storehouses, for instance, grain, wine, gold, or silver (1Ki 14:26; 15:18; Mt 2:11; 6:19).

Figuratively, treasure depicts God's resources in nature, God's peculiar people, piety, the Gospel, and Christ-centered wisdom and knowledge (Ex 19:5; Dt 28:12; Is 33:6; 2Co 4:7; Col 2:3). See pp. 26, 124, 142, 374, 447.

TREASURY. The place in the temple where gifts were received (Mk 12:41; Jn 8:20; cf. 1Ch 9:26; Lk 21:1). See p. 319.

TRESPASS. *See* SIN, II.

TRIAL. A testing, usually accomplished by a painful process, for the purpose of purifying or achieving good (1Pt 1:6–7; cf. Ps 7:9; Zec 13:9). See pp. 103, 160, 252, 433.

TRIBE. The 12 tribes of Israel (Jacob's name in Gn 32:28) came from Jacob's 12 sons, with Joseph's sons, Ephraim and Manasseh, forming two tribes (Gn 48:5; Nu 26:5–51; Jsh 13:7–33; 15–19). No tribal territory was given to Levi. The heads or elders of each tribe had great influence (1Sm 8; 2Sm 3:17; 2Ki 23:1). See pp. 17–21, 426.

TRIBULATION (trib-yoo-LAY-shuhn). *See* SUFFERING.

TRIBUTE. *See* TAXES.

TRINITY (TRIN-uh-tee). The church's term for the coexistence of the Father, Son, and Holy Spirit in the unity of the Godhead: three distinct Persons in one Divine Being, or Essence. The term *Trinity* does not occur in the Bible, but many passages support the doctrine of the Trinity (Dt 6:4; Is 48:16; Mt 3:13–17; 28:19; Jn 10:30; 2Co 13:14; 1Tm 2:5). See pp. xxix, 296, 426.

TROAS (TRO-as). A city of Asia Minor in the district of Mysia about six miles south of ancient Troy. It was founded by Alexander the Great (Ac 16:8–11; 20:5–10; 2Tm 4:13). See pp. 294, 360–61.

TRUMPET. A wind instrument made of metal or from the horn of a ram or goat (Nu 10:2). Trumpets were played to provide music; they were also sounded in battle and for other signals, such as an alarm or when a new king took the throne (Jgs 3:27; 1Ki 1:39; Is 18: 3; Hos 8:1; Am 3:6; 1Th 4:16). See p. 168.

TRUTH. That which is eternal, ultimate, secure, steadfast, reliable. God is truth; He cannot lie (Ps 31:5; Is 65:16; Jn 17:3; 2Tm 2:13; Heb 6:18). Everything that comes from God is true (Ps 33:4). God has made known all that humanity needs to know for life and salvation. Truth is manifested supremely in Christ (Jn 1:14, 17; 14:6). The Holy Spirit imparts the truth of Christ (1Jn 2:20–22). God's Word is truth (Jn 17:17–19; 2Co 4:2; Gal 5:7; Eph 1:13; Jas 1:18). See pp. xxv, 160, 239, 244, 297.

TUBAL-CAIN (TYOO-buhl-kayn; Tubal the smith). A son of Lamech who worked in brass and iron (Gn 4:22). Tubal-cain represents the ancestor of all metalworkers.

TURBAN. A head covering worn by the priests as part of their official vestments. The words "Holy to the Lord" were written on it (Ex 28:4, 36–39; 29:6; 39:28–31; Lv 8:9). See p. 150.

TURTLEDOVE. A common type of pigeon in Israel that poor people used for sacrifices (Gn 15:9; Lk 2:24). See p. 331.

TYCHICUS (TIK-i-kuhs; fortune). A disciple, messenger, and spokesman of Paul (Ac 20:4; Eph 6:21–22; Col 4:7–8).

TYRE (TIGHR; rock). An important Phoenician city on the Mediterranean coast. It was built partly on the rocky mainland and partly on an island. Alexander the Great constructed a causeway to connect the two parts.

Tyre was a powerful merchant city (Is 23:8). David formed an alliance with Tyre (2Sm 5:11; 1Ki 5:1; 2Ch 2:3). A number of the prophets spoke against Tyre and its inhabitants (Is 23:1–17; Jer 27:3; Ezk 26–28). Jesus visited its region and was well received (Mt 15:21; Mk 7:24). Paul once stayed in Tyre for seven days (Ac 21:3–4). See pp. 193, 293–94, 360–61.

U

UNBELIEF. A lack of faith; the rejection of God's promises and threats as found in His Word, and especially the refusal to believe and trust in Christ (Rm 11:20; Heb 3:19; cf. Jn 3:36). See pp. 257, 303, 428, 448.

UNCIRCUMCISED. 1. Those who have not submitted to the Jewish rite of circumcision; Gentiles (Gn 34:14; Jgs 14:3; 1Sm 14:6; Rm 4:9).

2. Ears that do not hear the truth (Jer 6:10; Ac 7:51).

3. Hearts that are not open to God (Lv 26:41; Jer 4:4; Ac 7:51). *See also* CIRCUMCISION.

UNCLEAN. 1. A number of food items were considered unclean in Bible times: animals that did not part the hoof and chew the cud; animals and birds that ate blood or the flesh of dead bodies; insects that did not have hind legs for jumping; and water creatures without scales or fins (Lv 11; Nu 19; Dt 14:1–21). See pp. 54–55.

2. Other forms of ceremonial uncleanness included leprosy, sexual dis-

charge, and contact with the dead (Lv 11:24–15:33; 17:15; Nu 19:16–22).

UNICORN (YOO-nuh-kawrn). *See* WILD OX.

UNKNOWN GOD. While Paul was in Athens, he found an altar with the inscription "To the unknown god" (Ac 17:23). This was an altar built to appease any god that may have been overlooked.

UNLEAVENED. Bread without yeast. The Israelites ate unleavened bread at Passover as a reminder of the Exodus (Ex 12:8; 13:3–10). See p. 38.

UNRIGHTEOUS. *See* RIGHTEOUS; UNBELIEF.

UPPER CHAMBER, ROOM. *See* HOMES.

UR (UR). Abraham's native city. It was located in southern Babylonia near Uruk and was called Ur of Chaldees (Gn 11:28, 31; 15:7; Ne 9:7). Today it is Tell Muggayyar. See pp. 18, 193.

URIAH (yoo-RIGH-ah; flame of Lord). 1. A Hittite, the husband of Bathsheba. After David committed adultery with Bathsheba, he arranged to have Uriah placed on the front line of battle so that Uriah would be killed (2Sm 11; Mt 1:6). See p. 79.

2. A prophet who was put to death by Jehoiakin after he predicted the destruction of Judah (Jer 26:20–23). See pp. 79, 118.

URIM AND THUMMIM (YOO-rim and THUM-im; lights and perfections). Objects placed in the breastpiece of the high priest. Their exact nature is unknown. They were used, however, to determine the will of the Lord (Ex 28:30; Lv 8:8; Nu 27:21). See p. 150.

UZ (UZ). The land of Job. Although its site is uncertain, Bible scholars usually locate it in the Arabian Desert next to Edom (Jb 1:1; Jer 25:20; Lm 4:21).

UZZAH (UZ-ah; strength). Son of Abinadab. When the oxen of the cart bearing the ark stumbled, Uzzah was struck dead for putting out his hand and touching the ark of God (2Sm 6:3–11; 1Ch 13:7–11).

UZZIAH (u-ZIGH-ah; Lord is strength). Also known as Azariah, he was the son of Amaziah and the tenth king of Judah. Uzziah became king at the age of 16 and ruled Judah for 52 years (2Ki 14:21–22). He fought successfully against the Mehunim, the Arabs, and the Philistines. He strengthened his kingdom by developing agriculture, fortifying Jerusalem, and organizing the army (2Ch 26:1–15). "And his fame spread far. . . . But when he was strong, he grew proud, to his destruction" (2Ch 26:15–16).

Uzziah decided to burn incense to the Lord and went into the temple with that in mind. The priests told him to leave, for only they were set apart to burn incense. When Uzziah became angry with them, God struck him with leprosy. Uzziah remained a leper until the day he died (2Ch 26: 16–22). See pp. 125, 189–90, 233.

VANITY. 1. Something that is not profitable (Ec 1:2). See p. 178.

2. That which is empty, nothing, worthless, futile, such as idols and lies (Ps 4:2; Jer 46:10–12; cf. 2Ki 17:15; Is 41:29).

3. Human help is vain (Ps 60:11).

4. Sin (cf. Ps 119:37; Rm 8:20). See p. 178.

VASHTI (VASH-tigh). The wife of Ahasuerus. She was the queen of Persia (Est 1:9–22). See p. 154.

VEIL. 1. *See* DRESS.

2. The curtain that separated the Holy Place from the Most Holy Place in the tabernacle and temple (Ex 26:31–35; 2Ch 3:14; Mt 27:51). See p. 40.

VINE. 1. *See* VINEYARD.

2. Figuratively, a vine often depicts both Israel and happiness and contentment (1Ki 4:25; Ps 80:8; 128:3; Mi 4:4). Apostate Israel is pictured as wild grapes or a strange vine (Is 5:2; Jer 2:21). An empty vine is a picture of spiritual unfruitfulness (Hos 10:1). The vine of Sodom refers to godless people (Dt 32:28–33). The vine and branches is a picture of Christ and believers (Jn 15:1–6). See pp. 226, 253, 351.

VINEYARD. The soil of Israel has always been good for cultivating grapes. When the Israelites arrived in Canaan, they expanded the grape industry already there (Nu 13:23–27). They cleared the land of stones, terraced it, planted choice shoots, and carefully cultivated and trained them (1Ki 4:25; Is 5:1–2; Hos 2:12; Mi 1:6). Often they built a wall around the vineyard and erected a tower (Is 5:1–7; Sg 2:15).

When harvesting began in June, bunches of grapes were gathered in baskets and taken to the winepress (Jer 6:9; Rv 14:14–20). The winepress was usually cut from solid rock, 6 to 12 feet in diameter and 1 to 2 feet deep, with a trench leading to a smaller container. Grapes were put in the winepress and trampled by men until the juice flowed into the lower container. This was one method of pressing grapes.

The grape juice was taken to the peoples' homes and allowed to ferment. The dregs were poured off, and then the wine was stored in large jars of stone or bottles of goatskins (Mt 9:17).

Fresh grape juice was also boiled down to make grape honey. Grapes were eaten raw in season or dried in the sun to make raisins (1Sm 25:18). See pp. 62, 184.

VIPER. *See* SERPENT.

VIRGIN MARY (VUR-jin MAIR-ee). *See* MARY 1.

VISION. An inspired dream or apparition (Nu 24:4; Is 6; Ezk 1; 8–10; Dn 7–8; Ac 10:9–16; 26:13–19; 2Co 12:1–4). See pp. 200, 235, 260, 263, 447.

VOW. A voluntary promise to God either to do or not to do something. The Mosaic Law did not require vows, but it did regulate them (Lv 27; Nu 30; Dt 23:18–23). See pp. 110–11.

WAGES. In early times wages were often paid in trade (Gn 29:15, 20; 30:28–34). According to Mosaic Law a hired person was to receive his wages at the end of the day (Lv 19:13; Dt 24:14–15; Mt 20:8). Withholding wages was condemned (Jer 22:13; Mal 3:5). See p. 238. *See also* LABOR; SERVANT.

WALL. 1. *See* HOMES.

2. In Bible times city walls were often made of clay (cf. Ps 62:3; Is 30:13). Fortified cities, however, were surrounded by enormous stone walls (Ne 4:3; Is 2:15; Zep 1:16). See pp. 85, 121, 272, 445.

3. In the Bible walls are a symbol of strength, protection, and salvation (Is 26:1; Jer 15:20; Zec 2:5). *See also* FORTIFICATION, FORTRESS.

WAR. Before going to war, the Israelites consulted God's will and sought His help through prayer and sacrifice (Jgs 1:1; 20:2; 1Sm 7:9; 14:37; 1Ki 22:6).

As they were about to enter into battle, the Israelites, their commander, or a priest gave a shout or battle cry (1Sm 17:52; Is 42:13). Fighting was carried on by hand-to-hand combat (2Sm 1:23; 2:18). Strategies employed included double attacks, ambushes, surprise attacks, false retreats, and night attacks (Gn 14:15; Jsh 8:12; Jgs 7; 20:36; 2Ki 7:12). Some wars were decided by a single combat (1Sm 17).

After a battle, countrymen and enemies (if they were on their own soil) were buried and mourned (2Sm 3:31–39; 1Ki 11:15). Triumph was expressed, captives were killed or sold into slavery, and the booty was equally divided (Dt 20:16–18; Jsh 10:24; 1Sm 30:24–25; 31:9; Am 1:6, 9). See pp. 59–60. *See also* ARMOR, ARMS; ARMY.

WASHING. Cleanliness is stressed in the Bible. Frequent bathing or washing was necessary because of the warm climate. After a journey the people washed the dust from their feet, and before meals they washed their hands (Gn 18:4; Ex 30:19, 21; Jgs 19:21; Mt 15:2; Mk 7:3; Lk 7:37–44; 11:38; Jn 13:5–14). See pp. 317–18. *See also* BATHE.

WATCH. 1. A guard (Jgs 7:19; cf. 2Ki 11:5; Ne 4:9; Mt 27:62–66).

2. A lookout (1Sm 14:16; 2Sm 13:34; 2Ki 9:17; Is 21:8).

3. The Hebrews divided the 12 hours of night into three watches (Ex 14:24; Jgs 7:19; Lam 2:19); the Romans, into four (Mt 14:25; Mk 13:35; Lk 12:38).

WATER. Because of the scarcity of water in Israel, it was greatly valued (Is 3:1; 33:16). Finding water was an important event; scarcity of water, a serious problem (Gn 6:7; Dt 28:12; 1Ki 17:1).

Water is also a picture for the messianic age, good news, life, and grace (Ps 23:2; Pr 25:25; Sg 4:15; Is 30:25; 32:2; 35:6–7; Jn 4:7–15). Negatively, it is a picture of trouble or misfortune (Ps 66:12; 69:1; Is 8:7). See pp. 34, 306, 376, 444.

WATER FOR IMPURITY. Water that was mixed with the ashes of a red heifer to remove impurity or sin (Nu 19).

WAVE OFFERING. The rite of waving the sacrificial portion before the Lord was regularly performed in the peace offering, the guilt offering of lepers, and the meal offering of jealousy (Lv 7:30, 34; 9:21; 14:12; 21; Nu 5:25). The sheaf of the first ripe grain as well as two loaves and two lambs at Pentecost were also waved before the Lord (Lv 23:10–11, 15, 20).

WEAVING. *See* TRADE.

WEDDING. *See* MARRIAGE.

WEEDS. *Tares* in some translations. Probably a poisonous plant known as the bearded darnel. It is a grass that cannot be distinguished from wheat until the two are full grown (Mt 13:25–30).

WEEKS, FEAST OF. *See* PENTECOST 1.

WEIGHT. The Hebrews used stones for weights and balances for scales (Lv 19:36; Dt. 25:15; Pr 16:11). For the most part they followed the Babylonian system of weights where 60 shekels (.36 ounce) equaled 1 mina (about 1 1/12 pounds) and 60 minas equaled 1 talent (about 65 pounds). These were the regular weights and were called light shekels, minas, and standards.

There were also heavy shekels, minas, and talents which were exactly double the weight of the regular standards above.

WHALE. *See* FISH 2.

WHEAT. *See* AGRICULTURE; FOOD.

WIDOW. Widows were protected under Mosaic Law. They were to be treated with justice and special consideration (Ex 22:22; Dt 14:29; 24:19–21; 27:19; Ps 94:6; Ezk 22:7; Mal 3:5). If a married man died without a son, his brother was obligated to marry the man's widow (Dt 25:5–6; Mt 22:23–30). *See also* LEVIRATE MARRIAGE.

The New Testament church also cared for its widows (Ac 6:1–6; 1Tm 5:3–16). Older, pious widows who had neither children nor grandchildren to care for them were enrolled, probably for special service (1Tm 5:9–10). See pp. 98–99, 410.

WIFE. *See* MARRIAGE.

WILDERNESS. Either a desert or a wild, thinly populated, uncultivated region used for pasturage. One of the chief wildernesses the Bible refers to is the place where the children of Israel wandered in the Sinai Peninsula (Nu 14:33; Dt 1:1; Jsh 5:6; Ne 9:19; 21; Ps 78:40, 52). See pp. 63–65, 82.

WILD OX. An animal, now extinct, that was known for its ferocity, strength, and speed (Nu 23:22; 24:8; Dt 33:17; Jb 39:9–10).

WILL. 1. Inclination or choice. God's will is that which He determines (Eph 1:11). It is revealed in His acts, His law, and especially in Christ (Mt 6:10; Ac 22:14; Rm 2:18; 12:2; Col 1:9).

Humanity's fallen or natural will cannot will good (Rm 8:7). God's grace alone is able to incline a person's will to good (Php 2:13). See pp. 69, 92, 195, 232, 427. *See also* ELECT, ELECTION; PREDESTINATION; SIN, II.

2. *See* TESTAMENT 1.

WIND. The Hebrews recognized four winds (Ezk 37:9; Mt 24:31). The wind that blew from the south was hot and dry; the wind from the north, cold (Sg 4:16; Lk 12:55; cf. Jb 37:22). The west wind brought rain (1Ki 18:43–45; Ps 148:8).

WINE, WINEPRESS, WINESKIN. *See* VINEYARD.

WINNOW, WINNOWING FORK (WIN-o, WIN-o-ing). A fork to throw threshed grain into the air to clean it of chaff (Is 30:24; Mt 3:12). See p. 96. *See also* AGRICULTURE.

WINTER. In Israel the winter season proper (December–February) is short. Scriptural references to the winter season, however, often include fall and seasons of seedtime (Gn 8:22; Ps 74:17; Zec 14:8; Mt 24:20). Although winters are usually mild, snow and hail occur in the higher regions. See p. 304.

WISDOM. Skill, intelligence, judgment, understanding (Pr 10:1; 1Ki 3:28; 5:12; Dn 5:11; cf. Ex 31:6). Wisdom is an attribute of God (Pr 3:19). It is the completeness and perfection of His knowledge (cf. Jb 10:4; 26:6; Pr 5:21; Is 31:2). God's wisdom is seen in creation, especially His creation of man (Jb 12; 38–39; Ps 139:14). God's wisdom is far above that of people (cf. Jb 11:6–9; Is 40:14, 28).

God gives wisdom to people (Pr 2:6). The fear of God is the beginning of wisdom (Pr 9:10). Since God's ultimate purposes in history are revealed in Christ, Jesus is wisdom (1Co 1:30; Col 2:2–3).

By faith in Christ, this wisdom becomes one's own and is expressed in one's life (1Co 1:19–24, Eph 5:15). The Bible contrasts this wisdom to a worldly understanding (1Co 1:19–26; Mt 11:25). See pp. 175–77.

WISE MEN. Those who served in the ruler's court to provide him with knowledge and insight (Jer 50:35; Dn 2:18). They were categorized together with sorcerers and magicians (Dn 2:27). It was these Wise Men who came from the east to see the infant Christ (Mt 2). See pp. 328–29. *See also* MAGICIAN.

WITCH, WITCHCRAFT. *See* DIVINATION; MAGIC.

WOMAN. The helpmate of man. Together with man she forms a unity, created in the image of God, to rule over creation (Gn 1:26–28; 2:18–23). See pp. 99, 173, 181, 227, 409. *See also* MARRIAGE.

WORD. God created the heavens and the earth by His Word (Gn 1). God's Word is His revelation to people (1Ki 6:11; 13:20; Jer 1:4, 11). By the Word, faith is created and the Church is built (Jn 14:26; Acts 4:29, 31).

God's Word came to people in various forms, for example, through speaking, writing, visions, and symbols (Jer 1:11; Jn 3:14–15; 20:3 1; 2Tm 4:2). His Word now comes to us through its written form in the Scripture (2Tm 3:16) as problaimed by His people. God's Word is dynamic, creative, and functional (Ps 147:15–18; Is 55:10–11; Mt 8:24–27; Rm 1:16).

Jesus Christ is the supreme revelation of God. He is the living Word (Jn 1:1–5; Rv 19:13). See pp. xiv–xv, xxi, 5–6, 232, 415.

WORKS. 1. The works of God include creation, preservation, and redemption (Gn 1; Jb 37:14–16; Ps 104:24; 107; Jn 5:20–36; 14:10–12). See pp. 4, 57, 396, 414.

2. Whether a person's works are good or bad depends on that person's relationship to God. Only a person who believes in Jesus Christ as Savior can do good works in God's eyes, since good works are a fruit of faith (Jn 6:28–29; Rm

6; 14:23; Gal 2:20–21; Col 1:21–23). See pp. 11, 27, 414. *See also* FAITH; JUSTIFICATION; SANCTIFICATION.

WORLD. 1. Universe (Jn 1:10).

2. The human race (Jn 3:16; 2Co 5:19).

3. The wicked; unregenerated; those who are opposed to God (Jn 15:18; 1Jn 2:15). The devil is the prince of this world (Jn 12:31).

4. The earth (1Sm 2:8; Jb 37:12; Is 18:3).

5. The Roman Empire (Lk 2:1).

See pp. 6, 15, 443, 445.

WORMWOOD. A bitter plant that grows in desert places (Pr 5:4; Am 5:7; 6:12; Rv 8:11).

WORSHIP (WUR-ship; to bow down, kiss the hand to, revere, work, serve). The respect and reverence given to God or a god. The patriarchs worshiped God by building altars and sacrificing to Him (Gn 12:7–8; 13:4). Mosaic Law established the place for worship and set the times and forms for it. The prophets condemn empty ceremonies and people who try to cover an ungodly life (Is 1:11–17).

Worship in the New Testament is centered in and around the Word of God. It involved reading the Old Testament and psalms, singing hymns and spiritual songs, teaching, praying, and celebrating the Lord's Supper (Lk 4:16–22; Ac 2:42; Rm 12:7–8; 1Co 11:23–24; 14:26; Eph 5:19). See pp. 165, 167, 325, 354–55.

WRATH. 1. Anger of people. *See* ANGER.

2. The reaction of a righteous God to evil (Dt 9:7, 22; Is 13:9; Rm 1:18; Eph 5:6; Rv 14:10, 19). See p. 42.

WRITING. Probably invented by the Sumerians, who wrote in pictograms around 3000 BC. Their writing led to cuneiform, or wedge-shaped, letters written on clay. The Hebrews obtained their alphabet from the Phoenicians. Writing among the Hebrews was attributed to men of learning (Dt 17:18; 24:1, 3; Is 29:11–12). Writing materials included clay, wax, wood, metal, and plaster (Dt 27:2–3; Jsh 8:32; Lk 1:63). Later vellum, parchment, and papyrus were used (2Tm 4:13; 2Jn 12). A stylus was used to write on hard material; a reed pen, on parchment and papyrus (2Co 3:3; 2Jn 12). Ink was made of lampblack or soot. See pp. xxvi–xxvii, 32–33, 206–07, 359. *See also* ALPHABET.

XERXES (ZURK-seez). *See* AHASUERUS.

YAHWEH. *See* LORD.

YEAR. *See* TIME.

YEAST. *See* LEAVEN.

YOKE. A wooden bar or frame with thongs that went around the necks of two draft animals and another thong that fastened to a wagon or plow. The yoke was used to join the animals together so they could draw the wagon or plow (Nu 19:2; Dt 21:3).

Figuratively, a yoke depicts subjection; the removal of a yoke, deliverance (Gn 27:40; 1Ki 12:4, 9–11; Is 9:4; Jer 2:20; Mt 11:29–30). A yokefellow is one's co-worker at a difficult task (Php 4:3). See pp. 205, 394.

Z

ZACCHAEUS (za-KEE-uhs; pure). The chief tax collector of Jericho who climbed a sycamore tree to see Christ. Jesus told Zacchaeus to come down because He was going to his house that day. With joy, Zacchaeus came down. He became a follower of Christ (Lk 19:1–10). See pp. 85, 306, 325, 389.

ZACHARIAH (zak-ah-RIGH-ah). *See* ZECHARIAH 5.

ZADOK (ZAY-dok; righteous). A descendant of Aaron's son Eleazar (1Ch 24:3). Zadok was the son of Ahitub (2Sm 8:17). He was one of the young men, mighty in valor, who came to David at Hebron with the intention of making David king over Israel (1Ch 12:28). Later, after David had become king, Zadok was high priest with Abiathar (2Sm 8:17). He supported David during Absalom's rebellion and remained faithful to David in his old age when Adonijah tried to take over the throne (2Sm 15: 24–29; 19:11; 1Ki 1:7–8, 32, 45).

ZALMONAH (zal-MUN-AH; shady). A place southeast of Edom where Israel camped (Nu 33:41–42).

ZALMUNNA (ZAL-mun-ah; shade denied). One of the two kings of Midian whom Gideon put to death (Jgs 8:5–21; Ps 83:11).

ZAPHENATH-PANEAH (ZAF-i-nath-pah-NEE-ah; the god speaks and he lives, or revealer of secrets). The name Pharaoh gave to Joseph (Gn 41:45).

ZAREPHATH (ZAR-i-fath). A Phoenician town 8 miles south of Sidon (1Ki 17:9–10; Ob 20; Lk 4:26). When the brook Chereth dried up, Elijah went to Zarephath. There a widow gave him a home until the famine was over (1Ki 17:8–24). See p. 130.

ZEALOTS (ZEL-uhtz). A Jewish party organized by Judas of Gamala in the time of Quirinius (AD 6) to resist Roman oppression. The apostle Simon, a member of this party, was referred to as the Zealot to distinguish him from Simon Peter (Mt 10:4; Mk 3:18; Lk 6:15; Ac 1:13). See pp. 269–70, 274, 287.

ZEBEDEE (ZEB-i-dee; Lord has endowed). A fisherman, the husband of Salome and the father of James and John (Mt 4:21–22; 27:56; Mk 1:19–20; Lk 5:10; Jn 21:2). See pp. 286, 289.

ZEBIDAH (zi-BIGH-dah; given). Jehoiakim's mother (2Ki 23:36).

ZEBOIIM (zi-BOI-im; gazelles). One of the five cities in the plain whose king was defeated by Chedorlaomer. God destroyed Zeboiim with Sodom and Gomorrah (Gn 10:19; 14:2, 8; Dt 29:23; Hos 11:8).

ZEBULUN (ZEB-yoo-luhn; dwelling). 1. The tenth son of Jacob and sixth son of Leah (Gn 30:20; 35:23; Gn 46:14). In his blessing Jacob describes Zebulun as dwelling by the sea (Gn 49:13). See pp. 17, 19 21.

2. One of the 12 tribes of Israel that descended from Zebulun. After crossing over the Jordan into Canaan, Moses divided the tribes into two groups, one group to pronounce blessings and the other curses. Zebulun was one of the six tribes that stood on Mount Ebal to pronounce the curses (Dt 27:13). The territory allotted to Zebulun was between the Sea of Galilee and the Mediterranean Sea. It included Nazareth (Jsh 19:10–16; Is 9:1; Mt 4:12–16).

ZECHARIAH (zek-ah-RIGH-ah; the Lord has remembered). The name of numerous men in the Bible, including the following: 1. The 14th king of Israel. He came to the throne in the 38th year of Uzziah, king of Judah, and reigned six months. He was the son of Jeroboam II. Shallum murdered Zechariah in order to become the king himself (2Ki 14:29; 15:8, 11).

2. A son of Jehoiḍa, the high priest, and a priest like his father. He lived during the reign of King Joash of Judah. Zechariah was a reformer. On Joash's order Zechariah was killed in the court of the temple (2Ch 24:20–22). He is probably the Zechariah referred to in Mt 23:35 and Lk 11:51.

3. A prophet who advised King Uzziah (2Ch 26:5).

4. A minor prophet; the son of Berechiah and grandson of Iddo (Zec 1:1). He was a contemporary of Zerubbabel the governor and returned from the Babylonian captivity under his leadership. Zechariah also lived during the time of Jeshua the priest and Haggai the prophet. Along with Haggai, he exhorted the leaders of the Jewish colony to resume work on the temple. It is likely that Zechariah was a priest as well as a prophet (Ne 12:16). See pp. 139, 260.

5. The father of John the Baptist. Zechariah was a priest of the division of Abijah (Lk 1:5). He and his wife, Elizabeth, who was related to Mary of Nazareth, were godly people who lived in the hill country of Judea. One day while Zechariah was serving in the temple, an angel appeared to him and told him God had heard his prayer; he would have a son. And so, in their old age, Zechariah and Elizabeth became the parents of John the Baptist, the forerunner of Christ (Lk 1:5–25, 39–80).

ZECHARIAH, BOOK OF. The 11th book of the Minor Prophets. The prophet Zechariah wrote this book in 520 BC after the Israelites' return to Jerusalem from the Babylonian exile. The book deals with the destiny of God's people. See pp. 260–62.

ZEDEKIAH (zed-i-KIGH-AH; righteousness of Lord). The son of Josiah and the last king of Judah. Because of Judah's wickedness, God allowed Nebuchadnezzar to come to Jerusalem and take Jehoiachin, Judah's king, to Babylon. Then Nebuchadnezzar placed Mattaniah, whom he renamed Zedekiah, on the throne as king. When Zedekiah rebelled a number of years later, Nebuchadnezzar seized him, put out his eyes, and took him to Babylon where he died (2Ki 24:17–20; 25:1–21; 2Ch 36:10–21; Jer 21–39; Ezk 17:15–21). See pp. 121, 202.